D1228203

LOUIS LIPSKY/MEMOIRS IN PROFILE

"MEMOIRS IN PROFILE,

by
LOUIS LIPSKY,

JEWISH PUBLICATION SOCIETY OF AMERICA
PHILADELPHIA

1975
ISBN 0-8276–0069-0
Set and Printed in Israel by Keterpress Enterprises, Jerusalem

TABLE OF CONTENTS

PREFACE

A comment is required on what Louis Lipsky would have called the shape of the present book.

The very fact that his life was so active, in the deepest sense of the word so creative, has made the task of Louis Lipsky's biographers remarkably difficult. His most intense activities were performed with a singularly small admixture of egotism. During his most masterful moments he persisted in regarding himself as no more than the servant of the cause.

This self-abnegation—for which he was, indeed, celebrated—no doubt enhances his stature as a historical figure, yet it constitutes a well-nigh insoluble problem for anyone trying to disentangle his personality from his performance.

In his downright way he sums up this quirk, or disability: "It appears that I am incapable of writing a personal memoir of myself occupying center stage." (Page 56).

Nevertheless, he managed to produce a personal memoir: it comes to a mere 60 pages, dictated, with immense travail, toward the close of his life. It appears here in the opening section.

The rest of the book is composed of Louis Lipsky's *Gallery of Zionist Portraits,* first published in 1956 (Section II), and of writings scattered, as indicated, over a long period of time and in a variety of sources.

The Editor

ACKNOWLEDGEMENTS

Acknowledgement is hereby made, in wholehearted gratitude, of Ann Jarcho's assistance in preparing the manuscript of Louis Lipsky's *Memoirs in Profile*. The deepest thanks are also extended to Lillie Shultz, whose role in its assembly was fundamental.

Further acknowledgement is made to Meyer W. Weisgal, lifelong friend and follower of Louis Lipsky, and to Kalman Sultanik of the World Confederation of General Zionists, who made publication possible.

Special mention should be made of the devoted and intelligent labor performed by Binyamin Hoffman in correcting the proofs.

FOREWORD

BY BEN HALPERN

The memoirs, reports, articles, and addresses collected in this volume of
Louis Lipsky's writings cover more than half a century of intense political
activity. He was the most characteristic leader of American Zionism,
and of a major part of American Jewry, for two generations. The fathers
and grandfathers of present-day American Jews continually marked his
words and followed or violently opposed his views. He experienced,
in terms of a direct, personal responsibility, all the Jewish trials of half
a century of fathomless sorrows and unimaginable triumphs.

It was a time when American Jewry, until then the ward and in every
way the dependent of Europe, was thrust abruptly into global leadership
and responsibility. Amid two world wars, the Holocaust, and the re-
recurrent perils and extremities of the Zionist Restoration, American
Jewry fought its own decisive domestic battles to determine its identity
and shape its character. Louis Lipsky was probably more continuously,
devotedly, and significantly concerned with the management of these
American Jewish affairs, both in daily routine and in moments of crisis,
than any other man of the day.

When the First World War broke out, Lipsky, at thirty-seven years
of age, was completing his second year as executive chairman of the
Federation of American Zionists, other, older leaders having defaulted
this responsibility. He continued to carry out the central executive
functions in this organization and its successor, the Zionist Organization
of America, during the period of Louis D. Brandeis' control of Zionist
affairs, as well as afterwards, until he relinquished the presidency in
1930. He was a central figure in the group that induced Brandeis to
do battle with the American Jewish Committee over the creation of
an American Jewish Congress in 1915. Zionist success in this campaign,
more than any other factor, represented the crucial American element
that contributed to the British decision to issue the Balfour Declaration.

Lipsky led the rebellion that ousted the Brandeis group from Zionist leadership in 1921. He was the local leader of Zionism in the Weizmann era when the organization of pro-Zionist fundraising that still endures was instituted. He was a doughty fighter for the interests of the Jewish National Home during the Hitler years, when fundraising for overseas needs was a major dynamic force in the rapid growth of American Jewish communal organization, and when the shape and structure of the community were transformed in fierce battles over the principles of fund allocation.

He joined with Stephen S. Wise in the fight to maintain the American Jewish Congress as a permanent, democratically oriented representative organization of American Jewry. He played a role of cardinal importance in creating and directing the American Jewish Conference, which, like the American Jewish Congress in its time, served to cast the whole weight of American Jewry in the balance for a Jewish Commonwealth after the Second World War. After the State of Israel arose, he drew radical conclusions about the usefulness of further partisan Zionist activity, and, as an octogenarian, he inspired the creation of a new organization of American friends of Israel (the American Jewish League for Israel), in the form he approved.

His was an active, controversial life, one that demanded decision rather than contemplation, resolution rather than openmindedness. Few men can ever have received, or so well deserved, the stream of wrathful epithets with which the name of Lipsky is peppered in the correspondence of his eminent opponents. That is one side of the picture.

The other side is brilliantly revealed in the memoirs and vignettes collected in this volume, those brief, flashing illuminations of one of the most attractive, easygoing personalities that ever wandered into the hurly-burly of political controversy. Lipsky, the soft touch; Lipsky, the bohemian, with his table at the Café Royale on the Lower East Side of New York and later at the Tiptoe Inn uptown; Lipsky, with his sovereign disdain for pettifogging accountancy—this offbeat, lanky, angular profile of a man is an intimate part of the mass culture orally transmitted among whole generations of Jews who overlapped any part of his long and peculiarly appealing life.

Maurice Samuel, who knew him so well and who knew so well how to put things, has a brief and telling diagnosis of the paradoxical "core of Lipsky's personality." He "in fact [embodies] in equal measure the detached observer and fiercely committed partisan, the inveterate causeur and the man of action." Yet "these irreconcilable qualities, these utterly contradictory temperaments are not at war in him; they do not intrude

x

on each other, or spoil each other; they alternate harmoniously in what seem to be separate existences. . . . It is the only case of schizophrenia I have met which moves me to affection and admiration."

This impression of the man is certainly supported by the style—or the dichotomy of styles—apparent in the collected writings. In his autobiographical notes, Lipsky tells us, "I could never write well enough or find the time to do the writing, but it was very easy to talk off the cuff." One large section of his collected writings is, indeed, oratorical, editorial, written in the rolling periods of platform eloquence, exhortative, persuasive, or castigative. The style is vocal, dramatic, moving on a stream of sound. This he did well and, evidently, easily. But he did equally well, and with great pains, what he essentially wanted to do: that is, he wrote, as an artist and a litterateur writes. The vignettes and "memoirs in profile" of this volume exhibit his other, preferred style: concise and objectively perceived. The writing is visual, concretely imagined, impressionistic, or even pointillistic, in its flat, swift laying on of one sharp, unmodulated, positive impression after another.

None but primary colors appear in each descriptive touch. Often they score off the subject in a glancing flash of penetration at the very start. Thus, "Victor Jacobson was the most inarticulate diplomat I ever knew, but in the early days of the Movement he was a very useful man"; or "Even his earliest years—as a boy in *Cheder*—Chaim Weizmann was bemused by Zionism, the Promised Land and the Return"; or "Menahem Ussishkin was a Russian of the old school. He looked like a rugged Cossack and behaved like a medieval boyar—a challenger of czars"; or "Dr. Nahum Goldmann spent a great deal of his time in living out his youth"; or, of course, "Louis D. Brandeis became a Zionist too late in life." What follows these tart or affectionate stabs at the core of his models is a fusillade of swift, flicking brush strokes of primary impressions, filling out a rounded portrait. In each case, Lipsky's particular vision of the subject is boldly outlined against the gentle mist of the author's characteristically amused tolerance and unfeigned enjoyment of them all.

The combination of such disparate traits may well suggest schizophrenia to the observer, especially when both sides of the personality are so fully, uncompromisingly expressed. To live them out together harmoniously, in such civilized and solid sanity as Lipsky brought to his dual character, may well be a unique achievement. But the elements of Lipsky's character and style—less completely expressed on one or the other side, to be sure, than in his case, but tending either to dogmatic commitment or near-cynical detachment—were the common ingredients of the most typical intellectual type of Lipsky's youth, the muckraking journalists and realistic litterateurs of the Progressive Era.

In his twenty-fourth year, after a perfunctory attempt to enter the legal profession, young Lipsky came to New York City as a working journalist. This was his profession for fourteen years until he became a professional Zionist, after a dozen years of volunteer effort as an editor and agitator for the movement. New York at that time was the city of Lincoln Steffens and Hutchins Hapgood; and also of Abraham Cahan, who, along with Stephen Crane, was hailed by William Dean Howells as the harbinger of a new American realistic literature. It was a generation of hard-headed, coolly skeptical reporters, scoffing at pretense and pretentiousness. They were romantic only in their enthusiasm for whatever was vigorous, individual, and irregular in American life, qualities which they found in rich abundance in the slums of downtown Manhattan. It was an era that continued to mark Lipsky's style indelibly through all the long changes of his life and career. The hard, vivid factualness and telegraphic economy of a reporter are the hallmarks of his best literary profiles. Even his most Churchillian-seeming addresses are never as lush and sentimental as the great original, but are cool and hard in tone when angry, and light and buoyant when enthusiastic.

Louis Lipsky was one of a group of American Jewish journalists who made their mark as communal leaders. The Zionist movement was uniquely the home for such young sparks; and the veteran Lipsky was an older brother and boon companion for a company that included Bernard G. Richards, Maurice Samuel, and Meyer Weisgal. His intimate circle included also, next to the stars of the Yiddish theater in whom he delighted, leading Yiddish journalists like Abe Goldberg and Jacob Fishman. It was a colorful group with a distinct and characteristic role in American Jewish life and, particularly, in the Zionist movement.

Lipsky's maturity coincides with the decisive emergence of the East Coast cities, and above all New York, as the major and leading center of the American Jewish community. Until the opening of the twentieth century, the most important leaders, and the institutional core, of American Jewry were in the Middle West, and particularly in Cincinnati, the capital of American Reform Judaism. The concentration of Eastern European Jewish immigrants since the 1880's in the metropolitan East, not to speak of the unrivalled wealth and power of New York's German Jewish older settlers, meant an inevitable switch of the center of authority. Once the Schiffs and Marshalls in New York joined the Sulzbergers and

Adlers of Philadelphia in their patronage and concern for the new Yiddish-speaking immigrants, a struggle for authority set in which could only end in the predominance of the East.

To have Eastern Europeans as one's clients was the key to leadership in the twentieth-century American Jewish community. Those who became leaders on this principle varied widely in their relation to their following, and the nature of their concern for them. The German Jewish philanthropists, lawyers, merchants, bankers, and rabbis who were the pillars of Eastern Reform Jewry were anxious to protect their own good name, as well as enhance their clients' welfare, by "Americanizing" the immigrants. To attempt this in a simple-minded direct way, by imposing the established type of old American Jewry as their model, could seem feasible only to Middle Western leaders, relatively detached from contact with the newcomers. The more sophisticated Eastern approach involved a sincere and serious attempt to appreciate and preserve what was best in the Eastern Europeans' own traditional culture. But the approach remained a patronizing and basically authoritarian one.

Such men were not usually to be found in the American Zionist leadership, or at least only the religiously more conservative among them, and only insofar as Zionism was construed in a conservatively religious sense. It was in these terms that men like Solomon Schechter, or even Gustave Gottheil, were Zionists. Other Zionists drawn from the same professional and social circles were more detached from the religious establishment of American Jewry. They included religious men, like Stephen S. Wise, who were not more conservative, but more radical and consistent, in their religious and social liberalism than the Cincinnati Reform establishment; men who in many ways patterned themselves on the arch-rebel Felix Adler. They included also men like Louis D. Brandeis, Julian Mack and Felix Frankfurter, who, unlike their peer and rival, Louis Marshall, were never very much at home at the synagogue. For them, in their moments of self-awareness as Jews, Zionism was the only ideologically suitable form of Jewish identification that was readily available.

Such men, in either case, inevitably became rivals to the established leadership, whether in Cincinnati or New York, as soon as they seriously concerned themselves with the new immigrants and were hailed as their new leaders by downtown Jewry. Yet their relation to their followers, in spite of its ideological base, was not essentially different in type from that of the established philanthropists: it was a relation of patrons to clients. This made possible rapprochement with non-Zionists and coalition against downtown Jewry when Yiddish-speaking East Siders rose against their uptown leaders, asserted their independence, and claimed dominance in the councils and leadership of American Jewry.

What distinguished Lipsky and other Zionist journalists and writers, like Bernard Richards, Maurice Samuel and Meyer Weisgal, was that their relation to downtown Jewry was never one of patrons to clients. Men like Brandeis and Frankfurter were drawn to Eastern European Jews by sympathy, and often admiration, and by a partisanship based on a rather general ideological commitment. Lipsky and his circle were drawn to Eastern European Jews because they enjoyed their company. Like the Hapgoods and Steffens and other aficionados of the slum wards in American cities, they had a taste for the style and culture of immigrants and a partisan regard for the irregular elements of the underside of American society. But in their case the affinity was far closer, representing a rediscovery of their personal roots, of what was precious in their childhood, and the partisanship was correspondingly stronger and more intimate. It resulted in a deep-rooted, unremitting opposition to the American Jewish Committee and the rest of the uptown establishment, in full accord with downtown Jewry.

The attachment of such men to Eastern European folk culture has been fruitful indeed for American Jewry. Maurice Samuel made himself the channel by which the world of Sholem Aleichem was brought into American culture and given as a heritage to native-born American Jews. He translated Sholem Asch and I. L. Peretz—the latter a writer first made known in English translation by Louis Lipsky, as he boasts in one of the rare claims of personal merit voiced in these writings. Meyer Weisgal made of Zionist magazines, but above all the theater, a medium for conveying to American Jews, and to all America, a showman's Yiddish-tinted, cosmopolitan palace of wonders; and in this he too was a true disciple of Lipsky. Lipsky himself, however, found the scene for his favorite observations of *genus Judaicum* in the most unlikely of all places: in the halls, conference rooms, lobbies and corridors of the congresses of the World and American Zionist Organizations.

It is by no means odd or unusual for leaders from the outside to be stimulated, enlarged, and lifted out of themselves by the movements they join, by the fascination and force of the new social milieu that absorbs them. Such an experience was certainly common among Zionist leaders, from Herzl even unto Brandeis. Nor was it uncommon for Zionist Congresses and conventions—which, to be sure, were a sheer nightmare for Brandeis and some others—to take by storm young Jews

xiv

previously unfamiliar with the color, variety, and unbridled passion of the world Jewish scene. Nevertheless, Lipsky's enchantment with the conclaves, sessions and hectic assemblies of the Zionist movement has a special quality about it.

He makes constant attendance at such transactions little less than a litmus test of the quality of authentic involvement and Jewish commitment in Zionist leaders. Lipsky, who at one point faced Louis D. Brandeis with the rude challenge to give up the Supreme Court for the leadership of the World Zionist Organization, leaves no doubt as to his implied judgment when he sums Brandeis up in a passing phrase as "the American judge who never appeared at a Zionist Congress." The full profile which he wrote of the great jurist is generous and discerning in portraying the moralist who "in his last days . . . was a symbol of rectitude and wisdom," and whose "foundations in character could not be disturbed." But he does not soften by an iota the ultimate judgment of Brandeis, the Zionist leader, which is laid down in lines like these:

> [Brandeis] found himself in London for the first time in the center of a free Zionist discussion. This was new to him. Discussion in a real sense was not the habit in the American Zionist circle dominated by Mr. Brandeis. His disciples expressed their loyalty by agreeing or trying to agree with his conclusions. In London, however, the European system prevailed. Everybody talked at length without fear or favor, unconcerned by threats of points of order. The long drawn-out debates in a number of languages left Mr. Brandeis exhausted. . . . He felt he was talking to an alien audience. . . . He did not understand their conventions.

Lipsky adds: "Their endless discussions exasperated and bored him. He wanted to cut the cackle and proceed to action." About Shmarya Levin, on the other hand, whom he loved, he can speak approvingly notwithstanding that he "was never an orator at Congresses." What counts was that he was always there, and "spent most of his time . . . in the lobbies or coffee houses." To do this was, in Lipsky's eyes, no small thing and certainly no demerit. What he says about his own attendance at Zionist meetings gives the impression that he was usually listening enthralled to others, caught up in the show of the thing, rather than engaged in its business.

This, of course, is an impression very far from the truth, and refuted on page after page of this volume by the evidences of Lipsky's yeoman labors in matters of organization. For whatever else Lipsky was as a Jew and a Zionist, he was a professional in both capacities. In this, too, he was typical of the whole group of Zionist writers and journalists, whom he served as their exemplary leader.

It is no accident, but a fitting thing, that men whose craft was observing and reporting should serve any movement to which they gave their commitment not as lay leaders and volunteers but as lifelong professionals. The American journalist of those days, like his successors today, always felt like a craftsman. It was better to write speeches than to speak them; to gather and compose firsthand reports, than to copy-edit them. It was more noble to be a workhorse than a showpiece. Professional labor, evidenced by a written piece, was hard and real, but nothing was more inevitably phony than the amateur efforts of laymen elevated to leadership.

One may surely question the total absence of personal ambition in any political leader. Nevertheless, suggestions in this vein about Lipsky, such as occur in editorial remarks in this volume, have a solid foundation. He was a professional; and what happened to his personal ambitions in one or another of the frequent political overturns in the organization he served could not suspend his commitment to its constant service. Lay leaders might come and go with the success of their political fortunes. The commitment of a professional like Lipsky was full-time, lifelong.

Much, much more than is written in this volume represents the daily labors of Lipsky as a professional Jew, a Zionist leader. Drafts of resolutions, innumerable constitutional proposals, reports, memoranda, surveys, and correspondence in floods flowed from his pen; and the talk he expended at countless office meetings, conferences, negotiations, and confidential chats—not to speak of what he had to listen to—could tax the patience of angels. There are, indeed, traces of the impatience he must often have felt. He notes with mild remonstrance that Stephen S. Wise, in his multifarious interests, was inclined to leave him to carry the burden of work in the American Jewish Congress. His whole career in the Federation of American Zionists and the Zionist Organization of America gives repeated testimony to his steadfastness, to his unconditional picking up of responsibilities which others let fall when their conditions were not met.

In the midst of these distracting responsibilities, he somehow maintained the cool, disinterested, detached, and open receptivity of an observer, and was able to absorb and transmit the shrewd, perceptive impressions given us in these writings. Perhaps his very professionalism was what made this possible. However deeply and passionately committed he was to the cause he served, since he served it as a professional,

xvi

a craftsman, his ego was involved more in the style and authenticity than in the personal consequences of his activities. He had the values of a line officer, not a staff man. He did not judge the success or failure of a movement strategy in terms of his own promotion or defeat. If he took pride in his performance, it was in matters of tactics.

He gave himself fully to the general objects of the movement and community he belonged to and served. He found in this not only fulfillment but unending fascination.

Section I
A Memoir of Early Days

A MEMOIR OF EARLY DAYS

I never thought I would have a memory so long that it would be impossible for me to bring more than a fraction of it to life. I always imagined there would be enough time to accumulate memories. Now when I try to recall them it is a very difficult thing for me. I find I have a tremendous amount of baggage, which I drag along with me in the form of articles, speeches, talking.

The beginning is Rochester. Rochester . . . I look back at it through the eyes of a child. I seem to remember everything from the beginning, even the coal that was embedded in my forehead when as a child I fell down in the schoolyard. The teacher tried to wash it away, but washing couldn't do it. I've still got a blemish from it.

I remember I was left-handed from the moment I moved my hand; the teacher was frantic trying to get rid of my left-handedness. I seemed to have committed a crime. So she tied my left hand. It broke loose. She tied it again and I broke loose. She kept on tying it all afternoon. She said she'd tie it tomorrow, but tomorrow came along and she forgot all about it. So did I. And there it is.

From the first day I remember, I was aware that we were a peculiar people, that we were Jews, that Jerusalem was *our* Holy City. I was under the quivering influence of Zionist thought from my birth; it was to fascinate me for the rest of my life.

My father and mother (whose light complexion their children inherited), also my grandfathers and grandmothers and uncles and cousins, all came from Philipova, a village near Suwalki in Poland. My father Jacob came to Rochester in 1874 to join his only brother Isaac and his two sisters, and to become the second *shochet* of the community. In 1875 my mother joined him with my older brother, Abram, who had been born in Philipova. In the course of only a few years all my mother's relatives, and father's too, and their sisters and brothers, came to Rochester, as well as any number of other residents of the neighborhood

of Philipova. My mother's father was a blacksmith, but had to leave when a competing blacksmith was brought into town by the mayor, with whom my grandfather had a fist fight. But he didn't win it; shortly afterwards he had to leave for Rochester.

A hundred or more Jews from the same village came to Rochester and mingled with people from Suwalki who, by some telepathic communication, had also made their way there. Dozens of Polish *goyim* also arrived in Rochester, and miraculously found their way to our home, where my mother had an exciting time gossiping with them in their language. I remember her exclaiming, on greeting them: "Wanda!" "Maryushka!" "Anya!"

I never saw Philipova or Suwalki. I never dreamt of going near there. I hated the Polish language, for reasons of my own; but my mother never ceased talking of her birthplace. Her father had a share in the community land of the town and she and other Polish girls used to go out to dig the potatoes, sing songs and romp about. My grandfather was a very strong man but he had no luck in fighting with *goyim*. The Jewish boys of Philipova used to leave before the date of their conscription and cross over to Germany and then to Memel, from there to Hamburg and on to the United States.

My mother came to America in 1875, two years before I was born, on a ticket issued from Rochester by a ticket agent who was not a Jew to a subagent who was. She came with my brother Abram, and another boy, Israel Unterberg, who was delivered to relatives in New York. Later prosperity made Unterberg a generous contributor to Jewish causes.

The guardian who received my mother at the boat was Sendor Jarmulowsky, a little old man with a closely cropped beard. There was no Hias (Hebrew Immigrant Aid Society) in those days, no organized Jewish community. The immigrants came seemingly from the sky— and were forwarded by Jewish hands to their ultimate destination.

I bless the name of Sendor Jarmulowsky! His name stands high in the memory of our family. As far as we were concerned he was the "Hachnosas Orchim" incarnate. He was known to thousands of Jewish families. He lived in New York, with a bank on East Broadway, facing Seward Park, but so far as his immortality is concerned, he remains in the memory of thousands of American Jews as the man who freed them on the soil of the United States. I have met Jews from Pittsburgh, from Chicago, from Boston and other places, all of whom remember his name with warmth.

He considered it his duty to receive personally the immigrants on arrival at Castle Garden. He provided them with a night's lodging, a good meal, and then despatched them to their new homes, personally accompanying them to the railroad station to say goodbye. Few people remembered the bank, but they remembered Jarmulowsky, a modest, retiring man who did a holy duty with zeal and devotion. My mother, who was guided by him in her first steps to liberty in New York, and then in Rochester, never forgot him—nor did I.

Nobody ever noticed that the whole Jewish immigration, from 1880 to the end of the century, was actually a simple, self-supporting, self-relieving operation with Jarmulowsky as the magician who made all the works go round. Later, Hias was organized to continue this worthy work.

For some reason I always had the feeling that I was born in Philipova, and had come from there to Rochester with my mother and older brother. By a quirk of circumstance, he looked on his grandmother as his mother, for she had suffered the loss of an infant boy at an early age. All memories of Philipova were transferred by them to me.

I was never to forget Philipova; I listened to many stories about things that happened there. There were memories of the invasion by Napoleon's army. There were stories of Jews killed by the French as alleged spies, and of Jews killed by the Poles as spies. The highway was known as a "shosay", i.e., *chaussée*. Over the years many young Jews came from Philipova to Rochester—relatives who had evaded conscription and were brought by relatives to Rochester.

Although I visited Europe many times, I never went to Warsaw or Suwalki. I had a grudge against the Poles because of their anti-Semitism I could never rid myself of. I remember nothing of Warsaw now except for its destruction by the Nazis, which I cannot forget.

As far back as I can recall I peopled Rochester with Indians. The bay and the river and the far-off lake were not just a bay, a river, a lake, but places where hostile Red Men cast baleful eyes on the usurpers who were occupying their territory. There was no doubt about it, everything around Rochester sounded Indian. All the streets, all the bays and the rivers and the lake to the north and the names of fraternal lodges had Indian names, as did every town, every village, indeed every corner. There were tribes bound in a confederation for the defense of the land from which they were being driven. This one was the League of the

Iroquois. When I was alone at night in some street with trees, I would imagine I heard their war cries and their night signals. Their names occupied my memory. It was their white tents that beckoned to me from a distance and menaced the streets we occupied. They should have been visible, but I confess I never saw one of them. The only thing I had to remember them by were stories taken from books, fossils that I found in the fields, and shells, and the light of their ghostly figures intruding on the houses we lived in. Each house had a barn, each barn had a horse. There were many truckers collecting rags and metals.

Later (in my daydreams) I included the Mohicans among the Indian tribes around Rochester; I pictured the appearance of Deerslayer and Uncas, characters in James Fenimore Cooper's novels, and I thought that the Indians would some day return to Rochester and revenge themselves on the white people for what they had done to them during the uprisings and wars that seemed to be a daily affair of Indian life. But they never showed up.

For a modern city, Rochester had a peculiar structure. The Genesee River ran through the center of the city and under the main street. Every spring the river broke through the protection of its banks and flooded the lower parts of the city, especially the Hay Market where the farmers came with their produce. It would often break through the main street and flood the entire section and flow downstream to swell the Falls that fell a great distance into a ravine down below and were compared to Niagara Falls. In fact, it was claimed that Rochester Falls almost equalled Niagara; it was one of the boasts of the city. I was sure of it myself. We used to climb down the ravine, swim in pools there and walk alongside the river down the road to the village of Charlotte.

In the early days my impression was that the road from Rochester to Charlotte to the lake was dotted with cemeteries—and few of them were Jewish. Later on, most of the cemeteries were removed to Cobbs Hill to the north of the city, in which direction the Jews had moved. There were many orchards and nurseries on the way, and many of my summers were spent roaming in the vicinity of the orchards and the nurseries. In that neighborhood the Kodak works were built, and later the University was put up around Cobbs Hill. There was a suspension bridge across the Genesee River that led to the Falls, and the bridge was used to cross from east to west.

The Jews were always segregated in a little corner of the city, in the very heart of the densely populated community.

I remember the house I was born in. It was on a little crooked street and had a garret. The fence was always broken. There was room in the rear for a barn which was occupied by a horse owned by a Jewish rag-collector. The synagogue was right nearby; so was the school.

There were six Jewish kids out of a class of 32; one of them was my cousin, Davy Levy, who was to become Captain of the Fire Department in Rochester, and used to come to our house to play chess on Sundays. He was a crusader who carried on a single-handed fight with Stevie Brasser, the "Mecklenburger." I didn't know what that meant, but I knew he was a fighter who loved nothing better than to start fights with the Jewish boys. Once my cousin Davy established his superiority, Stevie lost all his zest for combat.

There was also another school up forward near the main street. On a Saturday it was a treat to walk from where we lived to this school along the main street, at the end of which the Powers Block building loomed majestically.

Jews found it convenient to live close together. When a new building was put up in that section, all of us rejoiced; it meant that our city was growing. There were two synagogues—one on Chatham Street and one on Leopold Street. One was under the management of middle class people of no special description; the other, peculiarly, was a *shul* donated by a group of brothers. It was called the Nussbaum Shul. There were always quarrels between the two *shuls*—the fight concerned the rabbis—and after a few years a group of Rochester Jews established an independent *shul* for "T'hillim Jews."

We lived on our own streets. Joiner Street, where my family lived, was inhabited solely by Jews. They were smaller houses, few of them with two stories, with grass in front and trees in the rear. The Jews all spoke Yiddish until the children grew old enough for public school; then they had to become aware of the fact that they were living in an American city. In fact, they soon became Americans except for the screen of Yiddish that separated them.

But they were all in the grip of a strange old way of life they could not easily get rid of. The memory of Zion was part of their daily life. It was registered in the rotation of the Holy Days. It was refreshed in the synagogue, in the *cheder* and in the home. The traditional prayer, "Next Year in Jerusalem" was often repeated; the Prophet Elijah was a familiar figure. When Yom Kippur arrived, you could hear the footsteps of the predicted Messiah. There were always Exoduses and there was always a Promise. It had started from Jerusalem and was to return to

the place of its beginning. The Fulfillment of the Promise was the ex-
piration of the Exoduses, the first and the last, the Persecution of Persecutions that our people had endured with faith in God from the Dawn
in Egypt, from the downfall of the Temple, from the downfall of Judea
and the beginning of the long years of wandering through many lands,
banishment from their places of domicile, and the expulsion from Spain.
It was a long drawn-out story of endless dreams that crowded my
memory before the realities of the city of my birth began to color my
life.

I had heard of the ghettos of Rome, of Prague and of its Golem. My
father read the Hebrew and Yiddish journals and I heard of the openings
of the windows of modern civilization to the self-sufficient villages of
Russia, Galicia, Poland, and Rumania. The first breezes that ruffled
the sluggish stream of Jewish intellectual life and animated the Dreams
of Redemption spread over the cluster of Jews huddled together in the
marked-off streets of Rochester.

We had faith in God, the First and the Last, and endured the riddle
of our life as we had to. There was no premonition of the modern
Jewish tragedy, more horrible than any that had preceded it. At that
time we were celebrating in our city a providential escape that had led
us to a land of freedom and democracy; we were accommodating ourselves to an era of freedom in that new land, in which we were being
refreshed and reborn.

Strange to say, there were no theories or ideologies or definitions to
be mulled over in order to understand what I saw or heard or guessed
about the direction of Jewish life: why there were Jewish streets, why the
"cheder," the "shul," the language my father and mother spoke, why
we turned our gaze away from crosses and were uneasy when we heard
the chants in Gentile churches. We were marked out for identification
and disdain by people we could easily identify for our own reasons.

It was years before I became conscious of American political life and
especially presidential elections. But I remember the election bonfires of
my childhood. We were little shavers when we collected the bonfire
materials. The wholesale destruction absorbed quite a number of weeks
and required great ability. Election bonfires were not made in a simple
way. They required planning, engineering work and meticulous preparation. The names of the candidates were conspicuous for a few days and
then completely disappeared. Grover Cleveland, James G. Blaine,

later on Benjamin Harrison, bands playing—it was immensely exciting.

As a matter of fact, we Jews lived in a blind alley, and every now and then would become conscious of having some interest offended or distorted. It was not until I reached the voting age that I felt that we were citizens of a Republic who had rights and interests and grievances in disputes.

I recall echoes of the Civil War and the parades of the war veterans and their diminishing numbers as they marched on the streets on the Fourth of July. It took a long time to become conscious of living in a democracy and in a state of freedom.

I lived to see a President of the United States speak of the Balfour Declaration. I lived to see the head of the Republican Party introduce a joint resolution adopted by a large majority and signed by the President of the United States. I saw Bryan when he was Secretary of State. I went with Sokolow to discuss events with him. I saw Teddy Roosevelt, and went there as Secretary of the Committee.* I saw President Wilson. I saw Coolidge and I saw Harding. In fact, I met all the Presidents personally from Teddy Roosevelt to Truman. I even remember when Grover Cleveland was elected, when I was seventeen. The bonfires, the bands, the celebrations—it is all still vivid in my mind.

My father taught my brother Abram to read the Bible—the first book of Genesis—and then my brother Abram would read it to me. Abram learned how to play chess, and also taught it to me. I, in turn, taught my father; but when I beat him at the game we stopped playing: he had lost interest. My father used to borrow my library books; he learned English through them.

My father was only about 18 years old when he came to Rochester as a junior *shochet*. It was the first work he had in his life. His older brother Isaac had arrived in Rochester before him and had gotten the job for him. I was not yet born. I soon learned that my father was a taciturn man and avoided conversation—especially with me. A number of years passed before I had the courage to provoke him to tell me something about himself and his troubles. Usually he drove to the slaughterhouse in the country in a wagon drawn by a brown, rickety horse, half starved.

*The Committee was a Jewish campaign committee for the election of Theodore Roosevelt as President. Ed.

Once he took me by the hand, raised me to the driver's seat, and gave me the reins to hold. He looked down on me and said: "You are really too young to ride with me in the driver's seat." And then he went on: "You have no idea how hard it is for a young *shochet* with little experience. I am afraid of this bloody work." "What is there to be afraid of?" I asked, and he answered: "First, it's the young chickens. Then it's the crowds of women clamoring for me to hurry up and kill their chickens. I can't bear to hear the cries of the women; I won't be able to stand this much longer. It is even worse when a larger animal has to be killed. In that case the older, experienced *shochtim* are the witnesses; and they watch me in order to find fault with my work. The worst is when the dead chickens come to me in my dreams and haunt me for killing them. Just imagine if all the chickens I've killed so far were to come to haunt me in dreams during the night! It is impossible for me to stand it much longer. But what am I to do? I am only a young *shochet*, but I see that killing chickens or larger animals is not my business. It is not for me. Let somebody else do it who is stronger."

But he went on being a *shochet*, getting older from year to year, until he was counted among the older men and his conscience was strangled under the load of his life of "sin."

My father's silences were heavy and unrelieved. I remember him keenly for one reason—he introduced me to James O'Neill in *The Count of Monte Cristo*.

One Friday evening when I was about seven, he took my hand and said "Come along with me." I followed docilely. He walked me up Main Street to the Opera House and there I saw announced: "O'Neill in *The Count of Monte Cristo*." It was unusual for him to go to the theatre, especially on a Friday night. To my amazement my father took me up to the second gallery and placed me beside him in the first of the three rows.

There I saw James O'Neill for the first time. I saw him as "Edmond Dante" standing on a rock in the middle of the stage, supposedly deep in the ocean, holding up a knife and shouting "The treasure of Monte Cristo—the world is mine!" I am sure it was. He lived for many years and fascinated theatregoers throughout the country, though he failed to please his own son, Eugene O'Neill.

Though my father never went to the theatre again, he had introduced me to a gallant actor; I remember him in his last years playing the father in "Joseph and His Brothers."

I learned how to become a baker's helper by serving my mother every Thursday evening as the kneader of dough for the Sabbath bread. I was a boy of about ten and would knead and punch the dough until it was moulded right. It was not an easy task, but it required no skill— only willingness; and this was my assignment for many years. Then, to the surprise of the entire community, a Jewish baker appeared, and a great change took place in the whole Jewish area of Rochester. From that time on there were "bagels" to be bought; there was "*cholla*" to be gotten; there was any amount of cakes and bread to be purchased— enough to serve the entire Jewish community. The enterprising baker's name was Janofsky; it is assumed that he became a well-to-do "bourgeois" by this sudden access to a big market. So I lost my job with my mother.

Janofsky's son, who was a shopkeeper on Joseph Avenue, won the right to become an intellectual. His father's success as a baker made young Janofsky ambitious to become a doctor. From the day the first bagel was baked, he thought of himself as a student likely to be admitted to the University of Rochester. He became friendly with my older brother and arranged to take lessons. In the course of a few years, instead of being the owner of a haberdashery store, he became a student at the university and a few years later, guided by his mentors, he graduated from the university, went to Buffalo, where he changed his name, and entered the medical school to become a physician. He claimed that he owed everything that he was to the tutelage of my erudite brother, Abram, though he never forgot to mention the fact that he owed his success to the invention of the bagel and its introduction into the communal life of Rochester.

I always associated the smells of Rochester with the change of seasons and our holidays. When the scattering leaves perfumed the air and made the Fall a fragrance unlike any other time of the year, there was no doubt that Succoth would soon be here. I remember how the Indian Summer pervaded the streets and outdoors; we knew then that Rosh Hashonah was coming. I knew the names of the Sedras as they were read off on the special days and special holidays. Everything we did circulated around the synagogue, which gave elevation to the days that were being celebrated.

Fall was the time when the cabbage was packed in barrels and the potatoes were put away for the winter; the time when the russet apples found their way into the cellar; the time we used to rob the grapevines on Cobbs Hill and eat apples before they were ripe. To me it seemed that all this could happen only in Rochester.

We measured the winter by the exciting days of snow and sleet and wind. We counted the weeks that would bring an end to the cold that made the parlor stove the most important fact of life. We had a feeling about the first of May, when we could go out walking. The school program provided for a May "walk" of seven miles to the bay and the lake and then to Charlotte, which is now part of Rochester. I remember the scene when I once made this trip on my bicycle. Part of the ride was through the cemetery; I pedaled furiously because I felt that the ghosts had arisen and were chasing me. When I returned home I found refuge in our big cellar where I kept my pets—little mice, big mice and rabbits. I remember that we had a very long yard where I had housed an extra large rabbit. He got loose one day and created havoc.

I spent the vacation months in the summer exploring the woods. We had a picnic ground up north where Germans found places to enjoy themselves on Sundays drinking beer. We found traces of fossils that reminded us of the arrows of the Indians.

I had a friend with whom I spent all my vacations; it gave me great pleasure. His name was Lazar White. He had great curiosity, with an intense interest in scientific subjects. He left Rochester when he was 14 and entered Columbia University. He became a well-known foundation engineer. We were both grieved when the day came for him to say goodbye. I remember him standing at the front gate, twirling his cap and saying "See you again."

In fact we did see each other again—ten years later in New York City. I went with him and his brothers and sisters to hear Felix Adler at Carnegie Hall. That was the time I was taking an eclectic course at Columbia, and I used to have dinners with them on Sundays at their home. I learned a great deal from the White family about non-kosher "kosher" meals, for his mother did not believe in Kashruth, although his father was very observant.

I remember the doubts that filled me the first day I went to a *cheder*. My father came over to me one afternoon when I was about five years old, took my hand, fixed my clothing and said "Come along with me to the Rebbe." I did not know what he meant, but docilely obeyed, anticipating something unusual. We went to a room in the *shul* where there was a desk; seated at the desk was an old man with white hair, wrinkled, and barely able to see. He adjusted himself to my presence, produced a stick of *lekach*, handed it to me and said: "Taste it"—which I did. It was sweet. My father said: "Remember this. The study of the Law brings sweetness." The old man began "Aleph, beth, gimmel, daled" and said: "Repeat after me—aleph, beth, gimmel, daled," which I did. He said: "Taste the *lekach* again and repeat the alphabet" and again I repeated after him. This performance was repeated five or six times. Then my father took my hand and said: "Let's go home now, but go to see the old man again tomorrow." After a while I became very efficient in repeating the alphabet. He praised me on every occasion and I reported to my father that all was going well. The old man continued to be my Rebbe for some time, adding new knowledge from week to week. My next Rebbe was a *chazan* of the *shul* who also functioned as the Rebbe for the younger pupils. My third Rebbe was a secular man who conducted a large class where the study was more intricate. He not only taught the alphabet but also the translations of the first chapters of Genesis. I remember verbatim his original version of the first few chapters of Genesis. Months went by and I became a candidate for higher studies. More pages were added to the translations. Preparations for my Bar Mitzvah required an aptitude for music. This gave me a headache for many days. I didn't know what my Rebbe was driving at since he was teaching a form of music that didn't touch my heart. It was routine, and the *niggun* required a great deal of attention. The day was approaching when I would have to appear in *shul* and deliver my version of the "*maftir*" assigned me. What I mumbled I can't remember at all. I know I ran through endless sounds assisted by the assistant Rebbe and finally came to the part where he said "Say the *brocha*"— which I did with great relief. That was the end of my Hebrew education for the time being; but I was condemned to "*lay tefillin*," which was the ritual required of me before I could get anything to eat in the morning; in fact it was an essential before my mother's bread box would be opened or before I could get any milk to drink. After a month of this I decided it was enough. My mother expostulated with me; my father sternly urged me to be a good boy; but I was obdurate, and thereafter received my Jewish education in my own way without instruction from anybody. The only one who looked at me blackly because of this was my father, who would never forgive my mother for giving me breakfast before "*laying tefillin*."

I made up for this neglect by being a good attendant at the *shul* on Sabbath whenever a *maggid* appeared. I liked to hear a *maggid* exercising his art with great devotion and a great deal of imaginative learning. I heard every *maggid* who came to our neighborhood for many years, and took a special delight in hearing Masliansky whenever he came, which was often.

I must confess that in my early youth I had a first-class record as an observer of Kashruth. Even when I occupied a desk in a law office, I always observed the Sabbath and never ate non-kosher food. My mother provided me with sandwiches to take along, and they were always kosher tongue sandwiches, which is probably why I acquired a preference for them that has lasted to this day. When I ate in a lunch-room, I chose cheese. My mother's tongue sandwiches went with me when I started working in cigar factories; I took them to every loft. The foreman was always a Jew.

When I came to New York City there was an Austrian who had a bakery on the next block away from the *American Hebrew*'s printing shop. There I learned the ways of iniquity. This Austrian, whose name was Antosh, made hot veal sandwiches, which became my favorite food. But I never was able, at any time, to get familiar with pork, which has remained my basic abomination all my life. Since the Jews in New York dominate the business of eating, I don't know any more whether I'm eating kosher food or *"trefe."* It all tastes the same now.

When my brother had a tubercular attack my mother broke all the rules and constantly fed him milk—whether he was passing from *"fleishik"* to *"milchik"* or vice versa. About three years after I had passed Bar Mitzvah, my mother applied her aberration, about exempting milk, to me, too. I was also served milk at any and all times, her reason being that I was too thin. I don't know how my mother squared this with my father.

One of the few bridges to the world of the Gentiles that we Jewish boys could cross was, strangely enough, a church, William Gannett's Unitarian Church.

I remember Dr. Gannett with deep affection (Lewis Gannett the literary critic was his son). I remember his benign smile, his soft voice, the beauty of his hymns, his recitations from Emerson's poems. His church was the only one in Rochester that had no cross. It was known as the church without a cross.

When I was a young man, Dr. Gannett attracted many Jewish boys and girls to the church. In fact, in most of the cities around the country the Jews felt that the Unitarian Church was akin to them in some form or other, and they were sympathetic to the ministers who served in those churches. Dr. Gannett was kind and friendly to the Jews. His church had an Evening Home for Boys, and he was responsible for securing funds to send two Jewish boys to the Hebrew Union College to become rabbis. They did their best to follow in Dr. Gannett's footsteps, but were not very successful. They seemed unable to get away from the thinking of Emerson and the impression made on them by Gannett. They did not know that Gannett stood for freedom and that he wanted them to follow their own ideals.

It was at Dr. Gannett's Evening Home for Boys that I met and became boyhood friends with Samuel Goldenson. Slightly younger than I, he sold papers after school and also belonged to a club of which I was a part, called The Judeans.

But unlike me, he was not interested in Zion. Born in Lithuania, the son of a learned Jew, Sam Goldenson later became one of America's leading reform Rabbis and head of Temple Emanu-El. Many were the ideological clashes in which we were in opposing camps, in our adult years. To the day of his death in 1962 he remained, as far as I know, an anti-Zionist.

How a boy is introduced to books is often a matter of chance. He may be steered wrong at the beginning.

I was given a present by a teacher of a book of travels in England. That should never have been done to me. It almost destroyed my life. For a time it created a repugnance with which I approached any new book handed to me. I never read a book with the eagerness and zest with which I read the first volume of Horatio Alger, accidentally shoved under my nose by some companion. After Alger, a book had to be really good to be worth reading. But Horatio Alger was nothing special in a large world of books. He was followed by Frank Castleman, Oliver Optic, Edward Ellis. Then I jumped across the ocean to George Henty, a marvelous writer whose stories were steeped in history and gave boys a feeling of heroism. He was the bridge that connected me with Dickens, Thackeray, Wilkie Collins and others living in England, all of whom became good friends.

I ran through what might be called the juvenile books at a tremendous clip, and soon found myself thinking of new worlds to conquer. I had already taught reading and writing at night to members of the Workers' Forum when I was about fifteen, and by the time I was nineteen, I had accumulated a friendly group of boys, most of whom had gathered around Dr. Gannett. It was at this time that we formed the club, The

Judeans, whose program was the advancement of Jewish and general knowledge. We ventured on a grand undertaking when we organized a performance of a one-act play called *The Witch of Endor*, which I wrote. The actors were some of the members of our club. I was King Saul, and the surprise of the evening was that I, who wrote the play, forgot all my lines.

It was at this time, too, that I became an amateur "reciter." We used to read plays (at one session I was Cassius, and Sam Goldenson was Brutus). We also spent many hours reading poetry—Tennyson, Browning and Walt Whitman, who blasted the music out of Lowell's cadences.

We met in the vestry rooms of the Leopold Street Shul—our *shul*—but objections were raised to the attendance of girls. The man who raised the objection was the *shamus*; he thought great sins were going to be committed under cover of this mixed membership. However, our influence overcame his, and the girls for the first time met in the same clubrooms with the boys to talk about books.

One member had conceived the idea of borrowing books from the Board of Regents, located in Albany. It seemed that under the pressure of progressive ideas, education was being shoved down the throats of the young people: a list of books had been compiled by a committee and a letter addressed to Melvil Dewey, then the librarian or secretary of the Board of Regents. I remember that one of the books on the list was Graetz's *History of the Jews,* and another by Condor. The books came to me, as secretary; I kept them in my room reading them all first myself and enlisting a number of the members to aid me in my excursions in pursuit of an education. I grew rapidly, and soon there were scores of books presented to me that were not on the list and that I read with great satisfaction.

On the invitation of a friend of mine, I went to a parlor meeting of a German class. At that time I had to acquire credits for the Regents' exam I was going to take and thought it would be a very good way to try out my German; but I was afraid to talk because I felt that the German I knew would be considered Yiddish—so I did not talk and never went again.

It is strange how life makes its own provisions for your future. I was pushed into doing things when I was a boy because my uncle provided a place for me as a stripper of tobacco, which enabled me to get a little pocket money to see the plays that came to Rochester. But what I remember most of my cigar-making days was listening to my uncle talk about the plays he was seeing. He was fascinated by them in spite of the fact that he was, for all practical purposes, an illiterate. But he knew plays and he could tell their plots without being aware of where these plots came from. He saw Edwin Booth in *Hamlet;* he saw John McCollough in the mad scene of *Virginius;* he saw another Shakespearian actor in an English version of *Rigoletto.* When he told the story of a play, he had no sense of the limitation of time or circumstance. He waved his hands and yelled at the top of his voice. He "improved" on Shakespeare, but he knew all the lines of *Richard the Third.* He shouted for "a horse! a horse! my kingdom for a horse!" All I had to do to get him going was to begin telling about a play and he would finish it. My mother's sister was also interested in plays; she would sit with me stripping tobacco, and he would roll the play out.

Thus the first years of my life after I left the Free Academy High School were spent making cigars in a shop. I also had a little shop of my own in the house, and would run around trying to sell the cigars in the saloons.

In a way it was my brother Abram who gave me the first practical introduction to the newspaper business. He became a free lance reporter, and when he left for college I became his successor.

I always had a smell for a printing shop, especially if it was connected with a newspaper; so did my brother. I used to go to the office of a newspaper and stand around, smelling the ink and looking at the table where the pages were being made up.

One summer my brother got a job on *The Herald,* a Rochester paper, and he let me come with him on his rounds. He got all sorts of assignments. He was once sent to interview a boy who had no hands, but managed to write with his feet. My brother wrote up reports on the sermons he was often sent out on; here, too, I would go along with him. The next summer, when my brother was busy elsewhere, I went over to see the city editor and asked him for a job. He said: "You can do what your brother did, if you have the ability. You can have the job but you're not going to get any money for it." I took it anyway. For some reason I was told to bring in a report on the weather the next morning; the editor told me to "make it funny." I have no idea what made it funny, but I looked at the make-up man and saw him placing it in the form. It didn't take too much space, but I became conscious of my identity with *The Herald,* and that made me proud; it gave me an interest in journalism.

I used to write my stuff standing at the stone, and see it placed in position on the page. In those days all type was set by hand so I had a chance to read the page-proofs. *The Herald* was Democratic; the other paper in Rochester was dyed-in-the-wool Republican from the first day it appeared and was the paper circulated among the farmers of the county.

After my summer job on *The Herald* there was an interlude of about two years when I almost slipped into becoming a lawyer. I used to like going to the courthouse and watching the cases being tried, and I managed to get taken on as a clerk in the law office of John Williams and then, through the influence of a certain woman, a member of the Unitarian Church, I was accepted in the law office of the distinguished Theodore Bacon.

Mr. Williams was a struggling lawyer who occupied offices together with another lawyer who had a considerable practice. He had a large number of shady clients: he held their securities when they were away on short "vacations"; they could come to him and borrow money when necessary.

Theodore Bacon, on the other hand, had a distinguished reputation in western New York. His firm represented the New York Central Railroad; he was a graduate of Harvard and a descendant of the Bacons of New England. In that office I read briefs written by Bacon; he had great style and a delightful skill in analyzing the legal principles of whatever he was talking about.

My work, for which I received only fees, consisted of reading law books, serving summonses and legal papers, and going to court sessions, from which I learned a lot.

To become a member of the Bar required only taking a Bar examination; but in Rochester a special examination was required to become a city corporation counsel. I did this and was put on a waiting list. About a year later I was informed that I had come out first in the examination for corporation counsel and was asked to let them know whether I was accepting the post.

By this time my whole life had changed; I had left Rochester, and was never to go back again permanently.

My attachment to journalism had proved too strong even for the entertainment of the law. I had gotten into the habit of going to a private library, the Reynolds, which specialized in periodical literature. It was there I first saw *The London Jewish Chronicle,* and I read it with devotion for years. I also read the New York newspapers and became familiar with outstanding writers on the theatre; I became acquainted with them at an early age. I also saw every Jewish newspaper that came to Rochester because my father was a subscriber to so many of them, both Yiddish and Hebrew.

I became aware of Jews beyond the reaches of Rochester.

I read about the 1897 Zionist Congress in Basle in *The Jewish Chronicle,* and I read Max Nordau's address to the First Zionist Congress. It was the first open speech in which the Jews seemed to be the audience. It thrilled me. I didn't know anybody else who read that paper in Rochester. The Yiddish papers had accounts of the Zionist Congress but they were not especially publicized. They had no regular correspondents over there.

It was around this time (1899) that I persuaded a friend of mine, whose father was a well-to-do metal dealer, to lend me the money to start a weekly paper. He gave me $300. I called the paper *The Shofar.* I can scarcely recall anything about it, except that my brother Abram, who was a Columbia post-graduate student, wrote the sermons and I wrote the stories. My brother was engrossed in religion and theological subjects, while I had a penchant for journalism, though I had not yet given up the law.

The Shofar lasted about 13 issues, until the money ran out. I forgot each number of it the moment it appeared, and have never seen a copy of it since. I have heard that it is still to be found in the New York Public Library, buried deep in the Jewish Reading-Room.

I was only an amateur and *The Shofar* made no pretense of competition with Louis Wiley's *Jewish Tidings,* which was a successful business venture in Rochester for many years. Louis Wiley later became the business manager for *The New York Times.* Nevertheless, *The Shofar* was responsible for a momentous shift in my fortunes. It helped me to get to New York.

I had gotten up a mailing list for *The Shofar,* and the publisher of the *New York Tageblatt,* who had received an issue, pointed it out to Philip Cowen, publisher of *The American Hebrew.* Cowen sent for me to come to New York.

Since at this time I was still on the waiting list for the post of a City Corporation Counsel, it is amusing to reflect that if Cowen had gotten the idea of putting me on *The American Hebrew* a year later, I might well have spent the rest of my life as a lawyer.

I vividly recall leaving Rochester in a blinding snowstorm at midnight and arriving in New York on a bright sunny morning in March, 1900, to assume my duties as Managing Editor of *The American Hebrew*. I found Mrs. Cowen at the printing shop at 43rd Street and Third Avenue. Mr. Cowen did not arrive until evening from Cincinnati where he had been attending the annual convention of the Council of Jewish Women. During this time Mrs. Cowen had taken over. She introduced me to the men of the shop. One was a stout Scotchman whose name was Cameron, the other was a spare tobacco-chewing Scotchman with a goatee like a brush and a strong aroma of whiskey that perfumed the air around him. The third was a Dane by the name of Johnson. They may not have looked very good, but they were first-class typesetters and printers. When Mr. Cowen arrived, bringing the news of the convention at Cincinnati, he had a long discussion with me and made me feel as though I had come to the right place.

Soon afterwards I was fortunate in being able to get into Columbia University. I was allowed to register as a special student and took an eclectic course, which meant I was not fixed to any curriculum. Thus I had Prof. W.T. Brewster for English composition and Prof. Hyslop for psychology. The latter believed in spiritualism. He had his own syllabus on the principles of psychology. It was unlike any other book on the same subject. He had a thick beard and a twinkle in his eye. His custom was to run through the names of the class asking questions and breaking off exactly at the moment the bell rang to end the session. Next time he did not remember exactly who had been called on the day before. I was very lucky in having been called upon only once during the entire semester. Clever students knew how to prolong the class by asking questions without end. There was also Prof. Seligman who taught economics and was assisted by Prof. Day (I saw Prof. Seligman only once). I remember a voluble history professor whose name was Sheppard; his method was to dictate the text of a lecture to the class and advise them to keep the record because what they would remember would be credited in the final exam. At the end of the semester Prof. Sheppard asked the students to pile up their notebooks, give them to him—and we never saw them again. He "passed" the entire class.

Those were the classes which made an impression on me: I don't remember the rest of the faculty or the studies I pursued. On the basis of this one year at Columbia University, I have been reckoned as an alumnus of the Class of 1902 (when I would have graduated) and during these many years—to this day, in fact—I regularly receive pertinent mail and notices, especially when funds are being solicited.

It was while I was attending Columbia and rooming with Jacob Goldenson, a brother of Sam Goldenson, my friend from Rochester, that I regularly attended Friday evening services to hear Rabbi Maurice Harris preach at Temple Israel of Harlem at 125th Street and Fifth Avenue. He was a popular Reform rabbi who came from London; he had a habit of preparing brief sermons and reading them in a low persuasive voice to an audience that seemed to be made up of good old friends. Every now and then I used to print one of his sermons in *The American Hebrew*. They were simple sermons that could have been written by a minister in a suburban church in London.

I was to remain with *The American Hebrew* for fourteen years. I learned the structure of the Jewish community, its rabbis, its leaders and congregations, the Yiddish theatre and the Yiddish press. Mr. Cowen did a great deal of job printing and knew communal affairs from the point of view of an incipient Young Men's Hebrew Association. In fact, *The American Hebrew* was representative of the interests of the community which had its center up nearer to Temple Emanu-El than to the Lower East Side.

The American Hebrew was a sprout of the YMHA. It was thought of as such by the young men of that institution who wanted to have a community organ as *their* publication. Cowen took over as manager because he was a printer, but the members of the Board very often contributed services and articles, and, on occasion, ventured criticism of their paper in letters to the Editor. They had their coterie of interested persons who regarded the paper as their own, although they had no financial interest in it. Cyrus L. Sulzberger was one of the ardent members of the Editorial Board, and often got angry and expressed his views. Dr. H. Pereira Mendes was pious and dogmatic, and very strict. Other members of the Board were: Frederick de Sola Mendes, Dr. Solomon Solis-Cohen and Philip Cowen. A majority of these men were Zionists in spirit, but had adopted a critical attitude toward the activities of Herzl.

My predecessor, Arthur Dembitz (a nephew of Justice Louis Dembitz Brandeis) was so pious that he could not stand it any longer. He left *The American Hebrew* and attended Gratz College in Philadelphia. He was an observant Jew, and he regarded *The American Hebrew* as being very far from as "*froom*" as it should have been. His "*yichus*" was

derived from his own father, Lewis Dembitz (after whom Justice
Dembitz Brandeis was named). Lewis Dembitz was a distinguished
lawyer in Louisville and a Zionist of considerable Jewish erudition. He
wrote articles for the Zionist press on aspects of law and studies of
Jewish lore; he came to a number of Zionist conventions and participated in a number of Zionist controversies. Though staunchly Orthodox,
he nevertheless helped in the organization of the Union of American
Hebrew Congregations, the Reform body.

It was on *The American Hebrew* that I formed an attachment with
Harry Scherman, "Cabby" to family and friends, that has endured
throughout our lives.

I met him through his mother, Mrs. Katherine Scherman, who travelled the country selling subscriptions to the Jewish Publication Society.

"Cabby," fresh from high school in Philadelphia, joined me as an
apprentice in the editorial department, while simultaneously continuing
his education. He was remarkably efficient. His silent steadfastness, his
regard for my affection, his own reflectiveness gave life to my Jewish
development and my Zionism.

After some years on *The American Hebrew,* Scherman developed a
talent for the commercial side of correspondence and became an admirable writer and a builder of clear-cut letters from which he derived
large profits later on. He became a publisher of books—at first cheap
ones, but always dainty and well made, and then fine large books into
which he poured his talents. He did not stay in the Jewish field at all,
but found a world of his own which he occupied with great skill and
wisdom. It was he who founded the Book-Of-The Month Club of whose
Board he is the Chairman. He has since poured many generous gifts at
the altar of the new Zion. Throughout his career and mine his sister
and his mother remained my steadfast friends.

A word about Philip Cowen, who was my friend for fourteen years,
as long as I remained on *The American Hebrew*. Cowen had no pretensions to journalistic ability, and no special interest in Judaism,
but he had a deep sense of loyalty to his people. He had the good fortune to be brought up in the midst of intelligent, respectable people. He
was a printer with his own printing shop, which sometimes employed
eight to ten men. He was a member of a group connected with the newly-
formed Young Men's Hebrew Association among whom were persons
who believed in new things in community life. They formed the first
YMHA in Harlem. Cowen was associated with Samuel Greenbaum,

Nathan Bijur, Cyrus L. Sulzberger and others who became members of a sturdy, loyal community. A group of them formed a corporation to organize a weekly Anglo-Jewish newspaper; this was to become *The American Hebrew,* and many became members of the editorial board and Cowen's advisers.

But Cowen made his own program. He managed to establish a friendship with the family of Emma Lazarus, who left a substantial heritage to American Jews, not only in the form of poetry, but also in her views on Jewish questions. He was also a literary friend of Mrs. Esther K. Ruskay, who was a teacher and writer of some talent. He was responsible for the introduction of Mary Antin to America; Her book, *From Plotsk to Boston,* was translated into English and made quite an impression.

Cowen was not greatly concerned with the literary interests of *The American Hebrew.* He wanted it to be a paper that was useful to the community, to the synagogues, to the rabbis and to the institutions. Cowen allowed me the freedom of the paper insofar as that freedom was good for Jews. He was not a partisan, and though not close to Zionism he did not mind my temperature rising whenever the question came up.

As a result I was able to use *The American Hebrew* for such purposes as were good for the community. I used it to translate Yiddish sketches into English. The first to do so, I created an interest in the Yiddish theatre, and for the plays of Jacob Gordin, whom I admired.

I grieved when the Yiddish theatre broke down; the interlude during which Maurice Schwartz brought about its renaissance did not last long.

Mr. Cowen could not maintain *The American Hebrew,* and when I left in 1914 to become a salaried officer of the Federation of American Zionists, he became a member of the Immigration Service of the United States for the rest of his life; he served the Jewish community well.

I have deep appreciation of Cowen's loyalty, his kindness and his devotion to Jewish interests. He had all the best qualities of a simple, pious Jew.

Another man I remember vividly from my *American Hebrew* days was Arnold Ehrlich. I have often asked myself—why did he come to see me so often in *The American Hebrew* office? It was not to explain his views on the Bible. I was remarkably ignorant at that time, but he liked to tell me the stories that were hidden away in the Biblical translations. He had worked with Delitzsch in Berlin, and helped him translate the New Testament into Hebrew. He had original and daring ideas in matters of language, and his series of Biblical commentaries in Hebrew display critical acumen. I might have become a pupil, but he was able to see at once that all I was good for was to listen to his explanation of Biblical texts, some of which were beyond me and not exactly fit for polite reading. He wrote an erudite book in German, *The Scriptures According to their Meaning*. It seemed that he had a genuine delight in breaking up the illusions of morality and decency taught by the classical texts which he was studying. I stopped seeing him with the excuse that I did not think I would make a good Hebrew scholar, and he said, "You certainly are right." However, he did not cease pestering me with his explanations, and I remember him as being an unsatisfied explainer who was going to tell me the Bible in his own way, whether I liked it or not. Not wishing to become involved in a serious controversy, I avoided him and broke off all relations. I understand he lived to a good old age; but his secret talent was never revealed to my dense mind.

Before I left *The American Hebrew* for the Zionist movement, I had an "affair" with Joseph Jacobs. I was going to leave because Shmarya Levin suggested that I devote all my time and become a paid official— Chairman of the Executive—and accept the same remuneration from the Zionist Organization that I was getting from *The American Hebrew*. I agreed and it was this that brought me into contact with Joseph Jacobs. He was to become the editorial writer and I would be free to take over my duties in the movement when he would return from England where he was living. He was a most interesting literary man, and a facile writer. He cared very little for Jewish affairs. He did his duty with precision and was a first-class worker. I had the opportunity to serve with him for quite a number of months and saw the ease of his performance. He could write the editorials of *The American Hebrew* (which occupied two pages) in a half-hour. I would provide him with the subjects, and he would provide the music—in other words, the words. If he did not have enough words, his first suggestion was to "lead" the articles. We were a good team; he represented the composition and I represented the motif.

Because of the war, Jacobs was delayed in returning to New York from his native London, and I carried on in both capacities in the interim. When he returned, I left, but he had given a lesson on how to write without getting excited or worrying that what anyone said mattered very much.

One of the most interesting personalities I encountered soon after my arrival in New York, and an early friend, was Abraham Solomon Freidus.

If you wanted to identify Freidus you would have to place him in the middle of the career of the Café Royale on the Lower East Side of New York—a rendezvous of intellectuals, strays and Yiddish actors. That would be before 1900, when he became a cataloguer of Hebrew books and soon thereafter Chief of the Judaica and Hebraica Divisions of the New York Public Library.

First you would know him as the collector of Jewish clippings of interest to Yiddish journalists or to his friends whose names appeared in the press. He had the habit of pulling a clipping out of his wallet and handing it, with a flourish, to a grateful recipient. Sometimes, too, the clipping was not at all coveted by the person who received it.

Then you might know him as the depositary of the budget that Judge Mayer Sulzberger of Philadelphia provided for the maintenance of Naphtali Herz Imber. When insatiable thirst made Imber indigent, as frequently it did before the next payment was due, Freidus was the patient target for Imber's caustic diatribes meant for Judge Sulzberger. I frequently served as buffer between them.

But if you wanted to see him really, he was a devoted Zionist who never found it necessary to join the discussions. If he was pleased, his cherubic face smiled, but he would remain silent. Born in Riga in 1867, he went to Palestine as a youth to serve as a farm hand in Zichron Yaacov. Illness forced his departure and he came to the United States in 1889. He spent his life in the Astor Library, at the Café Royale and among Jews.

Never married, he had a great admiration for the ladies, which was not expressed. He had few friends, but many admirers. He was fond of books, fond of readers of books, and pleased with Jews. He lived quietly, modestly, thriftily; what he thought remained with him.

An outstanding librarian, at his death in 1923 he had created at the New York Public Library one of the most important Jewish collections in the world.

Editing *The American Hebrew* did not occupy my full time, so I simultaneously made excursions into other fields.

Cowen assigned me to serve on the campaign committee for Teddy Roosevelt, of which Oscar Straus was the Chairman.

For a short time I was a press agent together with Harry Scherman and Herman Bernstein.

Louis Mann commissioned me to write a play for him and paid me $300.

For about three months, too, I was editor of an English page for *The Jewish Herald,* from which the editor resigned, by suicide, because of a quarrel with his wife, a famous Yiddish actress.

Also, for a period after my arrival in New York, simultaneous with my editorship of *The American Hebrew,* I served as secretary to Leo N. Levi, national President of the Bnai Brith, one of the finest American Jewish personalities.

My duties involved, among other things, taking care of the Settlement House, run by the President, and of its restaurant. We developed a Bnai Brith Club on the Lower East Side which was an animated center of sociability. There I learned the virtues of "wiener schnitzel," which I subsequently rediscovered in every capital of Europe.

Leo Levi died in 1904, within a year of my association with him, and left me an orphan in the Bnai Brith wilderness.

On the day we learned of his death, David Bressler, Morris D. Waldman (later Executive Secretary of the American Jewish Committee) and I walked all the way up Broadway, drinking en route, and mourning his loss.

Simon Wolf, successor to Levi's unexpired term, introduced me to Washington and mint julep both.

Simon Wolf, titles apart, was the unofficial representative on matters Jewish before official Washington, and was used as such principally by the American Jewish Committee.

He had come to Washington, a boy of six, with an uncle. When I met him, he was a lawyer hobnobbing with politicians; he lived on a fine, wooded estate.

In appearance he gave the impression of a dilapidated Army man, hovering about military headquarters on the edge of war. In fact, he served in no army, having been rejected by the Union Army, for which he volunteered, because of poor eyesight. He was the author of a book on the service of Jews in the Civil War, which had quite a circulation and also had some effect on the establishment of the American Jewish Historical Society. For more than 37 years Wolf served as a delegate of the Central Jewish Organization in Washington.

When I arrived at Wolf's home, he offered me a drink. I was not an expert; I drank it. It happened to be a mint julep, the potency and quality of which were unknown to me. I left him with fond goodbyes. While waiting for a streetcar, I suddenly became conscious that I was feeling very peculiar, confused and drowsy. Fortunately for me the ride was long. By the time I reached my hotel, I was more normal; and there were no lasting effects.

In this period I began writing for the secular press.

I wrote an article on James Barrie for a monthly magazine called *The Reader* in what I thought was Barrie's style. (Sinclair Lewis was the Managing Editor of this publication for a short time.) To my surprise, they published it and sent me $100 for it.

Following that I wrote a similar satirical article for the same magazine on Rudyard Kipling, for which I also received $100.

The article on Barrie prompted a letter of praise to the Editor, by John D. Williams, business manager for Charles Frohman (who was a great admirer of Maude Adams and whom Mr. Frohman brought before the American public during her stage career) "as the best pen portrait of Barrie either of us had ever read."

The strangest friendship I developed at that time was with the editor of *The Sunday Morning Telegraph.* For a period of about a year and a half I wrote a weekly piece for that racy newspaper on any subject that came to mind. Many of the stories were on Jewish subjects, most of them about the Yiddish theatre, but I never, during that whole time, ever met the editor to say "hello" to; nor later to say "goodbye." His name was MacMillan. He was a very dogmatic man, I learned, but he never inflicted a rejection on me. He seemed to be under the impression that I was infallible. This was obviously an error because the paper finally asked him for his resignation.

I also wrote for *The New York Daily Press.* These pieces were in the form of vignettes.

Aside from these deviations, I never ventured away from Jewish life in any way.

I believe I was the first translator of the beautiful stories of Isaac Leib Peretz. I was rather shy in approaching this task because I felt insecure—and rightly so. Nevertheless I think I captured many nuances of the word-pictures drawn by Peretz in the early days of his life. I can say, modestly, I had a high appreciation of Peretz's art long before he was well-known in this country. I put them in *The American Hebrew, The Morning Telegraph,* and various Anglo-Jewish weeklies. The Jewish Publication Society declined the privilege of printing these translations on the ground that I had neglected to make literal translations. This was true, but if I had, it would have been a miracle had I gotten the real flavor of these Yiddish stories. So I translated them with a certain freedom that made them understandable to anyone familiar with Yiddish.

When I came to New York I was profoundly impressed to discover that I could obtain sketches of I. L. Peretz in print with vowel signs, usually omitted to some extent in ordinary typesetting. Peretz had a printing library, so to speak, of his own. It was called *Literatur und Leben*, also, at other times, *Yonteff Bletter*. It stimulated me to translate a number of his sketches.

I still regard some of them as very good pieces of work. They indicated a writer of great sensitivity and imagination. I have always wondered why, in Yiddish literature, Peretz is not regarded as among the great storytellers but is always subordinated to Sholem Aleichem and to Mendele Mocher Sforim.

It was, curiously enough, my living in New York that reinforced the bonds that linked me to my people. When I came to New York in 1900 I felt as though I had gone back to Philipova, yet it was not the city itself—it was the Yiddish theatre.

When I saw the Yiddish theatre I felt that I had returned to the world I remembered from my boyhood in Rochester. That world was passing away; even in Rochester itself it could only be found in the cemetery.

But it came back again when I began seeing Yiddish plays. The people who spoke the language I first heard, who recalled the dark places wrapped in mystery, began to show themselves on the faces of those who played parts that were written in the language I only now began to understand properly. Yiddish was asleep in me, but the men and women on the Yiddish stage awoke memories that became animated and articulate and meaningful.

The men with the beards were the most fascinating. They all seemed to have the same name. They always looked something like "*der alter Shachne*" of my youth—the little old man with the short pointed beard who called me a "*shegetz*" when I was a little boy sick in bed with the measles and who would pinch my cheek in gentle reproach. They all looked to me like the Yiddish actor Mogulescu. Mogulescu looked like a rabbi who looked like a teacher. He could sing a song, he could dance a little, and he could always draw a tear when he wanted to and bring a smile when he thought the audience might be losing interest in his antics.

It was the Yiddish theatre that taught me Yiddish, or rather revived the knowledge of the language that had been dormant in me ever since childhood. Jewish life has always been associated in my mind with Yiddish—not Hebrew.

Hebrew came from a long way off. It spoke the words of the Prophets, of the Psalms. It was the Bible, remote and revered. But Yiddish was the *Golus*—the Exile—and even though I have spent my life in a movement that tried to restore the Hebrew language as the medium of a restored Jewish people, the Yiddish theatre always made me feel a part of the Eternal in the Jewish people. I was utterly absorbed in the Yiddish theatre, and saw practically every Yiddish play produced between 1900 and 1914.

The founder of the Yiddish theatre in Europe was Abraham Goldfaden. All of his melodramas and musicals were produced while he was abroad. It was the backbone of all the Yiddish theatres everywhere. Many of his songs were sung as long as the Yiddish theatre existed. The Yiddish actors from the other side came over here and established theatres on New York's Lower East Side. The plays were written by other people, the outstanding playwrights being Jacob Gordin, Shomer and David Pinski, with Hirschbein later.

The idea that one kind of Yiddish—Yiddish Yiddish—was spoken in the Yiddish theatre is a misunderstanding. At first a German Yiddish was spoken, then a Polish Yiddish, and then each man spoke the kind of Yiddish he preferred.

It was Jacob Gordin who created a common language in the Yiddish theatre. He was the magician who evoked theatre out of the Yiddish the Jews spoke in Russia. I knew most of his plays—the good and the bad; those he adapted, those he rewrote and those he mangled. Indeed, the spirit of Gordin was responsible, to a large extent, for the prestige of the Yiddish theatre, and when he died, it died together with him, though of course other factors contributed.

It is true that a few years later Maurice Schwartz tried to continue it, on his own, but the structure had changed. The benefit performances were not there and the audience was not there. Nobody knew whom the plays were being written for.

There were many fine actors in the Yiddish theatre. Among them were Jacob Adler, Kenia Lipzin, S. Mogulescu, Bertha Kalich and Morris Moscowitch, who spent the better part of his life on the American and English stage. The same can be said of Paul Muni, whose introduction to the theatre was on the Yiddish stage, where he was known as Muni Weisenfreund.

I vividly remember all the plays I saw. I knew all the actors and actresses personally or otherwise. It was a theatre maintained by a few talented writers, but mainly through adaptations from other dramatists.

I knew Jacob Gordin very well for a long time. He had come here as a Russian journalist aligned with one of the Russian political parties that played an important part in the Jewish life of New York. He was not successful as a journalist. He was more Russian than Jewish. It was by chance that his attention was directed to writing for the Yiddish theatre; one of his first plays had to do with Russian-Jewish life. He gradually came nearer to Jewish life, but though he acquired a reputation for adapting plays, he always had to struggle for a livelihood. He was not a very good party man of any sort. In the course of time he became the author of a number of good Yiddish plays that drew audiences from among those who remembered the old customs in Russia. It was said that many of his plays were taken from original Russian dramas. There was a great deal of truth in this; he never denied it. But, by devoting himself to the Yiddish theatre it became quite natural for him to find the Jewish form of a theme with more than a casual interest. His best plays were performed by Madame Kenia Lipzin. She made a lasting impression in *Shehitah*—a tragic play on a strictly Jewish theme. He was also the author of *The Jewish King Lear* which was successfully played by both Jacob Adler and David Kessler. In many ways his most interesting play was *Gott, Mensch und Teufel*.

I remember Gordin's rehearsing a comedy of Molière in which he played the part of the leading lady in spite of the fact that he had a Herzlian beard. He did not seem to have the slightest hesitation about it.

This rehearsal, which I witnessed in a building devoted to small meeting rooms, is indelibly engraved in my memory; it was there I met my future wife, Charlotte (Eddie) Schacht. She had come with her brother Gustav, who in the course of time became one of the ablest character actors on the Yiddish stage, and whom I had met on other occasions. It was here, too, that I met for the first time Joseph Barondess; he was the first Jewish labor leader who openly and courageously took a position with the entire labor movement in favor of Zionism, and in fact became a leading labor Zionist. Charlotte was cast to play opposite Barondess, notwithstanding the fact that he was a tall, brawny man with a classical head and no knowledge whatsover of acting, and she was a young, very pretty girl. She made a deep impression on me at first sight. She never again played in a theatre, but took singing lessons for a number of years; she had a lovely voice.

Samuel Shiffman, who later changed his name to Shipman, the name his successful Broadway hits are known under, was a young playwright I met at Columbia when we attended classes there together. He persuaded me to invite a number of professors from the university, interested in the theatre, to come down to the Thalia Theatre to witness a matinee performance of *Gott, Mensch und Teufel*. This play used the theme of Goethe's *Faust*. It tells the story of a scribe who is tested by the devil with good fortune; he becomes a manufacturer of *talesim* and commits a number of sins. He divorces his old wife because she has given him no children. He abuses his friends by making them work in his factory at starvation wages. He makes his second wife unhappy by his indifference. Finally he commits suicide. David Kessler played the lead; Mrs. Kalich played the second wife; Morris Moscowitch was the devil. These parts became star parts for members of every Yiddish stock company that had competent actors of the class of Kessler, Kalich and Moscowitch, and more particularly, the part for Mogulescu, the comedian, who played the father. Shiffman and I were responsible for having this play become well known on the higher level of Morningside Heights. Shiffman became a successful playwright. He was the author of plays written for Louis Mann and his wife, Clara Lippman, which had long runs on Broadway. He made a big hit in his play *East is West*, in which Fay Bainter was starred. He translated one of the plays of Jacob Gordin into English for Kessler. It ruined Kessler and killed his ambitions to leave the Yiddish theatre. Shiffman never was interested in writing for the Yiddish theatre; he made a lot of money on Broadway instead. He and I were close friends for many years.

For some reason I always had a deep affection for the Yiddish actor, Sigmund Mogulescu. He was such a simple man and he had such a pathetic, atrocious voice which he was able to use with deep tragic tones. He was a little fellow with a long nose and wobbly legs. You were never able to see him alone. He always played parts that required an older woman to play his wife. This stage wife was a necessary feature to his personality. In the beginning of his career he played the farces of Goldfaden and Shomer, and he would sing the melodies of the music halls. As the Yiddish theatre developed, he was a necessary personality for the parts of clowns, of poor people, of people with hoarse voices who could not utter any melodic sounds. He was a great success, and he was never aware of it. His modesty was remarkable in an actor. My friend Shiffman and I once appointed ourselves a committee of two to interview Mogulescu in order to persuade him to allow us to organize a benefit performance in which he would play his favorite part. That did not mean that he was in need of money—it was a token of respect and honor to the actor and, incidentally, provided him with a little extra cash. Mogulescu at once said to us, "The idea of a benefit perform-ance is a great one, but why should you do it for me? I am not an actor of great parts, like Adler. I don't compete with David Kessler. I'm just an ordinary actor that plays in farces and sings a song." So we said: "It's agreed. What do you say—what play shall it be?" He replied: "The best part I have ever done, the best there is in the Yiddish theatre so far as I'm concerned, is *Haman the Third.*" Both of us expressed our opinion by laughing out loud. "We're friends of yours and we mean to honor you, but allow us to say that we would not have the nerve to come before a theatre public and let you play in *Haman the Third.* You ought to be ashamed of yourself. You are a character actor as good as Adler in the right part. You are a better character actor than Kessler in any part. We suggest the appointment of a committee of dramatic critics to select the part for you." Mogulescu looked around like a trapped animal and said: "That will never happen to me as long as I live. I know what part to play—what do they know?" We tried to calm him down. "Don't get excited. The best part for you is Lazar in *Gott, Mensch und Teufel.* Don't argue—just listen. Lazar is a father who loves his son and doesn't want him to make a fool of himself; doesn't want him to divorce his wife, not only because he is a good Jew, but because she doesn't de-serve it. He doesn't want him to marry a young girl; that doesn't fit the son. He pities him; at the same time he loves him. Just remember the scene with the bride-to-be and the chant you sing. Remember your fears and your hopes and your chagrin as a Jew when your own son is compelled to commit suicide rather than carry on a life that doesn't suit him. Remember how all audiences that saw you have great respect and love for you, and how they will remember forever the great im-pression you made on them with this beautiful part." We watched the effect on the little man. We saw the look of desperation in his eyes. He turned away and looked at us as if we were his prospective murderers; then he said: "I don't want to be remembered for being that old father. I want to be remembered singing and dancing in *Haman the Third.* It's *Haman the Third,* or nothing!"

The fact is, it was nothing. He refused to play; we refused to give him the benefit performance; we went away deeply hurt but never able to forget the reason for his rejection of our offer to him.

When Mogulescu died there was a tremendous funeral. As usual, he drew a great audience. I have the impression they would probably have agreed with his rejection of our offer. They also loved the clown!

There was, also, of course, a thriving German theatre on the Lower East Side. It followed the models of theatres in Germany, and German plays (in German) were seen on the stage of the Irving Street Theatre for many years. It was a stock company, the actors who came over playing the whole season.

Russian actors also came and also had a stock company, but they could not play the season because the Russian theatre never became an integral part of the scene and the actors could not make a living. Alla Nazimova was wooed away by Frohman, and her co-star, Paul Orlenoff, did not stay long.

A story I can vouch for personally is told of Paul Orlenoff. He was not a Jew, but he was greatly admired by the Lower East Side as an actor; he was a fine one. The Jewish community, always a great supporter of the Russian theatre, gave a benefit performance for Paul Orlenoff. The performance was given in the Thalia Theatre, and Orlenoff drew a large audience. Unfortunately, he got good and drunk before the performance; he stood in the wings barely able to keep his balance while listening for his cue. He was surrounded by well-wishers who were panic-stricken when they saw his condition. It was obvious that he could not endure, but the women flattered him, the men praised him, and everyone said "Pluck up your courage." Nevertheless he shook on his feet.

Suddenly the announcer stepped to the center of the stage and announced how honored and gratified he was to present one of the great stars of the theatre—Mr. Paul Orlenoff. To the utter astonishment of everyone backstage, when Orlenoff heard his name, he straightened up like a ramrod, marched to the apron of the stage, forgot he was drunk, and delivered an extract from one of the classical plays of the Russian repertoire. There was not a trace of drunkenness in his brilliant performance. It was thought he had feigned his intoxication.

While it was in the Yiddish theatre that I found, resurrected before me, the Jewish life I had last seen in Rochester, when I came to New York the totality of American Jewish life was revealed to me by the network of Jewish social, educational and religious institutions springing up and enveloping rapidly the growing number of immigrants from

Europe. An assessment of Jewish assets in the early 1900's is vividly before me.

When I arrived in New York in 1900, the Rabbinate played a singularly important leadership role. Quite a number of the important Rabbis of this period spoke German and poor English.

For example, there was Kaufmann Kohler, head of the Hebrew Union College in Cincinnati and Rabbi of Temple Beth El in New York, who could not be clearly understood when he spoke English. He was more at home in German; so was Isaac Moses; also Dr. David Davidson, a humble, modest man, who subsequently left the pulpit and established a very competent school.

Samuel Schulman later joined Kaufmann Kohler at Temple Beth El, presumably to bolster the English-speaking element. Born and bred on the Lower East Side, and educated at the *yeshiva*, Schulman did the unexpected—became a candidate for the Theological Seminary of the Reform Temple Emanu-El and was sent for study to Germany. He returned a Reform Rabbi and an anti-Zionist—with whom I often tilted—a vigorous debater and controversialist, always interesting to read. He was the first Reform Rabbi with the audacity to criticize Israel Zangwill for introducing "Children of the Ghetto" on the New York stage with Milton Lackaye and Blanche Yates as the leads.

There was also George Alexander Kohut, the son of the eminent Alexander Kohut, who spoke German very well, and, of course, first-class English.

I knew George Alexander Kohut primarily as a young poet, frail, handsome, debonair and cheerful. When his father became a widower early in life, he married Rebecca Kohut who became the devoted mother of his family of children. She was a worker in the Jewish community in her own right and made a deep impression on many areas of Jewish life.

George Kohut was an educator, but he was also a practitioner of the art of writing sonnets and loved to write them for various occasions. I knew him also as a young man who was paying attention to the young daughter of my employer, Philip Cowen. She obviously did not encourage the young poet, for she married someone else.

George Kohut was distinguished for his special attention to the diary of Ezra Stiles, an outstanding minister who made voluminous notes of his encounters with scholars, especially Hebrew scholars. Kohut took a fancy to the Stiles diary and determined to make excerpts of references to all Hebrew scholars. This collection of commentaries was published in *The American Hebrew* and republished in pamphlet form.

Kohut devoted a great deal of time to copying the excerpts and saw to it that punctuation and spelling and various type forms necessary to reproduce them appeared correctly in his work. I had something to do with the reading of the proofs. It was amazing how Kohut copied Stiles' book—the caps and small caps and brackets all faithfully reproduced. The modern method of printing had not yet appeared in *The American Hebrew*. The fellow who set the type in *The American Hebrew* was himself a superior typesetter and he would not let any of Kohut's innovations pass his sharp eye. He insisted that what was ordained by Stiles should be acceptable to Kohut. At any rate I profited a great deal by the mania of Kohut. It made a first-class proofreader out of me. The only one I ever envied as a proofreader was Henrietta Szold.

Dr. Adolph Radin was a half-breed—he spoke German, but also some kind of English. He was a rabbi, a graduate of the Wolozhin Yeshiva, and a bon vivant with a strong sense of humor. In 1905, he took charge of the pulpit of the People's Synagogue. Later he became a passionate Zionist, involved in all the movement's activities. When he died, it was said that 40,000 persons followed his cortege.

There was also Henry Samuel Morais, a free lance Rabbi in New York, son of Sabato Morais. His specialty was to criticize violations of Jewish law and to write vicious letters to the press about the violators.

The better pulpits of the better Temples were held by Reform Rabbis. It was always strange to me that Gustave Gottheil, who spoke faultless English, and was a leading Zionist, should also have occupied the pulpit of the leading Reform Temple and the nest of anti-Zionism, Temple Emanu-El.

The Orthodox Rabbis were for the most part local individuals who had no decided public views that anybody paid attention to, because the rabbi was not a spokesman for a community; he was in fact merely an official.

I credit A.H. Fromenson with leading me towards Yiddish journalism. Fromenson was the sprightly editor of the English page of *The Tageblatt*. His wife Ruth, later a leader of Hadassah, was a native of Rochester, whom I knew very well. Fromenson's father was a *chazan* who sang with his sons in the Nussbaum Orthodox Shul in Rochester. Fromenson must have been a very young man when he came to *The Tageblatt* whose English page he made very readable and informative and loyally Jewish. *The Tageblatt* served, through its English page, as auxiliary reading for the general run of young people in the United States. Fromenson maintained its standards with a certain sparkle and carelessness. Later, he became a publicity man for many Jewish causes, Zionist and non-Zionist, including the J.D.C. (American Jewish Joint Distribution Committee).

From 1880 Yiddish papers were a matter of family ownership. The leading New York Yiddish daily, *The Tageblatt,* was owned by the Sarasohn family; *The Jewish Morning Journal* by the Saperstein family. *The Jewish Daily Forward* was collectively owned by the labor unions.

Saperstein had an editor who dominated him; his name was Peter Wiernik. The character of the paper emerged not from programs or ideologies, but from the nature of the persons running the publication. Gedaliah Bublick, editor of *The Tageblatt*, was a Mizrachi. Abraham Cahan, editor of *The Forward,* successfully established his influence over a staff of writers. Later *The Day,* published and owned by David Shapiro and Morris Weinberg, became one of the most brilliantly edited publications; subsequently it absorbed *The Jewish Morning Journal.* There was also *The Jewish Herald,* which had a good editor in Boukansky, who was also the Yiddish editor of *The Maccabean.*

Outside of New York there were also a number of Yiddish dailies, particularly in Chicago and Cleveland, but they never attained the circulation of the New York papers; all have since vanished.

At first the Yiddish newspapers were simply competitors. But as ideas became clarified, the papers adopted forms of class appeal. *The Forward* became Socialist, *The Tageblatt* orthodox, *The Day* progressive. On Zionism they reflected their basic views.

Today only *The Forward* and the *Jewish Day-Morning Journal (Tog)* survive.*

The professional Yiddish journalist came late in the life of the community. In the early days writers who created names for themselves hailed from the *yeshiva.* One of them was George Zelikovitch who wrote articles about "scientific" affairs—inventions, pure and simple, but always covered with the glamor of encyclopedic knowledge. Another, identifiable with *The Tageblatt*, was Johann Paley, who had some learning but depended largely on his own personal inventions. He was the beginner of sensationalism in Yiddish. Shaikevitch, whose pen

---

*Since then the latter has ceased publication. Ed.

name was *Shomer,* was the man who put his mark on serial stories. It seemed he was able to write sensational "*romanen*" in his sleep. He would keep two or three of them going in different papers at the same time. Abe Cahan, who was identified with the life of *The Forward,* did his best to transfer to the pages of the Yiddish papers the features of the English papers. He contrived a column "A Bundle of Letters" which kept going for years and was the most interesting part of the contents of *The Forward.* Abner Tannenbaum was the writer of encyclopedic articles for *The Tageblatt.* Abe Cahan had the habit of centering his attacks on particular individuals. He made the life of Jacob Gordin a perpetual misery and hounded him to the day of his death. He also attempted to ruin Sholem Asch for having written the life of Jesus Christ. His pet aversion to Gordin had to do with constant plagiarisms which were well known to Cahan, who came from Russia.

From the ivory tower of *The American Hebrew* to which all Anglo-Jewish exchanges came, I was able to scrutinize every one of them every week and weigh their value to *The American Hebrew,* as well as to the American Jewish community. The Anglo-Jewish press in those days had very little telegraphic news and very little need for it. It got along with the general exchange of news as it was carried by the daily press. If the general press gave attention to an item, the Anglo-Jewish press took notice of it.

Most of these Anglo-Jewish weeklies were edited by rabbis of local pulpits. Considering the resources of that period (between 1900 and 1914) and the absence of a sense of Jewish news values, it may be said that the balance sheet was not trivial—but also not exciting.

The most popular was *The American Israelite,* published by Isaac M. Wise, founder of the Reform Judaism in the United States. But there were others: *The American Hebrew* of New York, *The Hebrew Standard* of New York, and a number of other free lance publications. *The American Israelite* had a fair circulation from the beginning. It was the organ of Reform Judaism. It was a paper well read, too, because at that time members of Reform synagogues were interested in their Temples. Later they were much less parochial. Rabbi Spitz edited *The Jewish Voice* of St. Louis. Rabbi Isaacs was the editor of *The Jewish Messenger,* of New York City. Felix M. Gerson edited *The Jewish Exponent* in Philadelphia. *The Emmanu-El* in San Francisco was edited by Rabbi Voorsanger, and *The Hebrew Standard* by H.D. Solomon in Canada.

There was also *The Jewish Comment* of Baltimore, edited by Louis Levine, brother-in-law of Henrietta Szold. He was distinguished by the fact that, unlike other Anglo-Jewish editors, he paid a writer a fee for whatever he printed. The fee was not high; but it was paid regularly.

The Jewish Publication Society (organized in 1888) owed its first years of existence to the zeal and devotion of two women, Miss Henrietta Szold and Mrs. Katherine Scherman, mother of Harry Scherman.

Henrietta Szold was the dynamic center of the Society, and Mrs. Scherman was the traveling salesman who spent many years canvassing the country for subscribers. A publication committee was organized which was a creditable achievement, but the engineer of the achievement was, in fact, Henrietta Szold, who was the secretary and editor, the proofreader of manuscripts and everything else that was necessary to make the Publication Society work.

From the beginning to this date, it was always, insofar as possible, a non-partisan organization.

The Jewish Publication Society once rejected my original stories about "Joey." But only this year, the management of the Society has proposed that an anthology be built around them because "here is a story of Jewish adjustment in the United States without the bitterness and lawlessness which the modern Jewish author of fiction has dragged into that aspect of our history."

The American Jewish community earned the right to publication of a Jewish Encyclopedia in 1901, due to the energy, imagination and skill of Dr. Isidore Singer, a very able organizer, who had been born in Vienna. He secured the financial backing of Jacob H. Schiff and others. Further he interested Funk and Wagnalls in publication, and persuaded Isaac K. Funk to become Chairman of the Board and Frank H. Vizetally to become Secretary of the Board.

Singer himself had the title of projector and managing editor. The 400 members of the Board, scholars and specialists, included an admixture of Zionists and non-Zionists, among them: Cyrus Adler; Wilhelm Bacher; Gotthard Deutsch; Richard Gottheil; Emil G. Hirsch; Joseph Jacobs; Kaufmann Kohler; Frederick de Sola Mendes; Herman Rosenthal; Isidore Singer; Crawford H. Toy.

The article on Zionism was written by Richard Gottheil. In that first volume, not a great deal could be written about Zionism as ideal or theory, as the movement was still too young. The most active member of the board was Frederick de Sola Mendes, brother of Pereira.

The settlement movement came into existence in a number of large cities in which there was a slum element and people of means thought of Americanization as something that should be applied more especially to foreign sections where culture could be administered by specialists.

In the early 1900's, there was the Hull House in Chicago run by Jane Addams; there was Lillian Wald's Nurses Settlement and the University Settlement, both on the Lower East Side of New York. There were institutions in the United States which were supported by Baron de Hirsch. There was the Clara de Hirsch Club for Women, the Educational Alliance and the Woodbine Farm School. In these settlements visitors established a residence and sought to bring culture and modern ways into the experience and knowledge of the poor neighbors. Chauvinists of all groups resented the intrusion of these aliens, although they had the best of motives. The foreign neighborhoods all felt the suggestion of a melting pot, under pressure, but these settlements had little direct influence on the Jews.

It may be said that the Society of Ethical Culture, organized by Dr. Felix Adler, was also a settlement, in that its influence reached out of the synagogue and influenced young men and women to pursue their studies under the influence of personalities of integrity.

Felix Adler was a great ethical Jewish personality who deeply influenced American life when released to American service by his exclusion from the Reform Rabbinate over doctrinal disputes.

There was a Scotchman by the name of Edward King; a philosopher by the name of Thomas Davidson who taught at the Educational Alliance on East Broadway. After his death, his students, led by Morris Cohen, the philosopher, formed the Thomas Davidson Society. Charlotte Schacht, whom I married, was proud to be a member.

Some of these personalities moved groups profoundly in a way beyond the experience of a rabbi. The idea of friendly and social intercourse was a natural part of the Ethical Culture movement. Reform Judaism, which alleged that it too had a world mission, did not regard this aspect of social life as a part of it.

In the ensuing years the YMHA also proved to be a form of settlement.

I was once coaxed by a Rochester friend of mine to visit Miss Lillian Wald's Nurses Settlement. Although I had been invited several times, I was very shy and did not relish meeting people I didn't know. My friend from Rochester Miss Josephine Schatz, a school teacher, resided in the Settlement and introduced me to Miss Wald, who had already established a reputation as a competent, friendly social worker who used her connections in order to do good among the people she could influence. I knew quite a number of the people who were present— Yiddish writers, young lawyers, Zionist personalities, young students, and people just becoming known in the Jewish community. The atmosphere of friendliness overawed me. The evening of sociability was used by Miss Wald to strike up new friendships for her Settlement, which provided free nursing by visiting nurses who resided in the Settlement. I was surprised to find my Rochester friend behaving as though she were at home in this East Side milieu. I also knew quite a number of other young people who made the settlements the center of their intellectual and social life.

I remember vividly the impression made on me by the recital given by the Yiddish poet whom Miss Wald introduced. He was Morris Rosenfeld, the Yiddish lyrical poet and journalist, who was just then the vogue on the Lower East Side. He was the poet of Jewish labor. I had seen him as an amateur actor when I was a boy of 14 in Rochester. I remember paying attention to a girl and inviting her to come with me and hear Rosenfeld read his poetry. That was the first time I ever asked a girl for a date. My mother chided me for being too fresh and too young and admonished me not to do it again. He was a first-class poet, who gave a touch of Heine to his own poetry. He moved the audience visibly, and received tremendous applause. I knew him, too, as a man who wrote feuilletons for the Yiddish papers in which he interlocked his humorous observations with poetic lines in which he was very successful in expressing satirical comments on events of the day. Some time later I had the pleasure of reading a volume of Rosenfeld's poems translated into German by Berthold Feiwel, who made Rosenfeld well known and esteemed in Germany. Rosenfeld had his ups and downs in literature. He was successful in the Yiddish but he was always financially broke, and every now and then his financial situation called for support by his friends. He was known for his poems depicting slum conditions on the Lower East Side. He was not a Zionist, though some of his poetry touched upon the theme of wanderers.

I met American Zionists for the first time at a convention in Philadelphia in 1901. I wrote a report of that convention for *The Ameri-*

can Hebrew and gave distinction to Naphtali Hertz Imber, who was on the platform when the speaking took place. He was so careless, at that time, that he forgot to cover up a bottle of whisky sticking out of his coat pocket. That was very unfortunate for him, but fortunate for me, since the article I wrote about it attracted attention and brought about my becoming the editor of *The Maccabean*.

In the summer of 1901, I was asked by Dr. Stephen Wise to go with him to the office of the venerable Dr. Gustave Gottheil in Temple Emanu-El, where he asked me if I would agree to edit a magazine to be the first and official organ of the Federation of American Zionists. Dr. Wise had called to his attention the account I had written up of the Zionist Convention held in Philadelphia for *The American Hebrew,* which was the first time American Zionism had made the press.

The old rabbi was old indeed then (he died a year later); but I remember his rugged face, his resonant voice and his deep-set eyes. He looked like a picture I had seen of the Apache Chief Geronimo. He wore an ecclesiastical collar and a long frock coat. His hair was white and his nose very prominent; unlike his son, he had no beard. His smile was warm; he greeted me with encouraging words.

I accepted his invitation, and became the Managing Editor of *The Maccabean* (with no salary, since money was scarce and I had a paying position on *The American Hebrew*). It was the first Zionist paper in English published in the United States.

The first number of *The Maccabean* was issued in October, 1901. As I look back, that first issue had several interesting articles, and struck a clear Zionist note. When it is considered that it contained articles by Max Nordau, Henrietta Szold, H. Pereira Mendes, Jacob de Haas, Richard Gottheil, Moses Gaster, and a sketch by me that was a translation from Peretz, it will be realized that this was a very good beginning for a new magazine. It looked good, too, although I had great difficulties in getting it out because the printer didn't have enough type to run both forms at one time. It should be observed that in addition to the editors, none of the writers of the articles were paid anything for their work—which is nothing to brag about.

It was a tedious business. The publication was always in financial difficulties. It could not pay for articles or editorial services. It regularly skipped issues to save expense. It owed its continued existence to the devotion and patience of David H. Lieberman who, although engaged in an engrossing manufacturing business, spent all his spare time and

much of his money to maintain *The Maccabean*. Lieberman was a
remarkable personality; he applied to *The Maccabean* all his skill as an
experienced manufacturer. He scraped and saved to keep it going. He
himself kept its books; he supervised its mailings; he was its accredited
beggar. He went about with a little notebook in which, in very small
handwriting, he kept all the accounts, from year to year, tabulated,
classified, and could at a moment's notice tell you how much money had
been lost, how much less money was being lost, how many subscribers
there were—in fact, the little notebook was a complete bookkeeping set.

In the second issue of *The Maccabean* (November 1901) I republished
an essay written by Dr. Baruch Felsenthal, then a rabbi in Chicago,
and an active Zionist both with his pen and his voice for many years,
in which he presented a clear account of the principles underlying the
Zionist movement.

It said in part: "Judaism is more than a religion, more than a system
of ethics; more than certain racial qualities with which a peculiar people
are endowed. It is the composite of all the above mentioned qualities. It
is the synthesis of all the Jewish people have produced, experienced,
endured and have aspired to. It is this composite expression of Jewish
life for the preservation of which the Zionist movement stands." It was
the first time such an article appeared in the Anglo-Jewish press of the
United States. It was reprinted in a number of American-Jewish periodicals, and made a deep impression, especially upon anti-Zionist
Reform rabbis.

I was the Managing Editor for about a year, until Jacob de Haas
became Secretary of the Federation of American Zionists and also took
over the Editorship of the official Zionist organ; but I continued my
cooperation throughout, and subsequently, after the retirement of de
Haas, I again became Editor of *The Maccabean*. In fact this continued
intermittently until about 1913.

How empty the Jewish world would have been if the dramatic personality of Theodor Herzl had not appeared on the Jewish stage of the
Zionist Congress at Basle in 1897! If a Jewish Parliament had not opened
its doors for the first time; if a Jewish international debate, with delegates
from all over the world, had not discussed the solution of the Jewish
problem; if for the first time the words "shekel" and "delegate" had
not been used in an international assembly ringing to the declamations
of Max Nordau; if for the first time the Jewish people had not explained
themselves to the world and demanded the restoration of rights to an

ancient territory they had been excluded from for two thousand years.

I have always been irritated when asked how I became a Zionist in the first place. By the time I was identified with the movement I had gotten into a habit of never answering the question. I resented anyone who put it to me. My Zionism had always been, as it were, organic; it was a natural state of mind, so it seemed to me, for any Jew who was surrounded by Jews and interested in Jews.

My eye was accustomed to detect a Jewish name or a Jewish word in any newspaper that made reference to a Jew or a Jewish event, or a Hebrew or an Israeli. I was born with an intuition for things Jewish.

That was why when I came to New York in 1900 and found people who called themselves Zionists, who talked Yiddish, who knew of the things that I knew and liked, I was forever bound to the cause they were advocating, and clung to that cause all the days of my life.

This attitude of mine was of course typical of many Jews, doubtless the overwhelming majority, especially of Jews who came from the vibrantly alive Jewish communities of Eastern Europe.

But it was not exactly the same thing as the politically organized Zionist movement I was to spend so much of my life helping to shape. When I first came to New York there were no traces at all of an active *Zionist movement,* as distinct from the *Zionist state of mind* natural to most Jews. While potentially in existence, so to speak, the Zionist movement was invisible.

I met Zionists in clubhouses on the Lower East Side. Their counterparts occupied their own quarters in the Jewish section of Philadelphia; they could also be met in the Jewish quarter of Chicago; but it took some time to establish what might be called national headquarters.

The Federation of American Zionists never had meetings in the early 1900s. If Richard Gottheil, the President, wrote a letter, he wrote it from his own office.

The first public affair I remember was a shekel campaign with Jacob de Haas. I was not there, but was told about it by Jacob Fishman, Imber, and others who attended. I attended small meetings of Zionist student circles to whom I used to read stories.

The data of organized Zionism in the United States are very hard to get at. It was born in Chicago, but Zionists made themselves heard and felt in New York where there were greater facilities for speaking than in the Midwest. Leon Zolotkoff, Bernard Horwich and Max Shulman are usually given as the founders of Zionism in Chicago, but even in

RIPON COLLEGE LIBRARY
RIPON, WISCONSIN 54971

those early days there were more and better things done in New York than in Chicago.

Every day brought Zionists to the United States through Ellis Island. They came from towns that they were identified with, and when they met in New York they formed groups of their own selection from their own places. They had clubrooms; they had meeting places where lectures were delivered or debates conducted; they had names ready for them: They were Austro-Hungarian Zionists, Russian Zionists, Rumanian Zionists and so on. The leaders, on the other hand, did not spring into existence so easily.

As far as I recall, the Zionist movement at that time had only a few leaders. The venerable Gustave Gottheil, who was the rabbi of Temple Emanu-El, was one of them. Stephen S. Wise, too; he was one of the founders of the Federation of American Zionists and its first Secretary. Richard Gottheil, the son of Rabbi Gustave Gottheil, was the first President. I would add the name of Henrietta Szold as a Zionist because she had an educational influence in Jewish life as Secretary of the Jewish Publication Society. Judah L. Magnes came later; fresh from his studies in Germany, he entered Zionism through the excitement of the Kishinev pogroms. I think that this classification is fair enough about the situation as it was then.

In fact, the Zionist movement can be considered to have made its appearance through the reaction of the American Jewish community to the Kishinev pogroms of 1903; its leadership was assumed by Dr. Magnes. The Kishinev pogroms evoked a manifestation of self-defense. They also evoked the first fund raising campaign in which all Jews more or less participated in various ways, some through the American Jewish Relief Committee, some through the People's Relief Committee, some through working men's organizations, and some through the Federation of American Zionists, of which at that time Jacob de Haas was Secretary and then Dr. Magnes.

In those days, the Jews were deeply concerned with the Russian movement of emancipation. They had been looking forward to the liberation of Russia for many years. Their relation to the freedom movement in Russia was always cordial, friendly and very sensitive. Most Russian Jews were deeply concerned with the Russian revolutionary movement and in all its forms. They organized meetings and collected funds; their newspapers were partisans of the partisans of the revolution. I remember time and again being present at meetings at which emissaries of the revolution were received and acclaimed by the Jews of the East Side of New York. I remember "Babushka"; I remember Nicholas Tchaikowsky; I remember the various representatives of revolutionary parties coming to the United States and receiving a hearty welcome. When the Socialist movement split and there were Mensheviks and Bolsheviks, the Jews on the East Side split, too, and took part in the raging controversies. There were quite a number of Jews elected to the first Duma, among whom were Shmarya Levin and Simon Dubnow. I used to print pictures in *The American Hebrew* of these propagandists.

When Alla Nazimova and Paul Orlenoff came to the United States via London presenting the play "The Jews", the subject was one which made for divided opinion in the parties concerned with the revolution. The play had a great success in New York. It introduced Nazimova to the American stage.

As a matter of fact, Jewish concern was registered very strongly in the October 1917 revolution, out of which Lenin and Trotsky emerged. It is strange that this revolution, originally supported by Jews, eventually turned into an instrument of persecution of Jews. It pursued them with obstinate dogma and without the slightest compassion, even when Hitler appeared on the scene.

I remember vividly the Extraordinary Conference of American Zionists, summoned at the Hotel Marseilles in New York in 1914, in anticipation of responsibilities growing out of World War I. The call to the Conference was issued by Dr. Shmarya Levin, on behalf of the World Zionist Executive, and myself, as General Secretary of the American Federation of Zionists. This conference was attended by some 150 delegates, including members of the Mizrachi and the Poale Zion. It elected a Provisional Zionist Executive Committee, representing all branches of the Zionist movement in the United States; the first of its kind, empowered to act for American Zionists and for the World Zionist movement. It voted an Emergency Fund, with a goal of $200,000 for relief and other purposes.

The multiplicity of relief activities thus stimulated led to the formation of the American Jewish Joint Distribution Committee in November 1914, as a merger of The Central Relief Committee, representing the Orthodox groups; The People's Relief Committee, controlled by the Socialists, and The American Jewish Relief Committee, sponsored by leaders of the American Jewish Committee.

The most significant action of the Extraordinary Conference, however, was, in all probability, the election of Louis D. Brandeis as Chairman of the Provisional Committee.

It was through Jacob de Haas that I had come to know Brandeis some years before he was appointed to the U.S. Supreme Court in 1916 by President Wilson.

The first years of de Haas' arrival in the U.S. from England (he arrived in 1902) marked a period of close friendship between us. I knew him from his contributions to the first issues of *The Maccabean,* when I was editor. Also he had written for me in *The American Hebrew.*

I was in full agreement with de Haas in his plans to involve Brandeis in the Zionist movement and went with him a number of times to visit Brandeis in his office. Brandeis' consent to his nomination and election had been given in advance of the Extraordinary Conference.

I remember the first meeting of the Provisional Zionist Committee, where Brandeis took off his coat, rolled up his sleeves, took possession of the meeting, outlined its agenda and gave expression to his dynamic interest in the cause.

There was no doubt that de Haas looked upon the election of Brandeis as a great victory. He saw in Brandeis a successor to Theodor Herzl; his aim throughout was to bring about a combination of circumstances so that in the winning of the Balfour Declaration Brandeis was to act the part that was to have been played by Herzl. Fate decreed otherwise.

There is a general impression that the Zionist movement encountered the opposition of a great many Jews.

In the early 1900's nobody was greatly concerned about it. The American Jewish press had no views about Zionism even after Herzl held the first Congress. The labor movement in New York was Bundist. If a Reform rabbi were asked whether he believed in Zionism he might reply that it was not one of his interests—that he was first and last an American.

But the Zionists would not agree to let matters rest there. They said it was the duty of a Jew to be a Zionist. The issue was joined on that question.

Soon there were quite a number of people ranged on one side or the other. A pious Jew would be in favor of the tradition but not necessarily of the principle; a Reform Jew subscribed to the ideas of his rabbi. He was usually a "yes man." In fact, a rivalry raged within the two Theological Seminaries. The older, the Hebrew Union College, was American; the younger, the Jewish Theological Seminary, took the side of traditional ideas and was sympathetic toward old-country points of view. There were more vocal Reform rabbis than vocal Orthodox rabbis; but there were quite a few Reform rabbis who defied the attitude of their environment and whose voices rang out in the cause of Zion, principally the venerable Bernhard Felsenthal, the fearless Gustave Gottheil and the young, eloquent Stephen Wise.

When the Zionist movement, in its attempt to organize the latent Zionist piety of the great bulk of the Jews, took on an unmistakable political profile, those Jews who were still mesmerized by the American patriotic concept of the melting pot and the whole cluster of ideas associated with it took up an attitude of hostility to Zionism.

The Reform rabbis who came from Germany under the influence of emancipation believed that their mission to the United States required that they devote themselves to Americanization. For that reason they regarded any reference to the past or to tradition as being something that could not be harmonized with plunging into the melting pot.

In essence, Reform Jews were opposed to the Zionist movement because they actually felt uneasy about possible criticism of their interest in a special land claimed for the Jews. Some of the Reform Jews were friends of Zionists but opposed Zionism out of fear of being charged with dual loyalty to the U.S.A. and to Zionism. They were opposed to the Zionist Organization and its aims. They wanted to live their way of life in the United States, unoppressed by ideologies.

The actual Zionist situation was reflected when the Hebrew Union College forced the resignation of three faculty members because of their Zionist views. Professors Henry Malter, Max L. Margolis and Max Schlesinger were dismissed, whereupon Dr. Judah L. Magnes added to the sensation by resigning as Librarian. But even though this attitude of hostility grew, with the growth of Zionist influence, at root it was never as bitter and venomous as its debates suggested.

It took some time before a newspaper emerged that began to consider that its class interests required opposition to Zionism.

Just as the Zionists had to find themselves in their enemies, so their enemies had to find themselves in what they favored.

Slowly the movement in America was being prepared for the grandiose task that historic opportunity was later to assign to it.

In the first years of my interest in the Zionist movement, I was concerned with speaking—not writing. It is true that I was the Managing Editor of *The American Hebrew* and became the Managing Editor a year later of *The Maccabean* and that I was familiar with the machinery of a typewriter. But in the Zionist movement what was needed primarily was the speaker.

Often a speech in the plenum of the Zionist Convention by a Yiddish speaker was eloquent and emotional; it had respect for the intelligence of the meeting and was superior to a speech in stiff English with no persuasive power. In those early days Yiddish was the language of the public platform, and I was not a Yiddish speaker.

I might not have been able to write well, but speaking was a gift I soon acquired through practice. I could never write well enough, or find the time to do the writing, but it was very easy to talk off the cuff. So the words I spilled in the Zionist movement for about fourteen years were cast upon the water and never came back to me. Soon, a feeling of resentment arose in me, a sense of loss. I wanted to make what I said fit in form what I meant to say, with the result that I found myself writing my speeches and then delivering them as speeches. In this way I accumulated quite a lot of speeches on quite a lot of subjects.

But writing is a peculiarly hard taskmaster. Nothing ever sounded genuine; re-writing was a constant necessity. I have written in my life an incredible number of words and remember nothing of them except what was printed or typewritten. Nothing ever satisfied me when written. Rewriting became a fascination, with the result that I have rewritten more than I have written and can never feel the satisfaction of having finished anything in a satisfactory way.

In writing about the Zionist movement I never was able to think of myself as an actor in a play. I was one of the builders of a movement, the maker of a play. A large part of it was tragedy. It turned out to be a greater movement than we ever dreamed it would be. It grew faster than we ever thought it would be able to grow. It took a disorganized people, scattered, broken into fragments, with no center, no resources, pursued by disaster—and transformed this humble people into a miraculous agent for the revival of seemingly dead history.

I began these fragmentary autobiographical notes as an informal introduction to my life in the Zionist movement. But it appears I am incapable of writing a personal memoir with myself occupying center stage.

Perhaps my love of the theatre explains the detachment I require to view events in their proper perspective. I seem to see people moving about on a stage, and it is only then that I can record my impressions of them. But since it is difficult to be one's own spectator I cannot do the same for myself. I have always been quite fortunate in my selections of silences, and I feel that this is an appropriate occasion for one of them.

I must now stand aside and wave the reader on to survey, instead, the landmarks of my Zionist career as it unfolded.

Those landmarks are constituted by the articles I wrote, the speeches I made, and the people I knew. I think they keep pace with the organic development of the Zionist movement in America and the world. The Profiles and Vignettes are an indispensable counterweight to the abstraction of the articles, for the movement was, after all, borne by people.

So—Profiles, Vignettes, and articles recalled are my way of writing a memoir. I hope the reader will accept them as a more objective, if less personal method of recording living history.

New York City, 1962

Section II
The Stage and Its Players

THE STAGE AND ITS PLAYERS

INTRODUCTION

The best memoirs of the Zionist Movement are those colored by the lives of scores of unique personalities who occupied the Zionist stage in succession, each in his own way adding interesting chapters to the Zionist chronicle. Much has been written about the philosophy of the Zionist Movement, its achievements, its problems, its partisan controversies. Zionism became more and more vocal and heavily reminiscent with the years. It amassed a tremendous store of archives now resting in the Library of the Jewish Agency. In the last analysis, however, it was the creation of a generation of men of forceful personality and varied talents who, instead of being driven into alien fields, identified themselves with the destiny of their own people and thus were able to live out their lives with more dignity, with greater creativeness, among their own people. They made Zionism and, in turn, Zionism made them.

It does not serve my purpose to give an account of how I was diverted to its service, how it shaped and guided my life, how it made me feel a pulsating kinship with all things Jewish, good and bad. I was a contemporary of its pioneers in the United States and followed its development throughout the world with a pertinacity I cannot explain—in all kinds of weather, through all sorts of exaltations and defeats—down to the day when the State of Israel was clothed in sovereignty in 1948.

From 1913 onward I moved closer to the international scene and got to know the leading figures at Zionist Congresses—the propagandists, journalists, poets, organizers, the party leaders, the official and unofficial kibitzers who used the Congress as the stage for their self-display. The tenants of the larger part of my memory were these Zionists. I was in it at the beginning, and a wondering spectator through the years when, by a miracle, what could so easily have been an unrelieved and consummated tragedy, became the fulfillment of an age-old dream. In that world I lived the larger part of my life. I was attracted and repelled by its *dramatis personae*. They were my companions, my confidants, the objects of my admiration, the butts of my criticism. They fascinated and thrilled me. In the shadow of their performances I played the small part destiny assigned to me.

Leadership in Zionism had many facets. There were poets like Bialik, philosophers like Ahad Ha-am, and social reformers like A.D. Gordon who exercised a deep influence on the Movement, but were never an integral part of the life of the Organization. There were eccentrics like Hermann Schapira, the fumbling philosopher of Heidelberg, who came to the Congress with various projects and finally subsided (and died) when his proposal for a Jewish National Fund was placed on the agenda. There were men like Davis Trietsch, who brought the idea of having Cyprus serve as a temporary haven of refuge and heckled Theodor Herzl with the proposal at the early Congresses. There were men like the egocentric Alfred Nossig, the sculptor and poet, who crossed swords with Herzl and disappeared from the Zionist stage as if the earth had swallowed him. There were poets and artists who haunted the lobbies and the cafés and gave the Congress the disorderly aspect of a County Fair. Leadership in the usual sense came from the Platform, where Herzl was the first regal dominant figure. That Platform was reserved for the Advocate who, for the first time in two thousand years, not only aroused the hopes of a people for their Return and Redemption, but established the stage on which the drama of Redemption could be reviewed, criticized, rejected or applauded. The Congress was the World Theater of the Movement.

On the day Herzl first appeared in Basle it may be said that the curtain was raised on the spectacle of an organized effort to realize in modern terms the mystic hope of a long-delayed fulfillment. It seemed as if the ghosts of the ancient past had been exorcised and brought back to the living world as witnesses. The hazy background of the Stage reflected the rise and fall of the Jewish people from the days of Abraham, the Father, to the last struggle of the dying Hebrew Commonwealth. The witnesses in the shadow included Moses, the leader of the Exodus, the promulgator of the Law; Zerubavel, Ezra and Nehemiah who led the return from Babylon; the Maccabeans who fought for freedom against the Syrians; Bar Kochba, the leader of the last revolt against the Romans. Among the shadowy figures were the men of the Law, the men of piety, the philosophers and exegetes; the moralists and the preachers;

those who gave their lives for *kiddush hashem;* who suffered under the persecution of centuries and taught the Jewish people the arts of patience and restraint, and humility. With the last echoes of the expulsion from the Promised Land, all these heroes passed off the living stage and Jewish life took refuge in the underground, and so far as the world was concerned, Jews were strangers living under their feet, to all appearances plowed under, raising their heads only to be flogged back whence they came.

The French Revolution was the herald of a new day. The emancipation of all the oppressed was proclaimed, but the freedom offered to the Jews was not an invitation to re-create their own freedom in their own land. It was an invitation to join in the equalitarian procession, carrying the banners of other civilizations, merging in a pseudo-freedom which for them meant their national extinction.

The Zionist Movement challenged history. It called a halt to what seemed to be an inevitable trend toward self-effacement. It turned the flow of Jewish life into its ancient channels of self-revelation and redemption. The Jews were organized against the Emancipation through a desperate attempt to recall to life their own civilization hidden under the burden of neglect and obscurity. Instead of adapting the coloring of their environment, their demand was to be recognized as a living, aspiring people in their own garb, with their own language, with their own social conceptions, in their own land. They asked for the right to rebuild their own home in their own image.

The whole Movement converged toward the Zionist Congress—the stage on which the leaders played their parts—heroic, melodramatic, comic, too. There, the vocabulary of an organized people found utterance. In its plenum and committee rooms, in its foyers and cafés, in its newspapers and through their correspondents the vocabulary of the Jewish renascence was created—the clichés of a parliament, the forms of organized debate, the programs of contending parties. A propaganda that encircled the world was given wings. Out of the many languages spoken, gradually one language took possession of the scene. Out of the many legal systems and procedures they got to know a common method through experience. The intellectual conceptions of emancipation, as well as the doctrines of the Marxists, were modified and developed to accord with the demands of Jewish rebirth; for the new life was not to be built on the dogmas of alien civilizations; it was not to be a plagiarism or an imitation; it was to work out its own destiny in consonance with the revelations of its own sages and prophets and poets. The trend of history had to be reversed and brought back to the field of Jewish self-emancipation.

From 1897 to 1948, with brief interruptions caused by war, the history of the Rebirth was recorded in the Zionist Congress. Every issue that arose in Jewish life was exposed and discussed there or in the Actions Committee or in the Zionist press or in the party conferences. Every change in the conditions of Jewish life in Palestine or in the Diaspora found its record there. Every Zionist of note registered his appearance in its proceedings in person or through indirect participation. The Congress took notice of the organization of the Galut, the progress of the Aliyah from decade to decade, the advances and retreats in the political field, the achievements of the budget-makers and the fund-collectors. The portraits of the leading actors were limned in words, descriptions or in dramatic conflict, and the names of the workers in the fields, the builders of the communes and the cities, were called from the rostrum.

In Herzl's day there was grace and dignity in its proceedings; there was majesty which was seldom revealed in later days. The floor was taken by men like Max Nordau, Alexander Marmorek and Israel Zangwill who returned from the free world to the platform of their own people. But the first *besetzung* of leadership soon made way for others. The Russians, the Poles and the Germans came over and took possession of the floor and of the platform. The formidable Ussishkin challenged David Wolffsohn, the merchant of Cologne. The "democratic faction" was swept forward into commanding positions.

Then came World War I; Chaim Weizmann, the chemist; Louis D. Brandeis, the American judge who never appeared at a Zionist Congress; and the Balfour Declaration. Vladimir Jabotinsky made his stormy appearances, like the hero in an Italian melodrama. The strident, challenging voice of Robert Stricker was heard. The economist Arthur Ruppin came to plan its economy. The vanguard of the labor movement made its appearance. The general debate developed into a rowdy exhibition; the Labor party to the left and the Mizrachi, just as vociferous, to the right. Leo Motzkin demonstrated his matchless skill as a parliamentarian. In the ferment of events between the two world wars, the stage was filled with men from England like Joseph Cowen, Frederick Kisch and Harry Sacher; Americans like Henrietta Szold and Stephen S. Wise; Austrians like Rabbi Osias Thon, Senator Ringel and Rabbi Chajes; proletarian leaders like Nachman Syrkin, Ber Borochov and Berl Katznelson, S. Kaplansky and Chaim Arlosoroff. As the Movement grew, the whole stage became more and more proletarian in manner and method, and party strife brought its divisive problems to the arbitrament of democratic procedures with a great deal of creaking of the parliamentary machinery. The National Home took over more and more of the agenda. The "budget" absorbed more attention. It was the inevitable cause of terrific controversies of class interests. The underground defensive force of Haganah made its presence felt and when World War Two came, the State was ready to burst its undercover wrappings, step out into the open and take over the molding of its own destiny.

From the records of that bustling, crowded stage—from the memories of personal experiences of fifty years—I have selected for consideration two score or more personalities, mingling the high and the low, and described them as I knew them, without prejudice. I have tried to give meaning to their lives in the setting of the Zionist drama; less of history and more of personality. In some instances I may have followed a wrong angle; I may have disregarded the conventions and contradicted the official tradition of unrelieved eulogy, and I may have transgressed protocol and social tact.

These profiles are not put forward as substitutes for biographies. With the exception of the piece on Theodor Herzl, they are sketches and impressions of personalities I knew whose lives were implicated in Zionism, more or less—leading it, contributing to its progress or hovering on its periphery. I had hoped to recapture within the form of a Profile the lingering memories of a long life in which I walked in their company.

There are many important omissions, which I regret. Many interesting personalities have become shadows in Zionist history. Some of them I have been unable to revive, for they do not now register or reveal themselves in an arresting manner.

In my view, the subjects shown on the screen of my memory come out of the ordeal of affectionate scrutiny in proportions of far greater human significance than if I had followed the line of least resistance and accepted the stereotypes of the official record. Let them stand as my eyes saw them, as my heart remembers them!

THE FIRST THREE: HERZL; NORDAU; WOLFFSOHN

THEODOR HERZL (1860–1904)

I knew most of the leading personalities of the Zionist Movement for over half a century. But I never heard the voice or touched the hand of the Prince of them all. Echoes of the personality of Theodor Herzl reached us through Americans who met him at Congresses. He was revealed in the records of the early Zionist Congresses and the literature created at the time. He spoke through Manifestoes and public addresses and letters written to persons we knew. His name was the spark that ignited the Movement in the Diaspora. Stories were told of him by American delegates to the Congress. His photographs in various poses were circulated as media of propaganda. A literature about his leadership became available. Fragments of his *Diaries* were made public after his death. Today there is little of his Zionist life hidden from public scrutiny. The dust found in his grave in Vienna was carried to Jerusalem. Many years after his death he was a living influence in the Movement.

I hovered about the fringe of his Zionist career, touching hands with others who had touched his hands; though distant in time and place from the creation of the Movement, I felt close to him in some mysterious way as I became aware of the varying colors of his life.* This profile—if it may be called that—is an attempt to capture the features of his personality—to limn him from memory—and to draw in general terms an outline of his amazing career, which still casts a warming glow over Jewish life long after his disappearance from earthly sight.

In the few years of his Zionist life and leadership, Theodor Herzl renewed and revived an old Jewish legend. He was accepted by many

---

* In November 1901 Richard Gottheil wrote Herzl that a promising young Zionist named Louis Lipsky had taken over the post as editor of *The Maccabean.* Ed.

as the reincarnation of the Messiahs of the Middle Ages who raised the hopes of their people for a brief span of time and disappeared in mystery and were forgotten. It was wondered whether this new Redeemer would stay long enough to test his Mission. Those who believed in the tradition were disturbed that Herzl did not come from the halls of learning; that he was not pious or saintly; that he was bred in a worldly Vienna and was a writer for journals and the theatre. He never pretended to Messiahship, but his regal appearance suggested the role he was destined to play.

The story of his life—personal and public—has been told by Alexander Bein; it has been revealed in his amazing *Diaries*. When you have read all that has been written about him, you begin to understand why the new Symbol of the old Legend would not be the weird and futile story of another False Messiah, but the engrossing first chapter of the modern Exodus which led in 1917 to the Balfour Declaration and in 1948 to the rebirth of the Jewish State in the Land of Israel.

There were no indications of his later transformation in the beginnings of his life. Born in Budapest in 1860, he was matured in an alien environment. He was not part of the mainstream of Jewish life. His Jewish education came to an end when he was thirteen. What he knew of Jewish tradition was packed away in his memory and rarely disturbed him. He knew of Jewish disabilities only as an affront to an ancient people and as a personal humiliation. He was made conscious of being a Jew by the society in which he lived. He was educated in the University of Vienna. He studied law and was admitted to the bar. He practiced his profession for a while, and then turned to journalism and literature.

He was drawn to the press, to the theatre, and to the society of the elite. Like most young men of the time, he was first a Viennese, then a cosmopolitan. He looked through a small window into the larger world of culture and longed to be included in it. He was not troubled by the deeper problems of life; he was not "a soul in torment." He became a good reporter and commentator, and a writer of light and easy entertainment in the theatre. His security was assured by the generosity of his father. When he was twenty-nine he married. When thirty-two, he was well known as a journalist and dramatist, and reached the high point of his ambition when he was sent to Paris by the Vienna *Neue Freie Presse* as its correspondent.

Herzl was unaware that for several decades the Jews of Eastern Europe were engrossed in a national revival. They were emerging, in

spite of Russian oppression, from life in the ghetto, and were opening
their windows to modern thought and aspirations. They were greeting
the alien air. They welcomed enlightenment. In the course of their
spiritual and intellectual escape, they ran toward the liberating ideals
of the Russian Revolution, but at the same time the Hebrew language
was reborn and the old ideal of the Return experienced a revival. Hebrew
became the medium of a modern literature. It was revived as a spoken
tongue. Hebrew schools and academies were founded. Hebrew journals
of a high quality created a rejuvenated public opinion. The ideas of
Pinsker, who wrote *Auto-Emancipation* in 1882, took the practical form
of promoting Jewish colonization in the Holy Land. Societies dedicated
to the Jewish revival were organized in all Jewish communities in which
Russian Jews had influence. While assimilation was eating away at
Jewish values, national aspirations were being fertilized through the
medium of Hebrew culture and the work of Jewish colonization in
Palestine.

To all of this Herzl was alien. Paris was, in a sense, the birthplace of
his conversion. There, slowly, with uncertain steps, he found his way
back to his people through the provocations of anti-Semitism. He read
anti-Semitic periodicals and books with avid curiosity and rising indignation. He was present as a correspondent at the trial of Alfred
Dreyfus in 1894, and saw the ceremony of degradation. He heard the
cries of "Down with the Jews" in the streets of Paris. He followed the
intrigues and sensations of the Dreyfus Affair as it moved to its revision
under the angry challenges of Emile Zola. He was obsessed by an inner
unrest. He fell into a mood of feverish agitation which he could not
explain to himself. He wrote a play with a Jewish theme in which there
was sharp debate about the Jewish "problem." He described the state
of his mind at that time in these strange words:

For some time now, I have been engaged with a work of indescribable
greatness. It has assumed the aspect of a mighty dream. Days and
weeks have passed since it has filled me utterly. It accompanies me
wherever I go. It broods above all my conversations. It peers over my
shoulder at the trivial work I do. It disturbs and intoxicates me.

A fascinating description of his agitation is given by Bein in the
following exciting phrases:

Then suddenly the storm breaks upon him. The clouds open, the
thunder rolls and lightning flashes about him. A thousand impressions

beat upon him at the same time. He cannot think, he cannot act, he can only write. Breathless, unreflecting, unable to control himself or to exercise his critical faculties lest he dam the eruption, he dashes down his thoughts on scraps of paper as if under unceasing command. So furiously did the cataract of his thoughts rush through him that he thought he was going out of his mind. He was not working out the idea; the idea was working him out. It would have been a hallucination if it had not been so informed by reason from first to last.

His mental state was reflected in the restless inquiries he made of friends and acquaintances as to the validity of his ideas. He was not sure of himself. He even doubted his sanity. He composed *The Jewish State* in various forms. He sent the first version to Baron de Hirsch; the second was a revision addressed to Baron Edmond de Rothschild. In desperation, he wrote and rewrote the text to get the matter out of his system. He then decided upon the publication of his manuscript in order to validate the creation of his mind and to win, if possible, public support.

Herzl knew nothing whatever of Pinsker or Hess, the forerunners of Zionism. He seemed not to be interested in what had been written on the subject. He was the victim of his own intellectual unrest, his own imaginative adventures, his own dissatisfaction with the position of the Jews in the world. He was led by degrees to appreciate the abnormal aspects of Jewish life. He came to despise Jews of standing in society who could have done much to improve the position of Jews, but who sought instead their own well-being without giving a thought to their doomed brethren in the ghettos. He believed that it was imperative that the Jews be liberated, that the world should be made to see that the solution of the Jewish problem was one of the issues of modern civilization. He became the self-appointed promoter of the cause, and the rest of his hurried life was dedicated to its service.

Herzl's distinction was that he gave the Jewish problem form, dramatic content, and political reality. He provoked a general international discussion. The pamphlet he wrote—*The Jewish State*—was the first public expression of a dynamic concept of how the Jewish people could achieve their freedom, a land of their own, how their redemption could be organized and financed.

With startling self-assurance, on his own responsibility, he proposed the creation of a Jewish State and became its sponsor and advocate. He used all his friends to help him find a way to distinguished supporters. He won the loyalty of Max Nordau, then at the height of his international fame. He met Baron de Hirsch who rejected his plans. He submitted a memorandum to Baron de Rothschild who thought his enterprise would be dangerous to Jews in general. He established contacts with Jews in England, in the United States, in Russia.

At first, Herzl hesitated to identify the territory of the Jewish State. The Charter he aimed for made necessary, however, approaches to the Turkish Sultan, who held sovereignty over Palestine. The pressures of the Russian Zionists forced him to come down to *terra firma*. When he wrote the novel *Altneuland* in 1902 he had beyond doubt landed definitely and forever in Zion. But here he revealed, even five years after the First Congress, that he still had not penetrated the deeper meaning of redemption and rebirth. The Zion he saw twenty years after 1902 was a synthetic composition. It was made of shreds and patches, picked up from alien gardens. The home the Jews returned to was provided with modern furniture not of their own design. It had acquired no distinctive way of life based upon Jewish tradition or Jewish ethics or Jewish aspirations. The garments of the Ghetto were removed, social living was cleaner and roomier, but nothing distinctive had been developed. There was only a faint reflection of a new Jewish spirit. There was no evidence of the renaissance of Hebrew. Children sang Hebrew songs to welcome distinguished visitors. German was very much at home in Zion. The pioneer labor movement had not yet put in its appearance. How the State was created was not described except in general terms. There was no reflection of the spiritual and social ferment Zionism would generate in the process of becoming a State. The Jewish religion was in *status quo*. The Jewish "soul" was not even under observation. Only in the last year of his life did Herzl realize what creative power was hidden in the Promise.

The publication of *The Jewish State* was the first public step in his great enterprise. It was not submitted as a dogmatic finality. It was not a plan or blueprint. There were many improvisations subsequently discarded, but the objective was clear. It was to secure for the Jewish people the grant of sovereignty over a territory large enough for the requirements of a nation.

The magic title of the brochure evoked widespread interest and comment, rejection and acceptance. It raised the sights of many Jews and made them conscious of their origins, their depressed position, their servitude and the urgency for organized action. It was their first exposure to world scrutiny as a people. It made them feel that the world might be won for the cause of their liberation. It gave them courage and hope and liberated their spirit. It gave wings to their imagination and work for their hands.

When Herzl set out on his mission he had no sponsors or backers, no committee or organization. He was the sole promoter and advocate of an international project, and its leader. It was not his aim to create a mass movement. He was not concerned with democratic forms. His first thought was to seek the cooperation of Jewish philanthropy. When these efforts failed and he realized that political negotiation must be backed either by masses of people or by funds, he called the first Zionist Congress to be held in Basle in August 1897.

Through the Congress the Leader of a people emerged. When he stood on the platform at Basle it was said that "he was like a scion of the House of David risen from the dead, clothed in legend and fantasy and beauty." In the Congress he was the moderator in clashes with persons and parties. He curbed his natural impatience. He was gracious and considerate, sharp in retort, but quick to recover balance. He was aware of the dramatic. His interventions in debate were well-timed, arresting, but controlled. He became a skilled parliamentarian in a democratic assembly in which procedures and languages fought for dominance. He was seldom an orator. He spoke as if he were the First Minister of State. He gave the impression of a man convinced of the validity of his mandate which stood higher than the vote of Congress. Beneath his public calm and reserve a fierce restlessness beat against his strained heart.

All his unrevealed talents converged to provide the audacity to become the first Jewish diplomat, the first to negotiate the cause of re-establishing the Jewish State on practical, political levels. The man of letters became a political strategist and diplomat. He seemed to carry the credentials of an ancient people who had regained old political manners and came straight to the throne of public opinion, seeking not special favors or mercy, but the righting of an ancient wrong; on the record, not in secret treaty.

He was not an economist. He was not a financier. But he had the gift of an extraordinary imagination and an amazing resourcefulness. He was able to find harmony in discord, unity in diversity. It required great resoluteness at that time to face an arrogant Kaiser and to plead the Jewish cause with restraint and dignity. The effort to see and influence the Sultan of Turkey was an elaborate conspiracy of great ingenuity. The influence of the Kaiser died early, but Herzl played the gambit with the Sultan to the bitter end. The crafty ruler finally offered him Mesopotamia, Syria and Anatolia, but specifically excluded Palestine.

Herzl had proposed the refunding of the Turkish debt by a group of Jewish financiers. The consideration was to be a Charter for Jewish Colonization in Palestine. His effort to establish contact with the Sultan is a fantastic story of Oriental intrigue. He had to push his way through the meshes of a corrupt court. His own agents were not to be relied upon. Every step had to be paid for. Bribery was the order of the day. He was never sure that his messages were being received or that alleged replies by the Sultan were authentic. He seemed to be playing with an invisible adversary. Finally, in 1901 he succeeded in having an interview with the Sultan and spent two hours face to face with the ailing ruler. In his account of the interview, Herzl wrote:

"He stood before me exactly as I had pictured him—small, lean, with a big hooked nose, a dyed beard and a weak, trembling voice. He wore the uniform of the Selamlik, a mantle above his shield coat, diamond orders, gloves. He gave me his hand and we sat down. He sat on a divan with a sword between his knees. He took two cigarettes out of a silver pack, handed one to me and took the other himself. He said, 'I have always been and still am a friend of the Jews. I rely chiefly upon Muslims and Jews. I have more faith in them than in my other subjects.'

"I complained of the injustices that are committed all over the world against the Jews. He said that his Empire was always open as a refuge for Jews. I said, 'When Professor Vambéry told me Your Majesty would receive me, I thought of the old story of Androcles and the Lion. Your Majesty is the Lion. Perhaps I am Androcles. Perhaps there is a thorn to be drawn out. I consider the public debt to be that thorn. If this could be removed, Turkey would once more blossom in all her strength.' The debt had accumulated under his Majesty's predecessors and it had not been possible to get rid of it. If I could be helpful, it would be most gratifying. The Sultan smiled, shook his head yes and no, and made no comment. He gave the impression of crafty solemnity."

Herzl left the audience and touched many hands stretched out to him in the vestibule. He distributed gold pieces. The next day Herzl received a diamond stickpin. That was all he ever received from the Sultan. The Turkish debt was taken over by the French. When the time came for him to return to England, it was in fact the last available station on the zigzag march begun in 1895. The English offer of Uganda was the only definite proposal Herzl was ever able to bring to his people.

It was the summation of his life. It was a distorted climax and a mockery. He was being detoured to East Africa. The Movement would be called upon to cease reference to the Return. It would lose contact with tradition and history. Zion would become a receding memory. The Russian Zionists for whom the "haven of refuge" was intended, rejected it with grief and dismay. They said Zionism was the breath of their life and they could not stop breathing. Life could not be halted as a part of a political maneuver. Although the majority was with Herzl for the acceptance of Uganda, he knew from the start that the battle was lost. He went into the caucus of the Russian Zionists and saw them mourn over the betrayal of their hope, and realized for the first time how deeply rooted was the mystic relation of the Chosen People and the Promised Land. He was driven by the power of Jewish memory to abandon the uncertain territory of his first thought and to accept without question the Land of Israel as the objective of Jewish hope. He knew then that he was not destined to lead the Modern Exodus. He was the Forerunner. A new generation would have to be born to take over the burden.

He had come to the end of his life. For ten years he had carried on with an impaired heart. He was sustained by the provocations of the adventure, its frustrations, his superhuman obstinacy. When he launched the Movement he was a young man at the height of a brilliant literary career. At forty-three he was old and exhausted. When the proposed detour was rejected he stood where he had started: a larger following, instruments of action, a press, the beginnings of a bank, a Congress, an organization, but no nearer the political goal than when he published *The Jewish State*. One who saw him at his last Congress said:

The imposing figure is now stooped. The face is sallow. The eyes are darkened. The mouth is drawn in pain and wracked by passion.

His obsession had destroyed his personal life. The wife of his youth was estranged and unhappy. When she married the writer of plays, the brilliant journalist, she looked forward to a social life in the intellectual circles of Vienna. Instead she found herself in the excitement of a rude movement associated with the emotional disturbances of the Jews of Eastern Europe who invaded her well-kept home and took her husband away into the peculiar by-paths of a political struggle in which she could have no place. She resented the adventure. She was cold to its surprises, its passion. It was estranging the father from the children. There were disagreements and reconciliations. He had no time for the articles he should have written, and was too proud to receive payment for Zionist services. He preferred to borrow endlessly from his father. He left his family penniless, his children destitute and unprotected, scattered and under the guardianship of various friends. He did not pause even when his physicians advised rest again and again. To his last day his mind was excited by alternative projects. When he passed away he was under the impression that his life had been a barren failure.

The offer of a colony in East Africa had been rejected and he seemed to have suffered a major defeat. But the ideal of the State, which had been relegated to the background by the Lovers of Zion—whose program had lost its momentum and become a tired discussion—was transformed by his death and incorporated in a Zionist Movement infused by and infected with the ideal of the Jewish State, which would never again be obscured and washed out of the corporate responsibility of the Zionist Movement.

He did not know that he had fired a revolution in Jewish life and thought. He did not know that he had created the instrument of redemption which would live on long after his departure, and would ultimately reach the goal he had missed. In the first flush of revelation he had thought freedom would come through the contributions of Jewish philanthropists, through foreign influence bought and paid for. He organized the Jewish Colonial Trust. He set in motion the Jewish National Fund. He made the Zionist Congress the international voice of the Jewish people. In the final hours of his life he knew that redemption would come from the struggle of his people, their sacrifices, their belligerency, their obstinacy. It was his historic privilege to set the Jewish people on the road that would bring them to the Promised Land—not *any* land, not Argentina, not Uganda, but the land which finally found a living place in his bruised heart.

He said that the foundation of the Jewish State was laid at the first Basle Congress. He foretold that fifty years later the Jewish State would be a growing reality. The First Congress was held in 1897. The Balfour Declaration was issued in 1917. The Jewish people proclaimed the State of Israel in May, 1948.

The personality of Herzl is best reflected in his *Diaries*. It is the record of his Zionist life. It contains everything of him—his foibles and caprices, his human weaknesses and his resoluteness, his discoveries and inspirations. It is crammed with contradictions and deep understanding of human nature. You see his confused mental state in the process of clearing. You see the reflection of his hopes and disappointments with nothing hidden or disguised. You wonder at his courage and audacity.

He lived with the shadow of death in his heart. He was driven to move fast to avoid being overtaken. You see the emergence in this amazing record of a personality of great proportions, who was led by the mystic influences of a great ideal to act as if he were really the State Builder, really the Redeemer of an oppressed people. It shows how, in a maze of activities extended in various directions at the same time, he gave life to an ideal and forged an instrument that could not be broken. He was impatient with God and aimed to achieve in the few years of his own life what his people were unable to achieve in two thousand years of suffering and faith.

In his last will he asked that his remains be buried in the Jewish cemetery in Vienna near the grave of his father "to remain there until the Jewish people take my body to Palestine." When the Russians entered Vienna in 1945, it was found that the Nazis had overlooked the desecration of Herzl's grave. The new State of Israel—the reality of all Herzl had striven for—resolved to fulfill his wish. On August 17, 1949, the dust of Herzl was gathered together and brought from Vienna and interred in one of the hills of the Holy City of Jerusalem where the Memorial to his historic struggle will be an everlasting shrine.

MAX NORDAU (1849–1923)

When I went to my first Zionist Congress in 1913, it was suggested by a quixotic friend of mine, Boris Kazman, that I must see Max Nordau in advance of the Congress, for I would learn much from the Sage of Zionism who lived in Paris. At that time I believed in Katzman as an experienced traveler and a wise Zionist. (Affection bound us together for many years.) He came from Russia, had studied in Vienna and France, had many friends in Berlin, was a delegate to the First Zionist Congress, and then came to us. I took his advice. I left the boat at Cherbourg, and Julius Meyer of Boston and I blundered our way to Nordau's residence, to be told by the concierge that the Sage was on vacation in Spain. At the opening of the Congress a cablegram from him was read which provoked a point of order that a political cable-

gram even from Max Nordau was out of order. Obviously, relations
with headquarters were not good. I saw Nordau for the first time in
London at the first Zionist conference held at the end of the First World
War. He spoke to our American caucus and at the Albert Hall mass
meeting. He was still a remarkable orator. He was critical of the Zionist
leaders and of the Balfour Declaration, and did not hesitate to say so.
He favored a mass migration to Palestine, which startled most of the
delegates, but he went his own way and seemed to think that those
who disagreed with him were lacking in foresight. His experience during
the war in Spain had made him suspicious of the pious words of the
English, and he believed it would be good for the Jews to change over
from unqualified acceptance of the Balfour Declaration to a clamor for
deeds. His audience was not sympathetic. He was not well. There was
a grimness about his manner of speaking and many of the leaders resented his critical tone as not in keeping with the mood required by the
moment. He had grievances against the Zionist regime which had not
treated him with the dignity his historic service entitled him to. He left
London and returned to Paris, recovering some of his household property and his library. He really did not feel at home in the Movement,
which seemed to be satisfied with the smooth phrases of conformity
and lacked the passion of the earlier days. He had come to the Movement
when it was important that the world should hear its voice. He brought
with him an incisive mind, a sweeping imagination, and his words raised
the spirits and hopes of all Jews sensitive to drama and emotion. With
the Balfour Declaration a new message was required. You had to speak
of funds, you had to speak of rights, you had to speak with familiarity
of the Land as well as of the Promise. The voice of the author of *Degeneration* and *Conventional Lies* seemed wholly out of place. Nordau
must have felt that in the quiet moments of his privacy. All his comrades-
in-arms seemed to have passed away. They left him alone with the
thoughts of the incredible effect his voice must have made in those early
days when he was the central personality of the Movement.

Max Nordau was one of the first and the most powerful supporters of
Theodor Herzl. He was born in Pest, Hungary, in 1849. He was eleven
years older than Theodor Herzl. When Herzl came to see him in 1895
with the manuscript of *The Jewish State,* he was an established man
of letters. He was the author of *Conventional Lies,* published in 1884.
He had written *Paradoxes* in 1885 and *Degeneration* in 1893. He was
the author of a number of provocative plays and novels. He was on

terms of personal friendship with the leading writers of many lands. He was a striking figure in the highest intellectual circles of Paris. He had arrived as a thought-provoking journalist whose field was the civilized world, and he was fairly prosperous.

At fourteen, one of Nordau's sketches was published in a local newspaper and paid for. At sixteen, he already had a fair income from his writings and at eighteen, was a regular contributor to the *Pester Lloyd,* the leading Hungarian newspaper. He paid his own way through the university and graduated at the age of twenty-two. He was sent on two transcontinental journeys by the *Pester Lloyd,* which made his name known to the readers of that journal and resulted in the publication of two travel books which had quite a success. In 1879, he left Pest for Paris, where he practiced medicine as a psychiatrist. To be financially more secure he continued to write, however, and never for long devoted himself exclusively to the practice of medicine. From the start his books aroused an enormous interest. His *Conventional Lies* established his reputation as a fearless and original thinker. It provoked the thinking of friends and foes; it was banned in Russia and Austria and denounced by the Pope. *Degeneration* elaborated on the theories of Krafft-Ebing and Lombroso and served as the spearhead of a general attack on the decadent tendencies of the day. He hated the so-called "decadents" uncompromisingly. He was one of the most sensational writers in European literature.

Nordau was more conscious of his Jewish background than Herzl. He had a smattering of Hebrew and could speak Yiddish and possessed an intimate knowledge of the Jewish way of life. His father was a Hebrew teacher who was highly respected as a Hebrew grammarian and a poet, and had a marked influence upon his son's character. When he entered the university and began the study of medicine, he freed himself from the authority of religion and tradition. He was an emancipated Jew. His intellectual life had passed out of the Jewish environment. He rid himself of provincial conceptions and became a man of the world. He was an analyst, a critic, a moralist. He diagnosed all social ills and challenged all standards. Society was strapped to his operating table and he reported, without fear or favor, on whatever disease his scalpel revealed. He was essentially a physician and scientist. He was proud of his calling and paid homage to no authority but his own conscience.

Nordau's friendly reception of Herzl was therefore most unusual and indeed surprising. The keen analyst should have seen through him. He should have paid attention to Herzl's excitement, his exaltations and depressions, his self-depreciation and doubt. He should have appraised him as a patient, and everything said and how it was said should have been taken as material by the psychiatrist. But nothing of the sort happened. The two men talked for three days in succession! Nordau gave Herzl, as Herzl reported, "a lightning-like understanding." The older man had a strange paternal feeling toward the younger man who was struggling with an inner revolution. When the talks were over Nordau said: "You may be mad, but if you are, I am as mad as you."

Nordau gave a brief account of his "regeneration" in a letter he wrote to Reuben Brainin, the Hebrew journalist, in 1896, some time after he had met Herzl. He said:

My father was extremely pious, sternly Orthodox, and observant of all the rules and regulations pertaining to the Jewish religion. He did his best to bring me up in the same spirit so that I might heed all the Jewish commandments and become a pious Jew.

When I turned my fifteenth year, I abandoned all the Jewish rules and the Jewish code of behavior, and from then on Judaism and Jewry became for me nothing more than a memory, but a pleasant memory, be it said.

Thus you will see that from my sixteenth year until my fortieth my way of life and my relationships were entirely alien to all things Jewish. By conviction, by emotion, and by philosophic conception, I was German through and through. My Jewish feelings slept in me; I believed that they had died completely and that all that had been Jewish was now completely destroyed, leaving not a trace behind.

Anti-Semitism opened my eyes and turned me back to the Jewishness which I had forgotten. The hatred of others for us taught me to love our people. And from year to year my enthusiasm and love of my people grew greater and greater, and my pride in my Jewishness grows ever stronger. Now I know that I am a brother of all Jews, a son of my people.

It may be that his encounter with Herzl, coming at a time of public excitement over the Dreyfus Case, made Nordau more sensitive to Herzl's psychic disturbances, released the impulses of his own youth to which he refers. The critic may have seen in Herzl the burning zeal of the martyred prophet and was dazzled by its incandescence.

From that day on Nordau became Herzl's most loyal and helpful friend. He had received the gift of a new faith. As Nordau said later, Zionism gave his own life "its aim and content." He was no longer the emancipated man of letters. He was no longer alien to the hopes and aspirations of his own people. He was the captive of Herzl's mission. No matter what differences arose between him and Herzl—and there were many—Nordau was always tolerant and forbearing, often aiding in spite of disagreement, always loyal and affectionate. He was never part of the organizational structure of Zionism, preferring to maintain his personal independence. But he was the ablest and most belligerent interpreter of Herzlian Zionism, appearing as its advocate in Zionist Congresses and on the platform, fighting off the influence of the "practical Zionists" many years after Herzl passed away.

It was Nordau's opposition to a conference of notables which Herzl proposed to call that led Herzl to call the Zionist Congress in Basle. Nordau was the chairman of the committee which formulated the Basle Program. He proposed an inventory of Jewish resources as preliminary to planning the Jewish State. He emphasized the physical training of Jewish youth and thus was the inspirer of the youth movement in Zionist life. He wrote some of the more important memoranda of Herzl. He introduced Herzl to many of the leading men of the day—writers and statesmen and philanthropists. He was the most effective propagandist of Zionism during the formative years of the Movement. He carried on the Herzlian tradition with audacity, even in the days after the Balfour Declaration was issued.

Herzl was the incarnation of the leadership of the Zionist Movement. Nordau was the resonant voice of the Zionist Congress. At ten Zionist Congresses in succession—the last at Basle in 1911—Nordau spoke for the Movement. In these addresses he spoke for all Zionists. His were the first public addresses in which the renascent Jewish people set forth its cause in all its nuances, with form and color and passion. They were addressed to and heard by a world audience and evoked world interest. They thrilled all Jews with a common emotion and hope. They set the Zionist Movement on its difficult way.

When he called attention to the blindness of Jews and their indifference to the call of destiny, the theme was novel and daring and never before uttered with such eloquence and directness and dignity. There was no pulling of punches, no conventional diagnosis. He showed the emptiness of the French Revolution, so far as Jews were concerned, in that adoption of the formula of equality did not change the fact of anti-Semitism, which at that time showed itself in its crassest manifestation in the Dreyfus Case. Read those addresses today and you will marvel at their clarity and daring, their dignity and wisdom. Time has not washed away the glow of his words.

Many leading Jews had emancipated themselves. They were to be found in London, in Paris, in Vienna, in Berlin, in St. Petersburg. They left the masses of Jews behind in their varied ghettos and made the pretense that *their* emancipation would soon be shared by all other Jews. But full emancipation for the Jewish people was not coming anywhere. There were social and political and economic discrimination and persecutions, cold and hot pogroms and general disdain. Here was an emancipated Jew in the person of Nordau—a defender of modern civilization, a bitter critic of its derangements, who was part of that world—declaring that only through freedom in their own land as a people would they be restored to equality among the nations.

By all standards Nordau was an amazing orator. He spoke freely from notes without manuscript. There was nothing theatrical about his appearance. He was short and stocky. He had a massive head and a patriarchal beard which hid his features. But his words cut through sham and circumlocution. Words came hurriedly at his bidding. When he spoke (his gray eyes flashing, his arms upraised, his voice every now and then rising in a gust of passion, sharp anger or sarcasm), it seemed as if he were conscious that he was speaking to the whole world, that he wanted them to understand what he meant—to feel the depth of his indignation and the heat of his truth.

I heard him in London at Albert Hall in July, 1920. Those who were there then saw him at seventy-two, still retaining his intellectual vigor, majestic in appearance, still capable of deep insight into the realities of the political situation. There was drama in his appearance on that platform, for he was the only untarnished relic of the days that had produced Herzlian Zionism. His faith and confidence were amazing. He said at that time with a total disregard of the practical situation, the views of his colleagues, and the official atmosphere in which he spoke:

Only political Zionism has a simple and clear doctrine of salvation: We need Palestine, not disinterestedly but effectually; and not a Palestine occupied by individual owners. We need it for the people, that we may establish there those millions of our brethren who are being threatened with massacre or rapine in the Ukraine, whom Poland is trying to strangle slowly but inexorably by means of economic boycott, and whom Austria, Hungary and Germany want to push back into the ignominy of the Ghetto.

"It is not possible, there are no houses to live in!" No houses? They will live in tents to begin with. Rather that, than to have one's throat cut in pogroms. "They will have nothing to eat!" We will feed them until the first crop. During the four years of the war twenty-two million troops, who neither sowed nor reaped, were fed. "It will cost billions!" No, but many millions—and they must be found. The Jewish people will give the required money when they will know for certain that it is to be used in a manner that will produce lasting results.

We claim Crown lands in Palestine. We want to establish our fellow-Jews on it; first hundreds of thousands of them, later millions, not in fifty or a hundred years, but quickly, to save them from the assassins and to make them a valiant vigorous Jewish nation, rejuvenated, planting deep their roots into the nourishing holy soil; realizing the moral ideals, the ideal of justice and brotherly love, as preached by the Prophets of Israel; giving to the world, for the first time, the example of complete man, cultivating the earth, and at the same time, their minds, handling the plow and the book, producing material values, living intensely the full intellectual life of their times, forming a vast elite of work and thought.

That is the program of political Zionism as Herzl and his collaborators always understood it.

There are not several, there are not two, there is only one single method of overcoming this difficulty; we must by all means and with the utmost speed see to it that our numbers are equal to those of the Arabs in Palestine, and that we outnumber them as fast as possible, however large the difference may be at first.

Nordau's audacity in the expression of his views, regardless of the climate of public affairs at the time, wholly unaware of the practical difficulties, can be appreciated by the fact that he spoke in the presence of Arthur Balfour and other English statesmen. He spoke with the same freedom that characterized his first Zionist Congress addresses. He spoke as Herzl had spoken in 1897. His body was broken, he knew what war meant now; but his backbone was as stiff as when he denounced the "degenerates" of his younger days and he was no respecter of persons and disdained formalities. He appeared as the dauntless tribune of his people.

The First World War was a personal tragedy for Nordau from which he never recovered. He had lived in Paris since 1879 but remained a national of Austro-Hungary. He never acquired French citizenship. The French Government regarded him as an enemy alien, a journalist working for an alien journal, and confiscated all his property. He was first imprisoned and then allowed to go to Spain, where he spent the war years in Madrid under great difficulties. When the war was over, permission was obtained for him to go to England. He came to London in 1919, and found himself in an atmosphere not to his liking. In his view, the Balfour Declaration was inadequate for the creation of a Jewish State; it should have been more explicit. In addition, he found himself in a circle in which none of his old friends, except Joseph Cowen, played a part, and the leadership was in the hands of men who in prewar times he regarded as being merely "practical Zionists." Generally speaking, Nordau always resisted, consciously and subconsciously, the eager desire of the "practicals" to proceed with the colonization of Palestine regardless of the political conditions. He was irked by an inadequate practicality. He wanted action even on the Balfour Declaration to be held up for further elucidation. Nor was Nordau's advice sought on many important problems under discussion. He felt himself slighted. He had no part in the planning of the future. He could find no adequate place for himself at 77 Great Russell Street (headquarters of World Zionist Organization). The movement seemed to have passed him by. Being a proud man, he never raised the personal issues and suffered in silence.

He advocated the settlement in Palestine, without delay, of 600,000 Jews taken out of the Ukraine, Poland and Rumania. He was in deadly earnest about it. He spoke of it on a number of occasions, but his views were not accepted. Nordau felt a great mistake was being made. The redemption was being delayed for a hundred years, if not forever. In disappointment he returned to Paris in 1921. He was old and quite ill. He would not accept Zionist assistance and tried to resume his literary labors and practice his profession. His devoted wife and his daughter Maxa did their best to make his life easy. So did a number of friends like Joseph Cowen and Jean Fischer. He worked as best he could almost to the end, and died in 1923.

He was never personally concerned with the building of the Jewish National Home. He left that to the practical men. It was his business to analyze the Jewish problem and suggest the remedy. He remained true to the old line of the Charter and to the grand, moving ideals of

Theodor Herzl. He challenged the trend of history that seemed to be passing the great moment of liberation. He never saw *Eretz Yisrael* with his mortal eyes. His remains rest side by side with Ahad Ha-am and Bialik in the old cemetery of Tel Aviv.

DAVID WOLFFSOHN (1856–1914)

The last Congress David Wolffsohn attended was held in Vienna in 1913. He looked well but it was rumored that he had suffered recurrent heart attacks which made him an invalid for periods of time. At the Congress, however, he was vigorously aggressive and at his best in the give and take of debate. He came to the Congress, he said, to protect the financial institutions of the Movement, which had the effect of angering his opponents to the point of frenzy. Was he needed to protect the finances of Zionism against Otto Warburg, Julius Simon, or Dr. Arthur Hantke? He had no great orators on his side. The old guard— men like Nordau and Alexander Marmorek—were not present. The last of Herzl's disciples were not an impressive group on a platform. I remember Jacobus Kann of The Hague. He was a tall, thin man, a dry, matter-of-fact speaker, incapable of using his imagination or of giving anything to an audience or drawing anything out of it. There was Jean Fischer of Belgium, who had a way of shrieking in falsetto and making German sound like a strange jargon which could not be understood by the Germans or by those delegates who had come to know Congress German. Wolffsohn was himself the best advocate of his cause. He had been elected chairman of the Congress as a result of a quarrel between Ussishkin and the Zionist Executive. He won the American delegation because he seemed to be talking good sense. He was also cordial, witty and passionate in his pleas for segregating the Zionists' funds from the control of the Zionist Executive, the same Executive marked for re-election. Elect them, he advised the Congress, but don't give them the keys to the safe. This seemed irrational but sounded sensible to most of the delegates for they had acquired a deep affection for Wolffsohn in spite of the propaganda conducted against him. We Americans left Vienna with the feeling that Wolffsohn, ill as he was, his days being numbered, was the strongest man in the Congress. He had followed Herzl loyally and with pride. He had reluctantly taken on the leadership, knowing that he had few years to live and that he lacked the experience to lead the Movement. He was not equipped by education or training for leadership. He was not a writer or experienced orator. But he accepted the Mantle worn by Herzl and died in the service, if not in the leadership. He had no children. He provided as best he could for Herzl's orphans and left all his possessions to Jewish institutions in Palestine.

David Wolffsohn was never at ease as the successor of Theodor Herzl. His admiration for the great leader never waned nor was he able to rid himself of the specter of his influence. He thought of himself as the guardian of the Herzlian heritage. When he came to see him in Vienna for the first time, he was surprised to learn that Herzl had never heard of nor read Pinsker or Moses Hess, that he knew nothing at all of the Choverei Zion Movement in Russia. And yet, so impressed was he by Herzl's majestic presence, his self-confidence and the daring of his program that without hesitation he said: "All that I am and all I have is yours without condition." He never lost that glow of discipleship. He lived in Herzl's shadow. Others have followed Herzl when they thought he was right, but Wolffsohn followed him—as he wrote—even when he was convinced Herzl was wrong.

He lost his guide and mentor when Herzl died. He did not feel fit for leadership. He was not a general; he was not a speaker or writer or politician; he was a rough man of affairs, plain, simple-minded, without experience or special talents, but he was capable of unbounded devotion. He urged Max Nordau to accept the leadership. But that astute individualist was obstinate and said again and again, "Thou art the man." Escape was impossible. Wolffsohn was bound to the servitude of Zionist leadership.

The death of Herzl was the finish of an exciting decade of Zionist history. The political opportunity had passed. The Sultan of Turkey turned away from Herzl and made terms with France. The offer of Great Britain had been rejected by the Zionist Congress. The Leader had fallen on the battlefield and his partisans had retreated in disorder. A new procedure, a new orientation or a new inspiration was called for. The Russian Zionists pressed forward to take "power" and Herzl's disciples were being overwhelmed by the life forces of the Movement which had its source in Russia and among the Yiddish-speaking Jews. The heritage of Herzl was slowly being retired to the pages of history and new forces were coming forward to fill the vacuum. There was a half-hearted defense against the clamor of the "practicals." The call for action had the right of way and petty enterprises of all sorts were being blown up to large dimensions. The questions were, what kind of action, where shall we get the funds, where do we start. Regardless of the Charter of Right, basic to Herzl's program, the Jews were to begin the slow penetration of the Promised Land. No power on earth could prevent the inevitable drift toward the fulfillment of the Basle Program. Nor was Wolffsohn himself interested in checking the drift, for he was in fact during this entire period, in spite of his veneration for Herzl, a Chovevei Zionist of the earlier days.

Strangely enough, the Russian Zionists looked askance at David Wolffsohn because they said he was a German Jew. But he was born in Lithunia near the Prussian border. His father was a Hebrew teacher; his childhood and youth were formed by the orthodox life of the community. He knew the Bible; he had a smattering of the Talmud. His memory was filled with Biblical and Talmudic citations. His way of life in his formative years was determined by the simple habits and customs of orthodox Jews. He knew Yiddish. He was the youngest of a family of sons who, as they reached maturity, crossed the border into Prussia to evade military service. For the same reason David left Lithuania when he was fifteen and joined his brothers in Memel, which was a way-station of the underground leading to freedom for the Russian Jews. Many of the refugees remained in Prussia, many of them moved on westward to other European countries or to the United States.

Wolffsohn remained with his brothers. He had an aptitude for business. He was cordial, good-humored and quick in business transactions. He worked for a while with one of his brothers and then branched out as a salesman in Libau and then in Lyk in East Prussia. He became a lumber merchant. He made friendships with the men of standing in the community. He got to know Rabbi Isaac Ruelf, the author of a Zionist pamphlet entitled *Healing of my People,* based on Pinsker's *Auto-Emancipation.* He was intimate with David Gordon, the publisher and editor of *Hamagid,* a well-known Hebrew periodical. He overcame the hardship of being an *Ostjude,* but never lost consciousness that Yiddish was his mother tongue. He was interested in all communal affairs and was appreciated for his good sense, his integrity and generosity. Love for Zion was a part of his Jewish education. He was interested in Hebrew literature and the organization of a Zionist group in Cologne. It was said that he never spoke German well, that he never overcame the handicap of his origin, and yet he made the impression of a substantial member of the German middle class. He was a merchant and he was proud of it.

Theodor Herzl laid the foundation of the Zionist Organization, but it was not much of an organization. The leadership was concentrated in his own hands. He and his friends had to provide the funds. He was both the leader and the administrator. His office was the bureau of the Organization. There were few checks on his leadership between Congresses. The "democratic faction" was formed to register disapproval of Herzl's policies, but its dissents were limited largely to demonstrations at Congresses. It was Wolffsohn who developed the Organization. He became the president of a democratic organization and was responsible to his constituents. By this time he was a very prosperous man in Cologne. To that city he transferred the head office of the Zionist Organization. He enlarged the editorial forces of *Die Welt,* adding Dr. Berthold Feiwel and Dr. Abraham Coralnik to its staff. He built up the *Juedischer Verlag* in Berlin of which Dr. Feiwel was made the director. Nahum Sokolow was appointed the general secretary, and Israel Cohen, of London, English secretary. A quaint Russian character later known as Avadio (Davidovitch) was the controller, remaining in office through the Weizmann regime as the financial member of the Organization. Max Bodenheimer, a young jurist, became the head of the Jewish National Fund, taking the place of Johann Kremenetzky of Vienna. He drew into the Zionist service Dr. Arthur Ruppin. He won the support of Franz Oppenheimer, a leading German economist, who was the founder of the colony Merhavia. He established a branch of the Jewish Colonial Trust in Constantinople with Victor Jacobson as its manager and chief of the political work in the Turkish Empire. He ventured on diplomatic missions to Constantinople and St. Petersburg. He visited many Jewish communities, engaged in many controversies with his opponents and in the course of time had to be accepted as the leader of the Movement.

But he was not able to give the Movement the magic touch of leadership, to raise it to its previous state of Messianic excitement. The mood inspired by Herzl never returned. Wolffsohn may have lacked imagination, but there was nothing to inspire him. He had no material for the building of a homeland and saw no need to make plans which would not go beyond the blueprint stage for lack of means and men to execute them. He had to resort in effect to the methods of the "practicals" for which Herzl's followers were being criticized by the "practicals" themselves.

He carried the weight of Zionist responsibility, like Herzl, until he fell under the burden. His heart gave way as did Herzl's. In 1911 he left office undefeated, resisting what he regarded as an attempt by his successors to use the financial resources of the Jewish Colonial Trust and the Jewish National Fund to serve wildcat party politics. He wanted to conserve the assets of the Movement, to live thriftily, honorably, with patience and faith, not to be excited by illusions, not to risk what one had for the unknown. He grew in stature with his experience. He refused to join in opposition to the new regime which succeeded him. He guarded himself against bitterness and disciplined himself to be just to his opponents. He lost interest in winning the partisan battle. He remained for the rest of his life the target of an organized propaganda conducted by the Russian Zionists. They thought they had to destroy him in order to defeat him. They wanted to show Wolffsohn as a man of ordinary education, without ability, without judgment, lacking *schwung* and leadership, who did not understand the Herzlian ideal of which he professed to be a disciple, an *Ostjude* masquerading as a *Yehudi*. This rabid propaganda extended to the United States. All our European visitors had the same story to tell about Wolffsohn to American Zionists.

The writer attended the Vienna Congress in 1913. Wolffsohn's official pictures showed him to be a tall, robust, bearded man with good-natured features. He always seemed to be wearing a Prince Albert coat. At Vienna he was not robust. Illness had given him an appearance of emaciation and fatigue. His Prince Albert coat hung loosely over his large frame, but his eyes shone with great eagerness. He seemed to be burning himself out in the course of this Congress. All our preconceptions of his personality were untrue. He appeared at the caucuses as a commanding personality, a fairly adroit debater, a good story teller, quick in repartee. Although he sat among the delegates, he was the center of the Congress. The issue was, should this ex-President of the organization be made President of the Congress? His opponents said "no," but they were divided on the issue. Finally, the Executive was defeated, Ussishkin won, and Dr. Weizmann as chairman of the permanent committee presented Wolffsohn's name as the President of the Congress.

Wolffsohn sat among the delegates while his successor, Otto Warburg, delivered the President's address. He heard the speaker outline the new policy and realized for the first time that they were dethroning Herzl and consequently himself. Warburg said that there were three periods in Zionism. In the first, all work in Palestine had to be subordinated to the great political ideal. In the second, as political difficulties arose, work in Palestine had to be regarded as a concession to the impatient.

In the third, work in Palestine had become an end in itself, an integral part of policy. Wolffsohn heard Warburg praise Herzl and Perez Smolenskin, without even a formal reference to the name of his own predecessor. Wolffsohn realized his loneliness when he saw Nahum Sokolow ascend the platform to take the place of Max Nordau as the orator to describe the Jewish position in the world. He heard Shmarya Levin speak of Baron Edmond de Rothschild (whose philanthropy Herzl had proposed to destroy) as a great man, the protagonist of "a heroic method." At this, his last Congress, he found himself without a group to defend his life's work.

But in the general debate which followed, Wolffsohn scored a personal triumph with his own magnificent speech. The deterioration of his heart had reached a dangerous stage. He was fearful it would not sustain him. He certainly was not an illiterate; he certainly knew what he was talking about. He argued his case with great conviction, but he did not know how to conserve his strength. Yet his address was a masterly attack on his adversaries, moving, persuasive, passionate and with interludes of humor. He dominated the scene. He asked the leadership to consider the organization as a whole and not to act for a party, whatever its majority. He said that he took the floor to protect Herzl's legacy from being dissipated, to save "the sacred pence of the poor." He defended the integrity of the Bank in London and in Jaffa. He recalled how hard it was to get together the capital to establish the Bank, how it lacked the confidence of the banking fraternity and how it slowly acquired a certain prestige which should not be frittered away. He said that his health was poor, that he did not know how long he could continue, but he was determined to be present at the Congress, to save the Bank and to prevent it from becoming the football of party strife.

The sentiments of the Congress were with him. They forgot all that had been said by the able speakers who preceded him. They arose in applause and the session had to be adjourned. It was felt that Wolffsohn had vindicated his cause, that he had established a human relationship with the opposition, which he had never done before.

It was Wolffsohn's bad luck to be too loyal a follower of Theodor Herzl and at the same time a Zionist whose love for Zion could not be hemmed in by the formula of the Charter. It was his bad luck that he had to be loyal to Herzl, which meant to be loyal in defense of Herzl's policies, while the trend of history demanded a new orientation, the synthesis of work and political effort. It was his misfortune that he could not inspire the spirit of partisanship among his friends, that he himself was no partisan and therefore found himself standing alone as Herzl's disciple while the Movement and himself were being forced by historic circumstances to take another road.

He was a friendly, generous man. Whatever fortune remained with him at his death he left to the movement and to Palestine. He was a fatherly man, taking over the guardianship of Herzl's children and providing for them while he lived. He could not see himself as a leader in a movement in which party advantage had priority over its larger interests. He passed away before partisanship became the rule of conduct in the Organization to which he gave his best. He died as the opening guns of the First World War shattered the world in which he lived.

FROM HERZL TO BALFOUR: THE RECORD

The dynamism excited by Herzl was exhausted when he came to the Sixth Congress. The East African offer was the last card he was destined to play. He had turned from door to door, seeking in vain the Archimedean point on which to base the Movement to which he had given life. In an enigmatic figure of speech in his *Diaries* he said: "Great things need no firm foundation. An apple must be placed on a table so that it should not fall; but the Earth swims in space; the secret is to be found in movement." He may have been playing with the idea that it might be possible for Zionism to get along for a time without *terra firma;* that he need not be overtroubled about a specific land. But whatever his thought may have been, he finally arrived at what seemed to be a formal exit from the dilemma of a territory in the blind alley of East Africa.

Not for a long time were Zionists again to be quickened by the excitement of discovery. Not for a long time were they to experience the sensation of touching the fringes of the garments of the Messiah. The glamor and the excitement were on the wane. Their sights were lowered. Zionism grew in substance, in dimensions, in complexity and color; but it moved at a slow pace, with shoulders braced for a long pull. It was prepared for a dull prosaic existence and waited for the ultimate miracle which would have to come some day.

The East African project died in Herzl's stiffening hand. In due course, it was pushed off the agenda. The first Congress after Herzl's death—in 1905—pondered the report of a commission of experts sent to explore the territory. The two Jewish members rejected it as a suitable territory for Jewish colonization. The English member was of the opinion that in time and with patience it might accommodate about 20,000 settlers. That should have dismissed the subject. But the Russian Zionists were determined to extirpate every trace of the territorial heresy. They organized themselves for a long relentless siege. Their preparations for battle were excessive beyond reason. In fact, the East African offer was dead even before the discussions in the Congress were registered in a vote. The English themselves were not as keen as they appeared to be when the Foreign Office made its offer. However, the controversy within the Zionist ranks outlasted the relevance of the problem. Israel Zangwill, a fervent supporter of Herzl, made an "ideology" of territorialism and set out to win adherents. His brilliant advocacy was not successful, for he was not adept in political debate and thought more of a striking phrase than a persuasive argument. Nor did he understand how to approach his opponents. The more he talked, the more the Russians were convinced that he was indeed a *goy* trained in *pilpul*, who by accident had wandered into a Jewish movement.

The Russians won the verdict of the Seventh Congress which reaffirmed the Basle Program and rejected any form of colonization beyond Palestine and its vicinity. It brushed aside the British offer and tabled it indefinitely. But the issue remained a thorn in the side of the Zionist leadership for a number of years. Zangwill and his partisans seceded from the Congress and initiated an organization which continued a running fire against the Zionist Movement from a distance. The Zangwill group set forth to locate a territory for Jewish settlement anywhere in the world. They were ready to consider any reasonable offer, but they never found a suitable territory and dwindled down to a Movement in miniature and decided to send Jews for settlement in Galveston, Texas. Some of the territorialists returned to the Zionist fold. Many of them, loyal to the memory of Herzl, spent their time heckling the Zionist leadership, and used their devotion to Herzl to punish those who had not been loyal to him while he lived. They intended never to forget that sin.

The novelty of the Zionist Congress wore off and the glow of its first years could not be restored. Congress sessions became normal calendar events, occasions for stimulating the propaganda of Zionism in the Diaspora. The Zionist leaders lost their skill for the dramatic, and the formalities of parliamentary action cramped their style. The mood of looking for miracles vanished. Many Zionists who had been fascinated by the personality of Herzl lost their keen interest. They lived on the memories of Herzlian Zionism which seemed to have lost its meaning, but they had reason enough to find fault with Herzl's successors on general principles. They returned to their normal pursuits and flared up only whenever Herzl's name or ideals or slogans were mentioned. Many of them were chagrined, perhaps, because they had been taken off guard by the glamour of a dream or the fascinations of a dreamer. They were still political Zionists, but the dream was a cliché, not a definition—a manner of speaking. In fact, work in Palestine became the order of the day without a charter or legal guarantees, even without a plan or blueprint.

The pogroms in Russia that Herzl had feared finally came soon after his death. In the light of subsequent Jewish history, they were insignificant. They raised the immediate fears of Jews for a brief period; they stimulated Jewish charity and organization, but had no lasting effect on political events. They brought to life a Jewish reaction favorable to solidarity that had not been present before, but the Jewish question was not raised through them to the level of an international problem. Zionism had a long way to go to that end.

Of greater significance was the Turkish Revolution, which broke the empire through unseating the Sultan and placed the Government in the hands of the Young Turks, who undertook a revolution on modern lines. The Zionists welcomed the Young Turks and their revolution. They anticipated that the new regime would be reasonable with the nationalist aspiration of the Jews, that they would welcome peaceful infiltration of Palestine by Jews. They were mistaken. The Young Turks resisted every form of supporting Zionism and were jealous of their sovereignty. They did not intend to give freedom to any minority except under strict control. Their own native Jews were resentful of the attempt to segregate them as Jews and were opposed to the intrusion of Jewish nationalism in their domestic affairs. The Zionists took countersteps to influence the Turkish Jews. In 1908, they opened a branch of the Jewish Colonial Trust in Constantinople with Dr. Victor Jacobson in charge. Several French periodicals were subvened. At the 9th Congress in 1909 David Wolffsohn said that Zionism was compatible with loyalty to the Ottoman Empire, and gave assurances that Zionist objectives would be pursued in harmony with Turkish law. This was a fatal impairment of the charter idea. Surprisingly, Dr. Nordau also shared the view that the charter idea was no longer useful or necessary or relevant. He argued that there really was no need even to amend the Basle Program, for its text had no reference to a charter. Although these explanations made no impression on the Turks, they had the effect of modifying the waning conflict between the practicals and the politicals in the Movement. In fact, all party differences on this score were apparently washed away by the realities of life. Dr. Weizmann's formula, enunciated in 1907, which was called "synthetic Zionism," was generally accepted as a statement of indisputable historical fact. It was something all Zionists could live with. Furthermore, there was nothing else in sight to absorb their interests or their loyalties. They could no longer live on verbal abstractions. They developed new party differences which were highly interesting and provocative of dialectical entertainment. They quarreled about Palestinian projects. But the earlier disputes were passed over in an agreed silence, broken only by the echoes of the old controversies.

The problem of the Jewish State perforce took a back seat; but the foundations of the organization and the beginnings of the Jewish settlement were laid in this period which seemed barren of political significance. David Wolffsohn did not allow his affection for Herzl to violate the habits of a man of affairs. He knew the value of credit at the bank. He cherished the title of merchant. He adhered to the slogans of political Zionism after Herzl's death largely as a matter of piety, but was drawn closer to the program of work in Palestine. It is difficult to understand why his opponents had less prejudice against Herzl (the alien) than against Wolffsohn (the *Litvak*). Wolffsohn was from first to last a member of middle-class society and should naturally have been found in the ranks of Russian Zionists. But for more than a decade, the Russian Zionists carried on a vendetta against him. From 1904 to the beginnings of the First World War, when Wolffsohn died, they were determined to eliminate the symbol of the Herzlian legend, if possible. The more devoted Wolffsohn became to the practical ideas connected with Palestine, the more determined they seemed to be to give expression to their rejection of Herzl by rejecting his successor. But they were the inevitable heirs of Wolffsohn's practical efforts in the fields of organization and finance. When he died, there was a substantial estate to take over which they never acknowledged in adequate terms of appreciation.

He made the Cologne office the active headquarters of an international organization, not a personal bureau as it was under Herzl. Nahum Sokolow, an outstanding personality in the Hebrew renascence, became its Secretary. Dr. Berthold Feiwel was the editor of *Die Welt* and the manager of the *Juedischer Verlag;* Dr. Max Bodenheimer, Wolffsohn's friend, headed the Jewish National Fund. The Zionist Congress assumed the feature of a permanent institution. Wolffsohn was personally interested in the management of the Zionist funds. He avoided sensations and dramatic appearances, political adventure and prophecy. On several occasions he ventured into the field of political action but con-

fined himself largely to the obvious steps that could be taken by a
sensible person to acquire economic and cultural positions in Palestine.

In this formative period, Dr. Arthur Ruppin, a German economist,
was attracted to Jewish work in Palestine. He became the administrator
of colonization and industrial enterprises. He was the planner of the
Zionist work, the central directing agency in all economic endeavors.
From 1907 until his death in 1943, Dr. Ruppin was the theorist of
Zionist practical work. He had a keen vision, a deep sense of responsibility, rare intellectual integrity and an unusual talent for interpreting
the plans he had in view for the development of the land. He was not a
partisan. Economics was his profession. When he first went to Palestine,
he was not even an avowed Zionist, but gradually and thoroughly
became the master of the facts in Palestine, which he endeavored with
skill and intelligence to shackle to the Zionist cause.

He reported in 1913 that when he first traveled through Palestine as
a tourist in 1907, what depressed him most was the lack of energy and
courage in the colonies. He described the condition as premature age.
The colonies were on the average 20 years old. Those who had once as
young men founded the colonies, had been worn out in hard and futile
labor, and the succeeding generation was missing, for the youth had
not inherited either their parents' enthusiasm or their hope for gain,
and many of them left to seek their fortunes in the towns or in foreign
lands. Many colonies looked just like homes for the aged, Ruppin
reported. He was convinced that there was only one thing that could
improve matters. The colonies would have to be regenerated by new
young enthusiastic Jews from Europe.

Reinforcements came to Palestine in 1905 in the form of the Second
Aliyah, which left a permanent impression on the future of the Yishuv.
These were young Jewish workers from Eastern Europe who had lost
their hope for freedom under the Czars after the pogroms and the suppression of the first revolution. They were inspired by collective ideals.
They made "work" their religion. They wanted to recapture national
traits lost in the Diaspora. They were determined to find their future in
the Promised Land, and it was to be a future unlike the past. They were
not welcomed by the Turkish authorities. A substantial number emigrated from Palestine. Those who remained endeavored to find work in
the Jewish settlements, but the early settlers preferred Arab labor, which
was seasonal and therefore cheaper. The newcomers contrived their
own forms of colonization and forced the Zionist organization to come
to their relief.

Dr. Ruppin centered his interests in the Palestine Bureau which began operations in Jaffa in 1908. It is surprising what he was able to do with a meager budget. The income of the Jewish National Fund was at his disposal, but it was always insufficient. He established the Palestine Land Development Company as the central land purchasing agency for all Jewish interests. The company acquired large tracts of lands, prepared them for cultivation, divided them into small holdings, provided water and laid the roads. Through this agency, cooperative land purchases by other Jewish concerns were regulated. The company took over the management of several colonies. It organized the founding of the city of Tel Aviv, neighboring the old city of Jaffa. It aided in the development of the Herzliah Gymnasium, the first modern high school in Palestine. The Bezalel Art School was founded by Boris Schatz, with American Zionist support.

The outlines of the Promised Land began to appear. The Zionists became aware of the difficulties of their national task. They had been preaching Zion and Promise and Redemption for over a decade with a dim appreciation of the land that had to be redeemed. For the first time they saw the people who were to be their neighbors and felt the hatred directed against them and prepared themselves to grapple with defense. They saw Arabs divested of legend in the clear light of day. They drew upon their memories of Zion from the Bible, from the Talmud, from the modern romances written by new writers and saw that the present had no points of identity. The propagandists and orators in the Diaspora carried the message of rebirth to the distant lands, where ignorance of the realities of Palestine was dense, and indulged their fancies to their hearts' content, fearing no contradictions. Small groups of pioneers spread out over the land, collided with the Arab peasants, jostled them in the city streets. They had to deal with Turkish officials and learned the ways of bribery. They settled in the Jordan valleys and worked the ancient roads and began the building of villages and cities. The dedicated Jewish workman and farmer appeared. The cooperatives dug deep into the soil and clusters of green trees marked the places the Jews intended to make their homes. The Jewish *Shomer* on horseback was silhouetted against the sky, taking his chances with Arab marauders in the dark of night. Soon, oases of labor and culture became visible in Galilee and in the Sharon with the help of the Jewish National Fund. Tel Aviv grew with amazing rapidity and excelled Jaffa in every respect—in size, culture and the amenities of social life. An agricultural experimental station was established at Rehovot, supplementing the school at Mikveh Israel. The first cooperative colony founded in 1909 was Merhavia; it was initiated and directed by Franz Oppenheimer, a well-known German economist. In this colony the workmen received fixed wages. It was directed by an appointed manager with whom the workmen could not agree. Soon, however, Merhavia became a cooperative which seemed destined to become the most appropriate colonizing form of settlement for the Jews in Palestine. Franz Oppenheimer came to the United States to speak of the ideals of Merhavia and to collect funds. Then the *Moshavim* appeared and other colonies based on individual enterprises were developed. The Jewish National Fund undertook large-scale afforestation and became responsible for the planting of trees in every available section of the country. Plans for a Hebrew University were being discussed.

Under the influence of the Second *Aliyah,* the Hebraic elements in the colonies, and Eliezer Ben Yehuda's pioneer work in the development of the Hebrew language, a network of Hebrew schools was established in these years. A technical institute was built in Haifa which became the center of a foreign language controversy, through which Hebrew was forced into the educational program, and from year to year the influence of Hebrew as a spoken language penetrated the life of the Jews in Palestine. There were about 60,000 Jews in Palestine in 1904. Their number was estimated at 85,000 in 1914. These were the roots from which there grew a new political situation. It was always Dr. Weizmann's thought that if the "things" were provided, a reflection of them would be revealed in political situations.

The Balfour Declaration was the climax of this period of development. It was not a promise of a Jewish State. It marked the birth of a new form of national life within a prescribed autonomy. It gave the recognition of the Allied Powers to the historical connection of the Jewish people and the Promised Land. It placed a seal of approval on what seemed to be Herzl's *Endziel.* As the war was coming to its conclusion, it seemed to most Zionists natural and even predestined that England would take the initiative in a political situation in which it could exercise effective leadership, not only because it had sentimental and religious interests in the Return, but because it looked forward to the opportunity to enter the field of the Middle East, for which it had been preparing. The break-up of the Turkish Empire was inevitable, and the question was who would occupy the vacuum and replace the authority of the Turks; who would take over a region largely inhabited by Moslem Arabs? During the war, England sought to enlarge its social and political connections in the area. The Turks were allied with the Germans. The Arabs were not united, and their national spirit was below par. England was able to find only one Arab connection of value. Due to the efforts of Lawrence of Arabia, a mysterious Englishman who was alleged to have enormous power over the Arabs, the friendship of the sons of Husein, the Sherif of Mecca, later the king of the Hejaz, was won to England's side. Their military support was negligible, but the significance of their friendship had a large influence in the Middle East. England made liberal and even contradictory promises to both sides as was its wont in such situations. The French were its rivals in Lebanon and Syria and had to be eased out of the situation. The Arabs and the Jews were both tools with which it could operate.

The friendship of Joseph Chamberlain extended to Herzl was related in a vague way to the general interest of England in the future of the Jewish people. The return to the Promised Land was a familiar theme in England's liberal and religious circles. England was the land of the Bible. *Daniel Deronda* was written in English. The Earl of Shaftesbury urged the Jewish restoration in 1840 but found no support in government circles. He returned to his hobby in 1876 and noted the growing bond of union between the Jewish people and Palestine. Herzl's first political efforts were directed to Germany. He thought of the ambitious young Kaiser; but soon realized that he was an unstable symbol of interest in the Jewish people. Herzl realized that when war would come—as was expected—England would be called upon to take the lead and would lend itself without too much persuasion to thoughts of the Promised Land. His love for and interest in England were reflected in the fact that although educated in law in an Austrian university, he insisted that the Jewish Colonial Trust and the Jewish National Fund be incorporated as English companies. He frequently used English legal phrases. In 1898 he wrote to the English Zionists:

"From the first moment I entered the Zionist Movement, my eyes were directed towards England, because I saw that by reason of the general situation it was the Archimedean point where the lever could be applied."

The knowledge that England was considering the Jewish problem also evoked an interest in Germany and its allies. The Germans thought that it would be wise to endeavor to win the good will of the *Ostjuden* and Jews in general, by promising Jewish national rights in Poland and in other lands to the east in which Jews were numerous. A Zionist committee was organized in Germany which, with the support of the Government, sent emissaries and propagandists wherever it was thought possible to reach neutral Jews. Such a propagandist found his way to the United States.

From the beginning of the war, Jews in neutral lands sympathized with the Germans because of their remembrance of Russian persecution. They did not want Russia to win. In the United States, Jews were pro-German until the negotiations with regard to the Balfour Declaration were initiated and became known. The committee in London was headed by Dr. Weizmann, who took the lead in the discussions and formed an influential committee of Zionists and non-Zionists, English and Russian Jews and some of the leading English statesmen. A neutral office had been established in Copenhagen which acted as a propaganda center on both sides of the war front. In the United States, representation of the Zionist cause was taken over by the Provisional Zionist Committee of which Louis D. Brandeis was the chairman. After a considerable amount of negotiation, formulas presented and rejected, new formulas being considered, at long last, on November 2, 1917, the Balfour Declaration was issued in the form of a letter signed by Balfour and addressed to Lord Rothschild:

> I have much pleasure in conveying to you, on behalf of His Majesty's Government, the following declaration of sympathy with Jewish Zionist aspirations, which has been submitted to and approved by the Cabinet:
> "His Majesty's Government views with favor the establishment in Palestine of a national home of the Jewish people and will use their best endeavors to facilitate the achievement of this object, it being clearly understood that nothing shall be done which may prejudice the civil and religious rights of existing non-Jewish communities in Palestine or the rights and political status enjoyed by Jews in any other country."
> I shall be grateful to you if you would bring this Declaration to the knowledge of the Zionist Federation.

It was the first authentic political success of the Zionist Movement. It expressed sympathy with Jewish Zionist aspirations and favored the establishment in Palestine of a national home for the Jewish people. It pledged England's best endeavors to facilitate the achievement of this object.

The Declaration had a difficult road to travel before it was validated as the Mandate and issued to England by the League of Nations. By that time peace had revived old ambitions and reminded the peace-makers of old scores they had forgotten to settle. The war had just been put to sleep. The agreement made by Dr. Weizmann with Prince Feisal was soon broken, and the Arabs were engaged in civil war and especially in violent behavior toward the Jews settled in Palestine. Opposition developed in England and in the House of Lords, which rejected the Declaration. As the Mandate finally emerged in 1920, it differed substantially from the terms of the Declaration. The vision of the first act was doomed by what followed. It became necessary for Lord Balfour to appeal to the Arabs not to "grudge that small notch in what are now Arab territories being given to the people who for all these hundreds of years had been separated from it." Most of the amendments to the Declaration were incorporated in commentaries on it in the Mandate and in the White Paper which was issued and bears the name of Winston Churchill. The White Paper dismissed the rumor that Palestine was to become as Jewish as England was English. It reassured the Arabs that their language and culture would not ever be subordinated to a Jewish majority. It said that it was not contemplated that Palestine as a whole should be converted into a Jewish National Home but that such a home would find a place *in* Palestine. It kept Transjordan under the jurisdiction of the Mandate but excluded it from the Jewish National Home and in effect created a new Arab state under the domination of the English. Thus, a throne was provided for another son of the Sherif of Mecca.

In a conference with an Arab delegation about that time, Churchill rejected their demands to annul the principle of a Jewish National Home. He said it was right for the Jews to have a national home and reminded the Arabs that they had been freed from the Turks by British arms and that a Jewish success would be good for all the inhabitants of the land. In May 1921, after an attack by the Arabs on the Jews of Jaffa and vicinity, Jewish immigration was stopped.

Despite the mutilation of the original purpose of the Declaration and the Mandate, it gave the Jewish people an opportunity to develop the National Home in Palestine under the guardianship of England. Having guided the negotiations with all parties concerned, Dr. Weizmann's leadership was assured.

The Mandatory Government was the first school in which the Jewish people were prepared for statehood. They had their struggles with High

Commissioners and Administrators of Government. They acquired political acumen and experience in dealing with the Colonial Office. They learned the art of preparing memoranda for the Mandates Commission of the League of Nations. Their temperament was subdued by their contacts with the British. They acquired a sense of national responsibility. Zionists in the Diaspora followed the example of their leaders in Palestine in developing public relations with their fellow citizens and the governments of which they were citizens. They learned how to conform to protocol and diplomatic forms. They learned how to apply their democratic procedures to political conversations. They learned how to build a National Home under corporate and collective responsibility. From a scattered group of colonies they became a federation of colonies. They recovered the soil through the National Fund. They learned how to establish farming villages and how to deal with the problems of economic life, how to make labor pay, how to defend their property and their rights. They learned how to provide the budgets which were so essential in the building. The National Home was prepared under the roof of the Mandatory regime, which gave it slight protection in times of storm but was an adequate formal defense at all times, enabling the growing organism to flex its muscles, to use the intelligence of its citizens to enlarge the scope of its endeavors and consistently to win with the years an ever larger Jewish and non-Jewish support in the Diaspora. It was the House of Refuge which was prepared to receive the refugees from Hitler's barbarism when the time came. But there was no force on earth, Jewish or Christian, that was able even when willing to intervene to prevent the massacre of 6,000,000 Jews which preceded the birth of the State of Israel.

PROFILES OF THEIR SUCCESSORS

EUROPE

CHAIM WEIZMANN (1874–1952)

From his earliest years—as a boy in *Cheder*—Chaim Weizmann was bemused by Zionism, the Promised Land and the Return. He lived in an environment where Jewish life was the only atmosphere in which one was free to breathe. Whenever he left home to study elsewhere he always returned, certain of finding the rich family life of his people, as if no interval of absence had intervened. He followed the growth of Zionism at first merely as a student, a debater, a critic, a member of the audience. But from the days he caught hold of the political threads in England until the day of his death, he was the only man who identified himself with the burdens of leadership and who regarded Zionism as the inescapable center of his life. He was a member of no party. He was sensitive to all the ills of Zionism like a mother to the ills of her growing child. He was perplexed and worried by its problems. He looked ahead and never saw the end of the road. His scientific training forced him to think that his tortured people had a long way to go to reach even the shadow of the goal of freedom. Who could tell how many generations? He thought of the Movement as a process of planting seeds of national life in the ancient homeland and in the hearts of the Jewish people in the Diaspora. Quality was as important as quantity. Patience, creativeness and sacrifice were of the essence. He was the guide and protector. Ever after I crossed the ocean and saw with wonder the new life Zionism had brought to the ancient soil and heard the voice of Weizmann in Vienna, in London, at Zionist Congresses through the introductions of Shmarya Levin, he guided my life in the support I was able to give to his struggling leadership—its successes and failures. He remained faithful no matter who was faithless. Not that what he did was always wise, not that he always spoke with strength when strength was required, but he was the symbol of the struggle and the carrier of its burdens. In office or out of it he could be relied upon to do his utmost, to do his best, to endure. He was always true to himself and on great occasions often rose to heights as if he were the reincarnation of the spirit of Jewish prophecy.

The grand tradition of Zionist leadership was restored by Chaim Weizmann. He was not a disciple of Theodor Herzl. In his early days he had no faith in diplomacy or the quest for a political charter. Unlike Herzl, he did not have to return to his people from alien ways of life. He was born in the heart of the Galut. He was at home among his people. He knew their languages and traditions and shared their hopes. He studied in Jewish schools—from the *Cheder* to the Yeshivah. He was never estranged from Jewish life. He experienced the traditional love for Zion from his earliest days. His childhood was enriched by the memories, the legends, and the mystic hopes associated with Jerusalem and Zion.

He was nurtured in a normal Jewish home only slightly touched by alien culture. He was one of a brood of brothers and sisters who left home at an early age to complete their education abroad. He was one of the many Russian students who departed from their homes to study in Germany and Switzerland. From his youth, he had an irresistible ambition to become a scientist. While in Switzerland he joined in the long drawn-out debates between Mensheviks and Bolsheviks, between Jewish Bundists and Zionists. He missed being a delegate to the First Zionist Congress; but at the Second Congress he was one of the leaders of the Democratic Faction and became known for his wit and audacity as a debater. In a mild way he was a follower of Ahad Ha-am. He spoke of youth and culture. He participated in literary movements but was not a writer. He prepared a program for a Hebrew university to be established in Palestine. He was a lieutenant in the Russian Zionist group of which Menahem Ussishkin was the leader. He was Jewish in gestures and manners, in his way of speaking.

His destiny led him to England, where he cultivated tact and dignity and the value of understatement. In the course of time he became the friend of political and intellectual leaders in England. He was a stranger to the English way of life, but proved an apt pupil. The Zionists of England resisted his influence for many years. They were Herzlian Zionists and regarded him as one of the group responsible for the miscarriage of the Uganda project; the man who had crossed Herzl in the Congresses. He made a deep impression, however, upon the young

men of England and was welcomed by the Yiddish-speaking community and acquired a place of distinction in Jewish and Zionist circles,
where he was appreciated for his original contribution to Zionist discussions. He became known in Germany, in Austria, in Poland and in
Rumania, and his name was carried over to the United States.

His leadership matured when he took over Zionist affairs at the time
when the Balfour Declaration was under discussion. He was spurred
to action by the imminence of Israel's recognition in an international
covenant; when it became possible, for the first time, for the Jewish
people to undertake the building of their National Home. He was the
leader of the Zionist forces during the entire period of the Mandate.

I remember Dr. Weizmann at the Vienna Congress in 1913. He gave
the impression of studied indifference to what was going on around
him. He was easily bored. He was still the promising young man who
had joined in debate with Theodor Herzl at the first Congresses and
with the followers of David Wolffsohn. As chairman of a Congress
sub-committee, he was called upon to settle internal disputes and to
bring in a list of nominations. The writer was a member of that committee. Dr. Weizmann's rulings were a study in temperament. He was
impatient with *pilpul* and sharp in procedure. He had a mordant sense
of humor. He was scheduled to address the Congress on the Hebrew
University. The imperious Ussishkin took the ball from his hands,
announced the beginnings of a fund, and Dr. Weizmann's *referat* was
a matter of academic interest. The older men dominated the caucuses.
Dr. Weizmann stood in the rear of the hall, his eyes half closed, listless.
He was a ready debater and liked to speak; but in Vienna there was no
drive in him. He seemed to be listening and waiting. There were few
intimations of the coming war. The burden of all speeches was: Get
along with the work in Palestine as best you can. The last I remember
of the Vienna Congress was the tired appearance of Dr. Weizmann
reporting the nominations at the end of the Congress.

The First World War projected Dr. Weizmann into the political
field. The Zionist leadership was scattered. Dr. Weizmann moved into
the vacuum without opposition, for he was in control of the political
situation in London. He had been meeting the men who were to mold
the immediate future of England and of the world. He touched a sympathetic chord in the mind of Arthur James Balfour. He stirred the
imagination of David Lloyd George who believed in the prophecies.

He made a lasting friendship with C.P. Scott, the editor of the *Manchester Guardian*. He won the cooperation of H.L. Brailsford, a journalist who thought that England's imperial policy should include Zionism. He had acquired friends in France. Together with a group assembled in London, and with the cooperation of American Zionists led by Louis D. Brandeis, he carried through the long and tedious negotiations of the Balfour Declaration to their final issue.

By now he was a distinguished chemist who had made an important contribution to the conduct of the war. His early years in England had been spent in privation. His reputation as a chemist became known in England and France. His success had freed him of financial worries. The Weizmanns now maintained a commodious home in London where many distinguished personalities of the political and scientific world found hospitality. He was in a position to absorb himself completely in Zionist affairs. His public utterances in England revealed a stately approach to the Jewish problem and commanded world attention. He was conscious of standing on a high platform. He was no longer listless and indifferent. He had banished the trivial and spoke as if the Jewish cause were using him as its medium. He made the impression of a man prepared to walk a long distance.

His leadership was confirmed at an international Zionist conference held in London in 1920. The democratic structure of the organization was revived and revised there. It was a reunion of the survivors of the war. Max Nordau, the majestic voice of the early Congresses, came from his exile in Spain. Otto Warburg, no longer the affluent member of a great family, came from Berlin. The Russians did not know where they belonged—in Soviet Russia, or in Palestine, or in the limbo of any country that would receive them. They were represented by Ussishkin, the Goldbergs, Naiditch and Zlatopolsky. Yechiel Tschlenow died there. Nehemiah de Lieme represented the Dutch Zionists. There were Stricker and Boehm from Austria. There were about forty Americans led by Louis D. Brandeis.

England was prepared to accept the Mandate, but the building of the Jewish National Home was to be the responsibility of the Movement. The miracle of propaganda was to be followed by the even greater miracle of securing the manpower and gathering the material resources for the task of creating the National Home. The funds of the Jewish Colonial Trust could not be used for hazardous enterprises. The meager resources of the Jewish National Fund were limited to the redemption of the land. There were no reserves. In London, the Keren Hayesod was founded. An appeal was issued to world Jewry. The level of giving was raised. The era of fund collecting set in. A tremendous wave of popular excitement passed over all Jewish communities. The funds raised, however, were always inadequate. There were chronic deficits and strange bookkeeping procedures. Dr. Weizmann had to devote himself to the continuous grind of collecting funds in every part of the world. He became the most effective of all Zionist propagandists.

American oratory has its own standards. Foreigners do not appreciate it. It stems from the rough and ready West. Its dependence upon sound suggests the open spaces. Dr. Weizmann did not qualify as an American orator. His voice was not resonant. He had few gestures. He used no groping introductions or exalted perorations. He hated the impersonation of emotion. He had no ear for the rhythmic phrase. He acquired the English gift for understatement. He did not propagandize himself as a person. He was not made for stage effects.

In spite of these limitations, no Jewish speaker ever made the same deep and lasting impression—even in the United States. Dr. Weizmann spoke as if his words were the issue of suffering. He made the impression of a murky flame that had to be fanned to give heat. Shmarya Levin had burning passion; Sokolow was a master of brilliant narrative and analysis and of sly humor; Ussishkin took his audience by storm with sledge-hammer blows; Bialik spun exciting ideas and fascinated his listeners with figures of speech that did not require form to make them live. Dr. Weizmann had none of these qualities. He established an identification of himself with what his words were trying to convey. He seemed to be able to capture the wisdom of Jewish life. He drew his thoughts out of an invisible responsibility. There was prophetic significance in his phrases—a mystery striving to explain itself. There was a stateliness in his speech which was unique. He seemed to speak ex cathedra for the silent Jewish people. He was their interpreter and advocate. A cause had found a voice for a people emerging from the clouded past and demanding justice from the modern world.

He grew with his responsibilities. His personality acquired stature. It was formed by his intimacy with Jews the world over, as well as by his adjustments to the non-Jewish world. He sensed difficulties before they appeared. He was overcautious. He never took refuge in formulas or programs. He coined many formulas but threw them away with great unconcern. The return to Zion was indeed a vision of redemption, but it had to be worked out in the terms of hard reality. It was the longing of a people scattered in exile to be free and to be Jews in their own land. Whither these longings would lead them could not be foreseen or foreshadowed. The road would be hard and the directives never clear. It was the business of the leader to avoid the dogmatic phrase and not to allow illusions to lead action. All slogans had to bend as the strategy of the movement demanded. To be controlled by definitions and clichés and nostalgic sentiment would be fatal. Time was not of the essence; growth was.

One of the most dramatic episodes in his life—and historically of the greatest importance—was the American conflict. Zionist opinion in the United States was divided in its support of the Keren Hayesod (Palestine Foundation Fund), upon which the Jewish Agency depended for the initiation of the new tasks offered under the Mandate. No Zionist agency could operate without funds. Dr. Weizmann had no reserves. The future of the Movement was tied up with the American conflict. It involved the authority of leadership, the traditions of the organization and the possibility of meeting a budget for the work in Palestine. Dr. Weizmann was called upon to carry the issue to the United States for settlement in public discussion. He was a man of compromise and peace. Yet, his credentials as leader had to be vindicated and established in an area of open dispute and controversy.

When Dr. Weizmann entered the waters of New York Bay in the spring of 1921 to launch the Palestine Foundation Fund, the controversy was in full bloom. The breach with Mr. Brandeis, scarcely apparent in London, had been widened. A bulky record of misunderstandings had been piled up. There were letters and memoranda, and messengers going to London and returning with grim reports. Eventually, the two sides seemed to be speaking different languages. The issue was forced when Dr. Levin initiated a Keren Hayesod campaign without the approval of the American leadership, who believed that by holding the purse strings of the largest Jewish community in the world—which they thought they could control—their views should be taken into account regardless of votes at congresses or conferences.

But the masses of American Jews were not controlled by such views. In fact, they were prepared to meet Dr. Weizmann as the victor in a movement which had brought recognition of the age-long Jewish hope. He had helped to make the dream of Herzl a political reality. They gathered at the Battery and awaited the moment when he touched

American soil. They cheered him on his way to his hotel, lingering in the lobby for him to appear. The largest mass demonstration ever held in New York greeted him when he was given a public reception by a national committee. These audiences were not impressed by the debate. They were impressed by the historic facts Dr. Weizmann symbolized.

When he spoke to them he saw before him not a fractional part of Jewish life but a microcosm of all Jewries. He saw more Jews from his home town than he had ever seen in Motele or Pinsk. These were the relatives of the Jews of Vilna, of Warsaw, of Bucharest, of Krakow and of Vienna. They were waiting for him to speak and they would rise and greet the historic opportunity he would describe. They were thirsting for his words. A leadership that could not speak to them in the language they understood, that persisted in going its own way without considering their feelings, prejudices and ideals, would not be able to lead them in the great period of building. These Jews declined to raise any barriers between Zionists in America and Zionists in Europe. They were not aware of any dual loyalties. They had become Zionists through the passion of their leaders in Russia, in Poland and in Rumania. They had not been separated from other Jews by time and distance. They were not the lost tribes of Israel. They were kinsmen who had wandered from home and who had found freedom in a new land, but they remembered their origins.

Dr. Weizmann might have accepted compromise and let time settle the issues, but Palestine could not wait. The Americans wanted to negotiate and Dr. Weizmann felt that he had no authority to negotiate. He was dealing with a challenge to the organization maintained intact from Herzl's day as the corporate responsibility of the Zionist Movement. To have departed from that line would have created two Zionist centers, two Zionist authorities, two Zionist funds, and thus would have made the task of the Jewish Agency impossible.

There were peacemakers who sought to adjust differences. There were turbulent conferences. At times it looked as if Dr. Weizmann was about to yield, but his resistance was stiffened by pressures from London and Jerusalem and by his colleagues in New York. He was faced by a man who had great qualities of endurance, who had fought a powerful railroad group with amazing tenacity, who had evolved his own idea of how Palestine should be rebuilt, and who would not easily be deflected from his course. Mr. Brandeis seemed unable to appreciate what the democracy of the Zionist Movement meant in terms of economic resources. He seemed to have in mind a planned economy for a people not yet organized, for whom a land had to be prepared, who did not have to be consulted as to what kind of a home should be built for them. His hand was not being forced by time and need.

In the last analysis, American Zionists did not go along with him. They were not impressed by his American experience. By an over- whelming majority they repudiated the position taken by Mr. Brandeis and his friends and elected a new leadership. Following an un-American tradition, the defeated party retired from the organization, abandoned the struggle and awaited the time when their cause would be vindicated. It never was.

In the course of years, with great patience and skill, Dr. Weizmann led some of the dissidents of 1921 back to active Zionist service. But his aim was the winning of the philanthropists and assimilationists. Mr. Brandeis had won a number of such converts, but they were not in the leadership of Jewish communal life. The American Jews could be reached only through their responsible organizations, which were grow- ing in influence and resources. Their leaders, however, maintained the traditional opposition of the Reform movement. The implications of Zionist ideology alarmed them. However, when President Wilson gave his approval of the Balfour Declaration and a joint resolution of the American Congress accepted it, the same desire to be loyal to the United States led them to greet the Declaration and to approve of Palestine as the Jewish National Home. Tremendous popular excitement prevailed. There were parades and mass meetings. The Balfour Declaration was regarded as a great historical event. The prejudices of the past—espe- cially against Zion—were softened, but the Zionists were by-passed. The ideal was ignored but the fact was accepted. The armor of many non-Zionist Reform rabbis was pierced and their hearts were touched. They now became friends of the Land. Nathan Straus, the big-hearted humanitarian, was interested in several Palestine projects. Samuel Untermyer, the corporation lawyer, became the head of the American Keren Hayesod. The aging Jacob H. Schiff, the militant, outspoken opponent of Zionism, publicly reversed himself and expressed his faith in Palestine as a Holy Land, the center of Jewish religion.

The new trend toward Palestine gave Dr. Weizmann the opportunity to push forward with his proposal for an enlarged Jewish Agency. He found a powerful friend in a man of strong convictions who was re- garded as the leader of the non-Zionist group. Louis Marshall was a distinguished American, but unlike Mr. Brandeis, was deeply involved

in Jewish communal affairs. He was the chairman of the American
Jewish Committee and an officer of the Jewish Theological Seminary.
He was stubborn and had strong prejudices; but he could be persuaded
by reason. He was greatly influenced by his contact with Jewish leaders
when he went to Paris as a member of the American delegation to the
Versailles Peace Conference.

He was a provincial in the best sense of the word. He was born in
western New York. His home town was Syracuse, where the smell of
hay filled the streets and farmers came to market in the center of the
city. He knew how the city lived—what its merchants, farmers and
workmen were thinking of. In fact, all his life he remained uncontami-
nated by the large city in which he rose to eminence as a lawyer. When
he was once convinced of the justice of a cause he became its partisan.

Dr. Weizmann found in him a loyal friend and a stubborn supporter,
without whose influence and aid he could not have succeeded in winning
non-Zionist cooperation in the Jewish Agency. Marshall was the spearhead of the enlarged Jewish Agency. He drafted most of its legal documents. He was responsible for its constitution—a rigid, unworkable
instrument. He solved many of its legal difficulties. He defended the work
of his hands with vigor and enthusiasm. In 1924, he said:

"It is no longer a theory but a condition that confronts us. The
Balfour Declaration is no longer a mere pronouncement of one nation.
It was adopted by the Peace Conference as a part of the Treaty of
Versailles. It has been set in motion and effectuated by the League of
Nations . . . We are no longer confronted with the question as to
whether this should have been done or should not have been done. It
is an achieved fact. The question is whether the Jews of America who
are not Zionists should remain indifferent to the situation which exists,
the continuance of which is guaranteed by the action of the Great
Powers, and which has the endorsement of the Congress of the United
States. We have no right to be indifferent . . ."

Dr. Weizmann brought the non-Zionist delegates to Zurich in 1929,
when the extended Jewish Agency was formally established. That was
a scene without parallel in Jewish history. The leaders of the Jewries
of the world were present on its platform. It awakened high interest
through the world. The Zionists met in their Congress and—with
difficulty—ratified the constitution of the Agency. Then the non-Zionists
followed suit; the American non-Zionists uniting with non-Zionist
groups from all parts of the world. Finally, both sections met, and with
impressive exercises all agreements were sealed.

The year 1929 saw the beginning of a rapid deterioration in international relations so far as Palestine was concerned. The Passfield White Paper was the first of the black papers which recorded the obvious effort of England to escape its obligations under the Mandate. The Peel Commission in 1937 proposed the partition of Palestine. The failure of that proposal led to a final effort to adjust relations between Jews and Arabs at a conference held in London, and then came the act of desperation known as the White Paper of 1939.

Under these circumstances, it was impossible to develop the Jewish Agency or effectively to engage the non-Zionists in the affairs of Palestine. The riots of 1929 not only shocked the neophytes, but the death of Louis Marshall left them bereft of leadership. Felix M. Warburg, his successor, was a genial, sympathetic sentimentalist who had no inclination to lead and was embarrassed by responsibilities. Mr. Marshall might have saved the Jewish Agency. He knew how to work with men. He had the patience and intellectual skill for negotiation and adjustment. He might have solved the problems of geography involved in an international council with members scattered over three continents. Such non-Zionist leadership did not emerge in the hectic period following the 1929 riots. The extended Jewish Agency disintegrated.

The survival of any leadership through such a time would have been a miracle. Dr. Weizmann had a way of carelessly stimulating opposition. He loved to indulge in wide-range speculation. He tested his theories in formal and informal meetings. He saw the long road ahead and engaged in imaginative fabrication of future events. He realized that Jews had no power to restrain a world bent on self-destruction. He saw the beginnings of the march of Italian fascism; he saw Japan invading its Chinese neighbor without interference; the Nazis growing in strength, power and arrogance; he saw the League of Nations disbanded. There were no defenders of the right. The free world was in retreat.

How would the Jewish National Home fare? Would full betrayal be preceded by a Palestine partitioned or by a bi-national state? Dr. Weizmann weighed these prospects and vacillated in his choice of one of the two evils. He thought we would have to live through the storm and make the best of a crumbling world. He was prepared to maintain, on the barest minimum of national existence, the Sanctuary that had been set aside for the fulfillment of the ancient hope. He had faith that another day would come, no matter how dark the night. He believed in struggling for the Return, no matter how narrow the road to freedom would become, how thin the line would be worn down to, for Justice would triumph in the end. You had to live through the night.

But this was not the temper of the Movement. It did not want to be reconciled to what seemed to be the inevitable. It felt that its frustrations and despairs should be registered in its leadership. Unable itself to act in the arena of public life, it wanted its leader to be vocal above the din of conflict. It was willing to take out in sound and fury what it could not give expression to in action. It was exasperated by immobilized faith. It refused to make terms with reality. It rejected the peace of supineness. It began to develop its underground fighters. The thoughts of youth were turned to violence and vengeance. The leadership became the scapegoat of this dilemma and thus, in Zurich, in 1931—two years after the establishment of the Jewish Agency—Dr. Weizmann was forced to retire from office.

The futility of his retirement was reflected in the fact that Nahum Sokolow, Dr. Weizmann's close associate during the entire period of the Mandate, was named as his successor. Morally as well as politically, however, Dr. Weizmann was the leader during the four years he was not President of the Organization. He retained his office, his desk and his secretary at 77 Great Russell Street. He went to South Africa for the Keren Hayesod. He became the head of the *Aliyah* of German refugees. He appeared at the World's Fair in Chicago. He absented himself from the Prague Congress in 1933. In 1935, the organization had no alternative but to recall him to leadership.

His return meant the acceptance of the crown of martyrdom. It revealed the unseverable roots that bound him to the destiny of his people. The Movement was the heart of his life. He knew that a hopeless situation faced him. The lights were going out in the world. It was to be a war, total in its effects. Engaged in that war would be the fighters at the front and civilians at home. All the rules of what used to be called war would be ignored. The aggressor would risk everything on the gamble of the winner taking all. In such a war, fought under such conditions, the Jews would not find friends, or protection, or even a semblance of security. They would be the first to be sacrificed. Their rights would be the last to be considered, for the free world was engrossed in the problems of its own survival.

Dr. Weizmann resumed his difficult journey. He made his memorable address to the Royal Commission and received the proposal for the partition of Palestine. He saw the failure of the Arab-Jewish discussion at the St. James Conference. He received the White Paper of 1939. He endured the intolerable administration of a High Commissioner who had determined, in spite of the tragic circumstances of Jewish life, to enforce the White Paper. He saw English officials turn Jewish victims of the war away from the welcoming shores of the Promised Land to perish in the sea. He saw the failure of every political mission he undertook. He was called upon to witness the destruction of his people and the disinclination of all professing friends to come to their rescue. He knew that he was waiting in the anteroom of history, that the door might not even be opened. He was unable to hear the conversations that were being held in camera, and did not even know that the fate of Israel was deliberately being bypassed.

He clung to the Rock of his Faith. The validity of that Faith was revealed in what Jews had achieved in Palestine during the years of the struggle in connection with the Mandate. He had always felt that freedom would come through self-liberation, and that the masters of the world would be asked to contribute only free passage to freedom. Here was the great demonstration:

Along the narrow path of a shrinking Mandate the National Home had become visible, potent, colorful and exciting. Its 85,000 in 1914 became 600,000 in 1944. The malaria-ridden pioneers had produced a generation of youth that had gone out on the battlefield to die for the honor of the Jewish name. Dead cities had been given new life, new forms, new hope. The eastern shores of the Mediterranean were dotted with night lights that carried a message of resurrection to all parts of Europe and Africa. The dead soil had been fertilized by the sweat and blood of thousands of Jewish pioneers. A great university had been established on Mt. Scopus, the center of a network of Jewish high schools, technical institutes, agricultural schools, elementary schools and kindergartens. The Hebrew language had come to life, singing the songs of Rebirth. When the war came, these victims of a cruel world had become builders of an arsenal of great resources which they placed at the disposal of the Allies. They even had to fight for the right to fight under their own flag, but nevertheless fought bravely on every battlefield.

At the age of 70, clear of mind, vision dimmed, but firm of body, he waited to see his faith in statesmanship justified or sealed in frustration for decades to come. England, which had made the Promise, had plunged into a state of utter forgetfulness of its greatness; giving way to the pressure of evil spirits; fearful of arousing its youth to the inevitable arbitrament of force; conniving with the chicanery of diplomats; and almost wholly forfeiting its place in world affairs. He lived to see the bankrupt leadership of Neville Chamberlain supplanted by the personality of Winston Churchill, in whom England renewed its strength, recovered its hold on its heritage, and, summoning all kindred forces of earth to rally against the enemy, finally drove that enemy into the shambles of defeat and dishonor. Dr. Weizmann had suffered for his faith in England. He was derided for it. He was humiliated when England was contemned. Now, his hope was that through Churchill a new England would emerge from the silenced battlefield.

Dr. Weizmann could not rid himself of his tradition and his habit of relying upon England, but again his hope was wrecked by the government which took power in England after the war. It was not headed by Churchill. The leaders of the Labor Party, however, were committed to the hilt to the cause of the Jewish people. They were fellow-travelers of Zionism for two decades. They had spoken of their friendship and written of their friendship, but within a few days of taking office it was evident that their purpose was to continue the White Paper of 1939 to its bitter conclusion. They did not have the moral courage to support their convictions and their pledges. Ernest Bevin was the symbol of their perfidy. He was an unfeeling man, a brutal opportunist, discreditable not only to the English Government but to the honor of that England which had given life to the Balfour Declaration.

Thus ended Dr. Weizmann's faith in England. He gave up his British citizenship, his home in London, his friends in England, and settled in Rehovot, finding escape in the great work of the institute which bore his name. He left the Zionist leadership at the Congress of 1946. He appeared as a witness at the Anglo-American Commission hearings in Jerusalem. He participated in the deliberations at the United Nations. He completed his memoirs. The State of Israel was proclaimed in May, 1948. He became its first President. He last visited the United States in the spring of 1949. He was an invalid in the last years of his life and died in 1952.

The Jews pouring into the free State of Israel vindicated his faith in Zion. The Zionists had rejected his leadership of peace and patience and restraint. They had refused to wait on goodwill and brotherhood and took up arms to meet arms, violence to meet violence, brutality to meet brutality. Weizmann was the builder of the Homeland, but they won its freedom with blood and sacrifice, and made the emergence of the State inevitable. They raised the flag of Zion over the New Jerusalem their hands had built and their arms had defended. They defeated their enemies in battle and forced the acceptance of an armistice. They began the building of the State and opened its doors to the hordes of refugees from Europe and Africa and Asia.

In the long fitful reveries of his sickbed Dr. Weizmann saw a free generation of Jews, their roots deep in the soil, their arms at attention, prepared to go forward valiantly with the redemption of Israel, down the long and difficult road of national rebirth. The dream of his youth was being fulfilled in his old age. He never really expected that to happen. He was not pleased with the national trend. He was frightened by the speed of its growth. He never thought that his eyes ever would see the reality of the Jewish State—but there it was. He could see it (when his eyes were good) from the window of his home in Rehovot.

By his own choice, he was buried, not in Jerusalem, but in Rehovot, the child of his Vision, which he had designed as the creative center of Israel's future.

NAHUM SOKOLOW (1860–1936)

Nahum Sokolow was a pioneer in Hebrew literature and equally prolific in Yiddish, Polish and German; but he maintained an attitude of aloofness toward the Zionist Movement which made the early Zionists suspicious of his sincerity. At one time he contributed to Polish as well as Hebrew journals; in his Polish work he wrote little of Zionism, and with his usual graceful style in the Hebrew press but avoiding commitments. He was the one Zionist in all Poland who carried off the illusion that he might be a Polish nobleman. His manners were impeccable. He spoke Yiddish with a Polish accent and seemed to have no genuine interest in Jews as a mass, but only in such Jews who achieved the credentials of Hebrew learning or social prestige or wealth. He was in effect a perfect specimen of a diplomat, bordering close to the type of the familiar *Shtadlon*. He was older than Dr. Weizmann and had a recognized position in the world of letters when Herzl first came to the Jews. But he hesitated too much and too long in deciding whether he should go along with Herzl or with the Russians. He always found it difficult to land his thinking on a firm decision. He had a low opinion of the reliability of the Russian Zionists—he, who could talk for hours and entertainingly, thought the Russians impractical because they talked too much. He regarded Dr. Weizmann as a talented young man, but was never reconciled to the idea that his colleague could conduct a proper diplomatic conversation with statesmen. Dr. Weizmann was always too young for him, and he was sure he could never overcome the handicap. Before the Balfour Declaration, it was Sokolow who talked to the French and Italians and had an official conversation with the Pope, which was also done by Herzl. He never got over the disappointment that Dr. Weizmann—and not he—should have gotten close to important English statesmen who sponsored the Jewish National Home. He could not imagine how Dr. Weizmann was able to do this. Nevertheless, Dr. Weizmann was always the President and he was always the Chairman of the Executive Committee. His lingering ambition was satisfied when he succeeded Dr. Weizmann as president in 1931, but his victory came too late and lasted too briefly. He costumed his activities in the conventional garb of diplomats and never missed a point of propriety or protocol. He enjoyed life best when he moved in an atmosphere of diplomatic deportment. He was capable of serving Zionism in many fields, but made the mistake of wanting to keep too many fires actually burning at the same time, with the result that he missed greatness in any one field.

Nahum Sokolow was in the Zionist leadership for many years, but always gave the impression of being a "fellow traveler." He spent the larger part of his early life in Warsaw and from his youth, as an infant prodigy, he was an integral part of its domestic affairs. He was a prolific Hebrew journalist and wrote equally well and voluminously in the Yiddish and Polish press. He knew many Jews of diverse intellectual interests and was the center of many Jewish discussions. When Herzl appeared on the scene, Sokolow decided to go along with the Herzlian stream only after long and cautious deliberation. He went to the First Zionist Congress as a journalist and there was persuaded to become a Zionist. He was not a man to get himself excited too quickly. He had measure and calm. He seemed to lack passion. He maintained a calm demeanor to the end of his days.

When he took the plunge and became a professional Zionist, he offered his services to David Wolffsohn, the successor of Herzl, taking over the editorship of *Die Welt* and the secretaryship of the organization. He went to live in Cologne, the seat of the Zionist administration. He went with Wolffsohn to Constantinople in 1909 on a political mission. In fact, he could not be held down to a seat. He liked having a roving commission. He traveled extensively and made friends for Zionism

among prominent men of letters and politics. He did not have to remain
in Cologne to edit *Die Welt,* just as later he did not remain in Berlin
or London to edit *Haolam,* the Hebrew organ of the movement. Although a protégé of David Wolffsohn, he did not hesitate to join the
Russian Zionists in overthrowing him. At that time he was the one
Zionist—aside from Victor Jacobson—who could boast of some experience in political affairs. Victor Jacobson was left to concentrate his
attention on Constantinople. The rest of the world seemed to belong
to Sokolow.

Sokolow was one of the members of the Zionist Executive who
found himself in London at the outbreak of the First World War.
Other members were marooned in Central Europe. Shmarya Levin was
in New York. When Dr. Weizmann began his negotiations with the
British Cabinet, a committee was formed in London to consider the
proposed statement of the British Government. It was inevitable that
Sokolow should be a member of the group. He could name with familiarity dozens of leading European statesmen.

It is a curious fact that throughout Dr. Weizmann's long career as a
political leader he was destined to have Sokolow as his partner. They
were jointly representative of Zionism in the political field. This was
not agreeable to either party. Dr. Weizmann disliked the double-headed
leadership and the incongruous combination. He felt that Sokolow was
a little too easygoing in his political conversations, that Sokolow was
too much of a *raconteur;* he put too much emphasis on manner and
too little on substance. On the other hand, Sokolow, who was the elder,
placed no great reliance on Weizmann's skill or knowledge of history.
Dr. Weizmann, in his view, was a novice in the field of politics; Sokolow
had knowledge and experience. He felt that Dr. Weizmann also lacked
savoir faire. He never would concede that Dr. Weizmann's personality,
such as it was, was an important asset and that his different method
had its own peculiar value. But the two men managed to get along
with each other, each in his own field, each in his own manner, each
with his own limitations and rare qualities. Dr. Weizmann won lasting
friends in the political field. Sokolow helped to maintain friendships.
The one was serviceable in the Anglo-Saxon countries; the other had
his value in France and Italy.

As journalist and political representative, Sokolow was urbane, un-
hurried and sagacious. He never could be forced into a partisan position.
He was always found in no defined position at all. In any alignment

of opinion he never could be claimed by either side. He held himself in reserve and when the talk warmed up and he had time to think the matter over, he was prepared to come to the rescue of the disputants and suggest a workable compromise, thus restoring order and peace. This led to the charge that he never knew his own mind and had no convictions of his own. This was unfair, for on a number of occasions he was able to make the best defense of policies for which he had assumed responsibility. He was by nature even-tempered and judicial, and hated quarrels. In the growing party disputes which gave Zionism its colorful effects he was above the battle, not as a pretense or convenience, but with sincerity. That was why he seldom failed to find a middle course which was attractive to both sides. He once explained: Why should the partisan who hurries to a conclusion be credited with principle because his mind is easily prepared and runs fast? That was no virtue. He believed that the principle of restraint was more important and that it was better to be guided by prudence than by emotion.

He lacked temperament as a speaker. His blood pressure seldom rose when he spoke. He liked to talk in a conversational tone of voice. On the rare occasions when he lost his balance he made the impression of hollow emotion. But his addresses always had form; he had the light touch of a feuilletonist; his universal knowledge was always on tap; he was always good-humored and pleasant to listen to. He rejected rhetoric and dramatic points. Even his speeches to raise funds were sprinkled with apt historical allusion and anecdote.

He was an extensive traveler and was never discommoded by any form of transportation. He went by sea or plane or train with indifference. He was never known to be seasick on the roughest sea, and in the midst of a storm could be seen jotting down his notes for the encyclopedic dictionary he was writing the last years of his life. When over seventy, he made trips to South Africa and the United States. His home was in London where his motherly wife awaited him in spite of the fact that he was seldom there.

Sokolow visited the United States for the first time in March, 1913. He spoke at a mass meeting in Boston, at which Mr. Brandeis appeared for the first time as a Zionist. It was he at that time who tried to interest Mr. Brandeis in an investment corporation. This was, indeed, a strain on Sokolow's versatility. Mr. Brandeis thought it queer, too. When he reported on his talks with Mr. Brandeis at the Zionist Congress in Vienna that fall, some of the Socialist delegates interrupted and shouted: "This is no place for *reklamen*." He came over in 1922 with Vladimir

Jabotinsky and Dr. Alexander Goldstein to conduct the Keren Hayesod
campaign. The American Zionists had introduced a joint resolution in
Congress, endorsing the Balfour Declaration. The resolution was
adopted and signed by President Harding. Both Sokolow and Jabotinsky
frantically urged American Zionists to withdraw the resolution; they
were sure it would be defeated. Such fears could be expected of Sokolow,
but not of Mr. Jabotinsky. They were in good company, however,
for Dr. Stephen S. Wise and Judge Julian W. Mack also condemned
the American Zionists for taking such a rash step. It was indeed rash,
but there were really no difficulties. The resolution of 1922 served as
an important political document. In subsequent years it was pointed to
as the authentic record of the Zionist policy of the American Government, which was continued with varying interest by all subsequent
administrations.

When Dr. Weizmann resigned his office in 1931, having been refused
a vote of confidence, Sokolow, who was his collaborator for over a
decade, agreed to accept the presidency and was elected to succeed
Dr. Weizmann. Sokolow found himself in a very difficult position. Dr.
Weizmann had resigned, but he was still regarded by Zionists the world
over as the Zionist leader, and Sokolow remained, as heretofore, one
of the sagacious representatives of Zionism who was not destined to
reach the height of practical leadership. Early in life, he was regarded
as an Elder Statesman. These embarrassments did not faze Sokolow at
all, who went along as usual, making hard trips to various lands for
the Keren Hayesod, leaving the work to the secretaries, but always
insisting upon all the titles which were his. He carried these titles with
dignity for 4 years, when Dr. Weizmann was recalled to the leadership.

Sokolow was adroit and impressive and sagacious in political conversations with European statesmen with whom manner and form
seemed important. He made a number of visits to the Vatican and was
on good personal terms with some of the learned scholars who had
influence with the Pope. He met American Presidents and Secretaries
of State. His memory of persons, their public achievements, their personal idiosyncrasies, was accurate and comprehensive, and full of
vivacious description. He would often astonish his listeners with appreciations of off-the-record foibles of people he knew. In discussion he
was not profound, but he had a light and easy touch. All history was
at his command. All literature and gossip and anecdote seemed to
float into his memory and stay there, and he suffused all his knowledge

with a wisdom that left a lasting impression of a charming gentleman. He practiced a French style after leaving Poland and settling in London. He dressed the part he played with meticulous attention to detail and to the etiquette of social and political relations. He often wore spats and a monocle. It was his privilege often to close a Congress in full dress. At the Prague Congress, he waited in his diplomatic uniform from ten o'clock at night to nine the next morning, emerging fresh and debonair to make the closing speech.

He was a remarkable writer in many languages. His mind wandered over a wide field; his memory of the written page was amazing, and everything he thought of he put into a book. He wrote a textbook on natural geography in 1878. He wrote a history of anti-Semitism in 1882. He wrote a historical novel in 1883. He wrote a geography of Palestine in 1889. He wrote a treatise on Baruch Spinoza in 1929. He wrote a book on mass psychology in 1930. He published essays on personalities in three volumes. He wrote a two-volume history of the Zionist Movement in English, with an introduction by Arthur Balfour. He is said to have written over forty-five hundred articles and thirty books in Hebrew, Yiddish, Polish, German and English. He was the first Hebrew journalist to introduce the feuilleton. He edited *Hatzefirah* from 1884 until the First World War. He was the founding editor of *Haolam* in 1907, which was continued and concluded in Jerusalem by Moses Kleinman. Bialik, the Hebrew poet, once said that if you gathered together all the books Sokolow had written, it would take three hundred camels to carry them away.

He grew old with grace. The man who wrote volumes upon volumes and was known everywhere as a scholar and an author of political history, in the last years of his life accepted a degree of Doctor of Hebrew Letters from the Jewish Institute of Religion in New York and ever after insisted that he be called Doctor Sokolow. He was proud of being President of the Jewish Agency and also President of the Palestine Foundation Fund. He insisted on occupying the best suite of rooms in the hotels he visited, not because of personal comfort or ostentation, he said, but anything less than the best was a derogation of his official position. He had to radiate affluence in order not to put the Jewish Agency to shame. For years he suffered from diabetes and had to be taken care of by his devoted daughter and companion Selena, who was a physician. He died in London on May 17, 1936. After a long delay—the State of Israel had passed its eighth anniversary—he was buried in the Promised Land.

Sokolow contributed to the Zionist Movement a clear understanding of its ideals, with the ability of communicating them to non-Jews. He had an encyclopedic mind and an ease of manner which had a soothing effect upon all those whom he tried to persuade to accept Zionism during its more hectic days. He maintained his dignity and prestige until the day of his death, a remarkable product of the Hebrew renascence and the modern Zionist Movement. It was aptly said of him that he was born an *Illui,* but never became a *Gaon.*

MENAHEM USSISHKIN (1863–1941)

Ussishkin always had the reputation of being a "man of iron will." He usually came forward as the last participant in a debate, when his views stood up against the whole assembly. He was also noted for strong and enduring antipathies. He had far-reaching ambitions which were invariably frustrated because of his rough disregard of the views of others, thus creating for himself walls of opposition that had nothing to do with his theories. He had a great reverence for Jerusalem and looked down upon Tel Aviv as a reflection of an upstart polyglot *Galut* creation. He was fanatically Hebraic but seldom qualified in the taste of the elite either as a writer or speaker of Hebrew. He was chock-full of grammatical errors in every language he knew. At first he suspected the motives of Herzl and rejected his leadership; he resisted Herzl's influence with implacable energy; but he was soon reconciled to Herzl's leadership when he learned of his devotion, his lofty vision and his unseverable attachment to Israel's hopes. In spite of the limping languages he used, however, his presence in a debate dominated the discussion and what he said—not how he said it—made the deepest impression. By nature he was a tyrant, but off the stage he was a man of simple tastes, and with a thrifty sort of friendship. He seldom was able to get rid of prejudices of a personal nature. This was true not only of Herzl but also of Tschlenow, who was his rival in Russia, and, who, to his last day, was the object of Ussishkin's antipathy. He thought that Weizmann was too easygoing, too loose in language and prone to compromise. Strange to say, he had a genuine affection for Jabotinsky. He was an outstanding figure in the Zionist Congresses. He was the dominant personality in Russian Zionism. He made a slight impression in the United States when he came here with Weizmann in 1921. He was not a theoretician of Zionism. He was, however, one of the strongest pillars of Zionism on occasions of conflict or controversy. He was the head of the Jewish National Fund in his later years and lived in Jerusalem, where his home attracted all those who esteemed and respected him for his great services to the cause and for his obstinacy in defending his views.

Menahem Ussishkin was a Russian of the old school. He looked like a rugged Cossack and behaved like a medieval boyar—a challenger of czars. There were many obstinate Zionists in the early days but none had his arrogance. He was rude and despotic, paternal and sentimental; and humor never touched him. He liked to throw a bombshell of blunt dissent into a debate and defied the majority to overcome his vote. What opponents did or said never disturbed him in the security of his own views.

Ussishkin settled in Palestine when the Bolshevik Revolution overwhelmed the bourgeoisie. He would have been at ease with the Czar or with Kerensky, but he could not abide the Communist dictatorship nor would they have been pleased with him once they got into their dictatorial stride. He left before they had screwed up their courage to undertake wholesale purges. He came to Palestine as the head of the Zionist Commission (1920). Had he been asked he would have said he could not stomach the Arabs or the English. He ignored them both as long as possible.

To his way of thinking the English had no business to be in Palestine at all. God had made a promise to the Jews and there was no need for the English to endorse the promise or help to fulfill it. The Arabs were the Ishmaelites; obviously they had no share in the covenant, and they should be made to know their place. When he was asked in those primitive days to wink an eye at the softening of the petty Arab politicians in Jerusalem with coffee and cake in the cafés—as the primitive beginnings of Arab-Jewish relations—he turned down the suggestion with hot indignation. He dismissed the young corrupters of Arab morals from his office and told them never to darken his door again. That they never did. They were his enemies for life. As far as he was concerned he would have no truck with the British at all. He tolerated them. He wanted the whole of Palestine, on both sides of the Jordan, and nothing less. He would never agree to a bi-national or federated state in Palestine. He wanted the Land of Israel as established in Jewish tradition and would make no compromise with that sacred dogma.

But he managed to live through all these difficulties in spite of his prejudices. He lived in his own world of tradition and was never disturbed by the clash between his austere views and the realities of the life he had to lead in Jerusalem. Herzl may have thought of Haifa as the great international center of the future Jewish State. Ahad Ha-am, Bialik and Shmarya Levin preferred Tel Aviv. But Ussishkin planned his future in Jerusalem and became the dogmatic partisan of the primacy of the Holy City. His eyes flashed anger when anybody mentioned any other Jewish center as comparable to Jerusalem. He resented the pretenses of Tel Aviv, the upstart city built on sand. There was nothing holy about Haifa. His sanctuary and his fortress was Jerusalem where he lived until he died in 1941.

This man of granite seemed made to rule. That was what he thought, too. He had the nature of a czar whose opinions issued in the form of edicts. He was deadsure that he was always right and no one else could be as right as he. But he found no kingdom at hand to rule. He had his Zionist origin in the slow-paced days of *Chovevei Zion* in Russia. Pinsker was its ideologist and leader, and Ussishkin was the heir-apparent, who never took over the succession. He was a follower as late as 1906. He greeted Herzl with doubts and reluctant admiration. He could not be expected to welcome Herzl with open arms, for how could a man so alien to the Jewish way of life lead the Return? He had no faith in any *Daniel Deronda*. Grudgingly he came with the Russian Zionists to the First Congress and challenged Herzl from the start. They heckled him month after month, year after year; Herzl had a trying time with him all his Zionists days. Ussishkin was the chairman of the Kharkov Conference in December 1903, which threatened a revolt unless Herzl undertook "in writing" to abandon the East African scheme and confine himself exclusively to Palestine. They struggled for a voice in the affairs of the Vienna Committee. They attacked Herzl's *Altneuland* for its views on Hebrew, for its misunderstanding of the quality of their Zionism, for not perceiving that the new Zion must witness a Jewish rebirth; not a Zion on a German base. But when Herzl at the Uganda Congress vowed never to forget Jerusalem, Ussishkin forgave all his mistakes and paid him tribute in a gracious speech. But he never overcame the feeling that Herzl was not exactly the anticipated leader. He suspected that he himself might have filled the bill with better results, but that history had passed him by. That was his fate.

Ussishkin also resented the leadership of David Wolffsohn, who was a Lithuanian Jew and knew Yiddish and Hebrew, and the Jewish way of life. Wolffsohn was suspected because he had transferred his allegiance from the Russian Jewish world to the German. Wolffsohn was too much the businessman, although Ussishkin was somewhat of a merchant himself. Wolffsohn was not a fanatic about Hebrew or nationalism or Zion. It is true Wolffsohn made one of the first gifts to the Hebrew University and was always mindful of his responsibilities toward Hebrew literature. Subconsciously, however, Ussishkin felt that there was something about Wolffsohn which invalidated his leadership. He was too much political and too little practical.

The same pattern of relationship may be discovered in Ussishkin's attitude toward Yechiel Tschlenow, his Russian rival. Tschlenow also stood in Ussishkin's way; he was the soft, persuasive, friendly man, devoted to any task he assumed, modest and humble. Ussishkin was no conciliator, no hand-shaker. In a pinch the choice was always Tschlenow in preference to Ussishkin. When Wolffsohn retired, Tschlenow—not Ussishkin—was elected to the Executive and it was he who was in London when the Balfour Declaration was under discussion.

That historic moment found in Chaim Weizmann, the young chemist, the leader to take over Herzl's heritage in what appeared then to be the consummation of Zionism. In Ussishkin's eyes Weizmann was a novice, too easygoing, not firm enough, too eager to make friends with the English, too diplomatic and not aggressive enough. The curse of the situation was the English language, which Weizmann knew and which remained a secret code to Ussishkin all his life. He nursed a grudge against Weizmann, which only his honesty and integrity forced him to modify on many occasions. He came with Weizmann to the United States in 1921 and aided in the struggle for the recognition of the Keren Hayesod. He was a member of the Zionist Executive for a while and finally passed over to the chairmanship of the Jewish National Fund, which became the main Zionist front he defended for the rest of his life with an amazing concentration of purpose and possessiveness. For there he was, for the first time, the undisputed master of a situation. He was the defender of the *Land* of Israel.

He wanted to be known—in those days—as the Redeemer of the Soil. Dr. Arthur Ruppin and Joshua Hankin, the pioneers of the National Fund, were shifted into the background and Ussishkin stood out after all his years of service, after the death of all his political ambition, as the man who did the most to acquire the land of Israel as the everlasting possession of the Jewish people.

He was all of one piece, in private and on public view. On the platform or in committee he was dogmatic, thrifty with words, hard to alter once his views were expressed, and lacking in the social graces, unable to turn a corner with good humor, nursing grudges with great consistency and fervor.

Ussishkin spoke Russian, Yiddish and Hebrew, and a sort of German, but in none of them did he stick to syntax or to the use of words in their proper relations. Nevertheless, he was capable of great passion in speech and often touched heights of classic oratory excelled by none of his contemporaries. In his home he was the lord and master but capable of deep affections. He was generous and considerate of others but his prejudices were formidable. His love for Zion was unshakable. It was the obsession of his life.

He was still the head of the Jewish National Fund when the Second World War came. Weizmann had offered Zionist cooperation to the British in spite of the White Paper of 1939. Palestine was being threatened by Rommel from the west. The Arabs had laid down their arms before the war began. They defended none of their cities. They waited for the conqueror to enter, ready to receive him with open arms. They had all their flags ready to be unfurled the moment Rommel entered. Ussishkin could not oppose the offer of Weizmann to help defend Palestine. He had to admit that Hitler must be fought with all available allies.

The whole of Palestine was in a state of excitement, conscious of revolutionary changes, anxious about what the revolution would bring and eager to put themselves in the vanguard of those changes even if they and their children would die in defense of their rights. The larger number cooperated with the British. A group of determined Irgunists fought the British. They all feared civil war with the Arabs who, in frustration, might have turned against the Jews, but Ussishkin was no longer physically able to participate in that struggle. He had spoken for the last time at the Zionist Congress in Geneva in 1939. He died before the State was proclaimed. Had he lived he might have raised his voice against the partition of Palestine. He would have stood alone with God against that sacrilege.

SHMARYA LEVIN (1867–1935)

The profile of Shmarya Levin which follows is inadequate. It does not reflect, as I recall, the personal side of his influence upon a generation of American Zionists. The larger part of his life was spent with us, when he was mature and we were groping youngsters. He was a Messenger of Emancipation—equally known in Russia, in Germany, and all of Eastern Europe—but we had the impression that he was most at home with us. His whole life, it seemed, was an endless tour except for the years he gave to us toward the end of his life and the years in Palestine. His first appearance was connected with his career when a member of the Duma, which we made the most of. But he was the catalyst of Zionism in many segments of our society, even among those who protested that they were our opponents. He was on close terms of friendship with Julius Rosenwald, visiting him in Chicago as his guest at his place of residence, which was called Tel Aviv. He was a companion of the professors at the Hebrew Union College and the Jewish Theological Seminary. His passionate, colorful speeches and conversations fascinated many who rejected the dynamism of his ideas. He was one of the earliest advocates of the leadership of Chaim Weizmann, for whom he had a special affection he never disguised and never lost. He often spoke of himself as Weizmann's forerunner. He was with us when the war erupted and it was our good fortune that the ship on which he left for Europe was turned back and he had to spend the war years with us. His authority as a member of the Zionist Executive was utilized to call the Provisional Zionist Committee into being, and he had the privilege of traveling with Mr. Brandeis on his first speaking tour. Dr. Levin often wondered at the intuitions of the great man of American Law who had missed being born in a Jewish environment. With Dr. Levin, I escorted Bialik on his first trip to the United States. The poet was sick all the way over. Shmarya rushed about the decks looking for a chess partner and marveled at Bialik's amazing resources in curse words garnered from Hebrew literature. Shmarya was never an orator at Congresses. He was often discounted as a *Maggid,* but on his own platform, with his own audience, he had no peer. He did not like controversial political talk and avoided it. He played chess not as one seeking perfect moves or games. He played to while away the time, and insisted on playing fast, and was impatient when any player mooned over the board as if the best move was of any importance. He was a sick man many years before he left for Palestine. He had to speak often while in great pain, and he was impatient with friends and guests on such occasions. He knew he was going home to Zion to die and was prepared to spend the rest of his days near Bialik, playing chess with General Wauchope—kibitzing his way along. But his work was cut out only for the Diaspora. In fact he was always on vacation in Zion and felt that he had nothing to do there. He brought his daughter Anna with him to the United States on several occasions. She resembled him in many ways. She was married and died in Palestine at an early age. His son, Boris, is a practicing chemist in Israel. It was Shmarya who persuaded me to leave the editorship of the *American Hebrew* forty years ago to enlist in the Zionist Movement. I shall always remember him for that with gratitude.

Shmarya Levin was one of the great preachers of modern Zionism. He was a pre-Herzlian Zionist of the Pinsker school. He carried Zionist thought to many parts of the world. His public career began in Russia where he was one of the pioneers of the Jewish renascence. He spent many years in Germany and developed a school of intellectual and political disciples who were the leaders of Zionism in Germany and Austria. He came to the United States soon after the Kishinev pogroms and was the inspirer of a whole generation of American Zionists. He was not merely a propagandist; he was a teacher of great ability who drilled his ideas into the minds of his audiences with eloquence and force, with wit and humor. He was a vigorous writer in Yiddish and Hebrew, but he loved speaking best. Nor was his speaking confined to the public meeting. He practiced his art with extraordinary vivacity in the drawing room and in cafés, where he drew eager listeners to his conversation.

He was born in Russia in 1867 and received his early education in Jewish schools and in a secular school. He studied at the Universities of Heidelberg and Berlin and after receiving his doctor's degree, returned to Russia where, from 1896 to 1906, he was a "government rabbi" at Grodno, Ekaterinoslav and Vilna. He was elected a deputy to the first Russian Duma and was a member of the liberal Cadet Party. His powerful addresses in the Duma made him known to all Jews who read the Yiddish and Hebrew press. He was one of the signers of the Viborg Manifesto, protesting against the Czar's dissolution of the Duma, which made it necessary for him to leave Russia for good. He established his home in Berlin. He won the support of the *Hilfsverein der Deutschen Juden* in 1908 for the Haifa Technical Institute in Palestine and then became the leader in the language controversy when the German organization wanted to use the Haifa Technical Institute for the promotion of the German language. It was as a deputy of the Duma that Levin first came to the United States.

Levin became a member of the Zionist Executive in 1911. It was as one of the leaders of the Zionist Movement that Levin came again to the United States in 1913. He was marooned in the United States during the period of the First World War. He initiated the organization of the Provisional Zionist Committee of which Louis D. Brandeis was the chairman. When the war was over, Levin returned to Berlin but visited the United States repeatedly in the interests of the Keren Hayesod. Levin was responsible for launching the first Keren Hayesod campaign in the United States. He was a member of the Weizmann delegation to the United States in 1921. He induced Bialik, the Hebrew poet, to visit the United States with him in 1923. He was always talking of Zion, but his work and his interests kept him in the *Galut*.

He was the teacher of a whole generation of Jewish educators and Zionist officials. His schoolroom was the lecture platform. He had no textbooks or charts but delivered his message in impassioned, illuminating addresses on all the Zionist problems of the day. He was able to make what he said glow with fire and passion. He was a master of invective and sardonic humor. He was remarkable in castigating his own people for their lack of vision, their disinterest in organized action. He was savage and relentless in his indictments. He was capable of terrible anger. He excited his audiences with his descriptions of what was being done in Zion—it was not much then—and how it was transforming the Jewish personality. No other Zionist propagandist gave as much as Levin to the spirit and intellectual life of American Zionism.

He was not noted for his addresses at Zionist Congresses or meetings of the Actions Committee. He spent most of his time at Congresses in the lobbies or coffee houses. He was disparagingly referred to as a *Maggid;* and that he was. But he surpassed many a Congress orator in his ability to excite the mind and spirit of his listeners and to persuade them that what he was saying was an echo of what they would find in their own hearts if they would only search for it.

He had none of the tricks of oratory. When he came to the end of what he had to say he stepped back off the platform. He would start his discourses with a stray observation and slowly find his way to his central theme, rushing along at top speed to drive home the idea which had burst into expression. He was like a spraying fire reverting to old thoughts and finding a new form for them, giving them forth as a new revelation. Old thoughts and old stories always were given new life in his repeated addresses. Whatever he said sounded as if it had just been thought of.

He was an agitator in a literal sense. He provoked thoughts and feelings against the will of his listeners. He was angry with Jewish life, and like Bialik, felt humiliated by Jewish indifference and lack of self-assertion. He was a panegyrist of Zion and spoke glowingly of the sprigs of new life that had appeared. He exalted the work of the pioneers, but glowered upon those who clung to the fleshpots of Egypt. He made the few green spots in Zion look like the beginnings of great forests; but did the Jews of *Galut* really deserve those green spots? He brought with him a nostalgia for all things Jewish. He was able to find Jewish quality in many things gathered under the moss of *Galut*. Zionism was the preserver and protector; it was the builder of the Temple of the Jewish future. The world had covered Jewish life with indignities and humiliations; the emancipation would drive Jews into assimilation and extinction; Zionism was the destined liberator.

He came into our American life to burn out the unclean. His voice would break through formalities and tear apart the pretenses and deceits of the contented, the indifferent, the short-visioned, the ignorant. He was always a wanderer, never at home, but only contented in spirit when he found in far-off places kindred souls who shared his vision. One felt that he came from an ancient shrine filled with un-forgotten traditions and that he was inviting the whole Jewish people to worship at that shrine. He lived in strange hotels, underwent the cruellest physical hardships, spoke when every word was pain; but one felt that all of this pain was being self-inflicted in order to earn the right to return home and there to find rest.

Many American Zionist conventions were made memorable by his closing addresses. He would stand alone on the platform, the hour would be late, and the delegates would be fatigued; but when he began to talk, with his hands in his pockets, he created an electrifying interest. They remembered him as he stood there, looking remarkably like Lenin, the communist revolutionary. They remembered the lather of excitement in which he was immersed. They remembered the tone of exaltation which rang in his voice, the sarcasm, the rebuke. He appeared like a Mephisto in reverse, speaking like an angry Prophet of God.

Levin was older than Weizmann and Bialik, but among the three men there existed a deep personal affection, based on a fraternal relationship which did not exist in other Zionist groups. Levin was a political disciple of Weizmann. He never pretended to the possession of political qualities. He lacked patience and understanding of political conflicts. He was led by Weizmann. In 1910 he let people know that he thought Weizmann was the coming political leader. He told it to American and German Zionists as if he had found the new Leader. Levin had the greatest reverence for Bialik's genius and humility. Only in the presence of Bialik did Levin retire to the position of a listener. Bialik was an incomparable storyteller and if you wanted an identification of any literary reference, Bialik could give it with remarkable accuracy, but he was always shy about his resources. He had to be coaxed to reveal himself. Levin treated the poet with great tenderness.

He was an inveterate chess player and played with a vindictive desire to win. Not that he was a good chess player; he never concentrated strongly enough; but he played for intellectual exercise, to pass the time and in order to overcome an adversary. He loved the play of skill. If he lost he became ill-humored; when he won his vanity was childishly jubilant. When he crossed the ocean—before there were planes— he was never affected by storms, but ran about the decks incessantly, looking for someone to talk to, or for someone to play chess with. He would get terribly cross with a chess player who played patiently and slowly to win. Facing such an unreasonable adversary, he would prod him with sharp urgings to move, reminding him that life was short, that chess should not be taken too seriously. He was always restless.

Although Levin was one of the Russian group who overturned David Wolffsohn, he had no appetite for the party struggle in Zionist affairs. In his later years, he retired from the political field altogether and was devoted to the promotion of Hebrew literature. He was one of Bialik's colleagues in the organization of the Dvir Publishing Company, to the affairs of which Bialik and he gave a great deal of personal attention while serving the Keren Hayesod. Levin always had his own favored campaign, his own extracurricular interests for which he was a remarkably persistent and successful solicitor of funds. He specialized in discovering patrons of Hebrew literature.

He was a writer of talent, an essayist, a publicist. He was editor of a number of Hebrew and Yiddish journals. He founded the Yiddish *Volk* in Vilna. His articles appeared in *Hashiloach, Hamelitz, Der Fraind* and other important publications. He shared in organizing the Hebrew monthly publication *Hatoren* in the United States and was a frequent contributor to the *Day* in New York. He gathered the best of his articles into three volumes which served as his autobiography. They were admirably translated into English by Maurice Samuel. His style of writing resembled his speaking in many ways. He was terse, direct, cruel to the irrelevant, and knew when his work was finished. Nor did he ever overstay his time on the platform.

He was always reserved in personal relations. His wife lived a retired life in Berlin. There were two children, Boris and Anna. Anna died in Palestine at an early age. Boris became a scientist in the Hebrew University and later an industrial chemist. The greater part of Levin's life was spent away from home. His children grew up in his absence. He knew them when they were adults. His wife died in Berlin before Hitler came.

Levin returned to Palestine suffering from a serious chronic illness. His home was a rendezvous for visitors from the *Galut*. Dr. Weizmann never failed to visit him when in the country. Friends from the United States and Canada and Germany knew where to find him.

They found him a restless prisoner in Zion. He could do nothing to help in the building. His thoughts reverted to the *Galut*—his many great moments in Russia, in the United States, in Germany. His future was where he had spent his past. His historic task was to awaken the *Galut;* now he was an invalid in Zion. Around him a new life was being built, but he had no personal relation to it. Life did not feel good. Hitler was on the march. Incredible dangers threatened the *Galut,* but the Land was not prepared, the political situation was unfavorable. He was impatient and bitter. His occupation was gone, and living was painful and empty. Henrietta Szold saw him ten days before his death, "speaking with the same bubbling fullness as always." He passed away in 1935 on the Carmel, topping Haifa, surviving Bialik by about one year.

AHAD HA-AM (1856–1927)

Ahad Ha-am was the founder of a school, the representative of a philosophy of Jewish life, and a personality of great intellectual strength and integrity. This frail old man, in whom the vital spark was with superhuman effort retained for many years in a tortured body, stood out as one of the most impressive of all the figures of the Jewish renascence. With Theodor Herzl and Max Nordau, Leo Pinsker and A.D. Gordon, he was the molder of modern Zionist thought. He was the most austere of all Zionist philosophers. From the beginnings of the *Chovevei Zion* Movement down to the latest phase of Zionist development, his sage words attended every Zionist act with warnings, analysis and appreciation. The quality that distinguished him was his intellectual sobriety and conscientiousness. From his early youth he disdained the temporary advantage of rhetoric, fine writing and casuistry. He was a perfectionist in thought and form.

Meticulously seeking the truth, unwilling to be deflected even if it seemed to contradict what the whole world thought, he developed into a personality with a strange stoic strain, calm and unyielding, reiterating in various forms, with marvelous restraint, the basic thought which has become associated with his philosophy. His style reflected the austerity of his intellectual methods. The truth with him was the product of knowledge, meditation, of cool reasoning. It was the postulate of intellectual experience, and therefore could not so easily be harmonized with the new truth which Jewish life, awakened, was in the process of creating through the Zionist Movement. He did not believe in taking risks; he had no sympathy with adventure. He could not endure loose thinking, the easy invention of the *Batlon* mind. He was often inflamed with prophetic anger against attempts at building, which were doomed, according to his keen analysis, to topple over. He refused to go the way of mere enthusiasm or aspiration. He was no sentimentalist. In the intellectual realm he was capable of originality and of daring, but in the things that had to be done in this world he had an intensely practical and conservative mind. Even in planning the future he wanted firm ground under his feet. Curiously enough, he was associated for many years with the tea business of the Wissotzkys in Odessa. He was not harassed by the element of time, for the Jewish people to him were an eternal people. He wanted Jews to exemplify in their national action the restraints and the wisdom of ancient times. He would have liked to have them revert to their Hebraic personality.

Naturally his methods led him to a conscious and subconscious opposition to the idealism of Herzl. For Herzl was the remaker of truth in the world of reality. He was the breaker of precedent. He was the daring adventurer. With all his practicality, Herzl dealt with dream, fantasy, drama, sentiment. What was not in existence, he aimed to create. He was willing to take a chance and to force the game. A rhetorical call would gather the scattered remnants of the Jewish people. Would they respond? (Reason was against it. *That* was not the way.) A Congress was to create a body to assume responsibility for the Jewish future. Would a Congress, lacking unity of speech, lacking common customs, with disparate cultures, endure? (Reason was against it. *That* was not the way.) Herzl placed reliance upon the fiats of governments, negotiations, interviews with potentates, the granting of charters. Would the fiat of governments bring the Jewish people to life—a depressed, scattered, hopeless people? (Reason was against it. *That* was not the way.) Herzl wanted to create an atmosphere of legal approval and sanction—then the vessel to hold and carry the physical body of the Jewish people—and out of this revolution he hoped that a new Jewish life would emerge. What Jews had neglected to do was no criterion of what they would do if the right conditions were created. Herzl depended largely upon inspiration and improvisation, without estimate of strength or resources, relying upon Providence or historical combinations plus the Jewish people in whom he had faith, to meet any emergency or to take advantage of any opportunity. He was the statesman, not the philosopher; the actor, not the commentator.

Ahad Ha-am was shy in speaking. He spoke through his writings. I remember him at the Vienna Congress of 1913. He sat with the Russians at their caucus. He was silent throughout, listening, with his head bowed over his cane, a medium-sized lean man with a light beard, absorbing the Russian words of his disciples, and indicating no immediate reaction.

To his contemplative, sober mind, the Herzlian maneuvers were distressing. Clay was not gold and could not possess the functions and qualities of gold. The redemption of Zion must be preceded by the regeneration of the Jewish people. The emphasis must be placed upon spirit and culture and the creation of a Jewish soul capable of visualizing and desiring the transformation of the conditions of life. All premature action would prove fatal. The foundations must be laid securely. And so Ahad Ha-am, throughout Herzl's career, held to a critical, neutral attitude, granting a point here, reserving judgment there, feeling entirely at a loss how to bring the new truth that was developing within the range of his own reflections. He was greatly disturbed when Herzl wrote *Altneuland* and exposed Herzl's lack of depth in understanding Jewish life by a merciless criticism of the book. It was the *Kultur-*Zionism of Ahad Ha-am that weakened the foundations of the political Zionism of Herzl.

The First World War overturned all prophecies. It radically affected all systems of thinking, and had a tremendous influence upon the Zionist Movement. Out of that maelstrom came the Balfour Declaration, in the making of which Ahad Ha-am, then residing in London, was an impressive and valuable influence; and with the Balfour Declaration came the opportunity and the pressure of life to push forward in the conquest of the land. The door of Zion was opened. Not now the time to hesitate. The charter that seemed a visionary thing in 1900 had become an act of the Allied Governments. The recognition of the Jewish right to Palestine was sanctioned by the League of Nations. The whole structure of thought, involving an evolutionary development of a Jewish cultural center—to some extent separate and apart from the establishment of the Jewish National Home—was disturbed. What the Jewish world saw was an opportunity to bring consolation and amelioration to a race that had suffered terrible injuries during the period of the War. Involuntarily, persuaded not so much by his intellect as by his Jewish intuition (for essentially, he was "one of the people"), Ahad Ha-am found himself for the first time in harmony with Zionist action, swept into it by the force of Jewish life, becoming a party to its difficulties and successes, becoming involved in the welter of self-criticism in which the Jews of Palestine were immersed, and out of which new life was being created.

Ahad Ha-am settled in Palestine, and at once established a position there which enhanced the services he had rendered to the Jewish people in the first Zionist decade. He was the Sage of Tel Aviv, witnessing with his own eyes a physical regeneration progressing on parallel lines with the spiritual rebirth. What he had posited as the essential emphasis was swept away by the force of human needs and by the need of taking prompt advantage, with all strength possible, of every opportunity. His teachings became the classical approach. In the actual rebuilding of Palestine, which he witnessed for a number of years, he found reconciliation with that mightier stream of Zionist thought which was represented by Herzl. He always had a fondness for Chaim Weizmann who was the exponent of synthetic Zionism and with whom he had a natural kinship. He came to see the great beauty of spirit which animated the new Aliyah, combining spiritual ideals with devotion to hard physical labor. He came to see how simultaneously the face of the earth might be transformed by the will of the pioneers. He saw simultaneously the conquest of the Emek and the founding of the Hebrew University. His last days in Palestine made him feel the greatness of the Jewish people, which overturned all precedent, made necessary revision of all estimates, built the roof before the foundation, and yet, through persistence and endurance, was able to mold a harmony which was representative of the unity of the Jewish spirit. Endeared to all, regardless of party, respected as sage and teacher, his body weakening day by day, although his mind was ever alert, he was privileged to witness the flowering of a new Jewish life which owes much to his teachings and which progressed from the Jewish National Home to the State of Israel.

ELIEZER BEN YEHUDA (1857–1922)

Eliezer Ben Yehuda gave his life to the task of resurrecting Hebrew as the vernacular of his people. From early youth he was a prolific Hebrew writer. In 1870 he pleaded not only for the return of Jews to Palestine but also for the revival of Hebrew as a living tongue. Born in Lithuania in 1857, he left for Paris in 1879 to study medicine, but fell a victim to tuberculosis. He was advised to seek healing in the warm climate of Algeria, but in 1881 went to Jerusalem as his cure-place. There he fell under the spell of the thought that he, by his example and his writings, would transform Hebrew into a language Jews should speak, not merely a language struggling to express ideas in the traditional forms, avoiding as sinful its awakening for everyday use, but as a living form of expression. He was not greatly interested in the Zionist Movement and stubbornly concentrated on his self-imposed task. During the First World War he had to leave Palestine with his family under Turkish pressure and lived in the United States for a number of years. When the war came to an end he returned to Palestine, concentrated on the writing of his Encyclopedia of ancient and modern Hebrew, and died in Jerusalem in 1922.

To his zeal, to his intolerant, forceful and controversial propaganda, to his exalted feelings of national pride and faith in the renaissance of his people, and also to his natural genius for the language—is due in largest measure the re-entrance of Hebrew among modern languages and its adoption by a new generation of Jews as their everyday speech for all purposes. He stood almost alone. There were others who cultivated the written Hebrew word, but they were dealing with the dry bones of a retarded language, browsing among the antiquities of their people, looking back with reverence to what it used to be and refusing willingly to accept the invitation to make it the servant of the New Day. They were fed by the Torah and its commentaries; its restraints and its pieties; bound by its archaic forms. They venerated and served a Holy Language. Ben Yehuda was determined to make that language secular, fitted for the new world where Jews were called to live and to be reborn; and to have it express the thoughts and desires, the hopes and tragedies of men of this generation, engaged in a desperate struggle to maintain and develop their identity. Without perceiving the vastness of the world that would have to be integrated in the living Hebrew, the prodigious task involved in giving the stiff, old language a flexible body, a living vocal expression to include what the world had created since

Hebrew stopped growing, Ben Yehuda dedicated himself to its rebirth in spite of his physical frailty, in spite of the rejection of his mission by those for whose benefit it was to be reborn; and made his mission the sole obsession of his life.

He was a superb fanatic with a fixed idea burning in his heart like a hot coal. He conceived of spoken Hebrew as the soul of a living people, without which it could not live. It was the essence of the Jewish renaissance. Without a language capable of expressing all the nuances of life, ancient and modern; capable of free intercourse in its own idiom, in all areas of human expression, the Redemption was a grotesque and meaningless anachronism, especially in the light of a growing, colorful Zionist Movement both in the Diaspora and in Palestine. He derided the contention of the older generation of Hebraists that you could find all the Hebrew you needed in the ancient writings, in the archeological remains of what had once been the vessel of speech of the prophets and the lawgivers. Disregarding technicalities, law and order—the stiffness of the language, the rigidity of its joints, the hardness of its roots—overcoming the barriers of time and place—he poured his life with amazing recklessness and disregard of physical and material interest into the great task of the renaissance of Hebrew. He was the living symbol of the revival. He was the fountain from which the words came with amazing variety. Many of the words he coined were rejected as artificial at a glance; some of them were brilliant improvisations that caught on to the tongue of their users; many of them were reflections of a genius for sensing what was the true word. He broke the hardened shells of the old roots, tore them apart, appropriated sounds from alien tongues, set them together in new formations and flung them into a new vocabulary. His scholarship and his talent for deduction enabled the Hebrew language to tread the rocky path of renaissance, adjusting itself through practice to the vast resources of written and spoken languages civilization had given birth to since Hebrew had ceased to be alive and fertile. He had to span centuries to make up for so much lost time. He had to absorb in the new language the techniques and the practices of new civilizations. He had to feed the needs of the Promised Land and its people now involved in the process of discovering their old language for new uses. He had to find the new words to express the variety and the novelty of the speech of those generations that had long since passed the point where Jewish life had started.

Jerusalem was his fortress. There he began the compilation of his all-inclusive dictionary of ancient and modern Hebrew. There in 1889 he founded the *Vaad Halashon* consisting of scholars and experts who cooperated in coining whatever new words were needed and publishing them in a quarterly journal. He lived in the center of fundamentalist orthodoxy where his innovations were regarded as heresy. He was ostracized and condemned by the pious who were under the deadening influence of the *Chalukah* and followers of immobile tradition. He felt that he was bringing freedom for his people; they thought he was undermining the foundations of religion. He thought that he was showing them the way to emancipation from the thrall of foreign speech. They preferred Yiddish to Hebrew as the vernacular in their schools. The freedom Ben Yehuda spoke of—they felt—would lead to assimilation and apostasy. It was the example of his life—forswearing the use of any other language but Hebrew, inhibiting the use of any other language by his children in his home—that evoked allegiance to Hebrew in Palestine so that it became dogma in the Jewish schools, in the colonies and in the labor movement, and ennobled the Second Aliyah, giving it a distinction never before achieved by any group in the Zionist Movement. It laid the foundation for the Hebrew school system which, when Palestine became Israel, was to become the national school system. Ben Yehuda had prepared the way for the language controversy in 1907 when the Jewish educators revolted against the hegemony of foreign languages and created their own autonomous schools.

His work was continued by his widow Hemda and his son Ittamar Ben Avi. Hemda took over the practical side of the Encyclopedia. She secured the material support for the enterprise. She was successful as a fund-gatherer in the United States. She was executrix of her husband's literary remains; engaged competent editorial assistance for the Encyclopedia and was responsible for the publication of its 15 volumes. Only six volumes had appeared during Ben Yehuda's lifetime.

Ittamar was a fiery, colorful orator and an able polemical writer. He seemed to be driven by the same passion which inspired his father. He, however, was articulate and capable of forensic exposition and enjoyed himself greatly in controversy. No matter what language Ittamar used he always began his speech in Hebrew. He had a way of making the words of any language sound like Hebrew. He liked to show his skill in appropriating foreign speech to Hebrew expressions. Once the writer was in Tel Aviv at a public affair and made a few remarks in English. Ben Avi eagerly undertook to translate and made the few

stiff English paragraphs used sound like an oration by Demosthenes.
[The language was more important to Ittamar than the content of his speech. He loved it for its own sake. He reveled in its sounds. He was born in Jerusalem in 1884, studied in Berlin and Paris and went into exile with his father during the war, collaborating in his publications and returning with him to Jerusalem when peace was made. Ittamar spent many years in the United States as a propagandist for the Jewish National Fund and died in our midst in 1943.]

Ben Yehuda struggled to free the language for use in everyday life in natural and artificial ways, and prepared for its use by the first generation born in Palestine. He removed the fear of innovation from the heart of the orthodox. He was responsible for the birth of a sturdy generation that tackled every problem of language and emerged with new words in authentic Hebrew to fit into the pattern of life. It had room in which to shelter new idioms taken from everyday life, scientific terms, words created by the intercourse of daily life. The new generation took what Ben Yehuda gave them with gratitude; then, later, with a certain disdain and arrogance; they kicked away the ladder on which they had risen. They seemed to wish to forget Ben Yehuda whose whole life—and what he had done with it—was imprisoned in his Encyclopedia where his personality is revealed to all who seek to find it.

LEO MOTZKIN (1867–1933)

It was said of Motzkin that as a young man he was a mathematical wonder, but that legend faded away as he settled down to the status of an "everlasting" student, always studying but never getting anywhere. After the Kishinev pogroms he was asked to compile a historical account of those tragedies, which he did after several years of laborious concentration. It was the heaviest task he ever undertook. The rest of his life was spent as a public figure in Jewish affairs. In the founding of the Committee of Jewish Delegations he played an important part and then drifted into the position of being Representative of the Committee at Geneva. But he spent most of his time in Paris, from which he refused to be dislodged. Whenever required, he went to Geneva, where he hobnobbed with representatives of other crippled minorities, and then returned to Paris. In fact, he was more influential in helping the *Goyish* minorities than the Jewish. His name was associated with the Delegation for the rest of his life, but being a transient, so to speak, he was open for Zionist service when and as required. In the course of time he became known as the chairman of the Committee of Jewish Delegations, the chairman of the Zionist Actions Committee, the chairman of the Presidium of the Zionist Congress, to which he finally attached himself as the master of the gavel. In that chair his imagination rested and was exercised on occasion. He was a routine speaker, had no fire in him, but was an interesting raconteur; in the cafés and lobbies he was a colorful and arresting personality. He was ingenious, resourceful and witty as a chairman and could be relied upon to prolong discussions instead of curtailing them. Thus, he was popular with all debaters, past and present. He enjoyed life best when he sat in the chair and ordered the procedures of discussion.

Leo Motzkin never could be hurried. He preferred to stroll through life. He loved the warmth of meetings. He always expected to be tagged to take the chair. So he was often made the *Vorsitzer,* for he sat so well and looked so wise and genial. In a real sense, he was a moderator— turning to the right or left, and eventually, after a great deal of fumbling, finding a true balance somewhere in the middle. The center was where he fitted—in the Russian Revolution and in the Zionist Movement.

Russian by birth and education, he came to Berlin when he was fifteen. He aimed to be a mathematician. The legend was that he abandoned his career to follow the light of Zionism. The certainties of mathematics would have suited his temperament, but he was too weak to resist the temptations of Zionism and to run away from its blandishments. Thus it was always said that mathematics was one of his lost illusions, which was due to the magic of Zionism. (His son was to follow in his footsteps and become a professor of mathematics at the Hebrew University of Jerusalem.)

Zionism captured his mind at an early age. He was a Zionist long before Herzl sounded his trumpet. He was a member of a youthful group in Berlin which published its manifesto to students in 1888, calling for a Congress to formulate the aims of "Pan-Jewish" Zionism. The manifesto criticized the slow-paced Lovers of Zion. Even at that time these young men said: "Give flaming youth the right of way!" Motzkin was then sixteen.

He was proud of his mastery of German and loved the German way of life. That was when educated Russian Jewry opened their windows to "enlightenment," looking longingly to German philosophy, science and worldly knowledge. Many became devotees of Russian culture, but more turned to Berlin and Vienna and the Swiss universities. Motzkin addressed Zionist Congresses in German. The delegates were *meine Damen und Herren*. Much later he was able to call them *Rabotai*. Of course, he knew Yiddish well. It suited his purpose, however, to pose as a German professor, and he always seemed dressed for the part in a careless way. He liked German cigars.

He was one of the first to respond to Herzl's call. He was impressed by the dignity of Herzl's bearing, the beauty of his German and his success in journalism. But he was not one of his disciples. He was a leader of the "democratic faction" in the earliest Congresses. He believed that if a Congress had no opposition, an opposition would have to be created, for uniformity would be fatal. The "democratic faction" was small, but it had audacity which it kept within bounds. It had no intention of refusing Herzl a vote of confidence or of forcing his resignation by its behavior. It used its right as a group to heckle the great leader, to challenge the procedure, to embarrass Herzl in order to show him how correctly and courageously these talented young men conducted their opposition.

With the defeat of the Uganda proposal and Herzl's death, the "democratic faction" lost itself among the "general" Zionists, who never could be charged with having a program or an ideology. Nevertheless, the "general" Zionists were to lead the Movement for a number of decades, maintain its financial solvency, and, through Dr. Weizmann, carry it to the edge of the liquidation of the Mandate. In the course of time, the Party Zionists waxed strong. In 1933 the Labor Party finally joined the Jewish Agency; the Mizrachi ceased being the religious party and became what may be called "clerical" politicians. The "general" Zionists in self-defense were driven to organize a quasi-party, whose chief trouble in later years was to find a reason for its being. Personally, Motzkin raised his head proudly above and beyond party, always.

Motzkin's specialty developed with a gradualness almost invisible. Following the Kishinev pogroms, he was asked to write a book about them. Looking back to that startling episode, one wonders at the violent emotions raised by what, in the light of subsequent events, seemed to have been a minor incident. Those pogroms took the lives of less than 100 Jews. The property destroyed was not impressive. But the fact that it was possible for such murders to take place at all, just as Jews were expecting more liberty (not less), made Jews feel that civilization was reversing itself.

The Russian pogroms followed the revision of the Dreyfus Case. The French outburst of anti-Semitism found Jews spectators of an old tragedy, but themselves inactive. The pogroms aroused Jews to action. Protest meetings were held in all Western countries. The pogroms were the signal for the awakening of slumbering Jewish communities the world over. More money was collected for relief than could be used. Jews in democratic lands turned their heads to look backward with apprehension, wondering whether they were really on the verge of universal emancipation.

Motzkin tackled the task of gathering material for his report with great energy and spread himself without reserve and produced two heavy volumes in German. He gave five years of his life to the project. On the basis of that performance he was regarded as a professional, as a political analyst and an authority on political affairs. He read a lot of books and reviewed Jewish current events from an international podium. He criticized statesmen, foretold political developments, and came to conclusions with solemn precision. He pontificated with delightful self-assurance as if he were a judge of a high court.

Motzkin did not indulge in rhetoric or lyricism. He was not an orator. He was not a sentimentalist. He could not rhapsodize about Zion. He was too reserved to get himself into a lather about the historic monuments of the Promised Land. He was in no sense a propagandist. He refused to ghettoize Zionism. Like Herzl, he thought of the Movement in international terms. He saw the Jewish world as a whole. He wanted Jews to build a homeland with their own hands, but he also saw Jews scattered the world over, denied their rights, suffering persecution. He saw Zion as a hill; the Diaspora Jews as in a dark valley; sometimes trailing clouds of glory, sometimes dragging their glory in the mud of poverty and persecution, but all bound together in the same destiny. He believed in one God, one Torah, one People; but not dwelling in only one land. He thought that the Zionist Movement should face both ways—towards Zion and towards the Diaspora—and should maintain a balance. Unfortunately, Motzkin did not live long enough to see the State of Israel and to tackle the realities of this fantastic conception. Diaspora nationalism split Motzkin's personality as it did a number of other leading Zionists'.

Thus, never able to connect his life with Palestine, he got to occupy two chairs—one at the Committee of Jewish Delegations, the other at Zionist Congresses. He was absorbed in the problem of Jewish disabilities, the political state of the Jews in Russia and Poland, in Rumania and Hungary, in the Oriental lands; and incidentally, as it were, in the political affairs of the Jews with regard to Palestine.

When the First World War overwhelmed Europe, Motzkin was sympathetic to the Allies and had to leave Berlin. He went to neutral Copenhagen to take charge of the Zionist office. He shared responsibility with Victor Jacobson. They made Copenhagen an important Jewish center for relations with Jews of all lands during the war. They were in touch with Arthur Ruppin, who had been removed by the Turks to Constantinople. The Bureau was visited on occasion by Zionists coming from Berlin. Emissaries of the American Zionists maintained relations with Copenhagen. Correspondents from all parts of the world flocked to the Danish capital, which became a buzzing center of all sorts of political information and intrigue. Motzkin's political horizon was broadened by his experience in Denmark. He acquired a universal outlook and aped the manners of diplomats. He learned how to dress as befitted his station, but he was guilty of many lapses. He was never like Victor Jacobson who was a diplomat to the manner born, but he was a patient student of protocol and learned a great deal from the Germans, the Swiss and to some extent from the French.

After the First World War, the scattered Zionist authorities assembled in London. Sokolow and Motzkin were appointed to organize the Committee of Jewish Delegations, which was formed to speak for the European Jewish communities. Sokolow took his assignment in his usual Olympian manner, but Motzkin was a *Litvak* who took his work seriously. He put his mind to the study of the problems of minorities. He gathered around him leaders of many Jewish communities. In fact, before the League of Nations was liquidated, he was the leader of all the minority group representatives in Geneva. He filled his portfolio with briefs, drafts of speeches and correspondence. The Committee of Jewish Delegations moved with the League of Nations to Geneva, but Motzkin hovered between Paris and Geneva and London and did not know where he should hang his hat permanently. In 1920 he organized the first international conference, which became a front for relief, but had no money in its treasury. When the Joint Distribution Committee was about to discontinue its work on the ground that there was no further need for relief, Motzkin came to the United States and threatened an independent relief campaign. The threat caused the Joint Distribution Committee to change its mind and to continue its work until the Nazi terror gave new life to Jewish relief and to all other forms of Jewish endeavor.

Motzkin could not settle down, however. He was unable to go back
to postwar Berlin. He could not acclimatize himself in London. He got
to like Paris best of all. There he had his restaurants and cafés and
he could speak a modicum of French. There he could meet Jews of all
lands. If you sat at the Café de la Paix any afternoon, you would see a
panorama of Jewish life pass by. He was beginning to adjust himself
to French ways—its language, its climate, its restaurants, its boulevards.
He seemed to have lost his affection for the Germans and their culture.
His duties required him to be in Geneva, but even when the Committee of Jewish Delegations, dominated by the American Jewish
Congress, voted that the headquarters of the Committee must be in
Geneva, Motzkin remained in Paris, defying the Americans.

In appearance Motzkin was not glamorous or imposing. He lacked
platform personality. At public meetings in the United States his addresses were too professional to stir the audience. He was a stout little
man with a rasping voice and a tangled beard. His features suggested
Emile Zola. When he was not pompous he had a merry twinkle in his
eyes as if warning one not to take his dignity too seriously. When he
got to Paris his beard was trimmed but it always got out of hand and
helped to muffle his voice. He spent more time drinking tea than at his
desk. He loved good company and was a good listener. He read heavy
literature and nothing light and easy ever crossed his eyes. He never
seemed to have time for home life and could be relied upon to pack a
grip and on a moment's notice go to London or Vienna or New York—
wherever a Jewish cause beckoned. He disliked quarrels and partisanship. He was never at a loss for alternatives in an argument ("on the one
hand" against "the other hand"). He was rather complicated in making
his points clear, but he worked hard to do so.

It was as a presiding officer that Motzkin became a legend. He was
the "Master of the Gavel." His career as a chairman may be said to
have started with Carlsbad in 1921. It should not be inferred that he
was a brilliant parliamentarian. He had a peculiar talent which Americans and Englishmen would not appreciate in a chairman. He was the
master of the agenda, he was the moderator, he was the logician and
analyst of *Antraege*. He had a genius for reconciling contradictions.
His wit was labored, but no matter how muddy a parliamentary situation became he was able finally to emerge holding the most general
Antrag between his two fingers, prepared to put whatever remained of
the idea to a vote. He did not function like Sokolow, who could preside
at meetings large or small and never breach the amenities or allow

disorder to get the best of him. Sokolow was brilliant at committee meetings. He would sit like a sphinx, listen to all the speakers, take no notes, and at the end of the debate was able to summarize everything said with meticulous accuracy and summarize unerringly the consensus of opinion and then suggest the common-sense action which was in most cases accepted.

Nor was Motzkin like Weizmann as a chairman. Weizmann presided in the Anglo-Saxon way; he kept the debate down to essentials. He did not hesitate to call a man to order and to put the motion to a vote with clarity and precision, undisturbed by heckling; in fact, disorder was abashed by Weizmann's disdainful attitude toward repetition and foolish talk. He was not fitted to preside, however, in moments of great heat or controversy. That was the specialty of Motzkin.

He was a Master in the sense that he gave a good performance. He intruded with his own shrewd observations. He was guilty of facetious remarks. He was loved for his casuistry. He directed the meetings with a keen eye for logical order and the general impression of the debate. He was like the leader of an orchestra who every now and then played some music of his own. He never gave the members of the presidium a chance to develop their talents. He monopolized the chair even when another occupied it, for he persisted in guiding the novice and suggesting ways out of difficulties which could not be refused. He always took the chair at an important moment in the Congress. He acted as if he were the president of the faculty and dispensed favors to his colleagues on the presidium. He was jealous of the status of his office and did not hesitate to join debate on issues of procedure beyond his authority. He had a slow way of talking, but he was quick at seeing a point. He was tenacious in the order and phrasing of a sentence until he got it just right.

At the Prague Congress of 1933 he got into a ludicrous conflict with himself. He was the chairman of the Actions Committee and was also to be the chairman of the Congress. As usual, the expiring Actions Committee held its final meeting before the opening of the Congress. A fierce controversy had arisen with the Revisionists over the Arlosoroff murder case, in which one of the Revisionists had been charged with the murder of the political officer of the Jewish Agency. For reasons difficult to reconstruct, Motzkin was of the opinion that certain questions were involved which came within the jurisdiction of the Actions Committee. As a rule, this committee had well-defined constitutional functions at its final session. It had to approve the agenda and nominate the president of the Congress. With the opening of the Congress its standing committees took over jurisdiction of all Congress affairs. Motzkin got the Actions Committee entangled in jurisdictional questions, and insisted that it should pass on certain aspects of the Arlosoroff case and prolonged the debate by raising new refinements of the issue and releasing all control of the debate. He seemed to be delighted with his own casuistry. He hypnotized hardened members of the Committee with his brilliant disintegration of the issues and their reformulation. The members allowed themselves in their helplessness to be led from one dead end to another and were persuaded that they had a right to meet even after the Congress opened. It was a fuzzy, bewildered Actions Committee that emerged, wondering how they could allow themselves to follow the music of Motzkin's harsh voice. That incident established Motzkin as a legend.

As he grew older, his views became rigid and it was hard for him to change. He went along with his destiny. His double-barreled Jewish views—on Zion and Diaspora—tangled, alternated in importance, and finally he himself could not disentangle them. He used to say the Committee of Jewish Delegations he led was only a *provisorium;* it was the forerunner of the democratic parliament of the Jews of the Diaspora. The Zionists had their Congress. The Jews of the Diaspora should also have their Congress. Strange as it may seem, however, the closer the World Jewish Congress came to realization, the more hesitant Motzkin was about going forward with it. He did not relish the idea of having his personal life interfered with. He dreaded the impact of American Jews, i.e., the American Jewish Congress, upon the enterprise he had made his own. The Americans were beginning to invade Europe and also Geneva. They would certainly wrest control from Motzkin's arthritic hands, or at best, subordinate him to their superficial and barbaric notions. Of course, he believed that the World Jewish Congress had to come to life, but it might be better to delay its coming for a while. He postponed its birth by various delaying actions, but time was working against him. The League of Nations was losing its vitality; it was being badgered by the Italians; the Nazis were pressuring on all fronts. He saw the court where he was speaking for Jewish rights dying on its feet, with none to mourn its demise except —at that time—the Russians.

Motzkin suffered a stroke and died in 1933. The World Jewish Congress was formed in 1936 in Geneva. When the State of Israel was proclaimed years later, Joseph Sprinzak, the first Speaker of the Knesset, took over the gavel Motzkin had wielded in the Zionist Congresses with skill, warm humor, and sagacity. Motzkin was not forgotten in the Knesset. Indeed, he was a tradition in the Knesset when it was born.

VICTOR JACOBSON (1869–1935)

Victor Jacobson was the most inarticulate diplomat I ever knew, but in the early days of the Movement he was a very useful man. His first assignment was to Constantinople where he went ostensibly to represent the Anglo-Palestine Company, but really to make Zionist propaganda among the Turkish Jews. He worked his way into the confidence of many diplomats, subvened several French journals, and established social relations with a number of prominent Turkish Jews. For these tasks he was well qualified. He was sensitive to art and was a good musician. He became the center of a circle of friends who were impressed with his conversation. Later, he was sent to Geneva in the period of the League of Nations and became, in effect, the Jewish ambassador. He was a delightful companion, guileless, courteous, and incapable of harsh anger. He was Russian born and bred but was familiar with French and German literature. His first wife was related to Ussishkin; the divorce which followed earned for him the eternal resentment of Ussishkin. Jacobson lived through that crisis in his life and became the father of two gifted daughters who inherited his talent in the arts. Jacobson's participation in Zionist Congresses was a time of unhappiness, for he had strong political views but was unable to communicate what he thought to others and was condemned to listen while he suffered the agonies of the inarticulate, for he knew the answers but could not express them. I once sat with him for days at an Actions Committee meeting in Jerusalem. I was immune to the boredom of Zionist discussions in various languages I did not understand, but loved to listen and guess what the speakers were driving at. But Jacobson was helpless; he muttered to himself, fidgeted, frowned, looked down and up, turned around, expressed anger, impatience, and knew very well that when he finally got the floor there would be nothing left for him to say, for by that time he would have worked out his frustrations and be completely exhausted. He had a small circle of intimate friends with whom he could discuss problems that escaped him at public meetings. He was an utterly selfless man whose friendship we enjoyed at Congresses, at Zionist meetings in London and finally in Jerusalem.

Victor Jacobson was the first Zionist who aspired to be not a Zionist leader but a "career" diplomat. Nurtured in an atmosphere of assimilation and revolutionary agitation in Russia, he manifested keen interest in the revival of the Jewish nationality at an early age. He organized clubs and wrote about Zionism in Russian Jewish newspapers. With Motzkin, Weizmann and Shmarya Levin, he was one of a group who plunged into university life in Switzerland when it was a hotbed of revolutionary movements. It was there he sharpened the edge of his Zionist sword in combat with Social Democrats, Bundists, and Universalists of all kinds, and emerged chastened for work in the larger Jewish world and specifically for the promotion of the Zionist cause. He was not a brilliant debater, but had a thorough knowledge of international political relations.

In the early days of the Zionist Movement, he was sent to Constantinople, then a frail center of political attention. He had the manners and the equipment. He was placed in charge of a bank established in the Turkish capital by the Anglo-Palestine Company. He soon acquired a large circle of friends and invaluable experience in diplomatic affairs, for he had a pleasant personality and was experienced in the ways of the Levantine world. With the retirement of David Wolffsohn as head of the Zionist Organization, Jacobson became a member of the Zionist Executive headed by Otto Warburg. This was the first functioning Executive elected by a Zionist Congress. It had a policy and a program. It was not a leader and his cabinet, but a group of men sharing collective responsibility. It was a homogeneous body and not overawed by a dominant personality. It was then possible to speak of leaders, without offending the notion that the Zionist Movement had to have an individual leader, around whom the organization revolved, and to whom Zionists bowed the knee.

In this new administration which represented the victory of the "practical" over the "political" Zionists, Jacobson devoted himself to diplomacy and politics, a portfolio he shared with Nahum Sokolow. During the war, he left Berlin for Copenhagen, then one of the few refuges of neutrality; and after the war continued his work in France, Italy and other countries in which German or French was the dominant language. He acquired personal friendships with many of the leading statesmen of Europe. When Dr. Weizmann became the Zionist leader and the League of Nations was organized, Dr. Jacobson was largely responsible for building up, in Geneva, those precedents of Jewish right to participate in international institutions, around which the

Committee of Jewish Delegations operated, and which was the source of an ever-widening influence. At the Prague Congress in 1933, having been theretofore merely a diplomatic agent of the Executive, he was elected a member of the governing body, but pursued his habitual course with the same modesty which characterized his entire career.

He was at first practically only a "shtadlon" and propagandist. I remember him in the last pre-war Vienna Congress, how excited and proud he and Sokolow were when they were given an opportunity to confer in person, without *baksheesh* or subterfuge, with the Turkish Consul in Vienna; maybe it was the Turkish Minister to Austria, but it really did not matter at that time. They revealed their success in secret, cautiously; it was the event of the Congress when it became known.

But he emerged from the chrysalis stage of diplomacy as the volume of his experience grew. He mastered international law and procedure. He came to appreciate that mere diplomacy was not politics, and acquired a boldness of thought and action that was entirely foreign to his former habits. He often reverted to the practical aspects of the conception of a Jewish State, wondering at the remarkable progress of the Movement from the time when the Young Turk revolution was regarded as the end of Zionist striving. In the last years of his life he believed in the possibility of building up the conception of a Jewish State in practical forms of preparation. I recall when traveling with him in Palestine in the spring of 1929 how eager he was to find an echo for his hidden thoughts of "empire"; and how avidly he absorbed the suggestion that the political situation could readily be influenced by mobilizing our economic resources for the support of a six- or seven-year plan to develop the National Home. As a diplomat, he never spoke of a Jewish State. As a Zionist, however, "daring" plans absorbed his mind, whenever they were placed on the agenda. The fact is that discretion and understatement in Zionist diplomacy were never as important as Jacobson thought they were.

He was a man of unusual talents. He loved music passionately, and was a fairly competent performer on the piano. He was sensitive to poetry. He had the refinement of one who lives in the exaltation that comes from the contemplation of the intellectual beauty of life and is not afraid of sentiment or ideals. He was a fastidious lover of books, and spent his leisure time hunting for out-of-print volumes and rare editions. He was a soft-spoken man, with a diffident smile, rare sensitiveness and modesty. He shunned the heat of controversy and the brawling of parties. Never a speaker in a real sense, what he said always had form, and he could be relied upon to speak the moderating word without prejudice or rancor and often contributed to the solution of vexatious problems. He loved quiet talk and quiet argument and was devastated by the later noises of the Movement. He loved to express his thoughts in a sort of reverie, waiting to hear the soft echoes of his words. He was always a poor man.

He was the pioneer of Jewish political representation, acting not in his own name, but as an emissary of his people. Under the Turkish regime he had to use the Levantine method, building up political connections through social contacts; always avoiding the sharpness of a direct issue; and waiting in patient oriental fashion for the insidious seed of propaganda to fructify. That was the era of the direct and indirect bribe and the contact man. You dealt not with national policies but with the whim or self-interest of a ruling oligarchy. After the First World War the methods had to be altered. You had to meet the interests of nationalities, their diplomatic representatives being their attorneys and advocates. There were briefs that had to be controverted. There was press propaganda that had to be met by stronger counter-propaganda. There were ideas to be implanted, facts to be communicated. The tactics and the maneuvers of the budding Jewish nationality had to be organized and directed.

In this new world into which Jacobson was thrown, he labored with the delicacy and concentration of an artist, not of a partisan or fanatic, not of a man interested in immediate sensation, but working persistently and with vision to build up an interest in the cause. He had to win sympathy as well as conviction. He was an unusually careful man, knowing full well that he carried a heavy responsibility and could not afford to be isolated by his manner or by his over-intensity, which so easily becomes the cause of irritation and revulsion of feeling and which logic and reason very often cannot overcome. To that growing body of political precedent in which Jews appeared for the first time in all the seeming garments of a political entity, Victor Jacobson was an important contributor.

He was at all times intensely interested in the development of Jewish national culture, but he was not in any sense a *Maskil;* most of his intellectual interests were derived from the non-Jewish world. His youth had been formed in the Russian pre-war revolutionary period—the period that expressed itself in the form of constitution, parliament, liberalism. He was engrossed in the literature of the Romance languages, and after the war acquired an easy fluency in English. Only in later years did he approach the Hebraic world and the culture of his own people. It was with difficulty that he spoke Hebrew. He stuttered and stammered his way through its intricacies. It was only in his last years that he established personal contact with Palestine. He was in all practical matters a gentleman of continental quality and interests.

In the last few years of his life one could observe an eagerness to integrate his life with the new life in Palestine. At one of the meetings of the Actions Committee held in Jerusalem, he sat next to me for days and listened intently to all the discussions in Hebrew. There was a pathetic eagerness in his eyes to follow what was said and to appreciate the mood and the emphasis of the discussion.

At that time I felt the great power of the national revival. It had taken this youth from a strongly assimilated environment, ripped him out of Russian culture, thrown him in middle age in an atmosphere of oriental deceit and shallow manners, carried him over to France and its brittle logic, then to England with its sober forms and traditions, to place him finally in a land built up by his own people speaking their own language, recovering their own aboriginal personality—making a valiant stab at it, anyway. And although he could not so easily feel at home there, the sense of loneliness, the resurgent nostalgia of a man a long time away from home, gave him the authentic feeling of a return and a recovery. In the warm embrace of that return he spent his last tired years. He died soon after the Prague Congress at about the same time that the Jewish world lost Leo Motzkin, Bialik and Shmarya Levin.

VLADIMIR (ZEV) JABOTINSKY (1880–1940)

Vladimir Jabotinsky was a remarkable performer on any stage, at a Congress or mass meeting. He was not at his best in a private meeting or conference. He was easily led astray by procedures. He could attract large audiences in Berlin, Warsaw or New York, but in the organization of his party or in the techniques of politics, he lacked understanding of the psychology of his opponents and was lost in skirmishes with them. His inferiority in this area led to his adopting dictatorial habits. His disciples seemed to know his weakness and practiced upon him the tactics he inflicted upon the Revisionist Party. He was doubtless influenced by his admiration for Mussolini, not as a political theorist but as a performer. Jabotinsky's opponents were personally greatly attracted to him. At one time, even Dr. Weizmann established cordial relations with him on a social level. The same was true of David Ben-Gurion, who on several occasions was on the verge of making peace with him, but was held back by his own party. Dr. Stephen S. Wise enjoyed himself for some time as a defender of Jabotinsky's plans, and then one day, without notice, switched over to a vigorous attack on the Revisionist Party, to which, as I remember, Jabotinsky made no serious reply. There were too many leaders in his entourage, and in the course of time, his ideas had a wide circulation and his party grew, but his leadership dwindled. He did not know how to take care of himself in the struggles of politics, but pursued his perilous course bravely, blind to the dangers in his path. When he left the Congress with a dramatic gesture, he left the stage where he had won universal distinction. He had always concentrated on Zionism. He was not greatly concerned in the *Galut* Movements of the Committee of Jewish Delegations, and lived his life among the Jewish people as a Zionist leader. He would have distinguished himself and his party, had he lived to the days when the Yishuv rose in conflict with the Mandatory regime, and the power of the Revisionist Party was taken over by the Irgun. Without his presence, the Irgun was able to shatter the influence of the Revisionist Party and transform it into a bundle of splinters, shooting at the enemy in many directions at the same time.

Vladimir Jabotinsky was cast in the role of opposition in the Zionist Movement from his first to his last appearance. I remember him as a writer as far back as 1900, when I used several articles he had written in Russian in the early numbers of *The Maccabean,* of which I was then the managing editor. Being young and uninformed, I thought that all European Zionist writers must be older settled men, bearded patriarchs, for they wrote with such erudition, assurance and dogmatic conclusiveness. Especially was this so in the case of Jabotinsky, whose name had appeared frequently in the Zionist press. Later I learned that he was at that time only about twenty years old. Behind the seeming maturity in Jabotinsky's writings, there lurked traces of that youthfulness which he never lost. He seemed always filled with the daring of youth, its vigor and cocksureness. He refused to let age master him.

In the early days, Russian Zionism lived within its own confines. It reluctantly joined the Herzlian movement. The Russian Zionists had their own controversies and their own programs and their own ambitious leaders. They were the formulators of Zionist ideology. They had their own views on *Galut* politics. They were involved in Russian political issues. They developed the renascence of Hebrew and lived in a circle of their own, slightly influenced by what Herzl and his Actions Committee were doing in Vienna. Their talent for criticism and nonconformity was given abundant exercise in their own conferences and then at Zionist Congresses, where they were often at odds with the "western" Zionist leaders. They were Herzl's "opposition" as well as his admirers. They wondered how a *Yehudi* could have ideas of his own on matters which they believed came within their jurisdiction. To a large extent, their language was Russian. I attended the Vienna Zionist Congress in 1913 and strolled into the caucus of the Russian delegates. There were over four hundred men present, and I remember Tiomkin holding forth in Russian, at great length. Ahad Ha-am was present, but I did not hear him speak at all.

It was in this Russian world—liberal, not revolutionary—that young Jabotinsky lived, and from which he was recalled to his people. He was not a product of the Yeshiva or of a Hebraic environment. He passed as a youth straight into Russian life, swimming with ease in its literature, sharing its hopes and ideals. He did not return from this brief adventure empty-handed. He had the equipment of an educated, liberal Russian. He proceeded to apply his intellectual experiences to Zionism, and looked upon the achievements of the Zionist Movement with Russian eyes. He was always an "outsider" looking in. They said that he had a *goyish* head, and they were right.

He was a child of emancipation, and saw in Zionism the reflection of an awakened *Galut* seeking national freedom, but using the old methods of the *Galut* to pave the way for the *Geulah*. He hated the chains of *Galut,* and hoped that through Zionism the Jewish people would throw off the spirit of submissiveness, inferiority, opportunism, and that Jewish life would become bold, proud and aggressive. He also hated the isolation of Jews and their refusal to be like the *goyim* on the battlefield, in the athletic world. To him Zionism meant revolution in earnest. It meant freedom not through grant, but through self-emancipation, and for that emancipation Jews must profit by the example of other peoples who had won their freedom. He had found his intellectual freedom through the culture of another people. Jews could learn from other people how to liberate themselves and how to maintain their freedom in self-government.

Jabotinsky was not born to be domesticated. He was always restless, inquisitive, longing for change. He loved adventure, movement. He began to move about the world at an early age. After he had become saturated with Russian culture, he moved on to Italy, where he studied for a number of years. He admired Dante, Alfieri and D'Annunzio in literature; Mazzini and Garibaldi as creators of Italian unity. The liveliness and grace of the Italians impressed and influenced him in many ways. He was a good speaker in Russia; in Italy he became a brilliant dramatic orator, with a flair for the theatrical. Under the Italian skies, stirred by the vivacity of its people, his style of oratory changed and the Italian influence was recognizable in his speech and abided with him for a long time, no matter what language he used. He had learned how Italians had forged their democratic unity on the field of battle; he had studied the teachings of Mazzini and found much the Zionist Movement could learn from him. Later he was impressed and influenced by Mussolini. He was slow in seeing that the Fascist leader was a hollow, theatrical imitation of the great revolutionary leaders of Italy.

During the First World War he went to England. All Russian Zionists were attracted to England as the land destined to be of help in the realization of Zionist aims, and also as the mother of parliamentary government. Jabotinsky learned English rapidly and made many friends in London. They were not among the upper classes; they were of the restless, protesting middle class—dissatisfied army officers, politicians of the minority, liberal journalists and artists. These friends he enlisted in the work for a Jewish Legion. He got his martial slant in the recruiting of that first group of Jewish fighters for the freedom of Palestine. His service in the Legion gave him a military bearing.

It was his English fixation that made him a profound admirer of the English people, and at the same time the dogged opponent of British policy in Palestine. The authentic Englishman was a non-conformist and "agin" the government. So was he. In England he saw the Parliament in session and learned how parliamentary speeches should be delivered, and parliaments managed, but he did not imitate the English in his speeches or parliamentary behavior. He saw how "muddling through" was useful in maintaining democratic balances; and envied the English their ability to cut loose from all serious problems at intervals—for tea, for weekends, for the hunting season. He appreciated the qualities of English sportsmanship; he learned how to be bulldogged; what it meant to be an English gentleman.

The fruits of his threefold adventures—in Russia, in Italy, in England —he laid at the feet of the Zionist Movement. It is curious that of all

Zionist leaders he owed least to German influence. But when he appeared in Zionist circles and spoke of his adventures among the aliens, he found himself more of an alien than ever before. He could not understand how the Movement launched by Herzl could remain bogged in middle-class achievement or in the dialectics of the German Karl Marx. He imagined that at least a suggestion of Garibaldi would find its way into the Zionist Movement. He thought that Zionists would act something like Englishmen, once they became partners of the Empire in the Mandate.

To his profound disappointment he found that it was not easy to persuade Jews to accept alien methods and manners. Jewish freedom would have to come in a Jewish way. The other nations had had a long history of struggle for freedom on their own soil. The Jews had had a long history of struggle for survival in the teeth of oppression, always on alien soil. The older Zionists argued that self-emancipation would have to come through an inner revolution, new conditions producing different national traits. They saw Zionism as evolution which at the end of the road would be seen as a cycle of a completed revolution. You could talk to them of the English but they were not Englishmen; you could talk to them of Mazzini and Garibaldi but they were not Italians. Nor was the Promised Land on the fringe of the Arabian desert comparable to England or Italy. They would have to learn through their own experience how to govern themselves. They would have to learn the arts of war only when war became an essential requisite for national survival. They could not become like other nations in the spirit of imitation. They would become like other nations only when driven to it by their own destiny.

But Jabotinsky was simple and direct. Personally he was a shy man, but in expression he was audacious and belligerent. He saw the idea but overlooked its practical implications. What was lacking in the picture of the Jewish State he pieced together from his study of history. Plant the seed; a flower would emerge. Set the idea in motion and its realization would inevitably come. A Jewish Army—small, one battalion, one company, a flag, a bugle—you needn't worry about the National Army. A Jewish State on both sides of the Jordan—demand it, declare it, act as if you had it—and one day a trumpet would be blown and the full structure of an integrated State would be visible for all eyes to see, a few ships at first, then fleets; a few sailors, then a navy. Make the beginning and the seeds would multiply. He stood for Jewish national rights in Russia long before it had the slightest chance to be regarded as a practical issue. He believed in a large-scale immigration to Palestine; then became an advocate of the unsystematic, sporadic, illegal immigration.

He was a stormy petrel. He disturbed minds. He disturbed the bureaucracy of responsibility. He disturbed the leadership of the corporate obligations of the Zionist Movement. He had a personality of charm but not of persuasion. He provoked but did not soothe. When he stood up in the Vienna Congress of 1925 and launched into a grand criticism of Zionist policy—satiric, courteous, denunciatory—he was like the angry conscience of the Movement. He poured acid on open wounds. He reminded us of the goal and made us ashamed of the results.

I remember what Jabotinsky said in Philadelphia in 1923 about the Shekel. He used the illustration of the water-carrier of Warsaw. He painted a picture of a ragged, starved, unidentifiable victim of the *Galut*. The water-carrier was anonymous; he did not count; he suffered in silence. But when the Zionist Movement awakened him to the consciousness of belonging to a living people, with a destiny of their own, with national burdens of their own, that man stood up and bought a Shekel, conscious of the fact that he had a place in the State that was "in the process of becoming." It was that same Shekel which Jabotinsky many years later, angry and disappointed, tore in shreds on the floor of the Zionist Congress when he left the organization.

Even when he was at peace within the Zionist Organization, he was at war with himself. He entered the door of the Executive, signed the Churchill White Paper, and walked out in a hurry. He could not for long remain a member of the majority. It irked him beyond words to be bound in the responsibilities of the Zionist Executive. Just as he broke Zionist discipline, so he broke Revisionist discipline. He was a man who played best as a soloist, as a lyricist; he did not fit into any ensemble and was at his best when he spoke his own mind devoid of any collective responsibility. For he never lived in the regular time of day. He had his own time. While we Zionists saw the clock at six, he saw it at twelve. He did not know what was meant by premature; whatever was true was timely. He saw the cycle of Jewish emancipation as a thing complete and was blind to reality.

The last years of his life were days of disillusionment. He saw the trampling underfoot of all Jewish rights, and had to abandon emancipation for evacuation. He had fought against the Mandatory Power for many years and was compelled to become an advocate of helping

England defend itself against Germany. He came to the United States when it was frozen in the spirit of isolation, and died before American isolation became defense and aid for England. He preached to his last days for a Jewish army and Jewish flag (Jews as allies of the fighters against Hitler), but he did not live to see the fulfillment of that hope.

He was dazzled by a Light. He saw his people once more like the other peoples of earth, at home in freedom, the masters of their own land, no longer suppliants and pariahs, no longer enduring inferiority, but bravely and courageously fighting for their freedom. That Light never got out of his eyes. Even when closed in death they seemed to see the coming of the day. He was a bold, imaginative, brave man. Practically alone, he marched ahead. He was sure the army would follow him some day.

CHAIM NACHMAN BIALIK (1873–1934)

I got to know Yiddish fairly well by living with it, but had only a remote familiarity with Hebrew, because there was no way to get close to it. Bialik was the most colorful personality in the Hebrew renaissance, but I knew him chiefly through his delightful use of Yiddish, which was his best language. He loved it even more than Hebrew. His Yiddish had a heavy background of Hebrew and he could put into Yiddish ideas and descriptions with such idiomatic twists and allusions, as to make it sound like Hebrew but more than that, for the Hebrew helped him to find what actually fitted the Jewish tongue. He was the friendliest Zionist whom I ever knew. His stories poured from his mouth with a perfection of form and phrase and sound that made his conversations exhilarating, as if one were taking part in the creation of a poem in prose. Many a trip I made with him among the Jewish communities— big and little—and marveled at his resourcefulness and patience in explaining complex ideas to miscellaneous audiences with such good humor and keen enjoyment, with quotations from the Bible and Talmud, with stories from his childhood and tales retold of his memories of his grandfather. But, like Levin, he seldom participated in Zionist Congresses and was content to move around in the lobbies looking for a congenial friend with whom to pass a few hours in conversation. He was a meticulous editor and publisher, and was known so thoroughly to have corrected many a manuscript that often its own authors were unable to recognize it. He had style not only in prose and poetry, but also in editing manuscripts and compiling anthologies and talking at length, never tiring, never losing his form or misusing a word and never even forgetting the proper punctuation or style of type to be used. His love letters to his wife, who survived him, are remarkable for their tenderness and deep affection. He had moods in poetry. There were long periods when he neglected poetry and took refuge in editing the works of others and in speaking on Saturday afternoons to large audiences in Tel Aviv. He had the temperament of a poet, but he could be just as temperamental in berating an author or a typesetter when his wrath was provoked. He was gentle with ignorance that was cloaked in modesty, but he could not abide ignorance panoplied in arrogance or conceit. He loved the company of the humble, for he, too, notwithstanding his genius, was also humble.

Chaim Nachman Bialik was the poet laureate of the Jewish renaissance. The Hebrew language was not his master; he mastered it to serve every need of his mind and spirit. He molded it to express light and shadow, sound and color. Nor was he disloyal to Yiddish, his mother tongue; he used Yiddish whenever he felt the need for something to be said in simple, homely form. He loved Jewish humor, Jewish folkways, Jewish wisdom, Jewish books—even the feel of them—and marveled at the beauty of Jewish children. (He had none of his own.) No other poet in Israel was accorded such universal esteem and affection.

He was born in Volhynia in 1873, one of many children. His father died at an early age and the orphans were distributed by his mother among a number of relatives. It was his good fortune to be placed with his grandfather, an erudite Talmudist and a lover of books, who had a deep and lasting influence upon Bialik's life. While with his grandfather, young Bialik was left free to roam in the nearby forests and to discover for himself the mysteries of nature; to read books of secular knowledge found in his grandfather's library.

At the proper age he was sent to the Yeshiva at Volozhin and remained there until his grandfather died, when he went to Odessa and became a Hebrew teacher. In that active Zionist center he made friendships with Ahad Ha-am, Lilienblum and Rawnitzki, who at once recognized his talent as a poet. He published his first book of poems in 1901. He married and went to live with his wife's family. In 1905 he organized the Moriah Publishing Company which issued several Hebrew classics and a series of textbooks. To the surprise and dismay of his large circle of friends, his desire to write poetry congealed in 1908 after he had written a passionate lamentation on the Kishinev pogrom.

He was devastated by the pogroms. His descriptions of the massacre of Jews have seldom been surpassed in Jewish poetry for their unrestrained and savage denunciation of the brutality of the attacks and the scorn he felt for the Jews who were the unresisting victims. The pogroms left him speechless. He turned to translations and the editing of Hebrew classics. He translated *Don Quixote* and Schiller's *Wilhelm Tell*. He edited three volumes of Ibn Gabirol's poems and one volume of the poems of Moses Ibn Ezra.

He was still in Russia when the Bolsheviks succeeded in wresting the government from the Kerensky regime. At that time Russia still had some sort of freedom and Bialik intervened in public statements against the persecution of Hebrew and of the Jewish religion and against anti-Zionist propaganda. His freedom and his life were in danger. Through the influence of Maxim Gorki, he and other Hebrew writers were given permission to leave Russia in 1921. He went to Berlin, organized a publishing company, and in 1924 reached Tel Aviv, which was his home for the rest of his life.

Bialik came to the United States in 1923 as a speaker to aid in a fund-raising campaign. Scores of American communities got to know him. He endeared himself to a generation of Zionists who were never aware of the deep sources of Hebrew tradition and had never seen or heard a personality of such varied Jewish quality. At that time they knew Levin, Sokolow, Ben Zion Mossinsohn and Chaim Weizmann. But Bialik was unique in every way. He was good-humored, unconventional and without pretensions. He did not look like a poet. He was more like a peasant. He seemed at that time to be most at ease speaking Yiddish, probably because his listeners were far removed from an understanding of Hebrew. He was not a master of Sephardic Hebrew, and referred to modern Hebrew as a *sabra*-mangled language. To him speaking Yiddish was like coming home and taking your shoes off and unloosening your tie. He loved a Jewish anecdote, but only one that came out of the ground covered with the dirt of plain living and simple thinking. He would engage in flights of fancy that led him far into the future, but he never lost track of the present.

With Shmarya Levin, the writer crossed the ocean with him and remembers his stupefying seasickness which led him to give vent to imprecations of lurid phrases drawn from the Book of Jonah. He was sick from beginning to end and only when the ship was docked in its berth was he able to rise and walk into the Land of Freedom.

When he settled down in Ramat Gan he persuaded Mr. S. Bloom, an American Jew—a manufacturer of artificial teeth—to dedicate a building for use as a meeting place, where he instituted Oneg Shabbat lectures and discussions in Tel Aviv. He was the leader of the exercises. I came to one of his lectures with Jacob Fishman on a hot Saturday afternoon. The place was jammed. At the far end, at the center of a long table, stood Bialik speaking in a conversational tone. It was pleasant to listen to him. Twilight was near and as he went on with his rambling discourse, his voice rising and falling with soft cadences, a few slivers of light came through a side door left open for air to relieve the closeness of the summer heat. A faint light fell on his bald head. All eyes were turned to him. They could have listened to him far into the night.

Bialik had none of the pretensions of a poet; he was conventional in manner and dress; he loved wholesome things; he loved Jews with a strange affection. He knew their memories and traditions, the cut and turn of their minds, their appetites and inhibitions, what was genuinely their own and what was pilfered from others, their ruthless desire to destroy false gods, their seeking in pain and struggle to make manifest the Oneness of God and His world.

He had the ardor of an artist who lives and creates with an intense desire to communicate his excitement to others, to have them share his emotions, his vision. He was no recluse consuming himself in isolation and refusing to open windows through which others should be able to see what his eyes beheld. And he was modest and humble and shy. He had to be persuaded to reveal himself, and when he emerged from his privacy his conversation created a great and lasting excitement. His closest friend, Shmarya Levin, could hold one fascinated by his conversation, but his hearers had no room to move about. Bialik opened the doors wide and invited all to follow him. He led one into the open fields of thought and provoked self-expression. Thought and image and color and reminiscence *sprudled* through his conversation. Discussion was raised to a higher level, exciting but not disturbing; bringing light but none of the dazzling effects of pyrotechnics in discussion. He made Jewish learning humane and homely and simple, and gave it a touch of nostalgic sentiment, freed from verbal complexities. The sacred and profane were mingled in him in even balance.

In his voice there were tones of an endless exile, of a struggle against an unhappy fate. God was close to us in our exile, sharing it. In his words—Yiddish or Hebrew—you heard the curses and the prayers of the slaves in Egypt; the revolt in the desert before the Promised Land was revealed; you heard the despair of the Shepherd King for his sins, his reconciliation with God after prayer and confession; you heard the harsh castigation of the Prophets. His muse was a harp that gathered echoes of the long past and mingled them with the tears of today and leavened them with the hopes of tomorrow. The Jews of Spain suffered the agonies of the Inquisition only yesterday. Through his soul and mind you heard the mystic songs of the Chassidim, the sharp dialectics of the Yeshivot, and the songs and sanctifications of the Ghetto.

He was born in a Jewish world that was narrow and confined, straining against the walls that encircled it. It was a world beginning to pour itself out into alien capitals, seeking free expression. He turned the *Haskalah* back again into the ancestral groove by reviving the things that seemed to be dead and quickened the spirit wherever it gave promise of a future. When he died the Jewish world was large enough and strong enough to hold in its grip all forces seeking freedom.

He was a peasant hewn out of the granite of Zion. He could not rid himself of the clouds of memory pouring into his mind out of the genesis of his race. He had a prophetic austerity and a rare sensitiveness. He was close to all Jews in brotherly love and at home with all Jews in the dust and dirt of everyday life. He brought light and warmth and hope into thousands of Jewish homes. He was a tree with widespread branches, roots that forked their way back into the ancestral soil, fed by hidden springs.

He should have lived to a good old age but he died early in Vienna in 1934. The surgical operation went unexpectedly wrong. Ramat Gan and Tel Aviv and Jerusalem were orphaned. Jews all over the world mourned. They would no longer feel the warmth and comfort and security that came from his life. Those who had the privilege of touching merely the fringe of his being, rejoiced that this luminous personality lived his mortal life in their time and that they too knew him. They were built up through knowing him and were strengthened through his strength.

DR. YECHIEL TSCHLENOW (1864–1918)

The Zionist Movement has, among other things, produced for the Jewish people a galaxy of outstanding personalities. Theodor Herzl was the herald of the new time. He was a novel personality, a vibrant force, electrical, imposing. He was the first Jewish figure whose personal influence spread over the Jewish world as the symbol of the renaissance of the Jewish people.

But the background of the movement was composed not only of the stars of the firmament, the favored sons who had grace, presence, eloquence and the attributes of outspoken leadership, but of the men who in reality were of the stuff of heroism. Their strength lay within. The boundaries of their influence were limited; they were in a sense more provincial; they were reserved in manner—or at least reserved on the larger, demonstrative occasions of Zionist life—and they retained the allegiance of a large following chiefly by the unequivocal sincerity and loyalty which inevitably animated all their actions.

Dr. Yechiel Tschlenow was of the latter class. Averse to the broad methods of appeal, he was not eager to push himself forward, preferring rather to concentrate upon the idea in which he was interested. At times it seemed—at least to one not privileged to know him intimately—that he was torn between a natural inclination to lead, and an innate sense of modesty that restrained him from reaching out for the supreme leadership. As a physician and scientist, he was always objective and possessed a certain detachment even with regard to important Zionist issues, a trait in his character that always made him the pacifying center of every conflict or controversy. Gusts of enthusiasm found him inexpressive and inarticulate; only when the spiritual intoxication had been dissipated would he find his voice.

He was a Zionist of the pre-Herzlian days, of the days of Pinsker and Smolenskin. The early Chovevei Zionists were also political Zionists. Their views were remarkably similar to the views of Herzl, but lacking political experience and the imaginative daring of Herzl, they preferred out of necessity to drive in the direction of achievement in Palestine.

Through this pre-Herzlian period, Dr. Tschlenow labored with devotion, and when the inspiring figure of Herzl appeared on the Jewish stage, Dr. Tschlenow was among the first to reach out a welcoming hand, and to pledge support. He understood Herzl and worked with him. Of the many Russian Zionists who played an important part in Zionist history, Dr. Tschlenow was least affected by the strident conflicts that often engaged the attention of controversialists in the first years of the movement. When others gave vent to acrimonious criticism, it was Dr. Tschlenow who became the guide, leading turbulent elements to an amicable understanding.

He was the actual leader of the Russian Zionist organization because in him were combined all the qualities that made leadership possible in Russia. Extreme in nothing, devoid of pretense and exaggeration, wholly absorbed in the cause and its ideals, and tolerant of all phases of Zionist thought, his influence in Russian Zionist circles was widespread, coming as a cooling breeze among those whose opinions were often expressed with heat and acrimony. While men spoke of the leadership of the "iron hand," in truth it was Dr. Tschlenow's hand that was always on the lever, bringing into coordination all elements, no matter how diverse in method and aspiration. Others may have fascinated the popular mind, Dr. Tschlenow inspired confidence.

In every emergency, Dr. Tschlenow appeared on the scene, bringing with him peace, understanding and capacity to do whatever was required. He was European in his understanding of organization problems. He was not wedded to the Russian method, nor did he prefer it when occasion presented other instruments that could be wielded for Zionism. When it appeared evident that the Wolffsohn administration must be succeeded by an administration representing the influence and the power of the Russian Zionists, Dr. Tschlenow's name was the one first thought of by all, friends of the Russian contingent, as well as its foes. His was the name that could be conjured with to bring about a solid front. But at that time it was impossible to create the situation that made his entrance into the actual leadership of the movement politically feasible, and it was not until the Vienna Congress that he became vice-chairman of the Inner Actions Committee. All were hopeful that with him at the helm, a powerful, new force would spread its influence into all parts of the Zionist organization. With that devotion which characterized his entire career, he gave up his lucrative practice in Moscow and prepared to take charge of the Zionist affairs in Berlin. Only a few months did he remain in Berlin, when World War I broke out, and as a Russian subject, he was forced to return to Moscow.

There he plunged into the nerve-racking work of relief. About him he saw the debris of the great war, and felt within himself a superhuman fury to overcome the enormous difficulties of Jewish life. He became the head of the Moscow relief section. In 1915 he went to Copenhagen and London, playing a prominent role in Zionist political activity. He returned to Russia for a short period after the Revolution in 1917, in an endeavor to convene a Russian Zionist Conference.

Throughout, he was intimately taken up with the progress of the Zionist movement. Out of the war there had come unprecedented opportunities. The Committee in London needed advice and guidance.

This he gave regardless of the physical consequences to himself. He took charge of the work in Copenhagen, and frequently moved from Copenhagen to London and back again, in spite of the physical hardships of travel. The consolidation of the Zionist organization was effected largely through his influence, for he represented the tie that bound together the Zionists of Russia, Germany, and the neutral European countries. When, finally, the British Government was prepared to issue the Balfour Declaration, he had the supreme happiness of being present at the consummation of his effective work.

BERTHOLD FEIWEL (1875–1937)

Berthold Feiwel met Herzl as a student in Vienna. He knew Herzl as the distinguished feuilleton writer of the *Neue Freie Presse.* When Herzl began the publication of *Die Welt,* Feiwel was a "piccolo" in Journalism, who used to hover about its editorial offices to rub elbows with writers. Finally he attracted the attention of Dr. Herzl who- added him to the staff of the Zionist weekly.

Feiwel attended the first Zionist Congress. He was by temperament obsessively a man of letters, a fairly good minor poet and a connoisseur of the fine arts. Even as a young man, whatever he wrote had a smooth, graceful style. He also pursued, from the days of his youth to his later years, the art of good living and was irrepressibly attracted to what was then called the Bohemian way of life. He made a good impression on Herzl from the start and was recognized by the Zionist leader as one of the ablest of the young men who came under his influence.

Feiwel was later one of the founders of *Ost und West,* the earliest and the best of the Zionist illustrated magazines produced by German Zionists. In 1902, with Martin Buber and E.M. Lilien, the artist, he founded the *Juedischer Verlag* and was the editor of the *Juedischer Almanach* and *Junge Harfen,* a youth magazine. He had an intense love for Yiddish and was the first to make an excellent translation into German of the Yiddish poems of Morris Rosenfeld, the first Yiddish poet to achieve international recognition.

Although Dr. Feiwel was never impressed by Zionist politics, he joined with Leo Motzkin and Dr. Weizmann in the Democratic Faction at the first Zionist Congress and became known as one of the good-humored supporters of that party. He seldom spoke in the Congresses and had no ambition to be known as an orator. As a matter of fact, he used to speak in muffled tones and it was hard to appreciate what he was saying. He was a facetious but comradely critic of what was going on in Zionist affairs. It might be said that he was a light comedian who blunted his barbs of opposition and therefore was never taken seriously.

He preferred the easy company of café attendants, artists, actors and *Literaten*. He was never suspected of having an ideology, but he used to think of quaint and wise things to contribute to conversation. He never fitted into any partisan mold, in literature or politics. He was a good dresser; there, too, he had a style that distinguished him. He was also a connoisseur of wine and food.

What attracted him both to Herzl and Weizmann was the fact that both of them had grace and personal magnetism. Dr. Feiwel was disturbed by deep thinkers who thought so deeply that it was hard to find the depths where they rested. At any rate Dr. Feiwel never tried to follow them.

In the second half of his life he found himself thrust into the world of finance, and became in a sense an expert on the problems of the Zionist budgets, banks and funds. Whatever he knew of business affairs he acquired in Germany and Switzerland before the First World War. He had held a position in a German bank. When the war ended he found himself in Switzerland where he made a connection with a mortgage bank. He was associated with Julius Simon in a real estate operation.

Dr. Feiwel's friendship with Dr. Weizmann led him, as it did Julius Simon, to London, where, after the First World War he and Simon were engaged in Zionist financial affairs. Dr. Feiwel was one of the first directors of the Keren Hayesod and later director of the Jewish Colonial Trust. None of this was in harmony with Feiwel's temperament. He experienced way-stations of unrelieved boredom. He felt he was losing his freedom and individuality in London. He married a girl of a fine Jewish family, established a home, but never felt comfortable in family life or in the London fog. He was always a Bohemian in spirit.

He was used by Dr. Weizmann on numerous occasions to draft political documents and memoranda in German, which he did very well. He was able to stimulate a political discussion even if he did not feel it. He was exasperated by the dullness of his surroundings. Dr. Weizmann was engaged in the endless journeys of his mission to collect funds or in the pursuit of his political interviews, and Dr. Feiwel missed the spirited conversations and the companionship of his friends. He was chilled by the routine and draftiness of the small office he occupied at 77 Great Russell Street. All financial problems were being dealt with by him as well as by Dr. George Halpern, later the founder and manager of a successful Palestine life insurance company.

He would come to his office late in the morning with a carnation in the lapel of his coat, a wet cigarette hanging from his lower lip and find a vase in which to place the flower. He would take as long a time as he dared for lunch and then wait for the murky tea passed around to all offices at tea time, anxious to lose himself in the fog of London streets. He took his vacations in Switzerland and would leave London as if chased by a west wind. The British capital was the symbol of the tragedy of his life. Finally, in 1933, sickness drove him from England to the sun of Palestine.

His health was shattered. He withdrew from active life and established a home in Safed. He was pursued by domestic troubles. It was said that he recovered an interest in literature and on his sickbed wrote poetry of unusual delicacy of feeling. His youth gave evidence of literary talent of a high order. His middle years were interludes of prose and *ennui*.

But in the prime of life he was a gay and witty man with fine interests, generous sentiments and a capacity for serious friendships. He was a sincere and devoted Zionist. Back of his badinage he felt deeply the influence of Herzl's spiritual leadership. He remembered the early days with Dr. Weizmann and later often wondered at Dr. Weizmann's ability to identify himself so ruthlessly with the minorities in Zionism.

The Promised Land came too late seriously to affect Dr. Feiwel's way of life. He and Dr. Weizmann were much alike in their youthful years. They were both touched with humor, with youthful cynicism and romantic aspirations. They were both infected with the joy of life. But Dr. Feiwel in the evening of his life saw all things of this world with heavy eyes and doubts and with no interest. He had lost his feeling for laughter. He was 62 years old when he died in 1937 in Jerusalem.

MOSES GASTER (1856–1939)

Dr. Moses Gaster, whose last parish was in London as *Haham* of the Sephardic Community, made a curious impression of a wayward scholar, straining to get into controversy and filled with the vanity that afflicted all great orators.

He was born in Rumania, the son of a Dutch diplomat, and studied in Germany under Graetz.

In England, he was recognized as a great authority on Slavic languages and given a chair in Oxford when not quite thirty-five. Before he was fifty, he acquired an international reputation as a master of Romance Philology, and as the greatest living Rumanian philologist of the time. Although expelled from Rumania for his liberal activities and for his protests against the treatment of Jews, the Rumanian Government bestowed upon him the Gold Medal of the Rumanian Academy for the services he rendered to the cause of Rumanian Philology. In addition, the Haham acquired an international reputation as master of Folklore, and was for many years President of the Royal Folklore Society of England, an extraordinary honor to be bestowed upon a foreigner in England.

The Haham also made great contributions to the cause of Rabbinic learning, and published many treatises and dissertations on ancient and medieval Jewish history which shed light upon many obscure phases of the Jewish historical process.

This industrious, many-sided scholar always found time to participate in the affairs of his people and to take an attitude on every Jewish movement. He was an eager participant in public discussions and wrote continuously. As a great orator, as an internationally famous scholar, and as a man of position and authority, he lent weight and dignity to every Jewish movement he supported. Nor was he hesitant in claiming credit for his superior talents.

One of the pioneers of the pre-Herzlian Zionist era, Dr. Gaster became a distinguished figure in the movement when it began to assume the realities of a world-wide political force through the activities of Theodor Herzl. Although in conflict with Dr. Herzl in the early days, because of differences on questions of policy, he exercised a major influence in the development of Zionist sentiment in England. He preached Zionism at a time when all the leaders of English Jewry regarded the movement as revolutionary and harmful, and in defiance of opposition even within his own congregation. He endangered his own position as Haham of the Sephardic Jews in order to uphold the Zionist cause. His elders at that time demanded that he discontinue Zionist activity but he ignored their demand and continued to work for the movement until he succeeded in raising a Zionist generation in England.

He never had many devoted followers or disciples for long. His biography would be an interesting story of a great man of temperament and self-appreciation. He was a proud man, an egotist, talented in many areas, a great speaker and florid debater, but never deeply interested in the subject, which he saw always with the eyes of a great performer. As he grew older, his opinion of himself reached lofty heights.

In the First World War period, Dr. Gaster played a prominent part in the negotiations which culminated in the issuance of the Balfour Declaration. It was in his home that leaders of the British Government and of the Zionist Movement met to formulate the text of the Declaration. Because of differences which later developed between him and Dr. Weizmann, regarding the conduct of Zionist affairs, he withdrew from the circle of leadership, and, in his last years, handicapped by illness and blindness, was prevented from active participation in Zionist affairs.

REUBEN BRAININ (1862–1939)

It is about time the Zionist Movement reassessed many intra-Jewish misunderstandings that arose during the Russian Revolution, especially the treatment of Reuben Brainin, the Hebrew writer whose 100th anniversary was celebrated in the Jewish literary world in 1962. Enough time has elapsed since these distant events for reconsideration and re-evaluation to be given in the light of history. The old slogans have lost their tang and partisan meaning. They no longer correspond with the emotions of those who were then concerned, and the passions that moved Jewish life have passed on to another plane.

Reuben Brainin was a delicate personality of the first period of the Hebrew renaissance. He remained a man of letters all his life, except for a few excursions into other fields.

He came into the Zionist Movement at its very beginning and was one of the first Hebraists to worship at the shrine of Theodor Herzl. He remained Herzl's bold and skillful partisan the rest of his lifetime. He had become an emancipated Jew at an early age and sojourned in the Western world, studying and appreciating its art and literature. He was a "European," and proud of it. He had a great capacity for absorbing and translating into Hebrew the things he read and heard of in the literatures of other peoples. His Zionism was bound up with a high appreciation of the literary side of the life of both Herzl and Nordau. All he wrote in Hebrew was colored by his surroundings in Vienna and Berlin. He was never provincial. As a Hebrew writer he was inspired by the fashions of the great writers of the Western world. He never really belonged to any local community or Zionist organization.

When he came to the United States, everything from Vienna and Berlin had to be discarded, except as memoirs, and he established himself as a writer in Yiddish, with Hebrew literature as his avocation. He served as a literary critic and publicist in the *Jewish Day* (New York) for many years, and continued in Hebrew literature as the editor of several Hebrew journals. But the old European flair had disappeared. He could not maintain himself strictly within the field of the belletristic. He had to be a publicist and was called upon to discuss a wide variety of subjects. He was caught in many controversies, and overthrown in some of them. He should have remained an essayist, a judge of literature, a reviewer of policy and belletristics, and avoided "debate" as bitter experience and the disturber of calm thinking. But he did not know how to protect himself.

In the last years of his life, he became entangled in controversies in which the Communist regime in Russia was involved principally in support of Jewish colonization in various parts of Russia. These efforts ran counter to prevailing Zionist and Jewish opinion. He found himself in a sea of dialectics; he was influenced in his judgments by the cunning propaganda of his new-found friends. At first he was merely a friend of Soviet Russia, and tried to explain away certain harsh and oppressive measures the Soviet Government had invoked against Zionists. It was clear that he was out of his element in those controversies. He outraged the sentiments of scores of his best Zionist friends who had held him in high esteem as a Hebrew writer. But it seemed that he was unable to go back and begin over again a discussion that had become greatly involved, vindictive and personal.

He was a victim of the dialectics of the time. In the last years of his life, frail and feeble, he found himself isolated from many of his Jewish friends, and forced to consort with crafty pro-Soviet elements who did not understand him and who were unable to appreciate him. This must have made him feel frustrated and defeated and alone.

It is good to remember the Reuben Brainin of the days when he stood out as a symbol of Hebrew culture, a gracious and refined personality, a writer of keen insight and literary sensibility, a slave of the right word and correct form, a good listener and a sensitive interpreter of books and their makers. All that he did for modern Hebrew literature and for the Zionist renaissance should be remembered with gratitude.

ROBERT STRICKER (1879–1944)

The martyrdom of Robert Stricker softened the harsh impression of the earlier Zionist who was the breaker of parliamentary china and loved nothing better than a scandal on the floor. He liked to be in opposition and expressed his dissents in denunciation, from the hurling of verbal insults to general disorderly behavior. As a matter of principle, he refused to pay attention to the amenities of debate. He enjoyed nothing better than to be called to order by an exasperated chairman and to resist the order to his last breath. He sometimes sided with Gruenbaum's splinter party; then he marched along with Jabotinsky for a time; then he was a primitive free-lance Zionist. His greatest delight was to be on the lookout for an opportunity to attack Dr. Weizmann which he would do with relish and keen satisfaction. I remember only a brief interlude when he spoke affably to Dr. Weizmann, but he soon repented that softness of spirit. He had no fundamental doctrines except to rise to the defense of Herzl or Nordau, to praise Wolffsohn when he was attacked, and to take the side of any minority simply because it was a minority. He was a well-built man whose black beard fanned out from his face, then was clipped short and trimmed, and his voice was loud and raucous. But he was a powerful orator, capable of reaching heights of amazing denunciation. Once, in Berlin, at an Actions Committee meeting, he pounced upon an interview thoughtlessly given by Dr. Weizmann to the Jewish Telegraphic Agency on the problem of a bi-national state. Stricker tore the statement to shreds and proposed the impeachment of Dr. Weizmann. He raised his audience to a pitch of such excitement that they were unable to appreciate what it was all about after the thunder of Stricker's voice had subsided. Personally, he was wholly unlike his public impersonations. He had all the good manners of a Viennese; but he loved the boisterous and unruly. He had a quiet sense of humor, and whenever he talked with a certain sharpness of expression it was only because he felt himself perpetually in the midst of a debate. He acted with great nobility in the concentration camp where he and his wife lost their lives.

In his middle age Robert Stricker was a Vienna café politician and free-lance journalist. You thought of him as a heckler at public meetings, as the leader of a crowd, as the rude intruder in communal meetings and as the shrill opposition at Zionist Congresses. You thought of him—mindless of the time of day—sitting at a table in a café surrounded by motley characters, talking volubly about foreign affairs, about the quarrels of newspapers, what was going on in the theatre and about the politics of the Jewish community. In the hurly-burly of free conversation Stricker's strident, ringing voice could be heard above them all. He sat there long hours, eating his meals, drinking his tea or beer, writing his editorials and articles, smoking his cigarettes, looking out at the world from the center of European civilization which was then Vienna, soon to be rubbed out.

Then came the terrible days of the First World War and its aftermath of misery and want. Vienna was stricken and bankrupt. Stricker added Jewish communal affairs to his agenda, again took up his crusade against Jewish assimilation and became a frequent delegate to the Zionist Congresses where he held the flag of Herzl high.

He was a true Viennese, rude and gracious, but squandered his amazing talents on the Jewish community and the Zionist Movement. He should have delivered his impassioned protests in a parliament, but he lived his life in the affairs of a stuffy *kehillah,* in the Zionist Actions Committee and the Congresses. He had the audacity of a Danton but played his part in the Zionist Congresses as an unruly member of a small opposition party. He poured out his heart in Jewish journals where he blazoned the word *Jude* defiantly in the city of the *Haken-kreuzler.* He never concentrated on a major issue. He was taken up with the details of life.

He was interested only when he could declaim against the majority. He felt at ease speaking for himself. When chance maneuvered him into a formal position as a member of a group, he was embarrassed. He was brilliant in attack, sharp of tongue, often vulgar and defiant of law and order. It was then he enjoyed himself most. He loved public life as an exercise in the technique of discussion.

He was young when Herzl came, and was swept off his feet by the grace and dignity of the leader, and followed him without reserve. He was proud of being a *Herzlianer* and thought of himself as the last of the tribe of Herzl's loyal and unquestioning disciples. To him, a man's Zionism depended upon his loyalty to Herzl. When the leader died, he reverted to his natural status of freedom, and although protesting his loyalty to Herzl's legacy, he made temporary alliances for tactical advantage but always retained his freedom—an improviser of dramatic surprises in discussions, never adhering to any party line or any order of business.

When parties began to emerge in Zionism, and the "party key" determined one's right to speak, Stricker had to find a party to which to attach himself. Standing alone he had no status. He joined Isaac Gruenbaum's radical group which was a party of leaders—Gruenbaum, Margulies, Nahum Goldmann, Moshe Kleinbaum (now Moshe Sneh).

When Gruenbaum crossed the line and struck a truce with Weizmann, Stricker said goodbye to him and joined the Revisionists led by Jabotinsky. When Jabotinsky walked out of the Zionist Congress, Stricker remained with the remnant led by Meir Grossman, where World War Two found him.

Stricker was an engineer by profession. He was born in Moravia in 1879 and graduated from the German Technical High School, and entered the service of the Austrian State Railways. There he was regarded as an efficient engineer and was transferred to Vienna, reaching the status of a Surveyor of Railroads. He remained in the service of the state until his retirement on a pension, when he was free to devote himself exclusively to his Zionist avocations.

He made his first appearance as a speaker at 18. He called Zionism, in 1897, *Makkabäertum*. He adhered to his political faith, as then enunciated, for the rest of his life. He underwent few basic changes. He used Herzl's doctrines to test any new proposal and fought any change in Herzl's dogma with the tenacity of a fanatic. He was proud of being a Jew and called the first publication he edited a *Judenblatt*. On one occasion when he was a deputy of the Austrian Parliament, he addressed his colleagues as *"meine Herrn Antisemiten!"* His Zionism included the fulfillment of Herzl's injunction to conquer the communities. He helped greatly to conquer the Viennese community and never let up heckling the assimilationists. He did this through the newspapers he edited, the public meetings where he expressed his views, and at the Café Astoria where he maintained his table for many years. He wrote in a popular style, vigorously and with precision, and had a common, even vulgar, vocabulary. He spoke with dramatic gestures and voice and often startled his audiences with the audacity of his ideas and the rudeness of his suggestions. He introduced himself to the Austrian Parliament with the words "I am a Jew." He had violent clashes with the Christian Socialists and the Social Democrats.

He was one of the most persistent and effective of the opponents of Weizmann whom he supported for only a brief period. He was opposed to Weizmann's defense of the Mandatory Government. He rejected the Weizmann proposal for the inclusion of non-Zionists in the Jewish Agency. He was the leader of the attack when Weizmann expounded his theory of bi-nationalism, which brought about Weizmann's retirement in 1931. He became an ardent supporter of the World Jewish Congress, but internationalism did not seem to attract him. He was too much of a provincial Viennese.

He and his wife died in Theresienstadt. That was the last mile on the long road the poor man and his wife had to travel after Hitler came. He could have saved his life. He was urged at Paris before the *Anschluss* not to return to Vienna. But he insisted that his place was with his family and his community. On the day the German Army marched into Vienna he could have saved his life again and friends begged him to leave the country. He said that his place was with the poor Jews of Austria; that as a private man he could have left, but as a leader he had to remain.

His life was ennobled by the three years he spent in concentration camps where he and his wife finally passed away. Though his health had already been impaired when he arrived in Theresienstadt—at Dachau and Buchenwald—he brought comfort and consolation to all whom he met in that tragic situation. The Strickers gave away their spare linen and clothing. They shared the gifts which they received from the outside. Stricker delivered lectures to small groups. On Saturday afternoons old friends met in their one small room. Stricker spoke of the past and the hope for the future of the Jewish people. It was amazing how clearly he foresaw the turn of events. He was positive that a Jewish state would become a reality and soon.

The Vienna free-lance journalist, the fiery speaker at Congresses, the intrepid defender of Jewish rights shared the fate of six million of his brethren with dignity, integrity and faith.

PINCHAS RUTENBERG (1879–1942)

Pinchas Rutenberg came to us from an alien world. His personality had matured in the Russian Revolution. He was a solid mass of rebellion, with absolute convictions. We were never certain of the part he had played in the Revolution or what present mission he might be pursuing. There were many other crypto-rebels coming to the United States at the time for refreshment, for renewal of vision, for propaganda, or for funds which they gathered from sympathetic Jews. They spoke for a bewildering chain of related parties. Rutenberg's pockets seemed to be stuffed with secret communications, plans and orders. He walked the streets of New York furtively, glancing over his shoulder to see whether spies were following him. In company he stood by in long silence; but in intimate circles he would dilate in the commanding tones of a ser-geant-major on wide-ranging plans, and speak of world-encircling strategy in which his listeners were invited to help turn the world upside down. But such outbursts would simmer down to a flat breathless silence; for far from the field of action—in New York—not knowing where or when or by whom the floods of revolution were to be released—Rutenberg was as helpless as a sailor lost in a foreign port.

He was born in a village in the Ukraine, where he attended *Cheder* until he was twelve. He was then admitted to the nearby secondary school, and at seventeen passed an examination which gave him a place in the St. Petersburg Technological School. He was one of the few Jews who made the grade that year. Here he immediately joined the underground revolution, and as soon as that fact was disclosed by the authorities he was summarily expelled. He went to Ekaterinoslav where he secured employment as a workman in a metallurgical plant. He returned to St. Petersburg a year later and was reinstated in the Institute. When he graduated in due course he entered the Putilov armaments plant and was given a responsible position. But his revolutionary zeal burned hot and he cast his lot with the workers in the plant and became one of their leaders. He was active in the first flare-up of the revolution in 1905. He had cut away from his own people and enlisted for the duration with his Russian comrades. As far as could be seen, he was a Jew with a Russian soul. When he first arrived in the United States he was credited with having liquidated the notorious Father Gapon who led a popular revolt in 1905 and was unmasked as a government agent. Rutenberg never admitted or denied his connection with the incident, but it provided him with credentials which served well among the American radicals who welcomed him. It was after the Father Gapon incident and the pogroms that Rutenberg reaffirmed his identity as a Jew. He organized a Jewish group in Zurich known as *Pro Causa Hebraica,* wrote a pamphlet in Russian which was translated into Yiddish, and not only confessed the error of his ways but gave expression to a positive creed and berated all Jews who did not admit the truth as he saw it. He had believed that Jewish freedom would come as part of the freedom of the Russian proletariat, but overlooked the incident of pogroms. When the pogroms came, his *Weltanschauung* was shattered and he returned to the Jews angry with himself, with those who did not follow him, and disappointed with the revolution. He could not understand why his Jewish comrades were so obstinate. He was as arrogant and intolerant a Jewish nationalist as he had been when he was fighting the Czar. He insisted that the Jews were a people, that they should have a land of their own, and that they should stand up and fight for their rights in the new world which the revolution was about to give birth to. But he never looked back to his previous doctrine or discussed it. It seemed to have been washed out of his mind. He settled in Italy where he devoted his time to the study of bridge- and dam-building, and became proficient in that field. He returned to Russia, however, when the ultimate revolution at the end of the first war destroyed Czarism and when Kerensky became the head of the shaky government.

Half his life Rutenberg spent in the revolution; the rest he lived out in the Land of Israel. He returned as a prodigal but his career was at its creative beginning. He brought to the Promised Land the great gift of light and power, a task he was well prepared for. But his work was not only that of an engineer. He had to acquire the franchise and the capital. He came to the United States on several occasions seeking a fund for "harnessing the waters of the Jordan," as his prospectus had it. He had to seek the favor of the Mandatory Government. He was aided by Dr. Weizmann, Alfred Mond and Rufus Isaacs. The Mandatory Government forced him to share his franchise for Jerusalem light and power with an Englishman who claimed a prior concession from the Turks. Rutenberg overcame all the formidable obstacles. He was not only a good engineer, but in spite of his curt manners he was also a good negotiator and an able organizer. He built his home in Palestine and settled down as a staid citizen of a new society, with an address of his own and a circle of friends. In the course of time he became a man of property.

The party man of the Revolution cast off the uniform of group discipline and found freedom in the Promised Land. He was irritated and depressed by the excessive partisan spirit which then prevailed in the National Home. His friends of the Labor group seemed to be anxious to create a simple, natural, free Jewish life in which all would share equally. But by their party maneuvers they forged weapons that could be and were used to impose the will of the majority on the minority, without kindness.

Rutenberg was an impartial friend, welcoming all with equal affection. He maintained an area of restraint in the expression of his personality. He did not indulge in memoirs. He wanted his privacy respected, his thoughts, his desires, his outlook on life. He wanted to live in a society of free men not chained by dogma. A man may not be a writer or speaker; he may be a plain workman, but his soul may find occult ways to communicate with others and to reveal himself. Rutenberg was that kind of a silent man. His way of life spoke for him.

At home, he seemed to have lost his interest in agitation and partisanship. He moved without resistance toward the quiet years of his life. He was at times at odds with Dr. Weizmann whose political methods he disparaged, but he seldom entered the field of controversy. He was regarded as a man above party and was held in reserve as a "dark horse" who might be saddled for a run to power, against his will, should the right time come. It never came for Rutenberg. He was in fact a middle-class man in all practical ways. After he had aided in stimulating the revolution in Russia, a mood of repentance seemed to overcome him. He could make a decision in the political field only with the greatest difficulty. He hesistated on the brink of choice. He had forgotten the vocabulary of political life. He was probably held back by memories and old habits. The blood had slackened in his veins.

Of the two prospects which changed the economic face of Palestine at that time, it was said that "mentioning Rutenberg's power and Novomeysky's potash, it would be difficult to say which encountered greater opposition in quarters which were loath to see the country emerge from its ancient sleep."

When he died after a lengthy illness he left a will that tells more of the man than any words he ever uttered. In his last testament he wrote:

"The division of our people and communities into parties and sects has always caused disaster. Civil strife has brought us to the brink of the abyss. If it does not cease, ruin confronts us. Therefore, it is my desire and will that the Yishuv and the Jewish youth growing up in its midst should always remember that it is not this or that Jewish sect or party which is persecuted or downtrodden, but the Jewish people as a whole. Whether we want it or not, we are all brethren in distress. Let us realize this and be brethren in life, in creative effort, and in action. Our youth is our hope and future. Its proper education is the guarantee of our existence."

He left his estate, which was not inconsiderable, to an endowment fund, the proceeds of which were to be devoted to the education of Jewish youth. He urged that no collections should be made to perpetuate the endowment, and that no forests or villages be named for him. He asked that he be buried on the Mount of Olives "among the graves of humble workers and tillers," that his funeral be held in accordance with Jewish tradition without flowers or speeches, and that his nephews say Kaddish at his grave.

That was a strange homecoming and ending indeed when one remembers that Rutenberg as Kerensky's military chief in St. Petersburg threatened to arrest and imprison Lenin when the leader of the Bolsheviks returned to Russia in April, 1917. Rutenberg was not there when Lenin arrived.

ELIEZER KAPLAN (1891–1952)

Eliezer Kaplan came out of Russia before its revolution had settled down firmly in its totalitarian forms, and came to Palestine in 1923. He was immersed at an early age in Zionism and associated with the leaders of young Zionist labor groups. His father was an active Zionist. The revolution made Eliezer realize that he would have to hurry to Palestine to save his life and the ideals which had become part of it.

From the start he made the economic aspects of the Movement his special interest. He had an aptitude for financial problems. He was a pioneer in the organization of labor. He worked his way up from the economic areas of the labor movement to the Treasurership of the Jewish Agency, and, finally, to the Ministry of Finance in the State of Israel. Twenty-five years of consecration to his self-imposed mission made him the outstanding personality in the economic life of Israel.

He was not an orator or politician. He made few contributions to Zionist theory or ideology and seldom ventured from the field of his special interests. But when he spoke or wrote on what was generally taken to be a dull, prosaic subject, he made you see the human factors involved in the budget he analyzed, in the financial problem he wanted you to know about and understand. To him, the figures of the accountant were the reflection of life itself. He talked of finances and economics with a strange animation, as if here was the heart of the cause. The problems tormenting him, however, were never merely the financial statements, but the tortured body of the State he was helping to create. He knew that no mystic word could give life to the State. He knew that freedom had to be won through hard work. It had to be buttressed by economic resources, production, material security, credit and prestige. He was impatient with the easy calculators who would inflate a budget figure and then want him to make the budget work.

He was a man of simple tastes, and lived frugally and was capable of deep and loyal friendships. He clung to his views with tenacity regardless of who opposed them. He was a bold critic of his own party.

But when discussion was ended and action was called for, his resistance relaxed and he moved along the middle course of uncharted economic and financial practices, making the best of the pressures that were forcing his decision. He was a partisan within limits. He fought valiantly for the place of labor in the Homeland, but orthodox socialism was not his guide. He realized that only with a healthy, thriving, self-sufficient labor force could the Zion of our hopes, based on the social justice of the prophets, be reborn. But he was tolerant and imaginative; worried a great deal; had few moments of relaxation; and possessed a provincial sense of humor which often revealed itself even in the heat of controversy. He had none of the arrogance of leadership that looks for self-vindication at the expense of the public welfare. He was seldom the victim of his partisanship.

In the first decade of his life in Palestine, he was passionately absorbed in the labor movement. His aptitudes for economics and management were recognized at once. He was one of the Directors of the Solel Boneh—at first a school for the training of workers, and later the most powerful economic agency of the labor movement. He was one of the organizers of the Histadrut and a member of the first central committee of Mapai when it was organized in 1930. He was elected Treasurer of the Jewish Agency at the Prague Congress in 1933, when Mapai for the first time assumed a direct official responsibility in the Zionist Administration.

The tasks that confronted him as the Jewish Agency Treasurer were formidable. The effects of Nazi persecutions in Germany were penetrating Palestine's economy, and new problems of great magnitude demanded study. The political waywardness of the Mandatory and the growing Arab intransigence were becoming intolerable. And the hope that the Agency budget would increase with its enlargement was not being realized. It was the beginning of the revolutionary period in Zionism. The Mandate was losing its authority.

Kaplan created the Agency treasury. He made the funds the springboard of financial reorganization. All the resources of the Homeland were coordinated within the authority of his office. The reports of the Treasurer for the first time disclosed the total resources of the National Home. He learned how to operate without adequate resources, with deficits falling over his ears; and maintained poise and sobriety and firmness of purpose, as well as solvency, through many threatened catastrophes.

He won the confidence of the *Yishuv* in his integrity, in his reliability as a man of affairs. He raised the prestige of the Agency in banking circles in England and with the fundraising agencies in every part of the Jewish world, especially in the United States. The structure of the financial administration he created was the foundation upon which the State of Israel was able to begin its life.

The startling change of Homeland to State found Eliezer Kaplan inevitably the Finance Minister. He was the only outstanding man of financial experience who was at the same time a leader of a powerful political party. By now his health was seriously impaired. But nothing in the world could restrain him from immolating himself in the grinding machinery of the new State. There were the means of defense to be provided. The return of the exiles was forcing the gates and presented enormous bills that had to be met. There were the hundred and one needs of the State structure which had to be established. He learned the ways of State finance in the hectic confusion of unpredictable new demands. He had to train himself to quick decisions and the assumption of heavy burdens, depending upon the miracles which had thus far sustained the national struggle. He was responsible for price controls, controls of exports and imports and austerity programs. He was forced to make and revise policies to suit recurring emergencies. He was the target of popular disapproval time and again, but undeterred and undismayed made his way laboriously through one difficulty after another with amazing skill and audacity.

He gave himself no rest. He wanted to live through the crisis and to see Israel emerging out of the storm into calm waters—strong and unafraid. That was what kept him alive. He was like one obsessed by his responsibilities.

I remember his excited appearance at a conference in London after the Arab riots in 1929. He came hurriedly from Palestine to report on the outbreaks to an emergency meeting at 77 Great Russell Street. Many Americans were still there, lingering after the Congress. Some of the leading non-Zionists were present. Kaplan looked as if he were being pursued by horrible memories he could not shake off. His vivid description of brutal destruction and murder, told in staccato sentences, as he gasped to catch his breath, aroused such a spirit of protest and determination as was never before manifested at an official Zionist meeting.

Death took Eliezer Kaplan before his mission in life was completed. He would not accept the summons. With great difficulty he was persuaded by his friends to leave his harassed desk and rest for a while in a quiet retreat in Switzerland. At the end of the journey, as he was about to disembark, his heart refused to carry him further. He did not die on a battlefield, but in a real sense he was a casualty in the struggle of the Jewish people for their national freedom.

NAPHTALI HERZ IMBER (1856–1909)

The last years of Naphtali Herz Imber, the author of Hatikvah (the Jewish National Anthem), were spent in the United States. He was born in Galicia in 1856 and died in New York in 1909. He might have lived to a ripe old age, but nothing could stop him from drinking himself to death. He knew where he was going and made a thorough job of getting there quickly.

He came to the United States in 1892. When his father died he left Galicia and became a traveling Hebrew poet. He stayed a while in Vienna, in Constantinople and in London. As a youth he had charm and wit and ingratiating manners. He knew how to flatter and serve a patron. He became a protégé of Laurence Oliphant, the English traveler who was interested in the Jewish settlement of Palestine. He went with Oliphant to Palestine and lived there for six years. He had the credentials of a Hebrew poet and made the most of his meager opportunities to live on his talent. His first poems were collected under the title of *Barkai* and dedicated to Oliphant. In this volume appeared "Hatikvah," which became the Zionist song, and "Mishmar Hayarden," another poem which was more popular with the early settlers in Palestine. After Oliphant's death Imber went to London where he lived a precarious life. He was a burden on all lovers of Hebrew. He always thought Hebrew literature owed him a living. Israel Zangwill made a caricature of him in the character of Melchizedek Pinchas in *The Children of the Ghetto*. It was an idealized portrait of Imber. Many stories were told of his escapades in London which were later enlarged upon by his admirers, who in their youth were fascinated by Imber's bizarre personality.

Wherever he appeared he told tall tales about himself, not many of them truthful or convincing, especially those with which he regaled whoever was willing to hear his amorous adventures. There was nothing in his appearance when we knew him that warranted belief in the authenticity of his romances with women for whom, he declared, he had a fatal attraction. Before he finally settled down on the East Side he traveled all over the United States, sometimes as a Hebrew Troubadour, sometimes disguised as a Mahatma and fortune teller. He wrote strange articles in English on esoteric subjects. He pretended a knowledge of theosophy and Hindu and Chinese lore. For a time he published a theosophical magazine in Boston under the title of *Uriel*. A second collection of his Hebrew poems appeared in 1902, a third in 1905 after the Kishinev pogroms. It was as a Hindu fakir that he appeared in San Francisco where, it was said, he married a Gentile woman impressed by his mystic behavior. This legend was never verified. He wanted to be known as the Jewish François Villon but he was not the scoundrel Villon was nor did he write such good poetry. His past was always obscure just as his present always seemed to lack the substance of reality.

I first met him in 1901 in Philadelphia at a Zionist convention. He was certainly not an attractive character. He had the head of an Indian, his face was bronzed, his hair was long and his clothes were always in tatters. He was indescribably dirty and always exuded the aroma of stale whisky. He was on the platform at the mass meeting. When they sang Hatikvah he rose unsteadily to his feet and accepted the applause as meant for him, with a grin of self-satisfaction as if to say, "It was I who laid that golden egg." A bottle of whisky stuck out of his coat pocket. No one in the audience seemed to know him. They marveled at his grotesque behavior.

Once having identified me as an easy mark for curiosities, which I was, he made it his business not to let me off and clung to me like a leech. He would write articles in English on large foolscap sheets and come to the *American Hebrew* to sell them to me. Every visit was an emergency. He wrote about the quaintest things in a strangely alien English and was never concerned with form or continuity; he avoided the usual Jewish themes of that day. Every now and then I purchased one of these articles, rewrote them and published them, but he never remembered how many had been purchased or when they were published. He was only interested in the fee. He would never accept an invitation for lunch; he abhorred food; but would take the money given to him and scuttle away to the nearest saloon. He preferred to drink from a bottle, not from a glass. He haunted the East Side cafés, but no one knew where he lived. He was often disorderly at public meetings. He once came to a Yiddish theatre where a Zionist play was being given in which

Hatikvah was sung, but he was not allowed to enter the theatre. A. S. Freidus, who was in charge of the Jewish section of the New York Public Library, interested Judge Mayer Sulzberger in him. The Judge knew of Imber from Israel Zangwill and agreed to give him a meager monthly allowance to be disbursed by Freidus. He was always over-drawn before the first of the month and pestered Freidus for days to give him an advance on the next month's check.

He was really not much of a poet. When he first wrote, Hebrew poetry was still rigid and traditional; there was more interest in lan-guage than in originality. Hatikvah was made the text of a song which struck a responsive chord by reason of its sentiment and melody. He had no philosophy nor was he really a "lover of Zion." In fact, he was not interested in Palestine overmuch. He mocked the seriousness of the Zionists, their romantic ideas, their tendency to mourn over the past. When I knew him he was certainly not a man of gallantry. Poetry could be written about Zion and Jerusalem, about the *Galut,* more especially about romance. The best poems, he thought, could be written only about wine and women. He had translated—so he said—Omar Khayyam into Hebrew. He made believe that Bacchus was his favorite god and that he hated Niobe for her tears. He was a sardonic jester. To those who listened to him he spoke of vines, of fig trees, of Turks, of myste-rious veiled women, of the drinks of many lands, of the Jordan and Jerusalem. He knew all the clichés. He pretended to joviality, which did not become him. His laughter was horrifying. It was hard to explain why we were interested in him; he had none of the geniality of the latter-day vagabonds of the Café Royal. It must have been that we were interested in him only because he had written Hatikvah.

I once visited him in the summer in Vineland where he was spending an enforced vacation in the country. He was the guest of Weinblatt, the Yiddish actor, who had retired to a chicken farm in his old age. Imber certainly looked queer in the company of chickens and cows and trees. He was embarrassed. He defended his presence on a farm by poking fun at the old actor. I saw the room he slept in. All he had of his own was a collection of grotesque canes and a stack of dusty manuscripts. He had no clothes except those he wore. He could have put everything that belonged to him in a handbag. He did not know what home meant nor was he conscious of being homeless. His escape was drink. He drank to stimulate his imagination or to dull his senses. Whatever it was, he never wrote what he was thinking about, really, and never spoke of what troubled him if anything did trouble him. He was no wandering minstrel; you never heard him sing. He was the perfect vagabond. The only thing that lives after him is Hatikvah, which is now being sung as the National Anthem of a reborn people. The words are his, but the Jewish people gave the words and the music life and meaning.

SELIG BRODETSKY (1888–1954)

I always thought that the worst thing that happened to Prof. Selig Brodetsky was that he was awarded the Senior Wrangler Prize by Trinity College.

It was this prize (a title given to the top candidate in the mathematical honors examination for the degree of BA) that made him known all over England. He stood out as a Jewish young man who acquired, in a most difficult science, an outstanding reputation which went along with him throughout a fruitful life. It made him the man he became— not in a perfect sense, but as a leading Jewish citizen of the British Empire. He was oppressed by it instead of stimulated and uplifted. He felt that it placed obligations on him; he had to make good as a man of scientific distinction. In 1920 he became a Professor of Mathematics at the University of Leeds. He worked very hard at it until 1949.

He felt heavy obligations to his family and he labored with a deep sense of responsibility to discharge them, especially to his father. It seemed as if the whole family was oppressed by poverty, and what he earned had to be distributed to all the members thereof without favor or reserve.

As a Professor he was a hard-working man. He made important contributions to aeronautics. As a Jew, by choice he was an overworked man all his life. He was a member of the World Zionist Executive and of the Jewish Agency Executive from 1928, and a generous speaker whenever called upon; a loyal colleague.

He became President of the Board of Deputies of British Jews and discharged his functions with great zeal.

He felt an inferiority which he did not in any way deserve, for he was a thorough scholar. His colleagues were not always fair to him, but he never resented unfair treatment. He kept his ambitions under the cover of his feeling that he should not ask too much.

He was not well treated by Dr. Weizmann for the better part of the service he gave to the Zionist movement, but he was a man ever ready to help the cause, to do what was required of him, and never to complain.

In the final years of his life he was appointed President of the Hebrew University in Jerusalem, but it was a stricken man who took that position in 1949. In 1952 he returned to England. He wrote an autobiography while he was ill and made a record, with remarkable fidelity and detail, of all the things he had done. His autobiography was published in 1960.

In his autobiography, Dr. Selig Brodetsky added interesting information on the death of Theodor Herzl's grandson, Stephen Herzl Neumann. The young man was the son of Herzl's daughter Trude. Brodetsky had brought him to England thirteen years before. He ultimately went to Cambridge where he worked for a law degree. Stephen looked very much like Theodor Herzl in his youth. He had been an officer in the British Army, and after the war received an appointment in Washington to deal with German inventions that might be useful to the Allies. Soon after he arrived he learned that both his father and mother had been killed in Austria by the Nazis. The news plunged him into despair; one day he jumped to his death from a bridge in Washington.

Herzl's son Hans and his daughter Pauline died unmarried. Stephen was Trude's only child. He was the last member of Herzl's family.

NAHUM GOLDMANN (1894–   )

Dr. Nahum Goldmann spent a great deal of his time in living out his youth. For a long time he was regarded as a remarkable young man. He went through all the best schools; he learned many languages, and he emerged a man without a party and almost impossible to dictate to as a party man. Nor did he join any Zionist party until he met with a small one where he could exercise his skill at maneuver.

Thus it was as a non-party man that he made an identity for himself in Zionist circles. He was an arresting personality from the moment he touched the Zionist Congress.

He was there a member of the party created by Isaac Gruenbaum of Poland which had five or six members. It was first called the "Democratic Group" and afterwards the "Radical Party". This assured Goldmann of his place in any general debate that arose. His eager and vibrant voice was heard in concert, at the beginning, with the heavier voices of veteran leaders; and he held his own for a long time with a remarkable audacity, passion and reasonableness.

Often he was on the losing side. On occasions he found himself in political isolation, but he was resilient enough to survive and to treat them as trivial and, with good humor, to always recover for the fight that came the next day. He was a veteran who received medals on many occasions, but was also proud of the many scars he bore.

He lived long enough to become the successor of Dr. Chaim Weizmann, as President of the World Zionist Organization and of the Jewish Agency. Now he finds himself in the tradition of the older Zionist leaders who, to their glory, always resisted being pressed into a party mold. They were themselves first, moving freely, reflecting their own ideals, creating their own enemies and winning their own friends, giving vent to their natural temperaments, pursuing their own real thinking and finding in Zionism the only freedom they could possibly enjoy in Jewish life.

In his earlier years, Goldmann made his mark in journalism. His was a fresh young voice in German, in Yiddish, and then in Hebrew. What he wrote had form and style and content and temperament. He had a keen sense of humor and showed a lively interest in all phases of Jewish life—scholarship, literature, art, politics and practical debate. But he could not limit himself merely to writing about life. He felt compelled to become one of the molders of Jewish history in a period of revolution; to occupy a place on the public platform and in all the political diversions of the Jewish world.

For many years he was regarded as one of the younger generation and was naturally eager for promotion, but spent some time sharpening his weapons for debate. Isaac Gruenbaum's Party was so small that it was not difficult to achieve distinction there rapidly. That Party was a simple device for saving a place for ambitious young men in Congress debates. It was not so difficult to devise a program, to acquire a status, to find an issue; it was not so easy to obtain numerous followers. Thus it remained a party of leaders. Here it was that Dr. Goldmann functioned for a number of years as speaker and parliamentarian. Here it was that he first became internationally known as a Zionist debater and participated as one of the opponents of the Extended Jewish Agency, which failed to accomplish its purpose. He was the ablest and the most persuasive and the most attractive participant in this debate which continued over many years and came to an end in 1929. After the Jewish Agency issue was settled, the Radical Party had nothing further to do, so it was dissolved in 1933. Gruenbaum made friends with Dr. Weizmann and so did Dr. Goldmann. They took their places in the natural grouping of the General Zionist Group.

In those formative years, Goldmann revealed, in all his utterances, a keen appreciation of the political difficulties of the Zionist movement. He saw the Jewish problem as one, but plagued with two battle fronts to defend. He was a close friend of Leo Motzkin, who was a protagonist of Diaspora nationalism. Dr. Goldmann had a keen understanding and appreciation of the political philosophy of Dr. Weizmann, but alternated in supporting and opposing his policies. His amazing knowledge of languages, his capacity for absorbing the intellectual and political ways of many European states, his protean skill in making himself at home anywhere, in any group, led inevitably to his becoming a political personality and a practitioner of the artistry of diplomacy.

In 1935, with the passing of both Motzkin and Victor Jacobson, Dr. Goldmann moved to Geneva, where he became the political representative of the Jewish Agency and later of the World Jewish Congress, and also a supporter of Dr. Weizmann.

Today he is not only the successor to Dr. Weizmann, as President of the World Zionist Organization, but he is probably our best-equipped student of international political affairs outside of Israel; his debates with Ben-Gurion are frequent, controversial and history-making.

He is the keenest of analysts, the least dogmatic and the readiest improviser in Zionist public affairs. His advantage lies in the fact that he is not weighed down by ideology. A pragmatist with a glowing imagination and a keen mind, he is ready to abandon an issue when faced by obstacles that will not bend to any design, and has faith that solutions will be found and new principles will be discovered by trial and error. He is never impressed by the loss of a battle, for in his mind's eye there is always projected the long-range strategy, not clear or definite at first, but in the end it can be relied upon to reach the goal desired, if you have the stamina to continue.

Issue can be taken with the view that Dr. Goldmann's eagerness to get away from difficult issues leads him to close the debate with hurried compromise. This is seldom true with regard to basic issues, on which he has been remarkably consistent and enduring.

The record shows that he had battered away at the enlarged Jewish Agency brilliantly with great energy, almost alone, until the last vote was taken in defeat in 1929. For two decades the movement wrestled with the problem of the *Endziel*. It avoided the formulation of the unpleasant, unavoidable conclusion which was finally expressed in Partition. Zionists dreaded reference to a Bi-National or Federated Palestine, hated to face the truth; and only in 1937 was a guarded resolution on Partition accepted by a divided vote in the Zionist Congress. Dr. Goldmann fought for Partition when it was as yet an unsanctioned and unacceptable doctrine. He believed in it as the only solution of an impossible situation. It was his daring and the forcefulness of his argumentation that led to the acceptance of the principle of Partition by the then American Secretary of State. The recommendation by the United Nations Special Commission on Palestine and its final acceptance by the United Nations Assembly in November 1947, was brought about, in important part, through his ardent support.

His boldness was also shown in his advocacy of and victory in connection with the German reparations being paid to Israel in partial repayment for the crimes of Hitlerism. He braved the attacks of partisans in Israel and in the Diaspora with remarkable courage. He stood his ground against an excited Israel populace and the denunciation of a number of Israeli political parties and their friends in the Diaspora. He was not deterred by threats. He succeeded in organizing a united international Jewish front as the sponsors for reparations negotiations and as the trustees of the funds involved. His genius for negotiation and statesmanlike behavior throughout the development of this whole delicate transaction won for him the commendation of Jews the world over.

The birth of the State of Israel not only shook the Jewish world and brought all its fragments together in a dynamic union for defense. It also seemed to split the Zionist Movement. Speculation ran riot as to the relationship of the State to the Diaspora, the relationship of the State to the Zionist Organization. If a viable balance has been established between Israel and the Diaspora, it is due largely to the steadfast leadership and tenacity of Dr. Goldmann, whose refusal to dogmatise, to draw hasty conclusions, to freeze a fluid situation, is responsible for the better relations that now prevail. All this could be done only by a man of his deep understanding of Jewish history, his sagacity, and his skill in negotiation; and with his impersonality of approach.

The Jewish world begins to give the impression of internal order and a genuine appreciation of the long pull that is needed in union and the suppression of partisanship, and in determination to stand firmly on its own feet.

It is clear that equally to be recognized are the sovereignty of the State of Israel and the autonomy of the Diaspora. There are mutual responsibilities. Respect for both has to be accepted by both. There must be fraternal cooperation of all free Jewish communities recognizing common responsibilities. On the one hand there is the State of Israel, led by its Prime Minister and his cabinet. On the other hand, there are the organized communities of the Diaspora. Of these, Dr. Goldmann is the acknowledged leader.

It takes no special gift of prophecy to foresee fruitful years ahead for his great gifts to shower benefits on both.

AMERICA

HENRIETTA SZOLD (1860–1945)

The traits of her character, molded in her youth, shone clearly throughout her long life. She changed little. Once her interest was captured,
her time and thought abided with it tenaciously. Her earliest memories
were detailed and could be relied upon as a reflection of a living reality.
When she was associated with the Jewish Publication Society, she
extended her interest from the simple to the all-inclusive, so that in
time she was editor and translator, proofreader and critic and the
symbol of its program. To every task she undertook she brought a
meticulous perception. When later, her correspondence increasing, she
was prevailed upon to dictate her letters to a stenographer, she had to
proofread them again and again, for she could not bear to pass even a
typing error. The same painstaking attention she gave later to the
Hadassah budget, to her work in the Youth Aliyah, and to her duties
in the *Vaad Leumi*. She was the obedient slave of her assignments.
Discipline to her seemed to be a moral command, and the clearing of
her desk at the end of the day a primary duty. She seldom fought to
have her views prevail in the presence of authority. Every now and
then, the higher morality prevailed and she joined in controversy on
issues she felt deeply, and her temper, once aroused, became a flame.
She could not abide orthodox casuistry, the authority of clericals, and
resisted their dogmas and procedures with a deep resentment. Her
piety was not going to be dominated by the dialectics of piety! Her
life was a chain of habit which she was unable to break; and as her
habits accumulated and became a formidable mountain, she found
herself more and more trapped in the ways of life she could not, or
would not change. I remember her correspondence with me in my
youth, regarding a manuscript. How patiently she explained in long
letters why the manuscript had not been accepted, why this member of

the publications committee, or that member, had refused to be influenced in its favor! She certainly spent an excess of her precious time to explain a situation, which, so far as I was concerned, was so simple and comprehensible. That was a fine excess of a great virtue; she had to be kind. She could not be persuaded to rest awhile in her old age, but worked on according to schedule close to the last days of her life. Life was work! When she could not find any work for her hands to do she folded them in her lap and found peace in death.

An army of American women followed Henrietta Szold; the Jews of Palestine loved and revered her; but she was not the conventional Zionist leader—the orator on the platform, the ready writer on Zionist themes, a controversialist in the "general" debate. Her life was devoted to service—not on the battlefield or in the hospital. She was the humble maid of all work, the housewife whose work is never done, having no personal diversions, no special hobbies, very little of a life of her own.

In her youth she had romantic dreams, but she was always diverted by duties which her conscience would not let her pass over. She wanted to be a teacher, a writer, an editor, a preacher of liberal ideas. She had warm, affectionate parents and five sisters. All the normal interests of a healthy, vivacious young girl were reflected in her early years. She was eager to hear learned discourses. She loved a good story. She was stirred by good music and was a fair dancer. She was absorbed in good literature and loved flowers inordinately. She had the added spiritual delight of being regarded by her father as a good substitute for the son he never was blessed with.

But her life diverted her course. Early, she was interested in Zionism, but only as one of the items on her program of life. What she thought would be her pleasant avocation became her inescapable vocation. Zionism grew to be the dominant tenant of her conscience. She thought that she would be able to subordinate it, but as the movement grew she found it to be an unrelenting taskmaster whom she could not deny, not even when she was over seventy and felt that she deserved a rest.

She served with humility. The burden of the Youth Aliyah was thrust upon her shoulders when she was seventy-three. She was overwhelmed by the agonies she had to go through in the discharge of her duties. She had to see the mothers in Germany prepared to have their children go to Palestine to avoid the threatened dangers, and never to see them again. At that age she began a new chapter of service. I suggested then that the time had come for her to relinquish the terrible exactions of her new mission; that this dedicated servant of a great cause should unburden her heart of its accumulated grievances, impart her wisdom to the heavily pressed Movement struggling with vital problems; or at least, write her memoirs. (Who does not write them nowadays?)

This she never did. It was too late for her to change. She never violated the part she was destined to play. Habit had become too rigid. Prodigal in service, she remained humble and restrained in public speech throughout her life.

In private letters to friends or in conversations off the record she spoke her mind in bold terms. Marvin Lowenthal wrote of her life, as illustrated by letters to her sisters and to others in Hadassah; but none of them reflects her revolt against dogma and partisanship in the Movement. None of them gives evidence of the sharpness of her tongue in criticism. All her life was absorbed in the drudgery of administration, of recording and corresponding, drawing up budgets and spending them; talking to visitors; speaking at Hadassah meetings; collecting the nurses and physicians for the medical unit; working from sunrise to midnight in the affairs of Youth Aliyah. In the halls of discussion, in the councils of leadership she was rarely heard. She rejected that sort of leadership. She was a grand exemplar of consecrated service. That was her metier. For that service she was loved and respected by the citizens of the Homeland and by all Zionists the world over.

She was a Zionist before the advent of Theodor Herzl. Her love for Zion welled up from her love for things Jewish. She was an omnivorous reader. Any Jewish book, in German or English, or later in Hebrew, had an irresistible attraction. She was an ardent and wondering admirer of Emma Lazarus, the young American girl of Sephardic parentage who wrote impassioned Zionist poetry long before the days of Herzl. When she taught English in an evening school for immigrants in Baltimore she met *Chovevei Zionists* who sat at her feet in the classroom and repaid her in full measure for her friendship with their loyalty and devotion to Zionism. The Messiah and the Redemption were an integral part of her Jewish faith. Her intellectual life was guided by the noble example of her father, a Zionist of the old school, a man of wide learning, a personality of great integrity.

She moved out of her normal life to identification with Zionism in gradual stages. She gave voluntary aid in the founding of the Jewish Publication Society and in 1892 joined its staff as secretary and editor, and remained chained to its service until 1915. Through her hands passed some of the most important early publications of the Society. She was the translator of a large part of Graetz's monumental *History of the Jews.* She translated and edited several volumes of Louis Ginzberg's *Legends of the Jews;* Moritz Lazarus's *Ethics of the Fathers;* Nahum Slouschz's *Renascence of Hebrew Literature.* She was more than translator and editor; she selected the paper and the type; she read the proofs; she "sold" many of the manuscripts to the conservative board of editors of the Society. She was one of the first to aid in publications for Zionist propaganda. She wrote and translated articles for the old *Maccabean* founded in 1900. She edited or translated a number of pamphlets issued by the Federation of American Zionists. She drew together a small circle of young women and founded a study circle out of which emerged the Hadassah.

She came to Zionist public meetings and attended several Zionist conventions. She finally was persuaded to take on the duties of the Secretary of the Federation after Dr. Judah L. Magnes had retired from office. Dr. Magnes was responsible for his immediate successor, who was not adequate and had brought the finances of the Federation to the verge of bankruptcy. It was characteristic of Miss Szold that when she was told of the financial disorder, she agreed to become the Secretary on a voluntary basis and for a limited period. She was determined to bring the finances back to normal and was outraged by the fact that the receipt of contributions to the Jewish National Fund had not been acknowledged. Night after night, for eight months, she was absorbed in digging out the names and addresses of contributors, sending them proper receipts and adjusting matters with the head office of the Jewish National Fund in The Hague. She spent long evenings at the musty Zionist office on East Broadway and finally had the satisfaction of knowing that every contributor had been identified, given a receipt, and his account closed. That duty being performed, Miss Szold returned to her normal pursuits. But she was finally won over completely to Zionism at the beginning of the First World War when the Provisional Zionist Committee was organized under the Chairmanship of Louis D. Brandeis and she was asked to serve as Director of its Education Department.

When she severed her relations with the Jewish Publication Society in 1916, her Zionist work filled her whole life. She was the inspiration of the first group of Hadassah women. She prepared and equipped the first two Hadassah nurses who went to Palestine. Her assignment to the field of education of the Provisional Zionist Committee became a major operation. She organized a group of educators to assist her and at one time threatened to absorb in her bureau a full program of educational propaganda (as well as a larger part of the budget of the Provisional Committee). She had the advice and cooperation of Reuben Brainin, the Hebrew writer; Kalman Whiteman, the Hebrew pedagogue; and Emanuel Neumann, then a young man in the teaching profession. For the first time in its history the Zionist Movement was equipped with an educational apparatus that commanded respect. The work continued until 1919 when Zionist policy was diverted to accord with Mr. Brandeis' views as to the future of the organization. Education was to be directed exclusively to service of specific projects. Political propaganda was to be discontinued. There was an interval of uncertainty as to Miss Szold's future which was solved by sending her on a mission to Palestine which she had not seen since 1909. Together with Dr. Seth Hirsch and Jacob de Haas she had organized the Hadassah medical unit. Now she was to go to Palestine as liaison for Hadassah with the medical unit and to share direction with Dr. Isaac Rubinow.

That assignment settled her course. The rest of her life was spent shifting from Palestine to the United States and back again. She continued her interest in the medical unit and the growth of the Hadassah in the United States. She made a number of American speaking tours. She participated in Zionist and Hadassah conventions. On the other end of the line she joined the *Vaad Leumi* (Jewish National Council) in charge of Palestine's social service. In 1927 she was elected a member of the Zionist Executive, serving with Frederick Kisch and Harry Sacher. In 1933 she took over the Youth Aliyah which was her last, long assignment.

The curious thing about Miss Szold was that in spite of her deep love for Palestine, her great interest in every phase of its development, her intimate friendships with hundreds of people in Palestine, she never could rid herself of the longing to return home to Baltimore. Her mind and body were occupied in Palestine, but her memories clustered with deepest affection and sentiment around her life in Maryland—her father, her mother, her sisters and their children. It was an incurable nostalgia. She was always promising to return home to remain, to spend her last days with her surviving sisters and their children, to index her father's library for shipment to Palestine (a pious pledge she was never able to keep). She wanted to see and smell the flowers of Maryland. But there she was in Jerusalem, the beloved foster mother of thousands of orphaned children, and the captive of the Cause to her last day. She died in Jerusalem in 1945 at the age of 85.

She remains imbedded in the memories of Hadassah women. She remains a warm and sympathetic personality in the history of the Zionist Movement in the United States. She will be remembered in the free State of Israel for what she did for thousands of men, women and children. She will be remembered for her great devotion, her wide sympathies and her understanding of the difficulties of a mass of human beings, coming out of servitude to freedom; she was a mother to them all.

STEPHEN S. WISE (1874–1949)

The first period of Zionism had to win Jewish recognition of the Promise. The seeds were brought over from Eastern Europe. But Stephen S. Wise was the first American Apostle to the Gentiles. In those days he was eager to find a cause to fit his ardent nature and give him scope for advocacy. He used the platforms available for his oratory also to serve Zionism. He was a liberal in religion and in politics, but he was not a theologian or a politician. He fraternized with American leaders and got a hearing for his views, for he had a great capacity for friendships. His stay in Oregon made him well known as an orator and a reformer on the Pacific Coast. He was a leader in exposing municipal corruption and stood out with other religious leaders for the reform of municipal government. He achieved a prominent place in the Democratic Party and soon was accepted as a formidable leader. He seldom overlooked an opportunity to further Zionist interests or Jewish causes. He carried the message to far-off places and made the press in effective headlines. He was the only outstanding Zionist in that field until the advent of Louis D. Brandeis, who was also known as a leader and reformer, but in a more impersonal way. Mr. Brandeis reflected liberal ideas but he never actively cooperated in any political party. When the great lawyer became known as a Zionist, many new doors were opened for our cause, and Dr. Wise naturally gravitated toward him and joined forces with him in the interests of Zionism. The prestige of Mr. Brandeis and the oratory of Dr. Wise led to the conversion of many in the group which was then backing Woodrow Wilson for the Presidency. Dr. Wise was accepted as a Democrat in good standing, but he seldom allowed that fact to bind him when he thought Jewish interests demanded freedom of action. He had many collisions with Franklin

Delano Roosevelt, but maintained an unbroken friendship with Harry S Truman. He grew mellow with age and began to seek peace and friendship where formerly peace was his least concern. He welcomed the State of Israel with fervid exaltation. He felt that his life had been given to the greatest Cause one could experience in Jewish life. My friendship with him had its ups and downs. I was the victim of formalism and always liked to play the game according to the rules. He was the incorrigible improviser, and was ready, without hesitation, to follow the beckoning of opportunity, if it led to immediate startling results. He went along with Mr. Brandeis in the Keren Hayesod controversy, but soon came back to serve the Fund he had rejected. I worked with him in the American Jewish Congress during the exciting period when the menace of Hitler aroused, in gradual stages, the American Jewish Community. I stood with him in the organization of the American Jewish Conference and then of the World Jewish Congress. He lost his interest in the American Jewish Conference quickly and I was left to carry that burden until its affairs were liquidated in 1948. We were comrades-in-arms when the State of Israel was born and when Dr. Weizmann retired from the Zionist Organization. He was a generous friend and a forgiving foe and capable of magnanimous behavior. American Jewry has never had another leader of his stature and gifts.

Stephen S. Wise was one of the founders of the American Zionist Organization and its best known leader for half a century. But it would be unfair to claim that his colorful personality was limited to one area of public life. He followed many lights. His was not a single-track mind. He was a leader of many causes. To Jews he was a commanding figure in and out of all parties. Wherever he took his stand, he had his own accent and was likely at any moment to breach the program and the tactics of the issue in which he was interested. He was a Reform rabbi, but seldom conformed to the dogmas and strategies of Reform Judaism. He was often at odds with Orthodox Judaism, but as he became older he had a reluctant sympathy for the old piety and old customs. He used to say that he was a "general" Zionist, but he ranged freely from one party to another and the end of his life saw him embrace all Zionist parties in an upsurge of sentiment, when the flag of Israel was raised.

So too in American life. To his non-Jewish friends (and they were legion) he was the broad-minded American rabbi who "raised his voice" for every humanitarian cause, regardless of creed, nationality or race.

He was an admirer of Theodore Roosevelt. He was a Wilsonian Democrat. On occasion, he stood with the insurgents of both major parties. All his life he fought municipal corruption under whatever banner it masked itself; and he was relentless in opposition to Tammany Hall. He was as ready to fight as to support the party in which he was enrolled. He was never frightened by the bogey of consistency. He followed his own *daemon*. He waited for the spark that ignited his spirit to free his speech. It was a sense of justice or humanity; it was friendship or prejudice; often it was excess of indignation or temperament; and more often it was the glimpse of an inspiring phrase which he seized with swift passion and made the most of. He could not endure shackles. He would not walk a straight line. He had no respect for logic. But, in the last analysis, no matter what might have been the aberration, he was the prodigal son returning to his own people in every crisis, marching along with them wherever they were going.

When Herzl's *Jewish State* startled the Jewish world, Wise was a young man just out of college. He was a postgraduate student at Columbia in the Semitics Department, studying under Professor Richard Gottheil. His father was a learned rabbi and wanted Stephen to follow in the family tradition and also to become a rabbi. Through his father's influence Wise secured his first pulpit. It was the B'nai Jeshurun Congregation of New York. The writer was a stranger in the city at the time and by chance heard Wise preach on a Sabbath morning. It was a modified Orthodox service. In spite of his youth, Wise was an impressive figure in a gown, a mitred hat and a High-Church turned collar. He was even then the master of ritual and form and knew how to use his resonant voice. But he was not at home there. What kind of a rabbi he was to be—whether a rabbi at all!—was not clear to him then. He was not a graduate of a rabbinical seminary. His father wanted him to turn his mind to scholarly pursuits. His education did not include more than a contact of courtesy with Hebraic or Talmudic tradition. He was more at home with the New England Transcendentalists, with the leaders of the Unitarian Church, with the son of a rabbi—Felix Adler—who had rejected Judaism and founded the Society for Ethical Culture. The larger part of Wise's cultural equipment was American. He had not found the springs of the Jewish renascence which were then effervescent in Eastern Europe. He was an isolated figure looking to the right and to the left, uncertain of the way he should go.

The Jewish community of that period—as he saw it—was drab,

parochial and unattractive. The older settlers from Germany were shep-
herded by rabbis educated in Germany, many of whom were still speaking German and preaching an easy unresisting assimilation and a uni-
versalism based on the prophets, a "mission" which had no missionaries.
The newcomers from Eastern Europe were crowded into the East Side,
with their own language, their own traditions, their own press, struggling to find a place in the new world, but determined to do that in their
own way. The two groups seldom met as brethren. Philanthropy was
the only bridge that brought them together, but not as equals. They
had different standards and clashing hopes. The Hebrew Union College
was graduating young rabbis who were sent forth to Americanize their
congregations. The Jewish Theological Seminary, based on conservative
ideas, was in the first stage of its development. The East Side Yeshivas
were merely inadequate replicas of their East European models.

The call of Theodor Herzl determined Wise's destiny. Herzl's pro-
nouncements in the European press, the support given his views by
Max Nordau, the press agentry of Israel Zangwill, the calling of the
First Zionist Congress, the protest of the rabbis of Munich, the attacks
of the Anglo-Jewish community and of Orthodox rabbis everywhere
gave Wise his cue for action. Here was a cause which was in need of
militant advocacy. He offered his services to Richard Gottheil, who
was its first official Zionist spokesman in the United States. He got to
know the American rabbis whose sympathies were with Zionism, the
Jastrows, the venerable Gustave Gottheil, Benjamin Szold of Baltimore,
Bernhard Felsenthal of Chicago. He met Herzl and other Zionists in
Europe. The isolation of Wise (as well as of American Jewry) was broken
by the advance of Zionism. Thus, while in a general way Wise had a
cursory knowledge of Jewish theology from German sources and from
his father, his Jewish masters were not theologians or rabbis. They were
Theodor Herzl and Max Nordau, whose sensational utterances at
Zionist Congresses stimulated an evergrowing Jewish interest in Zionism
throughout the United States. That movement thus conceived became
the guide of his life, colored his thinking (but did not monopolize it) and
gave what he said when he spoke on Jewish subjects a tone and dignity and
purpose it could have acquired from no other source.

In the issues of the *American Hebrew* of over fifty years ago will be
found the contributions of Wise which were tolerated by that publication because they were official communications. Zionism was being
attacked on the editorial pages of the *American Hebrew* with consistent
resentment of its intrusion on the American scene. But Wise did not

remain long in New York. He left in 1900 to occupy a Reform pulpit
in Portland, Oregon, where he remained for six years. It was a voluntary
exile, for he could have remained in the East had he chosen. In Portland,
he matured as rabbi, preacher and social worker. He was now a full-
fledged Reform rabbi. He was interested in labor problems and municipal reform and national political issues. His qualities as an orator
became known from coast to coast. He would return to the East on
brief visits. He won friends in non-Jewish as well as Jewish circles. His
going to Portland was due, it seems, to his secret hope that by serving
as the rabbi of a Reform congregation, he would qualify for the pulpit
of Temple Emanu-El of New York—proud citadel of Jewish wealth and
social exclusiveness. He had a friend at court in the person of the venerable Rabbi Gustave Gottheil, but he was opposed and rejected by
most of the lay leaders of the congregation. Fortunately for him and
his people, he was not destined to be chained to that golden chariot,
to be cribbed and cabined in thought and action. Upon the frustration
of his ambition, he hit out for freedom through the Free Synagogue.

He was never intended to be the rabbi of a parish or congregation.
He was more than a minister, whose sermons were incidental to parochial duties. He always saw himself standing on a platform addressing
a multitude, arousing them to war against injustice, stirring the public
conscience, preaching the brotherhood of man, regarding nothing human as alien to him. And he was determined that not only should his
congregation hear what he had to say but that his words should push
their way into the press, and win the larger audiences.

The Free Synagogue was his platform for fifty years. He became the
boldest, the most exciting commentator on American and Jewish affairs.
He took Felix Adler's place at Carnegie Hall. He sponsored lost causes
with the fervor and fire of consecration. He was irrepressible and unpredictable, but always spoke his own mind. He could always be depended upon for audacity of attack, as the master of winged words,
never to be controlled, reckless of the consequences to his own personal
career. It was from the platform of the Free Synagogue that Wise took
his stand on all the issues of the day. He was concerned with national
and state government. He was savage in his attacks on the municipal
rottenness in New York and Philadelphia and all our large cities. He
was a leader in defending civil and religious rights, in demanding that
racial and religious discrimination cease. The suppression of minorities
anywhere in the world aroused his denunciation and stormy protest.
He associated himself with the apostles of freedom in all lands.

But the central theme of his varied interests, the most sacred of all causes which he served was the Zionist Movement, in which was included not only the ideal of a Jewish State in Palestine but the rebirth of the Jewish nation. In Zionism was included, so far as he was concerned, Jewish rights everywhere, Jewish democracy, Jewish survival. It was the American Jewish Congress and the World Jewish Congress; it was the structure of the Jewish community; it was Jewish education; it was resistance and protest all along the line against Jewish inequality; it was Jewish pride and dignity.

The first phase of modern Zionism was determined by Theodor Herzl. It was a matter of political negotiations and propaganda. Herzl's failure to win support from Germany and Turkey and the rejection by the Zionist Congress of England's offer of Uganda followed by Herzl's death closed that chapter of Zionist history. The successors of Herzl were unable to restore the political objective as the center of the Movement until the beginning of World War I.

Wise was a political Zionist. It was Herzl's adventure and mission which stirred his imagination. He thought of Zionist leadership as associated almost exclusively with political propaganda. Of all Zionists in the first decade of the movement in the United States he had the qualifications and the desire to be of service in the political field. He became a political force in American life. He associated with political movements. He assiduously cultivated American political leaders. He had a deep interest in winning non-Jewish support for Zionism. In due course he had a large circle of political friends in every party and in all liberal circles, especially, who were sympathetic to the Zionist views of their favorite rabbi. He was a political friend of Woodrow Wilson as well as a leading Democratic campaigner in that period. His name went a long way to help make Zionist ideals popular, although during that first decade he was more often than not on less than speaking terms with American Zionist leaders, whom he classified as *kultur* Zionists.

He was never able to rid himself of the overwhelming influence of Theodor Herzl and the prejudices of that early period. He regarded the spiritual Zionism of Ahad Ha-am as a form of opiate for the Jewish masses, which would keep them in the bondage of a culture that never would lead to political rebirth. The fact that members of the faculty of the Jewish Theological Seminary were the new leaders of American Zionism and that Judah L. Magnes was their spokesman did not help to reconcile Wise with what he regarded as new trends in Zionism. He sulked in his tent. He complained bitterly of the influence of Magnes and the Seminary but made no effort to counteract that influence. He went his own way as an ambassador without credentials, relying upon his own platform in the Free Synagogue.

When Louis D. Brandeis came to Zionism and headed the Provisional Zionist Committee, Wise returned to the Zionist fold. He saw Zionism again becoming a political force. His large influence in the Democratic Party and with President Wilson had a great deal to do with the final decision of the American Government to approve of the Balfour Declaration. Wilson recognized the intellectual leadership of Mr. Brandeis, but it was to Wise he looked for the political advocacy necessary to win public opinion for the cause and the Democratic Party. Thus Wise became one of the molders of Zionist policy in the United States in one of its most critical moments. He was its most outstanding propagandist in non-Jewish circles. He was its most effective advocate with government authorities. From 1922 until the death of Franklin Delano Roosevelt, he was the most impressive Jewish public figure in Washington. He had taken on at that time the leadership of the American Jewish Congress, whose destiny he guided as well as the destiny of the World Jewish Congress which was organized in 1936. His great influence continued unabated through the Second World War, when he was the Chairman of the American Zionist Emergency Council and later its co-chairman with Abba Hillel Silver. When he withdrew from official leadership in the Council, relinquishing his authority in favor of Dr. Silver, his voice was not muted. Again he reverted to his own platform, to his own audiences, to his own circles of influence and to the last days of his life retained his freedom.

He was an orator and preacher of the old school. His voice was deep and resonant and changeable. He had the equipment of a grand actor and used the platform not only for oratory but to present a dramatic performance, always thrilling, always moving and always loaded with effective phrases. He was capable of winning the applause of tremendous audiences. His name was on the list of speakers of many of the great meetings held in the largest halls for causes which stirred the whole country. He preached many a sermon well; he delivered many a eulogy with great pathos; he was good-humored and captivating at dinners at which he presided with grace and dignity; he was a tempestuous political orator comparable to the best in American political life. But he was superb when he freed himself of form and manuscript and gave unbridled sway to his emotions. He often missed the bull's eye of accuracy; his logic was faulty, but the range of his vocabulary, the power of his invective, the wrath he was able to pour into his polemics gave these improvisations the quality of incomparable oratory.

Who will forget the period of his angriest mood, when the sinister figure of Adolf Hitler broke through the crumbling walls of the Weimar Republic and the Nazis began their march of destruction with the silent consent of the world, and in the course of their horrifying progress destroyed millions of helpless Jews? He was beside himself with savage moral indignation, and spoke in thousands of meetings and "raised his voice" so that he was heard in every corner of the earth. At that time he was beyond question the unrivaled spokesman for the appeal and protest of the Jewish people in the greatest tragedy of their history.

He was allergic to discipline in the Zionist Movement. As was indicated, he regarded the spiritual Zionism of Ahad Ha-am as disloyalty to Theodor Herzl. He was won over to the leadership of Mr. Brandeis, and regarded any opposition to his leadership as deserving of public censure. He went along with Mr. Brandeis in the controversy with Dr. Weizmann. He was opposed to Dr. Weizmann's political methods for about fifteen years and believed that these methods were the cause of the failure to convert Britain to Zionist friendship. He was against the enlargement of the Jewish Agency for Palestine. He opposed the partition of Palestine in 1937 but was reconciled to partition in 1946. He played for a time in the orchestra under Jabotinsky's direction and with de Haas wrote an indictment of British policy under the Mandate called *The Great Betrayal.* Very soon thereafter he reversed himself and denounced Jabotinsky for his attitude toward labor in Palestine in a terrific attack. He was a hard opponent, but was always prepared to admit error and make generous amends. When the heat of anger cooled, his natural friendliness and good humor returned. In the last years he walked side by side with Dr. Weizmann, ignoring past differences, seeking in loyal friendship to be of service. In 1931, he had joined in helping to unseat Dr. Weizmann, but in 1946 at Basle he stood with Dr. Weizmann's friends to prevent his defeat.

Although he seemed a man of storms, the word "peace" had a curious effect upon him. He hadn't the heart to resist appeals for peace and unity. Even while engaged in what seemed to be a relentless controversy, he regarded it as incidental, episodic, in the nature of an interesting game, unrelated to the real thing in which he was interested.

He never was able to fight to the bitter end of decision. He always seemed to be praying for a peaceful way out of the difficulty, as eager to fight for peace as he was to break it.

He was not concerned with foundations or monuments. He founded institutions and organizations and gave little thought to their future maintenance. He organized the Institute for Jewish Studies as a national seminary for the training of rabbis; it was a rival to the Hebrew Union College. A few years before his death, it was merged with the College. He gave twenty-five years of his life to the American Jewish Congress and was its champion in many a public controversy, disturbing the barons of Jewish philanthropy, running counter to their efforts to dominate Jewish life. But gradually the Congress moved away from its original moorings. He could not resist the encircling peace movements. He could not maintain a stand of belligerency against men who were his personal friends; and so he left the Congress unprovided for, dependent in effect upon the generosity of the Welfare Funds. The Free Synagogue was the foundation of his life; it was not only a platform; it was a social service with a large program. Only a few years before his death was he able to ensure the erection of a permanent home for the synagogue he had created.

In its early years Zionism was a propaganda movement. The practical work in Palestine was resisted for political reasons. There were few activities in Palestine that made an appeal for financial support. But as the Movement grew and deeper interests were aroused, more and more appeals reached the United States. There was then the Haifa Technical Institute, the Bezalel Art School, the Merhavia cooperative colony, the Herzliah Gymnasium in Tel Aviv, and, of course, the Jewish National Fund. The Keren Hayesod followed in 1921. Wise was one of the most effective campaigners for Palestine funds. He served all phases of the work indiscriminately, overgenerously. He saw Palestine on a number of occasions. He greeted the beginnings of the homeland and then saw its later development. His name appears in the Golden Book of the Jewish National Fund. Thousands of trees have been planted in his name. A village has been named Gan Shmuel in his honor. Like Herzl, however, he adopted none of the institutions in Palestine as his own; he had no favorites; he served them all in an all-embracing love. He was always the unrewarded servant of the cause.

LOUIS D. BRANDEIS (1856–1941)

Louis D. Brandeis became a Zionist too late in life. His personality was matured and fixed, and his way of life was trained in habit. It was not easy for him to learn new ways of thinking or of living. His was a liberal approach to the problems of American life. He had been greatly influenced by Lincoln, by Emerson and the New England thinkers. He looked American, he lived American, and the future of his country greatly concerned him. He was already distinguished in that way of life as a fighting lawyer for public causes. In all of his past his Jewish heritage had played no real part except as auxiliary to his basic concepts. He had to be recalled to his memory of the Jewish past that lived in his subconscious self. He had to return to his own people. It was a long distance to go. He had to be reintroduced to their living counterparts. He had to be sensitized to the tragedy of their lives, to sympathize with their aspirations and their hopes. He had to rediscover the Jewish people. The unfortunate feature of his return was that his knowledge was acquired not directly at firsthand but through the interpretations of others. These things had to be translated to him; they had to be explained. His questions had to be answered by third parties unrelated to the content of his soul. Therefore, when he passed over to the Jewish side and joined hands with his own people, he met them with fixed preconceptions, habits of thought and of speech by now rigidly his own. He had to leap over the processes that led him back to the birth of Jewish traditions, of ideals, and relate them to the Jews of his own day. Clashes were inevitable, for his mind was powerfully aggressive and seeking clear answers to his pertinent questions. He could not easily be reconciled with the forms in which the Jewish revival was being incorporated; the methods and standards of which were foreign to his experience, to his language and his social behavior; out of harmony with his personality. He got more from papers than from people. He could penetrate the meaning of intellectual conceptions; he was adept in the use of logic; but an understanding of personal relations was quite beyond him. His briefs were intended for the High Court of Justice, not for a jury or a general debate. His first defeat in the Movement was therefore his last. He retired from the Zionist field with displeasure and grief which diminished only as the years passed and as he was more and more enfolded in the silences that grew with the years. In his last days he was a symbol of rectitude and wisdom. His foundations in character could not be disturbed.

Louis D. Brandeis was the leader of American Zionists during the First World War. He was born in Louisville, Kentucky, in 1856. His parents were of Bohemian origin. He was molded by American life and there were few alien mixtures in the quality of his personality. He was taken by his parents as a youth to Europe and studied in a high school in Dresden, Germany. He returned to the United States and entered Harvard Law School. He was an exceptional student. He had a retentive memory and a keen orderly mind. He worked his way through the Law School and took his law degree when he was twenty. He went to St. Louis to practice law, but decided to accept the offer of a classmate to open a law office in Boston. When Brandeis was thirty his reputation as a skillful and resourceful lawyer was already well established. When he identified himself with the Zionist Movement in 1912, he was rich in legal experience and his name was linked with liberal causes and public service.

The traditions and standards of New England were integrated in his character. He acquired the habit of "plain living and high thinking." He disliked luxuries and excess in comforts. He had no itch for personal possessions and was simple in his food and clothing. He was reserved and restrained in speech and gave the impression of not revealing the workings of his mind freely. He was a Puritan in spirit and conduct, naturally thrifty and cautious. He hated ostentation and pride all his life. He was thoroughly American, feeling himself a product of its history, grateful to its great men, and endeavored at all times to measure up to the obligations of American democracy. He emphasized in all his public addresses the distinction of America as not being in its bigness but in the quality of its democracy; its doors were open to all on a basis of equality. His democracy was not soft and abstract, but resolute and practical. He was a moralist. Boston was the hub of his universe; he always came back to it as his home. He was a Jew, but did not regard it as his duty to assert the fact unless a situation called for it. He belonged to no Jewish religious body. And yet unrelated as he was to all forms of Jewish life, unread in its literature and unfamiliar with its traditions, the heart and mind of this man were captured by the ideal of the rebirth of a Jewish State and he became one of the few American Jews who understood and appreciated the genius of Theodor Herzl.

The identification of Mr. Brandeis with the Zionist Movement lifted it out of a narrow circle and enabled it to take advantage of the new political conditions which matured during World War I.

A decade of Zionist work had produced a substantial layer of Zionist life among the new settlers and their children. But the settlers of the older period were hostile to the new trend and fought it with harsh resentment. They regarded it as a disturber of their peace of mind; it was an offense to their Americanism; it was an obstacle to Jewish adjustment in a democratic environment; it revived memories they wished to forget. The orthodox at that time were steeped in their traditions and rejected innovations; they believed in the Messiah and the Redemption of Zion, but God had to utter the word. The Jewish labor movement accepted the materialistic conception of history that came from the mind of Karl Marx; they had already written off Jewish nationality as one of the sacrifices the Jews would have to make for the world-revolution; and they regarded Zionists as benighted reactionaries. The Zionist pioneers in the American field found it hard to overcome this formidable triple-headed opposition.

Through his position in American life Mr. Brandeis was able to develop a Zionist Movement colored by American standards and ideals. He had made a place for himself in American life without emphasizing his Jewish identity. His return to Jewish ideals therefore had an enormous influence upon all Jews—orthodox and reform, labor and liberal.

He took command of Zionist affairs in 1914 and held his control until he was named by President Wilson to the U.S. Supreme Court Bench. He became the master of Zionist facts. With the single-mindedness and tenacity for which he was distinguished as a lawyer he made the organization of the movement his special task. By "organization" he did not necessarily mean a democratic organization. He meant establishing law and order, planning, securing the resources for action, depending upon masses of people. The brief was in his hands. All believers were expected to cooperate. He prepared himself to assume the responsibility. He read modern Jewish history. He heard witnesses who told him of the facts of Jewish life. He listened with great patience and remembered all he heard accurately. He met Aaron Aronsohn, the discoverer of "wild wheat," who lost his life in the intelligence service of the British in the First World War. He had long and exciting discussions with Shmarya Levin, who was a sagacious analyst of Jewish thought and history. He met Nahum Sokolow, who had an inexhaustible fund of Jewish knowledge and recollection of historic fact, whose erudition made a deep impression on him. He knew little of the Jews of Eastern Europe or, for that matter, of Jews in general. He read up on Palestine and Zionist achievements. In general, he was a relentless cross-examiner and once he began questioning any man about Jewish affairs, his witness was in for a terrific raking of memory and a testing of its accuracy.

He was fresh and eager when he became head of the wartime Zionist agency which was charged with management of the larger part of international Zionist functions. The official world leadership had broken up; Sokolow and Tschlenow were in London; Shmarya Levin was in the United States; Victor Jacobson was in Copenhagen; Hantke and Warburg were in Berlin. Dr. Weizmann was not an official member of the leadership. He was the unofficial negotiator with the British Government on the proposed Declaration. Thus, Mr. Brandeis was the leader in fact of all Zionist affairs and procedures. The legal responsibility had been assigned to the Provisional Committee by Dr. Levin, with the approval of all Zionist authorities.

Mr. Brandeis took over with zest and enthusiasm. He would come to the Zionist offices in New York early in the morning and remain for hours, receiving visitors, questioning them and assigning tasks. He presided at the frequent meetings of the committee and won general admiration for the cogency and subtlety of his questions and the sagacity of his conclusions. He was innocent of vanity or conceit and unconventional in his behavior. He had a cordiality that won confidence. He was seldom direct in attack, but with rare subtlety insinuated the trend of his thinking into the discussion. But he could be merciless in judgment too, and his indignation could be devastating. You did not feel that he was forcing his views; he drove them home by logic and dominated the situation with tact and reason. He would take his coat off, loosen his tie, ruffle his hair, use his hands actively and twist his body in the chair as he carried on a hearty discussion with infinite patience.

The Provisional Committee assumed direction of every phase of Zionist activity. All Zionist groups were brought under its wing. Mr. Brandeis established a control over all funds. He set in motion a relief activity to reach remote corners of Jewish life in the war zones. He organized the sending of money from the United States to Poland and Palestine. The transfer department of the Provisional Committee was a large apparatus, occupying an entire floor in a loft building, with several hundred employees. He had a tremendous appetite for reports; nothing provoked him more than an executive who was reluctant to provide him with reports on request.

He joined Shmarya Levin on the platform and together they drew large audiences wherever they appeared. He was not an orator, but his directness and clarity, his moving sincerity, his use of illustrations drawn from American history made Zionism for the first time a matter of interest to all Americans and Jews. He was a controversialist on the platform. He challenged the opposition of the Reform Jews of wealth. He provoked to reply men like Jacob H. Schiff and Judge Mayer Sulzberger. He gathered a coterie of personal friends—men and women theretofore alien to Zionist and Jewish thinking—who served him with loyalty and reverence. He had Judge Julian W. Mack help him. Mrs. Joseph Fels became an interested member of the inner group. Men of affairs like Louis Kirstein and Eugene Meyers placed themselves at his disposal. Julius Fohs was interested to investigate the oil possibilities of Palestine long before oil was found in Arabian lands. Bernard Flexner, of Chicago, gave his skill and experience to financial problems.

He inspired confidence and optimism with rare skill. He believed from the start that the Allies would win and that one of the fruits of their victory would be the fulfillment of Herzl's program. He excluded all sympathies with Germany. He rejected every suggestion that came from German Zionists for testing German offers to give national group rights to the Jews of Poland. He barred pro-German and pacifist Jews from Zionist councils. He had a British orientation all his life. He was deeply convinced of the Anglo-Saxon desire for justice and fair-dealing. To no Zionist was Britain's subsequent violation of its pledges as devastating as it was to him. He was unable to see the value of the American Jewish Congress until he realized that it could be used as an instrument to further the Zionist cause. It was at his suggestion that the Congress adopted the resolution inviting England to accept the Mandate for Palestine. He was opposed to the involvement of the United States in the Mandate. As early as 1914 he had received verbal assurances from President Wilson and the British Ambassador in Washington as to the intentions of the Allies with regard to Palestine. He was on terms of close friendship with Colonel House, President Wilson's confidant; with William Hard and Norman Hapgood, liberal democrats, writers and lecturers. He was the American correspondent of the Zionist group in London headed by Dr. Weizmann and every step taken in connection with the Balfour Declaration was cleared with him.

His closest adviser during these years was Jacob de Haas. In fact, it may be said that he was converted to Zionism by de Haas, who came

to the United States in 1901, served as Secretary of the Zionist Organization for several years and then went to Boston, where, in 1910, he
had his first occasion to hold a conversation with the man who, at that
time, was deeply interested in a plan for placing life insurance in the
hands of savings banks. The conversations were protracted. Mr. Brandeis was led to inquire into the basic problems of Jewish life. The personality of Theodor Herzl was revealed to him through de Haas.
Through de Haas he was prepared for Zionist leadership, and when
he accepted the chairmanship of the American group, de Haas was
his closest adviser, seeing him more often than did any other man in
the Movement. It was Mr. Brandeis' habit to call de Haas before breakfast, regardless of time and convenience. De Haas' life was no bed of
roses; but he was dedicated to strengthening Mr. Brandeis' position
in the Zionist Movement and in American life.

In later years, after de Haas had led his friends in revolt against the
Zionist Organization and his alignment, to a degree, with Revisionist
elements, Mr. Brandeis' close friends sought to break the spell of de
Haas' influence. They did not succeed. In 1928, Judge Mack, then a
past President of the Zionist Organization of America, wrote to Mr.
Brandeis, suggesting that de Haas was using Mr. Brandeis' prestige
for ends that led to separating him from his Zionist friends. The complaint was made that members of the group, including Henrietta Szold,
were unable to discuss Zionist problems with Mr. Brandeis and were
being referred to de Haas. This was a fact. Mr. Brandeis preferred to
conduct his affairs so that all facts on any given problem could come
to him through one person who knew his mind. Mr. Brandeis rejected
Judge Mack's complaint and wrote to him: "No one whom I have met
has been more devoted (than de Haas), more knowing and on the whole
more clear-sighted in all the political aspects and in his judgments of a
political character." He said that de Haas was responsible for his political views on Zionism and it would be the height of folly in the strenuous
times ahead to get along without his knowledge and experience. He
acknowledged his indebtedness to de Haas on a number of occasions.
At 68, he called de Haas "his teacher and companion." He was conscious of no reason to doubt de Haas' reliability. De Haas was the first
to reveal the mystic ideals of Zionism. He had touched the mantle of
Herzl. He knew how the First Zionist Congress had been assembled;
who were its leading figures; what were the issues. Mr. Brandeis was
delighted to hear all de Haas had to say and kept it in his memory as
the first deposit of Zionist instruction. The verbal extravagances of

de Haas were an oriental quality, a part of his Sephardic heritage. There was something strange in the relationship. De Haas was the antithesis of Mr. Brandeis; he was complicated in his thinking; he could never tell a tale simply and made no effort to clarify his theme. He loved to dramatize political situations. But there is no doubt of the authenticity of the close personal relations established between these two antipodal men.

Mr. Brandeis went to Palestine with de Haas for the first time in the summer of 1919. The Balfour Declaration had been issued on November 2, 1917. A Zionist Commission headed by Dr. Weizmann had been sent to Palestine. The British Army was in charge of Jerusalem and British officials with experience in Arab lands were being assembled to set up the Mandatory Government.

Mr. Brandeis found Palestine a promising land, with much to be rebuilt, much to be created. He was amazed and distressed by the prevalence of malaria. He was disturbed by the anti-Zionist prejudices of the British officials. He found little encouragement in what the Zionist Organization was doing. He returned with an accumulation of devastating criticism. He found the Zionist group in London an assembly of refugees in a state of nervous anxiety, uncertain of the future, lacking funds and groping in the dark as to where the means could be found now that the road was open for the Return. The older Zionists seemed to be obstacles in the way of the new course Zionism would have to take. Their endless discussions exasperated and bored him. He wanted to cut the cackle and proceed to action. He was impatient with Zionist dialectics. He had become used to the terms employed by Herzl and was unaware of the burden of ideologies that already encumbered all Zionist thinking. He could not make order out of the "practical" programs submitted without any conception of the important factor of budget. He did not meet Arthur Ruppin, the pioneer of Zionist colonization, who had written what was to become the basis of the colonization program. Dr. Ruppin was in Turkey at the time. Mr. Brandeis had sharply criticized him for using the profits earned in money exchange with relief funds to bolster up the bankrupt Zionist corporations of prewar days.

He found himself in London for the first time in the center of a free Zionist discussion. This was new to him. Discussion in a real sense was not the habit in the American Zionist circle dominated by Mr. Brandeis. His disciples expressed their loyalty by agreeing or trying to agree with his conclusions. In London, however, the European system prevailed. Everybody talked at length without fear or favor, unconcerned by threats of points of order. The long drawn-out debates in a number of languages left Mr. Brandeis exhausted. He did not understand them, nor did they know precisely the meaning of the legal and political terms he used. It was difficult for him to articulate his thoughts. He felt that he was talking to an alien audience. He had the traditional English aversion to foreign languages. He did not understand their conventions. He did not know that agreement in private talks might be followed by violent disagreements in formal discussion. He wondered how American Zionists, and he more particularly, would be able to exercise an influence upon an international body so constituted. His American mind revolted against the confusion, against the dialectics, against the babel of languages, against the European parliamentary system which placed a premium on general debate and discounted the value of discussion of details. He could not imagine himself tied to that "wagon of Jewish renascence." He had a single-track mind; he saw Palestine as the objective; he thought of programs and budgets, of people and their redemption. He had been using the terms of Jewish nationalism. For the first time, however, he appreciated the embarrassing problems arising out of the acceptance of the nationalist ideal as interpreted by European Zionists.

His reactions were formulated in the plans later accepted by his group when he returned to the United States. These plans prepared the way for the controversy that arose between him and Dr. Weizmann, which came to a climax at the Cleveland Convention of 1921, when he and his group retired from the Zionist Administration. His views are succinctly expressed in his report on what happened in London, in the Zeeland document, in the memorandum adopted by the majority of the Provisional Committee, and in a number of addresses he gave at meetings of the dissident group which later organized the Palestine Development Council.

He could not stand what seemed to him the disorder in Zionism. He wanted to be free to serve Zionism from Washington, rather than from London or Jerusalem. He accepted the division of the Zionist Movement into two or more parts, provided it left American Zionism, and himself as its leader, free. He was eager to accept the fact of the Mandate as sufficient reason for the liquidation of certain features of the Zionist program. He said in the Zeeland document that Zionism was no longer a propaganda movement "except the propaganda that comes from undertaking concrete enterprises." He said that the Zionist Organization as such should not assist, directly or indirectly, migration to Palestine! It was not clear what this meant, for he followed it with the statement that it might properly grant certain temporary aid to those who actually reached the country. The Zionist Organization in particular should not undertake to grant such aid, but the Joint Distribution Committee might be persuaded to do so. He thought Zionist political work in Palestine should come to an end. It was then being represented by a Zionist Commission in Palestine. In the appointment of Sir Herbert Samuel as High Commissioner, "true to the Jewish cause as well as the British cause," we had reached the culmination of political achievements so far as the present was concerned. All political questions should be solved through the Mandatory Government and its proposed Advisory Council on which Zionists and other Jews and Arabs would have representation.

He had no faith that campaigns for gift funds would produce the budgets for the rebuilding of Palestine. The forms used during the war had become obsolete in 1920. His judgment on this matter was not supported by subsequent experience. The Keren Hayesod campaigns (conducted in its own name or in partnership with others) produced ever-increasing returns from 1921 onward to 1949. He thought an appeal for investment funds would bring larger returns. He would have liked to have each local community adopt its own project. He thought individual Jews could be persuaded to engage in export and import, which would create the commerce of Palestine. He wanted to give his attention to the American end of the enterprise. He was looking for stability, fixed objectives and blueprints. That was what he was good at, but he was distressed by the emotional agitation of Zionists and their emphasis on sentiment. He found it difficult to adjust his thoughts to an international organization. The stage was too vast and too complicated. He did not accept the concept of Diaspora Nationalism. Once the Homeland was an accepted fact, the internationality of the Jewish people would be liquidated and merged in the liberated nationality settling down in Palestine.

All these ideas were the material out of which the controversy between Mr. Brandeis and Dr. Weizmann was born and developed. Mr. Brandeis was then on the Supreme Court Bench. He was not the attorney of record in the controversy at Cleveland which led to his retirement, but he was in fact its leader. He provided the strategy and the reasoning. His views were reflected in the documents issued by Judge Mack and his colleagues. His advice was freely offered and accepted without demur. He wrote many of their letters. He saw many people on their behalf. He was responsible for the drafting of the Memorandum, the adoption of which by the ZOA Administration led to the organization of the minority group. He was in no sense the "silent" leader. He did not appear on a public platform, but he was the director of the controversy until it reached its climax at Cleveland, when he and his associates retired from the scene. To assume that Mr. Brandeis was an impartial judge at that time, or for that matter at any time, when he was not on the bench, would be a misrepresentation of a great, self-revealing personality who in all his life never avoided a battle in which he thought he was right and who in this instance showed the same zeal, audacity, magnetism and polish he gave proof of in all the legal and public issues he fought before he left the practice of law for the Supreme Court.

His interest in Zionism came too late in life. He was already a man of fixed habits and acquired few new ones after sixty. Zionism was the one object of his affection and interest which he clung to and developed in the last two decades of his life. He refused the crown of world Zionist leadership in London when he was sixty-four. He then said that as a Jew he could not withdraw from a post in government upon which liberal opinion depended, for the sake of Zionism which had better and more experienced men to lead it. When he donned the robes of his judicial office, he was deeply conscious of his obligations as a liberal and as a Jew, but he felt most his responsibilities toward the High Court of which he was a distinguished member. Privately he served Zionism and Palestine. He gave of his means with calculated generosity. He judged causes in Palestine on their merits and had no party interests or prejudices. He would not use the prestige of his office to further any cause privately, but he emerged on a number of public occasions to serve the Jewish cause. The fact of his association with Zionism and the Jewish people contributed to our prestige and influence through all the years of his life. He was the friend of Woodrow Wilson and Herbert Hoover. He was an elder statesman to Franklin D. Roosevelt who called him Isaiah. He made a deep and lasting record as a judge and was bracketed with Justices Holmes and Cardozo among judges of that court who contributed to its prestige at a time of great change in American trends.

As the influence of Hitler in the world became powerful and the menace to Jewish life assumed appalling forms, his isolation from Jewish life, his physical absence from the battlefield, made his position more and more difficult. He shared the Jewish protest and indignation, but he was bound by his own way of life, now almost rigid. He maintained his position with dignity and reserve. He spoke with forceful words as the situation required and identified himself clearly and unmistakably with the destiny of his people. His visits to President Roosevelt seemed to the younger man like the appearance of an ancient Hebrew Prophet reminding him of what justice required of him. But Mr. Brandeis did not join the throng or the leadership. He was perilously near to living in an ivory tower except for the gusts of passion in the interest of his people which, on occasion, drew him out of his seclusion and gave refreshment to his soul for brief moments.

To the American public he was one of the great liberals of his generation, one of the great judges of a great court. To Jews everywhere he was a superior moral personality whose heart and mind were engaged in the Jewish tragedy, who shared their grief and hopes. But he was bound by the chains of the conventionalities in which his American ambitions had led him and was always mindful with integrity and exactness of the position he had achieved in American life. His interest in Zionism never abated. To his last days he read the reports coming to him from Palestine, received visitors who told him of how Jews were reacting to British injustice, how they were establishing themselves in the land in spite of the mean-spirited and ungenerous conduct of the British Administration. He never forgot Zion.

He passed away in the fullness of years on October 5, 1941, just as Hitler intensified his rampage of destruction. It is doubtful whether Mr. Brandeis was able to foresee in all the confusion of the war the possibility that out of the debacle would come the establishment of the Jewish State and the fulfillment of Herzl's dream.

RICHARD GOTTHEIL (1862–1936)

That Professor Richard Gottheil should have been the first leader of an American Zionist organization is one of the curious incidents of early Zionist history. It was disconcerting that a student of dead languages should be called to lead the Zionist renaissance.

An earlier organization in Chicago, of which Bernard Horwich and Leon Zolotkoff were the organizers, antedated the Federation of American Zionists. The first was a merchant—*maskil;* the second was a journalist editing a Yiddish newspaper, later the editor of the *Tageblatt* of New York.

When the United States heard the voice of Theodor Herzl it was obvious that the center of American Zionists could not be Chicago. It would have to be New York, where the foundations were being laid for an amazingly varied Jewish community. Moreover, Professor Gottheil was a "better name."

He was a Professor of Oriental Languages at Columbia; head of the Oriental Department of the New York Public Library; a member of the Board of Editors of Funk & Wagnall's Jewish Encyclopedia. He was also the author of its comprehensive article on Zionism. Not the least, he was the son of the distinguished Rabbi of Temple Emanu-El, Gustave Gottheil, who in his old age had become excitedly interested in Zionism.

Richard James Horatio Gottheil was born in Manchester, England, and was eleven when his father brought him to New York. He studied in the universities of Berlin, Leipzig, Tuebingen, Columbia, and at the Hochschule für die Wissenschaft des Judentums in Berlin. He had rejected his father's suggestion that he become a rabbi.

He liked to take life leisurely. He was never a platform speaker. He had the habit of reading his lectures and seldom spoke without due preparation. He loved to browse in old libraries and to converse with scholars. He avoided the exciting issues of the day.

He was far removed from the dynamic phase of Jewish life which Herzl inspired, in spite of the fact that he had established personal contact with Herzl, Nordau and Alexander Marmorek at the Second Zionist Congress. In fact, he was never touched by the passion of Zionism. He put brakes on his emotions and at all times was calm, self-possessed and reserved.

He became a Zionist and then the Zionist President due to the dominating personality of his father and the persuasion of his wife, who was born in Turkey, lived in Paris and knew the ways of Eastern European Jews. She was, in fact, the first President of B'not Hadassah formed in 1900.

In 1898 a small group of East Coast Zionists induced Professor Gottheil to accept the Presidency of the new Zionist Federation. But he took the office with reluctance and did not alter his interests or his way of life because of it. He remained the student of books, the teacher of languages, leading a cloistered life from which he emerged from time to time to intervene indifferently in the practical aspects of Zionism.

He was always the professor—tall and erect, prosaic, precise, unruffled, seldom allowing his feelings to influence his writing or his speaking.

As Zionist President he was troubled by the birth pangs of the new organization. Its income was insufficient even to pay the salary of a part-time secretary or the rent of its own office. Both he and young Stephen S. Wise (who was the Federation's Honorary Secretary) were, at that time, untrained in the art of raising money or creating a nation-wide propaganda for the new movement, nor was the time favorable for Zionism. Finally they hit upon the idea of publishing a Zionist magazine, *The Maccabean.* A few hundred dollars were gathered, a few hundred dollars were pledged, and I was invited to be its managing editor.

Professor Gottheil shunned publicity; he did not mind the trickles of adulation accorded him as President; but his official duties irked him beyond endurance. He hated to preside at meetings. He was careless in procedural matters and embarrassed by ceremonies in which he had to take part. He was horrified by emotional debates. He felt that his status as a professor was being sullied by his being President of a propa-ganda organization. He ran away from official duties. He usually limited his official addresses at Zionist meetings to the necessary items, speaking briefly. He became more and more nerve-provoked by his status, especially as the practical affairs of the Zionist Federation made no visible progress.

Finally he found his opportunity for release from the burden placed on his shoulders in a letter he received from Theodor Herzl, in which the Leader, whom he venerated, suggested that the Federation should give a chance for service to Jacob de Haas, who was one of the Secre-taries of the First Basle Congress and an active Zionist worker in England. Herzl suggested that Mr. de Haas become Secretary of the Federation.

The President grasped the opportunity. In his opening address at the Boston Convention of 1902 he informed the delegates of Dr. Herzl's suggestion, seconded the proposal and put the question to a vote practically without delay. There was some discussion, but the recom-mendation was accepted. Subsequently, in due course, Mr. de Haas was invited to come to New York. Although Professor Gottheil was re-elected as President, to serve until 1904, his problem was solved. He left at once for Europe and disappeared from the Zionist scene for good.

When de Haas arrived, he found himself burdened with the responsibilities of office and Professor Gottheil nowhere in sight. He did leave a number of scholarly articles which were usefully employed as part of the Zionist propaganda, and especially the article on Zionism written for the first edition of the Jewish Encyclopedia.

In fact, Professor Gottheil never did return to the Zionist Movement. He continued his scholarly pursuits, his courses at Columbia, his occasional lectures, his writings on the Syriac era, and his intimate social life. More than a decade later he made a startling brief appearance when the Provisional Zionist Committee was organized and Mr. Brandeis became its Chairman.

He was seen, from time to time, at his reserved table at the New York Public Library, and remained in memory—to those who once knew him as a Zionist leader—as a gentleman and a scholar who, in his time, had served the cause of Zionism to the best of his ability, with integrity and modesty. But he never again caught up with the living Zionist Movement.

His last work was a biography of his father, published in 1935. When Professor Gottheil died in 1936, many Zionists wondered where he had been keeping himself in the years of his self-imposed exile.

HARRY FRIEDENWALD (1864–1950)

Harry Friedenwald was indirectly—and long ago—the cause of a caucus brawl, which made possible the loosening of my tongue for Zionist speech. In that far-off day I was shy and tongue-tied. I used to intrude in debate on points of order and I could be liberated to speak up only by the excitement a debate provoked. I had to be hot with anger. I was afraid, in beginning, that I would be paralyzed by a loss of memory and the inability to hit quickly the target of my hate.

It was in the course of the first election campaign for Harry Friedenwald in 1904 that I recovered my freedom. Jacob de Haas, A. H. Fromenson and I were determined to put an end to Professor Richard Gottheil's absentee presidency at conventions, and hit upon Harry Friedenwald, whom we did not know, except as a son of the veteran Zionist, Dr. Aaron Friedenwald of Baltimore. I saw Harry Friedenwald in advance and got his acceptance, but to my astonishment he stated he would not come to the convention under any circumstances.

Dr. Friedenwald was a member of a prominent Jewish family of Baltimore, of German origin, and was strongly influenced by his father, who was orthodox in the Jewish faith and way of life. His grandfather

(Jonas) arrived in the United States in 1831 at the age of 31 and became a successful merchant. His father, Aaron, was a widely-known physician, specializing in diseases of the eye and, at the same time, was interested in all phases of Jewish life. He established the Zionist tradition in the Friedenwald family.

Dr. Friedenwald was always more of a physician than a communal worker or leader. Like his father, he was reared in the Zionist tradition. He was restrained in speech and shy on the platform, preferring the brief, laconic statement to the oratorical or expansive form of expression. Never was a Zionist so handicapped. He never desired to lead and never attempted to. But he performed an historic service to the cause of Zionism in the early period. He was dignified and bearded. He was generous and amiable. He brought American manners and dignity, the German-Jewish sense of responsibility, and deep Jewish religious faith, to the service of the Zionist cause.

His presence influenced sympathy for Zionism in many unfriendly circles. When Dr. Judah L. Magnes returned from Germany, Dr. Friedenwald and Henrietta Szold led him into the movement and persuaded him to become Secretary of the Federation, succeeding Jacob de Haas. Through their joint influence the leaders of the Jewish Theological Seminary were persuaded to take a more friendly attitude toward the cause. Professor Israel Friedlander and Dr. Solomon Schechter became publicly known as Zionists. Dr. Friedlander later became chairman of the Executive Committee of the Federation and Henrietta Szold its Secretary.

When he was President, Dr. Friedenwald rarely intervened in administrative Zionist affairs. He remained, however, the titular head of the organization for fourteen years. In those difficult days this successful physician, this model Jew in a vigorous Jewish community, this self-effacing head of a turbulent movement, helped to establish Zionism through his personal integrity, his deep Jewish faith, and his loyalty. He was too good a Jew to be a partisan. He had a general sympathy for the ideas of Ahad Ha-am, which he acquired through his friendship with Dr. Friedlander and Henrietta Szold. But he loved Zion deeply— its past and present, and believed in its future.

He was not greatly affected by political programs. He was not interested in ideologies or parties. In the Keren Hayesod controversy he sided with Mr. Brandeis. He believed that Mr. Brandeis' prestige was of the greatest importance to the movement.

At the end of the First World War, he went to Palestine as the acting chairman of the Zionist Commission, assisted by E. W. Lewin-Epstein, Robert Szold and Rudolph Sonneborn of Baltimore, then a very young man, who served as its secretary.

When the Zionist Organization of America was established as successor to the Provisional Zionist Committee, Judge Mack was elected President, and Dr. Friedenwald and Dr. Stephen S. Wise Vice Presidents.

Dr. Friedenwald was patient and good-natured. A good listener, he was not easily persuaded. His features were immobile and his innocent look was deceiving. His emotions were always under control. Also, he was frugal in speech, a serious defect for a leader. One of his first speeches as President was written on a sheet of note paper and took five minutes.

His sentiments and interests were easily engaged. He was won by Boris Schatz, the founder of Bezalel, and any Jewish artist could get his warm sponsorship. He became a friend of E. W. Lewin-Epstein of the Carmel Wine Company, and of Aaron Aronsohn, who came to the United States with a dramatic story of having discovered the seeds of the original wild wheat in Palestine. He was a patron of Palestinian arts and music.

Together with his charming wife, who was a woman of rare intelligence and great vivacity, and who shared all his interests, his home in Baltimore was the mecca for all Palestinian visitors to the United States. His wife died many years before him after a lingering illness. Dr. Friedenwald was blessed with two children, a son and a daughter, both of whom followed in his footsteps as Zionists. His son Jonas is, as were his father and grandfather, a distinguished eye specialist.

After the Balfour Declaration, Dr. Friedenwald became interested in the work of Hadassah in Palestine and in the Hebrew University. He visited Palestine often and was known in many circles as a kindly, sagacious man with wide interests, with deep Jewish feeling, a man capable of great affections which he seldom revealed in words.

JACOB DE HAAS (1872–1937)

Jacob de Haas was a Jewish journalist in London who went to the first Zionist Congress as a reporter, was named as one of its secretaries and subsequently served Theodor Herzl with diligence and loyalty as one of his general correspondents. He enjoyed a good quarrel. He was so involved in communal disputes in London that he decided it would be better to emigrate to the peaceful shores of the United States.

Herzl gave him a letter of introduction to Professor Richard Gottheil, first President of the American Zionist Federation, in which he suggested that de Haas' organizing talent could be used for the Movement in New York. Professor Gottheil proposed de Haas' name to the Convention in Boston and he was elected unanimously as Secretary of the organization. He was compelled to take over immediately. Professor Gottheil was never again seen at a Zionist Convention in the United States. The burden of the Movement was taken over by de Haas with unusual courage, for it was a flimsy organization that was handed to him. He carried on for a year or two, until Dr. Harry Friedenwald was elected as President, when de Haas came to the conclusion that he could not carry the burden any longer and should look out for himself. He went to Boston and acquired the *Jewish Advocate* of which he was editor and publisher. I was his regular New York correspondent.

He was a Herzlian Zionist in an environment which, in his view, was more cultural than political. He felt himself alone, and in spite of the efforts of a group of us to bring him back to the organization, he was at odds with the Federation until he met Mr. Brandeis and began conversations with him that led to his gradual conversion, which officially occurred when the Provisional Zionist Committee was organized. To be near Mr. Brandeis, who then lived in Boston, de Haas was appointed Secretary of the New England Zionist Bureau and became Mr. Brandeis' confidant, guide and representative, finally returning to New York to become Executive Secretary of the Provisional Zionist Committee. Just as he had been a loyal follower of Theodor Herzl, so he now, in his middle years, became the disciple of Louis D. Brandeis. He had the tenacity of his Dutch ancestors, and once having committed himself to an issue, or a personality, was unable to relax or give up his position or change its terms. He fought against Dr. Weizmann until the last remnant of influence had oozed out of his hands. He was inexorable and probably fanned the embers of Mr. Brandeis' prejudices. De Haas returned to the Zionist Organization of America in 1930, remained for a year or so, but found himself an alien in an environment in which he had always been at home. In his desperation he joined the cause of Jabotinsky, but was too late to render effective service in the leadership of the Revisionist Party. Throughout all his years in the United States until the Cleveland Convention, we were close friends, but his star led him to follow Mr. Brandeis away from the Zionism which had its source in East European Jewish life, and from which I derived my Zionist convictions. After the first Zionist

Congresses, de Haas was never again able to identify himself with
any Zionist Group or Party. He lost his interest in the Congress after
Herzl's death. He lost his interest in the American Zionist Organization
after Mr. Brandeis' retirement and could not contract a perfect loyalty
to the Revisionist Party. His last years were darkened by disappointment
and fruitless endeavor and protracted illness; but none doubted his
integrity and the sincerity of his loyalties, and all deplored the ruin
of a personality destroyed by excessive loyalties to personalities and
dogmatic issues.

Jacob de Haas was sent to the United States by Theodor Herzl on a
Zionist mission, became an American citizen and lived ever after as
an American. He was born in London in 1872 and was descended from
Dutch Sephardic Jews. He attended the Stepney Jewish School and
was an eclectic student in a number of high schools before he became a
journalist. He remained English in manner and speech all his life; he
never rid himself of the London fog in his throat. As a young man he
was a member of the London Fabian Society, frequented public meetings
and heckled the speakers, acquiring a talent for debate which was good
preparation for a Zionist propagandist. He would take the "word" in
Hyde Park on Sunday afternoons, breaking into the addresses of the
free and easy haranguers in this forum of democratic discussion. He
also attended Jewish communal meetings and participated in the discussions, carrying the same chip on his shoulder he had with him in Hyde
Park. He began to write for the Anglo-Jewish press and soon was a
regular contributor to the *Jewish World* which was then the only rival of
the more prosperous *Jewish Chronicle*. He was a rebel and took delight
in attacking the conservative leaders of the Jewish community. He was
contentious and loved to pick a quarrel. He was a restless romantic
Zionist before Herzl appeared on the Jewish scene.

He was one of the first in England to respond to the call of Herzl.
He went as a delegate to Basle and was named one of the secretaries
.of the First Congress. In spite of his contrariness he was a
hero worshiper. His first hero was Theodor Herzl. He accepted Herzl
instantaneously as the great leader of his generation. He believed that
Herzl was the embodiment of Daniel Deronda. He saw a mystic
significance in every word Herzl uttered in his proclamations, in his
books, in his personal appearances. He never was at a loss for a word
from Herzl's writings in his conversation. He was proud to be one of

Herzl's lieutenants. When he became Herzl's English correspondent it was a great event in his life.

When de Haas returned to London after the First Congress, the *Jewish World*, of which he became editor, was on the verge of collapse. He saw no place for himself in Jewish public life. He knew that he had powerful enemies in the community who looked upon him as a disturber of the peace. Herzl urged him to go to the United States to develop certain connections he had made. Herzl had opened a correspondence with Cyrus Adler and Oscar S. Straus. He had met a number of American delegates to the First Congress. He wrote a letter on de Haas' behalf to Richard Gottheil, first President of the American Zionist Federation. To de Haas' surprise, Professor Gottheil read the letter to the Boston Zionist convention in 1902, recommending de Haas' election as Secretary, and thereupon de Haas became the administrative head of the American organization. Having secured a competent Secretary, Professor Gottheil seemed to be anxious to rid himself of all official responsibilities at once, and before de Haas arrived, left for Europe on a summer vacation and remained away for many months, and thereafter was President in name only. De Haas had to carry the burden himself.

In those days de Haas was a picturesque figure. He made the most of a beard trimmed in French style. He carried himself with a Bohemian swagger, spoke of political affairs with mystic allusions to what he might reveal if he were free to speak, and had an endless fund of gossip about the leading figures in the Zionist Movement. He was a colorful talker and had decided views on many subjects. He put all Herzl's friends and followers on a high level and was cynical about the Zionism of many of the Russian Zionists who were not, in his view, political-minded or reliable. He smoked a pipe with savage intensity, drank beer like a German, and had a bizarre taste in matters of the theater. He had keen appreciation of the psychology of English men of affairs and discussed politics as if he knew the ins and outs of all the affairs of the Empire. His beard was trimmed down gradually to a mustache which, in turn, was clipped to a dark shadow and, finally, many years later, was removed altogether. The final mask was that of a New Bedford fisherman who could have served as a model for one of Rembrandt's paintings.

He was always a romantic Zionist, playing with political combinations. He was influenced by Disraeli's grandiloquent style, his

oriental imagery, his fantastic mixture of the ancient and modern.
As to many of the early Zionists, Zionism was to de Haas a
great adventure in which he found place for self-expression that was
denied to him in other areas of Jewish life. He believed that mystic
influences played a large part in Jewish history. Romance and politics
and mysticism were joined in a strange combination. He often dwelt
upon the significance of numbers, the recurrence of historic events
on the same calendar day, giving the impression that Providence was
tied to numerology and coincidence, and through them, shaped the
course of Jewish history. He often talked as if the Messiah were just
around the corner waiting patiently to appear at a moment fixed in
advance by the recurrence of a historic date. He saw portents in the
sky. He used to confide that he saw meaning in the fact that he, himself,
was descended from Don Isaac Abravanel who had found a haven in
Italy, and that one of Don Isaac's descendants had become Herzl's
lieutenant to help in forcing the coming of the Messiah.

He loved to talk at night in cafés and spent much time at meals in
restaurants in conversation. It was hard to tell what was truth and
what was fancy in his discourses. He was easily provoked to informal
discussion but was not so fluent on his feet. In those days I spent many
evenings with him and Jacob Fishman of the *Jewish Morning Journal*
in discussions of how Zionism was to be organized, how the communities
were to be conquered, how the Promised Land was to be taken, about
actors and plays, about decadent art. What impressed him most was
what Herzl signified in the life of the Jewish people. With such a leader
the long-awaited miracle could happen any moment. De Haas
was a dissident by habit, but he had absolute faith in Herzl. His thoughts
were usually involved and blurred, but in the midst of the fog there
was always a glow of insight and imagination. He resented the pride
of the mighty, but equally resented democracy when it did not go his
way. When he seemed about to win the approval of the majority he
began to doubt his own views and sought with all his skill as a dialectician
to keep himself in that minority, which included himself and God.
He felt safer in isolation.

He never thought that he would have to spend the greater part of
his life in the United States and not return to live in England. He had
brothers there and often visited them, but soon he felt more at home
in the United States than in England. He fancied that one day he would
perform his mission and return to Vienna and submit his final report
to Herzl. He found himself, however, with a struggling organization on

his hands, with few supporters in an uncongenial atmosphere. He continued the setting up of an administration, edited *The Maccabean,* and was on the way to freedom from worry when Theodor Herzl died.

The blow shattered him. It meant the frustration of his life. It cut the ground from under his feet. His eyes were no longer fixed on Vienna where the leader lived. He had lost his guiding star and Zionism was in eclipse. He wandered about in a wilderness of indecision. He was the Secretary of the Zionist Organization, but did not know where the Organization would go after the death of Herzl. He felt that he was being encircled by Zionists who lacked his loyalty to Herzlian methods.

More and more, *Kultur*-Zionists were entering the movement. The "practical" Zionists were in the ascendance. The Jewish Theological Seminary was becoming Zionist-conscious, but not in the spirit of Herzl. Israel Friedlander, Henrietta Szold and Solomon Schechter were expressing themselves publicly on Zionist questions. Judah L. Magnes returned from Germany and introduced a new note which struck no answering echo from de Haas. Dr. Magnes brought with him the inspiration of German Zionist groups. De Haas could not adjust himself to the leadership of Dr. Magnes who became Secretary of the Zionist Organization upon the election of Dr. Harry Friedenwald as President.

De Haas felt that his Zionist career was over. He was no longer at home in the Zionist circle. He returned to a few Zionist conventions but he was querulous, depressed and hopeless. He saw the "practical" Zionists taking over and the end of political Zionism. With Bernard G. Richards he edited a weekly publication called *The Chronicler,* which had a brief exciting life. He took a newspaper job on the New York *Commercial Advertiser* through the influence of Samuel Strauss, its publisher, but the speed of the American daily newspaper was too much for him to endure. He left for Boston and took over the management of a Jewish center. He made an attempt to enter Boston politics, but he was a Democrat in a Republican state. He became the publisher of a local Jewish periodical, the *Jewish Advocate,* which he conducted for many years. The turning point in his life was his encounter with Louis D. Brandeis.

He met Mr. Brandeis to discuss a plan for life insurance through savings banks. He became a regular visitor at Devonshire Street and in the course of time aroused Mr. Brandeis' slumbering interest not only in Jewish affairs but in political Zionism, and specifically in the personality of Theodor Herzl. It was amazing how eager Mr. Brandeis was at that time to absorb knowledge about Jews, how he remembered what de Haas told him—much of it touched with de Haas' vagrant imagination—how delighted he was with what he heard.

De Haas' imagination at once saw Brandeis as the inevitable successor of Herzl. De Haas, in turn, found his zest in life renewed by contact with the thinking of a man who was thoroughly familiar with the twists and turns of American political life and who, at the same time, was capable of appreciating the glamor of a leader like Theodor Herzl. Through Mr. Brandeis de Haas got to know Norman Hapgood, William Hard and other liberals. He was able to persuade Mr. Brandeis to greater interest in the movement. In 1914 he enjoyed his greatest moment when Mr. Brandeis became the Chairman of the Provisional Zionist Committee and leader of American Zionism. For some time de Haas continued to live in Boston as director of an office provided by the Provisional Committee, but acting throughout for Mr. Brandeis. Then he returned to New York as Executive Secretary of the Provisional Zionist Committee and Mr. Brandeis' "Secretary of State."

De Haas believed that the coming war would shake the foundations of the civilized world and create disorders and changes out of which the miraculous would be revealed. He believed that we were destined to realize the slumbering hopes of the Wandering Jew, and that the Galuth would be liquidated. He directed and guided the spreading activities of the Zionist Movement through the Provisional Committee. In the strenuous days when the Balfour Declaration was born, de Haas had moments of political clairvoyance. He organized the Jewish Legion that was sent to Palestine to fight with General Allenby. With Henrietta Szold he assembled the Hadassah Medical Unit. The S.S. Vulcan was sent with provisions for Jews and Arabs in Palestine. He expected that when General Allenby took Jerusalem the keys of the city would be handed over to the Zionist Commission and that the Jewish flag would be unfurled over the Tower of David.

Mr. Brandeis was the second hero of his life. De Haas found in him a reincarnation of Theodor Herzl. With Mr. Brandeis he believed that he could take over the whole Zionist movement. He thought of Mr. Brandeis as capable of the same devotion and service that had characterized Theodor Herzl. He established a mystic bond of brotherhood with the Puritanic Boston lawyer and thought he could create the leadership Herzl would have exercised had he lived.

But Mr. Brandeis was not of the same material as Theodor Herzl. He was not of the same age or temperament or background. Mr. Brandeis was not a poet led by his imagination, nor could he understand the psychology of a whole people as Herzl got to know it through his experiences. Mr. Brandeis shattered de Haas' hopes when in 1920, in London, he rejected the mantle of Herzl and decided to remain on the Supreme Court Bench. At that historic meeting Mr. Brandeis heard the convincing, cold voice of Felix Frankfurter. He did not hear the voice of de Haas or of the entire American Zionist delegation. At that fateful moment the purpose for which de Haas had lived ceased to be real. He saw the collapse of his dream. De Haas was responsible for defending Mr. Brandeis' position at the Cleveland Zionist Convention in 1921. He deceived himself into thinking that the Zionists of America would not reject Mr. Brandeis, that they would remember what he had done for the Movement during the difficult years of the War. De Haas was mistaken. All his calculations were wrong. A two-thirds vote overruled the position advocated by Mr. Brandeis who with all his associates, including de Haas, retired from the Zionist Organization.

The disillusionment of de Haas found expression in the same drift toward nonconformity and protest with which he began his Jewish career. He thought Theodor Herzl would bring the Messiah; Herzl died before his time, disappointed. He thought the Balfour Declaration was the fiat of destiny. But when fulfillment of the Mandate lingered far behind and Mr. Brandeis stepped over to the sidelines, the frustrations of de Haas issued as revolt along the whole course—against the faithless Mandatory Government, against the leadership of Dr. Chaim Weizmann who was the cause, in his mind, of Mr. Brandeis' retirement, against all Zionists who disagreed with his analysis of the situation. He stood away from the organization he had helped to establish. He questioned methods he had helped to create. He lost faith in prophecy. He felt that through another instrument he might give expression to the tragedy of the Great Betrayal. He came closer to the Revisionists, but never could merge with the heated, viscid climate which was so peculiarly the emanation of that party.

In his recoil from the ideology which had maintained him in his youth, the glamor of his personality was obscured. When he returned to a coalition administration of the ZOA in 1930 and appeared once more in a Zionist convention, few of the delegates knew or recognized him. His sojourn on the fringe of opposition had blurred his imagination, hardened his will, cooled his ardor and enthusiasm, and after two years of effort in an attempt to take the lead in the organization, no longer supported by the mind and name of Mr. Brandeis, he retired to isolation and opposition with fewer friends, sheltered by no organization, a free lance. He wrote *The Great Betrayal*, into which he poured invective against Britain. He wrote a brief life of Herzl which was, in fact, his memoirs of the First Leader. He wrote a brief life of Mr. Brandeis. Even the flame of wrath burned low and feeble, and he found slight comfort in what the pioneers were achieving in the Jewish National Home. The Homeland did not look like home to him.

The picture he thus painted of himself showed a man of dark features and dour forebodings—a man exalted by mystic influences that made it possible for him to reach out and often touch the fringe of the robes of the Messiah, and often depressed him into the bitterest reflections. He had few moments of exaltation. He seldom let his prejudices mellow; his dogmas were as rock and he clung to them with obstinacy and resentment. He was a defeated man, whose defeat was reflected in everything he did or said or wrote. He could not forgive the non-Jewish world for its betrayal, nor could he be kind to the Jewish people who had disappointed his ardent dreams and plans and prophecies. His frustrations killed him in the sixty-fifth year of his life.

JUDAH L. MAGNES (1877–1948)

I met Judah L. Magnes when he returned from his studies in Germany, probably in 1903. I was advised by Mrs. Philip Cowen, the wife of the publisher of the *American Hebrew,* to see an American young man who should interest me as a curious personality. I met Dr. Magnes the next day in a kosher restaurant on Canal Street. He insisted that it be kosher. He was a tall, spare young man with a light beard, who smiled generously with an easy friendliness, and confessed without provocation that in Berlin he had been converted to orthodoxy, that he had attended a Zionist Congress and knew Theodor Herzl, and that he was born in San Francisco. He was a charming man and wanted to see what was going on on the East Side, and in the Yiddish Theatre. Soon he was speaking at Zionist meetings. Soon he knew all the celebrities of the East Side, including Chayim Zhitlowsky, a famous revolutionist and Yiddishist. We asked Dr. Magnes to speak at the Cleveland Zionist Convention, where he made what was regarded as a militant speech. Against whom? It must have been against Russian Pogromchiks.

His theme was "Jewish Self-Defense," which he had also picked up in Berlin. In the course of a few months, he succeeded Jacob de Haas as Secretary of the Zionist Federation, and one year later abandoned that post to a young reform rabbi. It was evident that he could not be kept down to routine. He was greatly excited by life. He liked to be free and to change his music. His next public venture was to lead an organization, the New York *Kehillah*, which he regarded as a further reversion to Jewish tradition. He was probably the first popular hero of the Zionist Movement in America and was greatly admired by all classes of Jews. To the surprise of all his friends, he made his way to the pulpit of Temple Emanu-El, resigning that post shortly in a clash of opinion on liturgical practices in the temple. The *Kehillah* was the first expression of Jewish Democracy in America but Dr. Magnes was persuaded to give away its educational program to the Benefactors who were to provide its budget if they would be allowed to control education through Dr. S. Benderly. Dr. Magnes lightheartedly agreed, and thought the world was a nice place to live in. It was the first step in the wrong direction for Dr. Magnes. It led him to joining forces with the American Jewish Committee against the American Jewish Congress. It led to his withdrawal from the Provisional Zionist Committee of which Mr. Brandeis was the chairman, and to his devotion to the Jewish Relief Movement, which was regarded by Zionists as competition to the Movement. The Zionists were pro-Ally; Dr. Magnes was pacifist. When peace came, he left for Palestine where he represented Hadassah interests for a time, and then became interested and identified with the Hebrew University on Mount Scopus, an interest which occupied the rest of his days. For all practical purposes, he never encountered Zionism again except as the head of the University, and as the leader of a small group of Jews in Palestine who were interested in Arab-Jewish peace. He was a stranger to Zionism in Palestine as well as to Zionism in the Diaspora, but his pacifism was indivisible; he never fought with Zionists, or Jews, or Arabs. He lived all the days of his life in what seemed to be a state of wishful peace, except that when asked to describe what he meant by peace, you could not guess from his answer the meaning of the blissful state which for him reconciled the existence of all hates and all prejudices, all differences and interests.

It is difficult to interpret the contribution of Dr. Judah L. Magnes to Zionist history. For about ten years after his conversion he was nobly excited by its ideals and prepared to make Zionism his mission in life. Then he withdrew and was a habitual nonconformist and critic. His activities took a mild controversial form. He walked on the other side of the street and seemed to be moving toward the same goal but in a leisurely way. His life was an endless contradiction. His Zionist faith collided with what the Movement planned to achieve in practical terms. He made the impression of being insensible to the political and human realities of the Jewish position. He had an aversion for the Movement as if he could not endure the clash of ideas, the dialectics of parties, the dynamics emerging from ideological struggle; and his personality seemed to reject democratic responsibilities. He could not achieve an articulated ideology. You could never get him to understand the meaning of a nationalist Zionism. He was above the tumult of the struggle. He was more the preacher of morality than the practical statesman or propagandist.

At the same time, of all American Zionists he was the first to accept loyally its implications as a guide in life. He shaped his practice to accord with his ideal. He was a convert to Zionism in a real sense. It brought him closer to the Jewish religion, its piety and its practices. It did not mean merely affirming the Basle Program. He spent the last two decades of his life as a resident of Jerusalem. He was at home there and glorified the beauty of the Holy City and the kind of Jewish life one could live there. He brought up his family there. He became the head of the Hebrew University and gathered around him a group of sympathetic men and women devoted to the cultural and intellectual life of the community. He was integrated with its domestic affairs.

Without harsh words, peaceful in tone and manner, his political views—if they may be regarded as such—ran counter to Zionist tendencies in every crisis. He was a pacifist in the prophetic manner. He wanted to avoid struggle and violence. He thought it nobler to shed one's own blood than to shed the blood of another; to take a blow rather than give it. He advocated a bi-national state of Jews and Arabs in spite of the fact that there was no evidence that either side believed such a state was possible. He organized a small group called the *Ihud*, printed a number of pamphlets, wrote letters to the press, testified before political commissions, and gave the impression that he was convinced that in God's own time—and in an easy way—the solution of peace and good-will would prevail. He lived long enough to see the Hebrew University on Mount Scopus occupied by Jordan troops;

the Arab majority disappearing in streams of flight; and the State of Israel established in a part of Palestine. The consummation of the Herzlian idea in that form was the bewildering climax of his life. It was a complete reversal of what he had advocated without abatement from first to last. Not that way did he expect Zion to be restored.

Born in San Francisco in 1877, Magnes was typically American. He loved American sports and was interested in American baseball games even when in Jerusalem. He read the juvenile stories of Horatio Alger, Oliver Optic, Castleman and Edward Ellis. He loved to talk about these books as a fond memory of youth. (I was reading the same books at the same time in Rochester, New York, where I was born.) Instead of entering a local university, he decided to go to Cincinnati where he could get his secular education and, at the same time, attend the Hebrew Union College and become a rabbi. The College was founded by Isaac M. Wise, a vigorous opponent of Zionism all his life. It was then being conducted in the spirit of its founder.

Before settling down to the life of a rabbi he went to Germany to pursue his studies further. He was a postgraduate student at the Universities of Berlin and Heidelberg, and obtained his doctorate in Berlin in 1902. In Berlin he came in contact with a new Jewish world. He was gregarious by nature and sought company among congenial persons who could instruct and interest him. He made friends of Berthold Feiwel, Shmarya Levin, Martin Buber, Ephraim Lilien (the artist), Heinrich Loewe (the librarian), and others. He was fascinated by every manifestation of the Jewish renaissance. He read *Der Jude,* a magazine published by young Jewish literati. He felt that he was being reborn and initiated into a mystic brotherhood. He was impressed by Hassidic lore, by the philosophy of Ahad Ha-am. The old Hebrew prayers moved his spirit. He was attracted to Theodor Herzl and attended one of the early Zionist Congresses where he served as translator of the German and Hebrew addresses with great success. He was praised for this by Israel Zangwill.

His sojourn in Europe transformed him. When he returned he seemed like a man who had put on the shining armor of knight errantry and was eager to conquer the world. He wore a beard and observed the dietary laws. Everything Jewish seemed to fascinate him. In New York he found the contemporaries of the kind of men he met in Berlin (on a miniature scale). He frequented the East Side and saw Yiddish plays. He read the Yiddish newspapers with eager curiosity. He admired the Yiddish poets, Morris Rosenfeld and Yehoash. He formed the Society of Jewish Art which had a short life. His conversion was amazingly thorough. He joined the Zionist Organization and became one of its most popular orators. He was the Secretary of the Zionist Federation from 1905 to 1908. He became the rabbi of Temple Israel of Brooklyn and drew young people to hear his sermons. He often spoke on the East Side.

It was a travesty of consistency that Temple Emanu-El of New York, which in the past had rejected as its rabbi both Stephen S. Wise and Max Heller because they were Zionists, should now extend a warm hand of welcome to Magnes to become its religious leader, although Magnes was the glowing embodiment of a form of Zionism that contradicted all the tendencies of Reform Judaism. His success was due to the charm of his personality. He was a speaker with a pleasing, sentimental approach, disarming in its innocence. He used simple and direct language and had a flair for poetry and abstract ideas. He avoided controversy and recrimination, and loved peace. He won public favor by his modesty and not through organized publicity. He radiated goodwill and sincerity. But in spite of the impression of softness he was capable of great determination. He may have been helpless in argument but it was hard to get him to change his mind once it was fixed. His life followed a simple pattern, consistent throughout. He took life easily. The years did not change him much. He had the same youthful spirit when he was seventy as when he was thirty.

In the heyday of his youth he seemed to be concerned about organization. His leadership in the Zionist Organization led to that unique anomaly in American Jewish life which was called the New York *Kehillah*. This was the first attempt to organize a democratic community, pressured by the Yiddish-speaking group. Magnes' enthusiasm lacked the revolutionary spirit without which it was not to be expected that the philanthropists of Jewish life would agree to the introduction of democratic procedures. Magnes was excited about the *Kehillah*; it reminded him of a remote tradition; but he lost interest as soon as its problems were blurred by popular demonstrations, newspaper controversies and the insistent demand that the "masses" should have a determining voice in its affairs. These demonstrations were not to his taste, nor did he know how to manage the difficulties arising from them. He was at the mercy of controversialists and ideologists, and the practical side of the institution confused him.

As the *Kehillah* faded away it was followed by the Jewish Congress movement. As the Congress gained momentum Magnes found himself in a dilemma. His wealthy friends were opposed to the movement as a blatant exposure of Jewish nationalism. The Congress idea could not come in peace. It had to be forced upon a determined opposition. Magnes decided to take sides against the Zionist elements and to support the American Jewish Committee. He wanted to delay facing the issue for a later day. He was averse to any form of revolution. He did not like popular demonstrations or sensations in the press.

The *Kehillah* was Magnes' last experiment in leadership. Never again did he attempt to be a leader of men. When Temple Emanu-El refused to accept his proposals for a radical change in its ritual he tendered his resignation and withdrew to minister to the needs of the Congregation B'nai Jeshurun which had an orthodox tradition. But he soon lost his interest in preaching. He had already lost his interest in the Zionist Organization, the leadership of which had been taken over by others. He turned to the bureaucratic efficiency of the Joint Distribution Committee.

Magnes' peculiar relations with the Zionist Movement deserve special consideration. He never was a Herzlian Zionist. The glamor of Herzl's personality impressed him, but after Herzl's death political Zionism was in eclipse. When the Turkish autocracy fell and a new constitutional government was formed, Magnes proposed that the Basle Program be cast aside and that the Movement should adjust itself to a program of settlement in Palestine on the basis of equality of citizenship. His resolution to this effect was accepted by the American Zionist convention—with seven negative votes, but the resolution did not survive a fortnight of scrutiny. When the Zionist group supported the American Jewish Congress, as indicated, Magnes stood by the side of Louis Marshall, the President of the American Jewish Committee, in active opposition.

When the Zionist group, under the leadership of Louis D. Brandeis, held that Zionist, as well as American, interests required a pro-Ally orientation, Magnes was a pacifist and, in a sense, a pro-German sympathizer. He sponsored the activities of a German Zionist who came to the United States to persuade the Zionists to accept a German "declaration" favoring Jewish national rights in Poland if and when Germany won the war, in place of the Anglo-American Balfour Declaration. The First World War presented an opportunity for the first time in Zionist history to raise funds for Palestine work. Magnes gave his support to the American Jewish Relief Committee and helped to organize the Joint Distribution Committee which was, in effect, a counterbalance to the Zionist effort, emphasizing the priority of relief against constructive work in Palestine. He was opposed in his own mild way to the Brandeis regime. It was he who publicly challenged Mr. Brandeis on the propriety of a Supreme Court Justice participating in controversial Jewish issues and thus was the indirect cause of Mr. Brandeis' retirement to "silent" leadership.

It was Magnes' fundamental dissent on Zionist policy with regard to Arab relations which revealed his tragic incompatibility during the years of the Mandate regime. Over a period of twenty-five years he persisted in urging a bi-national state in Palestine, by agreement, on the basis of equality of all parties concerned. During this period the Jewish community of Palestine suffered bloody anti-Jewish riots at the hands of the Arabs. They had to deal with the malignant influence of the fanatically hostile Mufti of Jerusalem. During this period the Peel Commission's report recommended the partition of Palestine, which was shelved by His Majesty's Government; an Arab-Jewish conference was held in London with the British Government meeting the Jews one day and the Arabs the next; the Mandatory Government issued the White Paper of 1939 in which the Arabs were assured of majority control of the whole of Palestine; Hitler assembled his power and let go at all Jews in Germany, extending the empire of his malevolence over the whole of Europe; from 1940 to 1948 Mandatory Government maintained its inhuman blockade of Palestine ports to prevent the refugees fleeing from Germany from reaching their only haven of refuge. But without varying his proposals in any appreciable way, with the same unruffled and naive spirit which was evinced when he first began his propaganda, Magnes urged again and again that the problem be solved by a bi-national state in the whole of Palestine; he submitted his views to the Anglo-American Committee of Inquiry on Palestine in 1946 in Jerusalem, and was in no way deterred from reiterating them down to the day when the State of Israel was proclaimed.

He believed—looking beyond the realities—that the Jewish people could achieve their aims through an appeal to the ideals of peace and justice. He believed that right was on both sides and that peace could come only by agreement. He wanted to keep on reminding both Jews and non-Jews of the ideals of peace and good will, while those who should have harkened to his lofty words were trampling humanity under their feet.

Magnes spent the last years of his life in a troubled Palestine, administering the affairs of the Hebrew University, speaking of peace while students were enlisting in the underground Haganah. He was devoted to the University. He was devoted to the Hadassah medical work. He lived a simple, modest life with no discernible ambition and with an easy mind. He was angry with the Nazis, he was disappointed in the English, he resented the Irgun underground and condemned their bloody deeds. He was accepted as a good man, fair in dealings, upright in character, clinging with remarkable loyalty and guilelessness to conceptions that had lost all meaning in a world in which genocide had become the pattern of life for the Germans whose civilization had greatly influenced his youth. His mind was revealed as a mold that had frozen, and which he could not adjust to the changing world in which he was condemned to spend his last years. He was not a party to the jubilation of the citizens of Israel when the State began its life. He did not join in the anniversaries that were being celebrated. He was not elated or hopeful. He died while on a visit to New York.

SOLOMON SCHECHTER (1849–1915)

Solomon Schechter was an imposing, white-bearded, tousle-haired man with a ruddy complexion, whom Rembrandt would have loved to paint. He was absent-minded, but had a prodigious memory. He loved to talk, seldom listened and was a rough participant in discussions. Fragments of his provocative conversations may be found in his biography written by Norman Bentwich. The echo of his voice lingered for many years in the halls of the House of Learning he presided over in New York City. He was an interpreter of ancient manuscripts, a student of the Bible and its commentaries, a teacher of teachers, an essayist with a distinguished style, and an advocate of universal, traditional Judaism. Of greater interest here is the fact that he made a substantial contribution to the growth of the Zionist Movement in the United States in its early period when it was encircled by opponents.

He was born in Rumania and educated in German universities. He was fortunate that, subsequently, he was greatly influenced by his life in England and by the thirteen years he spent in the more unconventional environment of democratic America. The core of his personality was Rumanian, which abided with him throughout. He had none of the talents of the religious or clerical functionary. According to the best authorities, he was not a pre-eminent Talmudist nor a master of Hebrew; but what he knew radiated from a luminous, humane personality, the universality of his knowledge and his strong desire to inspire a love for truth and piety, which gave him distinction. What interfered with Schechter as a scholar in the field he made his own was his active imagination and his exuberant interest in intellectual life generally. He saw beyond the text of the Genizah manuscripts he studied and was able intuitively to perceive the implications of the clues that lead to discovery. Although a bookman, he was not bookish. He loved light as well as heavy literature. He was not a cataloguer, a librarian, a specialist interested in the biography of books. He looked for the writer's personality and would read a poorly written book because of his inquisitiveness as to how it came to be written and who was the man who wrote it.

He was at his best when he gave expression to spontaneous opinions; he was at his worst in formal arguments. Facing a dialectician he was helpless. He was a *Chassid* chafing against the rigidity of the text. He could not accept contradictions. His affections as well as his dislikes were abiding. He did not relish tameness in love or in hate.

He was orthodox because he felt at home in the Jewish way of life. He respected authority, which he found in the practices of orthodox Judaism. He avoided the practices his reason could not accept, but in the main he lived in the orthodox way. He was willing to waive intellectual acceptance. Join in the synagogue services, observe the Sabbath and the dietary laws and you will come to believe in the principles of conduct underlying them. And if, in the last analysis, faith should not come, what have you lost?

He did not appreciate, however, the mechanical observance of the Law, and had no affection for theology as such. He had no liking for the rabbinical "profession," although he trained a generation of rabbis. His love went out to the pious, unlearned man, who believed in God with simple faith and went about the business of being a Jew with devotion, confidence and humility. He was not frightened so much by ignorance as he was by lack of piety. He was not interested in what the Priests in the Temple were doing. Let every man be his own rabbi, do his own praying; keep his own account with God. Be satisfied with coming out at the end of your life with a fair balance to your credit. In the final reckoning there will be cause for rejoicing.

He was not at home in the formal life of his Seminary. His amiable wife always had to keep him in line with convention. He was impetuous in speech. Even when his hair was white, he was the redhead he was born; quick in anger; capable of keen sarcasm and good humor; hot in attack on sham and hypocrisy; but his anger quickly passing and leaving him contrite. He took pride in nursing his prejudices, which he regarded as a weakness to be tolerated. He was pious, but not bigoted. It was because he loved the ordered life of the religious Jew that he observed the Law, that he chanted the prayers, that he sang the traditional melodies. He had no grudge against the ungodly; he felt compassion for them. All his life he lacked the feeling for money values. He knew what poverty meant, but was not humble in poverty. He was humble only in scholarship and in piety.

Schechter was never a "regular" Zionist. He always resisted regularity. His Zionism was a reflection of his religious faith. It was the incarnation of the Promise. The Return was the expression of God's mercy; the sinful people were to return to the Land Promised and to be re-enfolded in the arms of the forgiving Father. He loved the Hebrew language and its literature; it was a "sacred" tongue and therefore should be immunized against alien dross. He knew that the writers of Hebrew could also practice a sort of idolatry. He had a dislike of the Hebraists who poured into the old vessel the disintegrating influences of the modern world. He hated the pornographists who wrote in Hebrew.

Although for some time he made no profession of interest in the Zionist Organization, he exercised a paternal influence upon the young men who came to the Seminary to study for the rabbinate. He gave them the feeling that the great tradition of Jewish scholarship was the shield of their Zionist faith. His fresh, hearty, rude voice breached the wall raised against Zionism by the "Reform" graduates from Cincinnati who were presumed to be going the American way and not the way to Zion. In those days Zionism—whatever there was of it—came from the quarters of the newer settlers through their Yiddish press, their own social life, their own customs derived from the old country. The Anglo-Jewish press was dominated chiefly by Reform rabbis. The pulpits where English was spoken disseminated the ideals of a Jewish mission, but provided no missionaries. Every manifestation of differing Jewish life was condemned as disloyalty to the Land that had received them as refugees.

In spite of his sharp criticism of Reform Judaism, however, Schechter won the admiration of many of the Reform rabbis who derived their culture from Germany. In fact, they admitted that the crown of Jewish scholarship deserved to be placed on the head of the rough and ready Rumanian who came to the United States via theological seminaries in Germany, and more than that, clothed in the scarlet robes of a Cambridge doctor. They could not easily resist him. He crossed swords with many of them in the English manner of controversy. He won respect for his erudition, his literary skill in English and his genuine faith. Thus Schechter weakened the ideology of the mission the Reform movement preached. The mission finally became an empty phrase.

But he remained the scholar in Zionism, restless and eager to enter the field of dignified controversy. He was not a joiner or endorser of causes. His friends in England were never able to enlist his interest in the Zionist Organization. He waited until 1905 before he joined the Zionist Organization in the United States.

He raised the tone of Zionist discussion in the United States at a time when Zionism was sealed off from the gentile world. He was not reluctant to reply to Jacob H. Schiff's frequent letters to the *New York Times*. He always wrote such letters with great care, as he did all his correspondence. He made not only the students of the Seminary his disciples, but for a number of years spent his summer vacations in a summer resort where the Zionist conventions were held, and loved the company of the young people he met there. The unclerical atmosphere pleased him. He knew no order of business and interrupted the proceedings whenever the spirit moved him. In conversation with them he was overbearing. His disagreements were frank and unconventional and sometimes cruel. He disported himself in Zionist company on such occasions with an amiable gruffness which deceived nobody, for they knew he enjoyed the rough and tumble of debate and could take a vigorous reply just as comfortably as he could deliver a savage verbal attack.

Whatever Schechter wrote had a personal style which was easily recognized. He was, of course, a foreigner, but he acquired English idiomatic forms with keen understanding and without the slightest error. Philosophical discussions were enlivened by his wit and humor. He never hit an opponent in controversy with blunt, harsh words; he made his effects sharply but with tenderness.

His first words about Zionism were written in a preface to a volume published shortly before his death.

"Speaking for myself," he wrote, "Zionism was, and still is, the most cherished dream I was worthy of having. It is beautiful to behold the rise of this mighty bulwark against the incessantly assailing forces of assimilation, which become the more dangerous, as we have now among us a party permeated by Christianizing tendencies, the prominent leaders of which are ever clamoring for a recognition of Paul, the apostle to the heathen—not to the Jews. These tendencies which, it must be said in justice, would have been strenuously opposed by the founders of the Reform school, are now thrust upon us on every occasion, and Heaven knows where they might have landed us but for the Zionist Movement which has again brought forth the national aspect as a factor in Jewish thought.

"But the dream is not without its nightmares: For in their struggle to revise the national sentiment, some of the Zionist spokesmen, calling themselves by preference Nationalists, manifest such a strong tendency to detach the Movement from all religion as can only end in spiritual disaster. There is such a thing as the assimilation of Judaism even as there is such a thing as the assimilation of the Jews; and the former is bound to happen when religion is looked upon as a negligible quantity. When Judaism is once assimilated the Jew will surely follow in its wake and Jew and Judaism will perish together. All this is a consequence of preaching an aspect of Nationalism more in harmony with Roman and similar modern models than with Jewish ideas and ideals. However, nightmares are fleeting and evanescent—the vision as a whole still remains glorious. The aberrations will, let us hope, be swept away quickly enough as soon as their destructive nature is realized by the majority of the Zionists, whose central ideas should and will remain God and His people, Israel."

Schechter's death was hastened by the First World War. He was a sick man when the war came. He could not bear to read of the first German victories. He detested the arrogance of the Germans. He hated imperialism of all kinds and of all ages. In his youth he was attracted to the liberalism of Germany, but soon discerned that although the Jews had been emancipated in Germany, they had accepted an intellectual and spiritual inferiority. All the trends in German philosophy, history, literature and science were being used to depreciate the nature and organization of the Hebraic and Jewish contribution to civilization. He was enraged by the superciliousness of the Higher Critics. He reacted against them with fervor. He rejected the attempt to make the Son the equal of the Father, the Second Chapter as the more authentic Revelation, reducing the First to the status of a *plagiat*.

He felt more at home in England. He was impressed by its conservatism

and stability, its respect for tradition. He loved the atmosphere of
Cambridge, its professors, its students, the scholarly dignity removed
from the tumult of secular life. He said that "what interested me most
(during the war) was the glorious prospect of England annexing Palestine,
with God's help. This is the only solution for which we should hope.
England is a Biblical country, reverential and practical, kind to our
people and able to understand their aspirations for and in the Holy
Land. Any other power would secularize it soon enough. England
in its sincerity and reverence would serve as a model to our radicals,
and would save us from all sorts of assimilation."

But he loved America most and saw in its history, and more especially
its attitude toward immigration at that time, signs of providential
intention toward the well-being of Jews. America was the apogee of
the democratic revolution; it was the ideal testing ground for a democratic life in which respect was accorded to varying cultures and
religions.

He was a voracious reader of American literature. He knew intimately
the history of our wars—the War for Independence, the Civil War. The
personality of Abraham Lincoln had a peculiar fascination for him.
He found in American history, in its early days, a revelation
of personality which had in it traces of Hebraic influence. He thought
the way should be found to natural recognition of common origins,
the Hebraism of New England, the influence of the Old Testament,
the Hebraic coloring of the Christian religion. When he thought of
the Jewish "mission," not as mere doctrine of Reform, he considered
how properly trained Seminary rabbis could become a defensive force
in the process of reconciliation.

He made a study of the life of Lincoln. He used to tell how the figure
of the Great Emancipator became known in Rumania when he was
a youth through the medium of Hebrew journals. He was attracted
to the "Rail-Splitter" in whom he recognized a likeness to Hillel, who,
legend has it, was engaged in the occupation of wood-cutting. In a
lecture delivered in 1909 at the Seminary, he quoted a characterization
of Lincoln by Alexander H. Stephens that "the Union with him (Lincoln) in sentiment rose to the sublimity of a religious mysticism."
Schechter said of Lincoln's mysticism:

No religious hero ever entered upon his mission to conquer the
world for an idea and creed with more reverence and a deeper feeling
of the need of divine assistance than did Lincoln when he was about

to leave his home and his old associates and associations, good and evil, for his new home and his new life in Washington as President.

Religious mysticism, said Schechter, has the defects of its quality. From these dangers Lincoln was preserved by his training and not less by his "divine" humor. His sublime faith in the cause of the Union, which he considered God's cause, made real despair impossible in the trying days of the Civil War.

Schechter died before England was given the Mandate over Palestine. He was spared the sight of England's double-dealing with the trusteeship over the Holy Land in which he had great hopes. He never heard of the Nazis and Adolf Hitler. The future of the Promised Land seemed assured under England's guardianship.

HIRSCH MASLIANSKY (1856–1943)

Death found Hirsch Masliansky dignified and honored in old age. He was reconciled with that status and spent his last years in sheltered peace. From time to time, unable to resist the temptation, he would return to the Stage, but he got to be afraid of what he might do and say there. It was pathetic to see the Grand Old Man watching his step, hesitant in speech, feeling for the right word and worried because he could not always find it. Finally he raised the White Flag and was seen no more by the great public that loved him. Unless he was one of the speakers, he had no interest in appearing on the platform. In his home, old friends came to see him; he was warmed by the affection of his children and grandchildren. He read the Yiddish newspapers; he went to his *Shul* in Boro Park; he raged and wept when he heard of the tragedies of Jewish life in the Hitler days. He wanted to raise his voice to console his people; he wanted to blast the enemy with blistering speech. But he could not risk the excitement. Nor would the desired words come at his bidding. Toward the end, it is said, he had one complaint—he was living too long.

The story of his life begins in Russia with the rise of the movement to settle in Palestine and, simultaneously, the great migration to the United States. He was a young man when the May Laws of 1880 fell upon the Jews in Russia, when the *Chibbath Zion* blossomed, when the Biluists went out to found the first Zionist settlement. He saw thousands packing their belongings and crossing the great ocean to find new homes in "godless" America. He became a teacher and made his first talk in 1881 in the *Beth-Midrash* of Pinsk. It was realized by the leaders of the *Chovevei Zion* movement that he had a way of speaking which could command wide attention. He had power and imagination. So he began to address Zionist circles and was sent into the provinces of Russia to stimulate interest in Palestine and Zionism. He was always at home in the synagogue; he had a natural piety, but his ideas and methods could not be confined within the limitations of the synagogue. He never liked to be called a *Maggid*. He did not want to be an itinerant preacher; he wanted to have a home and live attached to the Jewish community; but he was not free from some of the mannerisms of the *Maggid*. He had his own style of speaking, which clung to him all the days of his life. He had interludes of description and anecdote; he drew easily upon the Midrash and the Bible; he even had his own chant for many years. But there was also something worldly in his approach to the subjects of his discourses. He had to have a broader platform. He needed space for movement. He wanted to be free, while speaking, even of the restraints piety and synagogue convention might impose upon him. As a preacher, he was also an agitator and a propagandist.

I remember hearing Masliansky over fifty years ago in Rochester. He came to the *shul*, which was the *shul* my father and mother were part of. I cannot remember when I became a Zionist. It must have been so with me always, for I had an instinct for Jewish books in which Jewish identity, Jewish character, Jewish tragedies and hopes, and the incongruities of Jewish life were dealt with. These disturbed me greatly. The Hebrew print of Yiddish newspapers fascinated me and provoked curiosity. My father had a large Hebrew library which was circulated among the Maskilim. His conversation brought to life the novels of Smolenskin and Mapu and what he read in the current Hebrew and Yiddish newspapers. I lived in two worlds. Side by side with books of English and American literature were these books that brought into my life bearded alien Jews, redolent of memories of a distant past, whose descendants were now living in the incongruous American present.

In spite of all this, Masliansky had the fanciful idea that he had made a Zionist of me. As one would say, "It was I who made a man of you." It would be hard to prove that, but there was truth in his claim in a deeper sense. I remember how he looked, how he talked, and what he said in the synagogue that Sabbath afternoon. I have never forgotten that experience. He was so thoroughly alive as a speaker. He raked his audience fore and aft with invective, sarcasm, lamentation, sentiment, and with appeals to faith and loyalty. He drew pictures in vivid words of what had been in the old country, what was to become of us here, what was to be the Jewish future. He spoke of *Golus* and Zion, of wandering and return. He alternated from comedy to tragedy, varying his tone, the tempo of his sentences, and, in interludes, rested in a soothing chant. Time has blurred the details of what Masliansky said that day, but nothing in later years changed the pattern of that picture of a great and moving speaker, nor that feeling he gave of establishing contact through him with an endless Jewish tradition.

Thousands who left Russia brought the fame of Masliansky to the United States. That was the time when imported goods were greatly relished in our community. When he left Pinsk, he traveled through Europe and went to London. He received the acclaim of that poor Jewish community, but its poverty and its climate distressed him and made him unwilling to remain there. He had started out with a longing for free America and he could not rest until he had found his home in the land Columbus had discovered. When once he rested his feet on American soil, he became its most loyal patriot and most extravagant panegyrist. He never had any difficulty in painting a picture of Zion that brought back animated memories of regal pomp and majesty; he could tell stories of the past with quaint charm and intimacy, never troubled for lack of words; but he never had words enough adequately to describe what a blessing America was to Jews. He had the naiveté of a peasant in this respect; and his wonder never ceased. He used to contrast the furtive meetings in Russian cities, the dread of visitations by the police, the censorship of speech and press, with the freedom of movement, of speech and press here in the United States. He might be speaking of Golus in a spiritual sense, but there was not a trace here of the dreadfulness of the Golus in Russia. Everything that was spread out before his eyes was a gift from God and he was genuinely grateful for it. He overlooked all the blemishes in our democracy. He chanted praises for his heroes, Jefferson, Lincoln and Theodore Roosevelt. He appreciated American democracy with Walt Whitman's exuberance and fervor. Nothing, ever, shook this faith.

Soon after his arrival, he made a tour of many of our large cities, was the guest of many congregations, received the adoration of many

groups he had known in Russia, and set up his platform in the Educational Alliance, where arrangements were made for him to speak on Friday
nights. At that time, the Jews of the older migration—the so-called
Yehudim—believed that the immigrant Jews should be made to accelerate their adjustment to the American way of life. They were afraid
that assimilation was not going on fast enough, that the uncouthness
of alien methods and dress and speech—the abnormality and congestion
of the East Side—was not good for public relations with the *goyim*.
They hit upon the quaint idea of having Masliansky use his talents
to inspire the aliens with a proper understanding of what America
expected of them. Masliansky was asked to serve as the interpreter
of Americanism to the Jews of the East Side.

They builded better than they knew. He accepted the commission,
for he believed in having Jews build their lives here on an authentic
American foundation. His platform in the Alliance became a weekly
forum for the review of all things that passed through the minds and
souls of Jews in the great community. He fought against the radicalism
of the day that scorned and derided the Jewish tradition. His was the
one noble and dignified voice that protested against the vulgarities
of godlessness and the crude violation of tradition. A whole generation
of Jews who received their spiritual and intellectual sustenance through
Yiddish, found in him a source of continuing delight, instruction and
inspiration. Hundreds of them came week after week, never satiated,
never bored, but always glad to hear Masliansky speak again. His
pulpit in the Alliance was not intended for Zionist propaganda. But
it served as the best Zionist pulpit in the United States, to the chagrin
of those who had elevated Masliansky to this position. Masliansky
became a Jewish institution all by himself, like the Yiddish press or
the Yiddish theater.

It was in the Zionist Movement, however, that he found his complete
freedom. Many Jews who had come here during that period remembered
the old country, its customs and traditions, but their memories of
the past were being blurred and forgotten by the softening influence
of the new world. The new life distracted and misled them. They were
prepared to discard the old gods and to accept the shoddy ideals of
a hurried, superficial life. Masliansky had to make their memories
live again. He did not want Jews to throw themselves into the melting
pot without retaining the virtues and qualities that were the Jewish
contribution to modern civilization. He reminded them of Zion, of the
prophets, of Jewish law, of Jewish legend, and he attuned them to the

vision of a new Zion and a new freedom. He made them conscious of the ties that bound them to the millions who were living under the oppression of Europe. He appealed to them to remember Zion and to strive for Jewish freedom. Masliansky was the symbol of all the implications of *Chibbath Zion*, its sentiment, its vision, as well as its hesitating practicality. He lifted Jews out of the slums of the East Side and made them see the new Jerusalem Jews were rebuilding in verification of the ancient prophecies.

For years and years—four decades—at propaganda meetings, at dinners, and at anniversaries, at Zionist conventions and conferences, at protest meetings of all kinds, Masliansky gave the light of his presence, his spirit, his remarkable artistry in oratory. He improvised his thought and the pictures he used to illuminate it were drawn from an inexhaustible fountain of knowledge and experience. His affection for his people was never tarnished by doubt of their quality, and he never lost faith in Jewish destiny. His name, his voice and gestures—the stories Masliansky had used, the epigrams Masliansky had made—became a colorful feature of American Jewish life. He was heard on every occasion of crisis and commemoration. He led in the Kishinev protest, that first American Jewish manifestation of protest. He participated in the *Kehillah* movement and the organization of the American Jewish Congress. He was always the favorite eulogist at the annual meetings of the Hebrew Immigrant Aid Society and the Hebrew Free Loan, for whom he had a special affection. Time and again, he went out on long, fatiguing trips for Zionist propaganda and Palestine fund-raising. He was one of the celebrants in the glorification of the Balfour Declaration and of the San Remo decision, and in all the protests against the violations of the covenant England had made with the Jewish people. He led in the mourning, and he led in the rejoicing, of his kinsmen in America, over a period of forty years.

The seeds of Zionism were transplanted to the freedom of America from the lands of persecution. These seeds were hidden in the baggage of many an alien, who had forgotten to throw them into the sea. The remembered voice, the printed word, the ceremony in the synagogue, brought Zionism to life in our midst. Herzl and Nordau, Ahad Ha-am and Pinsker had many a disciple here whom they never knew, but whose spirit and mind and faith were sustained by their inspiring words. Many of these creators of Zionist spirit came to us in person and fructified the seeds that were sleeping in our consciousness. Their names are

registered in the Zionist history of three continents—Palestine, Europe
and the United States. Among these are the names of Chaim Weizmann,
Ben Zion Mossinsohn, Nahum Sokolow, Menahem Ussishkin, and
Vladimir Jabotinsky. They were with us and of us for a time. Heading
the group were Shmarya Levin and Chaim Nachman Bialik—Levin
who spent years among us, enriched our lives, gave Zionism three-
dimensional proportions, and turned a sleeping idea into a ball of
glowing fire; Bialik, who came later and not so often, but whose personality glowed in our hearts long after he was called away from us; and
Weizmann, who was both speaker and statesman.

Masliansky belonged in that gallery of Masters. He too was more
than a voice, more than a message, more than a guide; but of all who
have been named, he was the only one who was never a stranger, merely
paying us a visit. He came, he saw, and he was conquered, never thinking
of leaving the hospitable community that provided him with home.
He was a neighbor and friend. He was a co-worker and fellow citizen.
He was a dash of vivid color that became part of our American landscape.
He never had any pretensions; he never assumed that he was a philosopher or the discoverer of new thought. He was an artist who communicated the emotions of a man greatly excited by the prospect of Jewish
life being recreated in an ancient mold. He painted pictures even the
simplest could see and understand. He made the whole Jewish world
the frame of his adventures—from Pinsk to London, from London
to New York, back to Zion, to Warsaw and Pinsk and Kiev, and returning always to rest in his home in Boro Park.

He was not merely a speaker of Zionism; he was the chanter of its
song. He was a Zionist by birth, an optimist by nature, sentimental
by temperament, and a man of great faith. He did not live to see the
Jewish State, but he came mighty close to it.

ABRAHAM GOLDBERG (1883–1942)

Abraham Goldberg came to the United States from Russia where
he was born in the town of Yarmolinetz (Ukraine) and spent his life
as a writer and speaker in the land of his adoption. He spoke Yiddish
for the most part with a unique sparkle and fluency, but in his latter
years, when Yiddish in Zionist circles was waning, he preferred to
speak and write English in which he was not so proficient or successful.
He was a genial *yeshiva bocher* delighting in casuistry, always cheerful and optimistic. At an early age he threw off the *yeshiva* attitudes

and rushed forward with youthful enthusiasm to conquer the new world—the world of Jewish labor, the Yiddish newspapers, the Yiddish theatre.

He was one of the few American Zionists who had made a place for himself in the old country as a speaker and writer. He never forgot, however, that home was where you found a *minyan* of Jews, and he loved to browse in alien fields. On his travels he found Jews to hobnob with in London and Paris, in Berlin and Vienna, in Warsaw and Vilna. At the same time, he was curious to know how the other half lived. He went to theatres and museums and restaurants and night clubs. He read foreign books and magazines, knew about their writers and artists, but he never rid himself of the impression that however well he knew them, they remained *goyim*. The better he got to know them, the more certain he was that the world was divided into two unequal parts. The larger part was *goyish* unmistakably. Equality would be achieved only when we Jews had a state of our own; there we too would fill a stage—a small one—but our own.

The cause of all causes was, of course, Zionism. That was his settled dogma and the source of his life. He stood on a Zionist platform and subordinated all other interests to the ideals of the Hebrew writers he cherished, the learning he imbibed in the *yeshiva*, the instruction received from friends of his youth. Zionism was the mother who took to her bosom all Jewish interests. From the Zionist platform he held out his hands to all Jewish causes and made them his own, in his own frame, and integrated them in his conception of the Jewish renascence.

In his youth he was a partisan. The practical aspects of territorialism then advocated by Israel Zangwill captured his interest, fed his tongue and pen, and excited him no end. When he was a workman in New York he was a territorial Poale Zionist and tried to reach a formula that would put him at ease for the rest of his life. He did not like to live in a cauldron of partisanship. The discipline of party was really not for him. He was too good-humored and eager for popular acclaim to bind himself to the decisions of a caucus. He had a facile imagination and a quick mind. He was the victim of logic that often led him to heresy. These made his sojourn within the walls of any party an unbearable restraint and embarrassment. He was a Socialist, but could not accept the yoke of Marxian discipline. The lure of Zion led him to abandon the strict logic of the territorialist, and he soon found himself in the vast freedom of what was called "general" Zionism. What that meant he did not pursue too far lest it lead him into difficulties. When once he entered that heterogeneous company he looked back at his first loves with wonder, thinking of them as the aberrations of youth, for he was not born to be loyal to any dogma or doctrine except in the broad open ways of Zionism—the more abstract the better.

He found the freedom he needed in the non-party form of Zionism then prevalent in the United States, and from about 1912 until his death he stood with the Center. The Center was (and probably always will be) the eclectic party. It made its decisions as circumstances dictated, but was always controlled by what was regarded as the interests of the whole. It swerved now to the right, now to the left, and always maintained the balance, becoming the stabilizing factor in the Zionist Movement. Power, however, went over to the parties which talked much of ideology, but won through the labor of the pioneers. Their ideology was a screen for more practical objectives.

First in the Federation of American Zionists, then in its successor, the Zionist Organization of America, Goldberg played the various parts to which his talents entitled him, but he always claimed that he was never given his rightful position. He was the editor of *Dos Yiddishe Folk* for many years. He was one of the founders of the Histadruth Ivrith. He was a popular Yiddish speaker who became known in every city and hamlet throughout the country. He was a messenger of enlightenment, the analyst of policies, the commentator on personalities. He spoke before the meetings and after them late in the night in the cafeterias. He served for many years on the Zionist Actions Committee. He attended many Zionist Congresses and spoke in the "general debate." At Vienna in 1925 he was the chairman of the *Permanenz Ausschuss* (general committee or steering committee) which he regarded as a great distinction.

Many times he went to Palestine and spent months loitering about, familiarizing himself with the land and the people. He was an advocate of "practical" Zionism and approved many practical enterprises which he himself promoted with embarrassing results. He spoke to Jews week in and week out on the platform, in *Dos Yiddishe Folk*, in *Hadoar*, as a regular contributor to the *Jewish Morning Journal* and *Der Amerikaner*. He showed early promise as a poet, but he deserted the Muse for easier forms of expression. In the midst of these specifically Zionist activities he was always found with *landsleit*, serving them, advising them, participating in their festivals and their funerals. He was one of the prime movers in the organization of the American Jewish Congress and the People's Relief Committee during World War I. He was always at the beck and call of the Federation of Polish Jews. There was never any mistake about his being a Zionist primarily. He wore the Zionist insignia on his sleeve. His name appeared in the telephone book as "Abe Zionist Goldberg" to be sure that nobody made any mistake about it. It was that he was most proud of. He was a lover of people and could not resist the appeals of people when they came to him with their complaints. But, as he said, his greatness was never apparent to his closest friends. He never could get to the head of the procession.

He loved books but loved the writers of them more. He enjoyed the company of the creators of the literature of his people, in Yiddish or Hebrew or English, and regarded as priceless moments the hours spent in conversation with kindred literary spirits. He would go out of his way to find—in Vienna or Warsaw, Berlin or London or Tel Aviv—the men who wrote the books for which he was grateful. He was prodigal in praise of his heroes and in a quaint manner loved to be praised by them, fulsomely if possible. He often resented the lack of reciprocity in this respect, saying that generosity on his side called for an equal degree from the other side in order to balance the account. He overpaid in praise, expecting a balanced return.

His love for people led him to being a chronic peacemaker. He loved controversy, but disliked seeing brothers interlocked in controversy that could not be settled in peace and come to an end. Every war had to have its peacemakers. He got to think that all differences could be settled by men of good will. All you needed was a peacemaker with *sechel*. And that he had in abundance. He tried his hand at the game time and again, often succeeding, but often giving up the job as hopeless and receiving the pay the peacemaker usually receives. Thus in the Zionist controversy with the American Jewish Committee, at the time of the first American Jewish Congress, Louis Marshall was the head of the Committee. Goldberg admired Marshall and believed that because he had a good Jewish heart you could come to a compromise with him on every Jewish question. He believed that having a good Jewish heart, Marshall was, of course, almost a good Zionist. Goldberg sacrificed much at that time to this thought, which the Zionists rejected. In fact, he lost the editorship of *Dos Yiddishe Folk* on account of it. Later, when Marshall went to Versailles and pleaded the general Jewish cause, and Dr. Weizmann set out on his efforts to create the extended Jewish Agency with the non-Zionists, Goldberg was one of the zealous partisans of this Zionist compromise. To him, every compromise was a victory.

But Goldberg's zeal for peace led him into courses of action later on that gave him great pain and, in turn, grieved all his friends who loved him in spite of his waywardness. He wanted to make peace with Soviet Russia. He thought he could do it single-handedly. He was afraid that the Jews of Russia would be lost. To the amazement of all his old Zionist friends he became, in fact, a "fellow traveler" in the last years of his life. He persisted in his efforts regardless of the friends he lost and the queer new friends he won.

He was the victim of a subtle communist who was a lawyer who had once studied in a *Yeshiva*. Goldberg became the tool of that intriguer at Geneva in 1936, when he volunteered to get the American Jewish communists admitted to the World Jewish Congress. The effort failed. When Goldberg returned home, it was noticed that strange friends provided his company. Then he appeared at a few "fellow traveler" meetings, then his writings betrayed traces of communist aroma. Then he was making trips in the interests of Jewish communist organizations.

When I went to speak in Detroit at a Goldberg memorial meeting, quite a few Zionist friends were present, but the strange voices of his new friends were heard, to the embarrassment of the Zionists.

He was never at a loss for a word or an argument, fighting for his ideas, quarreling about them, but always striving to hold together friendships and good-will. He would always ask for the floor the moment he entered a meeting even before he knew what was being talked about and before he knew what he himself was going to say. He would push his way to the front, run his hand through his curly hair, hesitate only a moment and then speak freely and eloquently without regard for time. The words gushed out of his mouth. He was short and stocky. He had a round face crowned with black hair, and always looked cheerful. He was young in spirit and dreaded the thought of old age. He served the Zionist cause with prodigal enthusiasm and all the talent he had.

He felt that he could go on and on for countless years. There was so much work to be done; there were so many things to be said; so many articles to be written; so many political combinations that could yet be made. He was more away from home than in it and was thinking of the day when he could change his way of life and get to know his children better. They were growing up rapidly. They were entering the professions. They were getting married. His family was crowding in on him and he would soon have to make a final decision—should he cling to the "road" or prepare to stay at home for good?

He was destined not to face old age, not to feel the weakening of intellect and body. He died young at 59 in June 1942. He died looking eagerly forward. He was about to take a train to make a speech in Detroit. Death closed his eyes quickly. It was so sudden that his friends felt his spirit marching with them years after he had left them.

JOSEPH SEFF (1864–1919)

The nineteen years Joseph Seff spent in the United States did not fulfill the hopes he had when he left Russia. He expected to be a Zionist missionary to the *Galut* of America. When he arrived, he was not hailed by crowds in America as a great speaker nor was his path strewn with roses. His life was a hard, bitter, rancorous struggle. He was in exile and, in effect, his American years were the twilight of his life.

Seff was born in Slavuta, Volhynia in 1864. His father was a man of means who sent his son not to a *Yeshiva*, but to the *Realschule* in Rovno nearby, where he acquired a solid Russian education. He found his own way to Zionism and Hebrew. He went to Vienna and conversed with Perez Smolenskin, the Hebrew novelist. He joined the Lovers of Zion movement and became a belligerent partisan. Unlike other Zionists of the time before Herzl, who thought of returning to the soil, of the renascence of Hebrew, he grappled at once with the political aspects of the Jewish problem. His mind turned to the Turkish Empire in which Palestine was not so profitable a province. He thought the time was ripe for revolution there. Although not provided with funds, he went to Constantinople on his own and lived there for over a year. His aim was to organize the Jewish-Turkish youth who were already infected with revolutionary ideas. He frequented coffee houses and newspaper offices, and acquired a mass of information which he integrated into a plan for Jewish action. He had a hard time of it. He had plenty of ideas and plans, but was short in funds and friends. He could get no support from associates back home; they were afraid of illegal schemes.

He left Constantinople defeated and returned home where he was hailed as a man of great spirit, but privately regarded as a high-class *schlemiel*. He went about telling of his experiences and convictions. He had influence enough to secure an appointment as Crown Rabbi in Old-Konstantin, which he used to extend his Zionist activities. He talked at great length of what might happen to Jews in a reformed

Turkish Empire. He saw a Zionist chance in the anticipated revolution.
Many American Zionists who came from the other side remembered
what a powerful speaker he was at that time. He spoke Yiddish and
Russian with equal passion and descriptive power. He deprecated
the *Galut* as all Zionists did at that time. He led his hearers into the
new world of international politics. He came to know all workers for
Zion. He was a visitor in the home of the parents of Bialik, the Hebrew
poet. He was not a friendly man, but his intellectual equipment
commanded respect and admiration.

When Herzl published *The Jewish State*, Seff's mind flashed in-
stantaneous recognition. He accepted everything Herzl stood for.
He became Herzl's loyal and devoted partisan. He supported the
"call" for the Zionist Congress. He traveled about in many cities
speaking at mass meetings and urging the election of delegates. He
himself was elected a delegate from Berdichev. When he left Old-
Konstantin for Basle, he never returned to Russia.

He met Herzl at Basle and was advised to go to the United States.
(The same advice was also given by Herzl to Jacob de Haas and Boris
Kazman.) Herzl was sure that a man of Seff's talent would be able
to organize Zionism in the United States. As Seff told the story, Herzl
gave him a letter to Richard Gottheil, then President of the American
Zionist Federation. The letter was never delivered. It was stolen or
lost on board the ship. To his dismay Seff found his wallet also was
gone. The handicap of coming to a new land without "papers" or
pocket money was the tragedy of his life. He used to say that if he had
come to Professor Gottheil as Herzl's representative, if he had established himself in a good hotel, he might have had a chance. He would
have been accepted as an official Zionist speaker, as a delegate to the
First Zionist Congress, as the Crown Rabbi of Old-Konstantin, as
one of Herzl's disciples. But he was unsponsored. Who could vouch
for his identity in this godless country? He could not blow his own
horn and there was no one around to do it for him. He had two strikes
against him from the start.

He made the best of his embarrassment. He found lodgings on the
East Side. He suffered great privations and humiliations. He was
always clumsy in money matters. He did not know how to negotiate
a small loan nor did he have the crust to ask for a large one. He was
reduced to having someone pay for his meals and to speaking at local
Zionist meetings, calling the chairman aside after the lecture to tell

him his hard luck story. His American career was conditioned by this miserable start. He was never able to recover the position lost. He started out in life, he said, as a dubious character, without a Zionist "passport."

As we knew him then, Seff was a tall, blackbearded man with a magnificent head, who had a talent for controversy and partisanship. He was a rapid talker. He was the first real political Zionist we knew. He was adept in Oriental politics. He had the intrigues of the Sultan's court at his fingertips. Those were the days when the Charter was the key Zionism was to use to unlock the door to Palestine. He was a relentless political Zionist. He denounced those who would take less than a Jewish State. He believed a Charter could be gotten, if not from the Sultan then from the Young Turks who would overthrow him, which they did a few years later, but they had their own reasons for not giving the Zionists a Charter. He wanted a Jewish army organized underground, located perhaps in Cyprus. He took scant notice of what was going on in Palestine, although he had paid a brief visit to the Judean colonies. The territory was to be Palestine, of course, but that was the lesser part of the problem. His mind operated only with the political situation. That was what excited him when he lingered over his memories of Herzl.

He was a stubborn opponent of orthodox rabbis. He had a great desire always to pick a quarrel with rabbis and religion in general. He brought that allergy with him from Russia where the rabbis were his inveterate opponents. He also quarreled with modern Zionists who disliked his caustic and cynical references to piety and religion.

He lacked a relaxed touch and a friendly spirit. There was not a drop of humor in him on the platform or in private life. He was full of gall and bitterness. Life had not treated him with kindness, so he retaliated. He soon acquired an easy use of English. He did not want to be known as a Yiddish speaker. He was at home on the East Side and frequented Zionist meetings. His aim in life was to speak at large mass meetings, to be counted as one of the leading Zionist speakers, but it was hard for him to make the grade. There was something forbidding in the way he spoke, in his resentment and criticism of his audiences, in his harsh voice and gauche manners. They felt a cold wall between themselves and his words. You never could tell what he was going to say or how he would say it. He was more Russian than Jewish. He was envious of the popularity of Hirsch Masliansky.

He was an intimate friend of Abraham Goldberg, but regarded him as a young upstart. He could not endure Joseph Barondess, who came to Zionism as a convert from the trade union movement. He regarded every secretary of the Zionist organization as his mortal enemy, standing between him and the platform he wanted to stand on. He sensed a conspiracy against him in which all Zionists were joined and found solace only with a few journalists or Zionists from the old home who remembered his great past and sympathized with his grievances.

The Kishinev pogrom aroused American Jews for the first time to the thought of helping Jews abroad in an organized way. Of course, the new settlers sent help to those left behind and assisted in their reunions; they also remembered their home towns. But the pogroms were the turning point in that they aroused public demonstrations and public relief measures. The American Jewish community as a whole was concerned about the Jewish victims of the pogroms. Out of all proportion to the damage inflicted by the pogrom in Kishinev, they were excited and disturbed and went to mass meetings determined to give public expression to their feelings and to make their contributions. It was a time of great trouble when all personal differences and partisan quarrels were overlooked. Seff was active in these demonstrations. He seemed to undergo a serious psychical disturbance. He would give hysterical descriptions of the pogroms, telling with brutal realism what had been reported, shocking the sensibilities of his hearers beyond endurance. Women fainted at his meetings. Men reviled him for his brutality and left the hall. His persistent conduct along this line made it necessary to call him to book.

"Do you have to speak that way?" he was asked. "Your words are shocking." He said: "When I begin to speak I tell myself, 'Be calm, don't get excited.' But when I think of the horrible crimes committed against women and children, my indignation gets the best of me. I feel a moral satisfaction in telling exactly what these crimes are. I feel as Bialik felt when he wrote *The City of Slaughter*."

He lost his status as a speaker. In fact, he could find no place at all in the Zionist world. He wandered into the field of American politics. He became an admirer of William Jennings Bryan, "the Great Commoner," whom he resembled in features and was proud of it. He joined the Democratic Party and Tammany Hall. He hobnobbed with Irish politicians and Jews who lived on the fringe of the political machine. He was taken by some of them to be a rabbi. Finally, he got himself a job as an interpreter in the courts and was assured of a measure of security for the rest of his life.

His rejection by American Zionists made an orphan of him. Now and then he made a startling appearance on a Zionist platform, looked morosely upon the audience and lost himself in the lobbies. He lived on the fringe of the growing Zionist community. He never had a family or a home. He seemed unable to keep money in his pockets. There were a few friends who listened to his complaints, loved to hear him talk about Russia and the people he knew there.

But he was a figure out of the past long before he died. He had a habit of vanishing from view for stretches of time. His beard was removed early. Then it was possible to see his face and to observe how life had traced deep lines of suffering on his features. His lips were thin and drawn. His nose was long and sharp. He lost all his teeth and never replaced them with plates so that when his mouth opened in speech, an empty cavern was revealed. There was no truth in the slander that he drank or took drugs. He protested that he was not well and he certainly did not look well for years before he passed away. He was reduced to a shadow of the virile, eager, ambitious personality he was when he first came here.

He died in 1919 and was buried in a Brooklyn cemetery. A stone was placed on his grave by a group of Jewish journalists who thus paid their last respects to the man who was an eloquent pioneer of Zionism in Russia, and had been given his Zionist credentials by Herzl. Nobody ever saw his credentials.

PETER WIERNIK (1865–1936)

Peter Wiernik, editor-in-chief of the New York *Jewish Morning Journal* for 35 years, was more than a singularly upright journalist. He was a *Maskil* who had stepped down into Yiddish journalism. He was the last of the generation of founders. He was a writer who was at the end what he was at the beginning. He did not change in character, in style, nor did he shift the window from which he looked out at life. He was born in Vilna in 1865. He respected learning. He disdained ignorance. He retained, always, poise, sobriety of judgment, practical common sense, and was a non-partisan in the best sense of the word. Like many of the old-time *Maskilim*, he held himself aloof from personal embroilment in matters that were to him not primarily intellectual and moral. He was cold to political or organizational controversies, although he had strong convictions on many of the problems of Jewish life which disturbed its peace. He was in fact a cool-blooded Zionist, mainly because he was a lover of Hebrew.

Wiernik avoided agitation and emotion in discussion and controversy with a sensitive reticence of personality. The editorial page of the *Jewish Morning Journal* was Wiernik's corner in the world. He kept boisterousness, or loudness, or excess, out of it. He let no harsh or vulgar sounds intrude on its narrow columns, always simple, no display headings. no italics, no emphasis.

His editorials were the balance wheel of the *Journal.* On the first page of news, in the articles written, all Jewish issues were spread out from day to day. The austere Jacob Fishman was his columnist and managing editor. He was Wiernik's partner and successor. The news reflected the taste and purpose of other journalists who contributed to the composition of the *Morning Journal*; the articles were written by a variety of writers representing different viewpoints and parties, many of them out of tune with the spirit of Wiernik, but he looked at all of this with the tolerance and sympathetic interest of a man nurtured among books, whose horizon was much broader than the daily record of a newspaper, and who went on writing his own comments on the same life, using a standard of an era now passing into oblivion, an era that, as a matter of fact, had its finest expression only in some of the reviews published in the Hebrew press.

What saved Wiernik from moroseness or cynicism or peevishness was his rich fund of dry Jewish humor and tolerance of different views based on knowledge. He was endowed with a broad sense of appreciation of historic fact and anecdote. He lingered in the field of folklore and delighted in the habits of thought and fields of interest of the pre-emancipation of Jewish life. He loved Hebrew and Hebrew books for their own value. It was that spirit in his character which made it possible for him, intellectually and spiritually, to enjoy the society of Bialik and Shmarya Levin, that made him feel comfortable in the presence of any personality no matter what party he may have belonged to, who brought with him the baggage of the Haskalah or of the Yeshiva in its orthodox phases.

In American politics he was a Republican. As to many other Jews of the old school who became involved in a tepid sort of way in American politics, all issues to him were matters of intellectual analysis and objective sympathy. Wiernik believed in the stability of the middle class, in the stability of the accumulations of culture and reserves of spirit. He believed in orthodoxy as a form of conservation of energy. Let the world go left and more left, but in order to balance what seemed to be tendencies leading to destruction, it was necessary to veer over to the right to avert the success of the extreme left. He was no revolutionist in any sense. But he never got over-warm even in defense of his own special political views. All of this seemed to him a play of the intellect and the expression of the habits of a personality that wanted quiet and order in the world. He maintained his own world in the newspaper he directed and was never disturbed by what was happening around the corner of his newspaper.

In 1912 he wrote a commendable History of the Jews of America, based on accurate research and calm, non-partisan judgment.

Wiernik may be taken as the symbol of the old *Jewish Morning Journal*—now merged—and also of that larger form of journalism which is not confined particularly to a daily newspaper. He was a man of great affability, with a deep sense of justice and fair play, and endeared himself to journalists of all parties. When he passed away, a certain restraining influence which he had exercised over the field of Yiddish journalism in America disappeared without replacement.

JACOB FISHMAN (1876–1946)

Jacob Fishman was unique among the journalists in the heyday of the Yiddish press. He never had any extracurricular employment. He was not an essayist or feuilletonist or a writer of romances or a translator. He was totally the dedicated professional journalist.

He had a prejudice against using the editorial "we." He favored the personal pronoun. He preferred to be the columnist in the first column, sensitive to what was happening in the Jewish world, here or abroad.

In the *Morning Journal*, whose editor he became, he created the first foreign news service in a Jewish newspaper, He saw Jewish life as a whole, and the *Journal* as a whole. He read it, from the last column advertisement on the last page to the first column on the first page.

His best friends will concede that he had little humor, that his style was awkward; but he was always fair, objective and never vulgar in thought or expression. He had an invincible sense of integrity and a great respect for learning. He was restrained in whatever he wrote. He was, in a way, a disciple of Joseph Pulitzer, who founded and edited the New York *World*. He admired Pulitzer's directness, his flair for making the news live, and his journalistic integrity. Fishman and Peter Wiernik—each in his own way—made the *Morning Journal* a first-rate middle-class, loyally Jewish morning paper, without neurotic impulses or sensational fevers, firmly rooted in Jewish tradition. His only passion was Zionism.

Fishman was born in Poland in 1876. He got his only schooling in Russian Yeshivas at Volozhin. At the age of fourteen he arrived in New York to join kinsmen; and this great city was his home for the rest of his life. But he travelled much in the European Jewish communities, especially after the First World War.

As a newcomer, he loved to prowl the crowded, noisy streets of New York's East Side and was lured to East Broadway where the Yiddish newspapers were printed. He was fascinated by the clangor of the printing presses. The smell of printer's ink made him restless. He was excited by the turmoil and disorder in the streets when the newspapers were vomited forth, there to be snatched in great haste by the newsboys, who rushed with their allotments of bundles and scattered in all directions of the East Side to sell them. In the early days there were no newsstands and the newsboys were the most important labor force a newspaper could have. They were as important as the subscribers.

It was Fishman's luck first to be a newsboy, then a helper in the editorial rooms, and finally to get a job as a reporter, first on the *Tageblatt*. The *Tageblatt* was a rigid, orthodox sheet, owned by a rigid, orthodox Jew and edited then by an unscrupulous but brilliant journalist, whose name was Johann Paley. (It was said of Paley—as of many Yiddish writers who had spent some time in London—that he was at one time a "meshumed," but on the *Tageblatt* he defended the purity of the home, the sanctity of the Sabbath and kashruth.) That job on the *Tageblatt* fixed Fishman's destiny. After he had served his apprenticeship he was recognized as a member of the fraternity of journalists. He was at home in the Café Royal, which was their rendezvous and club, the center of attraction for vagrant intellectuals or artistic kibitzers or Park Row journalists looking for material about the Jewish Ghetto. It was important for an actor or artist or musician to be known at the club of journalists.

Fishman had no personal interest in the synagogue. He lost his taste for the discussion of religious matters after he left the old country. He respected religious institutions and quite a few orthodox rabbis.

He lived his life in the Bohemia of the East Side. He knew the players of the Yiddish theatres. He rubbed elbows with artists who began their careers on the East Side, wandered off to Paris and returned to make fame or fortune, so to speak, in the United States or get lost in the Ghetto. Fishman knew the "stars" of the East Side, of all kinds— its vagabonds and panhandlers, the theatre-ticket scalpers, the petty swindlers, the purveyors of lottery tickets, the young lawyers who later became judges, the Irish ward politicians. But strange to say, he never wandered into the field of writing sketches in which these human encounters could be incorporated. He seemed to lack the imagination to create literature. He was an honest chronicler, in plain words.

In the course of time, Fishman himself became a personality. Invariably he would come to his favorite café about midnight after the *Journal* had been put to bed and ruefully scrutinize his work, frowning at irretrievable errors, praising an assistant when something had been done well, but already planning his work for the next day. He never qualified as a wit or raconteur or philosopher or theorist. He came to be known as an intelligent, reserved spectator, with an affinity for journalism. He did not specialize in the impersonation of himself in his columns and had a natural aversion for self-advertisement.

Always he seemed to be searching for a way of life he never was able to find. Among unbalanced extroverts he was an introvert. He seemed to be burdened by depressing thought; he was never satisfied with his work. He never married, but had many transient friends in the world of women. He had a deep feeling of affection for the families of his friends, their children and seemed to love them for something he had missed in his own life. He had nephews and treated a number of them as if they were his own sons.

His humor was cold and he seldom laughed heartily. In his style of writing he was a puritan, but not in his way of living. He often reprimanded the loose-minded and coarse, and was uninterested in the sexual acrobatics of Yiddish litterateurs, poets and writers of prose.

All the more, therefore, the call of Zion gave color to his personality. He was young when Herzl's call was heard in the Jewish world. Zion was not a new word to him. It had been drummed into his memory in the Yeshiva and the synagogue in the old country. He knew the old Chovevei Zionists and had read Leon Pinsker's *Auto-Emancipation* and Lilienblum and Kalischer, and could read, not without difficulty, the Hebrew literature of the day. He became a member of one of the first Zionist societies in New York. His Zionist interests were reported in his writings. He was drawn to the Federation of American Zionists, then to the Provisional Zionist Committee, then to the ZOA, on whose executive committee he served for many years. He was one of its representatives on the Actions Committee on a number of occasions and a delegate to the World Zionist Congress after the First World War.

He was a Zionist of the old school. He was curious about the political maneuvers of Herzl and Weizmann; but did not believe in politics within Zionism. He was loyal to the Zionism of responsibility and intellectual integrity. Often he did not share Weizmann's views, but was nonetheless one of his most loyal supporters and worshipers. He could always be depended upon for defense of the higher levels of Zionist policies; he was never seduced by the orators who often fulminated at Zionist conferences and Congresses.

He was, however, an ardent admirer of Jabotinsky, the orator and essayist, and brought him to the *Morning Journal* as a respected and admired contributor.

He loved Rabbi Chajes, the saintly rabbi of Vienna, and Rabbi Osias Thon of Cracow. He admired many of the European journalists and brought some of them to form the *Morning Journal*'s foreign staff. He was, in fact, what his column revealed over the years, a responsible commentator on Jewish and American affairs, dignified, fair, austere in expression, but always to be depended upon for a just appraisal of Jewish events.

The Yeshiva had made a deep impression on his personality. In its standards he saw the reflection of the old way of life, respect for learning and piety, wisdom and good manners.

His friendships in Zionism indicated his traditional habits. He had the highest veneration for Bialik, deepest affection for Shmarya Levin, respect for Sokolow, admiration for the personality of Ussishkin. But Weizmann was to him the incarnation of Zionist personality and its leadership.

As he advanced in years his loyalties became more rigid. His judgments were fixed. His women friends being transients in his life, he soon acquired the habits of a confirmed bachelor. His affections deepened and although the circle of his friends was not enlarged, a large number of younger men, introduced to journalism through his interest in them, looked up to him as a Master. They were impressed by his probity, his startling integrity, but it was impossible to penetrate the mystery of his personality.

For many years his heart had been affected. But he was not seriously concerned. He attended meetings of the Actions Committee, sessions of the World Zionist Congress, Conferences of the World Jewish Congress, and made periodic visits to Palestine.

He arrived at his last Congress in 1946, after being urged by his friends to bypass it. But he was greatly disturbed by the knowledge that this Congress would attempt to change the course of Zionist policy and bring about the fall of Weizmann's leadership. He knew that the majority of the American delegates, led by Dr. A. H. Silver, were inclined to join David Ben-Gurion in forcing Dr. Weizmann's resignation. Fishman was a member of the American delegation's minority. He felt it his duty to go to Basle, regardless of his health, if only to respond to the roll call.

Weather conditions in Basle, that winter, added to Fishman's discomfort. It was bitterly cold and the hotels lacked heat. The drafts in the Congress Hall were cruelly distressing. Many delegates fell victim to colds, pleurisy and pneumonia. It was a Congress of confusion—parties were divided and all leadership was being challenged. Principles were reduced to issues of tactics. Ben-Gurion's own party had in it a substantial majority backing Weizmann. The General Zionists felt uncomfortable with their unofficial alliance with Ben-Gurion. There was little Fishman could do. His cables to the *Morning Journal* reflected his disturbed state of mind. He was irritated and excited when he came to the caucuses.

One night he went, with a few friends, to a scrubby vaudeville house, where they chatted for hours and consumed cognac to keep warm. The show was archaic and boring. At midnight the "party" broke up, Fishman leaving for his hotel with Robert Silverman of Boston and Jacob Hodess of London, editor of the *New Judea*. Late that evening Fishman had a seizure and was taken to a hospital.

The next morning at breakfast the writer of these lines heard of Fishman's death from an English newsman. Later, at a meeting of the Political Committee, Dr. Silver, its chairman, made the announcement of Fishman's death and expressed the sense of loss of the Committee. A crowded memorial meeting was held in the lobby of the Congress Hall. That day, in the plenum of the Congress, I was allowed to speak of Fishman. I do not remember what I said. I do recall that I referred to the heart pangs I felt, as did all his friends, in recalling his life of loneliness, his singular devotion to Zionism, and his noble, aristocratic loyalty to Dr. Weizmann, and to the fact that he was privileged to die in the company of the leaders of the international Zionist fraternity.

He was not privileged to see the birth of Israel. But his eyes had witnessed, at this dismal Basle Congress, the opening of the gates of the Revolution in Zionism which was to establish Herzl's dream of a State in 1947.

The best of Fishman may be seen in the Zionist records and in the Yiddish press. In whatever he wrote or spoke, Fishman guarded the interests of Zionism, and all the enterprises in which it was engaged. In Zionist councils he was always calm and objective and respectful of the views of those who disagreed with him. His respect for truth made him strong.

Fishman never thought seriously of collecting the articles he had written, or the memories he had gathered. He never saw himself in the Gallery of Zionist Immortals. He regarded himself as a fortunate man who had been given the privilege of serving an immortal cause. He was one of the humble servants of that cause, loyal in days of trouble and rejoicing in its achievements.

MENACHEM RIBALOW (1895–1953)

Menachem Ribalow was a man of spiritual vision who dedicated himself with singular devotion to the exciting task of restoring Hebrew as the living voice of Jewish life, as the carrier of its authentic culture, as the medium through which the highest ethical ideals of a great people were meant to be expressed.

He lived in the Hebrew tradition. Hebrew was not merely another language; it was the form of utterance through which psalmist and prophet had spoken and through which the great personalities of the Jewish Renaissance interpreted Jewish ideals and Jewish hopes.

His work had its spiritual compensations. He was the intellectual director of *Hadoar* (New York) for over thirty years. It was his creation. To serve it he dedicated his heart and soul. Not only was he its editor, and its propagandist, but he was also the man who always worried about its finances. He knew that his work as writer and editor enlarged the domain of the language in which the culture of his people had its life and being; that he was helping to restore the vividness and power of the spiritual treasures of his people. He saw the Hebraic influence not only in Hebrew, but also in every expression of the authentic Jewish way of life. But as a partisan of Hebrew he nursed chronic grudges against anyone who was indifferent to the value of Hebrew in the Jewish renascence. It was his obsession and his pride.

There are Hebraists who are proud and condescending. Menachem Ribalow, however, like Bialik, whom he venerated as man and poet, loved to speak Yiddish too. But when he spoke through that humble servant of the Galuth, his overtones were always Hebrew and bound to Jewish virtues and ideals. He was not a follower of the latest styles adopted for the ancient language. He sought to maintain the traditions of the great masters of whom he was a humble disciple. He avoided as sinful the vulgarities of the new and easy phrase and strove with restless curiosity to find the precise meaning in the ancient roots of the language.

Unlike many Hebrew writers, he did not wish to live in an Ivory Tower constructed by specialists. He marched along with the Jewish people, with the organized Zionist Movement, feeling himself at home in the discussions of common objectives into which he poured his vision of the Hebraic spirit. In every discussion in which he participated, you felt the integrity of his personality, the deep sources of his inspiration, and the influence of Hebraic style.

Every book he wrote or edited and every article he admitted to the pages of *Hadoar* was an expression of the restless desire of the genuine Hebraist to bring all Jews within the sound of his voice and the meaning of his words. His reverence for Hebrew made him meticulous as an editor. His appreciation of Jewish values made him resentful of the intrusion of the common world in the domain of the higher things in Jewish life which to him were incorporated in the Zionist Movement. He did not live long enough to mellow as a personality. but to his last days retained the feeling that Hebrew was the most sacred creation of the Jewish people. That was the thesis he defended throughout his life.

BERNARD G. RICHARDS (1877–1971)

I first met Bernard G. Richards in 1901 at a Zionist Convention in Boston, when he was being trailed by a tall youngster in short pants who later was to achieve distinction as a disciple of William and Henry James and as a philosopher: Dr. Horace M. Kallen. I have known him intimately ever since then, but somehow, whenever I think of him or see him, which is quite often, my thoughts go back, not so much to him personally, as to a book he once wrote. It was called *The Discourses of Keidansky*. I have not seen it for many years, but I retain a vivid impression of its contents. I remember "Keidansky" so well, just because that sparkling character represents for me the personality of my friend Richards.

The Discourses of Keidansky was published in 1903. Many of its chapters first appeared in the *Boston Evening Transcript*, the leading daily newspaper in New England. How Richards later got into the staid *Transcript* is an engrossing story of the ambition, aptitude and zeal of a young man who came out of a Yiddish milieu and learned how to write English in a few years with remarkable freedom and idiomatic skill. This young man from Keidan was able to turn the tables on those who were then engaged in telling the Jews of the East Side how to live the American way. Richards was one of the first of that generation to rid himself of the Yiddish idiom and to tell the so-called Americans, in good English, about the Jewish way of life, and to remind them of their origins.

His book was acclaimed by the literary critics of the day. Stories were written about Richards himself—where he came from, his struggle with poverty. He was a literary sensation. He was admired and praised and encouraged by a number of the leading American writers. Julian Hawthorne predicted that he would do important and useful work in the literary field. Mitchell Kennerley, a young publisher, started *The Reader* magazine, of which Sinclair Lewis was managing editor, and invited Richards to become one of its contributors.

The Discourses of Keidansky has gone the way of many good books. It is out of print. It is a relic of the history of the times. Its ideas are out of circulation. I read the book again the other day and found—to my surprise and satisfaction—that it retains the living tang, the surprise and the pleasure, that come from meeting an old friend who retains the old spirit, the old fascination and the tempo of youth. He talked of things that are no longer in the living world. But are not many of our thoughts of things and persons who are no more, but who are still alive in memory?

In *Keidansky*, Richards created a "character" who followed the manner of Peter Dunne's "Mr. Dooley", but "Keidansky" had his own line of talk and talked from his own changeable platform. The charm of the character was not its seriousness or timeliness. It was not supposed to be logical or erudite. Good humor and satire identified the bubbling of Keidansky's thoughts. That constitutes his charm.

There were the cafés, the Yiddish theatres, and the Yiddish newspapers and their writers. There were the characters who lived in the Ghetto, fed on ideas generated elsewhere, trying futilely to create their own world. Keidansky was talking of Pinero's *Second Mrs. Tanqueray*; of Ibsen's *Doll House*; of Tolstoi's *Art*; of Abraham Cahan; of Janowsky, the anarchist; of Jacob Gordin, the Yiddish dramatist. He was performing acrobatics with themes like *The Feminine Traits of Men, The Goodness of a Bad Man, The Tragedy of Humor, The Immorality of Principle*. He was sensitive to contradiction and allergic to logic. He was practicing the art of paradox, which was done to death by the brilliance of Israel Zangwill and the cynicism of Oscar Wilde. Keidansky was sitting on the fence with regard to Zionism, but if any Bundist or Comrade or Yahudi talked against Zionism, Keidansky got off the fence at once and let them have it good and plenty. How innocent all the talk about Zionism was in 1903! How far off it sounds now!

The Yiddish theatre is now dead. Gordin left no heir and Jacob P. Adler no successor. The descendants of the old Yiddish actors have left the East Side and may be found in the movies or on Broadway, and the Café Royale closed its doors forever about 1948. The old Ghetto made room for the clearance of the slums. East Broadway and Grand Street are no longer recognizable as Jewish streets, nor is the Boston ghetto what it was then. The old cafés have lost their identity. The kibitzers are not the same kind of people, and who would want to go to a café even if there were kibitzers, with the radio and television in the home and the movies just around the corner? Scattered on Broadway you will still find some of the old waiters of Schmuckler's, Zeitlin's and Gertner's, who have faint, inaccurate memories of the old café life. They tell the weirdest stories of the people they saw there.

Keidansky stopped talking because he had lost his audience and had nothing more to talk about. The scenery and the actors changed. In fact, the Ghetto graduated; its people scattered in all directions; they are to be found in Brooklyn, the Bronx, Queens, Westchester. Their children are on the American stage, in the American Writers' Guild, among the columnists and the commentators, the scenario writers and the writers of the latest novels. They are to be found on the faculties of colleges and universities, among the actors and the singers and the comedians on Broadway. If they have cafés at all they may be found at Lindy's or Ruben's or the night clubs. What has happened to them has happened to the cafés of Vienna and Warsaw and Berlin. Life has moved away from the old places. They were not destroyed by the Nazis; but just rotted and faded away.

Destiny forced Richards to abandon Keidansky and turn to Jewish public life. His puppet could not be relied upon for a stable living. For a time he was the editor of the *New Era* magazine; then with Jacob de Haas he got out *The Chronicler*, a weekly publication which struggled and died in its infancy. His connection with public affairs started with the *Kehillah*. He was its executive secretary, with Dr. Judah L. Magnes as its chairman. For a number of years he fought for the Kehillah movement and with Dr. Magnes on account of it. Dr. Magnes had taken up the Kehillah idea after his official devotion to Zionism had cooled off. He was the first banner-bearer of democratic revolt against the founders of the American Jewish Committee. Then he deserted the flag and was regarded as a "lost leader." Theoretically a democrat, in practice he had no confidence in what was called "the masses" and gradually became the representative in the Kehillah of the philanthropists, and was smothered there in their warm embrace. This put Richards and all supporters of the democratic idea out on a limb. The treasury was taken away from the "masses." But Jewish politics at that time were not as brutal as they became later, and Richards settled his affairs with the Kehillah in amiable fashion and moved into the American Jewish Congress, which was also a revolt against the philanthropists. There he remained for many years, going to Versailles with the Jewish delegation, holding on to the "rump" Congress with amazing tenacity until the advent of Hitler. When he retired from the Congress he was involved in the fortunes of the Democratic Party and had an office in Washington where he labored for the leadership of Franklin D. Roosevelt for many years. He was the Jewish specialist in Democratic circles. In recent years he built up the Jewish Information Bureau, from which he conducts his varied affairs.

From this sketch it is apparent that Richards lost contact with "Keidansky" because he was absorbed in other interests and never looked back to locate and find him. He wrote articles on Jewish themes; he contributed to magazines and helped compile several Jewish books; and having a retentive memory became an expert on matters historical in American Jewry. Keidansky receded into the distance and became dimmer and dimmer with the years. Richards did not write the promised novel, had no time to give to the writing of essays in which he was a master. He became, to all appearances, a staid burgher of the new day, wondering where in blazes he and the post-war world were drifting to! His humor lost its bite.

But if you get Richards aside these days—not in an East Side café, but somewhere further uptown—and you get to talking with him off the record, you see in his twinkling eyes the volatile Keidansky looking out at you. There Keidansky looks for paradox and makes startling references to causes and personalities; there he still is capable of hearty laughter (touched with cynicism, why not?). There with the eyes and spirit Keidansky reveals himself. He still finds fault and praises the young creative talents with cautious judgment, and so far as you are concerned, you will agree that when you see Richards, Keidansky is as young and as alive as he ever was.

CHONA* (1886–1966)

During the life he spent with us, the renowned Mr. Chona was frequently mentioned in the Jewish press, but he was never formally presented in a manner even faintly in accord with his dignity. His wisecracks were quoted, but exotic mystery veiled his engaging personality. Many who were acquainted with him were not so sure that they really knew him. He never appeared as a speaker on a platform, though he invited himself onto many a dais and often fixed orators with his inscrutable glare from the front row of the auditorium. The fact is that Chona was a vagrant. He was a jester who told the Truth which nobody asked for. He was the Ace Reporter in the Grapevine News Service.

Chona made his start in Warsaw, where he was born in 1886 of incredibly poor parents. He did not remember ever having gone to school, and to this very day he reads even a Yiddish newspaper with difficulty. (It is amazing to note what he was able to do with this handicap.)

His childhood was spent in the streets and alleys. He was an urchin when he joined a strike of Jewish workmen and sat in a Warsaw jail, unable to find a sponsor to bail him out. He grew into a sturdy, aggressive, bold and reckless fellow, and came to be known as Chona, the Terrible. His face and figure made him formidable in controversy. He crashed into meetings, jostling his way to the front. He loitered about the editorial rooms of Yiddish newspapers, finally becoming an errand boy. Then he was a revolutionist in the ranks of labor, often browbeating timid writers and dominating the scene in many cafés. Finally Warsaw became too hot - and too small - for Chona. He decided

* His full name was Elhanan Mozdof (Ed.)

to become a wanderer seeking world experience. He left his father's
house and travelled to Canada, where he joined an elder brother.
He had to disavow this blood relative as an exploiter of Jewish labor.
(His brother disowned him when he died, years later.)

After a number of sensational and bizarre adventures (it was even
rumored that he had married in Toronto, which he indignantly denied),
Chona travelled across the border into the United States. In leisurely
fashion he reached the great metropolis of New York where he rested
his tired flat feet for a long while. Here he cut a swath of unconventional
behavior. He was an unruly spectator at Zionist mass meetings, a
vendor of Zionist party newspapers and a *kibitzer* in cafés. He was
no respecter of persons, but had ceased to be "the Terrible"; instead
he acquired the title of Chona, *Der Bewusster* (the Renowned), and
began to consider the amenities of speech and social manners. He
hobnobbed with judges, writers, actors, lawyers, tailors and waiters.
He argued with Bundists and Zionists, high and low, and declared
he was no snob. He saw through the veneer of class, and could always
identify the Person under any and all disguises. He knew human nature
and guessed what it was good for and what evil it was capable of. He
could identify a charlatan from a distance. Blindfolded, hearing a
voice, he could tell whether it was the voice of a good Jew, of a good
Zionist, of a good Socialist, or of a "Yahudi." His verdict in such
matters was unassailable. He never missed the mark.

When he was saturated with American experiences, he took a trip
to the old country. He visited Paris, Berlin and Vienna en route. When
he returned to his birthplace, he brought with him gifts from the New
York *landsleit*, left a purse with his astonished old father and meandered
over to Palestine to see the *chalutzim* at work. He went to the Zionist
Congress in Switzerland, then returned to New York, evidently for
the purpose of arranging his affairs in order to settle in Zion. Having
been provided with a fund by a circle of admiring friends (who stipulated
that he could draw upon the fund only in Tel Aviv), he went away
—he guaranteed—to live out his days in the land of his forefathers. He
was to become integrated in the Promised Land. This happened long
before the British abandoned Palestine and the Arabs invaded it,
before the Jewish State was born.

While he admired the devotion of the *chalutzim*, providing loud
applause at all meetings where their achievements were described and
listening gravely to the discussion of their problems, he felt uncomfortable in a land where everybody without exception, identified Zionism

with hard manual labor. This was a doctine which he had never permitted to become linked with his brand of Socialism. It was not so easy to be an habitué of cafés in such a land. As a matter of fact, it was embarrassing: it jarred his self-assurance. He found it impossible to *kibitz* the players in this particular game. His ideology was confused, so his wisdom, too, dried up; his wit sickened and refused to function—and he realized that the *galut* needed him. Without regrets, he left Tel Aviv.

It was on the eve of World War II in Europe. He still had his American passport and, with some difficulty, returned to New York and once more breathed freely in the freedom of the American *galut*. This was where he belonged, and he decided that he would remain. His admiring friends, who had contributed to the fund which was to keep him in Tel Aviv, remonstrated with him: had he not agreed to avoid exile and stay put in Zion? But Chona had to repudiate his guarantee and —like it or not—his friends had to adjust themselves to the situation.

Chief among his virtues was Chona's loyalty. He was loyal to Jewish labor wherever it rose to the surface - but that did not mean that Chona's hands were meant for work. He insisted that the Revolution must provide a proper place for the Intelligentsia, and he most emphatically regarded himself as a member of that class. His eligibility was established by the fact that he lived by his wits. And in view of the fact that every poet was entitled to his Maecenas, why shouldn't Chona have the right to accept patronage when it was offered as a tribute to talent?

Friend and foe alike had to admit that he brightened the corner where he stood with sallies of wit and cynical gibes. He was loyal to Zionism, but he was very strict as to the kind of Zionism he gave his allegiance to. He had a long list of spurious Zionists whom he despised. But once his loyalty was aroused, he clung to it to the point of self-effacement.

His world was divided into two parts. The larger part was the world of *goyim,* and he had no share in it at all. The smaller part was the Jewish world, and that was where he belonged. He never mixed the two. He lived in *galut* and did not complain, but wished it were a little smaller for his own personal convenience.

But though he did no work, his was a busy life. He was on the move day and night. His chief business was to avoid responsibility: since Hitler had destroyed his *landsleit* in Poland, he owed allegiance to no kith or kin. His own life was a small bundle of thrifty habits. To see and hear, to understand and appreciate, to analyze and judge what others were doing—and to tell the truth about it—that was his function in this now-confused world. He had no hand in making or marring life in the diaspora. He had done a little to help in the building of Zion, but nothing to brag about. He was the witness, the bystander, the critic, the mocker. His aloofness enabled him to tell what was wrong with all that he saw and heard. He was so clairvoyant that he could often guess what you were thinking merely by looking you in the eye.

He kept all personal matters—even where he lived and the state of his health—in an inner vault which few were able to penetrate. The only financial situation he revealed was his ever-present deficit.

Second Avenue was his Champs Elysées and the Café Royal his Café de la Paix. Every morning at nine or ten he walked up the Avenue as if he had a business appointment with God knows whom. That was pretense. He had no appointment on hand; he had all the time in the world. His arrival anywhere, at any time, was sheer accident. By the time he ended his promenade, he had read the headlines of every Yiddish newspaper, had spoken to scores of Yiddish actors and writers, had hailed a number of passers-by, and had come to certain conclusions as to how matters stood with the Russians, what was wrong with the Zionist movement, the politics of Yiddish newspapers, and which Yiddish theatres would open or close. He lumbered into the Café Royal to rest his feet and called for a glass of tea; and whoever was within reach of his voice was welcome to hear what he had to say —and pick up the check.

The final chapter of Chona's biography was begun when he left for Palestine again shortly before the State of Israel came into being. He had decided that the time had come for him to make The Great Decision. Some Zionists were saying that with so much to be done Chona should join the revolution and go to work. Thinking of this prospect, Chona was choked with terror.

So he persuaded some friends to make an investment with the Jewish National Fund which would provide that the income should go to Chona in Palestine—*only* in Palestine. An extra bonus was added in view of the prevailing high prices in the Yishuv. He outfitted himself with a substantial wardrobe of shirts, suits and the specially-made shoes he required, and after arranging for the shipment of some food packages, he left these shores and settled down in the vicinity of Tel Aviv.

Hayarkon Street and the area surrounding the Habimah Theatre now became the scene of his new life and his daily promenades. But he had come at the wrong time. This was no period for contemplation or serene reminiscence. Chona had to live through the most turbulent period in the history of the Yishuv. He saw the "illegal" refugees pouring into the land, while the British tried in vain to stem the tide. He was there when the King David Hotel was blown up. He saw the British finally leave at Haifa, and he heard Ben-Gurion proclaim the independence of Israel. He dodged bullets and bombs during the war with the Arabs. He was present at the opening of the first Knesset, greeted the first Speaker, *Chaver* Joseph Sprinzak, and thereafter became a frequent visitor in thé Parliament's lobbies. He loitered about some of the "friendly" cafés and disdainfully passed by those which had not valued his presence and had shooed him away. At the same time he became a frequent guest of the Habimah and hobnobbed with the actors, whom he had met in New York.

He became, in effect, an unregistered dragoman, specializing in American and Canadian visitors. For Chona it was no great accomplishment to know just where and when to find these tourists—he possessed a highly-refined instinct in such matters. When he located a prospective client, he attached himself; and, as a man of leisure with no special business to transact, he indicated his willingness to go along wherever the vistor happened to be going. Having established good relations, Chona took charge of the victim: showing him where to go, where to eat, how to get transportation—and when the visitor prepared to depart, Chona would stand by with studied disinterest until he was offered a few pounds for his cooperation. When the sum was not large enough, he shrugged his shoulders and departed contemptuously, leaving his client conscious of having committed a serious social error.

He felt, however, that he was being transformed. He was no longer Chona, the Proletarian—that was certain. He consorted with the Bourgeoisie and mixed in circles that were above class and party. He was uneasy. Everything in Israel was hustle and change. Thousands of new people poured onto the streets. What party did he belong to? Was he American or Polish? His Hebrew was inadequate and Yiddish was not what it used to be. Not to work in New York was not the same as not working in Tel Aviv.

So far as Chona was concerned, he was still aware of a *golus* which was peculiarly his own. He carried his "exile" with him—even in Zion. It was in his blood.

In September, 1950, I was in Jerusalem. Chona honored me with a visit in the lobby of the King David Hotel, where Ben-Gurion was to greet about fifty American visitors. He looked good—burly, sun-burned, well-dressed and with a new set of teeth. He knew many of the visitors who had come for the emergency meeting, but his greetings were not as spirited or as cordial as they once were at Zionist Congresses or in New York. Austerity was dragging his spirits down. He had lost his pitch.

When I came to Tel Aviv, I found a book of cartoons waiting for me, in which Chona—his feet very conspicuous—occupied the page ahead of Weizmann and Ben-Gurion.

The last time I met Chona was in November, 1956, when Israel was engaged in the Sinai Campaign. Those were exciting days. The exaltation of all Israel was remarkable. After the few days of victorious conquest, it seemed as if a general holiday had been proclaimed. There were still blackouts, and a shortage of gas, excitement all day long, radio messages, and uniformed men moving about aimlessly. At a reception given to me by the Histadrut, Chona was present. He looked radiant. His face was ruddy. As usual, he pushed himself forward to a front seat close to me and spent the evening looking at me reproach-fully. I had neglected and forgotten him. It was rumored that he was married but his spouse was not present. It was said that he still had no occupation, but managed to find friends among the American tourists. He was isolated from the "fellaheen" and regarded by his Labor friends as a comrade who had to be explained. He was still unruly and intrusive and capable of grim humor. He was a custodian of the past and lived on the fringe of the present, clinging desperately to his vanishing world.

In 1957 I heard from Isaac Carmel that Chona had provided himself with a grave he preferred to occupy after he had finished with this life. It is a site near the grave of Trumpeldor, the hero of Tel Hai. He also left with Kfar Blum a reserve fund on which they paid him a fixed interest, with the understanding that on his death the money was to revert to Kfar Blum and a section of a library in the kibbutz was to bear his name.

CYRUS ADLER (1863–1940)

It may be incongruous to include Cyrus Adler in any gallery of Zionist profiles. He would have resented it and requested its exclusion. He was Zionism's critic from its beginning in 1897 to beyond the Balfour Declaration; and when the extended Jewish Agency came into being in 1929—and he had had some share in its creation—he thought he was entitled to heckle a movement in which he had no creative part.

He was a man of faith. The tradition of Zion and Jerusalem was woven into his Judaism, but as happened to others, the projection of the reality of the tradition was too much of a shock, and his first reaction was to reject it with anger. He should have been a Zionist by reason of his faith, for he was a Sephardi. There were many Sephardim in the American movement who affirmed Zionism, like Henry Pereira Mendes, Sabato Morais, or Meldola DeSola of Montreal, who could get terribly excited about Sabbath observance or *kashrut*. Cyrus Adler loved the formal, the ritual, the traditional; but emotion seldom shook him.

Therefore he was a stranger to the birth of Zionism and always resentful of its existence and its successes. It was something he regarded as illegitimate, premature, out of order, not ordained. He disliked Theodor Herzl from the start and, having lived in Constantinople for some time, he derided the notion that Turkey could be persuaded to consider granting a charter for Jewish colonization in Palestine. It irked him to think that a Viennese litterateur who was in no way recognized by him as Jewish was being hailed as a Messiah. The only thing that recommended Herzl was his beard, which was a Viennese convention.

Dr. Adler achieved prominence early in life as a social worker in educational enterprises and as a quasi-political observer of Jewish life. He was connected with the management of the Jewish Theological Seminary, with the American Jewish Relief Committee (the Joint), and in the affairs of the American Jewish Committee. He functioned under cover of various institutions. He was the editor of the *Jewish Quarterly Review*. He was the president of both the Dropsie College and, after the death of Solomon Schechter, of the Jewish Theological Seminary. He was the active chairman of one of the most important committees of the Joint, which dealt with the relief of Jewish religious institutions in Eastern Europe. After the death of Louis Marshall, he succeeded to the presidency of the American Jewish Committee. He was a very successful heir-apparent. At one time he was connected with the Smithsonian Institution in Washington. He must have regarded with embarrassment an aberration of his youth in the form of "Coffee House Sketches" written with Allan Ramsay about life in Constantinople. But through the affectionate interest of his uncle, Judge Mayer Sulzberger, he entered the field of Jewish educational enterprises. He had an aptitude for administration and great respect for order, plan, budget and sober deliberation—slow thinking, slow acting. He was first interested in the Jewish Publication Society, to whose modest beginnings he made a major contribution. He was what could be called a first-class managing director. He was the right-hand man—for specific tasks—of Judge Sulzberger, Jacob H. Schiff, Louis Marshall and later of Felix M. Warburg. Through association with these leaders in Jewish affairs and in loyal service rendered in the promotion of causes in which they were interested, Dr. Adler rose to the position of leadership.

Although in no sense of the term a theologian or scholar, he lived his life in association with the Conservative forces in Judaism. He resisted innovation. He refused to lend himself to any form of action in which overemphasis or sharp distinction or controversy was an ingredient. He felt that in any change in Jewish forms basic principles would be disturbed and washed away in time. He believed in ceremony and the habitual and hesitated to acquire new habits and to direct his life into new paths for fear that he might lose his way. He was old when he was young and became mellow when he was old. In his youth he was a cynic on general principles. He discounted the value of adventure or novelty or revolution in either intellectual or social affairs. He was a conservator, not a creator. Thus in the Jewish Theological Seminary he did not venture to replace Dr. Schechter, nor did he seek to dominate its intellectual life. He rendered great service in maintaining to the best of his ability the institute of learning Dr. Schechter had created and added greatly to its equipment and buildings, its library, its faculty and its endowments. He was the guardian of the temple of learning, not its prophet or priest.

He resisted Zionism for fear that it would lead to the secularization of Jewish life. He would have avowed his love for the Holy Land in the old traditional ways if there were no Zionists to take advantage of his confession. He was reluctant to be seen in their company or to be mistaken as a member of their fraternity or as an admirer of any of their leaders, even, for that matter, of the American leader, Brandeis, whose conversion to Zionism he always regarded as motivated by personal ambitions. But these negative views did not check his interest in and affection for every trace of Jewish influence in the Holy Land— his interest in the Yeshivot, its learned rabbis, its archaeological records, the Wailing Wall, about which he wrote a memorandum in 1930 submitted to the League of Nations on behalf of the Jewish Agency. Nor did it prevent his giving generous support to the new creative Jewish life in Palestine, especially those aspects that appealed to his religious sensibilities.

He refused to go along with the democratic trends in Jewish life. He favored the formation of the American Jewish Committee on a strictly personal basis. He deprecated the *Kehillah* movement, which aimed to organize the New York Jewish community on a democratic basis. He denounced the American Jewish Congress and was angry indeed when the World Jewish Congress was formed in 1936. In American politics he was a liberal Democrat and protested his liberalism on many occasions. But he seemed to think that democracy was an alien notion in Jewish life. In Jewish matters he was controlled by a communal tradition integrated in religious practices and in forms of defense that had their origin in the Middle Ages. He seemed to think that Jewish life should be ordered in the spirit and mood of a religious service in a Sephardic synagogue, where ritual and ceremony are hallowed by time and Divine sanction and where disorder and controversy are an offense to sanctity. It seemed to him that Jewish life had to be lived unobtrusively, bending before storms and avoiding struggle, and relying upon Divine guidance and intervention in all mundane existence. Where God presided, majority votes had no binding effect and should be disregarded as a matter of piety.

But all this did not restrain him from following the lead of Louis Marshall in supporting the Versailles demands of the Committee of Jewish Delegations with regard to Jewish minority rights. Dr. Adler was there unofficially for the American Jewish Committee and could not resist the influence of the Jewish nationalists and Zionists. Nor did he hold aloof from the efforts of Dr. Weizmann to enlarge the Jewish Agency for Palestine. Here, too, Louis Marshall set the pace, but Dr. Adler followed with a genuine personal interest and later became a devotee of the program of the Jewish Agency. In his later years—more especially after the untimely death of Marshall—he participated in a number of Zionist enterprises and was aligned with specific Zionist policies in matters bearing upon British interpretations of the Mandate. He soon was not so keen in dissociating himself from the ideological implications of his new course. He gave his name and support to many Zionist protests against the violation of our rights in Palestine and evinced a keen interest in every phase of Zionist development. But he continued to disclaim Zionism. Even the term non-Zionist irritated him. He did not know how to escape from his dilemma. Finally, he gave up trying. There was involved in his thinking

a chain of ideas nurtured in the days of his youth that ran parallel
with the second chain of ideas born out of the secular experience of
a lifetime. He loved the old concepts, the old ways; there was sentiment,
there was all that he venerated in life, and he could not let it go. But
life also had its pressures, so he often turned away from the traditions
of his youth and compromised with reality.

While leader of the American Jewish Committee, Dr. Adler did
not maintain the vigor and forensic skill which was the distinguishing
trait of Louis Marshall's advocacy of Jewish causes. In discussion
Marshall was splendid when he took the offensive, but in defense
he was often complicated and confused. Dr. Adler, however, was not
an advocate. He could marshal his case in writing with great effectiveness. He built up a better administration for the American Jewish
Committee. He extended its program and influence and kept his group
constantly within the lines originally laid out in its earlier days. He
never ventured in a big way and never gained much for the record.
But he also never receded from a position he had once taken. He refused
to bend to democracy. He was faithful to the old staid procedures.
He disdained open struggle in domestic affairs, although his world
seemed to crumble and new forms blocked his way more and more.

In his last years he sensed that a new world was being born, but
he seemed content to continue his old habits without protest during
the remaining days of his long life. When he was young he was critical
and caustic, dictatorial and intolerant, but with old age a desire controlled him to live among his brethren in an atmosphere of peace.
He became friendly with old adversaries, enjoyed a whisky and soda
in the English manner and was a good conversationalist. He hated
pilpul. Once the writer sat with him at a meeting of the Jewish Agency
and heard his comments on the speakers. Dr. Adler wanted the right
to intervene and make a motion to close the debate. When he was
told that to move to close the debate while the list of speakers was
not yet exhausted would be a hazardous undertaking, he snorted and
said, "What *are* we really coming to!" He could not imagine Jews
having a parliamentary procedure of their own. He did not know
that Zionist procedure was taken from Austrian practices.

PIERRE VAN PAASSEN (1895–1968)

As far back as November 8, 1929, Pierre Van Paassen's devotion
to Zionism was commended in *The New Palestine.* The note was written

by Maurice Samuel or Meyer W. Weisgal. Those were the days in American Zionism when praise of a friend was expected to be restrained. The editorial note was brief and to the point and read as follows:

"There is one journalist who stands above the mountains of dispatches as an observer of extraordinary keenness, as an analyst of unusual depth. His name is Pierre Van Paassen, correspondent of the New York *Evening World*. The name of Van Paassen is not new to the Jewish public. For many years he has been a close student of Jewish affairs, and has acquired a thorough knowledge of Zionist history and Zionist problems. In November 1929 he was sent to Palestine by the New York *Evening World* to survey what had transpired. His reports were models of sympathetic understanding of the crisis through which Palestine was passing. Van Paassen's dispatches had a background of facts that no other Christian correspondent seemed to have. He knew the significance of every colony, the intricacies of every Zionist problem, the history of Arab-Jewish relations. There were times when he criticized Jewish work; but his criticism was the product of an impartial, objective mind. . . . In Van Paassen the Jewish people have an important friend—not of the usual type, but of the kind rarely found in Christian circles."

Van Paassen was discovered by Isaac Carmel (then working for the Keren Hayesod) who found him chained to a journalist's desk in Atlanta, Georgia. Carmel claims that he recognized Van Paassen at once as a kindred soul. In those days Christian friends were scarce. I remember many years ago, a Seventh-Day Adventist from Scotland who went around the United States on his own, preaching the doctrine of the Return of the Jews to the Holy Land as the inevitable climactic event of Christian prophecy. Incidentally, he also collected money for the Jewish National Fund. The advent of Pierre Van Paassen, an American journalist on his way to fame and a Christian minister, was greeted with great satisfaction in Zionist circles.

Over the years Van Paassen has spoken to hundreds of Zionist groups in hundreds of cities. He has been with us at Zionist conventions and conferences, at Zionist Congresses and in Palestine, many times. But Zionists know him not only as a speaker on the platform, as the companion after a meeting in a coffee shop, as a guest in their homes. They know of the fascinating books he has written in which are reflected the life-studies of an eager mind, expressions of a deeply religious faith, a genuine understanding of Hebraic ideals; and also the temperament of a fast-burning crusader. They know of the obstinacy of his struggle to help in the defense of Jewish rights, and his advocacy of Jewish freedom from the first days of Hitler, through the war that led to the defeat of fascism and the victory of the democratic world. He has been author, lecturer, preacher and advocate in and out of Jewish life, at times bitterly critical and denunciatory, but more often full of faith in his vision of the great day that awaited the Chosen People. In fact his identification with Jewish destiny was so marked that it was suspected that he must be a reincarnation of a wandering Jewish soul that had lost its way and was going through the purgatories of time in various disguises in order finally to achieve his true destiny in the bosom of Father Abraham. He uses Hebrew with an ease that often creates the queer impression that he may even be a Conservative rabbi.

He was one of the valiant soldiers in our Foreign Legion, when his anger blazed up with the birth of Hitler's Germany. In that struggle the greatness of his soul was manifest in the way he fought, as if he personally were outraged and humiliated; he could not be controlled or coordinated or kept in order. He was a roving correspondent for the *Evening World*, which gave him his first opportunity to wander in and out of the European scene and to witness with his own eyes the growth of aggression and tyranny and destruction against people and things. He seemed to be standing on his own platform, turning from Christians to Jews, from statesmen to politicians, to public opinion in general, with impassioned warnings, the exposure of a bankrupt morality and the presentation of an angry indictment of Christian civilization for abdicating from the throne of spiritual authority it had once assumed.

His personality came from Holland. Its original colors still cling to him unmistakably, for he is Dutch in his courage and obstinacy, Dutch in his loyalty to God and to principle, Dutch in his sensitiveness to the demands of humanity. He spent seven of the most impressionable years of his life in a school with this inscription on its shield: "Here is a school with the Bible. The Fear of the Lord is the Beginning of Wisdom."

Who among us has not read his "Days of Our Years"? It was a startling revelation in 1939, and reached an international public of large dimensions.

His encounters with the Italian dictator Mussolini were written with remarkable attention to personal details, and his dialogue with Mussolini sounded like the makings of an exciting play. He exposed the actor behind the mask of the false Caesar. You read his interview with the aged Clemenceau and not only discover the features of a master of French political thought—but you marvel at the skill and insight of a greatly talented literary portraitist. Nothing like his description of the personality of the Mufti of Jerusalem has ever appeared in book form; or like his description of the Jewish villages pogromed by Arab hordes under the Mufti's orders, or like his sharp encounters with cynical British officials.

"Days of Our Years" helped greatly to establish Van Paassen as a political and social observer and a literary artist of the first order. It shows him as a man of vast knowledge and humility and compassion, unable to be gentle with wrongdoing, attacking hypocrisy and political chicanery without mercy.

We shall never forget his "Forgotten Ally." This tour de force was a timely and effective intervention in our struggle with the Mandatory Power.

In the present mad rush of historic events, we forget how England settled its affairs in Palestine, what irresponsible and cynical acts were committed before it gave up its trusteeship and shipped its army to other fields.

There was a direct connection between the concentration camps in Germany and the Promised Land: Jews were being destroyed at both ends.

Van Paassen has never been a conventional friend. He was never a conformist. He gave generously of his own thought, his own understanding of polemical strategy, but would not take directives. He created his own weapons of offense and defense and used them in his own way. He was unpredictable. On a number of occasions he intruded in heated controversy and seemed to be standing alone against the world.

He has his own ideals about the kind of state Israel should be. He is excited by the Fulfillment and has a vision of Israel's destiny. Is it to be a nation like other nations? Or a nation of prophets and priests dedicated to the service of God, lending a hand in evoking a New Revelation? Will it give a New Look to the Torah? Is Judaism to be reborn? Or is Judaism to remain tied to the rigid forms created in Exile? Instead of lifting themselves up to the heights will the Israelis now fall back into the confusion of the days of cold wars, the materialism of self-interest, looking to high grade bombs for salvation; will they make terms with the world as it is and sacrifice all for the sake of the security of their Statehood? Who or what shall rule in Israel reborn—a constitution or party or economic need—or shall God return to be the Shepherd of His flock?

Van Paassen seems to be nursing and nurturing a spirit of revolt and protest, thinking of entering a powerful dissent against the lowering of the sights of Israel and of Zionism. But whatever he may be thinking, we respect him in all his moods, in all his prophetic excitements, whether he be genial or angry, disciplined or free; for all his traits go to make a man of stature, a friend of great capacities, whose record of service illuminates the pages of Jewish history.

MEYER W. WEISGAL (1894–   )

It would be timely for Meyer W. Weisgal to abondon the prompter's box and appear in person. His way of life has not changed to any great extent recently. The Weizmann Institute grows more beautiful and important fron year to year. His habits are fairly stabilized; but the passing of the years since the death of his great Hero, with nothing to distinguish one semester from another, has become monotonous and unbearable. He sees nothing memorable for him to create; he cannot overcome the virus of ambition and restlessness. For his own good health, he should emerge from anonymity, wearing the livery of no cause, proclaiming no project and avoiding reference to any fund and speak in his own voice for himself. Nothing much has altered him personally except that his black hair is streaked with gray. There is more wisdom and humor in his features and he is a bit bowed down, but his energy is all there and his vision is clear. He is as effervescent as ever.

His hometown was Kikol, his first landing place the Bronx and his last Rehovoth, in the Weizmann Garden of Science. He started as a breezy, aggressive, argumentative youth, neither subdued by authority nor respectful toward law and order. He never believed in the still, small voice and does not now. He overshouts it. He is the master of the colorful vocabulary in Yiddish and English, shocking to the blue-stockings and delightful to the connoisseurs of jargons. He came from an apprenticeship in a Zionist group in the Bronx in which it was difficult to breathe. He was seduced from nibbling at courses at Columbia University and was taken into the Zionist offices on trial as a handyman, free to find his own destiny in the maze of Zionist activity which was at that time concentrated in the Zionist Federation and later in the

Provisional Zionist Committee. He flung himself into this jungle with a frown on his face, inquisitive, impatient, irrepressible, disputatious, with outbursts of hearty laughter, challenging queries and loud invective. By chance or design he discovered the way to the vacant chair of the migratory editor of "The Maccabean," our first English monthly magazine; he took possession of it without authority and held it against all invaders. He became the contact man with the printer. He found the copy, brought it to the linotyper, received the galley sheets and read the proofs. He was intoxicated by the smell of printer's ink. With the joy of the discoverer, he saw the first damp copies off the press; and then and there he fell in love with journalism and the art of printing. This was the exciting life that beckoned to him, this was his convulsive beginning in Zionism.

It was his good fortune to join the Zionist fraternity when its provincial isolation was at an end. The invasion of our shores by Europe's celebrities began to provide our activities with color and fascination and a vision of great Jewries far off, more advanced than we in knowledge of Zionism and things Jewish. They were the first to bring distant Palestine to us, and the intricate mesh of Zionist thought. Men of expansive personality came to our stage and were our guest stars. They were speakers and lecturers and promoters of Palestine enterprises; but more than that, they gave us the pleasure of their dynamic presence as guests in restaurants and coffee shops, in homes, in the lobbies after their meetings, and helped to make us feel like members of a great international fraternity engaged in a long heroic struggle, the end of which no one could foresee. They brought with them the smells and sounds and the wisdom and wit of foreign lands and of things almost forgotten, which they revived.

I think Shmarya Levin was the first. Our encounter with him was like colliding with a streak of lightning; he created unrest and was intoxicating in his effects; he nourished us with his wit and wisdom for many years; he made Yiddish a language of great animation. We greeted Franz Oppenheimer—tall, erect, his face marked with duel scars, looking like a Prussian colonel but telling the story of Merhavia, the first Zionist co-operative colony, and seeking funds for its operation. We saw Ben Zion Mossinsohn, who was distinguished by a beard like Herzl's and was the first public orator who harangued us in Hebrew, which few of us understood. We met Nahum Sokolow, the well-groomed diplomat who knew all languages and had a phenomenal memory for history and anecdote and a talent for shrewd descriptions of personalities. Boris Schatz, the sculptor, came to us to promote the interests of the Bezalel Art School and gave us our first Palestine art exhibit, most of it his own.

Meyer brushed shoulders with all these talented men. Listening to their speeches and conversations refreshed his knowledge of the old home; he was beside himself with excitement, unable to find words to express his delight at becoming a part of the wheel of Jewish destiny, and eager to turn with it, faster and faster, and go with it wherever God would take him.

His career really began the day he adopted *The Maccabean*. He did not like the way it looked. He hated its monotonous appearance. He altered its format; he gave it an illustrated cover and better paper. He began looking around for writers whom he could persuade to write for the glory of it, with no thought of money. He avoided having his name appear as editor, but the office staff knew that he was the man behind everything that appeared in the magazine—the words, the music and the color. He discovered Boardman Robinson, a brilliant cartoonist then on *The New York Morning Telegraph*, and later distinguished for his political cartoons in *The New York Tribune*. He induced Robinson to caricature some of the issues in which we were then involved. A domestic war was on against the higher bourgeoisie concerning the American Jewish Congress. Robinson's latent radicalism found a vent in this war, which he played up as a conflict of classes. He made the leaders of the American Jewish Committee look like traditional, well-fed capitalists. His zeal brought down on us the wrath of many of our own constituents who felt this was going a little too far, for were they not also on their way to becoming capitalists?

But Meyer fought back with savage resentment; having the last word with the printer he would present the finished product and demand to know what in the hell could be wrong with such brilliant cartoons and articles by celebrities that helped to make *The Maccabean* attractive, readable and controversial. How else would Zionism make headway? It was fortunate for Meyer that Robinson listened to the call of the wild; Robinson was on the verge of being guillotined by us when the wanderlust seized him and his stalwart figure disappeared from our Zionist world. He became a distinguished painter.

This might be called Meyer's apprentice days. He found that he had the skill of an artist, the eyes and ears of an editor, and that he could stand up for what he wanted. He was a very obstinate and demanding individual. (The first bonus he earned in Zionism was Shirley, one of the brightest and prettiest members of our staff, who married him.) When destiny led us to the Cleveland Convention in which the controversy between the Brandeis group and the Weizmann group was fought out in democratic fashion, it was inevitable that in our campaign we should use a newly launched publication called *The New Maccabean,* with Meyer as manager of the temporary enterprise. That was his grand opportunity. *The New Maccabean* appeared weekly until the day of the Convention. It had a circulation of over 30,000. It was edited for argument and conversion, for the discussion of principles, and for appealing to our constituents. It was lively, dignified and clear in text. It presented the issues without personal abuse, distortion, or vulgarity. It was strange that the Brandeis group, which included able lawyers, eloquent speakers and good writers should not have come out with a publication of their own; and that it should have been out-classed by our small opposition group. The Brandeis group not only lost in the vote; its prestige was substantially depreciated. To a large extent the victory at Cleveland was due to the propaganda of *The New Maccabean.*

If you look back at the old issues of *The New Palestine* (1921–1930), which was the successor of *The New Maccabean,* you will be impressed by the editorial skill and the good taste in printing that Meyer was able to produce at a time when all Zionist and Jewish publications were amateurish in content and in form. He maintained a dignified front; he had fine literary skill in the selection and editing of articles and in the general appearance of the magazine. Its contributors were drawn fron the best writers in England, Germany and the United States. There was nothing stiff in what they wrote. Its discussions were easy to read. It was excitingly polemical. Its news was objective, restrained and concise. Among its contributors were Winston Churchill, Ramsay MacDonald, Leon Blum, Leopold S. Amery, and Herbert Sidebotham. Meyer always looked for "star" writers and got them regardless of cost. Zionism began to have an expanding budget and a payroll. There were important special numbers, which were comprehensive discussions of timely subjects. There was a Hebrew University issue in 1925, which is still a literary production of substantial merit. He edited the Herzl Memorial Issue of *The New Palestine* (1929) which for the first time contained a large section of the diaries of Theodor Herzl in English translation by Maurice Samuel and included articles by some of the leading men of the world in tribute to Herzl, many of whom recalled his personal magnetism.

Unfortunately, the progress of the Z.O.A. was seriously affected at that time, first by the financial difficulties of the American Zion Commonwealth and then by the beginning of the Great Depression, which cast a deep shadow over all Zionist endeavors for a number of important years. The success of the enlarged Jewish Agency was climaxed in 1929 by the Arab riots and the beginning of the collapse of the Mandatory Regime. Zionism was in great crisis.

It was a desperate time for us too, and especially for Meyer. All his plans were based upon steady growth, success after success, with no intervals of inaction, no retreats. He could not get himself to recognize the Depression, even when it was fully upon us. He believed in riding the storm full steam ahead, right into the financial crisis, and overcoming it by audacity but when his counsel was rejected by a cautious financial committee, and the climate became too oppressive, he turned his back on the Z.O.A. he had served for almost fifteen years and never returned to it.

His voluntary exile led to his last fling in the field of journalism in Toronto, where an admiring friend gave him the opportunity to launch a metropolitan weekly publication called *The Jewish Standard*. It had the old flair of *The New Palestine*. It was bold and creative. But it was an anomaly in the provincial life of Toronto and absorbed more money than Meyer's sponsor was willing to provide. It lasted three years. In effect it was Meyer's farewell to journalism; it opened his way to the Theatre and Spectacle.

He was transported from the propaganda of the word to the magic of the theatre. He thought that the theatre could be made a more exciting medium for Zionist propaganda than any other instrument.

He was in fact a talented stage producer. He was a master of "show."

His first opportunity in this field was a Chanukah festival in Chicago in 1932. He had been invited to aid in lifting the cultural level of Zionism in the Midwest. He thought that could best be done through a unique Chanukah Festival. From that Festival *The Romance of a People* was born. There in Chicago he encountered Isaac Van Grove, an experienced musician and composer who understood the stage and the management of spectacles. He also persuaded Benjamin Zemach— a dancer of great skill—to join him. *The Romance of a People* was uneven in form, more vaudeville than spectacular in execution. Its central theme was drowned in "show," but it had animation, tradition, Chassidism, Zionism, Jewish music and dance; an abundance of color; and best of all, it had room for large audiences, which was Meyer's obsession. It was an event in Zionist circles and when it was brought in re-written form to New York, its success was duplicated on a larger scale. Here it earned the $100,000 that Meyer gave to Dr. Weizmann for the Refugee Fund. The success in New York gave wings to Meyer's ambition. He saw *The Romance* as a road show that would revolutionize Zionist propaganda. He started out bravely on a tour of the country. In Philadelphia he was received by a blizzard. In Cleveland the local committee and a leading Zionist rabbi refused to support the enterprise. When he reached Detroit, *The Romance* faced a grim deficit, for he could not retrieve the $100,000 skimmed off in New York for the Refugee Fund.

The climax of his career in the theatre was Franz Werfel's *Eternal Road*, which was a great moral and artistic success, but did not live long enough to get rid of the burden of its investment capital. In fact, the conditions were such that the longer it went on with its large payroll the larger its deficit became. The makings of financial success were not there.

Meyer had the assistance, from an artistic point of view, as well as from the point of view of the budget, of two brilliant men of the theatre—Max Reinhardt and Norman Bel Geddes. Max Reinhardt had reached his mellow age in the theatre and still followed his old way of life; he made *The Eternal Road* one of his grandest productions and practically his last. He was in the period of the hardening of the imagination, and incapable of new discoveries, but what was left with him was an exciting archive of great imagination. He was assisted by Norman Bel Geddes, stage producer, architect and engineer, who was never daunted by any problem of stage construction, and had a flair for the circus. Bel Geddes had no regard for practical consider-ations. Budgets never daunted him. He made *The Eternal Road* one of his most imposing productions, but very expensive. The whole stage was divided into scenic subdivisions, ranging from the depth of the orchestra, where the prologue was played, to the topmost ranges of the stage, where Abraham and Moses appeared to play their scenes. The lighting effects were remarkable and the stage management was one of the most unusual, considering the size of the stage, the number of people involved, the number of scenic changes, and the difficulties of the system of lighting in a run-down theatre. Nevertheless, it was one of the noblest illuminations of the Biblical story ever seen on a stage.

Franz Werfel was a poet as well as a skilful dramatist. His text was admirably translated into English by Ludwig Lewisohn. The music was composed by Kurt Weill, who had written the music for the *Three Penny Opera*, which continues to meet with popular interest and curiosity to this day. Strains of Jewish traditional chants ran through many of his compositions. It was Meyer who suggested the idea of the play and plot to Max Reinhardt, who in turn enlisted the interest of Franz Werfel and of Kurt Weill, and brought along with him to the United States many members of his staff who had worked with him in the German theatre for many years.

When everything was ready, the only theatre available was the old dilapidated Manhattan Opera House in which the first Oscar Hammerstein had promised to establish a rival to the Metropolitan Opera House. There was no other theatre of adequate seating capacity available. Bel Geddes took over with avidity. He tore out the entrails of the old Opera House, removed seats that obscured the stage, reconstructed the stage itself, dug a deep hole down through the orchestra for the personnel of the prologue, and to his surprise struck gushing water, which required repairs that more than exhausted all financial resources. When the production was finished it was found to be too long and a number of expensive sets had to be destroyed. Meyer's financial backers began to feel that they were in the hands of a financial madman. When the curtain finally rose on *The Eternal Road* it was given a unanimously favorable reception by the best critics in New York and was the talk of the theatre for almost a year. The money invested was lost.

The highest level of Weisgal's life was reached, however, through his devotion to Dr. Weizmann. He was more than a disciple. He was like a son whose filial affection was three-dimensional. Dr. Weizmann was the incarnation of all his Zionist ideals. He was crowned with an aura which reminded Meyer not only of Kikol, his birthplace, his childhood, his own father, but also of the dignity and wisdom and humor of Jewish life, and all that was noble in Zionist ideals. He was bound to Dr. Weizmann by chains that could not be broken. There was no need for a translator between them. Everything about Dr. Weizmann had charm for Meyer's eyes. He loved him for his weaknesses as well as for his strength. He imagined himself as fortunate to occupy so exalted a place in the movement to which he was dedicated. He became Dr. Weizmann's thrall.

Meyer met Dr. Weizmann first in the controversy that led to the Cleveland Convention. He saw him in the intervening years when he made his periodic visits to the United States. He joined his entourage after the Congress of 1931, when Dr. Weizmann retired from the leadership for a time and headed the refugee movement. He was constantly on the lookout for things he could do that would exalt Dr. Weizmann's leadership. He became the architect of Dr. Weizmann's projects, giving them dimension, color and animation, and winning for them the support of influential people in the United States, and later in England, France and Switzerland. He hated Dr. Weizmann's enemies and loved his friends. He became the promoter of all the ideas Dr. Weizmann advocated for the building of the Homeland. He directed the transformation of the Sieff Institute into an all-inclusive Institute which was to be called The Weizmann Institute of Science. Meyer was Dr. Weizmann's American representative from 1934 to 1946 in the work of the Jewish Agency in the United States. He was not only personally devoted to Dr. Weizmann, but helped to develop a Weizmann cult in American Zionism. It had taken Meyer years to find his *Rebbe;* when he found him his loyalty was invincible, immortal and exclusive.

It is characteristic of him that when he is involved in creative work, he is absorbed in a stream of hot excitement, which boils over into a steaming obsession he cannot control. He rides on one rail at a time to success or to failure. Once sparked to action, he is unable to alter his course in transit. When he is under the spell of his vision, he is able to command the willing obedience of his co-workers, out-classing them in devotion and resourcefulness and tenacity of purpose. He rides roughshod over individual opinions. But when the work is done and all concerned are exhausted, he is as incomparable in generosity and appreciativeness as a moment before he was ruthless in command. He makes a virtue of rudeness, which is the veneer of an emotionalism he requires to spur himself to the utmost of achievement. His colorful, strident and electrical language is incomparable in range and unpredictability. He seeks perfection and never rests until what he has produced is the best he is capable of, reaching out always to the more difficult task, to the wider spaces, to the more complicated forms, to the larger mass. *The New Palestine* was the most engrossing Zionist magazine the American Movement ever established. *The Romance of a People*, when it reached its final form, revealed new aspects of Jewish theatre. *The Eternal Road* was an imposing version of the immortal story of the Rise and Fall of the Jewish People—the moral leadership that gave them their unique personality, their kings with their virtues and vices, their prophets with their vision and moral courage. (The play by Werfel should become a permanent number in the repertoire of Israel's theatre.)

Meyer has almost always been like the invisible stage manager in his productions, wearing muffled shoes, never to be caught on stage while the curtain is up. What he has put together—light and color and story—speaks for him and he dare not intrude in person with his natural voice. There he is, incessantly busy, constantly excited, always dictatorial and subsiding only when physically exhausted.

In 1948, after the proclamation of the Jewish State, his vision led him to Israel. There he has remained. There his vision, devotion and relentless drive forged, in the Weizmann Institute of Science, the finest scientific institution in Israel. It has come to be recognized as one of the great institutions of its kind in the world. After 14 years of intense, imaginative labor Meyer does not regard his work for the Institute as completed. He is still cultivating the Garden of Science that reflects his great ambition to link his soul to that of his hero. The Garden is ever expanding, playing its destined role in the development of Israel and in stimulating the development of its African and Asian neighbors.

As Meyer builds for the completion of his Great Dream, he retains his faith, courage, and sense of comedy.

VIGNETTES

NATHAN BIRNBAUM (MATHIAS ACHER)
(1864–1937)

Nathan Birnbaum (Mathias Acher) died in 1937 at the age of 73.
He started in life as one of the intellectual supporters of Political Zionism,
and toward the end of his eccentric career found himself among the
supporters of the Agudath Israel, and an uncompromising advocate
of orthodox Judaism. He was a man of startling talents and obstinate
intellectual habits. He was extreme in every enterprise he undertook.
He had in himself the capacity to become distinguished in leadership,
but always within the Jewish orbit. He had protean obsessions. He
could not remain loyal even to his own ideas. It depended upon time,
occasion and the state of his emotions as to what facet of Jewish thought
he attached himself to. But once having espoused a cause, he concentrated upon it, for the time being, with great passion and extreme partisanship. He had a sharp pen and tongue and a penetrating mind,
and served all the issues he made his own with tremendous zeal and
self-abandon.

He was one of the founders of the Kadimah of Vienna, a student
organization, in which Herzl found many a staunch defender. Kadimah
was one of the first student manifestations of national pride and defense;
its members undertook to defend Jewish honor in duels on the campus.
Every cause had its rise and fall in him. But in the early days of the
Zionist Movement he gave valiant service in the fight for national
integrity, and to him, more than to any other man, is due the development
of the ideology of Diaspora Nationalism.

In his early days, the fight he conducted was directed against the
larger part of the Jewish world, which was alien to all his thoughts.
In his later years, he refused to compromise with the smaller world
he had made his own. The fascination of the early days of Zionism

was due, to a large extent, to men of the virile intellectual quality of Birnbaum. He made the impression of a star without moorings. He coined the term "Zionism," which became the western name of the Movement. After the Nazi advent to power, Birnbaum fled to Holland and died there in poverty.

FRANZ OPPENHEIMER (1864–1943)

Franz Oppenheimer was a pioneer in the field of cooperative colonization in Palestine. He was the theoretician and planner of the first cooperative colonies. He was remote from Jewish life when he was persuaded to become interested in Palestine by Theodor Herzl and Professor Otto Warburg. Originally a physician, he was one of the outstanding political economists and sociologists of Germany and occupied a high position in intellectual and literary circles. He antedated Dr. Arthur Ruppin, who was primarily a colonizer, economist and general planner.

But Dr. Oppenheimer's contact with Palestine soon turned him into an enthusiastic and devoted supporter. As an economist, he was a critic of Marxian theories. He represented a trend away from Socialism and toward economic cooperation. He was an ardent admirer of Henry George, the founder of the Single Tax Movement. He helped to popularize George's theories in Germany. According to Oppenheimer, Merhavia (where Golda Meir went from the United States) and which was the colony he organized in 1911, was to be a cooperative as a matter of pragmatic necessity. But the idea of the common ownership of the land was a basic principle of the first attempts at Jewish colonization; it was tied in with the ideals of the Jewish National Fund. Professor Oppenheimer's plan prepared the way for the Kvutzot (communal settlements).

Oppenheimer is remembered by his visits to the United States in the years prior to World War I. He held himself aloof from internal Zionist matters, and was, for all practical purposes, an observer of the scene, except for his being involved in the early history of Merhavia.

He came to the United States as the guest of the Zionist Organization of America. He lectured in many cities and endeavored to collect funds for the support of the colony of Merhavia.

First and foremost Oppenheimer was a teacher and a writer. A man of independent thought, he had many controversies with the economists in the Zionist Movement. He wielded a trenchant pen, vigorously attacking theories with which he did not agree. He looked like a German military officer, and was aggressive in tone and bearing.

The rise of the Nazis in Germany found him, at the age of seventy, a retired professor, with no place in the intellectual life of Germany. He then settled in the United States. In the leisure of the pre-war years, he was a guest in Palestine and a distinguished personality in many circles. He continued, upon his return to the States, to lecture and addressed academic bodies.

He is remembered as a man of vigorous speech, a personality of great charm, and a platform speaker who could be relied upon to make caustic and witty observations on many phases of life. He died in California where he found refuge with an only daughter.

MEIR DIZENGOFF (1861–1936)

Meir Dizengoff is a legendary figure in the history of new Palestine. His death in 1936 provoked an unusual flow of eulogy and reminiscence, but the lineaments of that Dizengoff whose life's story the future children of Eretz Israel will read, centers about the founding and growth of Tel Aviv, of which he was one of the pioneers. Beginning in 1921, he was not only repeatedly its mayor, but he became known as its Father. It was a fact that was never questioned. From 1925 to 1928, somebody else served as Mayor, but no matter who was elected Mayor, Dizengoff remained the Father of Tel Aviv, who was always given the first seat of honor.

He had the appearance of a Mayor. He was tall, well-built, always carried a cane, and had a good appetite for enjoyment. But he was not one of those city fathers who went about patting children on the head, speaking at ceremonial dinners, or handing out diplomas to students, standing at the Four Corners and giving advice to all and sundry.

He was one of the ablest businessmen in Tel Aviv. He was the pioneer, in his personal capacity, in the organization of banks, industrial enterprises, home building associations, etc. He was a director of dozens of corporations, for his connection gave standing and reputation to any venture with which he was associated. He never wearied of bragging of the possibilities of Tel Aviv. He was an unashamed booster. He always believed in an ever greater Tel Aviv. Any estimate of the population, no matter how extravagant, he used to say, would sooner or later become a fact. So engrossed in the city's welfare was he, that he regarded it as his child—he had none of his own—and made all preparations before his death for the transfer to Tel Aviv of all his worldly goods, his heirlooms, his pictures, his books. The love and affection he showered upon Tel Aviv made a tradition for Tel Aviv, which will influence generations of citizens, proud of the city in which they live, and eager to add to its beauty and to its virtue.

He had no eye or mind for Zionism—its Congresses, its parties or its troubles. He was not a speaker or a debater. He was no orator. He was what his title indicated—the Father of Tel Aviv. That was a title that amply satisfied him.

GERSHON AGRON (1893–1960)

Gershon Agron (Agronsky) belongs to my life and I feel I must bring him into these memoirs. I think of his youthful cheer, his deep love of Israel, and of me, which I shall always remember.

He began his career as a Zionist in Philadelphia, with a passion to take himself as soon as possible into the heart of Zion.

He had enlisted into that valiant army of the Jewish Legion, in 1917, together with Louis Fischer, David Ben-Gurion, Ben-Zvi, Joseph Brainin and others and marched with Allenby to liberate Palestine from the Turks.

He found Jerusalem, and in Jerusalem himself. In Jerusalem he remained the rest of his days.

There in the days of the Mandate he established, in 1932, with himself as Editor, *The Palestine Post,* which flourished as the only English language daily in the Middle East with a recognized position in the field of world journalism. His home in Jerusalem was the Mecca of all distinguished visitors, diplomats, journalists, artists and Zionists. The Agronsky open house Friday nights in Jerusalem, were famous for three decades, not only for their social significance, but for the opportunity for diplomatic and political exchange, not otherwise possible.

The Palestine Post and the Agronsky Friday nights were among the most significant landmarks of the political history of Jewish Palestine, and largely relevant to the development of the Jewish state.

When Ben-Gurion, the leader for whom Gershon had the greatest reverence, made his carping criticism of the slowness of the Aliyah from the United States, it was a pity he did not remember Gershon Agron, of whom he said: "He was a volunteer from the United States to the first Jewish Legion in our generation . . . He was one of the

most talented and upright journalists we have had during the last
few decades . . . my friend and colleague, a man of integrity and nobility
of soul."

Gershon's labors for Israel were crowned with his election as Mayor
of his beloved Jerusalem. When death overtook him he had already
translated some of his dreams for expanding the glory of the immortal
Biblical city.

JACOB HODESS (1885–1961)

The larger part of the long life of Jacob Hodess was spent in
London. He was a gifted journalist who was articulate in Yiddish,
Hebrew and English. He had a phenomenal memory for Jewish events.
This was tied up with a mind remarkable in its clarity and loyalty to
Zionist ideals. I knew him from my first memories of London. He
first served Zionist interests in England in the early Yiddish press.
Then he was connected with the Zionist propaganda that emanated
from 77 Great Russell Street, which was finally expressed in *The New
Judaea* which he edited during the entire 30-year period of its life.

The New Judaea was the editorial personality of the Zionist
Executive. It was the record of the parliamentary debates in the British
Parliament. It was always objective and devoid of partisanship. Hodess
was a man of great loyalty, and although an excellent interpreter of
the ideas of Dr. Weizmann's administration, he never hesitated to
express his own opinions, when he felt it necessary. I am proud of the
fact that it was through my intervention in the Zionist Executive that
Mr. Hodess' services, for a long period, were given to Zionism through
The New Judaea. He served through the hard days; he served
through the victorious days; and he was able to retire to Israel with
honor when the State was established. At that time I wrote in the official
organ "Zion," issued from Jerusalem (April-June, 1954) that succeeded
The New Judaea, the following:

"The decision of the Jewish Agency to discontinue the publication
of the magazine *Zion* closes an interesting and valuable chapter
of Zionist history. On Friday, September 26, 1924, the Jewish Agency
began the publication in London of a fortnightly journal called *The
New Judaea*. It was to assist in the recovery of a stronger central
direction in Zionist affairs, to review what Zionists the world over
were doing, to strengthen their ideals and to summarize the facts of
Zionist activity in Palestine. Its appearance was like one of the English

political journals of the day. In its first issue there were articles by Leonard Stein, Col. F. H. Kisch, Dr. Arthur Ruppin, Israel Cohen, Meyer W.Weisgal, Hans Kohn, Robert Weltsch and others.

"*The New Judaea* continued without interruption until the establishment of the State of Israel when it was transferred to Jerusalem, given a new ugly format and renamed *Zion*.

"Throughout its life the journal was edited by Jacob Hodess, an excellent journalist in several languages, who dedicated himself to the task of creating a worthy Zionist journal with singular concentration and devotion; and with unusual ability and good taste.

"*The New Judaea* survived many political and financial crises but maintained throughout its continuity and high standards and gave expression to the best traditions of Zionist literary propaganda. It matched in English the high level of discussion typical of some of the Hebrew periodicals issued in Russia in the early days. It made it a practice to publish in its pages regularly full reports of the important political debates on Palestine conducted in the British Parliament. It became a first-class Zionist political and literary journal, all of which must be credited to the devotion of Mr. Hodess, who clung with great tenacity to his duties as editor without interruption from the first to the last day.

"It was a difficult task to maintain the position of *The New Judaea* with taste and dignity and objectivity in a magazine designed to represent the views of a not always harmonious Zionist leadership. Mr. Hodess did that with great skill and honesty. He was never a routine commentator and always had his own personal look at ideas, policies and events. He never used *The New Judaea* to force his views upon the official trends of the organization. His literary reviews were easy and fascinating reading, replete with anecdotes and historic allusion. His memories of the past were one of the features of *The New Judaea*. They were full of charm and accurate and kindly. He was a gracious editor to his contributors.

"To maintain such a magazine for thirty years, often through stretches of painful illness and great troubles of his own, was indeed a high achievement due in large measure to his intellectual integrity and his dedication to the Zionist cause."

His wife, who was an invalid for many years, was the partner of his Zionist enterprises. He owed much to her loyalty and understanding.

Mr. Hodess maintained a long period of friendship with George Bernard Shaw whom he imitated in also being a faithful vegetarian.

ISRAEL COHEN (1879–1961)

Israel Cohen, the traveling Zionist, whose address for the larger part of his life was London, was one of the reliable propagandists in England for the Zionist Movement. He developed a talent for description of his travels and visited scores of Jewish communities in all parts of the world, lecturing and writing. He was a quiet, sedate man who made a deep impression on one with the sincerity of his observations and his loyalty to the Zionist cause at a time when it was received with a degree of traditional interest. Everywhere he went on behalf of Jewish causes, some description of the community he visited appeared, sooner or later, as his contribution to Jewish journalism. He wrote a history of the Zionist Movement; he wrote a book called "Jewish Life in Modern Times"; "History of the Jews in Vilna" and others. His books were illustrations of the story of his travels. At the same time he was an official of the Central Office of the Zionist Organization, first in Cologne and then in London. He was an honored member of the civil service of the Zionist Movement as it developed over the years, having been a member of the Secretariat from 1910 to 1940. As I write these lines, I learned of his death in Israel.

I remember having to choose between him and Jacob Hodess as to who was to become the editor of *The New Judaea* in London. I did not choose Israel Cohen although he was a qualified preacher as well as a writer, and knew many communities and their leaders. He was a man of intellect and integrity and maintained the principles of a serious effective writer of the Zionist civil service.

NATHAN MILIKOWSKY (1879–1935)

Of all the men who came from Israel before the State was born, Milikowsky was one of the first visitors from there indigenous to the soil. He stood out as an audacious shameless propagandist. He was a pleader whose good-natured face did not hesitate a minute to exaggerate everything he was pleading for. He made the little things of Palestine seem more than big.

Everything could happen in Palestine! He peopled the animal world of the Holy Land with animals of large, extraordinary talents. They all spoke Hebrew.

He assured his audiences that he was not exaggerating when he told a donkey to move forward, and without hesitation and as a token of respect to the man who spoke Hebrew to them, the donkey (or the cow or the horse) did so.

He was a most amiable man, and when he occupied the platform speaking in Yiddish about Hebrew, which was then the prevailing habit, he filled the atmosphere with his own confidence in what he was saying—and that it was the truth. He was a very good friend of mine, and in one of the frequent quarrels we had in conventions (this one was in Pittsburgh) he paid me the compliment of being on my side against learned judges who thought I had no business to be a leader in the Zionist Movement. Fortunately for me, Milikowsky won his case.

He was a fascinating "maggid," full of quaint anecdotes and capable of extraordinary love for Palestine. The members of his family, who are outstanding scholars, are all proud of his memory.

ROSE DUNKELMAN (1889–1949)

Before the emergence of the State of Israel, the Zionist Movement grew in mass; large numbers flocked to its banners; great enthusiasm was created among the many who, in former years, were indifferent or hostile. But this recent period did not produce, as in the near past, the sturdy individualist who made his imprint on Zionist events, not by merging himself with the mass, but making contribution of his own peculiar personality to the cause, giving it a color of his own, brave enough to take the initiative, forcing recognition and often a reluctant cooperation by the power of his own will and obstinacy.

Most of us like to join in the common pull; are eager to keep in step. But there are always exceptional persons who find conformity too high a price to pay for freedom and who, by the rebelliousness of their own natures and the excitement of their own example, left a deep impression upon the movement. Zionism was a mass movement but it was also the first to awaken the individualist in Jewish life and give him free scope for the exercise of his own talents.

Rose Dunkelman was, in her own way, in her own circle, such a vibrant Zionist personality, who played a fine part in the Zionist Movement in Canada.

Zionism in Canada made progress slowly and always was considerate of the amenities of communal conditions. It held in reserve the dynamic powers of revolution; for here, as in other lands, it did not come as the promoter of radical, violent change. It made terms with the status quo. It grew with the size and experience of the community. It did not challenge traditional leadership for quite a period of time. It coordinated its controversies with respectful attention to the demands of what is now called "protocol." It achieved its results by patient endeavor and by tact and decorum. It had a long road to go and there seemed to be no great hurry.

In those idyllic days you had quite a number of non-conformists who made life interesting and exciting and disturbing; but of none of them could it be said what in truth must be said of Mrs. Dunkelman: that she was at the same time the rebel and the conformist, breaking ranks and walking alone, and then marching shoulder to shoulder in step with the organized purpose of Zionist achievement. Her nature could not be confined to the conventional and routine. She was strong enough and daring enough to go her own way without breaking the solidarity of the Movement. At the same time, she had great respect for the conventional and disliked to work for long in isolation. She was by nature gregarious and social, but to everything she did she gave her own color and her own pace.

Her Zionism was not a public matter only. She made the ideals of the Movement the warm center of her home. There was her Zionist and Jewish workshop. It was a domestic partnership in which her husband David played the ever-sustaining, ever-admiring role of the co-worker and supporter. There, in her home, she gathered her Zionist mementos. There she made her plans with her husband and her children. There, her loyal friends came to be inspired by her personality and her Zionist plans. She was the grand hostess to innumerable Zionist personalities and leaders. Her faith in herself was contagious. She disarmed hostility by her devotion and zeal and forgetfulness of self; by her good humor and robust laughter. Even when illness kept her confined for a number of years, she worked with concentration of purpose for every cause to which her heart was attuned.

It was because hers was a Zionist home that her children remained always with her, loyal to the cause. Their young years were spent in the atmosphere of Zionist ideals and Zionist work. They were fed by Zionist thought and Zionist movement. Their playthings came from the beginnings of Jewish art in Palestine, and their songs were the songs of Zion. She was the staunch matriarch of a lovable family.

She lived to see Jewish life plunged into the valley of disaster and death, and then, to see it emerge out of the battle, undaunted, fighting every inch of the way up the mountain to Victory.

She had the deep moral and spiritual satisfaction of seeing one of her stalwart sons, Benny, inheriting her good humor and her great devotion, taking his place in the leadership of the defenders of Israel, and, through his valor, achieving high position among the heroes of the War of Independence which was won against great odds after many difficulties.

Many were the forerunners of the New Day who helped to lay its foundations in a land forsaken, overwhelmed by decay and lethargy, brought to life again by the self-sacrifice of a whole generation. Among those who distinguished themselves by their services during that great historic period, the name of Rose Dunkelman will stand out and be remembered for her good cheer, her warmth, what she loved and how she loved, her great kindness and her abiding faith.

LEOPOLD J. GREENBERG (1861–1931)

Theodor Herzl made friends in many parts of the world, more especially in England. Israel Zangwill introduced him to writers and statesmen he knew and paved the way for a public reception. One of the most useful men Herzl encountered in London was Leopold J. Greenberg, who was then connected with the London *Jewish Chronicle* in a business capacity.

Greenberg introduced Herzl to Joseph Chamberlain. He provided a reception under the sponsorship of The Maccabeans. He became one of his couriers in connection with one of the investigations Herzl was required to make for some of the proposals of Chamberlain.

Greenberg was a man of temperament and original views. Although he thought highly of Herzl's talent as a journalist and negotiator, he nevertheless pursued, on his own account, a number of personal hunches that led to difficulties at the time with Herzl, who had keen views with regard to the significance of his proposals. The Uganda proposition led to no results. It split the Movement.

After Herzl's death, however, Greenberg became the editorial controller of the London *Jewish Chronicle* and exercised a policy which was Zionist but yet not in harmony with the views of David Wolffsohn, who succeeded Herzl. In fact, after Herzl's death Greenberg was more critic than supporter. When I saw him in London in 1913 he gave me a very friendly reception and loaned me and my group transportation from London to New York. He was an irascible man. He had strong dislikes and great loyalties.

He regarded himself as being one of the genuine Herzlians and as a rule, other Zionists were, in his opinion, variants and not Herzlians, but in all probability, Ahad Ha-amists.

He died in 1931 at the age of 70.

AVROM LUBARSKY (1856–1920)

Avrom Lubarsky came from Odessa in the early days of Zionism. He was a friend of Ahad Ha-am and Lilienblum, of Mendele and Sholem Aleichem. He knew all the Hebrew writers by their first names; he loved them all. He was the American representative of the Wissotzky Tea Company. Of course Lubarsky was a lover of Hebrew and a Zionist. But he was the first broad-minded, open-pocketed man of affairs we had thus far encountered in New York. He loved to play the part of a Maecenas, but in spite of his bragging about his wealth he had not enough money to go around; there were too many of the *literati* who knew of his existence.

All Russian *emigrés* of the Zionist school passed through his home and—more or less—his checking account. He was a hearty full-blooded man with a rare sense of humor, oozing stories and anecdotes—some of them rather salty.

When stolid businessmen expressed a protest against the aggressions of the journalists and speakers in the Zionist Movement—a protest in later years lodged against paid Zionist officials—it was Lubarsky who fumed and spluttered against the argument. If it was necessary to collect a purse for an impecunious Zionist, Lubarsky held the bag.

He was friendly to all groups—with Dr. Solomon Schechter as well as with Dr. Nachman Syrkin, the Poale Zionist; with Jewish labor leaders as well as with Mr. Marshall.

He was a disciple of Dr. Magnes; he thought that Dr. Magnes was an exponent of the doctrine of Ahad Ha-am. He went so far as to join Temple Emanu-El when Dr. Magnes became its associate rabbi. In the Self-Defense movement he was a busy man. He liked to be in on political secrets. Revolutionists from Russia always found him an eager listener and contributor, especially if the work to be done had the earmarks of a conspiracy. He was not much of a scholar himself but had great respect for Jewish learning. He sought the company of learned men, of men of wit, and could easily be found at different hours of the day in the coffee-houses frequented by one class or the other.

He suffered business reverses during the First World War; and, what was worse, was overtaken by ill-health which pursued him with malicious thoroughness and killed him within a few years, after much suffering.

MAX SHULMAN (1885–1937)

Max Shulman died in his middle years in 1937, but in the Zionist Movement he ranks with the veterans of the First Period. For many years when Zionism was a seed that had to be nurtured by personal devotion and sacrifice, he was the most ardent and self-sacrificing personality in the Midwestern scene. It was not his wealth; it was not his scholarship; it was not his oratory or personal distinction; it was not his standing in the non-Jewish world. It was his undaunted pertinacity in promoting the Zionist cause under all circumstances and at all times that made him the outstanding Zionist personality in the Middle West. There was nothing too small for his attention. It was he who brought the message of Zion to hundreds of small communities in Michigan, Illinois, Indiana.

In spite of resistance, he organized meetings and linked the scattered hamlets with the center of Chicago, in which he was the moving spirit for over thirty years. He was there in the days of the old Knights of Zion. He was there when the Knights were linked up with the Eastern organization. He was valiant during the period of World War I. He was in the vanguard of leadership when the Keren Hayesod was launched, and during all the years of the building of the Jewish National Home under the Mandate.

It was to his home our European visitors came. He met them at the station, escorted them on their way. He was a Zionist with universal Jewish interests.

He was also deeply concerned in the growth of synagogues, Talmud Torahs and Yeshivas, for he was both orthodox and pious, and had a fair knowledge of Hebrew and the Talmud. In fact, his greatest influence in Chicago was exercised in the orthodox synagogues, where he was highly respected.

He was a Vice President of the Zionist Organization of America and attended a number of Zionist Congresses. He was well-informed on all phases of Palestine development. In later years it seemed that a new generation of Zionists had appeared on the Midwestern scene; new leaders, new teachers, a faster tempo; but Max Shulman, with a few of his older associates, stood by, rather disturbed by the changed scene, wondering what it would lead to, but with the same old Zionist loyalty and sense of discipline. To the last he stood out as the most dependable Zionist personality in the great city of Chicago. He remained one of the old guard to the last day of his life.

BORIS KAZMAN (1874–1933)

Boris Kazman, ardent friend and admirer of Herzl, came to the United States after Herzl died and raised the flag of Jewish National Restoration among the young men in Zionism with an intensity and passion they never before had experienced.

He had made his way out of Russia. He had a record as a duelist in the University of Vienna and had been expelled. He had gone to Palestine and worked as a laborer in one of the Judean colonies and had been dismissed for smoking on the Sabbath. He was a delegate to the First Zionist Congress. He had graduated as a chemist from the University of Montpelier. And here he was, preaching Herzlian Zionism, although not a preacher or orator, with an arrogance and sweeping conviction as if he were summoning an army to rise and fight its way to Jerusalem.

His language was Russian; he spoke Yiddish and English with great difficulty. He was in fact incoherent in every language he used. He was a handsome young man, tall and slim and graceful; he had fair hair and blue eyes; but never dressed the part of the man of gallantry and fine manners which he was. He was the most restless and impatient Zionist of all whom we knew, and self-effacing to the extreme.

He was a disciple of Theodor Herzl, in whose every word he sensed the spirit of prophecy. He always had a word or aphorism or thought of Herzl to bolster up his arguments on any phase of Zionism. He really believed, as Herzl said: "If you will it, it is no dream."

He came to a small group of Zionists to warn them of the coming of the revolution. They were harangued to throw off their chains and prepare to become pioneers in the realization of Herzl's program.

The only baggage he had with him was a certificate from Montpelier as an agricultural chemist and a letter of credit from his father in Russia.

We were then a small group of excited Zionists and Kazman came to us bubbling with life and excitement. He secured a position as an agricultural chemist in Michigan, then later on, in central New York and other places. He had the most curious ideas. He wanted to have

made a complete soil map of Palestine (which would have cost a fortune
to prepare and have taken many years of labor) to prove that Palestine
could hold the Jewish people. When Brandeis heard of it he said he would
be willing to go slow with such an ambitious plan, but Kazman was not a
man who could favor in principle taking his time. He used to pester me
day and night to write letters to the press embodying his ideas. A number
of them were published in the *New York Times* in reply to Jacob H.
Schiff.

Kazman joined a group of us who went as delegates to the Vienna
Congress of 1913. Among the delegates were Hyman R. Seigal, Julius
Meyer, Abraham Goldberg, Max Shulman of Chicago and a Hebrew
teacher from Pittsburgh by the name of Hankin. Kazman didn't have a
penny with him when he set out on this trip. His father and mother and
sister met him in Vienna and provided him with funds to continue his
way back to New York. Although determined to get to Palestine as soon
as possible, he stopped off in Berlin and married a young Russian girl
who, incidentally, was not a Zionist and who never intended to go to
Palestine. They returned to New York and set up housekeeping in the
Bronx. His first child was born there.

Subsequently Mr. Brandeis made a contribution to an enterprise
that Kazman had developed of getting oil out of shale, and Kazman
finally got to Palestine. But the discovery of oil in the Middle East
made the whole project of shale extraction impractical, and it had to
be abandoned. Kazman then turned to experimenting with the refinement of olive oil while living and working on his father's farm in Rehovot. He died in Palestine at 59 as Hitlerism began to overshadow
the world.

ISAAC CARMEL (1886–1972)

When Isaac Carmel was born in Dobrzin, Poland in the year 1886,
in effect his destiny had been created for him. He had all the signs
that foretold the beginning of the career of a long-enduring and greatly
sacrificing Zionist propagandist. It took him his whole life to become
what he wanted to be. He never lost faith in himself or his people or
in the sanctity of Jerusalem. He left his birthplace and joined relatives
in Leeds, England. From Leeds he went to London; from London
to New York. From New York he reached out into every part of the
United States and became a general propagandist with allegiance

to everything Zionist, and with skepticism toward all Zionists as a whole. He believed in himself as the symbol of Zionism and left footprints in every State of the Union. His special quality was his ability to be a free man in spite of his Zionist servitude: No one dictated to him, no one bought him, no one sold him. He helped build up every branch of every Zionist organization in his own time according to his own rules, and in defiance of every bureaucrat that endeavored to tell him what to do and where and how. He was at home in Ohio, he was at home in Florida; he was part of the Keren Hayesod; he was part of the Jewish National Fund. He was a valiant worker in the Z.O.A., the Sons of Zion, the Keren Hayesod, the United Palestine Appeal, and Israel Bonds, but he was never bound in pledge or promise to any branch of the rapidly growing democracy which was Zionism.

He had a personal life which nobody ever saw, except for a wife who died after a long invalidism and a young daughter who passed away before her time.

When he wanted to return to the land of the Jewish people, after the State was established, he could not find his way and thought that somebody would miraculously provide him with transportation and settlement. But there was no one who volunteered to make it possible for him to go and settle there. "Who are you?" they said. He could not identify, however, for whom all these sacrifices had been made during his long lifetime of service. Responsibility was rejected by every branch which had used his services and owed him a debt of gratitude. He was on no list. He had to find his own security. But he managed to get to Israel, and lived there for several years—and at a time when it was a great hardship, but not to Isaac Carmel.

When he wanted to come back to the States, from the galaxy of international bureaucracy only one candidate showed himself. It was the Israel Bonds. The name of Isaac Carmel was written into the register as an employee and from now until the end of his days Isaac Carmel will be listed as a staff member of Israel Bonds, due to the understanding and thoughtfulness of Joseph Schwartz, its Director.

LOUIS E. LEVINTHAL (1892–   )

Any biography of Judge Louis E. Levinthal must begin with his father. His finest qualities were derived from his loyalty to the family *"yichus"* he inherited. The source of his distinction lies in the memory of his beloved and distinguished father whose piety and wisdom, tolerance and sensitiveness to Jewish tradition belong not only to his direct heirs, but are included in the fine memories of American Zionism. His father, Rabbi B. H. Levinthal, was one of the shrines of Jewish learning and rabbinical authority in Philadelphia. He was a sturdy individualist whose responses to questions were accepted because of his integrity and loyalty to Torah. He was a Zionist of the old school whose Zionism was quickened to revival by the dramatic advent of Theodor Herzl. He greeted the new day of Zionism with wonder and pride that never ceased. For many years he joined in our own conventions, and he had the rare gift of brevity. He enjoyed the mingling of youth in the Zionist rebirth of the Jewish people.

It was the influence of his father that led Judge Levinthal to the discipline of modern Zionism in his boyhood. It was the love and respect for the traditions maintained by his father that gave tone and integrity to the Jewish personality of Judge Levinthal. The learned rabbi was a man who always wanted to bring peace in controversies. He was by nature a Judge whose authority among his colleagues stood high for many years. It was this aspect of his father's personality that found expression in Judge Levinthal's choice of a profession and in the years of exemplary and dignified service he gave to the Superior Court of the State of Pennsylvania.

With such a patrimony Judge Levinthal could not be a narrow or partisan Zionist. He has had a natural affinity for all things Jewish. He has served for many years as President of the Jewish Publication Society. He has been active in the Association of Jewish Education. He stands out in the Philadelphia community, rich in Jewish tradition, as a leader of the quality of Judge Mayer Sulzberger and Dr. Cyrus Adler. He is deeply interested in the cultural enterprises that incorporate American-Israel cooperation. He has a personal interest in a long list of activities that concern his community, the American Jewish community as a whole, as well as the State of Israel. He and his esteemed wife have a living stake in the building of Israel through their daughter and grandchildren who now reside there.

Here it is in order to speak with pride and admiration of Judge Levinthal's demonstration of bold Zionist loyalty. I refer to his withdrawal from the Zionist Organization of America, only a few years ago. An habitual conservative, he has never been deeply involved in our controversies. He had been a youthful pioneer in the ranks of the Z.O.A., which he always regarded as the moderate center of the Movement. He was the leader for years of his Zionist District and Region. He was the unanimous choice of the Z.O.A. as its President from 1941 to 1943, and led with modesty and distinction. Dignity and tolerance were characteristic of him.

Nevertheless, he did not hesitate to register his dissenting opinion with regard to the pressure tendencies in the Z.O.A. to form entangling alliances with political parties in Israel and their involvement in internal Israeli political affairs.

He expressed the view, which many of us share, that the interlocking of Diaspora Zionist groups with Israeli political parties is bound to impair the freedom of action of the Z.O.A. and reflect on the Americanism of its membership. It subjects the sovereignty of Israel to influences not directly affected by Israel's internal affairs and opens Israel to guerrilla warfare throughout the Diaspora, it commits the entire Z.O.A. membership to party alliances, misrepresenting substantial numbers of the Z.O.A. members and forcing them as a matter of principle to protest a breach of their basic individual rights.

Judge Levinthal was a party to the long negotiations with the Zionist Organization of America pleading for its withdrawal from these partisan involvements. Protests were not heeded. Then Judge Levinthal, together with others, gave active leadership to the creation of the American Jewish League for Israel, which incorporates a moral and constitutional protest against the Z.O.A.'s position and provides an organization where Zionists may perform their services for Israel secure in the knowledge that it is not identified with any political organization or party in Israel.

JACOB H. SCHIFF (1847–1920)

It is not customary to write biographical notes on a man whose life was practically a public document. Jacob H. Schiff was undoubtedly an unusually rich man, and a remarkably generous man, without limit in the giving of his money. His family, having settled in Frankfort in 1379, contained several distinguished rabbinical and scholarly men, the earliest of whom, Jacob K. Zedek Schiff, was *Dayan* at Frankfort. Among the rabbinical authors included in his family were: Meir Ben Jacob Schiff (known as "Maharam Schiff" who died 1644) and David Tebele Schiff, Chief Rabbi of the Great Synagogue of London.

He received his early education at the School of the Jewish Religious Society established in 1853 by Samson Raphael Hirsch. He came to

New York in 1865, at the age of 18, and married Theresa Loeb, daughter of Solomon Loeb, head of the banking house of Kuhn, Loeb and Company.

Although a Reform Jew, a member of two Reform Temples in New York and a supporter of the Union of American Hebrew Congregations, Mr. Schiff always retained his affection for and attachment to the traditional observances of his youth in Frankfort. He generously supported both the Hebrew Union College and the Jewish Theological Seminary.

There was hardly a single important charitable institution to which he did not contribute magnificently.

For many years he was an outspoken opponent of Jewish nationalism. He also steadfastly objected to Zionism without a religious platform. When, however, the First World War revealed the need for a refuge for Jews who could not live freely and happily in the countries of persecution, he readily admitted that he had been shortsighted and promised his aid in the rebuilding of Zion as a great cultural center. He purchased stock in the Jewish Colonial Trust Foundation and helped to finance loans for Palestinean wine growers. In 1914, when the War had cut off the Jews of Palestine from sources of support from abroad, Mr. Schiff contributed $50,000 to a fund for which Henry Morgenthau, Sr., then U.S. Ambassador to Constantinople, had made an urgent appeal to the Provisional Committee for General Zionist Affairs and to the American Jewish Committee. He gave $100,000 for the founding of the Haifa Technicum at the request of the Hilfsverein. When the Hilfsverein, which favored instruction in German instead of Hebrew, came into conflict with the Palestine view of Jewish education, Mr. Schiff sided with the Palestineans and withdrew from the Technicum. He subsequently financed the purchase of the Haifa institution for the Zionist Executive. It is impossible to list in detail the charitable gifts of Mr. Schiff to institutions in Palestine. It shows, however, that through his long life a liberal feeling existed in Mr. Schiff with regard to Palestine that was independent of his opposition to political Zionism.

FELIX M. WARBURG (1871–1937)

Felix M. Warburg was born in Germany, the scion of a wealthy Jewish family. He came to the United States and became the son-in-law of Jacob H. Schiff whose heir he was in public service. He maintained the Schiff standards and ideals with devotion and a high sense of responsibility. Mr. Schiff was—transcending the fact of his generosity—the leader and symbol of American Jewish philanthropy. Mr. Warburg enlarged upon what was handed down to him by his predecessor. He was more easily approached and won for great causes.

At the beginning of this century, the Jews of America narrowed their interests to their immediate surroundings. The more local the need, the more generous were the gifts. Only in the days of the Kishinev pogroms were American Jews first drawn out of their American obligations to a consideration of interests beyond the seas. Even then their gifts were meager. Warburg led American Jews into the brotherhood of universal Jewish responsibilities. He not only symbolized the idea of philanthropic federations, but through the Joint Distribution Committee, the Palestine Economic Corporation and the Jewish Agency for Palestine, he led, by his example, a large segment of American Jewry in appreciation of the whole Jewish problem. He was also a distinguished lover and patron of music and art.

With the death of Louis Marshall in 1929, Mr. Warburg became the leader of the American non-Zionist forces in the Jewish Agency. He was far ahead of his friends and associates, for he had an abiding interest in, and affection for, the Holy Land. He came to know it intimately and to love it. He made his contributions not promiscuously so far as Palestine was concerned, but with an affection for certain places and activities. Before long, he was a Chovevei Zionist in the best sense of the word. And although he hated ideologies and refused to be classified, in his death the Zionist movement suffered a great loss.

After Marshall's death Warburg's interest in the extended Jewish Agency was intensified; he was interested for a time in its organization problems and cooperated with Dr. Weizmann in various political problems. But he could not stand alone. He found few among the non-Zionists of his day to supplement his interests in cooperative effort. His heirs today are the American army of non-Zionists working for the success of the State of Israel. Among them, enrolled in its leadership, stands his son Edward, true to the Warburg and Schiff tradition.

HENRY MONSKY (1890–1947)

Henry Monsky was the convenor of the American Jewish Conference in 1943, which carried through to success a form of organization never before ventured in Jewish life. It was the rallying of communities and organizations, through democratic elections, for the single purpose of registering united American Jewish support for the establishment of a Jewish State in Palestine at the end of World War II.

Monsky was then the President of the Bnai Brith, the largest Jewish fraternal membership organization in the United States. It was Monsky's influence with the Bnai Brith which made possible the birth of the Conference. He threw the weight of his large organization to the side of the Jewish nationalist forces which were trying to re-enact, in a more effective way, what had once been attempted in the first American Jewish Congress in 1918. Monsky had been a delegate to that first American Jewish Congress.

A lawyer, with a successful practice in Omaha, Nebraska, of Russian Jewish parentage, he carried great weight with those organizations in Jewish life never before identified with the Zionist cause. Once having approved the principles for which the American Jewish Conference was to be organized, he helped bring into the Conference these large and important elements of the Jewish community, particularly the Reform congregations, the Temple Brotherhoods and Sisterhoods.

Tall, slender, lithe, affable, expert in the art of maneuver, an overcast of melancholy added mystery to his touch and parry.

Often in the preparatory period he chose compromise to avoid conflict; but his associates in the Zionist leadership had faith in his commitment to the fundamental ideals of the Conference, which he vindicated.

In 1943 Monsky was elected the first head of the American Jewish Conference and served it with devotion until he was stricken, on May 2, 1947 at a meeting of the Conference's Interim Committee, as the battle lines were forming in Palestine and at the United Nations, just six months before the United Nations was to adopt its resolutions partitioning Palestine, and authorizing the creation of the Jewish State.

HARRY SACHER (1881–1971)

Harry Sacher is my oldest English Zionist comrade. Though an American by birth, I can recall a close kinship to everything English from the time I could first read. England spoke to me, as a boy, through the books of George Henty, and later through the unforgettable prophecy of George Eliot, whose inspired book "Daniel Deronda" struck a chord in my heart never to be stilled in my lifetime. London was Disraeli; London was Montefiore; London was the *Jewish Chronicle*, which contained the first great oration of Max Nordau which I read with avidity in Rochester; London was the great theatre of the Anglo-Saxon world. London was the pubs, the fogs, the quaint street lamps, the spirit of its people, and the dirty windows of 77 Great Russell Street which later became the citadel of the Jewish National Home. London was everything liberal and advanced in the modern world, and gave promise of the fulfillment of our traditional hopes.

It was because I sensed in Harry Sacher the spirit of that England that I was drawn to him the day I met him at my first Zionist Congress in 1913. Though his first Zionist Congress was, he told me, in 1903 in Basle, I have always thought his career in the Zionist Movement an almost exact parallel of my own.

The first layer of the Zionist Movement in England was laid by the direct supporters of Theodor Herzl. They were succeeded in turn by those who rallied to the support of Dr. Weizmann. Among these, Harry Sacher was one of the foremost. He was a friend and co-worker, and remained faithful through the trying days of early idealism.

He represented the first generation of English Jewry. Totally English in education, he entered the public life both of England and of the Jewish community. Throughout the Weizmann era, Harry Sacher was a loyal supporter with a dedication that was wholehearted, experienced and responsible. He represented the solid, stubborn English community with deep understanding and vision. He has played the part of journalist, editor and advocate. He was an executive force whose energies were expended in supporting the new State that has been created in our lifetime. In a movement that has been harrowed by so many partisan conflicts, his gifts as a barrister and conciliator enabled him to avoid partisanship even on issues he had profound convictions about. His unwavering loyalty, one of his outstanding characteristics, never warped his practical sense.

When Dr. Weizmann came to England with his family he did not find a welcome in the Zionist circle. He was regarded by many as being a follower of Ahad Ha-am. In the course of time, however, he established a circle which profited by intellectual and social contact with his Zionist views. Among those who became an adherent of the views of Dr. Weizmann was Harry Sacher.

Sacher has been an editor of the *Manchester Guardian;* he was a barrister; he was a frequent contributor to the contemporary literature of the period, and wrote a number of books.

He was elected a member of the World Zionist Executive together with Miss Szold and Col. Kisch, and edited a number of pamphlets issued by the Federation of English Zionists.

For a time he practiced law in Palestine, then returned to London to become a member of the firm of Marks and Spencer.

During the War of Independence he wrote a first-class description of the whole campaign.

Now one of the leading members of the firm of Marks and Spencer in London, he participates in most of the good works of that corporation which has played an important part in the history of the London Jewish community. His latest work is a book of profiles called *Zionist Portraits and Other Essays*, published in London in 1959.

ISRAEL AMONG THE NATIONS

The objective of the Basle program was, in a measure, achieved on May 14, 1948 (5 Iyar 5708) when the representatives of the Jewish community of Palestine met in Tel Aviv, under the chairmanship of David Ben-Gurion, to proclaim the State of Israel.

The Proclamation was written under great stress and in haste. General Zionist opinion was divided. Leadership in Palestine wavered and swayed back and forth. Government authorities in the United States strongly advised against the proposed action. They feared the consequences in view of Arab threats. For these reasons the text of the Proclamation lacked the classic form and the lofty tone of a great historic document. It reflected the indecision that prevailed in Israel. It was calculated to serve an immediate purpose. It conveyed the views of the Provisional Government on matters of urgent political concern. It was intended to be communicated with dispatch to all nations who should hear what the new State had to say on the day of its birth. Speedy advantage had to be taken of the opportunity to give assurances to friends and to allay disturbance in hostile circles. There was no time to consider rhetoric or style.

On the record, a political victory was registered at the United Nations, but Israel had to be provided with the organs of state life. The world had to be told of the new nation's democratic intentions. It had to be impressed by Israel's aspirations for peace and justice. It had to convey faith and confidence in the promise of a useful future. The Proclamation served these purposes well. It is regarded as a document worthy of a great occasion. What is basic and relevant eight years after the event is herewith appended:

The Land of Israel was the birthplace of the Jewish people. Here their spiritual, religious and national identity was formed. Here they achieved independence and created a culture of national and universal significance. Here they wrote and gave the Bible to the world.

Exiled from Palestine, the Jewish people remained faithful to it in all countries of their dispersion, never ceasing to pray and hope for their return and the restoration of their national freedom.

Impelled by this historic association, Jews strove throughout the centuries to go back to the land of their fathers and regain their statehood. In recent decades they returned in masses. They reclaimed the wilderness, revived their language, built cities and villages, and established a vigorous and evergrowing community, with its own economic and cultural life. They sought peace yet were prepared to defend themselves. They brought the blessings of progress to all inhabitants of the country.

In the year 1897 the First Zionist Congress, inspired by Theodor Herzl's vision of the Jewish State, proclaimed the right of the Jewish people to national revival in their own country.

This right was acknowledged by the Balfour Declaration of November 2, 1917, and reaffirmed by the Mandate of the League of Nations, which gave explicit international recognition to the historic connection of the Jewish people with Palestine and their right to reconstitute their National Home.

On November 29, 1947, the General Assembly of the United Nations adopted a Resolution for the establishment of an independent Jewish State in Palestine, and called upon the inhabitants of the country to take such steps as may be necessary on their part to put the plan into effect.

Accordingly we, the members of the National Council, representing the Jewish people in Palestine and the Zionist movement of the world, met together in solemn assembly today, the day of termination of the British Mandate for Palestine, by virtue of the natural and historic right of the Jewish people and of the Resolution of the General Assembly of the United Nations, hereby proclaim the establishment of the Jewish State in Palestine, to be called ISRAEL.

We hereby declare that as from the termination of the Mandate at midnight, this night of the 14th to 15th May, 1948, and until the setting up of the duly elected bodies of the State in accordance with a Constitution, to be drawn up by a Constituent Assembly not later than the first day of October, 1948, the present National Council shall act as the Provisional State Council, and its executive organ, the National Administration, shall constitute the Provisional Government of the State of Israel.

The State of Israel will be open to the immigration of Jews from all countries of their dispersion; will promote the development of the country for the benefit of all its inhabitants; will be based on the precepts of liberty, justice and peace taught by the Hebrew Prophets; will uphold the full social and political equality of all its citizens, without distinction of race, creed or sex; will guarantee full freedom of conscience, worship, education and culture; will safeguard the sanctity and inviolability of the shrines and Holy Places of all religions; and will dedicate itself to the principles of the Charter of the United Nations.

We offer peace and amity to all the neighboring states and their peoples, and invite them to cooperate with the independent Jewish nation for the common good of all. The State of Israel is ready to contribute its full share to the peaceful progress and development of the Middle East.

Our call goes out to the Jewish people all over the world to rally to our side in the task of immigration and development and to stand by us in the great struggle for the fulfillment of the dream of generations—the redemption of Israel.

With trust in Almighty God, we set our hand to this Declaration, at this Session of the Provisional State Council, in the city of Tel Aviv, on this Sabbath eve, the fifth of Iyar, 5708, the fourteenth day of May, 1948.

The Partition decision of November 1947—the climax of the turbulent history of nine years—was backed by legal and moral authority. But it did not reflect the firm intention of the United Nations to see that what had been agreed should be realized in fact. It came as the result of a political squabble that ended in a favorable majority vote. What is agreed to on such occasions may sound convincing at the time, when the vote is taken under stress of passion or sentiment or intense self-interest, but when the irrevocable action is imminent, timidity and fear take over and a scramble ensues to undo what had been decided to be done, if retreat is at all possible. The Palestine problem had been one of the most difficult controversial items on the agenda of the United Nations. It was a football of international politics. It was the center of conflicting national interests. It was being used as the object of the vindictive and relentless policies of the British Foreign Secretary, Ernest Bevin. Opinion had swayed from right to left, from Yes to No, from loyalty to pledges to a frantic desire to undo a decision arrived at.

The U.S. State Department was bedeviled by pro-Arab and pro-British officials. No sooner was the vote on partition taken than forces were released to set in motion plans for retreat, revision, and the reshuffling of the cards with a view to inhibiting the success of any solution that might bring to life a Jewish state. It was doubted that the British at any time had a serious intention to solve the problem. They relied upon chance. They were waiting until the very end, thinking that something different would come up if they could only continue to muddy the waters of political action. It was not believed at any time that the British genuinely intended to evacuate Palestine. Many friends of Israel in the United States were frightened by the British and Arab propaganda. For the record, they had done what they had been called upon to do, but they had not anticipated the violent repercussions that shook the lobbies of the United Nations and the international press. In Palestine there were clashes between British and Jews, between Arabs and Jews. The disorder was tantamount to civil war.

At this time of hesitation the retreat was led by the United States. A Temporary Trusteeship was to be substituted for partition. The idea was to go back to where they had started. The trusteeship would undoubtedly bring Great Britain back again to the driver's seat in Palestine, supported by friendly governments. But by this time world opinion and especially the free discussion in the United States had become so incensed and inflamed with the obvious chicanery of change-eable "statesmen" and their irresponsible behavior that steps had to be taken without delay to set up the plan for the partition of Palestine.

Foreseeing that there would be an interregnum between the Mandate and Partition, a Commission of five was appointed by the United Nations for an orderly transition from the Mandate to Arab and Jewish states. The British in Palestine rendered the efforts of the Commission ineffective. The British rejected its request to open a port for Jewish immigration or to permit the organization of Arab and Jewish militia to maintain order after the British withdrew. The British would not permit the Commission to enter Palestine before May 1 on the ground that its presence in Palestine would lead to divided authority and stimulate Arab disorders. The British removed Palestine from the sterling bloc countries and its assets in Great Britain, amounting to 100 million pounds, were frozen in British banks. A large grant from the Palestine treasury was made to the Arab Higher Committee for the "religious" purposes of the Mufti of Jerusalem. The huge oil refineries in Haifa were closed and a fuel famine was imminent. Imports of essentials were suspended; railway traffic was halted; telegraph services were discontinued. The Lydda airport was closed and international air traffic came to an end. As the day of final evacuation approached, huge quantities of dispensable military vehicles and other equipment were either destroyed or sold by British soldiers to Arabs or Jews. Barracks, military camps and police stations were either abandoned or turned over to the Arabs. Ernest Bevin refused even to consider at that time President Truman's proposal to let 100,000 Jewish refugees into Palestine. The victims of Hitler were blocked at the ports of embarkation. They were harried on the high seas, on the beaches, in the air.

The Arabs were preparing to take advantage of the situation the day the British left Palestine. They stood at the frontiers with their armed forces like vultures ready to strike at their victims and tear them apart. They warned the local Arabs to vacate the fields where the battles might take . place. They advised them to get out of the way when the bombs burst, when the tanks rolled in, when the planes struck. They were promised a rich harvest of loot when they returned home after the infidels had been driven into the sea. What Great Britain had built up over a period of three decades was virtually dismantled and ruined before the last Englishman left the Promised Land on May 15, 1948.

The Arab States gave notice to the United Nations, to the press, through all the media of communication, that they intended to make war on Israel the day the British left. And sure enough, on May 15 the army of Egypt crossed the frontier of Israel. The United Nations failed to react. On the following day the Syrian army, reinforced by the Iraqis and the Arab Legion of Jordan, marched forward to seize the Jordan Valley from Lake Kinnereth to Beisan, and then to cross the Emek to Haifa. After a few minor victories the loud threats of the Arabs failed of their purpose. The Iraqis were routed and fled back across the Jordan. The Syrians were repulsed and fell back with heavy losses. In the north, the Lebanese suffered a prompt defeat and ceased to be a factor in the war.

The battle for Jerusalem was the most crucial and desperate struggle of all the incidents of the war. When the British left Jerusalem the Jews took possession of nearly the whole of the New City. They hesitated to attack the Old City, for nearly all the Christian holy places were there, and to attack them would evoke world repercussions. Likewise, the defense of the Old City under these circumstances was impossible.

On May 28 the few remaining Jewish defenders gave permission to the leaders of the community to surrender to the Arabs. There were then only 39 Jews in the Old City capable of bearing arms. But the critical front in the Battle of Jerusalem was still the road to Tel Aviv. The Arab Legion, holding Lydda, Ramle and Latrun, sealed off the road. It was clear that unless food, water and fuel as well as arms and ammunition and reinforcements could be kept flowing to the city, beleaguered Jerusalem, with its 100,000 Jews, was doomed. The city was saved by the fortitude of its people and by the ingenuity of their defense. They managed to change the character of the siege. The army of Israel hewed out a track through the hills south of Latrun and around a ten-mile arc about Bab-el-Wad which they held and along which vital supplies were carried by jeep and mules and men to the city. They called it their "Burma Road." The work was done at night and in secret, and only on the eve of the cease-fire did it become known that the siege of Jerusalem had been outflanked through this improvised road.

Israel's defense of its sovereignty and freedom lasted for eight months. There were periods of armed conflict, alternating with cease-fires ordered by the Security Council. In the first period, from May 15 to June 10, the Arabs felt certain of a swift and decisive victory, but they were checked on every front during this period. The first cease-fire was ordered on June 10 and continued to July 9. The war then continued for ten days, and again a cease-fire was ordered. When the second cease-fire was agreed to, Israel held more than 800 square miles in addition to the area included in the Jewish State under Partition. The second cease-fire lasted officially until the signing of the Armistice Agreements. The Armistice Agreements were arrived at in various stages. On Febuary 25, 1949, after six weeks of negotiations on the Island of Rhodes, Egypt and Israel signed an armistice agreement which left the disputed Negev in Israel's possession. In March of that year Israeli forces moved down to Elath, near the southern tip of the Negev on the Gulf of Aqaba. The Gaza coastal strip remained in Egyptian hands, but the strip had never been included in the Jewish State. An armistice with Lebanon was signed on March 23, and with Jordan on April 3. The armistice with Syria was not concluded until July 20, 1949.

Since its troubled beginning Israel did not see peace in any form. It is a nation encircled, compelled by vociferous and active enemies constantly to give thought and to spend resources on its security. The Armistice Agreements are honored more in the breach than in the observance. Nonetheless Israel has survived, grown, established itself as a sound democracy, harnessed its resources to achieve basic economic stability at home and to lend its services and know-how to other new nations. It has absorbed more than a million immigrants, coming in largest part from the D.P. camps of Europe and more recently from Arab and African countries under the spur of persecution. It has built for them schools, housing, retrained them for self-sufficient livelihood in their new home and educated them in the practices of democracy. Its scientific institutions have achieved world renown, notably the Weizmann Institute of Science. Sixty-eight countries of Africa, Asia and Latin America are being guided in their development programs by Israel. As it approaches its fifteenth birthday, though there are large internal problems to be resolved and peace with the Arab States still seems a distant hope, the permanence of the State is assured. Among the nations of the world the creative contributions which Israel can make to human welfare are finding increasing recognition.

GOLDA MEIR (1898–   )

Golda Meir (the greater part of her life was spent as Golda Meyerson) was a child of the Labor renaissance in the Zionist Movement in the United States. Born in 1898 in Kiev, Russia, she was brought to Milwaukee where as a young girl she served an apprenticeship as a teacher. In the Labor Zionist Movement in the United States, she was active, capable, bright, energetic and audacious. Milwaukee of her day was one of the few American cities ripe for socialism, and one of the first to elect a Socialist as its Mayor.

In her early days Golda gave an impression of reserve, even of shyness; her eyes seemed to reflect an inner sadness which was seldom hidden. She was uncertain of her resources. Her voice seemed touched with tragedy. But when she spoke it was awakened with conviction and certainty. She seemed to be groping to find the tasks she was fated for. Her superlative simplicity in the use of English came after great effort and practice and remained with her all her days as an important asset of her Zionist service.

Early she acquired the knowledge of the rudiments of organization for social action. She reached out for more complex activities and larger responsibilities. She was strangely restless; wherever she was she looked forward with impatient longing toward the East, toward a new life which was tempting her with its mysterious promise.

The Jewish people have lived through dark periods in their own underground world. Zionism drew them out of their ghettos into the open, liberated their spirits, gave wings to their hopes and summoned them to cultivate a vigorous ambition to live openly under the same sun that shines for all people. A goal was set for them to reach out to. They established their own stage on which their struggle was to be reflected.

Golda Meir was the child of that renaissance. It was a leap of spiritual desperation when she decided to leave Milwaukee for Merhavia in Palestine. Merhavia was a cooperative colony, entangled in the difficulties of birth, where food was scarce and the economy in the making; where the settlers were young learners who were being redeemed through hard experience. It was a greater stride, several years later, to pull out of Merhavia and become attached to a Labor office in Tel Aviv. To every extension of herself, she brought important assets from her previous experience; and her personality grew in stature from year to year. The young woman from Milwaukee made her way with great energy from one level of service to another, to what she believed was predestined for her personality and inescapable.

In those years, when the steel in her character was being forged, she earned her place in the leadership of the Labor Movement in Palestine. In 1934 she was asked to join the Executive of the Histadrut, Palestine's Jewish Labor Federation.

The Histadrut laid the economic and cultural foundations of the National Home. It came to the foreground of the entire Yishuv when the Nazis ran riot and when the Mandate was coming to its final phase and the State was in the process of being born. The men of labor had learned the business of management. They were the creators of whatever civil and military service was available when the State was hastily put together. They were, in fact, a trained group, weak in some of its links, but strong as a collective and capable of turning the wheels of administration for every purpose.

Mrs. Meir proved to be one of the most adaptable and dependable members of this group from the early beginnings. She acquired poise and a rare dignity, a mastery of the art of expression, and an almost immovable obstinacy in controversial discussions. She was not burdened with the weight of antecedent ideologies in the Socialist Movement. She was a revolutionist in the real sense. In the realm of ideas she exercised an unusual freedom of choice.

Many have been the tasks that she has performed, with thoroughness, intelligence, recklessness of self; a stormy figure in debate, a hard worker in the field and with a human touch, reflected in all her relations. She was the one member who was invaluable both at home and abroad.

She was often sent travelling to distant communities. She was an awakener of communal initiative in the Diaspora. She was the guide and the critic of labor groups. One of her first tasks was the organization of the tourist department of the Histadrut. She was placed in charge of mutual aid programs in 1936. When Dov Hos passed away she took his place for a time as head of the political department of the Histadrut. She came to the United States in 1937 to make known the work of Nachshon, organized for the development and building of maritime enterprises such as ports, fisheries, cargo boats, etc.

With the issuing of the White Paper in 1939 the Jewish governing body in Palestine—a combination of the *Vaad Leumi* and the Jewish Agency—was pushed into the foreground, and the shape of the State to come began to take form. The duties of leadership expanded, included an extension of powers into the European field where Jews were being martyred. In this situation, with the State attaining the climax of birth, Mrs. Meir's duties developed new elements in her growing personality. She represented the Histadrut before the Anglo-American Committee in March 1946 in Jerusalem and made a memorable impression with her simplicity, clarity and dignity. It was said that with her direct approach to the essence of the Jewish Problem, in her clear and unevasive replies, she dispelled the uncomfortable courtroom atmosphere, the irritability and boredom that pervaded the room. She brought the hearing back to its human aspects. When Mr. Sharett and other leaders were imprisoned by the British in Latrun, and Ben-Gurion was in Paris, she was acting head of the Political Department of the Jewish Agency and carried off her duties with grim attention to tact and protocol. When it was necessary to send a person of courage to see Abdullah of Jordan, Mrs. Meir was delegated. She made a deep and favorable impression on the wise and cautious King at her first interview in 1947. A year later, however, when she met him again in the dead of night on the Jordan side, Abdullah was depressed and nervous and reluctant to proceed along the road to friendship and decided to retreat.

She was the first representative of Israel sent to Soviet Russia and established contact with the silent masses of Jews in the muffled State. She was not able to alter political relations there, but her presence in Moscow had an electrifying effect not only upon the masses who saw her and touched her garments, but upon the repressed Jewish population of Soviet Russia. From Moscow she was recalled to become a member of the first elected Government of Israel and served from March 1949 to 1956 as Minister of Labor. In 1956 she was appointed Israel's Foreign Minister.

She possesses a quality rare in the leadership of Israel: She does not suffer the tensions of abstract thoughts. She lacks the terrible infection of ideology, the pale cast of thought that has sicklied o'er modern civilization to the point of reducing thought to inertia. She is a pragmatist. She is not worried by definitions. She is fascinated by ideas concerned with creative work. Because she seeks to locate her objective and her target has priority, her words are simple and clear. She is frugal in speech, which with her must always have a bearing upon action. Her words carry her emotions over to the listener who hears and understands what she says. She stands firmly on her feet and faces the problem under discussion without flinching, convinced that she is dealing with reality, and that the struggle cannot be avoided.

I have often wondered, remembering in detail the record of this remarkable personality, whether her intense desire always to be at work, to think of leisure as a state of sin, derives from a sense of guilt. Does she think she was tardy in finding her way to the Promised Land; that opportunities were not grasped in time; that there were years missed; that she did not heed the first call; that she should have come home sooner? It may be for these reasons that she was determined to make up for the lost years. At any rate, the record shows that she offered herself for service on many occasions when she deserved exemption.

DAVID BEN-GURION (1886–1973)

I conclude this series of profiles with the man who was the leader on the day the State was proclaimed and who, at this writing, continues with unabated vigor and courage as the Prime Minister of the Government of Israel.

David Ben-Gurion worked his way up in the Zionist Movement through the period following the death of Theodor Herzl. His distinctions in Zionism came originally from the labor movement, which he first nurtured in Poland, then organized, led and tyrannized over in Palestine. From his first days on he had his own dogmatic views on problems of Jewish life and of Zionism. It was never easy to dislodge any notion he had latched onto. He was a savage fighter who took advantage of every opening in a debate and remained unrelenting until battered down by a more powerful antagonist. All he knew of life he learned in the close comradeship of the labor movement. His education came from his experiences in that narrow world. He drew his inspiration from a keen knowledge of the ways of Jewish life, its history and its folk tradition. Although it is said that he was engrossed in the study of Greek and Greek literature and philosophy, the alien influence did not show in the pattern of his life. The student was not there. Least of all his comrades was he ever a disciple of Karl Marx, whose doctrine he outlived years ago. He fought side by side with labor comrades in a common cause, but above and beyond that cause the oracle he consulted most came from Jewish life, its wisdom and loyalties. Zion was his lodestar.

He was exiled from Palestine by the Turkish authorities when the First World War erupted. He came to New York and here, as elsewhere, devoted himself to the labor movement. Strangely enough, he was persuaded by Pinchas Rutenberg to join the American Jewish Congress movement and in the preparations for a Jewish Legion to join General Allenby against the Turks. Marching side by side with tall, lanky and awkward Itzhak Ben-Zvi (later on President of Israel) he returned to Palestine and helped remove the debris of war when peace came. He also spent two years in London and then returned to Tel Aviv, which was his home from then on.

In the Homeland he was propagandist and leader of power. He was a doughty fighter in partisan struggles. He was the most aggressive one of the brilliant group who created the Histadrut and its economic and cultural enterprises. He was not a theorist like Borochov, or Dr. Nachman Syrkin, or A. D. Gordon. He was not a scintillating journalist or a personality of charm and winning manner, like Berl Katznelson. He was not an adroit political analyst like Chaim Arlosoroff. He was not a Yeshiva student, turned practical, like David Remez. He seemed to think that most theorists were bores. But he had what none of the others had—a vision of where he was going. He elbowed his way through opposition and always expected to come out the victor. But when he lost he retired to his tent, licking his wounds, sulking, and preparing for the next round. He was obsessed by his work and could not be diverted. His mind followed one track. In fact, he was by nature dictatorial but fortunately he was bound in discipline to the party of which he was the leader, whom he could swear at, berate unmercifully, but with whom—that was his fate—he had to live as a brother-in-arms. He had to bow to the democratic spirit of Palestine, which gave a dissident the right to answer back, to swear back and to denounce the man whom he acknowledged as his leader. That was what made Ben-Gurion leader in office or out of it.

His hold on the Jewry of Israel came from the fact that he had the right to appeal to a higher court. The interests of the nation were above the interests of Jewish labor and the interest of Marxian socialism. He believed labor to be the instrument for the fulfillment of prophecy. Without labor, the co-operatives and the collectives, without labor as the crown of the State, one was bound to fall into the morass of competitive struggles in which Jewish national destiny would find a miserable death.

He gradually worked his way into the larger interests of Zionist authority in Palestine. He was driven in that direction by the tragedy of Jewish life. He foresaw that the Hitler massacres would inevitably lead to the opening of the doors of Palestine to the refugees and also inevitably bring about the creation of the Jewish State—in the whole of Palestine or a part of it. Its size did not concern him. If not big enough at the beginning, then later it would expand to provide welcome to those who needed sanctuary.

The first labor representative in the Jewish Agency was Chaim Arlosoroff, who accepted the political portfolio with Moshe Sharett as his assistant. Eliezer Kaplan graduated from the Histadrut and became the Treasurer of the Jewish Agency. David Ben-Gurion seemed to be free-lance in the Jewish Agency, then became its Palestine Chairman and served as liaison with London. He was once on the verge of a pact with Jabotinsky, which his party rejected. He and the labor movement went along with Dr. Weizmann through the enlargement of the Jewish Agency in 1929 and the Partition resolution at the Congress in 1937. But it soon became clear that David Ben-Gurion's hot blood, his uncontrollable indignations, his egotistical drive, his impatience, could not long endure the moderation of Dr. Weizmann. He wanted the Jewish people in its pain to cry out and to denounce the betrayers of the Promise. He was unable to accept restraint as a policy or patience as a virtue. He was unable to accept Dr. Weizmann's timeless program, his reliance on faith and his readiness to carry burdens endlessly while waiting for the redemption. Still, Dr. Weizmann remained the political leader until 1946. He was honored as the Elder Statesman and President of Israel until he passed away.

But David Ben-Gurion was the *de facto* leader of the Jewish settlement through the period from the White Paper of 1939 to 1946, when, with an intensity and ruthlessness difficult to understand, and against the will of over half his own party, he forced the official retirement of Dr. Weizmann and became the Chairman of the Executive of the Jewish Agency at the Basle Congress in 1946 and then the head of the State in 1948. It is a heavy crown that rests on his head.

Section III
Organizing the American Jewish Community

ORGANIZING THE AMERICAN JEWISH COMMUNITY

INTRODUCTION

Although the first Jewish settlers arrived in America from Holland in 1654, the American Jewish community of today, largest, richest and most powerful in the world, is actually no more than some 80 years old.

In 1876, when Louis Lipsky was born, there were fewer than 250,000 Jews in the whole of the United States.

Four years later began the great waves of immigration that for four decades poured into the United States millions of Jews, largely from Eastern Europe, seeking freedom and a haven from poverty and political and economic oppression, exacerbated by periodic pogroms.

By 1900 there were one million Jews in the United States; in 1914, at the outset of the First World War, three million; in 1928 their number had increased to 4,228,000.

Lipsky entered this populous arena when he arrived in New York from his native Rochester in 1900 to edit the American Hebrew. *He was 24 years old, unknown and self-educated, with some legal and literary experience. In love with literature, the theatre, writing, Jews, and American democracy, he was seeking a career as a writer.*

For fourteen years he pursued that career with perseverance, as the editor of The American Hebrew, *as drama critic, book reviewer, short story and feature writer for such leading American publications of that day as Reader Magazine, the Morning Telegraph, the New York Press, the Associated Magazines. Privately he wrote plays and short stories.*

Simultaneously, he was drawn as by a magnet to the Herzlian dream of a Jewish State for a renascent Jewish people. In 1901 he began to serve that dream as the editor of The Maccabean, *organ of the Federation of American Zionists, the first Zionist publication in English to appear in the United States.*

But he found himself most at home in the simmering life of the new immigrants.

It was a life constantly astir with a striving to create roots, to provide livelihood and education, to learn the new language. It was heady with freedom.

Yet it was a parochial community, despite its size and despite a lively Yiddish press. Few Jewish institutions existed, other than religious and philanthropic. The landsmannschaften *dominated the community. Everything had to be created—and it was, in the succeeding decades.*

The Zionist Movement in America was still in its cradle. A Federation of American Zionists had been formed in 1898 at an interstate conference of some 100 organizations held in New York City. Professor Richard Gottheil was its President, Stephen S. Wise its Secretary. Individual membership was unknown and activity limited.

The American Jewish Committee was spokesman for the Jews. This was a group of notables, established in 1905 under the spur of the Kishinev pogroms three years earlier, self-appointed and unchallenged until 1015. It was opposed to Zionism.

American Jewry was a community ripe for organization; World War I provided the incentive.

For nearly five decades the great struggles of Jewish life in the United States revolved around two basic issues:

1. *The building of a Jewish State in Palestine.*

2. *The right of Jews to organize their own institutions for the defense of Jewish rights at home and abroad, and fund-raising, by democratic methods, on the local, national and international levels.*

The building of the Jewish State, and the organization of representative Jewish institutions created by the democratic vote of their constituents, became Lipsky's twin passions. He devoted his life to them.

At the outset, the protagonists of Zionism, of the Jewish State, and of democratic organization were one and the same. They were: Louis D. Brandeis, Stephen Wise and Louis Lipsky, later joined by others. Their opponents were the leaders of the American Jewish Committee.

*

On May 14, 1948, a Jewish State was proclaimed in Palestine, sanctioned by the United Nations Partition Resolution of November 29, 1947. This historic climax had been achieved by a tremendous Jewish effort, after two wars, the Hitler holocaust, and the murder of six million Jews.

In this effort, American Jewry played an increasingly important role by reason of its organized power and its wealth.

But before that power could be wielded, organizations had to be created.

The Balfour Declaration and the Mandate had to be won; the wavering Mandatory Power both wooed and castigated; a Jewish Yishuv established in Palestine, nourished and developed; a war of survival and rescue fought.

A Zionist movement had to be created, with an organizational structure and with fund-raising institutions of substance; an articulate and influential press had to be developed.

To support the Zionist goals at the crucial moments involving the Balfour Declaration, the Palestine Mandate, the U.N. Partition Resolution, Israel in its battle for survival in the War of Independence, instruments expressive of American Jewish unity had to be forged. And they were in the American Jewish Congress in 1918 and in the American Jewish Conference in 1943.

Jewish life abroad had to be protected against Hitlerism and its aftermath. A World Jewish Congress was established in 1936.

The challenges of Nazism abroad and anti-Semitism at home required a struggle by courageous and representative Jewish spokesmen on the national and local level. The American Jewish Congress renewed its mandate in 1938 through direct, popular, democratic elections. By 1943, it had established itself with such strength, locally as well as nationally, that at the American Jewish Conference its delegation was the second largest.

The menacing charge of dual loyalty was used for 40 years by the opponents of a Jewish State and of democratic organization. It was rejected and disproved.

The struggle was constant, often bitter, until 1948.

Lipsky's life and work spanned this entire period. From 1901 he was involved in the struggle: from 1913 to 1930 as an official of the Zionist Organization; thereafter as a volunteer. For more than half a century he was at the helm of these distinct yet concerted movements—the Zionist Organization; The American Jewish Congress; The Keren Hayesod; The United Palestine Appeal; The American Jewish Conference. He was in large measure the architect of the great achievements in the period of upbuilding. He was theoretician, parliamentarian, propagandist and fighter.

On the international scene, he served the World Zionist Organization as a member of its Executive Committee from 1923 and as the American member of the Jewish Agency Executive from 1933 until 1946.

His literary career was abandoned for the Jewish cause in 1926, when he became President of the Zionist Organization of America. His literary talent was devoted to the movement for the regeneration of the Jewish people, and has preserved the great drama of that regeneration.

In the succeeding pages various chapters in the great struggle to forge a potent, democratically organized Jewish community in support of a Jewish State and the defense of Jewish rights wherever threatened are presented in articles and speeches by Lipsky over half a century. They constitute a unique historical record of a turbulent epoch by one of its principal figures.

The Editor

THE EARLY YEARS

THE ZIONIST CONVENTION*

It cannot be said that the American Federation of Zionists displayed any sign of vigor at its Convention this week. It is true that there was a rally-meeting on Sunday night at Cooper Union, where enthusiasm and nationalistic sentiment ran riot. But this was not due to the inspiration of the Convention, but rather to the orator, whose presence and utterance, whatever the topic, always win a large audience, which he invariably moves by his eloquence. On this occasion he touched the racial pride of those present by his use of the sacred tongue, with a fire and feeling that touched the most callous. Then there were some songs that the vast audience snatched up in a way that thrilled the onlooker though he understood not a word.

But all this does not prove the strength of Zionism. Cooper Union crowded to the doors by our downtown brethren is no new experience to us. It is an annually recurring occasion when the closing exercises of the Hebrew Technical Institute take place. Yet who will point to this as an indication of the strength of that excellent institution?

The Convention gave evidence of the need of a strong hand at the helm; the hand of a Herzl, who can impress his individuality upon those coming in contact with him.

There are two things in connection with Zionism that must strike the unbiased observer: That there is but a single Jewish journal in the world, published in the English language—none in this country—favoring Zionism, at least as expounded at Basle; and that among the new adherents to the cause in this country since the inception of the Movement there has not been a single person prominent in Jewish life.

The venerable Dr. Gottheil said, when presiding at Sunday's mass

* *The American Hebrew*, June 15, 1900.

meeting, that every Jew must be a Zionist. We presume he meant that
the most indifferent Jew must look with some regard upon that land
which was the cradle of his ancestors. If that sort of passive Zionism
suits Dr. Gottheil, well and good; but it must be small comfort for
Dr. Herzl, his banking scheme, and his aspirations towards
colonization.

THE DUTY OF AMERICAN JEWS *

Zionism is not merely a solution of the Jewish question. It is not like
the atomic theory, or the Darwinian theory. It is not merely an argument
which logically proves a certain thing, and which you must, as a logical
being, accept and cease combatting. If you see the truth of it you are
not saved. It is not merely a program. If it were, discussion, education,
argument, etc. would be the simple method of propaganda, and it
could get along without orators, songs or displays, without appeals
to the imagination, without poetry or enthusiasm.

Theodor Herzl expressed it right when he said that a return to Judaism
would precede the realization of the object of Zionism, but by the
word Judaism, I take it, Herzl meant a return to the fervor
and enthusiasm, a return to faithfulness, which has always been associated with religion in its larger sense.

Before Zionism, which is the means of escape from the *Galuth*, can
become a reality, it must be preceded by the rebirth of emotion, which,
among Jews, will take the form of religious enthusiasm. You may talk
for centuries of theories, of certain truths—as Reform Jews talk of the
Jewish mission—but until the souls of the persons appealed to have
been quickened, until the idea has become related to their own being,
the idea, or the theory, or the truth, is just so much junk in the intellectual
treasury of the world and nothing more.

An annual exhibition of spiritual and intellectual squinting and
dodging is given by the Central Conference of American Rabbis, who
also speak of truths, Jewish ideals, etc. It is not many years since that
dignified body of wanderers in the desert of barren ideas and empty
phrases declared that the Jews do not constitute a nation, that Washington
is our Jerusalem and the United States our Zion, and yet, that idea, unrelated to the life and thought of the Jewish people, actually untrue to
Jewish life, has floated about the United States, the object of ridicule, a

* *Read before the Nordau Zionist Society,* January 23, 1909.

gratuitous fling at the aspiration of loyal sons of the Jewish people, a useless impudent, foolish idea, for it never had a basis in the lives of Jews who have the right to speak as Jews. The force of spiritual necessity has even brought into the fold of Zionism a large number of the very men who at the time stood by and passively permitted the rabbinical stupidity to speak.

The Jewish mission has dwindled down to a mere whisper, and is heard now only in apologetic terms, for the force of circumstances has swept it off the boards, and it is now properly taking its place in the archives of American Jewish history, which our alert American Jewish Committee is compiling for the edification of future generations. It was an artificial thing from the start, but it was puffed up into the semblance of life by the army of ranters, who contrive to hold the right to the pulpits of Jewish temples.

The trouble with the Jewish mission was that it was an unreal interpretation of the meaning of Jewish life, promulgated with a dishonorable motive. In their souls the Jewish missionaries knew that the theory that the Jews were chosen by God to live in *golus* and to be a light to the nations, to whom they were to preach a pure monotheism, was an audacious brag, an artificial imposition on Jewish history, a contrivance to permit Jewish life to be sapped by assimilation without a struggle on the part of the victims. It was a contrivance to prolong the Jewish Galuth by inertia. It was a conception which struck truth at no point in its career. It was something to which no honest, unprofessional Jew would subscribe. The Jewish mission was an apology for existence, which no dignified man or race or nation would ever consent to make. The mission of any individual, race or nation, is, first and last, to be true to its own self, which from the start was denied by the mission theorists.

Nor are the rabbinical exponents of race and national dishonor the only organized body in the field, pretending to speak for the Jews. The Union of American Hebrew Congregations met last month and again the empty pretence was pressed to the fore by the same class of professional Jews, who have never understood the people whom they are supposed to represent, that the Jews are not a race or a nation, but a religious community. If the Jewish mission means anything, it should aim to express not only Jewish principles of religion, but the Jewish principles governing all the relations of man, yet every opportunity they see to limit the Jewish mission to something more ethereal, more unrelated to life, they grasp with the enthusiasm of makeshift statesmen.

When the Union of American Hebrew Congregations makes a declaration like that it does not go back to the records for proof of its assumption; it does not consult the Jewish religion to see whether it is consistent with it on that subject, for its primary object is to lull to rest the slumbering national and racial feelings among the Jews, and thus make easier, from a crass material point of view, their present existence. When it speaks of religion, so obtuse are these professed theologians that they do not see that they are speaking of religion in the Christian sense, as a creed, which the Jewish religion never was, for it has always considered religion and life one and indivisible.

Wherever you see Jewish life in its undiluted, unassimilated state, no matter how deformed or abnormal it may be, it is always bounded in every detail by the Jewish religion, and there is no more un-Jewish conception than that the Jews can eliminate all national and racial elements in their lives and actually remain exponents of Judaism. In every genuine Jewish town, or community, the Jewish religion means law, civil and criminal, hygiene, charity and philanthropy, education; in fact, all of life is governed by this version of the Jewish religion, for the value of Judaism, its future development, as well as its past, lies in just this combination of law and life, which has made it an indispensable factor in the civilization of the world, and which the Zionist Movement has come into being in order to conserve for future uses.

Dr. M. H. Harris, of New York, who for a brief period was regarded as somewhat of a nationalist, but who has since retired to reconsider the question and to listen to the dictates of an enlightened conscience, recently said that all Jews who have no faith in Judaism and do not practice it, should get out of the fold. That was a bold thing to say for a rabbi whose congregation stands so close to the precipice of advanced reform. Dr. Harris' audacity has not been denounced as it should be. His impertinence has not been called by its right name, and, although his views have appeared in print, not one of the many rabbis and prominent Jews of this city have been keen enough to take offense at the insulting, un-Jewish, inquisitorial proposition made by Dr. Harris in the statement that if Jews cannot or do not believe in what he calls the Jewish faith, and do not practice Judaism, it were better that their children be brought up at least in the Christian faith.

This teacher of ethics and religion, who writes books on Jewish history where he condemns the efforts of Jews to maintain their own nationality against the Romans, forgets, however, that while there are many Jews who cannot utter the words of prayer, and who cannot regulate their lives according to the statutes of an arrested nationality, these same Jews wish to base their lives in Jewish thought, Jewish religion, Jewish tradition, but the conditions of life hamper the expression of their desires, and because they cannot get out of the fold without repudiating the Jewish brotherhood, which they hold dear, they prefer to reserve to their own homes the expression of the religion they believe in. They are not as glib as rabbis are, who so easily compromise with even the trivial incidents of life, who so easily formulate a pallid, empty monotheism, modelled on Christian forms. Jews who are Zionists are not so facile in forming their religion to suit the exigencies of a professional career.

We Zionists face Jewish life, see the abnormality of our position, admit that the Judaism we know cannot live in *golus* unless we create a national center in Palestine, observe the demoralizing effect of the *golus* spirit, the insidious inroads of assimilation, the dilution of Jewish ideals by alien forces, and we demand of the Jewish people that they assert their national or racial strength in order to give reality to our projects and to destroy these abnormalities and dangers. We are not so positive even that the Jewish people will respond. When Bar Kochba took up arms against a magnificent Roman army, he was not so certain that his brethren would respond to his call to arms; but his cause was just, it was necessary, and he was bound to take up the fight. We are not victims of self-deception; we are not dreamers in that sense. We expect that there will be thousands of assimilating Jews, who, short-sighted and complacent, will take up arms against us, and denounce us, but we hope and we have the right to expect that they will have the decency not to invoke the Jewish religion or Jewish tradition against us.

A double dilemma confronts every American Jew, the Zionist as well, who is not orthodox. He sees before him an immobile Judaism. The law decisions and the statutes of an arrested nationality, congealed in a religious form in order to conserve the Jewish people, are repugnant to democracy and especially to the American youth filled with impulses to have life reflect his own individuality. The hygienic regulations of the Jewish state, which have also become enslaved to religion, he would have scrutinized by science and rejected if they do not stand the test.

The detailed methods of worship, the legislation that prescribes every movement on the Sabbath, cannot have any actual authority, wherever the Jew is free, and inner pressure does not demand it for ulterior reasons. Even the ideal of God, who once selected the Jews as his bearers of light and law cannot, unless there are reasons of national interest, be accepted without a protest against the arrogance of the claim, the absence of humility in it. Unless you admit the national authority, you are bound to deny the validity of Jewish law. Those who deny the existence of the Jewish nation, and live the Jewish traditional life, are like the blind fish in the mammoth cave in Kentucky who would insist having eyes, where there is nothing to see.

The traditional law was effective while the world erected barriers against us, and we could not escape from the Jewish world. Here in America the barriers have been removed. But you cannot touch the traditional religion without destroying the form that had been created to preserve the Jewish future. You dare not remove one form of Jewish life, without creating another.

Before you can be free to create your own religion, with variations on the Jewish original, as it must be, you must free the Jewish religion of all its national elements, allowing those national elements to develop under normal conditions. Jewish life must be made to mean more than Judaism, in order that Judaism may not tremble at every danger which affects Jewish life.

Therefore the Jewish youth of America, who are not materialists, who are not atheists, who have faith though it does not conform, who hope to reconcile the phenomena of life with their religious hopes, are unable to go very far without an encounter with this peculiar situation. On the one hand the American Jew sees an anomalous form of arrested religion, and, on the other, a form of religion which has repudiated all those national elements without which Jewish life becomes a ghost without a habitation, without which our heritage from our fathers is given away, denied, compromised, for the sake of conformity, assimilation, adjustment, etc. He has the choice of subduing his natural longing to have religion express his conception of truth, his relation to God and man, or repudiating all those things in his own soul, which he has had from his forefathers, and which he does not wish to deny, give away, compromise or lose.

That is the religious dilemma of every progressive, thinking young Jew. The rabbis may not wish to see it, but we choose not to pass it over with pretence and hypocrisy. The American Jew must meet the issue. When life in all its complexity confronts him, he must get out of the dilemma, he must state his relation to the problem, he must adjust his life to the great past, which holds him, not in bondage, as so many think, but as a willing servant, in order to realize the best in his own individuality, and pass on to his children something of the heritage of which he is proud.

Nor is the religious cause the only one that must prompt the American Jew to become a Zionist.

There is plain, ordinary, every-day gratitude to your parents, and through them to your ancestors. You are compelled to an interest in all the difficulties of the race, whose son you are. Not because they are over there and suffer, but because you yourself are so much less in value, as they are reduced in value. It is not altruism; it is ennobled self-respect. You bear the name Jew, and wherever a Jew is ill-treated, oppressed, contemned, despised, you are ill-treated, oppressed, despised. You feel their hurts, just as you feel the hurt of your own natural brother when he is hounded and maltreated. They strike you when they strike him. You cannot hold your head erect here, while over there Jews are being thrown to the ground and trampled upon. You may live far from the scene, but you cannot live your own life unless you have righted your brothers' wrong.

Your parents have implanted in you certain affections, certain hates, certain aspirations. They have breathed into you the traditions of Jewish life, of Jewish lore, of Jewish conceptions of nobility, of virtue, of dignity. Wherever those virtues, that dignity, that nobility is attacked, your own dignity, your own nobility, your own virtue vibrates in sympathy, and is seriously affected. The destruction of the Jewish people means the destruction of everything you hold to be noble in life, which you hope to transmit to your children. You cannot live a full life without having lifted your hand to redress the wrongs which the Jewish people endure, *for your own personal interests are at stake.* These interests may not be your own bread and butter, your goods, but they are the higher interests of your individuality, which, if you are a Jewish nobleman, you will defend at the cost of your life, if need be.

Judaism is one of the manifestations of Jewish life. It is not the only manifestation when Zionism has entered into Jewish life. Judaism has preserved the identity of the Jewish people; it has been the form of communal unity, which held all that was valuable in Jewish life. Until we have re-established Jewish life on the model of its fomer national life, we Zionists shall not raise a finger to minimize or destroy the Judaism which has performed such a valuable function in Jewish life heretofore, but we shall devote ourselves to the enlargement of Jewish life so that it will be possible for all Jews who feel the ties of brotherhood to be included in the ranks of the Jewish people.

If you are Jewish noblemen, American citizens, you are bound to heed the call to defend the interests of Jewish character, of Jewish ideals, of Jewish aspirations. And when you see the victims who have suffered in those interests, it is not only sympathy you feel, but also a feeling of greatness, for you will find that the outraged kinsmen who are about you here, as they are over there, are not the victims of diseased ideals, not dumb beasts, not the scum of the world, but men and women who have been everlastingly treated unjustly, and it thus becomes not only your duty, but also your willing mission, in order to relieve the everlasting injuries of your people, to become a part of them, to merge all your interests with theirs, to take into yourself all that they have to teach of the ideals of life, which have been perpetuated among the Jewish people, not merely in response to a caprice of nature, but in order that some day it may obtain its freedom and develop under normal, natural conditions.

When you are once under these influences, as all self-respecting American Jews are bound to come, then you are on the road to become a full-fledged Zionist. You open your soul to the waves of life which Jewish national life has set in motion. You take your knowledge and culture from your own people, for you know that your own people have produced that which best adjusts itself to your individuality. You gradually permit yourself to be enveloped in Jewish life, and you naturally arrive at the Zionist solution, for you see that all these abnormalities in Jewish life, all the dilemmas of your soul, can never be adjusted while the Jews are in exile or are not in a land which they feel is their own, in an environment where only Jewish influences are radiated, where a political form of life shuts off, for a time, the intrusive alien ideals.

And thus, if you open your soul, your taste for Jewish literature is developed. You do not, naturally, take it at its face value, for you understand that it reflects, for the most part, the abnormality of Jewish life. But you appreciate that this reflects also the normal, and you hope for the day of redemption when literature shall become a free expression of the aspirations of the Jewish people.

You will see nothing incompatible in Zionism with the ideals of an American republic. Rather, you will find in American history analogies to confirm your faith in Zionism. You will see in the migration of the Pilgrim fathers the same impulse which animates Zionists. You will see in the American revolution the ideal of freedom, for which men have fought and died, and thus there will be nothing visionary or fanciful in the Zionist ambition to sacrifice material gains if need be in order to acquire those spiritual rewards for which, in many diverse ways, the Jews have died during the ages of exile. Zionists demand a separate national territory for those who by long tradition, by a common religion, by a common culture, have acquired certain traits that can best develop and purify themselves in a territory governed by representatives of that culture, tradition and ideals. That is compatible with American tradition, with democratic principles, with present American citizenship.

Let those who call themselves American Jews take warning. It is vital to the future of the Jews that they be honest with themselves. The difficulties, the alterations in character, which I have attempted to describe to you, are real, and the arrival at the ultimate solution cannot be stopped. Not all the resolutions of a central conference of Reform rabbis, or a union of American Hebrew congregations, or the utterances of shortsighted time-servers who occupy pulpits, will alter, in the least, the revolution in Jewish life which is going on in American Jewry. If these people were honest with themselves, they would confess that the troubles of life are their own troubles, that the religious dilemma, the racial dilemma, the national dilemma affects them also, and instead of trying to beat back the ocean waves, they will lend a hand to our movement, help to sweep away the brush of the forest, make the path to Zion easy, and aid Jews who wish to establish a nucleus of free independent Jewish life in Palestine. Instead of denying Jewish nationality and making desperate efforts to meet Jewish immigration problems by diverting it to Texas, Mexico, or North Africa, they would be among the first to aid us in our work of regenerating the Jewish nation in Palestine. They will find, from year to year, that the inevitable progress of Zionism, without an adequate relief in Palestine, will still further embitter their lives, and imperil their efforts to be the first of all the peoples coming to this country to jump into the melting pot which Israel Zangwill has imported into the United States.

The more our opponents protest, the stronger will Zionism become, for as their protests lose the value of novelty, and investigation proves that they are based on an unreal conception of Jewish life, the American Jew is bound to become a Zionist, and these assimilationists will be left as the unhonored remnant that refused to leave the flesh-pots of Egypt for the Land of Promise because they had become victims of their own social aberrations.

THE AMERICAN JEWISH STUDENT*

When Theodor Herzl uttered his first message to the Jewish people, he found the community where he lived antagonistic to his endeavor to call a Zionist Congress. The official community was opposed to him. The leaders were distressed by his persistence. But he found a sturdy backing in the Jewish student organization in Vienna, the Kadimah. These young men, conscious of the national struggle they had to wage in university circles, appreciated their kinship with the Zionist ideal. They became militant advocates of the cause.

The same conditions were to be found in the Russian universities. The young men of our people, flung into the vortex of life where anti-Semitic prejudices struck them with full force, became enthusiastic advocates of the movement that appealed to their manhood.

The Bilu was composed of students. They made a heroic fight against intolerable conditions, and in Palestine struggled like heroes to make life possible under the then unpropitious circumstances. Many of them died in Palestine as a result of exposure. Many of them emigrated, determined to return when conditions improved.

In this country, Zionism is a movement as yet directed by professional men supported by the middle class and the upper proletariat. We look in vain for the influence of the university men in our organization. In England, a group of young students has come to the front during the past five years, who promise much for the advancement of our ideas. In the United States, the army of university-trained men who will devote themselves to Jewish national interests has yet to climb up the hill and to be seen.

But they are coming. We already see the tips of their banners waving.

It may be that they have not come before because in this country the student has been regarded as a frivolous, athletic, fun-loving individual anxious to avoid the contamination of serious intellectual ideas. The American student has had his standard fixed not by American thinkers, not by strong enthusiasms, but by the ideas of the athletic field. Of course, there have been students who pursued their own intellectual and spiritual ideas, but the tone of the American university did not favor such pursuits; the atmosphere of the university seemed to be against enthusiasm of the spirit and mind. There was place in it for football, baseball, and other athletic games, but there seemed to be avoidance of active idealism. The university course was

---

* *The Maccabean,* November 1912.

the feeding period of our youth. They were being molded. They were not expected to take part in the serious affairs of life. It was considered the proper thing for the student to imbibe knowledge and build up a strong body.

This tendency is disappearing in American universities. Public life in America is also becoming more serious. The students are not all boys; they are acquainted with the intense competitive struggle. American politics is becoming more serious.

Our Jewish students are not backward in taking cognizance of the new conditions. They are forming, we are glad to say, their Menorah societies that will radiate light in Jewish circles. They are forming their university clubs, based on Jewish separateness, with a feeling that they owe something to, and will gain by affiliation with, Jewish interests. We may therefore hope that within a few years, when these young men will go out into the open fields of life, they will become active members of the cause which means so much for the future of the Jewish nation.

They carry the banner of our future.

They are beginning to feel their kinship with the Jewish liberation , movement. They are beginning to appreciate the lofty ideals that animate it. They are bound to listen when the clarion call of their people rings in their hearts. As Jews, as Americans, as men who have lingered in the halls of knowledge, they will come to us, and strengthened by their adherence, the Zionist cause will march from one outpost to another, from strength to strength, until we raise the flag of our nation upon the soil of our ancient people.

We see the tips of their banners waving. Soon we shall see their banners unfurled white and blue.

A REVOLUTION IN AMERICAN JEWRY*

To give an account of the Federation of American Zionists—in other words, a history of American Zionism—involves tracing the development of American Jewry during the past twenty years. It is not only the story of the progress of Zionism, but the history of a revolution in Jewish life, in which the protagonist was the Zionist Movement.

Zionism has not only captured the attention of American Jewry, pointing the way to a renascence in Palestine, bringing Palestine into the center of Jewish life, but it has evoked the revolutionary democratic forces of that life and turned them into the service of the Jewish people.

Take a photograph of American Jewry before 1895, and you will see a picture which is totally unlike what it is today. It then presented a flat surface, without color or animation. There were parochial organizations, unattached to general Jewish causes; there were no issues that aroused enthusiam or interest. There were no people, but just individuals. The obvious and the commonplace, both in thought and deed, were in control. Hospitals were built, orphan asylums were established, *chadorim* were maintained. The interest was wholly local. The Reform movement was busily engaged in adjusting itself to the new conditions, preaching the obvious and employing such means to fortify its position only as circumstances made necessary. The Hebrew Union College was not a first-class theological seminary; it was busily engaged in graduating rabbis to take the positions that were waiting for them. The Jewish Theological Seminary was leading a precarious life, not yet the object of philanthropic attention. The Jewish Publication Society had exhausted itself with its translation of Graetz's history, and was indifferent to that stream of life emanating from Russia, which was subsequently to overwhelm it and bring about

* *The Maccabean*, June–July 1917.

a change in policy. The Jews were not involved in struggle or conflict. Meetings were perfunctory. There were no events. The Jewish "street" was not audible.

The Anglo-Jewish press was placid, pliable and provincial, lending its support to the routine affairs of life, chronicling the births, marriages and deaths of the community, mainly concerned with the problem of the bread and butter of its publishers and editors. Most of them were the personal organs of rabbis, utilized by them to spread their own reputations, and there were no writers whose utterances were read or commanded attention. For the Yiddish press there was a sullen contempt. With Jewish life vociferously Americanizing itself, the Yiddish newspapers, then rather feeble enterprises, were regarded as the organs of alienism, introducing a discordant note which was disturbing. The Yiddish theatre was also exotic, to which pilgrimages were made as to one of the landmarks of a bizarre existence, which had as its western boundary the Chinese quarter, with its josses, restaurants and theatres. Downtown was the place to get away from. Yiddish was the language of the alien, to be rid of as soon as possible. The East Side was the chrysalis, which every Americanized Jew sloughed off at his graduation. Under such conditions the East Side had no part in Jewish life beyond local interest in a few institutions.

The parochial side of American Jewish life was thus a fair reflection of the poverty of resources and influence of the period. But, at the same time, there were national or international aspects to Jewish life, and these had to be dealt with as occasion demanded. These aspects of Jewish life, however, were treated as in other days. To the volunteer, free play was given. Whoever desired had a license to concern himself in such matters as were above and beyond the parochial interests of American Jewry. It was the era of the self-appointed leader, the unrepresentative spokesman. Out of this freedom and license, certain elements in American Jewry took possession of the political life of the Jewish people, deciding what should be and what should not be the position of the Jewish people in relation to other peoples. In effect, there was a Jewish Ministry for Foreign Affairs. Someone had to speak, someone had to act, at a time when most Jews were busy with their local affairs. This Ministry was at first composed of appointees of the Union of American Hebrew Congregations, which, through its Board of Delegates, established an Ambassadorship in Washington, which acted for the Jewish people on immigration and other political affairs that arose from time to time. Subsequently, the Union was given the support of the Independent Order Bnai Brith, whose leading member had been appointed the Jewish Ambassador.

For thirty years and more our Ambassador at Washington was the Hon. Simon Wolf, who is now publishing a book entitled "Presidents I Have Known." He came to know these Presidents by reason of his position. It was he who informed the United States Government what the Jews of this country wanted and what they were opposed to. In his opinion—and in the opinion of his colleagues—the Jews were not a nationality, but a religious sect; the Jews insisted upon being regarded solely as Americans; Jewish immigration was due to religious persecution; every trace of individual Jewish life was discord and not Jewish. In short, Mr. Wolf spoke unchallenged in the name of assimilation on behalf of the Jews of America.

The Jewish people had not elected Mr. Wolf to do this. He had no mandate from them. He acted for the few men who had appointed him, who, in lieu of an organization of all Jews, acted for all Jews in such matters. In default of a government, they were the government.

The group controlling Mr. Wolf had its center in the Middle West. About the time of the Kishinev pogroms, a new and more powerful group of influential Jews entered the field and disputed the position of the Western Jews. They felt that Mr. Wolf had outlived his usefulness, and that new blood should be infused into the Jewish government, or Ministry for Foreign Affairs. They represented the same policies. They were of the same element. But they had unbounded faith in their superior ability. This new group, entrusted with the distribution of the Kishinev relief fund, decided to organize. Five gentlemen took the lead. These five added twenty or twenty-five additional members. The twenty-five or thirty thus named selected forty or forty-five other men, and the enlarged group organized, adopted a constitution, was incorporated, and the American Jewish Committee was born.

The members of the new group were, in fact, much more active in the parochial affairs of American Jewry. They were responsible for many of the charitable and philanthropic institutions in New York. They had reorganized the Jewish Theological Seminary. They controlled the Jewish Publication Society, and other Philadelphia institutions. Members of the group were large contributors to Jewish enterprises outside of New York, and some of them were known to leading European Jews.

Soon Mr. Wolf ceased to be the sole Jewish spokesman and representative in Washington. He was not displaced, but he gave place to others on important occasions, and devoted himself more exclusively to the details of petty representations that had to be made to the American Government on behalf of Jewish immigrants. The sceptre of power slipped from him and his friends, and others decided the fate of our people.

The American Jewish Committee has acted as the Jewish Ministry for Foreign Affairs ever since the Kishinev pogroms. At its annual meetings, pretentious claims were made as to its participation in Jewish events, but it was felt that should any occasion demand a large and liberal-minded policy, the Committee would be in a position to act for American Jewry.

Autocracy, however, destroys itself by so reducing the surface of responsibility that, finally, only a limited few are interested, and then only one or two give the word of command and make the decisions and issue directions. In absolute control of the Committee, autocrats never made an effort to enlarge the sphere of interest and to bring in the forces of the people. By meeting in secret, it estranged the people from genuine personal interest in what it was doing or not doing. As an autocracy, it could nevertheless have become a popular autocracy, for a while, by riding into popular favor with a policy that reflected the ideals and aspirations of the Jewish people. But with a perversity which is inexplicable, the self-appointed leaders contrived at every critical juncture in Jewish life to speak exactly the reverse of what was in the Jewish heart. It was decidedly unpopular, not so much because of its undemocratic methods, but because it never actually spoke for those ideals that were becoming the ideals of the people, under the influence of the Zionist propaganda.

It had no faith in the competence of the Jewish people, and no confidence in the judgment of the rank and file. It treated the enthusiasms of the general run of Jews with disdain and contempt. It had no faith in the extension of Jewish life, but wished to restrain and fetter it so that it would fit exactly into its Procrustean bed of dogma and book theories. Instead of inviting the expansion of Jewish life, it wished to keep it within the bounds of a definition. It did not believe in Jewish nationality not because the symptoms of nationality were not present, but because in its opinion such symptoms should be eradicated. Whatever should not be, must not be. It had notions of order, progress, taste, language, and all of these notions the Jews were expected to adopt, and if they would not, they had to be remonstrated with until bullied into acquiescence. Not only did this self-elected leadership insist upon doing what it pleased, but it insisted that American Jewry must conform in its thinking to the thoughts of the leaders.

They were the weight that oppressed Jewish life, preventing expansion, making impossible color, animation, interest, responsibility. Had they prevailed, there would not have been a Zionist movement resting firmly upon the masses of the Jews; there would not have been that widespread interest in Hebrew education, in the Congress, in every popular movement of the day. The Yiddish-speaking Jews would have been a cowed, submissive, broken-English group, minus a literature, a press, a theatre, and a national life. The American Jewish youth would have been servile, lacking initiative, looking for the patronage of the wealthy instead of seeking to make Jewish careers for themselves. Our life would have been an unimaginative, unprogressive, wholly contemptible survival of a people unable to combat the forces of assimilation, and practically doomed to extinction.

The policy of the self-appointed leaders had two forces to contend with. First, such a form of life could not endure in an American atmosphere, where freedom and democracy are ingredients of every phase of social life. To the American young men bred in the public schools and graduated from American universities, autocratic representation could not be endured. It was obnoxious to the spirit of the times. What is characteristic of the American spirit is its assertiveness, its refusal to subordinate itself to codes formulated by others. The American does not minimize his powers; it is more frequently brag than self-effacement. The constant reiteration of submissiveness, the denial of Jewish characteristics and talents, the segregation of Jewish life into only one form of expression, the obsequious and vapid claims to patriotic ardor, the seeking of justification for Jewish life—all this the free American spirit could not swallow. The first to resist control of the American Jewish Committee were American-born and educated Jewish young men, who were active in the Zionist Movement.

Second, such a policy excluded from consideration the large, predominant element of Jews coming from Eastern Europe. A policy that refused to take them into account was doomed to failure. The Russian Jews knew what oppression and persecution meant, and contact with American institutions was bound to lead to a genuine respect for democracy. They increased in numbers so rapidly that they were compelled to establish their own institutions, unaffected to a large extent by American methods. They established their newspapers and theatres, their asylums and charitable institutions, and clung to

Yiddish long enough to enable that language to attain a fluency and an influence which gave content to their own national aspirations.

Little respect was paid to the new settlers, and plans were made for improvement without consulting them. Gradually there developed, thanks to the tactlessness of the self-appointed leaders, a feeling of estrangement, a feeling that the leaders were not related to them in their conception of Jewish life, and there ensued a conflict in which the self-appointed leaders were challenged to produce their credentials. The new settlers produced their own leaders, many of whom were at once first absorbed and then smothered by the American Jewish Committee. But there were too many who refused to be "co-opted." They formed the nucleus of the revolt. The Yiddish newspapers edited by radicals, directed their batteries against the Jewish government, until gradually, the prestige and influence of the Committee were reduced to such proportions that with the development of the American Jewish Congress movement, its power was taken from it, and now awaits the installation of the American Jewish Congress to be handed over to its successor, elected by and responsible to the people.

In this revolution in Jewish life, briefly indicated here—the Zionist Movement is largely responsible. Not that it held the self-appointed leaders in low esteem, but because it felt that unless the Jews of this country were liberated from the oppressive influence of autocracy, Zionism as a radical solution of the Jewish problem could not make the necessary progress. Zionism could not hope for success with the fate of the Jewish people in the hands of persons who declined to take the people into their confidence, and who refused to accept the basic principles of nationality in Jewish life. If the movement was to make headway, the people had to be aroused from their lethargy, from their ignorance, from their indifference to larger responsibilities. Zionism means democracy because only the Jewish people can save the Jewish people. Philanthropy is an obsolete cure, not only in Jewish life, but everywhere. The philanthropist acts from altruistic motives; a people may become free only through its own efforts. Unless Zionism secured a hold on the imagination and the will of the masses of Jews, the outcome would be a sentimental love of Palestine, but not the solution of the Jewish problem.

The Zionist organization during its twenty years of life was therefore unavoidably compelled to overthrow every force that consciously or unconsciously threatened to keep the Jewish people out of the councils that were deciding their future. But more than that, the Zionist ideal itself, with its implications, could not exist in an atmosphere of oppression and autocracy. Where it lives, all contradictions must die. The mere growth of the Zionist organization, its increase in membership and influence, was the wedge that destroyed the opposition. The splinters had to fly. As Zionism moved forward, the opposition had to recede and make way. And as Zionism moved forward, democracy came to the foreground, and all anti-democratic elements in Jewish life had to disappear or become innocuous.

We have built an organization which is the tangible expression of our ideal. It is democratic. It is progressive. It takes its cue from the aspirations and hopes of the people. We have placed Palestine on the Jewish map. The Jewish nationality faces its supreme test as it is about to be recognized. Men and women of influence and prominence are rallying about our blue and white banner, joining without condition, subscribing wholeheartedly to our program and our ideals. All this in the face of conditions that would have disheartened others, but thanks to the power of our ideal, we have moved forward in spite of all obstacles. But the greatest achievement of the Zionist organization in the past twenty years is the Democratic Revolution of Jewish life, which foreshadows the final success of our endeavors.

THE DISTRICT ORGANIZATION PLAN*

Introduction

The structure of the United States Government, in the performance of its functions, is the model used to build the Zionist Organization of America. Lipsky was its architect. The name he gave his model was The District Organization Plan.

The year was 1918; the plan was revolutionary.

It replaced group affiliation with individual membership, absorbed autonomous affiliates into one cohesive national organization, and established the geographical District as the basic Zionist unit, in place of the smaller groups called Societies.

Like many "firsts" it was fought by the organizations then constituting the Federation of American Zionists.

But the author of the plan, despite doubts of those who supported the idea, including Louis D. Brandeis, succeeded in piloting it through the 1918 Zionist Convention to its adoption.

Thereafter he was chiefly responsible for its implementation, first as Secretary for Organization, later as Chairman and as President.

The results created both the foundation and the edifice for the Movement, crucial to the role it was destined to play in helping create the State of Israel.

The Editor

A lively discussion is going on among Zionists on the District Plan of Organization, which is to come up at the Pittsburgh Convention. I hope critics of the plan will bear in mind that the Constitution as framed was not intended to cover all probable circumstances that may arise out of the acceptance of the fundamental principle. A written Constitution

* *The Maccabean*, June 1918.

cannot contain anything but the general rules. In the Constitution of
the District organizations themselves, there will be found amplifications
of the General Constitution that will throw light upon the reform that
is proposed.

We are now concerned with the general aspect of the Plan. What is
intended by the District Organization? Will it supersede societies and
make their existence impossible?

The basic feature of the District Plan is its individual membership, and
its usefulness in providing a form of organization which will allow for
the affiliation, free and unhindered, of all Jews who wish to enroll in
the Zionist organization. The District Organization is to be the vessel
into which all our Zionist resources are to be poured, and the sum total
of the strength of the District Organizations will be the strength of the
Zionist Organization of America. Just as the United States Government
is constituted, in fact, of the citizens who are politically divided into
States, or Congressional Districts, so the Zionist Organization of
America is to be divided into District Organizations, which are to be the
units of our government. Just as the United States Government, as
a government, is elected or established, by citizens voting in certain
Districts, so the Zionist administration will be elected or established by
the Zionist citizens enrolled and registered in a District Organization.

That does not mean that the Zionist citizen has nothing else to do but
to vote. He joins with other Zionist citizens in whatever work he thinks
will further the ends of the entire citizenship. He may form parties, engage
in educational work, and combine to further the interests of certain
Zionist institutions or funds.

But all fundamental taxes and obligations as Zionist citizens are discharged though the District Organization. Outside of that, there is
freedom of action, unless certain general laws, approved by all Zionist
citizens in their annual convention, may decide otherwise.

The situation in Pittsburgh may be taken as an example. What have
we there now? There are a Camp, an English-speaking society,
a Hadassah Chapter, a Young People's League which has for the most
part Yiddish-speaking Zionists, a new society of young people, and
probably one or two more societies, exclusive of Young Judea Circles.
These societies are combined in a Zionist Council, to which delegates
are sent by all the societies in the combination. The Zionist Council
takes up all the general Zionist business, co-ordinates the work of the
societies, and leaves to them their own specific activities. If a general
mass meeting is to be undertaken, the matter comes up before the

Council Executive Committee, which may then appoint a committee of representatives to assume charge of the meeting. If a Shekel campaign is to be undertaken, the Council through committees organizes the campaign, but the work is done by the active members in their societies and in the camp.

Suppose the District Organization Plan becomes law. A meeting will be called of the members of all Pittsburgh societies. (In fact, this is done now, I understand, at the Council's semi-annual meeting.) At this organization meeting officers are elected and an executive committee chosen. Inasmuch as the new Constitution provides for proper minority representation on the Executive Board, every active group through its members will be able as a matter of course to elect its proportionate number of members on the Board. The Executive Board will then take over from the Federation the duty of collecting from every member the annual per capita tax, remitting to the Federation. The member may actually pay as he does now to his society, but the remittance will have to be made through the District Organization. Of this per capita tax the District Organization will retain one dollar per member for District work. A rule may be adopted that District organizations may retain a certain fixed percentage from all funds collected in the District. It may, if it pleases, make allowances to the various active groups for some of their activities, for the maintenance of clubrooms, for libraries, etc. But that is a matter that is optional with the district, and is to be decided by its own members. The Federation will issue all official requests to the District Organization, but that will not prohibit such correspondence with individuals or groups on matters relating to special Zionist activities, as occasion may require.

Will the societies in Pittsburgh be destroyed? Not at all; the societies will be freed from certain technical burdens, and will share in the gains of Zionism in the District. Every member of the District becomes a good prospect for every Zionist group. Every added strength of the District means strength for the Zionist group. Because every member of the District, being interested in gaining members for the District, will be providing the groups with new prospects for their own personnel.

What will happen to the Camps? Every member of the Camp will be a member of the District, but the Camp being a homogeneous group, bound together by the strong tie of insurance interest, will continue its activity as heretofore. There may have to be an arrangement made with the Executive Committee of the Order with regard to per capita dues, but that is not insuperable, and at any rate does not affect the members of the Camps individually. The same holds good with Hadassah Chapters.

It becomes necessary for the District Organizations to elect delegates to the Federation annual convention. The annual meeting of all members will be called. But it may be provided that the active societies may have their members voting in a precinct by themselves, of course using the same ballots as are used by other Zionists in the District. Provision being made by proportional representation, the various groups will have the opportunity of electing their own delegates, as they desire.

The societies and Camps practically remain as they are; but in every city *one common representation will be created which is to be the unit of Zionist organization.* We shall have provided for the existence of our national organization, and for all of its branches. And, furthermore, we shall have an organization which is not made up of a heterogeneous group of societies, with all sorts of fantastic juvenile names. Every Jew affiliating with Zionism will know at once that his entrance into the District Organization means his naturalization as a Zionist citizen.

The power and jurisdiction assumed by the District Organization depends, primarily, not upon any authority granted by the New Constitution, but by the power and ability of the present local societies so to transform themselves as to become capable of carrying the burden of the Zionist Movement. I imagine that where the regular Zionist society is strong, and representative of the community where it is located, the regular Zionist society may be, *ipso facto,* the District Organization. Or, where a number of Zionist societies together represent all elements in the community where they operate, they, in conjunction, will form the District Organization, much as a Zionist Council now operates, with this difference, that the District Organization is composed of all the members of the District, while the Zionist Council is composed of delegates representing the societies in the District. But where the societies actually only touch the fringe of the Jewish community and include only a small section of it, it is clear that the District Organization will have the balance, and the larger part, of the power and authority in the District.

What seems to make Zionism a party affair is the fact that the Zionist organization is founded on the social or class divisions in Jewish life, and does not reflect the sum total of Jewish life. Our organization is divided into groups, classes and parties, so that if a convert comes along who does not belong to the group or class which holds Zionists of his neighborhood or city, he feels that in fact he is debarred from entering the Zionist organization as an equal citizen. An orthodox Jew in a city with only one Zionist society composed of boys and girls cannot actually join the Zionist organization unless he undertakes to form a society of orthodox Jews, for he would not feel at home in a junior organization. A Yiddish-speaking Zionist in a city which has only an English-speaking Zionist society cannot comfortably become an organized Zionist unless he organizes a group of Yiddish-speaking Zionists in a separate society. This cannot be expected of the individual Zionist. In other words, the Zionist organization would be open to all Jews only if in every city we had as many Zionist groups as there were elements or classes in that city.

To expect, therefore, under such a system the Zionist Organization to become the containing vessel of all the Zionist sentiment and allegiance in the United States is to expect the impossible.

THE APPROACH TO FUND-RAISING

MEN AND MONEY*

Of course, it is Money that is going to build Palestine. We din that into the ears of all who are to be interested. It is the chief burden of our song. The sinews of war, the arts of peace—Money! For the schools, the hospitals, the colonies, for the Chalutzim, for land, for water power, for irrigation, for the National University: we need Money, lots of it. Money makes the wheels go round. Money fills the aching void. It redeems the waste places, brings water to the desert. Without it, nothing happens; the Movement stops; the Ideal hovers in the air and cannot get down to earth.

There is fatal error, however, in regarding Money as the cause, and not as an effect. Without Money, the Movement comes to a standstill; but what dries up financial support, what causes it to come forward, involves a wholly different order of ideas. Money is a tool, the slave of an idea, of a spirit, of an emotion. It is not the Master; it obeys orders. It is the instrument that goes forth to do its Master's bidding. It is the Golem, the Robot, without a will of its own, expressing only that spirit which is poured into it. Money is metal, dull, mechanical, without intelligence. It glows when an idea casts its light upon it.

In our quest of the means wherewith to build the material forms of our ideal, we exaggerate and misinterpret the function Money has to perform in our creative work. From its inception, the Zionist Movement aimed to transform a Golus people into a people living in freedom on its own soil. We were concerned with people, the living forces that were to be animated with a new hope, to be inspired with a higher sense of duty toward the race, its culture and ideals. The material conditions were to be changed in order that the spirit of the race should be liberated for new creative work. The emphasis was on *people*. The interest was in human beings. We used the tools of democracy in order that the whole people

* *The New Palestine*, July 26, 1923.

might be awakened from inactivity. We spoke of Money as the handmaiden of the ideal. The revival was due to force of personalities, animated by soul-absorbing ideals. The merely money-owners held aloof. In the new world we were creating, the yellow pallor of Gold would have withered the free spirits that found exercise for mind and soul in the Zionist Movement. Devotion counted. Intellectual and spiritual vision counted. Dragging along in the rear came an occasional declassé, fortune-favored son, glad to be a party to the rebirth of his nationality, happy to be with the creators.

We have progressed from that primitive state. We are becoming businesslike. Money begins to talk, make demands, take up space, threatens (as Money always does) to place its mark on the altar, bringing into the conquered circle new standards, jostling the old out of place. The Shekel indicated the democracy of the Movement, whatever the Shekel might be. Every man or woman over the age of eighteen was expected to pay it, and thus become the equal of all others. We counted votes. Every man had a voice in the affairs of his people, not on account of how much he gave, but because by his enrolment and his vote he indicated that he claimed a share in the inheritance and in the responsibilities of his people. All Zionists were free and equal. We now hear echoes of a new time. The word first was, Men and Money. Discipline was added as a complement to Money. Discipline meant due recognition of obligation to obey authority. The first (Men) begins to be slurred over, and the second (Money) talks loud. It was heard at the London Zionist Conference, where, not frankly, the new emphasis was uttered. Authority and responsibility should be transferred from Men to Money, to those who could give or get it. The insidious influence of that thought found a way into the organization of the Keren Hayesod, with its donation and personal interest contrivance, with its voting rights to contributors. It appears again in the suggestion, made in Germany (finding also an American echo in London), that financial institutions working in Palestine should be given votes and power in the Jewish Agency. We shall hear it again at the Carlsbad Congress, from delegates whose frantic reliance is upon the Money which shall relieve immediate anxieties and troubles.

A Zionism that is whole and wholesome relies upon the strength and persistence of Men. It places Men first and foremost and beyond compare. Out of the wellsprings of a national enthusiasm, out of sacrifices, not only of money but of comfort and life, comes the generosity that places wealth at the command of a great cause. Not by wooing wealth, cajoling it, adulating it, but by seeking divine inspiration at the source of Jewish life, will Money come to the aid of our effort. Before there can be giving, there must be an understanding of identity of interest. Before there can be generous giving, there must be felt a sense of relationship, either personally or through descendants, with new life that is being created.

FIRST SIGHT OF PALESTINE

"NOW COME WITH ME TO THE PALESTINE OF THE JEWISH PEOPLE"

Introduction

Lipsky first saw Palestine in November, 1924. He was then forty-eight years old; had dreamed the Zionist dream for the whole of his adult life; and he had worked for it for twenty-four years.

He was already a member of the Executive Committee of the World Zionist Organization, a co-founder of the Keren Hayesod, Chairman of the Zionist Organization of America.

He had helped shape the events leading to the issuance of the Balfour Declaration in 1917, American support of it: approval by the Allied Nations in 1920 at San Remo of the British Mandate for Palestine and by the League of Nations in 1923.

He had helped to inspire and to organize the first American Jewish Congress, democratically elected, and to choose a delegation to the Peace Conference, representing all American Jewry, which in cooperation with the Committee of Jewish Delegations had helped secure recognition of minority rights for Jews and others in the peace treaties.

And he had fanned the nebulous interest of American Jewry in a renascent Jewish Homeland into a burning flame. He had created a potent movement, with organized membership and funds, in the face of formidable opposition and obstacles.

The sight of Palestine was the crowning event of almost a quarter of a century of service.

Of that visit, The New Palestine *said editorially, on November 14, 1924:*

". . . Mr. Lipsky has become, by reason of his extraordinary devotion, the symbol of American Zionism. For more than a quarter of a century he has made Palestine the keynote of his thoughts and acts, and it may be said quite literally, that not a single day in 25 years can have passed without his having spoken of the Jewish Homeland, without his having referred to it the great majority of his daily acts. Yet he had not had the "zchus" to see it with his own eyes. It may be easy to smile at the

paradox of it. But it is easier to smile at difficulties than overcome them. Today he stands on Palestinian soil and sees the physical replica of all the images which have spurred him on. Every place that he visits, every institution, every organization, must be at least as familiar to him as to the Palestinians. He knows their history, their growth, their problems, their needs. He knows their leaders, most of them personally through contact with the Galuth, all of them by repute and by correspondence. One wonders: how near does it come to this previsioning? How close is the reality to the image? What changes in his plans, in his views, will the personal contact make? What will he learn, and what unlearn? And what will he have to tell us on his return?"

Lipsky delivered the following address upon his return home at a reception in his honor by the Zionist Organization of America on December 14, 1924.

The Editor

It was from London, the city of fogs, that I left for Palestine. I had not seen the sun, really, for many months. If the sun ever shone in London, it must have been when I was immersed in the office work of the Zionist Executive. I crossed the Channel and found Paris in a pelting rain. It was night when my train passed through Switzerland. In the morning, I was rushing through a beclouded Italy, arriving late in the evening at Trieste. When I awoke the next morning, I found the sun pouring itself out into the beautiful Italian harbor. When I boarded the "Heleouan," I felt I was leaving the lands of fog and mist forever, their gloom and depression, and that I was moving toward a new world, in which the Sun was King, reigning with a prodigal generosity, a Sun of Hope.

It was also a new world in a different sense. As I left Trieste and approached Alexandria, I felt that other nationalities, imbued with the spirit of the blue Mediterranean, play an important part on the fringe of the Land of Promise. We do not associate Italy with our affairs. The Italians are the masters of the Mediterranean Sea, plying their boats with a rakish aggressiveness, bustling, turbulent, resourceful. It is chiefly their ships that carry the returning Sons of Israel. You feel

* Text of this Address appeared in *The New Palestine,* December 19, 1924.

in Alexandria, for the first time, the presence of the Arabic world. There
are the so-called Egyptians, puffed up with a resurgence of national
feeling, who bring back to consciousness a much larger world, which
extends through kinship of race, language and ancient custom to
Mecca, Damascus and Bagdad. I refer not to the Arabs of Palestine,
but to those inhabiting the surrounding lands, for the Arabs in Palestine
—nationally marooned—are the backwash of the great Arabic world
which encircles our land.

Not one word should be said of our Palestine without first referring
to the land itself. It is beauty not to be described in words. It is color
and architecture that seem to reflect the play of Divinity. The world
assumes magnificent proportions. The austerity of straight lines is
absent. Instead, you get a cubistic effect of nature. The mountains,
with Hermon and Jerusalem projecting themselves into the sky, wind
in circular lines. Measure distance not as the crow flies, but as the
eagle soars. The approach to Jerusalem is a winding ascent of hills.
You go up and up, returning again and again to the same mountains
under the changing light of the pervasive sun, and as you ascend, wondering to what heights you are being borne, there suddenly flashes upon
your sight a vision of a city of white, upon which the sunlight plays,
giving forth shafts of varying color.

And when you leave Jerusalem, the Regal City, the city of memories
embedded in stone, and pass over to the Plain of Esdraelon, the valleys
give an impression of fertility, of richness, which overbalances the
meager promise of the sand dunes to the South, where there is a touch
of desert and endless distances that hint of the presence of other peoples
and other aspirations. The Emek is not to be seen at one glance. It
softens the landscape for miles. Here, where in ancient times were
fought the great battles for the control of Judea, you feel as if only
peaceful husbandry has a meaning. All that went before is buried in
the bosom of nature and it is still warm and it still invites, and it has
hopes of becoming the home of that people once driven away from it.
The beauty of Tiberias is best seen at night, by moonlight. It seems to
hold the secrets of a great past. The mountains of Gilead rise stark on
the opposite side. There are clusters of white houses, new Jewish settlements that blink at you, rising along the slopes; and the lethargic
Jordan, near the colony of Kinnereth, begins its journey toward the
Dead Sea.

The impressiveness of the outer aspect of Palestine transfixes you.
Merely to have seen that is to acquire an everlasting memory.

Now, come with me to the Palestine of the Jewish people, where work is being done, where a new life is being created, where (under the influence of the ancient hills, the moon-ridden beauties of Tiberias, the fertile promise of the Emek) an ancient folk, rejuvenated, is engaged in recreating its own life.

It is Jewish capital and labor that are building the cities of Palestine, and only *Jewish capital and labor*. This is the striking effect in Tel Aviv, in Haifa, in Tiberias, in Jerusalem. Whatever is being done to bring about an enlargement of the ancient cities and their improvement in every direction, is to be credited to Jews. Tel Aviv, the city by the Sea, now boasting of 28,000 inhabitants (all Jews), represents what Jewish energy and daring and resourcefulness have been able to achieve under circumstances of great difficulty. Not a stick or stone in Tel Aviv, but has been cut and set by Jewish labor; not a street, not a pavement, not a building. Jests have been made at the expense of the economics of Tel Aviv, but this marvel of city building, disproving all rules, and contradicting all theories, starting from the roof, now begins to make its own foundations. Upon these sand dunes, yesterday traversed by caravans of camels, a city has been piled up. At first drawing its life from elsewhere, there now begins a stream of immigration of persons of means who seek to serve in avenues of industrial effort. The city becomes self-supporting. There are traces of a healthy industrial growth. A silicate factory, a weaving establishment (financed by Jews from Poland), a shoe factory, a tannery, a furniture factory, a candy factory and dozens of small enterprises have come to life. It is being fed regularly by the produce of the colonies nearby, and it is becoming a market-place to which the colonists come for their supplies.

The architecture of Tel Aviv does not seem to have any Jewish characteristics. It gives evidence of a marvelous eclecticism. Almost every house has been built in the image of the Galuth experience of its builder. The result is not impressive; it is awkward. But in every instance it represents what each man conceived to be the highest form of architectural art. Once convinced of this mistake, you will see a wholesale renovation of Tel Aviv, which will be not an expression of Galuth, but of genuine Palestinian experience. As it is, however, it is bright, it is clean, it is orderly, it is homelike and inviting. It is a Jewish city and it will yet become the city beautiful. Jewish enterprise will not cease there. On the southern side of Jaffa, a new development has begun. The old city will soon be encircled, a wall of friendship will surround it and that city which only recently refused to accept the light that was brought to illuminate its narrow streets will one day be part of a greater Jaffa.

Haifa is to be the port of Palestine. A few years ago, it was regarded as the citadel of Arabic influence. Walls of prejudice have been broken down and today Haifa takes its place among the cities of Palestine destined to be Jewish. Along the Mount Carmel, pushing its way into the sea, forming one end of the crescent, of which the other is Acre, along the slopes of that mountain to the south and north of the old city, there are Jewish settlements. But the houses are not walled in, the streets are not closed, there are pavements and all sanitary improvements. Soon there will be electric lights, for Rutenberg has already built his electric station. And it will be a new city. Look down today from Mount Carmel, up to Acre, and you will see land owned by Jews, houses built by Jews, settlements laid out by Jews. When the new port is finally built, it will be within a Jewish city. And even in the old city, with its narrow streets and lack of light, Jewish foresight has already cut out a business street opening to the sea, which is to be like the open spaces in the Italian seaport towns.

Tiberias is a sleepy city by the Lake of Galilee. It is destined to be the winter resort of Palestine. In the month of November it was as warm as Florida. Around the old city, however, you see clusters of Jewish settlements. An old Yeshiva lies in the distance on the slope of a hill. Nearby are Degania, Kinnereth, the Migdal Farm and Garden City. The hot springs, now dilapidated and hardly fit to use, will be cleaned and the building of new hotels in the city will become possible. Within the old city there are many old Jewish families, numerous enough to constitute quite a considerable portion of the population. With this foothold in Tiberias, the rest is merely a matter of work for a year or two, and then Tiberias will be, like Tel Aviv and like Haifa, a thriving city of a developing new Jewish life.

And Jerusalem. The city makes the impression of tremendous strength. As hard as its stones is the task that here confronts us. Within the old walls, the life is like a petrification of Biblical times. It is marvelous to see, with modern eyes, what seems to be the exact duplicate of times historical. It repeats old customs. It repeats an old psychology, and it is impervious to outer influences. It seems determined to be true to the mold in which it was cast. Excrescences, if they may be called that, of this life, appear elsewhere. In *Mea Shearim,* in the Yemenite quarter, you see, under little better conditions—at least, the sky above is clear— the same form of life repeated by a new layer of Jewish population. The

Wailing Wall is not a ruin, but rises high above the head of the worshippers; it is the foundation upon which the Mosque of Omar was erected. There and within the walled city, it is too difficult to break through and create a new city. New ground has been broken. You see it on the Jaffa road, extending beyond the Tower of David, miles beyond the city. The new King George Avenue, leading to the railroad station, is to be lined with new buildings, and along the Jaffa road nearby, plans have already been made for business structures that will give a new look to this thoroughfare. But beyond this development, you see Talpioth, a white settlement in a green sward, and Bet Hakerem and Ratisbonne. All of this is not as yet compact enough to exclude from view a sight of the environs of Jerusalem, the vision of the Dead Sea and the mountains of Moab, the glimpse of Mount Scopus and the residence of the High Commissioner. The same strategy employed in Jaffa is being used in the Holy City. The old city remains intact. A new circle is made, surrounding the old with buildings that retain the solemn beauty of the old Citadel. Let the moon come ten years from today and look down upon Jerusalem. It will still find a white city, but the circle will be larger and there will be a new people inhabiting it.

And in all four cities, Jaffa, Haifa, Tiberias and Jerusalem, whatever there is of new life comes from Jews. If there is enterprise, reverential and loyal, it comes from Jews. If there is labor, it is Jewish labor engaged in remaking the cities of the old land.

But Jews have built cities before. They have broken the walls of many an old city, created new suburbs, brought in new life, extended the horizon, and when their work was finished, they found that they were strangers within the gate. If you want to see that which is not to be seen in any other part of the Jewish world, you will find it in the Jewish colonies of Palestine. In winning back the soil for the people, *the Jewish peasant has been born*. In the older colonies, like Rehovoth, Rishon le-Zion, Petach Tikvah, you see the pioneer graduated into the landed proprietor. In Rehovoth, the man is on *his* land. It is *his* property. He has his own vineyard. But in the communal colonies you feel that something is involved which is of much greater significance. The work is imbued with consecration. It expresses the quest for the everlasting; not to make property for oneself, not to put a fence around that property, not to hold anything back as one's own, but to create that kind of Jew who will become a part of the land, *its serf,* and make it possible for Jews to hold their position everlastingly in Palestine. I saw them in Ein Harod. It is a busy hive of bees. They work like beavers. They are determined to make everything they require for themselves. They are at their task from morning until late at night. They eat sparingly. They are thoughtless of clothing and show. They look at the sky and they look at the land and their one thought is: We must make ourselves an integral part of this soil so that no force on earth shall ever be able to wrest us away from it. They have made a religion of their work, and it is religion in the highest form. It represents the sum total of their life's interest. Should some find fault and say, What of Judaism, you may tell them that in this consecration to work they fulfill the greatest *mitzvah,* for they labor not for themselves but for the generations to come, whom their eyes will never see, thus attesting to their faith in God, and in the immortality of the Chosen People.

That gives national color to the work in Palestine. With a class bound to the soil and willingly its servants, and thinking only of the interests of the whole Jewish people, you have an assurance of the firmness of the foundations of the national Homeland.

The same spirit of the land-worker is revealed in the city worker. It is superficial thinking that speaks of the monopoly of labor. There is the chalutz who goes on the land, and is absorbed there. The same kind of chalutz enters the labor organization, and is absorbed there. The labor organization discharges one of the functions of the Zionist Executive. It maintains the labor army, trains unskilled men for new crafts, seeks new avenues of employment, and puts the army into action. It has educated stonecutters, road builders, house builders; it is prepared to undertake the most difficult work and does the work now in a most satisfactory manner. There is not a thought of self involved. Every man works hard and receives barely enough to keep himself. They are trained to think of themselves as servants to the country and show a spirit of self-abnegation which is just as admirable in them as it is in the peasants on the soil. The absence of a strong middle class makes their position, relatively, rather anomalous, but that is not their fault. The middle class has as yet not arrived in sufficient numbers to be organized as a substantial factor in the development of Palestine. And therefore, if it becomes necessary for the Zionist Executive, through the Keren Hayesod, to pay deficits created by the army of workers, that item on the budget should be regarded just as essential as the expenditures that are made on the land for maintaining the colonists. For here, too, we are creating new forms of Jewish enterprise, filling up the interstices of the national life with productive forces.

When you see this beehive of activity which has been created in

Palestine, you lose your respect for the accountants who come with their figures and seek to estimate values upon the basis of annual balances. In laying the foundations of a new civilization, the cost is to be amortized upon the basis of a vision of the future. You have to see far in the distance, when the actual reckoning takes place. You cannot strike a balance every year and declare business is bad because the annual balance is bad, but you have to take into consideration the imponderable things that are slow in maturing, but when they mature, produce everlasting values.

Every dollar that has been spent in the making of the Jewish peasant who has become an integral part of the soil, *has been well spent*. Every cent it has cost us to establish Kinnereth, Degania, Merhavia, Ein Harod and Nahalal has been well spent, for out of that expenditure has come that which today gives us strength and faith in the future of our work.

When we speak of reconstructing Jewish life, it is usually in a figurative way. But a new life is just like a new garment. It has to be made piece by piece and every little detail is of importance because the whole is made up of many details. What we see in Palestine is the weaving of a new garment, which is not only a new economic life for the Jewish people, but a new national life. The threads are being gathered together. Every new industry involves going into the roots of life, finding where the industry begins, how the material is to be gathered, where the machinery is to be secured, how to find the markets, how to adjust the prices, where to get the capital, from the smallest thing to the largest, from the making of food to the making of cement, clothing, shoes, hats, details of machinery, export of oranges, almonds, olives, the making of oil, the resources of the Dead Sea, securing light, making roads, sewers, building houses—the whole complex of the *wirtschaft* of life is being remade and every Jew who comes to Palestine becomes a party to that restless energy which is seeking as rapidly as possible to transform every feature of Jewish life to conform to the new conditions.

In the interplay of forces, the language plays by far the most important part. It is the Hebrew language, the language of the street, of the school, of public life, of business, which stamps all effort as unmistakably Jewish and national. Without the language, Tel Aviv might be another Brownsville. Without the language, there would be felt no new ideal— the content of Zionism would evaporate. If we did not at once capture the children who go into the schools, we might have a Palestine resembling to some extent the architecture of Tel Aviv, a replica of the Galuth experiences of the Jews coming from various lands. That is why the schools are of fundamental importance. And just as we feel that the making of the Jewish peasant is the task of our national forces, organized for the Jewish National Home, so we must agree that it is of the utmost importance that we maintain an effective control over all the schools in Palestine, from the University down to the kindergartens. For in these schools the national features of Jewish life are being created *and maintained.* We cannot permit these features to be distorted even by the good intentions of a thriving colony or by any municipality that may desire to adapt schools to local, transitory needs.

We have said, for the past three years, that ways should be found to transfer the schools to agencies that would make them their special interest, and relieve the Keren Hayesod budget. I confess that this was a mistaken view. *The schools must be adequately maintained and controlled by the Zionist Organization.* There is nothing more national, in every respect, than the schools, and we would be making a fatal mistake if we were to eliminate them from the Keren Hayesod budget.

In parenthesis, I may say that the work of Hadassah, owing to the fine spirit of its management, comes under the same heading of national enterprise. For Hadassah does not content itself with merely establishing hospitals and clinics. It goes out to find new work, new avenues for its labors. It does not serve, as many other hospitals do, just the ordinary requirements of the situation. It is a creator of new standards and ideals of public health.

It is deplorable that this fine demonstration of Jewish power and national determination should be made the target of unfair criticism, and especially that representatives of religion should attempt to affect our status by depreciating the work and character of our pioneers. *There is no ground for this criticism.* It is well that the world should know that Jews have gone into Palestine, and are going in ever increasing numbers, under public assurances given by the nations of the world. They have been told that their place in Palestine is theirs as a matter of right, and not of privilege. These assurances have been approved and sealed by the League of Nations. That bond of understanding cannot be taken by indirection, by mean calumny, by evasion and depreciation.

The Mandates Commission struck a blow at the authority of the League of Nations, when it hearkened to voices hostile to the work of our pioneers in Palestine. The British Government, through its Secretary of State for Foreign Affairs, the Hon. Austen Chamberlain, took occasion at the first opportunity to protest to the Supreme Council against this unfair report. But it will doubtless be used again and again by vicious enemies, in spite of that protest, and in spite of its untruth. High dignitaries of the Catholic Church are engaged in creating the impression that Jews in Palestine desecrate the sanctity of the land by introducing modern amusement forms. This is absurdly untrue, as every impartial visitor to the Holy Land will attest. But the fact that this propaganda is going on is deplorable. It displays a perverse state of mind, a forgetfulness of pledges made, a forgetfulness of the ideals of that teacher whom these religious representatives profess to emulate. When Jews, suffering for generations, and to this day, at the hands of followers of that religion, suffering as no people have suffered, are painfully returning to their ancient home, and through their labor seek to serve a Living God, their advent on the hills of Judea should be greeted with satisfaction and encouragement by the sincere adherents of all religions and by all enlightened nations. Least of all should their sincere efforts to create a center of normal life for themselves be disturbed by representatives of that religion which preaches peace on earth and good will to all men.

Let us hope that the Jewish people will appreciate what is involved in this effort. The strength of opposition indicates its importance to Jewish life. We are engaged in a struggle, not only to win Jewish adherents, but also to overcome prejudices, hatreds and age-long jealousies, and to place ourselves in a position of equality as against the civilizations of the world. We must be prepared to put into the struggle all that we possess. We must not be content with mere lip-service. The time has come when we must consider every Jew who does not come forward to aid his people in regaining their national status as one who is false to his Jewish heritage, false to the covenant, and a contributor, by abstinence, to the destruction of the Jewish future.

THERE IS SINGING ON MOUNT SCOPUS*

Mount Scopus is the eye of *Eretz Israel*. Looking to the east, clearly outlined against the sky, you see the Mountains of Moab and the Jordan River winding its way sluggishly into the silent Dead Sea. To the north you see the port of Haifa, the crescent-shaped Bay of Acre, and the white city of Acre projecting into the Mediterranean Sea. To the west the plain of Esdraelon (broad, warm, fecund, carpeted with color), Jaffa, and again the Mediterranean Sea. Behind you, southward, not far from where you stand, you look down, somewhat, on the Old City of Jerusalem, rimmed by the great wall, the Mosque of Omar rising above the piles of corrugated stone. Mount Scopus is the all-embracing eye of *Eretz Israel*.

Upon this mountain, eighteen hundred and fifty-five years ago, the Roman general, Titus Vespasian, pitched his tent the better to direct the attack of his cohorts upon Jerusalem. It was from Mount Scopus the order came to pierce the walls with battering-rams, to place ladders against them, and for hordes of Roman soldiers to grapple with the brave defenders upon the parapets. Resistance was gradually broken down. The invaders set fire to the Holy Temple. Jerusalem was taken amid the slaughter of thousands of zealots, who resisted to the last. Masses of the vanquished were taken captive and dragged to Rome, where they were set in mortal combat with wild animals, and their blood crimsoned the sand of the arenas. As a memorial of victory, Titus Vespasian caused an arch to be erected in Rome, and a coin was struck in his honor on which were inscribed the words, *Judaea Devicta*.

The wandering Jew, bearing the stigma of national defeat, has traversed the world these eighteen hundred and fifty-five years, nursing the hope that in God's time he would return to the scene of his former glory. He bore with fortitude and patience the burdens of life rendered

* *The New Palestine*, March 27, 1925.

all but intolerable by continued oppression. The evergreen sprig of memory made suffering endurable. Faith gave incentive to struggle. Before the storms of adversity, conscious of his inner strength, he bent his shoulders and lowered his head, but his spirit was never conquered. He made terms with conditions, but never lost hope. He embodied his hope in precept, in prayer, in ceremony, in physical habit, in the everyday duties of life. He determined to outlast enmity. He pressed through adversity in order that when the Day of Days arrived, he would be identifiably the man of Judea, able to recover the straight back, the clear upright head, the ability to begin again the making of new life, with a consciousness of living traditions and ideals still virile and forceful.

The great Empire of Rome today is ashes. It is the dust of a dim past. The conqueror, Titus Vespasian, owes his place in history to the act that sent the Jews once more out of their land. Titus is tyrant forever in Jewish legend, a figure of incarnate cruelty. He is the god of the machine that intervened, unknowingly, in the drama of Jewish life, and through his intervention sent the ball of Jewish existence rolling into the tragic depths of a long and terrible exile. The Arch of Titus crumbles. And on the mountain which saw Jerusalem in flames, the descendants of *Judaea Devicta* gather in the year 1925 to dedicate an edifice which proclaims to the world the Return of the Exile, again head up, again shoulders erect, the light of renewed life glistening in his eyes. They dedicate the Return on Mount Scopus.

From Jabneh to Mount Scopus. The defeated Jochanan ben Zakkai petitioned the Roman usurper for permission to retain a Jewish school of learning, and the petition was granted. It was an act of grace. It implied admission of defeat. It was a supplication and a prayer. It gave opportunity within sight of the Hills that had been desecrated to gather together the debris of defeat, to preserve the learning of Jewish life, to husband it in order that life (quiescent, unoffending, unaggressive) might be retained. Self-restraint held the passion of hatred in leash; the battlefield was abandoned; the resistance of endurance supplanted the resistance of arms. Terms were made with the conqueror. Jabneh was a seed planted deep into the ground. At the very moment of destruction, it was the beginning of the Return inevitably to be realized.

Today, the noonday sun brilliantly illuminating the scene, in the sight of a wondering world, the Jewish people—Judea Victorious—return to Mount Scopus under right sanctioned by fifty-one nations of the world (not privilege) and in the presence of representatives of all that is liberal in our present-day civilization, dedicate the Hebrew National University, which is to assemble the renascent Jewish culture and ideals that have outlived all the devious turns and twists and degradations which Exile has imposed upon us.

It is the dedication of the university of a returning Jewish nation. Such an institution cannot be created *ex nihilo*, with words or high intentions. This edifice could not be dedicated unless beneath its visible props there had been laid a foundation upon which it could rest. All hail to the persistence of the writers of Hebrew, who, in spite of conditions that tried their powers of endurance, in spite of temptation, the pressure of physical need, followed the light of their souls and created for us a living literature without which a Hebrew University would have been unthinkable. All hail to the makers of the Hebrew language, who took the rigid words of the old language, rent them open with loving strength, gave them flexibility, vigor and fluency, and made it possible for the children, blossoming under the Palestine sun, to become the living carriers of the new Hebraic life. All respect to the Biluists who came to Palestine and with their lacerated fingers dug into the soil and established the first outpost of the Jewish Return. Every Chalutz who drained a swamp, laid a road, dug into the soil, built a house, contributed to the making of that brave, bold, creative hopeful life upon which the foundations of the Hebrew University are to be established. A university is the flowering of life. A university is the flowering of a culture. It is the treasure house of the wealth of a nation. It is the preserver and the interpreter of national ideals.

Gathering about Mount Scopus, crowded into the open arena, thousands of Jews, inspirers of the renaissance, will witness the ceremony of dedication. And the doors of the white building that rears its head majestically into the heavens, will open wide. They will come from all parts of the world—the scattered tribes, foregathered on the Judean hills, joining in the hymn of praise. Scholars, poets, educators, men of professions, philanthropists, leaders of communities, the men of toil, will unite in a Passover pilgrimage for the dedication of this imposing edifice.

In the foreground, clasping hands with the Zionist leaders, will stand the distinguished representatives of the greatest liberal civilization of our day. The Earl of Balfour, burdened with years, wise, forbearing, tenaciously loyal to his fondest aspiration, directs his faltering steps to Mount Scopus, eager to join a jubilant people in the resumption of the buoyant tasks of their civilization. He will bring a message of good will, not only on behalf of the people for whom he directly speaks, but also for the liberal brotherhood of intellect and ideals of which he is the superlative exponent. His word will be the first and it will be heard all over the world. The air will carry it into distant parts, and it will penetrate into circles that have not yet heard of the rebirth of a great old nation. It will speak to the heart and mind of Christendom. It will dispel hesitation in extending congratulations. It will develop appreciation of our race and aid greatly in establishing universal approval. The leading institutions of learning of America and Europe will be present either through persons delegated to represent them or through messages of greeting that will be read. Governments will send special envoys to register their presence, thus raising the event to the height of an international incident of highest importance. Pomp and ceremony will attend the exercises.

These will be the visible actors, and this the visible and audible program. But we imagine the dead awakening, an invisible chorus joining in the songs of praise with toneless lips, hovering about Mount Scopus. Those who suffered for the ideal and endured the pangs of physical and mental anguish, those who died in order that their people might live in some far distant day, will be present, pale shadows glowing with a renewed fire.

The Zealots who fell in the defense of Jerusalem will rise. They have been passively waiting for hundreds of years. In their graves they endured the sufferings of their people. The martyrdom of the Jews was their martyrdom. Once and again, their dust was stirred by a new breeze, the dry bones seemed about to begin to stir; but the Day was still in the womb of Time. When the Return began, a quiver of unrest thrilled them, and now, when they see their descendants gathering to rebuild the ancient highways and reclothe the bare hills of Judea, when Jerusalem is being redeemed, they rise from their cerements and partake of the joy that extends from Dan to Beersheba. Now they know that they did not die in vain. When they finished and fell, across the chasm of hundreds of years others arose, blood of their blood, flesh of their flesh, to weave the stronger bonds of an unbreakable national life.

The generations that kept the faith and retained the inner fire of Jewish devotion and passion—hiding their light so that none could see and, unseeing, could not destroy—that never saw the Promised Land, but died and were buried in alien soil, will forget humiliation and suffering; and their spirits, rising, passing through all the lands of persecution, will make their way back again to the land of their origin. And as the *shofar* is heard on Mount Scopus, they will join in the psalms of praise and jubilation that will resound through the Holy Land. They, too, will rise—the generations who died in the *Galuth,* their hope unrealized.

The silent witnesses of the Rededication join in the Celebration.

There is singing again on Mount Scopus. And there is rejoicing in the Holy City of Jerusalem.

ON BECOMING PRESIDENT OF THE ZIONIST ORGANIZATION OF AMERICA

THE IMMORTALITY OF THE JEWISH PEOPLE*

Introduction

In July 1926, Lipsky was elected President of the Zionist Organization of America for the first time, a position to which he was successively re-elected until 1930.

Twenty-six years of work for the Zionist ideal, beginning with his arrival in New York in 1900, thirteen of them as directing head of the work for Zion, under various titles, had brought him to this climax.

In this period he had helped forge a movement from the amorphous Federation of American Zionists; created an organization plan and structure which is the basis of the Zionist Movement until this day.

He had helped to secure American Government assurance of support for the Balfour Declaration in 1917, together with Louis D. Brandeis, Stephen S. Wise and Felix Frankfurter. He had helped to create the first great precedent of applying American democratic methods to the organi- zation of Jewish life which, after a two-year battle, produced an American Jewish Congress elected in 1917 by direct, popular vote that represented all factions of American Jewry, including the erstwhile opponents.

He had helped at the 1918 session of the American Jewish Congress, of which he was Zionist floor leader, to elect a Delegation to the Peace Conference which, in turn, had helped produce protection of minority rights in the peace treaties and support for a Mandate for Palestine.

Side by side with Dr. Chaim Weizmann he had helped found the Keren Hayesod, the Palestine Foundation Fund, that was to become the principal fund raising instrument of the Zionist Movement. He dared to challenge giants like Louis D. Brandeis and to split the Zionist Movement to achieve that victory.

Trusted friend and co-worker of Chaim Weizmann, he had three times

---

* Address delivered in Buffalo July 2, 1926, accepting the Presidency of the Zionist Organization of America.

been called to London for Zionist work; had attended two World Zionist Congresses and been elected a member of the Executive Committee of the World Zionist Organization.

In 1901, at the invitation of Stephen S. Wise, he had become editor of The Maccabean, organ of the Federation of American Zionists, a post he held until 1918. In 1912 he assumed the chairmanship of the Executive Committee of the Federation.

During this period, for fourteen years he had served as editor of The American Hebrew, a non-Zionist publication. In 1914 he left The American Hebrew—to become official Secretary of the Federation, a title which was changed to Chairman of the Executive Committee, a year later.

In 1924 he saw Palestine for the first time.

By 1926, he was the recognized architect of the Zionist Movement, its theoretician and leading propagandist, and had developed an extraordinary speaking and writing style in behalf of Zion.

In these same 26 years he had become a short story writer, playwright, drama critic, book critic, essayist, whose work was published in the leading American publications of the time.

For three years, from 1910 to 1913, he had been on the staff of the New York Morning Telegraph for which he wrote on the theatre, contributing as well drama critiques, book reviews, fiction.

For two years he had contributed a weekly article to the Sunday issue of the Morning Telegraph.

Articles and essays by him were published in The Reader Magazine of which Louis Howe was the editor and Sinclair Lewis associate editor.

The New York Press and Associated Magazine, both Sunday publications, the latter Sunday supplement of a national chain of papers, including the New York Tribune, published his articles.

Short stories by some of the great Yiddish writers, notable among them I. L. Peretz, appeared in their first English version, translated by Lipsky.

With his election as President of the Zionist Organization of America Lipsky abandoned for all time, a career as playwright and story writer begun so felicitously when he left Rochester in 1900. Henceforth, the distinguished writing style was to be put at the disposal of the Jewish people and their cause.

In his speech accepting the office of President, Lipsky tells why he chose Zion.

The Editor

In all my Zionist life I have avoided discussion of things personal to me. In an enterprise which touches the immortality of a people, the individual is naturally merged with the stream of creative life. His private concerns are petty and of no great account. To give them a public airing makes one experience a self-exposure that is indecent. So far as I am concerned, it is great embarrassment. To speak of sacrifices in connection with Zionism is pure exaggeration. What we are engaged in doing repays in ways unseen and inexplicable. I have given to the Movement much less than it has returned to me.

All the interests that once tempted me have given way to an overpowering and irresistible desire to be helpful in the rebirth of the Jewish nation.

I used to devote much time to playing chess—the King's game. I was intrigued by its opportunities for the exercise of the art of strategy and tactics. It gave scope to imagination. It developed patience and restraint. But was not that time-wasting? In the guiding of the Zionist Movement, we also dealt with strategy and tactics. For that you must have patience; for that you must exercise restraint; for that you need vision and dream. What formerly was played with carved figures in a game, we now play in real life with fructifying Ideas and People. The goal is not a checkmate, but a victory in which the destiny of a race is at stake.

There was a time when I dreamed of writing plays for the theatre. But what is the value of contrived drama in comparison with the great drama of Jewish life in which we have been privileged to enact a climactic scene? We have been working out, in terms of actual life, a drama which had been dragging, had become monotonous, and into it we have put the element of struggle and creation. We have given the Jewish people the possibility of enacting the hero in this living drama instead of the victim of blind, historic forces. We have given color and point to this drama.

I speak the frank truth. It has been a privilege and not sacrifice to be in a Movement which has won, through our effort, a status for our people that had been denied them for over nineteen hundred years.

THE AMERICAN JEWISH CONGRESS

The struggle for the democratic organization of the Jewish community of the United States through an American Jewish Congress, began in earnest in 1915, spurred by the outbreak of World War I in 1914. A year earlier, on May 19, 1914, Bernard G. Richards had projected the idea of "a Congress for and from all Jews" in an article in the Jewish Daily News. This was a modification of an earlier projection by Abraham Shomer.

A first, major victory was achieved on December 15, 1918, when the American Jewish Congress, representing all sections of the community, assembled for the first time in Philadelphia.

Present were 300 delegates, elected by direct, popular vote on June 19, 1917, in which 335,000 votes were cast, the first such election in the history of the American Jewish community.

The 1918 Session, in which national Jewish organizations were allocated 100 delegates at large, elected a delegation to attend the Peace Conference as the representatives of a united Jewish community. That delegation, whose names had been placed in nomination by Louis Lipsky, in behalf of a nominating committee, consisted of Judge Julian W. Mack, Dr. Stephen S. Wise, Louis Marshall, Harry Cutler, Jacob de Haas, Rabbi B. L. Levinthal, Joseph Barondess, Dr. Nachman Syrkin, Leopold Benedict. Bernard G. Richards was elected Secretary of the Delegation.

The delegation was instructed to cooperate with other Jewish delegations in seeking Allied support for the Balfour Declaration; for a Mandate for Palestine to be assigned to Great Britain; and for the inclusion of equal rights for Jews and other minority groups in the Peace Treaties.

As part of the Committee of Jewish Delegations, representing other communities, the Congress delegation succeeded in securing the inclusion of minority rights in the peace treaties. The Zionist objectives were also obtained, largely by the same personalities, although acting, by agreement, as representatives of the World Zionist Organization.

This unity was attained only after a two-year debate, in which the charge of dual loyalty was hurled at the proponents of democratic elections, and only after compromises had been made, principal among them that the Congress should be an ad hoc organization, representing the Jewish people at the Peace Conference, but adjourning after its mission had been accomplished and its delegates had reported.

Exactly twenty-five years and another war later, a similar battle was waged when an American Jewish Conference was proposed, elected through democratic elections; and opposed by the same people, i.e. the American Jewish Committee, inspired by the same fears.

Nonetheless, in 1943, an exercise in democratic procedure produced a united Jewry in an American Jewish Conference which adopted a resolution affirming a united Jewry's support for the creation of a Jewish State at the war's end, with the dissent only of the delegates of the American Jewish Committee who walked out of the Conference.

These two great achievements were produced by the same initiative and, in part, by the same people.

Between 1918 and 1943, the struggle for democratic representation, on national and local levels, continued on many fronts, particularly after the crises created by Hitler, when the need for coordinated defense of Jewish rights abroad led to the establishment of the World Jewish Congress in 1936; when the need became imperative for a single defense agency in the United States to deal with Nazi manifestations, fascism and anti-Semitism; when pragmatic logic urged that Palestine be accorded upbuilding funds, equal to the role which not only Zionism, but tragic current events, had marked out for it.

The organization of the first American Jewish Congress owed its initiation to the Zionist Movement and followed endorsement of the idea by Louis D. Brandeis at the 1915 Zionist Convention in Boston. Mr. Brandeis was then Chairman of the Zionist Provisional Committee and Louis Lipsky Chairman of the Executive Committee of the Federation of American Zionists.

The Jewish population of the United States then totalled some three million, the majority of whom had come into the country beginning in 1881 and in the fourteen years preceding World War I. This ebullient population, largely from Eastern Europe, was ripe for the assertion of its own views and leadership.

Since 1906, the reins of leadership had been firmly in the hands of the American Jewish Committee, a group of notables who exercised considerable influence by reason of their roots in the United States, their

*wealth and position. The Committee's authorization was derived only
from itself; its membership was limited and selected by its Executive
Committee from other notables in the communities and among national
Jewish organizations. Not until 1944 did the American Jewish Committee
invite individuals to join it and to form local committees in the
communities.*

*But in 1915 the Provisional Zionist Committee, looking ahead to
the end of World War I, began to wonder who were to represent the Jews
and the Jewish question were it to come up at the Peace Conference.
Lipsky describes the dilemma thus in his "Memoir of Thirty Years":*

> *"Suppose we were unable to rally, in due time, a majority of American
> Jews under the banner of Zionism; and the bulk of American Jewry
> remained unorganized; or, if organized, were marshalled against our
> interests?*
>
> *"In a way, the American Jewish Committee claimed hegemony in
> American Jewish life. The leadership might be challenged by the
> Independent Order Bnai Brith or the Union of American Hebrew Con-
> gregations. All three bodies could be relied upon not to be friendly
> to the Zionist program.*
>
> *"We therefore thought it of utmost importance to bring into existence
> a new American representative body, all-inclusive, if possible, demo-
> cratically elected, in order to insure, first, the creation of an authentic
> personality to speak for American Jewry; second, to mold that body
> into a likeness satisfactory to Zionist hopes; and, third, to have a forum
> towards which our propaganda might be directed. Toward that end, after
> some hesitation, we became parties to the organization of the American
> Jewish Congress. And thus we were plunged into the most interesting
> struggle American Zionism went through, in all its history."**

*With Brandeis' support of direct, popular elections for the Congress,
the interest and the opposition of the American Jewish Committee were
engaged.*

*By 1917, however, peace had been made, with Brandeis (who took no
part in the actual Congress) in a principal role, and with Louis Lipsky
as the Zionist officer in the peace negotiations with the American Jewish
Committee.*

The American Jewish Committee agreed to participate, and Louis

* Louis Lipsky: *A Memoir of Thirty Years*, Vol. I, page 51, Collected Works, 1927.

Marshall, its President, was elected a delegate. At the 1918 session of the Congress, Lipsky was the Zionist floor leader.

On May 30–31, 1920, the Congress Delegation reported on its mission to the Peace Conference at a second session in Philadelphia. After the report, that session, in accordance with its prior pledge, adjourned sine die.

Immediately, however, at a session presided over by Lipsky, it was proposed and voted that the American Jewish Congress be reconstituted. A new Provisional Organization for the American Jewish Congress was elected with Nathan Straus as Chairman, and Bernard G. Richards as Secretary.

Until 1933, the American Jewish Congress, committed to the idea of democratic organization in the U.S. and also to the idea of a world body for the defense of Jewish rights abroad, was circumscribed in its activities by the limited scope of its funds.

But in 1933 Hitler's rise plunged the American Jewish Congress into activities which virtually overnight made it the center of the anti-Hitler action in the United States, because of the courage and dynamism of its leadership.

Emergency action of protest and the mobilization of understanding that Hitler's crimes against the Jews were crimes against civilization and would overtake the world, were followed by a concerted program:

1. To establish a World Jewish Congress to defend Jewish rights abroad
2. To organize local community organizations on a democratic basis for coordinated effort
3. To unite Jewish defense efforts, in one central democratic agency, to eliminate duplication and competition and magnify potency
4. To renew its own mandate, through direct, democratic elections
5. To affirm the equality of Jews in the United States by giving public battle to any denial of that equality.

Under the leadership of Stephen Wise, Louis Lipsky and their associates, the Congress attained its objectives on four fronts.

1. A World Jewish Congress was established in 1936
2. Democratic elections carried out in 1938 gave the American Jewish Congress a new mandate
3. The Congress organized its own local branches and used them as spearheads for democratic local community organizations. So far had it succeeded in 1943 that the Congress delegation was the second largest elected to the American Jewish Conference

4. *It made great strides forward to protect the equality of American Jews by its bold, frontal, public attacks on discrimination—political, economic, social, cultural.*

In one respect it failed. It did not succeed in forming a united Jewish defense agency.

How the American Jewish Congress succeeded, and how it failed; the nature of the opposition; the lively debates in the communities constitutes one of the most colorful and important chapters in the development of the American Jewish community.

In the forefront of the debate and the battle was Louis Lipsky. The following articles, written while the events were in progress, mirror the struggle and the results.

The Editor

VICTORY OF JEWISH DEMOCRACY

(A Historical Event)*

The meeting at the Hotel Savoy on December 25th, when the United Congress Committee met to organize the American Jewish Congress, resulted in a victory for the forces that have been struggling during the past two years for the creation of a Jewish Congress on democratic lines, that shall effectually cope with the problems of the Jewish people as reflected in present conditions.

The fate of the Congress was in the balance. The fear was that the erstwhile opponents of the Congress, driven by the force of public opinion into the movement would, by reason of their influence and prestige, obtain the mastery of the situation and thus be in a position to make the Congress an ineffectual instrument for the purpose outlined. They were defeated in their endeavors. They were defeated openly and squarely in a manner which could not be mistaken. The Congress will now take place, and, within the limits of the peace agreement, will reflect the spirit and the aspirations of the progressive elements in American Jewry.

The first test of strength in the Hotel Savoy meeting centered about the election of a temporary chairman. The significance of the first act of the United Congress Committee made it imperative that the democratic forces join issue on the temporary chairmanship. Moreover, from a tactical point of view, it was important that the chairman, who exercises

* *The Maccabean,* January, 1917.

so large an influence in American assemblies, be one not hostile to the democratic forces. Mr. Marshall, the exponent of all that was being fought, the symbol, as was said at the meeting, of the *status quo* elements in American Jewry, was nominated by Judge Mack. Mr. Adolph Kraus, President of the Independent Order Bnai Brith, was presented as the candidate of the democratic forces by Dr. Kallen. Mr. Kraus was selected with a view to the avoidance of baldly taking the control of the organization for either the democratic forces or their opponents, for Mr. Kraus had occupied a neutral position in the Congress movement. He was offered practically as the peace candidate. By refusing to accept Mr. Kraus, the leaders of the American Jewish Committee flung at us a challenge and seemed to be prepared to take the consequences of a defeat on this secondary proposition.

For the first time in the history of American Jewry—they probably did not know it—the leaders of the American Jewish Committee were face to face with an organized opposition, understanding democratic procedure, and prepared to meet the issue of autocracy frankly and squarely. A roll call was demanded, in order that the public at large might know clearly the personnel of the forces involved. The procedure produced an interesting scene. The men voting for Mr. Kraus stood for democracy, nationalism, and for faith in the Congress. The men who voted for Mr. Marshall were either men who did not believe in democracy in Jewish life and in nationalism, and who lacked faith in the Congress, or men who preferred to regard the incident merely as an opportunity to express individual preferences. The latter wanted to perpetuate the control of the American Jewish Committee. Interesting was the fact that fourteen representatives of the National Workmen's Committee voted for Mr. Marshall, who, in Jewish life as well as on all issues in American life, represents principles they oppose. The explanation of this phenomenon may be found in the unofficial slate drawn up in advance of the meeting by a committee composed of representatives of the Workmen and of the American Jewish Committee.

The outcome of the roll call was foreseen by the democratic forces. When the election of Mr. Kraus was announced, it developed that beyond making an issue of the chairmanship, the minority had no program, except one of limitation. This was revealed in the second outstanding incident of the meeting.

Mr. Marshall was made the chairman of the committee to report on the question of constructive relief. He was a minority in that committee, a number of his own followers voting with the majority in favor of a free consideration of the problem by the Congress. Mr. Marshall made a powerful argument in favor of restricting the Congress to the consideration of constructive relief through the existing relief committees, pleading that to do otherwise would involve the permanence of the Congress. Against this argument, Dr. Wise spoke with remarkable eloquence, pointing out that the Congress ought not to be limited to a consideration of the problem through the existing relief committees; it should be free to do the work through them or through such other agencies as might be created or utilized. The vote on this question was unmistakably against Mr. Marshall's contention. Many of his own followers voted against him. The count showed sixty against him, and twenty-nine with him.

When the question of permanent chairman came up, it was hoped that the defeat of the morning would bring about the election of a compromise candidate, satisfactory to both parties. The leaders of the American Jewish Committee made the issue the candidacy of Mr. Marshall. His friends would not withdraw his name. Attempts were made to suggest other candidates, but only his name would satisfy his friends. Had they contented themselves with merely placing his name in nomination as the minority candidate, the conflict would not have aroused such bitterness of feeling. Instead of the simple procedure usual in such cases of making the minority nomination, the nominators of Mr. Marshall tactlessly and unfairly attacked Mr. Kraus by charging that he was the head of a secret Jewish organization. When they did this, it was clear that Mr. Marshall could not by any possibility be elected, and that Mr. Kraus would receive the overwhelming majority, for among the men on the other side were prominent members of the Bnai Brith, who knew that the charge was unfounded and malicious. But Mr. Kraus, with rare generosity, met the situation by offering to withdraw, provided Mr. Marshall also would withdraw. The challenge of Mr. Kraus was accepted by Mr. Marshall, and instead of electing a man who had been neutral on the Congress question, the meeting had the added pleasure of electing to the leadership of the committee a man who is identified with the Zionist movement and with the Congress movement as a representative of the original Congress committee. This was the penalty Mr. Marshall's friends had to pay for their tactless behavior.

The only other incident worthy of notice—or unworthy of notice, as tastes may go—was the incident of Mr. Meyer London. The Workmen's Committee took advantage of the strong desire for peace in the Congress movement to threaten withdrawal unless Mr. London was elected on the administrative committee. A majority of the delegates were determined not to permit Mr. London's election, on the ground that he had publicly insulted his own people in a speech delivered in Boston, and that he had not satisfactorily explained his remarks or apologized for them. The Workmen's representatives, however, under cover of the pretext, wanted to withdraw on the ground that they had not been given adequate representation on the administrative committee. This was an obvious evasion of the issue. Dr. Magnes' intervention on behalf of Mr. London revealed the hypocrisy of the threat, and brought the issue to a head. Mr. London was compelled to make his explanation to the assembly, which, while characteristic and only partly satisfying, was accepted by the majority, and the incident was closed by his election to the Committee.

The names of the officers of the new Committee reveal the quality of the control of the future organization of the Congress: Nathan Straus is chairman; Harry Cutler, Harry Friedenwald, Isaac Hourwich, Morris Hilquit and Leon Sanders, vice-presidents; Adolph Lewisohn, treasurer; Bernard G. Richards, executive secretary; Harry Cutler, chairman of the Administrative Committee; and Louis E. Kirstein, vice-chairman of the Administrative Committee. These officers constitute the executive branch. On the so-called administrative committee, we have a majority of nationalists and Zionists.

Congratulations are due to the well-organized Zionist group, including the Mizrachists and the Poale Zion, and to their allies in the Orders and Verbands, and especially credit is due to Mr. Kraus and his friends, for the victory here briefly recorded and commented upon.

POSTPONEMENT OF THE JEWISH CONGRESS *

The vitality of the American Jewish Congress is effectively demonstrated by the reception given the decision to postpone it. Before the Congress elections on June 10th, impatient friends of the movement were convinced that death had overtaken it. When the votes were counted, they were agreeably surprised; over 340,000 ballots were cast; a dead movement would not have aroused such a tremendous interest. When the Congress was postponed from September 2nd to November 18th, loud lamentations and fervid denunciations in the Yiddish press again settled its fate; for the second time the Congress died. But the discus-

* *The Maccabean,* November 1917.

sions and denunciations, the general fuss that was created, forced the Congress again to the forefront, and it was apparent that a movement that aroused so much strong feeling could not so easily be killed off. So it has been for the past two years; whenever a decision contrary to the popular impatient view was made, the men of little faith and patience, with tears streaming down their cheeks, made all their preparations to attend the funeral of the Congress. But the funeral has not taken place to this day.

The last postponement found Jewish public opinion a little more rational, a little less hysterical and with more self-confidence. The sworn defenders of the integrity of the Congress have not neglected spreading sentiment of pessimism, but the large mass of enlightened public opinion is not depressed. A surprisingly large number of men and women whose interest in the Congress cannot be questioned have expressed their unbiased judgment in favor of the postponement. They seem to be much relieved that the Congress will not be held on November 18th in the midst of liberal loan campaigns, military preparations, local elections and general national excitement. The postponement itself has evoked expressions of loyalty to the Congress from circles whose loyalty had been in doubt.

The history of the Congress movement is a record of progressive education. All the pangs of a new birth have been experienced in its organization. The delays, the hesitations, the many adjustments of partisan differences have created it. Out of the confusion comes light and leading. The bare idea of two years ago, which came as a response to the demand for immediate action, would not, if realized then, have produced the revolution in Jewish life, which is expressed by the Congress movement. Education was essential, and the progress of education is gradual and cannot be forced. It has taken all of these two or three years to bring about an appreciation of the implications of a democratic Jewish Congress. When the Zionists first promulgated the idea, it was only half understood. The slogan was: the organization of the Jews of America for the protection of all Jewish interests. Very few of the original Congressists had the patience or the farsightedness to wait for that idea to percolate through the minds of the Jews of this country.

The zigzag progress of the movement may be attributed to the lack of understanding of its underlying idea. The majority was so intent upon having an immediate public demonstration that they overlooked the more lasting benefits to be derived from an organized American Jewry. They pressed for action. The essence of the Congress was its absolute freedom. This freedom the demonstrators were willing to give up in order that a loud demand might be registered. Under the pressure of Jewish "pacificism"—there is no other good word for it— the idea of a free Congress was abandoned, and a Congress by agreement was set up.

But the education of the Jewish people could not be suppressed. The compromise was not satisfactory. It brought home to thousands the lesson of democracy, for when democracy is outraged, the reaction comes with a vengeance. The dissatisfaction was due, in large measure, to the belated realization on the part of many who had not thought much of democratic processes that a great sacrifice had been made. The free Congress had been given up for the sake of immediate demonstration and a so-called unity. This rankled. Agitation could not have accomplished one-quarter as much for the spread of democratic sentiments as did the compromise agreement. It came too late, however, for any retreat, and the Congress elections were hurriedly decided upon and held. This haste was due to the fear that a factitious unity might dissolve if held too long. The nominations, the election, and the party strife made clear the fact that the controversy raged about a Congress, which, if it was to be effective, would sooner or later be compelled to modify the Congress agreement. This produced the reaction. Thousands who came into the limited Congress were convinced that only a Congress that was free to frame its own program could adequately meet the situation.

Whatever the program of the Congress, it was clear that the liberating thought had been expressed in the fact that the Jews of America had been called upon to elect their representatives, and that notwithstanding the peace agreement, the Congress would have to express the fundamental idea involved in the Congress as first proposed, which was, that the Jews of America, for their own protection, interests and development had to take control of their affairs into their own hands. The peace agreement might limit their action, but the exercise of freedom even in a limited degree would necessarily, by common consent, soon result in the unhindered expression of Jewish democracy.

With the rules of election fixed, with the full quota of delegates elected, with all organizations bound to abide by the decision of the majority in the Congress, the Congress had been established. No delays could destroy it.

The writer was one of those who believed the Congress should be held on the date fixed, November 18th. He felt that, from a moral point of view, the future of the Congress should be placed in the hands of the delegates to the Congress. Whatever arguments might be advanced against possible exhibitions detrimental to Jewish interests should be lodged with the Congress delegates, for them to decide what to do under the circumstances. The fears of pacifism could be dealt with only by the Congress, which by its action would destroy the exaggerated notions that prevail as to the extent of pacifism among the Jewish masses. The Congress would show where organized American Jewry stood. No anti-Semitic propaganda could then utilize isolated facts of pacifism against the credit of the Jews. Further, the delegates could devote themselves to the internal organization of the Congress, and place a committee in charge of Jewish affairs, so that the power and authority of the Congress could be exercised by its elected representatives, thus taking authority away from all such organizations that have in the past presumed to speak as the representatives of American Jewry.

The future of the Congress being secured through the election of the delegates, the question of the date was not a matter of principle, but of judgment. The date of the Congress was at no time one of the principles of the movement. We challenged the attempt of our opponents to establish as a principle the right of any group of persons in advance to decide that the Congress should not be held before the cessation of hostilities. It was a constitutional prohibition with regard to the date that we combated. Mr. Brandeis felt that the Congress committee should be free to select any date, which, in its judgment, would best serve Jewish interests. Dr. Adler contended that the holding of the Congress before the cessation of hostilities was so dangerous that his group could not become a part to it unless it was agreed in advance that the Congress under no circumstances would be held before the cessation of hostilities. That was the issue. On our part, it was a defense of the principle of freedom; on the part of Dr. Adler and his friends, it was the assertion of a right to bind the Congress committee by a constitutional prohibition.

The writer is still of the opinion that the holding of the Congress on November 18th would have relieved the situation, not from the point of view of what could be achieved for Jewish rights, but from the point of view of our own internal affairs. There is no doubt that holding the delegates away from the exercise of their rights may weaken them in their Congress interests, and we shall have to hold them together by engaging in educational work related directly to their functions; we may have to provide some medium of communication, through which the delegates may speak. These countervailing efforts will entail a large amount of work, which otherwise would have been unnecessary. The future of the Congress in the hands of the delegates would have removed the fear of usurpation or misuse of authority on the part of the Congress committee, which has in its membership men who are still opposed to the Congress.

But the decision of the majority of the Committee was against this view. Having established law and order, to some extent, in Jewish life, it would be criminal on the part of the minority to engage in any revolutionary movement to overthrow the decision of the majority. The power was given by agreement to the Congress Executive Committee to fix the date of the Congress. It has acted within its powers. It is the duty of every delegate-elect and of every member of the Committee to abide by its decision.

It is deplorable, however, that the reasons advanced for the postponement at the meeting of the Committee held in Temple Emanu-El were of such a character as to compel many of those who were in the majority—in self-defense—to dissociate themselves from the view expressed. No one questions the sincerity of the men who advocated postponement, but it is clear that in spite of their protestations, they have thus far not caught the spirit of the Congress movement, and still hold ideas that have no place in the new regime.

Their views implied that Jewish policy was to be determined not by internal Jewish need, but by external pressure and opportunities; that the controlling factor was not the righteousness of our cause, but how, under the circumstances, non-Jewish public opinion would regard frank statement of Jewish views; that the organization of American Jewry could not take place if, as a result, prejudice and calumny might attack the good name of the Jewish people. Before the Russian Revolution, the same ideas were advanced with regard to the propriety of Jewish denunciation of Russian tyranny. No criticism of Russian misgovernment was to be allowed, for fear of the non-Jewish reaction. In this country, this view was an obstacle to the organization of American Jewry, and the cry was raised that if Jews organized, it would be said that we are forming a state within a state. Those who opposed the holding of the American Jewish Congress took advantage of the same argument to maintain their autocratic control of Jewish affairs. In every crisis in Jewish life, the fear of non-Jewish opinion—known in advance to be unfounded— prevented authentic utterances in the public defense of Jewish interests. That has been the block in the way of Jewish organization that has prevented the development of a sound domestic policy for the Jewish people, without which a clear international policy is unthinkable.

The writer does not charge all who voted for postponement with the possession of such views, but the spokesmen of the resolution dwelt with undisguised satisfaction upon such arguments as embodied this point of view and indicated that they took it for granted that the old plea would convince. They insisted that when the American Government was engaged in war it became the duty of American Jews to abandon all their separate interests and they warned the meeting of threatened attacks.

The Congress is not seriously affected by the indefinite postponement. But in the resurgence of the *Mah-yomru-hagoyim* policy in Jewish life there is a great danger to Jewish interests. It threatens the supremacy of the democratic principle in Jewish life, for it makes the democracy subservient to prejudice and calumny, and renders it incapable of dealing with its own problems as free men. This policy must be rooted out of Jewish life. From now until the holding of the Congress, a campaign of education should be conducted to enlighten those who have learned nothing from the Congress movement. If that is done, the postponement may have its compensations.

THE AMERICAN JEWISH CONGRESS *

The American Jewish Congress is a movement, and not yet an institution. The thousand and one newspaper articles and editorials written about the Congress have all failed to state clearly all the implications of the agitation which first threw the question into the arena of practical life, and have dwelt almost exclusively upon the direct achievement of the Congress. What will the Congress do for Jewish rights, for Palestine? is asked by the practical men. The illuminating question is, What is the Congress?

The writer recalls the first promoters of the Congress movement. A group of zealots, grappling with an idea which not one of them clearly understood, they tenaciously and persistently kept the idea alive, pushing it into one circle after another, until like a battered football it emerged out of the councils of the Kehillah and the American Jewish Committee and was given place in the deliberations of the Zionist Organization.

The fundamental thought was that the Jews of America had the right and duty as Jews to govern their affairs. Self-constituted committees

* Excerpts from *The Maccabean,* February 1919.

or conferences should not usurp the rights which belonged to the whole Jewish people. The Jewish interests should not be held in trust by any group of men, no matter how able, by means of holding corporations, which separated the trustees from the people for whom they were acting.

What made it so urgent that the holding companies be dissolved and made powerless was the fear at that time that in the consideration of the Jewish problem when the war came to an end, these trustees, not speaking for the whole Jewish people, would barter away the future of the Jewish race for the sake of some immediate benefit. For the most part, the trustees were anti-nationalists and anti-Zionists, and the great mass of American Jewry felt instinctively that the war was bound to settle the great national problem of the Jewish people.

Like every other political ideal, the Congress movement lost its original color by a chain of compromises, one leading into another, which reduced the Congress to the idea that there should be an assembly of American Jews to articulate the demands of the Jewish people, and which should then disappear. Reducing the Congress to an assembly with a limited program, in the course of time the leading motive was lost sight of, and every interest was concentrated upon the quality of legislation the Congress would produce. The question of what the Congress was to be in Jewish life became secondary to the program of Jewish rights that would be adopted, and too late came the effort of the radicals to turn against all compromises and agreements and to start afresh from the point of view of the East Side meetings, where the Congress movement was launched.

These radicals were themselves responsible for most of the compromises, the limitations that choked the Congress. They were the first to abandon the position taken by Mr. Brandeis in his illuminating discussion with Dr. Cyrus Adler. They were the ones to insist that the Congress devote itself to the question of rights, and eventually they were the most eager to obliterate the features of the Congress that resembled the ideal picture which was in the minds of those who set the ball rolling.

Now, in discussing the American Jewish Congress—the series of meetings that were held in Philadelphia last month—every one is told that the success of the Congress was due to the adoption of resolutions that placed American Jewry without a doubt in favor of national rights and the establishment of a Jewish homeland in Palestine. The great struggle that preceded the opening session is lost sight of, and what we are called upon to take notice of is the Polish resolution and the Palestine resolution.

As a convention, the American Jewish Congress was a success. It produced resolutions that satisfy every Jew who believes in a Jewish future. Its deliberations were orderly and it acted with fair intelligence. The delegates felt the serious responsibility that had been placed upon them, and acted like true Jews. A high level of discussion was maintained, with only occasional lapses, which were pardonable. Everyone felt that the Congress was acting as one of the many national assemblies, whose decisions would have to come before the Peace Conference for final ratification.

The finest piece of work produced by the Congress was undoubtedly the resolution introduced by Mr. Marshall's committee. This resolution—the result of three days' labor on the part of the committee of fifty-two men, the best men in the Congress—was worthy of a parliament. It was a bit of constructive legislation and gave a hint of the possibilities for constructive work in a Congress that would meet regularly and take care of Jewish interests with a feeling of continuous responsibility. Another resolution was that approving of placing Palestine under the trusteeship of Great Britain with a view to enabling the Jewish people to establish a Jewish Commonwealth. The compactness and clearness of this resolution deserves commendation.

On account of this Palestine resolution, a controversy has arisen, which is being used to undermine the authority of the Congress deliberations. It is said that the resolution was introduced by the Zionists, who failed to inform the Congress of a cablegram received from Dr. Weizmann, in which he expressed opinions contradictory to the resolution. It is claimed that Dr. Weizmann did not ask for a Jewish Commonwealth or State, and did not want to have Palestine placed under the jurisdiction of the Zionist Organization, but that the Zionists in the Congress failed to give this information to the delegates. The argument that the Zionists have abandoned the position taken by them in the Basle Platform, that Dr. Weizmann has abandoned it or that the English Zionists have beaten a retreat, is unfounded and manufactured out of whole cloth. It is typical of the inability to understand political action, which has been characteristic of the whole anti-Zionist propaganda.

The Zionist Organization is as one in support of the British Declaration, which states in principle what Great Britain hopes to achieve for the Jewish people, with their cooperation. The resolution of the American Jewish Congress goes one step further and attempts to define how the Jewish national home is to be established. There should be created a trusteeship under Great Britain and under that trusteeship there shall be established "such political, administrative and economic conditions in Palestine as will assure the development of Palestine into a Jewish commonwealth." This indicates how the Jewish commonwealth is to be brought to life. We know of no responsible Zionist leader who believed that a Jewish State would be created overnight by the fiat of any government. It was Herzl's idea, as well as the thought of every succeeding Zionist administration, that the Jewish home in Palestine was something the Jewish people themselves would have to establish. What was asked of the governments of the world was a recognition of the Jewish right to Palestine and a free opportunity to develop the homeland.

That the affairs of Palestine were to be turned over to some Jewish organization other than the Zionist, is a thought which Dr. Weizmann may be pardoned in expressing, and it is a thought that has a great deal of support in Zionist circles; but obviously until such an organization is created, the responsibility remains the responsibility of the Zionist Organization, which is ceaselessly being called upon from day to day to meet all sorts of material and other obligations. We have not got the time, with events pressing close upon one another, to divert our attention to the tremendous task of forming a new universal Jewish organization, and there is no other organization that has shown the slightest willingness to aid the Zionists in meeting their obligations.

Any attempt to distort the fact in order to make black appear white, to give comfort to individuals or groups who lack knowledge of the rudiments of international law and of Zionist policy by mendaciously reiterating statements that have no basis in fact, should meet with universal condemnation. The Zionist task is heavy enough. Backbiting and lying reports on the part of persons who have not been known to make any sacrifices for Palestine, and who now come forward to interfere with the great work that confronts the Jewish people, are beneath criticism.

It is with no intention of belittling the Congress that the writer speaks of his disappointment. Four years had been spent in the education of the Jewish people in the democratic control of their own affairs. We have been speaking of the Congress as the Jewish Parliament. We were thinking of an assembly that would put in the shade every other Jewish assembly ever held. The three hundred elected delegates were to come to the Congress conscious of the fact that they were the first democratically elected representatives of the Jews of America, and the Congress was to reflect this elevated spirit.

It cannot be said that the Congress measured up to these expectations. It was not as deliberative as it should have been. There was too evident haste, as if the business had to be disposed of as quickly as possible. The discussions were to a large extent superficial and not illuminating. The discussion on national rights, which resulted in an overwhelming vote in favor of national rights, lacked weight, because it was felt that the stupid arguments of two delegates had to be overcome by invective and the expenditure of elementary educational effort. Mr. Marshall's resolution or bill of rights was not discussed at all, but was immediately put to a vote. Mr. Marshall's address on the Polish situation was introduced to fill up a gap in the Congress proceedings; in fact, was out of order, and, thus, views that in all probability did not meet with general approval were passed by without comment. The incident of Dr. Schitlowsky was an unfortunate breach of decorum, and the avalanche of speakers who consumed the whole of Monday evening was certainly not in place before the Congress had concluded its business. So, too, the resolution favoring a Universal Jewish Congress was badly prepared, and when subsequently introduced in revised form was so framed that it was felt that a discussion would be futile.

The tone of a number of the addresses was not in keeping with parliamentary form. The opening session was a mass meeting with the usual addresses of welcome and replies, and there was a lack of consciousness that the Congress was indeed a Parliament, where the dignity of the assembly involved a definite method of discussion, procedure, etc. The delegates did not feel a sense of continuing responsibility, a responsibility to their constituency and a responsibility to the Congress itself. The difficulties of getting the delegates together and of holding them were indicative of this lack of individual interest.

In nothing was this shown more glaringly than in the abortive attempt to have the Congress elect an executive committee. The Congress as such was intended to be the spokesman of the Jews of America. Its resolutions were the laws that were to bind its officers, and no one could have a right to speak for the Congress except by direct enactment. And yet the insurgent movement at the Congress centered itself upon the proposal to elect an executive committee, which, if it had any power, would have to usurp it, for all authority in so far as the Congress had acted would be given to the delegation going to Europe. In fact, the election of an executive committee would have destroyed the Congress, transforming the ideal into the usual organization that meets once a year and hands over full power to an executive committee.

Luckily, the delegates were soon convinced of the dangers of the proposal, and the plans were abandoned. A few delegates moved about the Congress hall until the last day, muttering and threatening to bring in a resolution about the executive committee, and probably went away with the feeling that, because an executive committee had not been elected, a great wrong had been done to the Congress.

The personnel of the delegations going to Europe amply reflects the various elements and parties represented in the Congress. Critics of the quality of the delegates indulge in the same arguments that are used by all Bourbons who are against representative government. In all probability there could not be gotten a better set of men to set forth the vari-colored American Jewry than those selected.

The delegation will go to Europe and return to report to the Congress. Upon them rests the responsibility for the future of the Congress. If they return with a report that involves support on the part of American Jewry of plans for clinching the political advantages gained at the Peace Conference, if they have recommendations to make bearing upon reconstruction or any other phases of Jewish life that needs the material or political co-operation of American Jewry, it will not be possible to prevent the establishment of the American Jewish Congress as a continuing power in Jewish life.

CONGRESS REDIVIVUS *

The American Jewish Congress was extricated from a difficult position by the action of its conference in Philadelphia last Sunday. The uncertainty and lack of clarity that enveloped its program and its principles for the past year were removed. The declaration of principle adopted indicates, in unmistakable language, the purpose of the American Jewish Congress in American Jewish life. It was a declaration of high value and significance. The American Jewish Congress is not merely an organization for the maintenance of Jewish rights abroad, for the defense of the Jewish position; but regarding itself as representative of Jews who assert their determination to maintain the group existence of Jews everywhere, who are conscious of the need of increasing and strengthening the inner life of that group, it aims to establish in American Jewish life a creative agency that will stem the tide of assimilation by building up inner reserves based upon the Jewish outlook upon life.

* *The New Palestine,* March 22, 1935.

Its immediate program indicates that an important element in the building up of the defenses of the Jewish people is to create permanent forms of local support, through which the preparations for the nationwide direct elections are to be organized. In other words, the American problem is to be faced in an organized way. With the so-called community councils established as the representation of organized constituencies, the value of the direct elections, both as sources of popular support and inner education, is greatly enhanced.

The Congress will be further strengthened by the setting up of agencies for such specific activities as civil rights, legal defenses and economic research. Action in the Congress will hereafter be based upon authoritative studies of the facts, the recommendations of experts, which will help in the avoidance of that emphasis upon demonstration which, in the early days of Hitler, the Congress was forced to adopt as the only method available for the defense of the Jewish position.

In a word, the Congress has consolidated its position and is preparing to move forward in a more deliberate fashion. The present situation in Germany requires the consideration of new methods. New problems are in the offing, arising out of the outbreaks of the maniacs of Germany, which are being recorded day by day in the general press. New methods of defense will be required. It is entirely possible that the old policies will have to be scrapped and the radically new ones be given consideration in concert with the Jewries abroad.

There is no doubt that recent events in Germany and Poland have brought the idea of a World Jewish Congress or Conference into the field of immediate practicality. Revolutionary changes have taken place in the position of Jews throughout Europe. The walls of an extreme nationalism prevent certain Jewries from voicing their needs. It would be the height of unwisdom to neglect the possibilities of some form of united action by all Jews to deal with the immediate problems arising out of the prevailing unsettled conditions abroad. If each Jewry could deal with its own problems, such a Conference or Congress might not be required, but it is quite obvious that the moral and political support of the freer Jewries, united in action, is essential effectively to deal with the situation.

In this revitalized American Jewish Congress, the Zionists played an important and dominant part, as was their bounden duty. It was clearly the obligation of Zionists, responsible for the organization of the Congress in the first instance, to come forward with all their strength to make the Congress an appropriate and effective agency. It is now in order for the Zionists in every locality to take the initiative in establishing the American Jewish Congress upon a permanent basis through the organization of Community Councils which are to be the basic units of organization of the Congress throughout the country. The assumption of direct leadership by Dr. Stephen S. Wise is also a healthy sign of improvement. When the responsibilities for leadership are distributed, it is always difficult to maintain a straight line and a clear-cut policy. The concentration of authority in the hands of Dr. Wise, supported as he will be by a large circle of representatives of all constructive elements in American Jewish life, is bound to have a tonic effect upon the future course of the American Jewish Congress.

JEWS MUST STRUGGLE FOR SUPREMACY OF DEMOCRACY*

In this assembly—the second in our annals to consist of delegates given mandates by nation-wide individual vote—the record of the intervening years need be referred to only in passing. The chronicles of the past twenty years have given a full story of the contribution of the American Jewish Congress to the strengthening of Jewish life, to the defense of Jewish rights, and to the development of organized responsibility in the American community. Zeal and courage and daring were its distinguishing qualities. And a proud and unequivocal kinship with the whole Jewish people was the keynote of its program.

But under the pressure of the excitement induced by revolutionary changes in recent months, calm perusal of that record is well nigh impossible. The Europe we have known has fallen. All positions have been reshuffled. The center of the axis has moved from the Western democracies to the dictatorships of Rome and Berlin. The area of Jewish difficulties has enlarged with amazing rapidity; the *status quo* has deteriorated and worse follows. The colors are changing; but black sprawls over an ever-growing area. On that continent of calculated hatred and organized attack on modern civilization, the wheel of Jewish life has made a complete turn; and we are forced today to consider anew, in a greatly deteriorated world, the problems of our strange fate, beginning the struggle at the bottom of the hill, almost as if we had never risen.

It would have seemed incredible in the days of 1918, when the first American Jewish Congress met in Philadelphia. At that time, the

* *The Congress Bulletin,* November 4, 1938.

international world, stricken with remorse at the end of a devastating war, had given place to the Jewish problem on its agenda. It was a world in which you could speak freely of democracy; of self-determination; of justice; of righting wrongs. You could denounce evil without restraint or fear. The pressure of the new order had evoked international recognition of Jewish right. A status was given to the victim of ancient and continuing wrong. It could submit indictments and demand a reply. It was given the position of a legalized petitioner and could avail itself of all forms of approach to the International Council at Geneva. Petition and demonstration—the evocation of public opinion—controversies in the press and on the platform—the writing of pamphlets and books— the democratic organization of Jewish life—were placed in our hands as instruments of defense. The long night of Jewish exclusion, of endlessly standing as a stranger at the gate, voiceless in international discussion, seemed to be over.

For the first time, we were the recognized beneficiaries of an expanding democratic world. The rights spoken of were inscribed on the parchment of international agreement, in the records of international conference. A procedure was provided for the registry of judgment.

At the end of the war the position we occupied was given a dual recognition. There were equal rights in the lands where we lived. There was final achievement of recognition of our rights to establish the Jewish National Home in Palestine. In other words, the Allied victory at the end of the war gave us public opportunity to fight with our own resources, through our advocates, for ultimate and complete equality—not privileges through surreptitious approach to authority, but public equality in all phases of organized society.

It was to that task the Jews the world over addressed themselves. A large segment devoted itself to the cause of the Jewish National Home, to the implications of nationality and the Jewish renaissance. They poured labor and sacrifice into the foundations of the National Home. They created physical and spiritual defenses of the positions they conquered for themselves. They built with power and national purpose. They transformed the Balfour Declaration into the tissues of a national life.

Other elements addressed themselves to the task of maintaining rights in the lands of dispersion. They organized demonstration and petitions and made courageous efforts to have the rights, registered in covenant, integrated and maintained in the forms of life. They identified themselves with all manifestations of democratic ideals, with progress and liberalism.

These organized efforts finally achieved, on the one hand, the organization of the extended Jewish Agency for Palestine; and on the other, organization of the World Jewish Congress, in which the American Jewish Congress played a dominant part. In Geneva, Jerusalem and London, a certain status had been achieved.

The most powerful force in the reorganization of modern civilization—the first uprising in modern times which shook privilege from its seat of authority—was the French Revolution. The French Revolution proclaimed the rights of man. It was a flaming torch that spread over the face of Europe. The heat of that conflagration reached the American shore. It set in motion tremendous changes in organized society. Today, however, the rights of man are being dishonored and trampled under foot; and the dark torch of destruction of everything achieved in the French Revolution is being applied in all parts of the world by vandals and barbarians. New slogans are being contrived. New conceptions of state power and the significance of states are being imposed upon intimidated and misguided peoples. Totalitarian ideas compel the subordination of the individual. Force and violence are becoming the masters of the highways. Today, democracy is in retreat. Justice is a fugitive in hiding. Humanitarian impulse is regarded as escape for weaklings; the good Samaritan is a sentimental fool. The ideals of Machiavelli and Genghis Khan dominate the maneuvers of these engines of destruction.

And the temple of international justice in Geneva which had been dedicated to arbitration, conciliation, collective security and peace, has been dismantled and pushed off the scene of life. It has become the object of mockery and derision. It is pilloried and denounced by friend and foe. It has become the symbol of the tragic inefficiency of democracy. The saboteurs responsible for its failure point to the collapse of Geneva with pride and satisfaction, as justification of their own way of life. And the realists seem to agree with them.

The democracies are in retreat, and as they have given way to threat, uncertain of the next step, the Jewish position becomes worse and Jewish life in the conquered areas passes into the stage of complete and utter ruin. It is almost inert human material which is moved about at the will of the conqueror. They have no rights or title to respect. The elemental respect to be paid to human life makes no appeal to the honorless and shameless barbarians with whom the Western Democracies are prepared to strike a bargain of mutual interest. Thousands of human beings are ruthlessly driven into the night of despair—footballs of dictatorial sport—and the civilized world stands by silent and ashamed. But democracy struck to the earth will rise again. It is inconceivable that the madness of a few decades will succeed in vanquishing the spiritual accumulations of generations. The ghosts of the past stand by and encourage all the forces of humanity and democracy to make effective resistance, to re-establish in this world the ideals of justice and brotherhood.

In the army that is being organized for the recapture of world freedom, there must be a Jewish division equipped for battle, carrying the Jewish flag, making contributions to the pool of resources. It is to be an offensive on a universal scale, it is to be a battle that will decide the destiny of the world; and in that battle, once more Jewish spirit and Jewish sacrifice must be registered without equivocation, without evasion of responsibility. There can be no isolated defense for any segment of Jewish life. There can be no partial peace for the amelioration of a segment of Jews. The force of circumstances compels us to throw in all our resources without reserve in this struggle for the supremacy of the democratic ideals of peace and brotherhood.

There is an even greater task which we must perform in protection of the ideals of the great Republic in which we are citizens. The poisons of the European world are carried across the sea. They attack the lower elements in American life. They bring in sectional dissension. They arouse slumbering racial prejudice. These poisons undermine the foundations of the American form of government. They impair the efficacy of government as the agency for the protection of the equal rights of all citizens. They break the spirit and intent of the Constitution, under which America has become the leading and dominant democracy of the world. In this land, all races have found a haven of refuge. In this haven, they have accommodated themselves to the spirit of democracy and tolerance. The defense of Jewish interest in the United States must be organized in alliance with the democratic liberal forces that constitute the majority of the citizenship of the country. Just as it is important for us to defend ourselves against calumny and specific racial prejudice, so is it important for us as Jews to contribute strength to the maintenance of American democratic institutions.

This assembly will not pass in a perfunctory manner the great experience in Palestine. The quality of devotion revealed in the Jewish settlement in Palestine registers the only success which we have attained in the course of the past twenty years. The Balfour Declaration may have been a mere scrap of paper, just as were the covenants inserted in the

Peace Treaty for the recognition of Jewish rights in certain European lands. But the Balfour Declaration was taken up by living Jewish hands and, through organized resistance and creative resourcefulness, it was transformed into the substance of a vibrant and virile Jewish national life. Under the cover of the Mandate, the pioneers have built up institutions of cooperative Jewish life. They have maintained the ideals of social justice and democracy. They have revealed the quality and the temper of Jewish personality. They have brought back ancient virtues and given new meaning to the prophetic teachings. That experience is warming to the heart and soul of all Jews, the world over. It makes present misery less repugnant; it makes pain and struggle more meaningful; it gives substance to hope and faith. It is the living axis of a Jewish life which is now, for defensive and creative purposes, represented by the Yishuv in Palestine and the great American Jewish community. The attack that is being made on the Palestine front is doomed to defeat. The same feeble hand that signed the Munich pact may be prepared to capitulate to threats of violence, but the resistance of the Yishuv, supported by the American Jewish community, will make impossible repetition of the Munich Pact.

The reports to be submitted here will give summaries of the work of the American Jewish Congress. It represents an organized and continued attempt to wrestle with a terrific problem, which has worsened in the course of the years, in spite of unremitting efforts to stem the adverse tide. You will be called upon to consider new ways and sanctions for the development of new policies, for the accumulation of larger resources, with more effective coordination and broader communal response under a unified national direction. By your decisions and pledges of support, you will determine not only the future of our people, but the place and the significance of the American Jewish Congress in that future.

There are those who have no faith and who would make Jewish policy rest on inevitable Jewish weakness, inability to organize, absence of courage; who would prefer to reduce both the defense of Jewish right and cooperation in democratic reconstruction to a state of accepted inferiority through fearsome indirection. That does not reflect the traditions and the living faith of the American Jewish Congress. It is to be hoped that by your actions you will continue that tradition and maintain that faith.

DUAL LOYALTY AND DEMOCRATIC ORGANIZATION

Today the right of American Jews to organize democratically on the local, national and international levels, for philanthropy, social welfare, and defense of Jewish rights is considered axiomatic.

But it took more than 40 years of heated discussion and battle, two World Wars and the Hitler holocaust to defeat the concept that Jewish institutions, democratically organized to represent the Jews of America, involved a challenge to the Americanism of Jews and invited the danger of the charge of "dual loyalties."

The principal antagonists of democratic organization were the so-called assimilated Jews, largely of German ancestry, whose forebears had settled in America long before the first wave of Jewish immigration from Eastern Europe in the late 19th and in the first two decades of the 20th Century. Their principal spokesmen were the representatives of the American Jewish Committee, which until 1944 was a committee of notables not exceeding 400, hand-picked by its Executive Committee.

Opposed to them were the new immigrants who wanted to create their own institutions in America, elect their own spokesmen, delegate responsibility to help build the Jewish National Homeland in Palestine, protect their equality in the United States and to defend their brethren in other lands whenever attacked. And to do so by the democratic procedures which governed other United States practices.

"Dual loyalty" was the principal charge hurled at the protagonists of such democratic organization in the battles which blazed between 1910 and 1943.

The first major battle in which the charge of dual loyalty erupted, occurred when it was announced that an American Jewish Congress would be formed through direct, democratic vote of the Jewish population in the communities in which they lived.

Although the dissenters subsequently joined the American Jewish

Congress and were represented at the Peace Conference, the charge was only retired, not forgotten.

It came to the fore again in 1935 in a major community battle when the American Jewish Congress took the initiative in organizing the World Jewish Congress. Hitler had been in power two years. His "Aryan" policy had not yet culminated in the extermination of the Jews; but the Jews of Germany had already been deprived of all fundamental rights. Many organizations in many countries made sporadic efforts to help German Jewry, with resulting duplication, sometimes competition, and limited effectiveness.

In 1932, foreseeing what was to become the bloodiest chapter in world history, the American Jewish Congress approved the holding of a preparatory conference to study the manner in which a World Jewish Congress could be formed. It authorized Dr. Nahum Goldmann to organize such a preparatory conference, after explorations with European Jewish communities.

In 1935, discussions began in earnest about American participation in a World Jewish Congress. And, after a year of disagreement in the inner circles of the American Jewish Congress as to form and date of the elections, an Electoral Convention was held in Washington, D.C. in June 1936. The Convention was attended by more than 1000 delegates who had been democratically elected in 99 communities in 32 states. This convention in turn elected 52 delegates and 64 alternates to attend the first World Jewish Congress.

The first session of the World Jewish Congress was held August 8–15, 1936 in Geneva, Switzerland. Thirty-two countries were represented at the initiating session by 280 delegates. Dr. Stephen S. Wise was elected President of the World Jewish Congress; Dr. Nahum Goldmann, Chairman of the Administrative Committee and Louis Lipsky, Chairman of its Central Council. Lipsky had worked out the form of the organization and the election procedure for the United States.

Because the participation of American Jewry was indispensable to the successful organization of a World Jewish Congress, the opposition tried to prevent this participation by raising the spectre of dual loyalty. They failed.

After its first session, the World Jewish Congress set up and maintained a listening post in Switzerland throughout the war years; played a significant role in the work of trying to rescue Hitler's victims; in uncovering and exposing Hitler's extermination program; in supplying crucial evidence at the Nuremberg trials; in securing reparations from post-war Germany; in the formulation of the U.N. Genocide Pact; and in continuous protection of Jewish rights wherever assailed abroad since the war's end.

In 1938, the American Jewish Congress decided to renew its mandate from the Jewish community through direct elections. 351,674 votes were cast and 500 delegates elected in 30 states. This procedure too was labeled un-American by the American Jewish Committee.

That same year the Congress proposed the creation of a single Jewish Defense Agency in the United States to end competition, duplications, and to heighten the efficiency of the struggle against anti-Semitism at home and Hitlerism abroad. This, it proposed, be put to a referendum of the Jews of America. The hue and cry raised by the American Jewish Committee in association with leaders of the Reform Rabbinate, such as Rabbi Samuel Schulman, Rabbi Samuel Goldenson and Dr. Jonah B. Wise, effectively defeated the idea.

Jews moving democratically to organize for the representation of their interests were castigated for the last time as endangering their Americanism and their loyalties to the U.S. in 1942 when the American Jewish Committee again used the charge of "dual loyalties" to bolster its disapproval of democratic elections for the American Jewish Conference.

After a year of sustained opposition, the American Jewish Committee agreed to participate in the 1943 session of the American Jewish Conference. But it walked out of the Conference after the session adopted its resolution supporting the establishment of a Jewish State in Palestine at the end of the war.

Throughout the long span of years, the most indefatigable defender of the rights of Jews to organize democratically to defend themselves and their brethren, seeing therein an expression of their Americanism, was Lipsky.

Lipsky, a strong proponent of cultural pluralism, believed American freedom offered scope for the expression of Jewish brotherhood; and that democracy has meaning only if applied—and to the organization of Jewish life as well.

The following four articles reflect the nature of the battle and Lipsky's defense of American Jews against the charge of "dual loyalty."

The Editor

CAN THE JEWS ORGANIZE FOR THEIR DEFENSE?*

It is quite well known that leading American Zionists have a definite stand on the question of the World Jewish Congress. It was due to the action of the Administrative Committee of the Zionist Organization of America last year that the proposed World Jewish Congress was postponed. The American Zionists expressed their opinion that such a World Jewish Congress had not been adequately prepared for, nor had its purposes and program been clearly enunciated and accepted by those who were to be interested in it. At the Geneva Conference held in the summer of 1934, no representative of the Zionist Organization of America was officially in attendance. As a matter of fact, leading American Zionists challenged the authority of the Geneva Conference to fix the date of the World Jewish Congress.

In Dr. Cyrus Adler's report to the annual meeting of the American Jewish Committee, which was a comprehensive survey of Jewish conditions, there appears a paragraph using a principle against the World Jewish Congress, which, in my opinion, cannot be approved by those American Jews who believe in the urgency of some form of international cooperation in matters affecting the elementary rights of Jews. In this paragraph Dr. Adler said:

"The Committee believes that, as American citizens, Jews have the right, independently or associated in groups, to approach the Government of the United States and solicit its good offices in behalf of the betterment of the lot of oppressed Jews in other lands. The Committee does not believe, however, that it is consistent with these principles for them to associate themselves with the citizens of other countries in creating an international body which will assume or attempt to speak for the Jews of this country."

Is it necessary or advisable, in expressing dissent with the proposal for a World Jewish Congress, to put it upon the ground as indicated in Dr. Adler's report? The quoted statement has implications which, I believe, Dr. Adler himself upon reconsideration would agree places American Jewish citizens in a curious position. It raises far-reaching problems.

* *The New Palestine*, January 11, 1935.

The assumption is that the proposed World Jewish Congress is to be a World Parliament and that it will undertake to speak on all and every subject that may be regarded as of Jewish interest; it will have a mandate to include universal Jewish questions within the orbit of its consideration. It is true that some advocates of the World Jewish Congress have said things that lay them open to the charge that this is to be the program of the World Jewish Congress, but sober consideration of the matter by these same "tone-givers" will undoubtedly bring about a reduction of ambition and a limitation of scope. There is a strong sentiment among friends and adherents of the World Jewish Congress that the Congress would agree in advance to limit its right to speak for the Jews of any land unless express individual consent would be given. In fact, the Canadian Jewish Congress gave its adherence to the purposes of the World Jewish Congress with that proviso. So it may be expected that, should the World Jewish Congress acquire form and content, there will arise any number of other lands that will take the same position as Canada took in this respect. In other words, it is quite conceivable that a World Jewish Congress, if held at all, would start with a program agreed to in advance, in which provision would be made for the protection of all Jewries from encroachments by the Congress upon their own political or internal affairs.

Assuming, therefore, that the World Jewish Congress would be limited as indicated, and assuming that it would undertake, through an Executive Committee, to make representations on abuses of elementary Jewish rights (say in Poland or in Germany), what reasonable objection could be advanced to having American Jewry affiliate with a body with such limited objects? Or, as has been suggested, to such representations as would be made through a Committee of Jewish Delegations to be set up in place of a Congress?

It is quite evident that all the representations that would be undertaken by such a committee would have to be made and directed to the League of Nations. It is quite evident, from a practical point of view, that a cooperating Jewish committee appearing before the League of Nations would be much better than to have many representatives from various Jewries appearing at various times, with varying pleas, on behalf of the same cause.

I regard the point that we, as American citizens, have no right to join with Jews of other lands in an effort to alleviate the conditions of Jewish life, insofar as deprival of Jewish rights is concerned, as a concession which should not be made because, in effect, it is a limitation of our rights as

Americans. It is quite in order, as matters now stand, for other groups of American citizens to join in international action with groups of citizens of other lands on matters that are of their particular concern. There are League of Nations Unions, with branches in every part of the world, in which the citizens of one country join with the citizens of other countries for the pursuit of an international purpose. There is an English-speaking Union in which American citizens join with citizens of the British Empire for certain common purposes. There are international labor organizations in which organized American labor unites with organized labor of other countries for the purpose of defending the interests of labor. There are unions in the United States of former citizens of other lands for the legitimate purpose of nurturing and fostering such national cultures that represent legitimate common interests. Nobody seems to regard such international activities of American citizens as objectionable.

Why, therefore, should it be necessary, in expressing opposition to the World Jewish Congress at this time, to make such a radical concession as is made by Dr. Adler in his report, in a form and manner which practically advances the doctrine that American Jews have no right, in the opinion of the American Jewish Committee, to act together for the protection of basic human Jewish interests as members of the same race or religion or nation, whatever it may be called? Does it not place obstacles in the way of any form of cooperation?

As a matter of fact, American Jews have, with right, participated in quite a number of international conferences at which certain Jewish questions were considered. There was a Jewish Economic Conference held in London last summer, which was attended by representatives of the American Jewish Committee itself. There are international conferences of representatives of Reform Judaism that are held periodically either in England or in America. The existence of the extended Jewish Agency is, in a way, challenged by this statement of Dr. Adler, for the extended Jewish Agency is an international combination of Jews interested in the upbuilding of Palestine, and in this instance they are operating under a Mandate which has been recognized by the League of Nations and in it are represented Jews of all lands that have expressed a willingness to cooperate. No one raised this question, as a matter of principle, at the time the Jewish Agency was formed in New York, nor would anybody raise that question now. Why, then, should it be raised in connection with the World Jewish Congress, or by inference, in connection with the proposed formation of a Committee of Jewish Delegations?

There are so many other objections to the World Jewish Congress at this time that this sweeping objection in principle, in my judgment, might well have been held in abeyance, especially in these perilous days so far as Jewish rights are concerned.

In fact, Dr. Adler gives a series of cogent reasons for refusing to join in the World Jewish Congress. These reasons are based upon the practical considerations involved in the difference in value between a plebiscite and a union of existing organizations. The introduction of the principle I venture to criticize only serves to weaken the case Dr. Adler makes against the World Jewish Congress as proposed, which I have also criticized time and again in the deliberations of the American Jewish Congress.

A VOICE FROM THE PAST *

The interview of Judge Proskauer, which appeared in the *New York World-Telegram* on Tuesday, and was probably reprinted in all the Scripps-Howard newspapers, resurrects an old approach to the Jewish problem which life has made obsolete. It is reminiscent of what used to be said by so-called Americans of Jewish persuasion in the primitive days preceding the Great War. That Judge Proskauer knows the source of his creed and to what extent it is "dated," is indicated by his quotation of a statement made by Jacob H. Schiff in 1915. That statement was made at a time when the whole of American Jewry was absorbed in the American Jewish Congress movement, in which every statement made by Mr. Schiff was ultimately rejected and a new basis was found for American Jewish life. The trend of Mr. Schiff's opinion is indicated by this excerpt:

> "It is quite evident that there is a serious break coming between those who wish to force the formation of a Hebraic element in the United States as distinct from those of us who desire to be Americans in attachment, thought and action, and Jews because of our religion as well as the cultural attainments of our people. I am quite convinced that the American people will not willingly permit the formation of a large, separate Hebraic group with national aspirations . . ."

What serious-minded person would reiterate these views today, in the light of what has happened to Jewish life since 1915? When Mr. Schiff made that statement, it was the conventional utterance of a small

* *The New Palestine,* February 8, 1935.

group of American Jews who were content with the *status quo* of Jewish life, although at that very time external circumstances were already creating a revolution in Jewish affairs. There was no Balfour Declaration and Palestine Mandate in which the right of the Jewish people to the establishment of a National Home in Palestine was recognized. The Hebrew language was then struggling for dominance in the small Jewish community in Palestine, and it is today the mother tongue of a new, vigorous, aspiring generation of Jews in Palestine. There were then hopes that the doors of many lands would remain open for victims of political or religious persecution, but at this time practically all the doors have been closed. Instead of taking an adverse position with regard to Jewish national aspirations, the American people, through the American Congress and every President of the United States since 1915, have given their unqualified and unreserved endorsement of the scheme for the establishment of a recognized National Home for the Jewish people in Palestine. At that time, the emancipation of the Jews in Germany had not reached its tragic collapse through the development of a Fascist Government, and there was no Hitler agitating all of Europe with his frenzied anti-Semitic crusade.

The American Jewish Congress (the organization of which was started in 1915) established the principle of democracy in Jewish life and created a forum which was representative of all Jews in America; and although the spirit of democracy has suffered a temporary defeat, there is no person who holds liberal ideas who will question the principle of the democratic self-government of the Jewish people in matters that concern their own welfare. Judge Proskauer does the memory of Mr. Schiff no good service when he invokes a statement made in the midst of a World War, and proposes that that statement, without alteration or amendment, in exactly the same form, be accepted as the creed of all American Jews. The acceptance of such a creed by all American Jews at this time would be a repudiation of all that American Jewish life has achieved during the past twenty years in the way of self-development and self-expression.

It is not difficult to fathom the workings of Judge Proskauer's mind. There is reflected in his views an attempted evasion of responsibility for the universal calamity which has fallen upon the Jews of the world. What he has in mind seems to be a rejection of the ideal of Jewish nationalism in order to separate the Jews of America, in this time of stress and difficulty, from those Jews that are immersed in a sea of anti-Semitic flame. His thinking leads to the thought that American Jewry is to be established on an island of safety, far removed in interest and responsibility from those who are the victims of ruthless persecution, and he aims to envelop American Jews in the American flag in order to protect them, if possible, from a potential anti-Semitism which begins to develop also in the United States. To serve that purpose what Judge Proskauer proposes is that Jews should cover their faces with a mask in order to hide the truth about themselves. The mask shows what they would have the *goyim* think of the Jewish people in America. It is a social and political maneuver. It is a pitiful defense mechanism at work, unworthy of any self-respecting people.

The statement of Judge Proskauer would not deserve the attention that is being given to it were it not for the fact that he is a member of the Executive Committee of the American Jewish Committee and plays a leading part in its affairs. It would not deserve any attention at all except as an exhibition of muddled thinking and perversity, were it not for the fact that Judge Proskauer himself assumes to speak indirectly for the American Jewish Committee, which does represent in a way a substantial part of American Jewry. If Judge Proskauer speaks for the American Jewish Committee, it is the duty of the American Jewish Committee to indicate, in unmistakable terms, that the doctrines he enunciates are not shared by the large body of its own members, and especially by those leaders of the American Jewish Committee whom the Jews of America respect and esteem, in spite of disagreement on matters of policy and method.

"AMERICANS WHO ARE JEWS"*

You get the strangest feeling of unreality from the recent statement of the American Jewish Committee. Every impulse of your mind rejects it. What is said is not so important as what it avoids saying. Some words are significant not for their meaning, but because of the fact that they are used at all. The American Jewish Congress is not even mentioned, but it is intended that there should be no mistake about what group is meant. The Jewish good name must be protected; and all American Jews are "Americans who are Jews." The statement hovers on the edge of reality, but never touches it. It is as frank and direct as a diplomat's conversation. It avoids vulnerable admissions; cross-examination touches smooth, oiled walls. It is perfect in its evasiveness and in its innuendo.

* *The Congress Bulletin*, October 5, 1938.

Why was the statement made—its publication arranged for in the *New York Times,* the names of most of the members of the Executive Committee attached? You will find the explanation in the lead of the story. It is legal notice to non-Jews (as well as Jews) that the American Jewish Committee "disavows and disassociates itself" from the referendum of the American Jewish Congress. On the one hand, it warns Jews not to vote; and on the other, it wants non-Jews to know that a chasm of basic differences separates "these" and "those" Jews. The statement is both apologetic and self-defensive.

En Passant: the urbanity of the statement is marred by a streak of malice which should be noticed here. It is distortion of fact to insinuate that the proposed union for Jewish defense is an attempt to organize Jews as "a distinct political unit." There is no warrant for such an observation. In all their organizations—fraternal, educational, religious, philanthropic, social—American Jews have excluded political aims and interests; and in no Jewish assembly has that tradition been observed as scrupulously as in the American Jewish Congress. The insinuation that Jews in an organization for the defense of Jewish rights would give way to political temptations is a gratuitous insult to all the national organizations affiliated with the American Jewish Congress. The gentlemen of the American Jewish Committee—many of whom are actively engaged in politics—should be the last to venture this form of criticism.

If you think that the text of the statement reflects on the intelligence of the American Jewish Committee, you fall into error. Many of the signers of the statement are men of distinction in the legal profession. They are all principals or agents of a coterie that desire to control *Jewish* political affairs. Many of them are engaged exclusively in Jewish communal work. Of some of them it may be said that their only distinction (political and otherwise) derives from Jewish association. They are all good Jews; even those who feel oppressed by their Jewish ancestry; and their intentions are honorable.

They sincerely believe that they are acting for the good of Jews. They think it the safest policy for Jews to deny solidarity of race and nationality, a common brotherhood. It is better for Jews to say "Americans who are Jews." Jews must be very careful. They want to be careful.

Of course, they know that the Jews are a people; that they are more than a religious denomination; that they are the special objects of a world-wide wave of race prejudice; that this prejudice spreads even into the United States; that it does not discriminate between rich and poor, reform and orthodox, reactionary and red; that it is bound up with tendencies to impair and undermine the democratic foundations of the American republic; that it is better to be united than divided. *They know all this.*

The disparity between public utterance and personal knowledge comes from this fact. They are terribly afraid of prejudice; they are nervous about prejudice. It grows in surprising ways; it is a peculiar aberration; it is a craze that spreads. The least agitation on the part of its victims, the bold intrusion of Jews on the non-Jewish vision, making themselves conspicuous in defense, feeds prejudice. And it is the business of wise and cautious Jews not to provide cause that will feed prejudice. Keep under cover when trouble is brewing.

These gentlemen, assuming to act for the good of the Jews, believe they have the right approach to the problem; they believe in their tactics and methods; they are convinced that it is best for Jews that all these important matters should be entrusted to cautious, tactful, wealthy Jews. (They answer to this description.) The responsibility should not be thrust upon the shoulders of all Jews indiscriminately. Democracy should give way to efficiency. Democracy should be qualitative. Defense and representation should be left to the American Jewish Committee. The right people are selected as its members. The right tone of exclusion and segregation is mentioned. They know the right policy. They know what is best for Jews.

In their wisdom, they believe that you can lull the spirit of race prejudice into a state of calm, you can hold it in check, you can divert it by using the arts of camouflage and non-irritant statements. It can be neutralized and disarmed by tactful behavior. Truth will not serve; common counsel will not help; but policy and tactics, avoiding the pitfalls of truth, silence and avoidance (hire good lawyers!), that will do the trick.

Nor will they regard all anti-Semites as being fit for the psychopathic ward. They will agree that the Nazis are not all deranged, that the leadership aims to get control of political authority. Many of them are not as crazy as their writings seem. But caution is the word. Which makes the policy of camouflage all the more stupid. It does no good—with the Nazi ruffians—to prove that Jews are not Communists, that Jews are not criminals, that they do not control international finance, that they are not ruled by the Elders of Zion. It does no good to deny and sidestep. Let your false mirror show that which is unprovoking and inoffensive. It does not matter. Hate is unreasoning. It does not serve the self-interest of the criminal anti-Semite to believe you, and the crazy anti-Semite is likely to believe whatever his insane impulse leads him to believe.

What amazes one is that men of practical sense (sane and sober in all other matters) should in Jewish affairs believe that they are dealing with the lunatic fringe of anti-Semitism, which leads them to engage in maneuvers that give the impression of irrationality. In Jewish affairs, they allow fear to dictate the mood and the action. It is nerves, not reason, that prompts the American Jewish Committee to become unpleasant and unfair whenever an attempt is made to establish a sense of reality in Jewish affairs. It is the resistance of fatigued nerves that is reflected in the vicious attacks that are made whenever democratic means in the governing of Jewish affairs are mentioned. It is the false pride of offended leadership (feeling itself impotent in a troubled world) that resents the suggestion that all Jews—not merely the members of the Harmonie Club or the American Jewish Committee—should get together to consider what is to be done to defend Jewish interests. That men, honorable in all other things, should persist in thinking that pretense and camouflage can serve as defense in the existing terrible Jewish situation, is an amazing phenomenon.

The American Jewish Committee is not only defending its self-assumed leadership (which shakes in its feeble and nervous hands), but it is pursuing a tragic mistake in judgment. Its methods do not protect the Jewish position. The danger we face cannot be overcome by taking counsel of our fears. It cannot be overcome by camouflaging the realities of Jewish life, the quality of Jewish personality. It can only be met by organizing the courage and self-reliance of the Jewish people. It can only be met by confidence and truth, and faith in the power of these ideals. The identical policy the American Jewish Committee now pursues—the same ideas, the same methods, the same vocabulary—have been used in every land; in Germany, in Rumania, in Poland; and in every land it has had no substantial effect upon the development of the peculiar hatred of Jews that flourishes in these lands. *The policy of retreat and avoidance has proven bankrupt.*

For the good of their own souls, it is important that the members of the American Jewish Committee establish a reconciliation with the realities, which requires the abandonment of all self-deception and make-believe. For the good of their own souls, these futile tactics must be discarded.

It is due to faith in these tactics that a man like Dr. Samuel Goldenson, a preacher of morals and an expounder of theology, falls into confusion when he discusses the Jewish problem. Like a sick and apprehensive child, he preaches a philosophy based not on his faith, but on his fears. He exaggerates all dangers and sees things that do not exist, and ends in a fever of prophetic exaltation. This also explains the American Jewish Committee.

They want non-Jews to believe that there is nothing tangible about Jewish life—it is colorless, it is self-effacing—in order to put on record the plea that we are merely Americans who are Jews. This is the magic to exorcise prejudice. They will admit that there should be a defense of Jewish rights, but the fact must not be conceded lest the adversary be goaded into further excesses. Therefore, pledge yourself "to fight anti-Semitism", but "shoulder to shoulder with all other elements of our population."

The end of this futile discussion has come. It has been going on for over twenty-five years. The same arguments are repeated; the same evasions are presented as arguments; the same threats are made. Heavy clouds hover over the House of Israel. Never in Jewish history have we faced such desperate conditions. The hate of the world seems to be arrayed against us. Millions of our brethren are suffering unparalleled brutality. Jewish life is scattering in anticipation of the last blow. Academic discussion serves no further purpose. Legalistic pretense is travesty in the controversy. Action is called for. For their own good, the advice of the American Jewish Committee must be rejected, and the strength of the Jewish people must be mobilized, regardless of their warnings.

Courage will dispel the fears of the timid and the nervous. This display of courage (the acceptance of mass responsibility) will breed confidence and faith and evoke the necessary sacrifices. If the American Jewish Committee wishes to be helpful, it will have to cease its foolish remonstrances and its unworthy pretenses, and come forward as loyal members of an organized, democratic community to cooperate in the public defense of Jewish rights.

THE ELECTION AND THE JEWISH VOTE *

The fact that Jews in large numbers will vote for Mr. Roosevelt—which is assumed by many—is being used by Mr. Willkie's friends (especially his Jewish friends) as an indication of a "Jewish vote." Jews are being

* *The Jewish Day*, November 2, 1940.

warned not to expose themselves to this charge, which may be used against them in days to come. Those who make the charge advise Jews at least to establish a reasonable balance; let some of them announce that they are going to vote for Mr. Willkie; they should repudiate the idea of a Jewish vote; they should let it be known that it would be un-American for Jews to vote as a bloc.

This is political balderdash. It is designed to get Jewish votes by intimidation. It is being used to frighten the timid and confuse them.

There is no more a Jewish vote than there is a Polish or Irish vote, as there is a Catholic or Protestant vote—no more and no less. Everybody knows that there are as many kinds of group votes in the United States as there are groups. And every group is likely to react to the same stimulus, not in the same degree, but approximately in the same way. That it is natural and not un-American is shown by the fact that most Southerners who remember the Civil War to this day vote the Democratic ticket, and that Maine farmers, for reasons that probably have to do with local tradition, continue to vote the Republican ticket. If there is anything of significance or value in the idea of democratic freedom, it is that freedom of expression for a group is just as important as freedom of expression for an individual. In practice such freedom for groups to express themselves in various ways, and more especially in their voting, has always been recognized. In the political history of the United States, there has been much evidence of these colorful variations in reaction to public issues, and it has never been regarded as un-American. It is now being used offensively and for partisan purposes only in connection with Jews—often by Jews themselves in the spirit of self-effacement and subordination to suspected prejudice.

The truth is that there are among Jews, as there are among other groups, individuals of all sorts and classes. There are Democrats, Republicans, Socialists, Communists and congenital mugwumps. There are capitalists, workmen, and middlemen. There are snobs and plain democratic people. There are optimists and pessimists, philosophers and cranks. There are religious and non-religious individuals. And everyone acts in accordance with his own personal understanding of any issue that may arise in political affairs. Naturally they come under the influence of their class or group, taking or leaving whatever is compatible or incompatible with their own personalities or their own views. Whether there is a strong Jewish reaction on any issue depends largely upon the amount of Jewishness that may be found among any collection of Jews.

This is true also of many other national or religious groups in the

United States. It is said that most Italians will vote against Mr. Roosevelt because the President, in one of his addresses—when Mussolini took up arms against a tottering and defeated France—referred to Italy as having "stabbed France in the back." Many of the Italians who are thus influenced against Mr. Roosevelt may not be Fascists at all, or Republicans. They may be loyal, patriotic Americans. But as Italians, they are naturally resentful of any derogation of Italy, its Government or its people. They cherish a sentimental memory for the homeland, they register their protest as a matter of group pride, which is done in this case by voting against Mr. Roosevelt. But for every Italian who will do this, there will probably be another Italian who for wholly different reasons will vote for Mr. Roosevelt; because as workmen they may want to vote with their Labor Union; or because they believe in democracy and want to indicate their abhorrence of Hitler; and who are not at all stirred by memories of flag or the homeland.

The Jews of America have no such sentimental attachments. They have no territorial remembrance except, among most of them, a faded memory of an ancient Palestine. As far as they are concerned they have every reason to be loyal first of all to the America symbolized by the Statue of Liberty, incorporated in the Bill of Rights and in the ideals of Lincoln. With them America is something special—it is the land of freedom, the land of liberal thought, where they have found refuge and security. The Jews—all of them—have experienced persecution and oppression; the memory of that lingers. They are an immigrant people. They have brought with them much that had to be thrown away when they arrived. But what they were seeking in life they found to be exactly that which was typified in the America of their dreams. The Jewish ideal of democracy and tolerance, nursed in their souls during long periods of exile, is the prototype of the ideals underlying the American Republic.

Because of that tradition of democracy and tolerance, they have invariably been found giving support to the liberal Presidents of the United States. Their authentic Jewishness reacted to those traditions. I remember my mother telling me—years ago—that in her home in Poland, over seventy years ago, the only American they knew of and admired was Abraham Lincoln. Theodore Roosevelt was an exuberant, aggressive American. He was a Republican. It was said of him, too, that there was a Jewish vote behind him every time he ran for office. American Jews delighted in his frankness, his democratic manner, his sympathy with and understanding of the various groups of immigrants who had built up the United States. In fact, Theodore Roosevelt won the loyalty of all the immigrant groups. In their eyes at that time he was the typical democratic American. So, in the same way, it was said of Woodrow Wilson that he won the loyalty of a substantial majority of all classes of Jews. Not because of anything special that he did for Jews but because they saw that he followed in the tradition of Lincoln and Theodore Roosevelt—incorporating American ideals in speech and action, raising his voice so that the homelands on the other side could hear the message of America.

If today a large number of Jews—as is believed by many—are going to vote for Mr. Franklin D. Roosevelt, it is probably because they see in him a continuance of that great American tradition. It is that tradition which in our day incidentally works itself out in ways that are helpful to all minority peoples and more particularly in defense of Jews at a time fateful for their future. The synchronization is accidental. In the course of the past eight years the progress of America has led to an identification of American interests with a rejection of all Hitler stands for. In the creation of this identification the President of the United States has led the American people in the direction of a militant Democracy, establishing its inner and outer defenses in order the better to meet the vandalism that spreads over the world. Jews therefore see in him the American leader whose policies include not a narrow-minded selfish isolation, but an understanding of the universal application of the principles of law and justice. He defends all minorities, all oppressed, including among them also the Jewish people.

That in itself would not have sufficed to make Jews so deeply concerned in the re-election of Mr. Roosevelt. That in itself would not have brought about such an overwhelming interest on the part of American Jews to have Mr. Roosevelt continue in office at this critical time, in order to keep America aligned with the Democratic forces fighting against the domination of the world by the destroyers of modern civilization.

In addition to all that, Mr. Roosevelt has been responsible for the adoption of a program of social justice which makes a special appeal to all Jews conscious of what their race has contributed to the progress of a free humanity. In the deep concern for the common man, in the protection of the rights of labor, in the provisions for old age security, in the emphasis placed on people rather then property, Mr. Roosevelt has brought to American life—more frankly and clearly than ever before—the social idealism of the Hebrew Prophets. Under all the layers of veneer—the masks of Jewish bankers, Jewish merchants,

Jewish promoters—the authentic Jewish personality is always latent, and can be relied upon to react with amazing intensity to the call of humanity and justice.

The influence of Jews in all lands has been that of pioneers. Always there have been those who believe in maintaining the *status quo*—things as they are—the men of wealth or position; but the general run of Jews have always been susceptible to thoughts of how to make life better, to promote ideals that will bring the better day nearer. They were the dreamers of utopia and millenium; they were the vanguard of social reform. They knew what it was to suffer and therefore had a vision of the day when man-made suffering would come to an end.

Mr. Roosevelt represents that daring, forward-looking personality which is not afraid of change. He does not retreat in face of challenge, and persists in his effort to alter existing conditions as may be possible and in accordance with law and order. Forced by crisis in the national life, he plunged into work that aimed not only to save the economic edifice from ruin, but also to make an earnest endeavor to reconstruct our society, to bring about a better understanding of social relations, to develop the resources of earth for the good of all and not for the aggrandizement of a few. He had to break the shackles of the old tradition —breaking and building at the same time—until at the end of eight years he found that there had been created an environment in which the ideals of Freedom and Democracy had become the foundations of a better society. The issue in the election seems to be whether there shall be further building upon these foundations or that they shall be destroyed.

Nor has his leadership been limited to a vision of an isolated America. As always, America has exercised an influence on the whole world. At a time of great crisis in the affairs of the older civilization—lawlessness and violence rampant, vandals breaking down the restraints of civilization —the voice and influence of Mr. Roosevelt has encircled the globe bringing comfort and hope to peoples enslaved, to states in ruins; and throwing the weight of all that America represents on the side of Justice, Freedom and Peace. In the days of the Civil War, Lincoln said that no land could "endure half free and half slave."

In our day it has become clear that the world cannot endure "half democratic and half despotic." In this larger struggle, Mr. Roosevelt has not hesitated to place the American people indubitably on the side of World Democracy. That Jews are found supporting Mr. Roosevelt is a credit to their understanding of Americanism.

THE STRUGGLE FOR UNION *

There are rumors that conversations are going on between American Zionists and non-Zionists with a view to arriving, if possible, at some understanding for common action on a war and peace program. The idea is to lay the foundation for a united American Jewry to speak and act at a Peace Conference. The historic example of the delegations that went to Versailles is cited. All these conversations are "off the record," but the matters involved are in the air, and no harm is done by referring to them, here and now.

The difficulties were not so great in the first World War. There were organized European Jewish communities greatly impaired during the War, but still intact and capable of expressing their views; they sent their representatives to Versailles. A Zionist delegation organized in London was prepared to speak for the Balfour Declaration. A *modus operandi* was established in the United States. After a period of bitter controversy, all the interested parties were finally assembled in a democratically-elected American Jewish Congress, which agreed to limit its program and to dissolve after the return of its delegates from Versailles. Louis Marshall was the Chairman of the Committee on Program at the Philadelphia Congress. He was the final editor of the political resolution unanimously adopted by the Congress. This resolution endorsed the Balfour Declaration and invited England to accept the trusteeship of the Mandate for Palestine. Minority group rights were agreed to for such lands where these rights were recognized and the Jewish communities wanted them. At Versailles, a Committee of Jewish Delegations was formed, in which the American and Zionist delegates played the leading parts. An agreement was reached on all points. The representations made to the Peace Conference were unified, and there was only slight divergence from the agreed plan. The Balfour Declaration was incorporated in the Mandate for Palestine, which was entrusted to the care of England; and the minority rights clause was inserted in the constitution of all the states established or reconstructed by the terms of the peace treaty.

At this time, in the informal discussions referred to—according to report—the same pattern seems to be developing. The Jewish Homeland is not in dispute. In fact, it is said that there is no objection in principle to the new formula of "Palestine as the Jewish Commonwealth." It is

* *The Congress Bulletin,* May 1942.

almost incredible to hear that even the blunter phrase of a "Jewish State" does not shock the ears of former opponents of Zionism. But the dispute now centers—as it did twenty-five years ago—on the interpretations and implications of *Galuth* nationalism.

The question is, What emphasis do the Zionists or nationalists intend to place on the *Galuth* in connection with the universal brotherhood of Jews? There could be an easy agreement, it seems, on the old formula of 1919 as to minority group rights, but now many non-Zionists are uneasy as to a nationalism that will intrude upon their existence in various lands in which they anticipate following the line of assimilation, which is most comfortable to them as individuals. They imagine that the recognition of a Jewish Commonwealth dedicated to the development of Jewish life in a political form may seriously affect the political status of Jews in other lands; that is, of themselves. They are therefore asking for assurances that the Jewish Commonwealth of Palestine shall not implicate them in their *Galuth* relationships. The new phrase which has come up in these discussions is "universal political nationalism."

Where does this phrase come from? It has never been used in former discussions. Two or three decades ago, "divided loyalty" was the phrase that always recurred. It was argued that Zionism raised the question of loyalty to the state in which Zionists were citizens. This was one of the habitual objections of Jacob H. Schiff until about a year before his death. The phrase comes up even now in the propaganda of Morris Lazaron. But the "divided loyalty" referred to always meant something of a cultural nature. It meant that Zionists intended to create in the *Galuth* spiritual or cultural or religious ghettos, which would interfere with the status of Jews as citizens. The phrase "universal political nationalism" means something quite different. The new objection assumes that the establishment of a Jewish State or Commonwealth in Palestine would implicate all Jews, wherever they live, in a "political relationship."

From the days of Theodor Herzl down to the last Zionist Congress, in all the official and unofficial pronunciamientos of Zionists and Zionist Organizations, the position was always taken that Zionist political implications in Palestine applied exclusively to the Jews living in Palestine, and excluded from the Palestine jurisdiction all Jews living elsewhere. When this is pointed out, a case is sought to be made out against the World Jewish Congress, which is alleged to have taken a position which implies the exercise of political authority over Jews everywhere, superimposed upon whatever local citizenship they may have acquired. But officially and fundamentally, the promoters of the World Jewish

Congress never assumed for one moment that a universal political relationship between Jews was feasible or desirable. On the contrary, it was recognized from the very start that Jews had to concentrate on the idea of establishing a National Home in Palestine, and as far as Jews in other lands were concerned, upon equality as individuals and as members of a group. Recognition of a group status for others implied the right also of Jews to the recognition of their cultural, religious and political group status, but these minority rights never extended beyond the borders of the specific state in which they were claimed. The World Jewish Congress has never—in the record or in fact—stood for a universal political nationalism in any sense of the term. The idea was to establish an international organization dedicated to the purpose of mutual aid in the matter of Jewish rights by a federation of Jewish communities for such Jewish communities as were in need of assistance. The intervention of the World Jewish Congress in any territorial matter did not involve the exercise of any sovereign right, but, on the contrary, the exercise of that right was limited by a definite restriction that it should not be invoked in any state in which the Jewish community itself refused to sanction intervention by a foreign body. There is not the remotest indication of a common political tie. The interest is limited to such rights as are common to all citizens of the state. Nor did the World Jewish Congress, as a matter of fact, exercise any authority or discipline over any of its constituent members.

It is quite true that Simon Dubnow and Chaim Zhitlowsky carried on a propaganda for many years, in which they expounded views that lend color to the thought that nationalism implied a political world relationship between Jews. But the ideas of Dubnow and Zhitlowsky have never found fruitful soil in any Jewish community or among any reasonable number of Jewish writers or thinkers. The views of these two eminent scholars have been consistently rejected by Zionists from the beginning, and also by the large body of what is called Jewish nationalists who are not Zionists. Dr. Zhitlowsky prides himself upon the fact that he remains true to his ideals and principles regardless of the support he receives for them. He continues to preach doctrine without the slightest hope of having even a small group of disciples follow in his footsteps. He loves to be regarded as a voice crying in the wilderness, and no one would be more surprised than he to find that others share his relentlessly "logical" views on Jewish life.

If it is true, therefore, as rumor has it, that what troubles the anti-Zionists is a mistaken notion of Zionist identity with the wild idea of a universal political nationalism, what stands in the way of a united American Jewish front?

Twenty-four years ago the Balfour Declaration was endorsed by the American Jewish Committee and other non-Zionist bodies. Mr. Jacob H. Schiff accepted the Balfour Declaration. Since the issuing of the Mandate for Palestine to England, non-Zionist bodies on many occasions joined the Zionists in demands for the protection of Jewish rights under the Mandate. In 1929, after many years of negotiation, the so-called non-Zionist group in America joined the Extended Jewish Agency, and during the incident of the Passfield White Paper which followed the setting up of the Agency, was no less concerned in that threat to the Mandate than were their partners. Nor has there arisen in the matter of minority rights any serious difference of opinion or practice.

The Committee of Jewish Delegations, formed in Paris, was for a time active with an American Chairman, and then the Chairmanship was assumed by Leo Motzkin, who represented the Committee of Jewish Delegations in Paris and in Geneva until his death. The Committee of Jewish Delegations devoted itself to action at Geneva and elsewhere for the protection of Jewish rights as guaranteed in the constitutions of a number of the reconstructed or re-established states. This action on the part of the Committee was always taken in accord with the wishes of the Jewish communities affected. What was done on behalf of the Polish or Czech or Rumanian Jews never caused any serious difference of opinion with any Jewish body in the United States.

What has raised a cloud of obscurity about the whole question of nationalism has been the appearance in the world of the wrecker of modern civilization, Adolf Hitler, and his emphasis upon aspects of nationalism which have raised fears and misconceptions with regard to nationalism in general. The nationalism of Adolf Hitler is nationalism refined to the point of insanity. It is the mask behind which organized brutality and murderous invasion of the homes of many peoples has been organized. It is the word that is being used to cover blackmail, murder, the larceny of property, the larceny of the rights of people. The spiritual meanings of true nationalism have been lost in the hatreds against Hitler, generated by the destruction he has brought to the world.

There is no reason why American Jewry, in agreement on all points of practical interest, should allow itself to be disunited by misconceptions falsely attributed to Zionists and Jewish nationalists, which they consistently have refused to accept, and which, at best, are utterly meaningless in the world as it is and which it is in the process of becoming.

FOR A UNITED JEWISH DEFENSE AGENCY IN THE UNITED STATES

The first provocative discussions on creating order by democratic unification of Jewish communal efforts in the United States took place in 1938 at the height of the Hitler advance in Europe and of the inroads made by anti-Semitism in the United States.

In 1938 the American Jewish Congress sought to create a single unified instrument for the Jewish defense effort in order to magnify that effort, eliminate competition and duplication and to increase effectiveness in action.

With the advent of Hitler, a Joint Consultative Council had been established through the initiative of the American Jewish Congress which brought together with it the American Jewish Committee, the Bnai Brith and the Jewish Labor Committee. The four groups were never in accord on the tactics of fighting Hitlerism. This Council disbanded in 1937 in disagreement with the American Jewish Congress over the latter's initiation of a boycott movement against the goods and services of Nazi Germany.

In 1938, Edgar J. Kaufmann, a Pittsburgh philanthropist, together with thirty Jewish community leaders, prevailed on the four so-called Jewish defense agencies to co-ordinate their efforts through a General Jewish Council.

The American Jewish Congress sought to convert this Council into a single, unified agency. It failed. The General Jewish Council came into being, but functioned only as a consultative group, whose activities were further limited by the fact that action could only follow unanimous agreement, which was rare.

Subsequently their own competition led the American Jewish Committee and the Anti-Defamation League of the Bnai Brith not to unite their activities, but to form a Joint Defense Appeal for fund-raising unity.

In 1941 the American Jewish Congress again brought about the formation of a Joint Emergency Committee which, in 1944, led to the formation of the National Community Relations Advisory Council with its membership constituted by the four defense agencies and The Jewish War Veterans, the Union of American Hebrew Congregations and a number of Jewish Community Councils on the local level.

In 1950 Dr. Robert M. MacIver undertook a study of Community Relations Agencies for the National Community Relations Advisory Council; his report was made public in 1951. Dr. MacIver recommended re-allocation of some activities to eliminate what he called "wasteful competition and duplication."

A majority of the Council approved the report. The American Jewish Committee and the Anti-Defamation League refused to accept the recommendations and resigned from the Council.

In 1947, the American Jewish Conference, after a year of study by a committee headed by Dr. Maurice N. Eisendrath, President of the Union of American Hebrew Congregations, considered a plan that an organization "democratic in structure and representative of the American Jewish Community . . . be established to secure and protect rights and promote the general welfare of the Jewish people here and abroad; and to enhance the contribution of the Jewish community to American democracy." The plan provided for the maintenance of the entity of the participating organizations (of which the American Jewish Committee was not one, having left the Conference in 1943). The plan was adopted at the 1947 Session, subject to ratification by the constituent organizations at their own meetings.

A special committee of 63, designated by Bnai Brith to meet and consider the question of adherence to the projected new organization (the American Jewish Assembly) decided on February 1, 1948 that a substantial unity would be unachievable under the proposed plan. Thus it collapsed.

In each period, "sovereignty" was the issue that defeated unification.

Lipsky was Vice-President of the American Jewish Congress and Chairman of the Executive Committee of the American Jewish Conference when the efforts to attain unity were made, and an ardent advocate of it. In the following articles by him the issues are presented.

COMING REVOLT OF THE COMMUNITIES *

The combination of Jewish defense agencies formed at Pittsburgh in June, 1938, was finally given a name in September of that year. It was

* *Detroit Jewish Chronicle,* November 29, 1940.

called the General Jewish Council. But what this Council is, what it is doing, what it plans to do, is not known to the general public. Many explanations are offered, but these explanations are confusing and evasive.

There was an agreement at Pittsburgh. The text of the document was published. This agreement was taken to mean that at last the four rival defense agencies had decided to join in a "single group" for Jewish defense, which would assume full responsibility for all Jewish defense work in the United States; and that it would enlarge its membership to include representatives of other Jewish groups not already included.

It seems, however, that the Pittsburgh agreement was taken in hand by lawyers and reduced to writing in the form of a constitution and by-laws. In the course of "drafting" the constitution, what was set forth in Pittsburgh was radically transformed. Instead of a federation moving progressively in the direction of a united front, there was hammered out a structure which was designed to prevent that consolidation of agencies the Jewish public had a right to expect would be established. Instead of twenty members coming together, it was the four corporate defense agencies that met as a board of strategy—not strategy against the anti-Semitic forces, but the strategy of one defense agency against the other. The emphasis was on organizational autonomy. Autonomy was taken to mean the right of any agency to extend its defense program and to enlarge its budget; to listen to advice but to be free to disregard it. In the days before the Pittsburgh agreement there was free competition in the field of Jewish defense. After the Council was formed, the agencies were just as free, their rivalries were just as pronounced, but they had been persuaded to sit at a round table and talk together like gentlemen. That was taken to be a great achievement. An office was set up on Madison Avenue. Quite a number of meetings were held, but most of the time was spent discussing constitutional questions—matters of jurisdiction, what was the Council created for, what were its functions, what was meant by autonomy? The only thing created by the Council was a legislative committee which passed on bills in legislatures and recommended action; such action as was to be taken was left to the four defense agencies.

During the two and a half years the General Jewish Council has pretended to be alive, the whole Jewish world has fallen to pieces. The Jewish communities of one state after another were broken into bits and scattered to the four winds. There isn't a place today in Europe where Jews are free from the persecutions of Nazis and Fascists. The results of Jewish emancipation have been wholly annulled. Anti-Semitic agitation in the United States grew in virulence to an amazing extent. On various occasions, the American Jewish Congress appealed to the General Jewish Council to organize a united front for the defense of Jewish rights, to call Jews together in conference, to arouse the non-Jewish world, to revitalize the sense of organized Jewish responsibility. This appeal was consistently rejected by the majority in the General Jewish Council.

Not only did they refuse to join in common work, but, under cover of the pseudo union in the Council, they enlarged the field of their activities, increased their budgets and built up stronger partisan interests than they had before. Organizational pride and the desire to outdistance the others produced enlarged programs and budgets. Both the American Jewish Committee and the Bnai Brith used the situation to build up a special clientele whom they alarmed, on the one hand, by distorting the facts of anti-Semitic propaganda and, on the other, by saying that they were the only ones who were keeping Jewish defense "under control." Locally, Jews organized themselves for their defense; brought together all elements; consolidated their work under a single management. But when they demanded that the General Jewish Council take over national supervision and control of the local bodies, the Council declined to do so and, as a matter of fact, in a rare moment of frankness, adopted a resolution definitely repudiating the idea of a single local body for Jewish defense. They were afraid that local unity would force unity on a national scale.

At this time, all controversial questions have been removed from the General Jewish Council. It has ceased to meet for months. The discussions had produced a hopeless fatigue. Life was brought into the Council again, however, by the technical question of how to raise funds, a problem forced by the pressure of the local Welfare Chests. These have been demanding that one budget for defense purposes should be submitted, and not four. In order to meet this situation, a plan was devised by the Bnai Brith which, if approved, would have the General Jewish Council appoint a committee for the raising of funds for all four agencies together, in one pool, in one approach to the Welfare Chests. What should be the division of funds? Who should decide on the allocations? What would there be left for the Council to do? For months, these questions have been tossed to and fro. One form is suggested and withdrawn. Then an elaborate plan to have the Council absorbed by a joint Fund-Raising Committee is proposed and defeated. Months have been taken up with the problem.

Bombs are falling all over England. Millions of Jews are in flight. Problems of the present and future accumulate and weigh down the spirits of all Jews. We in America are the only free Jews now left in the world to deal with the problem of Jewish defense and relief. But the momentous question which agitates the leadership of the General Jewish Council is how to raise funds to meet their budgets, how to divide their income.

The truth must be faced. So far as Jewish defense is concerned, unity has been given up as a lost cause—a united front cannot be created. The tragic fact is admitted that, in effect, the Pittsburgh agreement has been liquidated.

It is forgotten that the General Jewish Council came into being because of local pressure. That pressure was exerted by Edgar Kaufmann of Pittsburgh, and about thirty local communal leaders. It was a response to a popular demand. It represented a public call for union and consolidation. In the deliberations of the Council, Mr. Kaufmann has not played the part of leadership which was expected of him. He has suffered months of illness and, when not ill, has been a busy man. He served as the chairman of the Council, but rarely put in an appearance. He was not experienced in Jewish political affairs. He was perplexed and amazed by the way simple things became complicated in the discussions of the Council. He was unable to lead. Nor were the local communal leaders who helped him to force the Pittsburgh conference upon the defense agencies of any great help in this matter. They had signed telegrams and letters and urged the leaders to come together, but that was the end of their job. They were satisfied to urge a united appeal for defense funds, a control of their budgets, co-ordination and consultation, and leave it to the defense agencies to fight it out between themselves.

But, in the matter of defense of rights, there are local committees in which all are united, and these committees are growing in power and experience. They are not chiefly interested in how the funds are to be raised. They are directly interested in a united front of defense not only locally, but nationally as well.

The failure of the General Jewish Council must be taken as the failure of American Jewish leadership. It is a reflection not of the mood and capacity of local leadership, but of the inept, egotistic national leaderships that lack courage and vision. The men of the "provinces"—of all classes and elements—are prepared for united action, for single communal responsibility. They are prepared for service. They are not obsessed by the traditions of organizations or parties. They are eager to play their part in discharging the obligations of the Jews of America in the solution of Jewish problems. But national leadership is lacking. Organizational loyalty stands in the way of union. The national leaders rely upon their prestige, the loyalty of Jews to the traditions of the organizations they represent, to hold the local communities in a state of submission. They hope to prevent the revolt of the communities.

But Jewish needs are becoming more and more pressing. They are bound to break through all traditions and all loyalties. These needs will break the "sovereignty" of the organized national groups that stand in the way of Jewish solidarity. They will set aside a leadership unwilling to adjust itself to the demands of these revolutionary days, that persists in narrowing the outlook, avoiding responsibility and controlled by dogmatic prejudices. The Jewish communities of America are preparing for revolt. That revolt the leaders of the past will not be able to suppress.

BURY THE DEAD *

According to all reports, the General Jewish Council—which is made up of the American Jewish Committee, the American Jewish Congress, the Bnai Brith, and the Jewish Labor Committee—is as dead as a door-nail. It has nothing at hand to do. From the start, it rejected all functions. Nor does it want to have anything to do. Nevertheless, it makes the appearance of having life. There are one or two stenographers in an office on Madison Avenue, New York. The office bears the legend "General Jewish Council." Certainly, it has a letterhead. There is a treasurer who pays the salaries of the help, the rent and incidentals. Every now and then—whenever the American Jewish Congress threatens to do something publicly which the American Jewish Committee might not like—the stenographer gets busy at its request and calls a special meeting. Sometimes the American Jewish Congress responds to the summons. When a meeting is finally gotten together, the chairman is never present, anybody who wants to takes the chair, and hours are spent in desultory, pettifogging talk which seldom comes to an intelligent decision. They have even given up the fruitless controversies which once enlivened the proceedings of the Council meetings. All the symptoms are of dissolution; *rigor mortis* has set in. Why is not the coroner called in to hold an inquest?

Members of the Council have, from time to time, frankly told the

* *Detroit Jewish Chronicle,* April 11, 1941.

public that actually the Council does not function; it is not what it was supposed to be; it cannot do anything because no agreement can be reached as to what it should do. It is dead, but not officially. Still, the Jewish public does not want to believe this. The letterhead still exists, rent is being paid for the office and for clerical service. No one seems to have the courage to do what is usually done in some old-fashioned European Jewish communities at funerals. A member of the congregation is supposed to address the corpse and tell him, in so many words, precisely, that he should take notice of the fact that, so far as the community is concerned, he is dead; stricken from the record; his seat vacated; and he should be sensible enough to adjust himself to the fact.

But this *pilpul* is not impressive. It is not frank. The conference held on December 29 was called by authority of the governing council of the American Jewish Congress. Invitations were issued to representatives of local Congress committees and the national organizations affiliated with the Congress. The conference was directed by the chief officers of the Congress, and the decisive resolution was introduced from the platform by an officer of the Congress. The resolution seemed to have official sanction. It was supported on the floor by leading members of the governing council. It is true that the resolution of the governing council, specifically opposed to the proposal to join the Inter-Faith Committee, was not read. But the President of the American Jewish Congress was the chairman of the conference, and although he did not express the official view, he gave his personal opinion, which must have had decisive consequences. It would seem that the Congress faces the dilemma of either repudiating its own officers, or dissociating itself from the responsibility for adopting the resolution to join the Inter-Faith Committee.

I recall the historic incident in the first American Jewish Congress where Louis Marshall was persuaded, after hours of discussion in committee, not only to approve a resolution endorsing the principle of "group" rights for Jews, but to undertake to draft the resolution himself. He was a very stubborn man, but fair in argument. He was surrounded by men like Nachman Syrkin, Isaac A. Horowitz, Chaim Zhitlowsky, Pinchas Rutenberg, Baruch Zuckerman and many others who fought for every word in the resolution, and by their erudition, logic and earnestness, brought Marshall reluctantly, but like a good sport, to accept the idea of national rights. But in the final adoption of the resolution, it was "group" rights. Marshall was adamant to the last in refusing to use the word "national."

That was over twenty years ago. Since then, the old world has been transformed. If we are to have any place in the new world, it will depend upon what we think we are, and what sacrifices we are willing to make for our conception of Jewish life. The word "national" has become dominant throughout the world. Our refusal to accept it will be decisive in turning our destiny.

The Old Guard in American Jewry—those who have come forward after Louis Marshall died—pygmies in intellect and spirit compared to him—are preparing themselves for a last stand in defense of their conception of Jewish life, which is to annul all Jewish national pretensions and to hide away, once again, in every national organism that will allow them to live. These defenders of the right of the Jewish people to commit national suicide have their fronts in every segment of the organized life of American Jews. They have their front in the relief; they are ensconced in the philanthropic federations. They have a strong minority in the National Council of Welfare Chests, and they have now succeeded in segregating themselves from the Zionists, whom they have forced into an independent campaign. They occupy the dominant front in the defense agencies, and, according to report, they are preparing to take absolute control in the American Jewish Committee, eliminating the sentimental from their midst, and coming out openly in a frontal attack upon Jewish nationality, upon Zionism, and upon all the implications of the Jewish renaissance.

The American Jewish Congress is the nationalist front in the field of diaspora rights. It cannot afford to play with its principles at this time. It cannot in this critical moment place tactics and opportunism above principles. More than that. This organism called the American Jewish Congress, which has lived through a period of thirty years of tragedy and achievement, success and failure, carrying the banner of the national hope, cannot afford at this time to raise any doubt as to how it stands on the crucial issue of Jewish nationality, and what it thinks of the place faith and religion should occupy in the totality of Jewish life. This doubt it has raised (needlessly, unwisely) in the case of the Inter-Faith Committee and the Conference which was held on December 29.

Again this year—since September—reports have come of the discussions carried on between the Joint Distribution Committee and the United Palestine Appeal for a renewal of the life of the United Jewish Appeal for 1941. And again, for weeks and weeks, varying rumors came of agreement through negotiation, peace through arbitration, common action through unanimous agreement. These are useless *ersatz* methods.

They lead to nothing of any importance or value. *The arbiter Democracy should be summoned to determine all differences in matters of Jewish public concern.*

That is why it is most desirable—if only as a matter of sanitation— that the corpse of the General Jewish Council be buried without delay. That corpse stands in the way of the effort which American Jewry should make for its own defense, which requires democratic responsibility in Jewish life.

THE FUND THAT SPLIT THE ZIONIST MOVEMENT

At midnight on May 14, 1948, when the British, after 28 years, suddenly relinquished their Palestine Mandate, three months before their planned departure, there existed on the record:

1. A November 29, 1947 U.N. resolution authorizing the partition of Palestine into an Arab State and a Jewish State, and making any armed attack on that resolution a breach of the peace subject to U.N. Security Council action;

2. A 1947 British statement to the U.N. refusing to cooperate in the implementation of the U.N. Partition Resolution;

3. A War on the Palestine Partition Resolution begun the day of its passage by the so-called Arab Volunteer Armies, which took the form of attack on Jewish Palestine.

Imminent chaos was anticipated by a United Nations which had been in almost continuous session for some six months as a result of the Palestine situation.

Two things happened simultaneously:

1. The State of Israel was proclaimed at the instant of British departure; a Provisional Israel Government began to function immediately.

2. On May 15, 1948, Egypt announced to the U.N. Security Council a War on Israel. The armies of Egypt, Syria, Lebanon, Iraq, as well as the British-trained Jordan Arab Legion, attacked Palestine; leaders of the Arab League called upon Palestine Arabs to evacuate their home areas in order to pave the way for a speedy Arab assault and anticipated victory.

But, to the astonishment of the world, the Provisional Government of Israel was able:

a. To arrange an orderly take-over of civilian authority.

b. To direct and win the war against the superior numbers and arms of the Arab official armies.

This "miracle" was produced by 28 years of training for government on the part of the Jewish Agency; the experience and skill of the Haganah; the passionate love of the Jewish inhabitants of Palestine for the land they had carved out of the desert; the support, financial as well as moral, from Jewish communities the world over.

For 28 years, the Jewish Agency, with its recognized status under the Mandate, had been functioning in Palestine, at first with the fervor of idealism and belief in the Mandatory. Later, as the Mandatory began to whittle away the pledge and purpose of the Mandate, with redoubled determination to create a Jewish Palestine, despite betrayal.

The Jewish Agency was in effect responsible for the existence of an embryo Jewish Government in Palestine during the Mandatory period; responsible for the enabling funds and institutions with which to buy land from the Arabs on which Jews could be settled; to bring the Jewish pioneers into Palestine, settle and retrain them; for a network of schools, hospitals, health services; for the upbuilding of colonies, the draining of swamps; the training of a labor force; incentives to exploration of minerals, industry; the reafforestation of the country; an irrigation system; for a system of defense in which virtually all adults could be mobilized, on short notice, against Arab attack, and for an army for that defense, the Haganah.

As Britain gave increasing evidence of unwillingness to accelerate the building of the Jewish National Home, the Jewish Agency assumed more and more responsibility.

What had been built up in Palestine in 28 years was made possible largely through voluntary contributions to various funds, of which the principal and official fund was the Keren Hayesod, or Palestine Foundation Fund, an international fund responsible to the World Zionist Organization which, in turn, made allocations to the various Jewish operations and institutions in Palestine.

Yet this was the fund whose founding split the American Zionist Movement.

In 1920, the Keren Hayesod was established as the international official fund of the World Zionist Organization by Chaim Weizmann, on the urging of European Zionists, under the pressure of necessity—i.e., the issuance of the Balfour Declaration in 1917; the agreement in 1920 at San Remo, by the Allied Powers, to establish a Mandate for Palestine with Britain as the Mandatory; the appointment of Sir Herbert Samuel as the High Commis-

sioner for Palestine—and the responsibility of the World Zionist Organization to assist the Mandatory in establishing the Jewish National Homeland, under the terms of the Mandate.

A fund of $25,000,000 to be contributed by the Jews of the world, responsible to the World Zionist Organization, was envisaged for the execution of a five year development program, with the entire program for building the Jewish National Homeland to be financed by it.

Lipsky was an American co-founder of the Keren Hayesod.

At this climactic moment for Zionist aspirations, the establishment of the Fund created a furor in the United States that in 1921 split the American Zionist Movement and produced the resignations of Louis D. Brandeis, then Honorary President of the Z.O.A., Judge Julian W. Mack, President of the Z.O.A., Stephen S. Wise, Felix Frankfurter and others, men who had been in the forefront of the effort to secure the Balfour Declaration and the British Mandate for Palestine.

Their resignations followed a bitter battle at the Cleveland Convention of the Zionist Organization June 5–8, 1921, which voted for the Keren Hayesod.

In the United States, Lipsky, standing with Chaim Weizmann, led the opposition to the so-called Brandeis forces. To lead that battle he resigned his post as Secretary of the Zionist Organization.

The Brandeis forces, beginning with their leader, Supreme Court Justice Louis D. Brandeis, opposed the Keren Hayesod because it was planned as a world fund, responsible to the World Zionist Organization. The Brandeis group favored territorial units, all over the world, each an entity unto itself, with limited functions and funds.

In an address delivered on June 6, 1921, Louis Lipsky, presenting the case for the Keren Hayesod, made two points that were to prove prescient. Said he, then, of the building power the funds of the Keren Hayesod would give the World Zionist Organization: "If we are to leave all the functions of government entirely to the Palestine Government,—how shall we Jews, without any knowledge in State building, develop the qualities needed for a National Home?"

Further, he said, only the enlistment of the support of the Jewish masses, not in separatist movements, but united behind the World Zionist Movement, could produce the resources in sufficient strength, financial and moral, to build the Jewish National Homeland.

So intense was the feeling and the power of the Brandeis group that Chaim Weizmann had been induced to come to the United States, for the first time, to bring his influence to bear in behalf of the Keren Hayesod. Weizmann, appearing at the Cleveland Convention a day after the affirmative vote had been taken, attacked defeatism and predicted: "You can have the form, gentlemen and lawyers, we shall have the substance." Of the necessity which forced him to create the Keren Hayesod, he said:

"After San Remo I repeated this slogan. I said: 'Now we are approaching the treaty of Sèvres, which may be ratified any day. Lloyd George had asked us that we shall speedily begin to work. Samuel (Sir Herbert Samuel) is being sent to Palestine. It will break Samuel if we won't work. Make Ready; Strip for Action.' And I insisted upon Simon going to America. And he went to America. . . . Not only as it was said yesterday to get dollars in America, but to get Jews, to get ideas. I believed that here were men full of experience and ideas, and incidentally money, and now the tragedy begins.

"When he arrived I asked him, 'What is the news? Are you ready?' And one reply and answer as you have heard was, 'Zionism in America is going down. There is apathy. There is no money.' 'I don't know,' he said, 'whether even the budget, the miserable little budget which we need for Palestine, whether this can be gathered, whether the quota which America is giving, a respectable quota in proportion to the budget, whether this will be forthcoming.' In vulgar language: 'nothing doing.' And here I was proudly promising Lloyd George, 'The Jews will reply.'

". . . There was Samuel waiting, pledged to the British Government, waiting and waiting, without a budget for the daily routine work in Palestine and the only program which was given by your leaders at the end of the conference after San Remo was 'Cut down expenses.' These are the auspices under which I began work.

". . . Why this indecision, why this demoralization, dry rot, which set into the organization when the organization was at the height of its achievements? . . . I have and I formulate here a definite accusation . . . not before the Convention but before the bar of history. American leadership did not understand the movement .They failed to grasp it. And that is the tragedy of the situation. They lost faith in their own supporters. Therefore, they came to Europe and they told us 'Bankruptcy.' Instead of coming to us with plans, with means, or telling us, 'Come and help us to provide these plans and means.' These very gentlemen who rendered yeoman service during the War when the business consisted of negotiating with governments, with non-Jews, have proved a failure when the business consisted of negotiating with Jews. Here lies the great truth. It is perhaps the fault of their education. It is perhaps the tragedy of Jewish life, yet

here it was and it came out for the first time. I felt it. Powerful as they might have been in speaking to non-Jews, they were powerless when they had to face the power which mattered, that is the Jewish people, and that is the only people which began to matter after San Remo . . . And here began the degradation of our movement . . . And the whole program consisted of things which cannot be done, which should not be done . . . These were the auspices under which work began nine months ago . . . I had to set off the Keren Hayesod . . . The organizations from all over, with the exception of America, have been clamoring intuitively for work. They knew that in the Keren Hayesod lies salvation . . . and they started work before we had statutes, before the executive could give them the signal.

". . . I set off the Keren Hayesod and in that I was right. You can have the form, gentlemen, lawyers. But we shall have the substance."

Brandeis never did recognize the Keren Hayesod. But most of the 1921 dissidents rejoined the Zionist Movement and assisted in the successes of the Keren Hayesod.

How far the funds of the Keren Hayesod had enabled the Jewish Agency to develop the operation of an embryo Jewish Government was set forth by Lipsky on June 7, 1940 in an editorial in The New Palestine. World War II was then already a year old; the Jewish refugee problem growing by leaps and bounds, and Jewish Palestine the only haven but enjoined from becoming such by the British White Paper of 1939.

"On the one hand, the Government of Palestine is concerning itself with the problems of the larger defense, but it is guided by a desire to maintain the ante-war balances as between Jews and Arabs, and to insinuate the purposes of the MacDonald White Paper, which still linger on after Mr. MacDonald has disappeared. These restraints hinder much of the work of the Government. It is more interested in policy than in performance.

"The larger field of Jewish interest thus becomes the almost exclusive concern of the Jewish Agency and the Vaad Leumi, the latter having been built up in this emergency to take over some of the responsibilities for the welfare of the Yishuv. The tasks that confront the Jewish authorities in the Homeland include: the problems of labor employment; of commerce and industry; of relief and social service; of credits and banking; of acquiring land for new settlement; of absorbing the new immigration; the finding of new paths for industry; the interlocking of all economic interests in order that a collective responsibility shall be created to protect the totality of Jewish interest; and last, but not least, how effectively to defend

the Jewish territory which is much more the concern of Jews than it seems the concern of the Mandatory Government.

"*In effect,* what we see in action in Palestine is the operation of a Jewish commonwealth, *unrecognized as yet, not legalized as yet; but it is an exercise which calls forth all the talent and experience and spirit of sacrifice of the whole community, deeply stirred by events and determined that they shall play a worthy part in the struggle which faces the civilized world of today. Our financial institutions are alive to all the problems of the country. Our colonization experts have not become routineers, but still retain the spirit of pioneers. Our labor force is not merely organized to protect labor interests, but is a powerful weapon of defense, eager to be used for all national purposes. Our immigration authorities are keenly alive to all the difficulties, the changing of routes, the fluctuations of exchange, and are rendering an enormous service in turning the flow of refugees toward the Promised Land. The many professional men who have escaped from the European hell—chemists, engineers, etc.—are thinking in terms of the Allied cause, and how their talents can be made to serve that cause.*

"*When we think of the plight of Jews in European lands, and of how difficult it is for us to lend them a hand, it should be a source of great encouragement to all of us that what we are doing in Palestine serves to redeem the name and credit of the Jewish people. It is not a band of refugees huddled together, requiring material relief. It is a growing state, defending what it has achieved. There, on the Eastern front, we are building and maintaining a democracy that is prepared, on behalf of the whole Jewish people, to carry its burden in the great cause which engages the interests, and the sympathies and the hopes of the whole civilized world.*"

By 1940, the Keren Hayesod had attained national stature in the United States, reflected in its inclusion as an integral part of the national Jewish fund-raising effort known as the United Jewish Appeal.

But the vital necessity of accelerating the development of the Jewish National Homeland had not yet been recognized in 1940; the Palestine Foundation Fund was subordinate to the relief fund encompassed within the U.J.A., with 23.3% of the funds of the U.J.A. going to the United Palestine Appeal (including the Keren Hayesod and The Jewish National Fund); 28.1% to the National Refugee Service; and 48.6% to the J.D.C., the American Jewish Joint Distribution Committee.

Five years of war, the extermination of six million Jews by Hitler were to follow before the primacy of Jewish Palestine was recognized.

The primacy of the Keren Hayesod in the upbuilding of Palestine was the cause which Lipsky continued to espouse, first in the context of the Zionist Movement, and later in the context of other national and local drives for funds in the United States.

In 1933, after thirteen years of effort by the Keren Hayesod, Lipsky was able to report a resilient and growing Jewish life in Palestine and to contrast it with the deterioration of Jewish life in Europe.

Three years later in 1936, when Hitler had already been in power three years, and the subsequent Jewish tragedy was already silhouetted, Lipsky was still of necessity pressing for larger funds for the Keren Hayesod in order to accelerate the tempo of development in Palestine. In 1941 he was a leader in a major battle revolving around parity for Palestine Funds and the right of the Jewish Communities of America to decide democratically how funds should be allocated, a battle which ended only with the establishment of the State of Israel.

The Editor

A FUND TO BUILD A STATE *

Behind the conflict which is culminating here this evening, there is a history. We are now witnessing the climax of a movement in American Zionism which represents to a large extent a breaking away from the fundamental principles of the Zionist Movement. In every movement for an idea it has happened that, when sufficient strength and momentum have gathered, a supreme effort becomes necessary for its success; at that moment there develop in the movement elements that have not the strength to make this supreme effort in the forward direction—and they break away from the movement and the ideal. That is what has happened in the Zionist Movement here.

You will remember that when the Sultan gave his people a constitution, there were at that time any number of Zionists who felt that the burden of the movement had come to an end—that no more effort was required. Politics was at an end, and terms must be made with the constitution. All that was left to do was to enter Palestine. And again with Uganda there came a period of doubt. At a moment when all the strength and determination and sacrifice of the Zionist Movement expressed itself in a forward motion, the same element arose: there grew up the Uganda problem and there developed some sort of movement away from Zionism and the Zionist ideal. And today we are facing exactly the same situation with San Remo and the Balfour Declaration. Should Zionists, seeing before them the achievement of the Balfour Declaration, feel now a lack of confidence? Yet there are men who, at this moment, unwittingly, and with no desire to leave Zionism, began to develop something which was not Zionism. And this movement has been going on since the Balfour Declaration. It has expressed itself in various ways. It was not conscious of its own progress. Many of us did not know whither it was tending, and probably did not mind as long as the things we cared for were maintained. And now this movement has found expression in the Memorandum; but the men that wrote it were not philosophers—they were legalists, and not interested in the truth absolute. There were inconsistencies innumerable—but you can see in the Memorandum the inevitable tendency. I do not say that those who framed it were conscious of this, but the Memorandum has in it the element of a movement, destructive of all that we have achieved till now.

I will trace it for you so that you can see it for yourselves. The first

* Speech delivered at 24th ZOA Convention, Cleveland, Ohio, June 6, 1921.

paragraph deals with *Gegenwartsarbeit.* Many of the members of the National Executive Committee thought this was a simple matter. We were against an appropriation for schools in Poland. I voted against that proposition. But I am not against *Gegenwartsarbeit,* and I believe that no Zionist can deny the principles contained in it. The thoughts here expressed concerning *Gegenwartsarbeit* constitute a denial of the essential unity of the Jewish people, for if we produce in Palestine a living Jewish nationality with a political status, and then deny our relationship to it, we break up unity, and create an American Zionism as distinguished from universal Zionism.

We come to the idea of Federalism as expressed in the Memorandum. I know where this idea comes from: it springs from a proposal to have a budget committee which should be made up of the Federations of the World. That is why you find in the addresses of our leaders so many references to American Zionism, to the American contributions to Zionism. Thence comes the idea of the separation of funds, and the idea of the limited responsibilities of the World Zionist Organization. And thus the World Zionist Organization is to become the holder of a small fund, to be used for certain purposes designated with the establishment of the fund. This is the reason that the Reorganization report was endorsed. But this report belongs properly to the Congress, as you know. Those who are affected by that report had a right to be heard in court, but we have taken that report and presented it to the American Zionist Organization as if we were the proper tribunal. We spread that report throughout the United States, knowing at the time that two individuals would be affected by that report: and yet those two individuals were never asked to give testimony with regard to the facts. And the circulation of the *New Palestine* was increased, so that those who were new to the Zionist Movement might also learn good news which the report contained.

There is another item in the report of the Organization Committee, an item which says that the Zionist Organization shall not assume any of the functions proper to the Government of Palestine or any of the functions proper to the Jews of Palestine. When it comes to the building of the Jewish National Home, when it comes to the laying of the foundations of that state, says the report, we must leave these to the Government of Palestine. But according to Dr. Weizmann, and according to any Zionist who knows what is involved, the only right which is given us by the Balfour Declaration, is that very right of proceeding at once with the laying of the foundations of the Jewish State which is subsequently to be confirmed by legal action in other ways. If we are to leave all the functions of government entirely to the Palestine Government, how shall we Jews, without any knowledge in state-building, without experience, develop the qualities needed for building a National Home?

We are told on the other hand that we shall not assume any of the functions proper to the Jews of Palestine, meaning the educational system: this is an assumption that the educational system of Palestine is built up only for the Jews of Palestine. But this is not the case: the educational system of Palestine is built up for the Jewry of the whole world, as an expression of the Jewish ideal: it is a center from which the Jewish spirit will stream forth. And yet we are told that we must limit that educational system to the bare needs of the Jews in Palestine, that we are through with supporting them—that only for one year and a half must they expect our co-operation in this gigantic task.

You see that the Memorandum, poorly as it expresses the real intent of the American Administration, reveals itself as a denial of our opportunity, reveals that our American leaders have become skeptical of the powers of the Jewish people. There is one great power that has moved the Jews of the world in the Zionist Movement, and that power was the chain which bound all Jews together. If they were weak in Poland, they knew that they were strong here. And because of that there was hope and confidence. But when we break that chain, when we say that we shall control our own work, they lose confidence and strength, and in its place there comes despair. And because of that weakness there arose the desire and longing to liquidate, to place the Zionist Organization in accord with the lowest terms of confidence. Our program is the expression of our faith, and our program goes down as our faith is reduced. In our program for the last year our faith in the Jewish people is expressed in terms of $60,000 a month. Now, when Dr. Weizmann comes to America, and our faith increases, you see that new faith translated into greater expectation and better results.

Why do you suppose that the Zionist Organization was not able to attract to itself the Jews of this country? It is because in the minds of our Administration there was a lack of understanding of their people. I have been in the organization twenty years, and when it was urged upon our Administration that they should appeal to the Jewish people, they thought that was a mistaken idea. You have the power of the press. But the papers, they said, do not reflect public opinion. They are made by journalists. And, in saying this, they ignored the Jewish people, and the

Jewish people felt it, and our office, which should have been the Mecca of all the Jews in the United States, became instead a branded thing—and that just at the moment when the Balfour Declaration comes, when San Remo comes. That is why there has been spread amongst Zionists the statement of our leaders, the instruction that our allegiance to Zionism is not for the World Organization, but for the American Zionist Organization. Now since the arrival of Dr. Weizmann our Administration has had an opportunity of seeing what the Jewish people felt about it, how its authority could not stop them in their enthusiastic support of the things they hold dear.

That separatist tendency has been exerted since the Balfour Declaration, since San Remo, since the London Conference. Though it was known well enough here for what purpose we were going to gather funds, we began by demanding plans, by demanding details first. Resolutions to this effect were voted at Buffalo, but no matter what legal minds may say, every Zionist felt at heart that if the London Executive undertook to differ from the Zionist Organization of America, the wishes of the London Executive should be complied with. And the London Executive did express itself on the Keren Hayesod, expressed itself in terms that were heard throughout the whole world. And Zionists and non-Zionists the whole world over, heard and were moved. The Keren Hayesod obtained a popularity in New York which a businessman would have paid a million dollars to get for his own enterprise. And, instead of taking advantage of this situation, we devoted ourselves to legal debates, out of which there arose only bitterness of feeling. Every act of the Administration with regard to the Keren Hayesod indicated that it did not understand what was before it. "How can you raise money?" was the cry—because they had not been able to raise it in December. Then, when Weizmann came, all the conceptions of the Administration were thrown into a controversy with the leaders of the Zionist Movement. The guilt for the damage which has been done lies with our Administration and with no one else. And now after infinite debating, after the reading of reams of documents, after the study of interminable reports, it is made clear by this Convention that the Zionists are firm in their allegiance to the World Zionist Organization, firm in their belief that through the Keren Hayesod the Jewish Homeland will be established. But, at the last moment, when it is certain that the delegates understand the purport of this Memorandum, understand that, in so far as it can be deciphered, it expresses principles and policies with which Zionists have nothing to do, then an appeal is made to the delegates, in the name

of peace, that no action should be taken, but the whole matter be left
to the Congress. But the Congress cannot decide questions we must
decide for ourselves. If our Administration has issued this Memorandum,
and taken a position that is illegal, the Congress is not going to settle
that issue for us. We have got to settle it right here.

I want to state clearly now that a vote of confidence is asked for all
of these acts of the Administration. If we give that vote of confidence,
the Keren Hayesod is voted away, the World Zionist Organization is
repudiated, the separatist policy as expressed in the Memorandum is
approved. That is what we are voting on here tonight, and when that
question has been settled, we shall know where the Zionist Organization
of America stands.

PRIMACY FOR THE KEREN HAYESOD *

There have been brighter years, but no year of service for Palestine was
ever given in which there was spent so much energy and persistent effort
in the face of handicaps unparalleled in our history. For these were the
most cheerless and distressing twelve months of a decade. When the
general Depression began, American Jewry was at the height of its
development, proud of its seemingly endless resources, struggling with
skyscraping plans, bursting with optimism. The fall was so sudden and
rapid that it dazzled and bewildered the vision. It was hard to realize
what was happening. The speeding deflation made it impossible to
sense what values would remain once the bottom was reached. All the
reserves of organized Jewish life were strained. The slogans that had
served to build up social energy and had sustained life during the past
decade while the curve was turning upward, were found to be inadequate.
Confidence in the future expressed itself by grandly spreading communal
obligations over into the future. And now, the mortgages placed upon
that future rudely began to harass the mortgagors, demanding immediate
payment in full, while the assets froze with lightning rapidity. It is
assumed that we are now at the end of the Depression—certainly, the
past year reached depths never plumbed before.

What effect this deflation has had upon the relation of American Jewry
to the larger interests of our people need not be described here in detail.
It was inevitable that the remote should be sacrificed for the proximate,

---

* Address as National Chairman, National Conference of United Palestine Campaign,
  January 12, 1933.

the intangible for the tangible, the general for the personal. Self-preservation is the first law of nature, and expresses itself in a spiral progression of decreasing temperature, extending to the outer circle of human relations. First, your own preservation, then, that of your family, then, that of your friends, then, that of the institutions and causes near you, then, that of the institutions and causes farther away. In an atmosphere of change and uncertainty, with all values falling, the whole social structure seems to be in a state of disintegration, and to let the home fires go out in order to keep the Eternal Light burning would seem to be fantastic to the ordinary mind.

As so it has come about that American Jewry which, not so long ago, prided itself upon being the providential saviour of the broken-down Jewries of Europe, which was beginning to make itself publicly responsible on a large scale for the building of the Jewish National Home in Palestine, was now compelled to look to its own preservation, to prevent the breakdown of its own immediate communal life.

With the year 1915 began the great relief movement which, for the first time, brought American Jewry into direct contact with the general problems of Jews resident in other lands. It was said that this remnant in the House of Israel had been saved from the burning Galut of Europe, brought to a land of freedom and equal opportunity, in order to be the Deliverer of the captives, the harbingers of the *Geulah*. All the hopes of our people turned to American Jews, and nobly and generously did American Jewry respond to the call. Millions were expended to relieve distress, and delegations were sent to give personal cooperation. The Joint Distribution Committee was regarded as the guardian of Jewish interests, and it had unlimited resources. The relief organization set many European communities upon their feet. It kept the schools alive. It sought to organize the financial affairs of the communities. It enabled thousands of families to withstand the devastating influence of hostile governments and peoples. No part of the Galut was left unaided.

The interest of American Jewry was not only material and moral. It extended into the field of government and politics, and through the American Jewish Congress, representing all classes and elements in as public a manner as possible, it intervened in the political problems arising out of the war, and forced serious consideration of the rights of minority groups, securing the inclusion in the peace treaties of provisions to protect Jewish national groups' rights.

Our ancient hope with regard to Zion was also assumed as one of the major responsibilities of American Jewry. During the period of hostilities in the great War, the Jewish settlement established in Palestine, from the beginning of the Zionist Movement until 1914, was preserved and maintained, thanks to the generous interest of American Jewry, first through the Provisional Zionist Committee, and then with the cooperation of the Joint Distribution Committee. With the issuing of the Balfour Declaration and the subsequent ratification of the Palestine Mandate, all division among American Jews as to doctrinal beliefs were merged in the practical work of upbuilding, and the larger part of what is now the Jewish National Home owes its existence and development to the cooperation of a united American Jewry.

It is with no thought of invidious comparison that I call your attention to the pictures of Galut and of Palestine as they now appear, contrasts in two fields of Jewish collective endeavor, into each of which the same sincerity, the same spirit of devotion and the same hopes were poured by American Jews, and which may now be brought under the scrutiny of friendly evaluation.

The heart of faith becomes despondent, for all the good will and brotherly interest contributed to Jewish life in the Diaspora by American Jewry seems to have been spent in vain. The need of the hour was alleviated. Life was kept moving. The dawn seemed often on the verge of breaking. But the new day is darker than the old. Of all the lands included within the scope of our relief and reconstructive measures, there is not one which does not present a spectacle of tragic hopelessness and helplessness. As we have plugged a hole, evil hands have come and rend it open again. There has not been a constructive effort which enemies have not undermined and rendered futile. The area of distress does not diminish, but becomes endemic to the whole of Europe, as witness the blossoming within the past few years of that destructive anti-Jewish force in Germany known as Hitlerism. The Galut is not a fortress, the Jews living within their own protective walls. The Galut is an open field in which the winds of prejudice and the storms of hatred have free play, and there are no shields to protect, no shelter in the ground in which life may take refuge. The Depression, which is now reaching its climax, has served only to expose, in raw frankness, the prevailing condition of incessant economic and political war against Jews, which is being waged in Poland, in Germany, in Austria and in Rumania.

He would not be worthy of the name Jew who would wish to see the Homeland flourish upon the ruins of the Galut, or to profit by its miseries and defeats. The Zionist spirit grows out of appreciation of the affirmative values of a Jewish life maintained and developed on its own soil. It is the expression of the free choice of free men and women. It is aspiration and self-realization, not the expression of oppression and wretchedness. The Homeland is the relief and end of the Galut, not its competitor.

It is solely, therefore, as consolation and compensation that the contrasting picture of Palestine is presented. A good experience offsets a bad experience. Whatever we have put into Palestine—invested at the same time while everything humanly possible was being done to bolster up the Galut—should, regarded with the eyes of reality, give us immense satisfaction.

Only in passing do I speak of the economic conditions in Palestine. For centuries Palestine had been neglected. Its agricultural life was primitive. It knew little or nothing of the ways of industry and commerce. Its natural resources were unknown to its dominant population, whose wants were rudimentary and who were ignorant of the progress made in the outer world. The coming of enterprising Jews from Western lands, imbued with national zeal and spirit of self-immolation for the sake of an ideal, brought progress to the land, led to its rapid development, and gave Palestine a place on the modern map. This progress is of such modest proportions that the currents of commerce and industry and finance deriving from the Western world could not affect it materially. The Depression seems to be passing over it as a plant too lowly to be reached. Its banks are solvent. Its industries are expanding. Its commerce grows by leaps and bounds. There is no unemployment, and a reasonably strong immigration has been resumed right in the midst of the Depression. It is possible now to consider Palestine as a port of entry for a reasonable number of Jews coming out of the Galut.

Palestine is not immune, however, against the probable reactions that will follow excess in any direction, industrial or commercial. It is subject to the same laws of economics as prevail everywhere, and ultimately the force of world crisis and markets will also reach it, and it will be impossible to avoid the usual alternation of rise and fall that seems to be an inevitable feature of modern social organization.

But what is significant is the fact that whatever we have invested in this land, moral or financial, has not gone to waste, but is preserved in permanent Jewish experience and assets; that it has placed a foundation under Jewish feet, built a fortress for Jewish self-defense, has created and maintained an authentic environment, and that every advance made has become opportunity for further growth.

It is a picture of romance and of healthy outdoors, not of tragedy and congestion, airless city streets. The Yishuv is the master of its own fate, and not the victim of conditions to which it is bound. There we are an organized people, not exposed to alien winds and storms, to the political entanglements of other peoples, but enveloped and protected by our own collective strength, capable of self-defense and in a position to use it, united by bonds of national determination in a common enterprise and a common destiny. The economic life we are creating is not built within an alien economic structure in which we play a fractional part, and from which we may be easily dislodged. Our feet are planted in the soil, and the soil we labor with is our own. We are not tenants living on mortgaged property. We are not merely living on the surface of a social organization, but we ourselves are responsible for everything that is done for the reclamation of the land, from draining of the swamps to the tilling of the soil, to the making of the roads, to the building of the houses, to the labor in the factories, to the construction and the maintenance of the Electrical Corporation and of the Dead Sea undertaking.

In other lands, more Jews mean added difficulties. In Palestine, more Jews mean more strength, and whatever may be lost by the individual or sacrificed by him for the common good, finds its way into the Jewish treasury, ready to serve the interest of other Jews. Nothing that we produce there can ever really become *Hefker*.

Furthermore, here for the first time the Jewish people the world over stand united, responsible in a corporate capacity for a national task. The settlement of Palestine is not an accidental movement of individuals, not made up of evicted Jews moving from a land of oppression into another of comparative freedom, making a trek on their own. A united Jewish people has assumed the responsibility for building the Jewish National Home in the full light of day, registering its acceptance of the obligation in an international tribunal. The undertaking has the sanction of the great nations of the world. To this aim we are solemnly and deliberately committed—all Jewries, all parties, Zionists and friends of Palestine. To the end that the enterprise may be effectively carried on, the Zionist Organization entered into a compact with friends of Palestine to extend the Jewish Agency in accordance with the terms of the Mandate, and all Jewry now acts through legally constituted Jewish authorities: the Zionist Congress, the Council of the Jewish Agency, the Executive Committee of the Jewish Agency. Not unlike governments, we have budgets and deficits, parties and controversies, all of which indicates that the corporate responsibility assumed is not a mere abstraction or formal arrangement, but a reality in Jewish life, subject to growth and change, but functioning in accordance with the laws of its own life.

It is in the development of this picture that the Conference of today calls upon the Jews of America for cooperation. The Depression will not continue forever, but there is a continuing responsibility involved in the maintenance of this movement. For the Galut, it is hoped that the relief measures will be continued and that the organized attempt to arouse public opinion against governmental neglect and oppression and anti-social outrages will be furthered. But in Palestine we have a responsibility which is peculiarly our own. The continuity of the work is of vital importance for its effectiveness.

If the present state of economic security in Palestine is to be turned into immediate advantage in the way of increased immigration, if we are to avoid the petrifaction of the Jewish population of Palestine in its present small size, if we are to make possible, through our collective endeavors, the enlargement of the base upon which private enterprises are to be built, the modest quota set for American Jewry for the 1933 Keren Hayesod budget should be contributed without fail, in spite of the difficulties which admittedly exist in American Jewish affairs.

At any rate, those who are members of the Zionist Organization, and the friends of Palestine who have joined in organizing the extended Jewish Agency, should appreciate the importance and urgency of making the Palestine interest as represented by the Keren Hayesod budget, that interest which is entitled to primacy and priority. It is our obvious duty to maintain the solvency, the integrity and the effectiveness of the Jewish Agency, upon which the credit of the whole Yishuv is based. The obligations of the Jewish Agency should be regarded as sacred responsibilities that involve every person or party or organization that has been, directly or indirectly, responsible for the adoption of the Keren Hayesod budgets from year to year.

This Conference signalizes the beginning of a new campaign, but it is also the beginning of a restoration of the morale of American Jewry, the return of faith and hope. There is not general disintegration of the Jewish world. Jewish standards are not falling everywhere. Despair and gloom do not prevail in every corner of the Jewish world. A beginning has been made to re-establish contact with our ancient soil, and to build a new life there. Out of the loins of an ancient, harassed people, a new generation of youth has been born, which is engaged in enriching the ancient land with the sweat of their labor. They are building cities and making a new Jewish civilization. They are bringers of peace, and they

know the arts of self-defense. They stand erect. What they have created
is an invitation to all Jews who are oppressed and who wish to live in
a state of freedom, to come over and join them and make themselves a
part of that home. To thousands of Jews the world over, this land
speaks of self-determination and self-emancipation through labor. It is
they who are giving new meaning to Jewish ideals, and spreading song
and beauty into all Jewish homes, in which mind and spirit are attuned to
the message of the new day.

If we come to American Jewry with this encouraging message and
with a realistic picture of that hope, it should not be difficult to discharge
our obligations to the Keren Hayesod budget of the Jewish Agency.

WHAT THE KEREN HAYESOD HAS BUILT *

In American Zionist life, the birth of the Keren Hayesod was attended
by a sharp controversy, the development of a prolonged partisanship,
the infliction of wounds that took years to heal, which was followed by
a long period of unparalleled achievement for the Jewish National
Home. During the period, it was American Jewry that provided the
larger share of the funds to lay the foundations of the National Home.
American Jewry provided more of the national capital required than
all other Jewries put together, owing to the terrible economic conditions
that prevailed in European lands at the time when American prosperity
was at its height. It was the contributions of American Jewry to the
Keren Hayesod that gave strength and power and authority to the
Zionist Executive, and subsequently to the Executive of the Jewish
Agency.

In European Jewry, the name Keren Hayesod, untranslated, embodies
the very essence of the corporate responsibility of Jewry toward the
re-establishment of the Jewish Commonwealth. There, the Keren
Hayesod is taken to mean the treasury of the Jewish corporate responsibility. It provided the Zionist Executive with instrumentalities to
effect its national purposes. It covered the maintenance of the Hebrew
national schools. It provided the means for the settlement of Jews on the
land. It enabled the Executive to organize and regulate the immigration.
It was through the Keren Hayesod that the labor forces of Palestine
were recruited and their institutions given their initial start, from which
developed the present Histadrut and its various branches. It enabled

* *The New Palestine*, October 30, 1936.

the Executive to conduct the long and difficult political activities of the Zionist Organization, in London, in Geneva and in Jerusalem. In other words, it was the Keren Hayesod that gave the outline of a corporate administration which made plans, assumed obligations and maintained continuity in the life of the Zionist Movement. So it was understood among the Zionists of Europe.

The Keren Hayesod continues as the fund-raising instrument of the Extended Jewish Agency. The budget adopted, derived from the income of the Keren Hayesod, is now fixed first by the Zionist Congress, and then by the Council of the Jewish Agency. Among European Zionists, the Keren Hayesod is a powerful instrument of propaganda as well as a source of income.

But so far as we in America are concerned, for a long number of years now the Keren Hayesod, as such, has functioned largely within the framework of campaign agencies. To a large extent, it has become an item—quite large, it is admitted—in united campaigns, sometimes composed of exclusively Zionist funds, but every now and then including also relief funds. More recently the Keren Hayesod as well as the relief funds have been sheltered within the framework of Welfare Chests, in which, in a number of instances, other funds and other responsibilities receive the larger part of the income. As a matter of fact, except for the first few years, the Keren Hayesod never made its appeal in America exclusively for itself. It was first involved in the quite ambitious program of the United Palestine Appeal of 1926. It then was included within another appeal called the American Palestine Campaign, and then, as American Palestine Campaign, it was alternately included within a United Jewish Appeal, and under other names.

In short, the Keren Hayesod (which in 1920 was launched as the all-inclusive fund which was to be representative of the entirety of the Zionist responsibility) is now, so far as America is concerned, a budget which is fitted into the campaign needs of American Jewry.

This is a distinctive loss to the Zionist Movement in America. The Keren Hayesod is not merely a fund, it is also a symbol. It represents a state ideal. It represents a corporate responsibility, and its propaganda should be the means of conversion of thousands of Jews who look upon the Zionist Movement merely as an appeal or as one of the partners in a campaign. The Keren Hayesod represents national capital operating in Palestine for collective needs. It stands for the totality of the corporate responsibility. It gives power and strength to the Executive, which is the representative of the Zionist Congress and of the Council of the Jewish

Agency. As such, it loses utterly by being thrown into a medley of funds and made to appear in the many-colored garments of a campaign in which miscellaneous interests are assembled.

Zionists who are interested not only in the amount of money raised, but also in the development of Zionist ideals, are coming to the conclusion that it is of the utmost importance that both the Jewish National Fund (Keren Kayemet) and the Keren Hayesod (Palestine Foundation Fund) should be kept free from entanglement as far as possible, in order that the Zionist movement as a whole may be presented to American Jewry, and that the campaigns that may be run for them should serve the purposes of converting American Jewry to Zionist idealism. Partnerships should be arrangements made between similar ideals and interests, and not a mere mechanical gathering together of diversified interests merely for the sake of avoiding a duplication of campaigns. The Keren Hayesod should be liberated from its entanglements. It should be given an opportunity to appear in America under its own name.

NATIONAL BUDGETING AND THE BATTLE FOR PRE-EMINENCE OF PALESTINE FUNDS

Hitler, destroyer of six million Jews, was also the catalyst that forced the acceleration of the democratic organization of American Jewry; advanced recognition of the importance of funds for Palestine development and finally produced a union of organized American Jewry in support of a Jewish State in Palestine at the War's end.

But this was not accomplished without continuous struggle.

A major aspect of this struggle involved the division of publicly raised funds; the allocation as between funds for Palestine upbuilding and funds for relief; and who should make the decision on apportionment.

By 1941 friction over this issue reached an explosive climax.

Hitler's successes had exposed the absence of any haven for his Jewish victims except in Palestine. Further, the holocaust had determined the Zionists to accelerate the pace of development of Jewish Palestine.

While Zionist funds had increased, the bulk of funds raised for overseas work was being allocated to the American Jewish Joint Distribution Committee (J.D.C.).

In 1930, 1934, 1935, 1939 and 1940 the J.D.C. had joined forces with the U.P.A. (United Palestine Appeal) in the United Jewish Appeal. In 1939, the U.P.A. had received 26.1% of the funds raised; in 1940, this percentage dropped to 23.3%.

In that year, when the negotiations for the 1941 U.J.A. campaign were resumed, the National Refugee Service for New Americans was brought in as a beneficiary of the U.J.A. by the J.D.C. The Zionists believed that they were being outweighed two to one, and that a resurgence of anti-Zionist effort was being planned.

Interlocking directorates between the J.D.C. and the American Jewish Committee, the principal anti-Zionist organization in the United States, helped to add fuel to the fire. Of the 42 directors of the J.D.C., 27 were directors of the American Jewish Committee. Of the 17 members of the

J.D.C. Executive Committee, 12 were also directors of the American Jewish Committee.

Rabbi Abba Hillel Silver and Lipsky were then the co-chairmen of the United Palestine Appeal. Lipsky was then also co-chairman of the Keren Hayesod and Chairman of the Governing Council of the American Jewish Congress.

Zionist fears were further stimulated by the Council of Jewish Federations and Welfare Funds, with a non-Zionist leadership, which announced a plan to establish a "national advisory budgeting service" to evaluate the relative importance of Jewish charitable institutions, on the basis of which allocations would be recommended.

In an editorial written by Lipsky, The Congress Weekly for February 14, 1941 called this "nothing less than a declaration of war against the Zionist Movement and more specifically the U.P.A."

On May 17, 1941, the officers of the Council of Jewish Federations and Welfare Funds announced that a nationwide referendum had been conducted by it and that the national budgeting service had been approved by a vote of 54 to 53 cities; and that, on the basis of this one-vote majority, it would proceed.

This vote was challenged, as was the entire concept of the Council. Lipsky led the battle both from the public platform and in a series of articles and editorials in The Congress Weekly, The New Palestine, The Detroit Jewish Press, and elsewhere that received national attention.

It was a battle for recognition of the primacy of Palestine and also for democratic procedure and action.

At the very moment when the Zionists thought they had lost, by a technical defeat, the non-Zionists compromised. An agreement was reached for a joint campaign whereby the U.P.A. was to receive 37% of the funds and the J.D.C. 63%.

This was the first major breakthrough for the U.P.A., and the beginning of acceptance of the role of Palestine funds, through the U.P.A., which by 1945 produced for the U.P.A. 45.5% of the national funds, and by 1949 more for the U.P.A. than the J.D.C.

The Editor

FAILURE OF LEADERSHIP *

Governor Lehman who, on numerous occasions, has shown a rare appreciation of the responsibility of Jewish leadership, is calling an emergency conference on June 10, in order to examine the status of the New York campaign of the United Jewish Appeal. By focusing attention on the grave situation that has arisen in New York City, Governor Lehman is performing a service characteristic of his long career and calculated to remind other leaders of the burden that should rest on their shoulders.

In a year that has witnessed the addition of hundreds of thousands of Jews to those for whom aid must be forthcoming if they are to be saved, the United Jewish Appeal should have had an unprecedented upsurge of support that would have made the $23,000,000 quota not merely attainable, but minimal. It has been disquieting, however, to observe that in a number of major communities there has not been observed that level of generosity which reflects a proper understanding of the extraordinary requirements facing the three agencies included in the United Jewish Appeal: the United Palestine Appeal, the Joint Distribution Committee, and the National Refugee Service. Many factors have confused the situation; the events abroad are not unrelated to a spirit of bewilderment and uncertainty; and yet to all who have been close to the problem, it has been obvious that not political red tape stood in the way of extending aid to our people in Palestine, in Europe, and in America, *but the lack of adequate financial resources.*

If the United Jewish Appeal is to receive funds commensurate with its goal, it is New York City which must give direction and inspiration. In 1940 the United Jewish Appeal seeks over $6,000,000 more than was raised in 1939. The quota of $23,000,000 was not lightly adopted. It was the result of prolonged discussion and reflection, which took into account the possibilities of the community and the continuity of the fund-raising program. But if American Jewry is to raise $23,000,000, it is the men of means, the leaders of Jewish life in New York City, who should have been the first to assume their proper share in the national task. With but few exceptions, however, those who should have issued a challenge to the compassion and the generosity of American Jewry, have contented themselves with the same standard of giving as in 1939. What is even more alarming is that all too many of those who are in a

---

* *The New Palestine,* May 31, 1940.

position to understand the needs of the hour have been niggardly and evasive, giving less rather than more.

An analysis of the gifts of some fifty of the leading contributors in the New York City United Jewish Appeal discloses a sharp ratio of decrease as compared with 1939. The givers in the middle brackets and in the lower brackets have once again, as always, shown their comprehension of duty toward the plight of our people. In the broad mass, the New York City campaign is showing a gratifying response, but we dare not overlook the ignoble example that is being set by a group of men who fail to understand the moral trusteeship of the funds they possess.

The time has not yet come to place final responsibility for this neglect of solemn obligation on the part of men of wealth and position and influence in Jewish life. It is to be hoped that the June 10th conference which Governor Lehman has convened, will remind New York Jewish leadership that they are not merely the standard-bearers and the pace-setters for the metropolis, but for American Jewry as a whole. It is not yet too late to repair the immense harm that is here done to the financial programs of the agencies in the United Jewish Appeal.

PRIMACY FOR PALESTINE FUNDS
(Prelude to a Real Union) *

Again this year—since September—reports have come of the discussions carried on between the Joint Distribution Committee and the United Palestine Appeal for a renewal of the life of the United Jewish Appeal for 1941. And again, for weeks and weeks, varying rumors came of agreement and disagreement; "never again" was supposed to be the position of certain obstinate friends of the Joint; "never again" was supposed to be the imperative demand of certain Zionist circles; but then there were interludes of reports of peace and harmony and a united front, and the bets were all in favor of a 1941 combined campaign. To the great surprise of most of us who knew that the differences, from a practical point of view, had been reduced in the course of discussion to a very narrow field, an official announcement was given to the press, signed by Dr. Jonah B. Wise and Dr. Abba Hillel Silver, declaring the United Jewish Appeal dissolved—the "overseas" union disbanded.

This put an end to all the rumors and makes possible a frank dis-

* *The Congress Weekly,* January 17, 1941.

cussion of the whole situation. It will bring to the surface a struggle which has been going on under cover for many years. The union reflected in the word "united" meant union merely for the sake of an adjustment of proportions in order that one campaign be conducted instead of several. It involved only the technical aspects of fund collecting for "overseas" purposes. With the inclusion of the National Refugee Service as a beneficiary, the term "overseas" was stretched to include expenditures for refugees in the United States. The National Refugee Service in the United States was regarded as a subordinate interest at the beginning, but on January 1, 1941, the National Refugee Service represented an item larger than the allotment given to the United Palestine Appeal for the building of the Jewish National Home.

The United Jewish Appeal had only the appearance of union. Beneath the smooth, noncommittal, neutralized words of the campaigns a more or less polite struggle was carried on to subordinate the ideals and objectives of the Zionist movement to the aims and desires of a small but influential group of Jews who are anxious to keep American Jewish life loyal to isolationist, assimilationist ideals, who are always limiting the Jewish interest, always avoiding Jewish identification, always seeking to have Jewish life adjust itself to the fears and negations arising out of an everlasting apology for Jewish existence.

On various occasions, this struggle was fought out in a more or less frank manner. It was the gist of the struggle in the self-defense movement at the time of the Kishinev pogroms. It was the very heart of the struggle that was reflected in the controversy about the American Jewish Congress. It appeared obliquely in the discussions about, and the help given to, Crimea and Biro-Bidjan. It is represented with historic consistency in the resistance manifested toward the Zionist ideal. This struggle sometimes takes place within the forms of relief, within the forms of Jewish defense, within the forms of communal organization, and in the field of political affairs. *But it is never fought out in a public arena.* Even to destroy the Zionist movement, for example, our friends (the enemy) would avoid publicity at all costs. The struggle must be carried on within the corridors of Jewish life. The disturbance must not reach the ears of *goyim.* If Rabbi Lazaron rushes to the press with an attack on Jewish nationalism, they are the first to condemn him, although they may fully appreciate his zeal and enthusiasm. Items in the *New York Times* are undesirable if they reflect, in any way, a ripple of controversy in Jewish life. All Jewish controversy, however, is confined to conversations in committee rooms, conferences in executive session, confidential letters circulated to a limited group of friends, couched in language which is the perfection of camouflage. This "kid glove" manner would avoid speaking of anti-Zionists or anti-nationalists, or of anything that indicates dissension.

This old struggle was held captive in the fund-raising field by the device of the United Jewish Appeal. In the United Jewish Appeal the differences in ideals were reduced to figures, percentages and ratios. In the United Jewish Appeal the slogans were kept within the limits of the lowest common denominator, which was found in the idea of "refugees," "overseas," etc. The literature of the united campaign reflected a colorless situation from which neither Zionist nor anti-Zionist could derive any comfort. The literature was given a bath of the deodorant, which took away all the flavor and color of an effort that was supposed to engage the zeal and enthusiasm of five million Jews.

For some time, leading Zionists in the united campaign have been conscious of living in a suffocating atmosphere. It was hard to describe. There was nothing definite about it. It was the way Palestine was spoken of by the non-Zionists; they were too friendly. It was the words used in telling of the building of the Jewish National Home. They were so nonchalantly avoiding the use of the word "national" and all the attributes that go with the building of a State. There was a feeling that between the non-Zionist leaders in the joint campaign and certain elements in the Welfare Chests, understandings were arrived at in a social, off-the-record way, which were more effective than any official agreement. The pressure used to produce the percentages allotted to Palestine, the strange eagerness to have impartial accountants criticize the book-keeping system employed in Palestine, the attempts made lately to bring in the National Refugee Service not merely as a beneficiary but as a full-fledged partner—all of these gave indication of what might be called, in a detective story, sinister motives.

It was true that most frequently the most effective speakers in the campaign were leading Zionists. But they were the showpieces at banquets and mass meetings, and no one could tell what went on in committee rooms or in the privacy of social relations between the non-Zionist leaders and communal leaders. No one could guess how many unofficial letters went out to preferred friends throughout the country, giving unofficial versions of differences of opinion that arose among the leaders of the campaign. One suspected that the partnership was a partnership of two antagonists, and that the one had better beware of the other. The Zionists naturally desired definiteness; the non-Zionists definitely resisted all attempts at definiteness.

In the history of joint campaigns there never was any serious effort to reconcile conflicting ideas. The late Felix M. Warburg was one of the most earnest advocates of unity in fund-raising. It was due to his intervention that on a number of occasions what seemed to be a threatened break, was transformed into a peaceful arrangement. But Mr. Warburg did not like discussion of ideas. He was opposed to any definiteness because he felt the closer you approached the definite, the more certain you would be of entering into controversy. Generally speaking, discussion was regarded as an irritant, not as a possible solvent of differences. It was resented as an attempt on the part of doctrinaires and theorists to lead the Masters of Business away from the practical into the realm of ideas. They prided themselves on being realists and did not want to have the realities troubled and disturbed by intellectual theories. They wanted to have the Jewish problem reduced to its practical aspects— the aspect of relief, of hunger and nakedness—and anything above the lowest common denominator was taken to be a flight into the unknown of speculation and aspiration.

Thus the cause of Zionism, of which the United Palestine Appeal is the material incorporation, was set in juxtaposition to the cause of elementary relief, and in the distribution had to be measured by the standards of relief. All aspects of nation-building had to be reduced to conform to the general plan. But the United Palestine Appeal symbolized a constructive national enterprise. That enterprise involved the building of a Jewish National Home as an enduring form of organized, self-governing Jewish life. It was the way to national freedom. It had all the attributes and qualities of a State in the process of becoming. It meant the buying of land and its settlement. It meant the building of roads and their use. It meant the reception of new settlers and their transformation into self-supporting, assertive Jews. It meant the stimulation of industry and commerce. It meant defense and military support of the land and its Protector. It meant the maintenance of schools, high schools and a university. Its success, from a practical point of view, was to be measured by its inner strength and its power to absorb new settlers. It dealt with a continuing institution on a long-range program.

This enterprise was compelled by the exigency of the joint campaign to justify its existence in comparisons with relief and bare emergency. It had to suffer the disadvantage of comparison with the immediate. It had to labor under a prejudice not only directed against its chief objective, but also against its remoteness from immediate distress. On a long-range program, relief would be reduced to infinitesimal values, but on a short-range program these infinitesimal values could be made to assume an aspect of greater humanity and deeper concern with Jewish welfare.

In addition to the "overseas" relief, there was insinuated in the campaign the problem of refugee relief in the United States, which assumed a priority both against the United Palestine Appeal and the Joint Distribution Committee. Why not? The refugees were here, in our midst. The responsibility could not be shaken off. Public opinion required that every Jewish refugee be taken off the main street of public benefaction and become a specific Jewish obligation. Soon, there was discussion in the United Jewish Appeal of the proposal to give the National Refugee Service its natural priority, for, it was argued, before any money could be sent abroad for any purpose, our obligations to the refugees here should be met one hundred per cent. In 1940 the National Refugee Service, for the care of refugees coming to the United States, will have received out of the United Jewish Appeal $3,500,000, against the receipt by the United Palestine Appeal of $2, 900,000; this exclusive of at least $2,000,000 contributed by local committees to the solution of their own local refugee problems. Thus, the objective of the Zionist movement had to swim in a pool with "overseas" relief and refugees just around the corner, and was placed in the impossible position of receiving its support at the expense of the hungry and the homeless.

It is important to point out that the local disorders that might have come years ago through independent action by the national fund-raising agencies are no longer a danger to be feared. This is due to the growth of the Welfare Chests. The Welfare Chests have created local pools in which allotments are made to a varied list of activities the community wishes to support; foremost among them, of course, are the "overseas" funds. The Welfare Chests organize their own single campaigns. They have their own Allotment Committees. They cover their own local expenses, and they are often strong enough to prevent a violation of the local order they have set up. An independent campaign by the Joint Distribution Committee or the United Palestine Appeal, from a practical point of view, means that the same local Welfare Chest campaign will be conducted, but the division as between the United Palestine Appeal, the Joint Distribution Committee and the National Refugee Service will be determined by the local Allotment Committee instead of by an agreement nationally entered into between the principal agencies. Instead of one check being sent to the United Jewish Appeal, three checks will be remitted; one to the Joint Distribution Committee, one to the United Palestine Appeal, one to the local Welfare Chests with their own propaganda and the ability to organize their supporters within the framework of the Welfare Chests.

The Zionists will have the first opportunity in years through a free campaign, to carry their propaganda into the communities, undiluted and free from distortion. They will have to abandon the tone of "appeasement" which has run through much of their Zionist work in recent years. They will have to be more courageous and more forthright in speech than they have been in joint campaigns. They have no interest in securing funds to enlarge or strengthen the Jewish National Home at the expense of relief or the American activity for the care of refugees. What is the specific ideology of relief or of caring for refugees? These causes are being used as fronts from which attacks are made upon the Zionist cause. Zionists have an interest in seeing to it that the Zionist cause once more swung by the accidents of time into the very center of Jewish life, again as in 1918 standing for the fulfillment of Jewish national hope, shall be considered on its merits and be given that adequacy of support which the overwhelming majority of American Jews—in our view—are prepared to give to the cause of building the Jewish National Home not merely as a haven of refuge, not merely as a relief measure, but *as the vessel of the rebirth of Jewish national life.*

It may well be that the discussion which will ensue in the course of the campaign of 1941 will lead to better understanding of the significance and value of the Zionist ideal than could be done through the methods employed in the joint campaigns. It may well be that this free campaign will prepare the way for a genuine cooperation of all American Jews in the solution of the Jewish problem on a national, territorial basis. The 1941 break may be the prelude to a more genuine union.

CONTROL OF AMERICAN JEWRY THROUGH ITS BUDGETS*

Declarations of war are no longer the fashion. There are no trumpet calls; no preliminary parades. The aggressor does not have to announce his intentions. His business is through pressure to force the victim to give the action a name. The fur is made to fly before the war cry is ejaculated.

Whether they know it or not—I think that even now they may be

* *The Congress Weekly*, February 21, 1941.

unaware of it—the leaders of the Council of Welfare Funds have given substance and form to a first class conflict in the American Jewish community. The stage was set at the Atlanta Conference, which promised at first to be, as usual, mediocre, proper and monotonous. Its program was of peace and unity and budgets. The bones of Jewish philanthropy were to be talked of; its spirit was to be banished. It was of an Advisory Budgeting Committee mention was made; ratios, relations, facts and facts again. But that was the formal palaver, the routine conversation. It did not reflect, in the slightest, the tense struggle which lurked in the background—the bitter partisanship, the class prejudices, the resurgence of old animosities between Yehudim and Jews. There was no allusion to any of these "facts of life." There was no intention to speak the name of the Devil lest it serve as summons or invitation. You could feel behind the Babbitt-like repetitions of banal clichés that something fundamental was in ferment, the indignation and resentment that were being held under control.

Nor were the alignments clear. There were many Zionists among the delegates from Welfare Chests or Federations. They were paired off with delegates from the same Welfare Chests or Federations who, when the divisions came, belonged to another grouping. The lions and the lambs (take your choice as to which is which) were snugly locked in fraternal embrace; and you had to have sharp eyes to see what was going on behind the glib discussions of ratios and accountancy forms; behind the formal etiquette, the foil of social intercourse. The experienced in public affairs sensed something vitally disturbing behind the impassioned arguments of Dr. Silver; in the nervous tone and high color of Sidney Hollander; in the rapid speech of the usually calm and diplomatic Dr. Loewenstein; in the impatience of Welfare Fund presidents who pretended not to understand why simple business proposals were being haggled over with such obstinacy. ("Give and take. You say 60–40; I say 65–35; you say $2,000,000 for the National Refugee Service; I say, let us set fact-finders to work and let them figure out what should be the last line; let us settle the deal and have a drink.") There was too much excitement about such simple "business" matters. It was kept within bounds at the public meetings, but from the caucuses and the unofficial conferences angry, strident tones could be heard in the hotel lobby.

The ghost at the banquet in Atlanta was the breakup of the United Jewish Appeal, the Joint Campaign. But the dissolution of the United Jewish Appeal was not due to disagreement as to ratios, or to the fact that the allotment to the National Refugee Service was in dispute.

That is the view reiterated by the Joint; but it is not warranted by the facts. It was due, in my view, to the determination of the leaders of the Joint (interchangeable, more or less, with the leadership of the National Refugee Service and the American Jewish Committee) to establish a "reasonable" control over the growing influence of the Zionist Movement.

Once again, as in 1917, world events were to come to a focus after a period of war and destruction. Once again, as in 1917, an international conflict was to produce its inevitable conclusion in discussions of peace; and once again the problems of Jewish life would emerge and demand public consideration and just settlement. In the climactic scene, the Jews of America—as in 1918—would be called upon to join with the Jews of other lands to unburden their hearts and identify their relation to world events and see what part Jews expected to play in the New World to be created. In that scene, Jews of wealth and prestige had come to the conclusion that the mistake of 1918 should not be repeated; never again would they go into a world delegation of Jews the world over to represent Jewish international interests. What the Zionists represent in Jewish life must be subordinated to the more immediate concerns of American Jewry; American Jews must conserve their own interests first.

This thought was not born out of the discussions which led to the desperate attempt of leaders of the Joint Distribution Committee, through the Welfare Funds, to incarcerate the Zionist movement behind the walls of a controlled budget. This conception of policy has been brewing for some time in high circles of "established" Jews, where "philanthropy" dominates, growing clearer with the days. It is seen in the constant reference to "American" Judaism, the burning zeal in a time of Jewish world catastrophe to shout "we are Americans first." It is reflected in the policies that have been adopted in Jewish reaction to world events. It was heard, curiously enough, in the addresses of Alan Stroock and Sidney Hollander in Atlanta; and also, quite unexpectedly, in the strange views uttered by Dr. Louis Finkelstein of the Jewish Theological Seminary.

The line runs thus:

It is left for American Jews to save themselves out of the debacle of Jewish life. The saving remnant, destined to be the carrier of the Jewish future, must be careful to identify itself, wholly and without reserve, with the life, ideals and future of the American democracy. American Jews should always act with due regard for their peculiar status, which prevents complete absorption in the great Jewish tragedy that occupies the world stage. A humanitarian interest in their miseries, in their persecutions, might be allowed, but not an identification with their ideals and their future. Whither America goes, we go—having no private griefs, no added loyalties. All that is to be done for the sake of preserving the remnant who are to continue the Jewish "mission." We are the generation saved from the flood in which European Jews—most of them—are doomed to perish. Like the Jews of Babylonia, said Mr. Stroock, who in exile built a Babylonian Judaism, out of which came the Talmud; living a Jewish life within the protected walls of an idolatrous Babylonia.

This conception has grown in the course of years that followed the advent of Adolf Hitler. It was being prepared for in the cowardly approach of Jews of this group to the problems of Jewish defense against Hitler. They would have nothing to do with the direct defense of the Jews of Germany—through boycott or public demonstration; and only when the Nazi poison seemed to be infecting the bloodstream of American life were they awakened to the dangers by which they themselves were surrounded; they were aroused to the need of self-protection; and even then, every move was taken in a spirit of subordination to the "climate" of American life—fear of Father Coughlin, fear of the persuasiveness of Nazi doctrine in American circles; fear to identify themselves as Jews who had a special reason for hating Hitler. There was a marked desire to isolate themselves personally (except through sympathy and humanitarian help) from the status and the destiny of the Jews in Europe.

When America seemed to be isolationist or neutral to universal causes, Jewish philanthropists frowned upon every manifestation of collective Jewish interest and regarded it as a violation of American policy. They were alarmed at the raising of Jewish heads above the subdued, cautious position taken, at that time, by the American Government. In their alarm they often ran to Washington to get Governmental advice approving caution and tact and avoidance. Many rabbis began to preach "adoration" of democracy, as if the Jewish religion had been created to serve democracy as the highest ideal in life, as if the Laws of Moses had been absorbed in the all-inclusive term "democracy." The same attitude was manifest in their reaction to the policy of aiding Britain in its fight against the Nazis. It was agreed that all aid should be given to Britain "short of war," but with no specific Jewish aid and no Jewish appearance on the scene.

But the greatest menace they saw in Zionism and the Jewish Homeland, which seemed to be growing in immediacy from day to day, and which seemed to be irrepressible, insatiable, seeking to dominate every field of Jewish life. The fear began to grow when the idea of a Jewish State emerged out of the plan to partition Palestine. Since then, Zionists have not hesitated to use the terms "Jewish State," "Free Jewish State," "Jewish Commonwealth." The Zionist restraints were removed, and without any regard for the feelings of Jewish isolationists they began to speak with a definiteness foreign to their earlier practice. It was evident that the problem of the Jewish Homeland would have to be considered—solved or disposed of.

It may be an exaggeration to say this. But the attitude taken by Jewish philanthropists toward the refugees in America showed a keener interest, a deeper anxiety, a more realistic sympathy, than was being expressed with regard to the homeless and hopeless refugees who had to remain in foreign lands. There was no lack of theories. It was said, in certain circles, that the aid to be given refugees in America must be continuous, adequate and convincing of the desire of American Jews to keep their refugees under adequate Jewish guardianship in order that the general Jewish position should not be impaired. The refugee in the United States was a major problem entitled to priority of attention. He represented an unavoidable responsibility. The National Refugee Service was one of the "musts" on the philanthropic calendar, for that burden had to be discharged with an eye toward appeasement of any prejudice growing out of these alien intrusions.

The problem our old friends—the philanthropic anti-Zionists—had to face was how to make the front of Jewish life fit into a strictly American isolationist pattern. It was a difficult task to maintain such a policy with Jews. This is a free country. A policy of silence and secrecy cannot be imposed upon 5,000,000 Jews. We are a talkative, argumentative people. There are national organizations, Jewish newspapers, Jewish forums, all kinds of movements in which free speech is a prized doctrine. If you want to control the American Jewish community you have to take public action, and public action in this case was most undesirable. In fact, Jewish philanthropy had never achieved freedom of action in the fields which they thought belonged to them—the fields of political and diplomatic intervention. They never could maintain a monopoly of political representation even in the earliest days of the American Jewish Committee. The American Jewish Congress successfully challenged the monopolistic aspirations of the American Jewish Committee, and now there are four organizations operating in this sphere of interest.

But the situation was otherwise in the field in which money plays the most important part. Here, Jewish philanthropy could achieve dominance through practices that are usually associated with financial influence. In order to meet the dreaded problem of Jewish life—how to build the Jewish future, or evade building the Jewish future—and to control the forces that were dealing with these problems, Jewish philanthropists were driven to the use of methods and devices that are derived from their experiences in the practices of corporations. Where there are ideas or ideals in ferment or collision, democratic procedure must have its way, more or less. But in the field of Federations and Welfare Chests, wealth and prestige have their privileges—the privileges that accrue naturally and normally to wealth as such—numbers do not count; but the control lies with the larger bank account or the larger contribution. In the Federations of Charities, budgets and accounting are important deities.

The way chosen by Jewish philanthropists in 1941 to dominate Jewish life, to keep it within check, to prevent the exposure of what might be regarded as unpleasant or harmful, was not the way of democracy, the way of the plebiscite, that could be invoked by the American Jewish Congress or the Bnai Brith. It was the way of the stock corporation. The club of large stockholders settled all discussion. The control is being exercised in the Federations. There money rules the roost. That success could be duplicated in the Welfare Chest. Therefore, the line of procedure was to control the budgets of the Welfare Chests.

Thus came the proposal in Atlanta that a small committee be given "advisory" authority to evaluate the funds included in the Welfare Campaigns. Through the exercise of this authority it would be possible, in the course of a few years, to evaluate movements (more particularly the Zionist movement) to the point either of growth or retardation or extinction.

In the past 35 years public controversy in American Jewry was always provoked by either the Zionist movement or the American Jewish Congress. This latest controversy is an attack and a provocation by the philanthropic group. They might have succeeded in their purpose had the so-called referendum been kept in "executive" session. Unfortunately for them, they have precipitated a public discussion, and there are Jews angry and resentful of what they propose to do. The attempt to put the creative movements in Jewish life under the tutelage of unimaginative Jewish philanthropy will be defeated by the clash of opinion now going on in every community throughout the land.

A REFERENDUM OF BIG GIVERS *

In 1938 a referendum became the subject of serious controversy in the American Jewish community. True to its traditions, the American Jewish Congress issued a call to the Jews of America, asking for an expression of opinion on creating one single, representative agency for defense purposes. The agencies of defense resented this intrusion upon their "sovereign" rights. It was felt by many that there should be a united Jewish front in defense against the growing menace of anti-Semitism in America, but the united front should be born out of common consent and not forced, as it was said, through a referendum. The general press was resorted to by the American Jewish Committee (and others) to scotch what was called the un-American proposal of the Congress. Dr. Samuel H. Goldenson of Temple Emanu-El delivered a lengthy sermon which the American Jewish Committee circulated all over the United States. So annoyed was the American Jewish Committee that "in person" it made a subtle allusion to the dangers of a referendum in the *New York Times*. Emissaries were sent to Washington to excite Administration circles against this dangerous step. The pulpit was influenced to express its unqualified condemnation. It was said that a referendum (which they called a plebiscite) was not only un-American; it was using the methods of Hitler! Finally the referendum was withdrawn at a conference held in Pittsburgh, where the ill-fated General Jewish Council was born. A united Jewish front was not created; the sovereignty of the defense agencies was not interfered with; and life went on as usual.

To our great surprise, the same groups who in those days fought the referendum suggested by the American Jewish Congress, are now engaged in the difficult task of carrying through a referendum of their own. It was approved at the Assembly of the Council of Jewish Federations and Welfare Funds held in Atlanta in the presence of the leaders of the philanthropic group. It was a unanimous vote. The suggestion was made by Dr. Abba Hillel Silver and was immediately accepted by Dr. Solomon Loewenstein. Instead of the Board of Directors of the Council making the decision, it was agreed that member-agencies of the Council are to fill out a questionnaire and to decide the questions: Shall the ratios, relations and budgets of the funds raised through Welfare Funds be fixed by a National Budgeting Committee; and shall the ratios and

* *The Congress Weekly*, February 28, 1941.

relations in the United Jewish Appeal for 1941 be fixed by a special committee?

Have the philanthropic leaders reversed their position? Have they come nearer to an appreciation of democratic procedure in Jewish life? Have they become soft?

Not at all. They are hard as they always were. They have not changed in the slightest. They have become even more resentful than ever of interference by third parties with the questions of what they are to do with their money. They would oppose today—especially in the field of charity and philanthropy—more vehemently that ever, the unseemly democratic procedure of voting in matters of Jewish interest in which their financial support is involved.

The fact is that what they are now doing through the Council is not a referendum in a real sense. It is the use of a form, but not of the substance of the idea. It involves only the member agencies of the Council of Welfare Funds. It involves, more directly, only the members of the Boards of Directors of their member agencies. All other Jews are excluded from the referendum.

When Dr. Silver suggested the referendum—which he did to avoid, I think, the inevitable acceptance of the idea of national budgeting by the Conference in Atlanta—it was immediately taken up by Dr. Loewenstein, who made the impression of an amiable gentleman eager to concede a valid point even when offered by an opponent. His approval seemed to dispose of Dr. Silver's suggestion. But no indication was given in Atlanta of what kind of referendum its proponents had in mind. It was left to the national office of the Council to find in the constitution such guidance as it might need in drawing up the form of the referendum. Obviously, every member agency should have only one vote, there being no grade or class of membership in the Council. There seems to be no provision in the questionnaire—at any rate, in the form I have seen— to record how many members of the local Boards are present at the formal meeting, how many vote "yes," and how many vote "no." Every member agency having an equal vote, such recording would not be necessary. Thus it would appear that regardless of the amount of money collected by any local Welfare Fund, it would have one vote against an equal vote by each and every other Welfare Fund. The city of San Francisco would have a vote equal to the vote of Nashville, Tenn.

If the members of the local Boards would vote, and every vote would be counted, you might then say that the majority and the minority were representative of communal opinion; provided these members had been selected locally, in accordance with some basic rule of representation; that they were selected as coming from the Orthodox group, the Labor group, the Zionist group, the Conservative group, etc., that there was proportional representation. But it is public knowledge that the members of the local Boards of the Welfare Funds are selected from among the "big givers." To qualify as a member of a local Board one must be included in the coterie of "big givers" in any community. This means that the Boards are composed of persons who are invariably found on the side of the philanthropic view of Jewish life. Representatives of causes, as such, are not included. Occasionally, a representative or two of what might be called mass Jewish opinion may be placed on the Board. But the general rule, followed almost everywhere, is that only the "big givers" are included in the local Boards. It is they who give the lead in the campaign.

The referendum, therefore, will not be a referendum addressed to the Jews in America. It will be addressed to a small group of "big givers" of Jewish philanthropy. It will not be addressed to the adherents of various causes and movements and interests that stir the Jews of America. It will be addressed exclusively to a class of Jews who are interested in a limited aspect of Jewish life. This means, in effect, that in every community from fifteen to thirty individual Jews will be called upon to vote in the referendum, the deadline of which is April 1.

No! The Jews of America are behind the fight of the democracies against Hitlerism; they are good and loyal Americans, upholding the ideals of the American Republic; they stand behind the foreign policy of President Roosevelt; but democracy is alien to Jewish life so far as the philanthropic group is concerned. It is the money that talks. It is the money of the largest giver that talks the loudest. All Jewish life is graded, with Wealth in the front rank and the Moneyless trailing in the rear. Stay where you belong—you idealists, you sentimentalists, you dreamers of a Jewish future worthy of the great Jewish past! Give way to the successful in the world of business! Those who have a large bank account, large business affairs, who know the value of money and how to use it, who deride the past and have no eyes for the future—these are to be the directors of Jewish life. Let them and their accountants, budgetmakers, executive directors, run the affairs of the Jewish people on a streamline basis. Let them run Jewish affairs in a period where faith and hope and imagination are indispensable for the maintenance of Jewish life.

The equality God recognizes, they refuse to accept. Such equalities have no place in business affairs. If they had the slightest democratic sensibilities or the least appreciation of the leveling revolution that is shattering modern civilization, they would not retain their Bourbon qualities in these days. They would—in this instance at least—call in the many thousands of contributors to the Welfare Funds and let them speak their minds on this referendum. They would give the least contributor equal right with the largest to say how the communal pool is to be divided, for the mite of the poorest is entitled to equal consideration with the bulging gift of the rich. It is their gifts that are to be divided. It is their future which is being decided.

It is estimated that there are about 4,000 directors of about 170 Welfare Funds throughout the United States (including overseas funds collected in New York, Chicago and Philadelphia, which are not exactly member agencies and do not qualify as Welfare Funds). It is further estimated that including New York, Chicago and Philadelphia, there are at least 450,000 contributors to the funds included in the Welfare Chests.

The 4,000 directors will decide how contributions of 450,000 contributors are to be divided—how much Palestine is to get, how much defense money is to be distributed, and to what agency; whether the Hias is to continue to live or to be absorbed in the National Refugee Service. This small group of men would arrogantly assume to act on behalf of so many hundreds of thousands of Jews who have responded not to the appeal of the individual philanthropists, but have responded to the appeal of Jewish causes in which they are interested. This small group of men propose assuming the right to decide the fate of causes and movements in which Jewish destiny is implicated.

It is a procedure not only undemocratic and un-American. It is a scandalous procedure, a *Chillul Ha-Shem* of the first magnitude.

TRAVESTY OF A REFERENDUM *

In these days of revolutionary change, even our language reflects the masks the revolution operates with. All of Hitler's wars are incidents of his "peace" program. He invades Bulgaria to protect its freedom. The Japanese bombard Chinese cities, occupy Chinese territory with armed force, but they carry the white flag of peace and good will. We Jews are affected by these language camouflages. We are no longer "defending" ourselves against anti-Semitic attacks. We are no longer protecting our

* *The Jewish Day,* March 8, 1941.

"civil status." It is undignified to defend ourselves. "Coordination," "reorganization" and "unity" are forms of political offensive in which aggression is reduced to a whisper, but peace is shouted from the house-tops. It is a Babel of words, with many of the old words serving new purposes. It is politic nowadays *not* to call a spade a spade.

The referendum on national budgeting, which is being submitted by the Council of Welfare Funds to its constituents, is not a referendum in the plain, ordinary sense of the word. It is not a broad inquiry as to popular opinion on the subject of national budgeting. It is an inquiry narrowed down to a limited circle. And even that narrow inquiry is being unfairly influenced by its official sponsors. This is shown in the official literature sent out, as well as in the form set up for the voting. Properly speaking, it is not a referendum at all.

It goes so far as to influence even the limited circle of voters. Whether the national budgeting system will become mandatory or will be, as proposed, merely advisory, time will tell. Formally, it is advisory. Time and again the emphasis is placed upon the word "advisory." How it will work out in practice, however, remains to be seen. It is inherent in the situation for a national budgeting committee's decision to become coercive without being technically mandatory. The National Budgeting Committee, as well as the Council of Welfare Funds, will use their influence, quite naturally, to have their report accepted. They will use all sorts of coercive arguments. They will plead for unity in American Israel, for order and system in our philanthropies, for the maintenance of authority in Jewish life. The setting up of a National Budgeting Commission will mean the setting up of a standard which will serve as effective restraint upon the independent action of every Welfare Fund in the country. Therefore, when the Council includes on its official ballot the following sentence: "Approval . . . does not in any sense imply any commitment on the part of this member agency to utilize the services or findings of these committees," *it is, in effect, attempting to influence the voting and to give assurances to the voters that nothing will happen in the future to bind them in their local budgeting*.

The peculiarity of the situation lies in the fact that the Council of Welfare Funds is not concerned with people. It is a loose federation of corporate bodies—Federations and Welfare Funds. These are its members. It has been dealing only with its own members. It does not see beyond the meeting room of the board of directors. All its members are more or less equal. It professes to be blind to the fact that some of its members are millionaire corporations, and others of its members are poor, struggling, self-sacrificing communities. When it was decided in Atlanta to refer the question of national budgeting to the Welfare Funds, the general impression was that in some way the Welfare Funds would make an effort to ascertain the views of their own members— the contributors. It was not imagined at the time that the referendum would be an inquiry limited to the Welfare Funds as corporate bodies; that the Boards of Directors of these corporate bodies would assume the responsibility for acting on behalf of their contributors. It was not imagined that the voting would be registered as so many Welfare Funds voting "for" and so many Welfare Funds voting "against" the proposals. It was not imagined that whoever happened to be a member agency would be given the right to register its opinion on the matter of budgeting of funds, for which the Welfare Funds were assumed to be responsible.

That is what is now being done. It is open and aboveboard. No deception is being practiced. The printed material is being distributed all over the United States by the national office of the Council. It is as clear as crystal.

The members of the Council are Federations of Jewish Charities, Welfare Funds and, it seems, also in some cities, Community Councils. Included in the material sent out is a published list of the member agencies and the number of votes assigned to each member agency. Who made these assignments is not indicated. However that may be, and disregarding the probability that all member agencies are given equal consideration, the following interesting facts are revealed by the "list of member agencies and the number of assigned votes":

The city of Greater New York contains almost half the Jewish population of the United States. It raises from one-third to one-half of the amount of mony collected for overseas purposes. According to the records of the United Jewish Appeal, in 1940 Greater New York produced $5,073,866.14 in pledges, and there was received at the end of the year $3,657,725, in cash. In the voting on the referendum, however, Greater New York is assigned 12 votes—6 for New York and 6 for Brooklyn. Next in size is the city of Chicago, which usually produces about one-quarter of what Greater New York produces for overseas and refugee purposes. In 1940, Chicago gave to the United Jewish Appeal $999,850. The city of Chicago is given eight votes. The city of Rochester gave in 1940 $50,000 to the United Jewish Appeal, but is given five votes. The city of Philadelphia gave $50,000 in cash to the United Jewish Appeal (collecting, however, a much larger sum for other purposes in the same campaign) and is given seven votes. The city of Scranton, Pa., contributing $35,000 in

1940 to the United Jewish Appeal, is given four votes. The city of Flint, Michigan, contributing $3,750 in 1940 to the United Jewish Appeal, is given two votes. And the city of Hartford, Conn., which produced $79,821 for the United Jewish Appeal in 1940, is given three votes.

There is no need to go further into this matter. There seems to be no rhyme or reason in these assignments, except on the theory that the votes have been assigned not on the basis of money contributed, not on the basis of the number of contributors, but exclusively on the idea of membership in the Council of Welfare Funds. In some cities the Council has a membership which consists of a Welfare Fund, a Federation of Jewish Charities and a Community Council. In other cities it has a Federation of Jewish Charities and a Welfare Fund. In other cities it has only a Welfare Fund which is affiliated with the Council. What the designers of the referendum had in mind was to give voting right to all of its members substantially on an equal basis, whether they were Federations or Welfare Funds or Community Councils, regardless of the fact that they were thus giving votes to corporate bodies not directly concerned in gathering the funds for the purposes included within the program of the Council. In other words, votes were given in the referendum to corporate bodies that are not concerned with the collection of funds. On the contrary, the community has assigned to a special corporate body the task of collecting these specific funds.

Thus, in the City of New York votes would be cast by the executive committee of the Federation of Jewish Philanthropies; also in the city of Brooklyn. How the committee in charge of raising the $5,073,866.14 (which was what was pledged to the United Jewish Appeal in 1940) will express their opinions is not revealed. In Brooklyn, the "member agency" is the Federation of Jewish Charities, which by no stretch of the imagination is related in the slightest degree to the effort which is made annually to collect for overseas purposes. In New York, the Federation of Jewish Philanthropies is not only not responsible for the raising of any of the overseas funds, but it has, from time to time, regarded itself, to some extent, as a competitor of the overseas fund. In a similar way in other cities, (like Camden, N. J., and Dayton, O.), it is a Federation of Jewish Charities interested more specifically in the local charitable work that will do the voting for the fund raising agency.

It is probably his own personal opinion, but if, as H. L. Lurie, Executive Director of the Council, says that in matters of philanthropy it is in order to act as corporations act, and every stockholder should be entitled to as many votes as he owns shares, or according to the amount of money he has invested in the corporation, then the referendum should have taken account of the great disparity between one corporate member 'or member agency responsible for, say, $10,000, and another corporate member or member agency responsible for $500,000. Nothing of the sort appears in the list of assigned votes. The amount of money contributed is unrelated to the number of votes that have been given to the various Welfare Funds or member agencies.

The Council could have adopted another rule that sometimes prevails in corporate bodies. It could have used the rule which prevails in trade unions. At their conventions, a delegate is given as many votes as there are members in his union. The council could have agreed to assign votes on the basis of the number of contributors. It is the contributors who have an interest. It could be assumed that they can assign the right to budget to their board of directors. And having assigned the right to budget to these boards, the boards could be given the right to cast as many votes as there may be contributors. But neither of these alternatives has been taken up in the assignment of votes. It is to be a referendum addressed to the members of the boards of directors of Welfare Funds and Federations of Jewish Charities and Community Councils in all cases where such corporate bodies have become members of the Council of Welfare Funds. It is a simple form. It is a simple procedure. No idea is even suggested that at the meeting of the boards of directors it should be recorded how many members were present, and how many voted "for" or "against" the referendum; the corporation, as corporation, is called upon to cast its vote. In some cases it will have the right to cast eight votes, seven votes, five votes, three votes and two votes. No member, no matter how small, is given less than two votes.

This is the height of absurdity. It is a travesty performed with a solemn face. A technical exercise is being set in motion, and the result will be merely a technical acceptance or rejection of the referendum. The Council must be aware of what is involved in this issue. It knows that, as a matter of fact, behind the directors of the Welfare Funds there is an army of contributors, of various classes and interests. It knows that it is their contributions to the causes they desire to support, which is involved in this hocus-pocus of a referendum. All these men and women scattered throughout the United States in about two hundred Welfare Fund cities, are voluntary contributors to causes and institutions. Any betrayal of their interests is bound to be reflected disastrously in the results of the campaign. They make or break campaigns. They can make or break the Welfare Funds. They can make or break the Council, which has assumed responsibility for the introduction of this dictatorial form of control. They are free to refuse cooperation with any Welfare Fund that will give its consent to the imposition of an outside control upon their generosity and goodwill.

The referendum will be meaningless; it will serve no good purpose; it will not reflect what American Jews want in the matter of national budgeting; *unless at least the contributors to the Welfare Funds are given a right to vote.*

HAS PEACE REALLY COME TO AMERICAN JEWRY? *

The perennial controversy over the renewal of the United Jewish Appeal has come to its predestined end. There is to be a joint campaign in 1941, under the same name and auspices, but under different conditions. This year's performance was drawn out for a longer period of disagreement and indecision. There was a fatal lethargy about the whole business. It was marked by the breaking off of relations and the definite announcement of independent campaigns to be conducted by all three agencies. It was made dramatically exciting by an interlude in Atlanta, where the Council of Welfare Funds attempted somewhat belatedly to play its part of peacemaker once more. Its peace offering was a referendum which served to pour oil on the fires of controversy. A furious Zionist attack was made upon the referendum. The Joint Distribution Committee pursued its usual tactics of trying to make it appear that the other fellow was the peace-breaker while it was the pious one, always eager for peace and compromise, but in fact it carried on a great deal of propaganda by mail and over the phone and through emissaries.

The denouement is a scene of peace and unity. The country is greatly relieved. There is joy unrestrained. Now, all the incriminating evidences of warfare must hurriedly be removed and the campaign of 1941 must be allowed to proceed soberly, dully and without discussion. Back to routine.

The first scene which was enacted in this curious play showed the Joint Distribution Committee insisting upon the ratios of 1940 and a fixed allotment of approximately $5,000,000. The ratios in 1940 were 23.3 per cent for the United Palestine Appeal, 28.1 per cent for the National Refugee Service, and 48.6 per cent for the Joint Distribution Committee. All balances were to go to an Allotment Committee.

* *The Congress Weekly,* March 21, 1941.

That scene closed with the declaration of the United Palestine Appeal that the status quo could not be accepted in view of abnormal needs in Palestine. The second scene showed a counter-proposal by the United Palestine Appeal as follows: $2,000,000 for the National Refugee Service, and the division of a balance of $7,000,000 on a 65-35 ratio between the Joint Distribution Committee and the United Palestine Appeal. All balances were to go to an Allotment Committee. This was rejected by the Joint Distribution Committee, but no counter-proposal was made or even suggested. There was a strange apathy and resignation to the inevitable. War! No peacemakers put in an appearance; the negotiations came to an end without protest. The third scene showed the signing of a public statement by Dr. Jonah Wise and Dr. Abba Hillel Silver, announcing the dissolution of the United Jewish Appeal. Skipping all the intermediate incidents in which interveners played a part in Atlanta and in New York, the last scene that ends this rather expensive drama shows an agreement for the division of $8,800,000 on the basis of $2,000,000 for the National Refugee Service (22.9 per cent), $2,525,000 for the United Palestine Appeal (28.6 per cent), and $4,275,000 for the Joint Distribution Committee (48.5 per cent). The balance will go to an Allotment Committee.

Why the proposal made by the United Palestine Appeal on December 17 of 65-35 was rejected by the Joint Distribution Committee, and why it accepted the last proposal of 63-37, is a question which will be discussed, probably, in the inner circles of Welfare Funds, but will be regarded as confidential matter by the Jewish press. It is one of the mysteries of high finance.

In principle, the Zionist Movement, of which the United Palestine Appeal is the instrument (representing, as it does, the Jewish National Fund and the Keren Hayesod) has always chafed against the joint campaigns into which it was forced by circumstances or need or policy. For a variety of reasons. The partnership was usually with the Jewish philanthropic group which was largely out of sympathy with Zionist aims, and always insisted that in any joint campaign a common denominator of propaganda should be used, which had the effect of slurring or hiding the Zionist objective included in the joint campaign. Second, in any combination with relief, the higher task of building the Jewish National Home was bound to become less important than the pressing need of relief. The Zionists in such a joint campaign always felt under the obligation of restraint and tact in order not to offend those who did not believe in Zionism. The protection of the joint campaign made necessary these restraints. Lastly, the joint campaign always made Zionists feel as if the movement were chained to partners who did not welcome or approve what it stood for.

What made the situation intolerable in 1940-41 was the fact that the protection of the Zionist position in Palestine had become a matter of paramount importance. It was not only funds that were involved in the defense of Palestine, but also matters of political import and significance. The defense of the Homeland was a Jewish contribution to England's defense. It had become a political act of supreme value. The Zionists were made to feel that the leaders of the Joint were disinclined to give any consideration to these circumstances. This was evident in their insistence upon maintaining the status quo, in which the United Palestine Appeal received only $23\frac{1}{3}$ per cent of the total income of the United Jewish Appeal. The Joint never wavered during all these months from the position of status quo. It rejected every proposal of the United Palestine Appeal. It maintained a stony silence with regard to its position after its first utterance, as if it meant, Take it or leave it. It made the impression that it was prepared to hear a discussion only of the terms of status quo. There were even rumors that this was due largely to the resurgence—in the councils of the Joint—of the more intransigent anti-Zionists. The Zionists had sacrificed the principle of independent campaign time and again. This was in normal times when, in deference to public opinion, any fair proposal for union could not be rejected. But when the Joint Distribution Committee persisted in demanding, in 1941, the unfair status of 1940, to the point of breaking the joint campaign, the Zionists realized that the only alternative, under the circumstances, was not further concession to the Joint, but a vigorous free campaign within the forms of the Welfare Funds. Thus, material interest and principle became identical.

Both the Joint and its unofficial ally, the Council of Welfare Funds, were anxious to avoid public discussion. More specifically, they wished for delay of decisions by the Welfare Funds communities. In his letter to the Welfare Funds, declaring his intention to have the Atlanta Conference authorize a National Budgeting Committee, Sidney Hollander strongly advised the Welfare Funds not to do any budgeting of their own until the Atlanta Conference had acted. Similarly, the Joint Distribution Committee pleaded with the Welfare Funds not to allot any of their funds to any agency until they had heard proposals from the Joint. The United Palestine Appeal was forced into the field and in the press to prevent the congealing of opinion in the communities, and their arrival at one-sided conclusions. It had to attack the national budgeting proposal, without delay. It had to present the issue of ratios direct to the communities in order to prevent the paralysis of the 1941 campaign. Delay was regarded as important for the Joint and the Council, but prompt action was essential for the defense of the interests of the United Palestine Appeal.

The struggle in the communities brought to life once more the frayed specter of unity. It was pointed out that, in effect, recognition of the integrity of the Welfare Funds made the whole procedure of independent campaigns a mere formality. Instead of drawing one check, the Welfare Funds would have to draw three checks to three different agencies. Instead of one ratio, each community would be called upon to decide for itself what should be the ratios between the Joint Distribution Committee, the United Palestine Appeal and the National Refugee Service. It was pointed out that all that was involved in the controversy itself was merely a friendly approach to the budgeting committees of the Welfare Funds.

This was in theory. In practice, however, the demand that the Welfare Funds decide the ratios before they begin their campaigns led to an animated partisan discussion, bitter, personal. Meetings were held. Pressure was brought to bear on individual members of the Welfare Fund committees. Articles appeared in the press. That semblance of unity which the Welfare Funds or the Community Councils or the Federations of Jewish Charities had set up was greatly shocked and disturbed by the reverberations of the controversy. It was a conflict. It was not merely a budgeting matter. It opened up old partisan wounds that had been healed. It revealed the basic, unrepresentative character of the Welfare Funds Budgeting Committees. It revealed also the anomalous relations between Community Councils, Welfare Funds and Federations of Jewish Charities. It revealed fundamental differences between Zionists and non-Zionists and anti-Zionists. It revealed to the Zionists themselves the fact that although they were playing important parts in the community, the control was in the hands of non-Zionists and anti-Zionists, who were not susceptible to public opinion and regarded philanthropic funds as coming within the category of trust funds. Whatever may be said as to the quality of communal organization, the controversy about ratios and budgetings made every party to the controversy feel that they were breaking the solidarity of the community.

In short, the peace now announced for the campaign of 1941 was brought about by the pressure of an overwhelming public sentiment coming from all groups and all elements. It was not due to peacemakers. It certainly was not due to the Council of Welfare Funds, which, in this instance, instead of playing the part of the neutral, took sides in the controversy and lost its status as a non-partisan body.

From the point of view of relations, the United Palestine Appeal made a decided gain in the arrangements for 1941. It is assured 28.6 per cent against both the Joint Distribution Committee and the National Refugee Service, and 37 per cent against the Joint alone. Its initial minimum exceeds its initial minimum of 1940, while the initial minimum of the Joint is reduced by about $1,000,000, and of the National Refugee Service by $1,500,000. The independent campaign, however, was not achieved.

All efforts to raise funds in the United States will have to be adjusted to the forms of organized life which the American Jewish community adopts. Experience has shown that the idea of communal solidarity has grown and is stronger than many believed. It is strong enough to make impossible a reversion to the old system of "free" campaigns of all sorts, coming at all times of the year. The new order is incompatible with the absolute freedom of movements and institutions. At the same time, it has revealed the value and need of communal organization based upon democratic principles. The more difficult it is for a free agent to approach an organized community, the more insistent will be the demand that that community be organized upon a democratic basis. The idea that "money" can take possession of communal responsibility and run things to suit itself has now been challenged and it will be challenged again and again. These "wars" will continue to break out until democratic communal organization is achieved. Through repeated shocks of violent controversy democracy in Jewish life will come.

Communal unity depends upon democratic procedure and democratic representation. To this state of affairs Zionists will have to adjust themselves. It is possible to "capture the Jewish communities" for Zionism, but only if they become democratic and representative. There is no alternative.

TWO WARS: TWO RALLYING CALLS

Lipsky's unshakable faith in the Jewish people is demonstrated vividly in two exhortations delivered twenty-four years apart.

The first was offered in 1914, three months after the beginning of World War I, in an article entitled "Let Us Not Lose Courage."

The second was written in 1938, one year before the formal outbreak of World War II, but after five years of a relentless war of Hitlerism upon the Jewish people.

In 1914 and again in 1938 this exhortation to fight was backed by tremendous labors to defeat the enemy and to build up Jewish Palestine.

The Editor

LET US NOT LOSE COURAGE *

Since August 1st, 1914, the civilized world has fallen from its high estate. Old standards have been demolished. A new world is being created for us, by the hordes of fighting men in Flanders, East Prussia and Poland. War on a scale imagined only by fantastic fiction-writers or obsessed militarists has returned, and now occupies the throne. Lucifer stalks the earth, searing the tie of brotherhood, and in his wake are piled the dead hopes and ideals of two generations of progress.

The din of battle intrudes everywhere. The terrible effects of war are gradually effacing the recollections of peace. War streaks the page red and all other colors are being obliterated. It has banished the universal appeal to truth; it has made science sectional; it has unseated all movements and is tending to reduce life to the level of brutality, with man-slaying as the badge of renown, and pestilential hatreds as the salt of life. We used to live in homes; now, it seems, we are living in trenches.

* *The Maccabean*, November–December 1914.

Our interest zigzags from Flanders to Poland, to East Prussia, to Galicia.
All other interests disappear like frightened pheasants before the heavy-
footed fowler. Our eyes turn with the pegs the German or French
strategist moves on his bleeding map.

In the face of this great world catastrophe what becomes of Zionism?
Our sense of values has been affected. Our cause seems so small in
comparison with the cause in which the destinies of European civilization
are involved, and in which our own destiny seems so insignificant. Do
we wish to establish another Belgium in Palestine? Do we dream of
a nation with justice as its armor and peace as its sword? Our Zionist
fire is a spark in the light of the glowing fire of war.

Like ants whose hill had been overturned, we scampered after the
first outbreak, trying to rebuild what the enemy War had destroyed. We
felt instinctively that Palestine—Zion must be protected. We called in
alarm to our comrades and to all Jews, clamoring for assistance in
patching the deep rent made by the belligerent powers in the life of the
Jews in Palestine. We thought only of bridging over the time till war
would cease, and we would be free to resume our normal course.

But no sooner had we pledged our efforts to this work when, as we
had surmised, the terrible situation of our brothers in Galicia, Poland
and Russia was forced upon our attention. Millions of our brethren
are in the center of the war maneuvers. Lodz, Warsaw, Kalisz, Cracow—
what are these but Jewish cities? Thousands are being ruined every day.
Every day Jewish widows and orphans are being made by the war. It
became also our duty to help. There was no one else to help. The Belgium
catastrophe, whereby a whole nation was scattered, aroused the interest
of the general public. The Jewish tragedy could not be seen—it could
not be felt—except by Jews. In this work the Zionists were in duty
bound to help. We were thus between two fires. Whom to save first?
Was it to be our Polish brothers, the buffers between two fires, now suffering at the hands of Russians, now at the hands of Poles, Germans and
Austrians; or was it to be the hopeful life in Palestine, our national
stake in the ground, upon which our future rested?

This was our dilemma, and we took both horns of the dilemma in
true Jewish fashion. But the tragedy of it all lies in that we feel that no
matter how much we Jews may sacrifice, we cannot make good the
losses in either section of the Jewish world. We shall lose much in the
golus, and we shall not save all in Palestine. Irretrievable loss, no matter
what we do! The growth of Palestine has not developed sufficiently to
become a real salvation in such a trying time.

But more than the physical distress we feel, Zionist policy—Zionist hopes, Zionist enthusiasm—has been affected by these conditions. The raw facts of the moment overcome us. Our vision is clouded. We feel for the next step. We do not know what it is to be. The dependable things have been shaken; and we have no props upon which to lean. Confidence and faith in nations, in law, in ideals, in the sense of justice of nations, have been lost. We feel, more than ever before, that our problems are solely our own problems, in which no other nation can have a share. Our battles must be fought by our own people, and we need not depend as formerly upon the altruistic interest of foreign nations. Israel must redeem Israel, and it must depend upon its own intelligence, its own ideals to find the way out of the morass of "civilization," in which we have been entangled.

What are we to say? How shall we advise our people, our comrades?

The Guardian of Israel sleepeth not! Through the smoke of battle we look ahead and perceive the line along which we must march. It is the same old line, the way back to Zion, although the protection we expected from other nations is now lacking. We have lost our faith in other nations; but we are bound to acquire a deeper faith in the Ruler of our destiny, and we expect, through His power, to be given intelligence and strength to deal with our own affairs, wholly in our own way.

We are an Eternal People. The war will pass, but we live on. Our ideals, the ideals of Jewish people, have not been dimmed by war. On the contrary, they stand out now more clearly than ever. We now know what we are not, and what the nations are. We are not a warring nation. Our mission is peace. We do not oppose force with force. We present our claims, and appeal to the sense of justice of nations. We continue our appeal in spite of the deafness of nations. We continue our appeal in spite of the deafness of nations, but in the meantime we work out our own program. The general in command of our army is not Von Kluck or Rennenkampf. It is the Chief, who showed our leader Moses the way through the Wilderness.

DO NOT DESPAIR *

In the gravest period of our history, with evil rampant, bent on forcibly excluding us from many lands in which we are living; with the springs of renewed hatred and prejudice gushing forth again and inundating all Europe; we gather to consider how to marshal our living strength to

* *The Congress Bulletin,* November 4, 1938.

defend ourselves, and our first word to Jews scattered the world over is:

Do not despair! Cease not to hope for redemption through the power of righteousness.

For despair would be the ultimate sin. So long as we stand up against attack with resolute faith, the destroyers are powerless. Thousands may fall, crushed under the feet of barbarians; the work of generations may be destroyed; but faith in survival is the essence of resistance. It is the keystone of defense.

The heirs of a long-suffering and far-seeing people look again into the eyes of catastrophe. We have succeeded in surviving because never in all that history has catastrophe been accepted as the fatal conclusion. Just as we dare not believe that the world is condemned to destruction, that its morality and humanity have lost their potency, that civilization will succumb to barbarism, so we refuse to accept the darkness of this day as the everlasting climate of the Jewish people.

We boldly declare that the Jewish people have earned the right to work and to create in the lands in which they live; that they have a right to equality of rights. Through centuries of suffering and humiliation and oppression; through centuries of work and sacrifice and contribution to the making of modern civilization, they have acquired these rights which have been registered in law and covenant. These rights we shall never renounce until they are completely established in every part of the civilized world. We look forward to the day when freedom and equality will become the law of all life. And we propose to summon the help of all liberal and democratic forces in burning out the poison of hatred and intolerance, which infects so large a part of the world.

It is our purpose to fight without relenting against any enforced emigration. We deny the right of any country to expel its Jewish citizens. The need for emigration as an incident in the stabilization of organized society has been recognized by Jews from time immemorial. The large Jewish settlement in the United States (which we have the honor to represent) is an outgrowth of voluntary resettlement on the part of the Jews of Eastern Europe. It was emigration that built up the Jewish National Home in Palestine and established other centers of culture and science and art in various parts of the world.

Nor shall we abandon the position we have established in Palestine, which we occupy as a matter of right and not on sufferance. Fully cognizant of our historic responsibility, we declare that the greater part of our strength and resources shall be concentrated to the diversion of the stream of Jewish emigration into the Jewish National Home. The ideal of a National Home in Palestine is an aspiration of the whole Jewish people, seeking to achieve national freedom. The right to strive for the fulfillment of that aspiration is fundamental to our existence and we shall never renounce the historic claim of the Jewish people to the status of a free nation living on its own soil.

To the Jews of the dispersion, we send our fraternal sympathy in the hour of their need and agony, and pay tribute to the spirit of resistance and endurance which they have manifested in the lands of persecution. In their suffering, they have not forgotten the stream of life which fed them in generations past. They have made invaluable contributions to the cultural life and the spiritual content of Jewish existence, which has helped to sustain the Jews of America. Thus, we are united in one stream of life; we are one people; their weakness is our weakness; their strength is our power. And it is our intention to concentrate as great a part of our resources as we can possibly contribute to the strengthening of their resistance and to their sustenance in the hour of their distress.

We send a word of encouragement and admiration to the Yishuv in Palestine for their heroic courage and sustained sacrifice. In the days of their creative joy, we stood with them; and in these days of warfare, we feel their suffering and admire their strength, for their devotion to the National Home makes more meaningful the vow that rises to our lips: "If I forget thee, O Jerusalem, may my right hand forget its cunning."

These tragic days impose a greater burden of responsibility upon the Jews of America. We have built up in this great Republic a Jewish community in many cities, with its own cultural and religious and social life. The European Jewish communities are being maimed and humiliated and treated as alien to the rights of the world. Through their healing, we shall heal ourselves. Through their salvation, we shall be saved. Through their defeat, we shall be defeated.

We call upon the Jewish youth of America to find places in the ranks of organized Jewry. Let them imitate their comrades in Europe and the example of their comrades in Palestine. The Jewish youth of all lands are not in retreat; they are not victims of despair; they are fighting the battle of their kinsmen the world over. It is their blood which runs through the veins of the Jewish youth of America. It is their example that should serve as incentive for the mobilization of the American Jewish youth in the defense of our entire national front. We are the reserves and the reinforcements and, most important in the defense of our frontiers, is the feeling of confidence created in the defenders that reinforcements are prepared to take their places in case they fall in battle.

It is our firm conviction and faith that mankind will overcome the evils of Hitlerism and anti-Semitism just as it has overcome plagues of disease and barbarism in times past. The new idols will crumble as did the old. Mankind will be stirred once more to self-recognition. It will once more appreciate the moral value of democracy in the progress of the human race and as it moves toward the new world which is to be created through resistance to the dictators, we shall again find our roots as a free people in a world of freedom.

BRITISH BETRAYAL OF BALFOUR DECLARATION AND THE PALESTINE MANDATE

The whittling down of the pledges of the Balfour Declaration and of the Palestine Mandate began in 1922 when two thirds of ancient Palestine was detached from it by Britain and the separate state of Trans-Jordan created in an area of 34,700 square miles over which Britain, too, became the Mandatory.

The area in which the Jewish National Homeland could be established was thus reduced to 10,400 sqare miles.

Although Britain was charged as the Mandatory Power with placing the country under such political, administrative and economic conditions as will secure the establishment of the Jewish National Home, Jewish settlement on the land was not encouraged, few agricultural state lands were made available, local self-government was not advanced by the Mandatory. So flagrant were Britain's omissions that in 1937 the British Royal Commission said the government imposed on Palestine— "is not a suitable or natural form for the Jewish section of its population . . . Crown colony government is not a suitable form of government for a numerous, self-reliant, progressive people."

This attrition policy reached its climax with the British White Paper of May 1939, three months before the outbreak of World War II, parallel with the rise of Hitlerism and the crescendo of Hitler's racist policies against the Jews.

In 1933, Hitler became Chancellor of Germany after three years of intensive preparation for that event. Within six years, he had gathered half of Europe into his orbit without firing a shot. Jews sought frantically to escape his dragnet. In 1938, an International Refugee Conference convened at Evian, France, of which Britain was a co-convener, had established that virtually no countries were open for Jewish refugees from Hitler. Palestine alone beckoned, through the Jewish community.

At this moment, Britain decreed (through its White Paper) that Jewish immigration to Palestine, already heavily restricted by it far below the absorptive capacity created by the Jews themselves, should cease at the end of five years. Transfer of lands to Jews, in certain areas, was prohibited; a year later Jews were prohibited from acquiring land in 63% of Palestine and restricted in another 32%.

Britain's 1939 White Paper was intended to appease the Arabs, who had been carrying on bloody riots since 1929, in the hope of thus rendering secure her bases in the Middle East and her oil concessions. Britain insisted on carrying out the White Paper despite the unanimous view of the Permanent Mandates Commission of the League of Nations in June, 1939, that "the policy set out in the White Paper was not in accordance with the interpretation, which, in agreeement with the Mandatory Power and the Council, the Commission has always placed on the Palestine Mandate."

Tens of thousands of Jews, who might have found haven in Palestine, were thus doomed to extermination by Hitler. That record was set forward in a memorandum of fact submitted, in March 1946, to the Anglo-American Commission of Inquiry by the Jewish Agency for Palestine. Said this memorandum:

"The blows came to the Jewish people at a time when the Nazi Government was intensifying its campaign against the Jews. But even the outbreak of the war and the capture of 3 million Polish Jews produced no change of heart.

"Before hostilities commenced, the Jewish Agency asked for the immediate admission of 20,000 children from Poland and 10,000 young men from the Balkan countries, the latter to reinforce manpower in Palestine. These requests were rejected; it was, apparently, feared that at such a pace the quota of 75,000 would be used up too quickly. The Polish-Jewish children went to Maidanek and Auschwitz instead, while of the young Jews in the Balkans many died and many were forced to work for Hitler. The fear of impending massacres expressed by the Jewish Agency at the time was written off as spurious. So the hopeless tug of war continued, the Jewish Agency trying to rescue Jews as quickly as possible, the Government trying to dole out the quota as slowly as possible.

"After the holders of pre-war permits had been admitted, a ban was imposed on all further immigration from enemy countries, on the ground that Nazi agents might come in. In May, 1940, the Jewish Agency appealed for the exemption of children and of certain adults

of assured identity. The decision took two years. No exemption was then granted in favor of adults. The concession regarding children came too late.

"Meanwhile groups of Jews had managed to escape from Europe and reach Palestine. Their entry was held to justify a complete suspension of the issue of new permits even to parts of Europe which were not yet enemy territory. Thus quotas were withheld for the half years October 1939 to March 1940 and October 1940 to March 1941. The latter period immediately preceded the German invasion of the Balkans. Only a few hundred emergency permits were granted for Balkan Jewries at the time, mostly too late. The Government actually advised the Jewish Agency to save permits for post-war use when they could be given to Jews from Germany, who were a better type than those from the Balkans.

"The search for boats carrying Jewish fugitives and the prevention of their landing became a major concern of the authorities. In November 1940, the Government announced that Jews coming illegally from Europe would not be allowed to land, but would be interned elsewhere and not be admitted to Palestine after the war. As a reaction, the 'Patria' with 1771 Jewish refugees on board awaiting deportation, was blown up and sank in the port of Haifa. About 250 of its passengers were drowned and the survivors landed and were interned. A further 1700 refugees, who had been landed, were, with a considerable use of violence, re-embarked and deported to the island of Mauritius. From there they were released and brought to Palestine only at the end of the war, after over 100 of their number had died of disease. In December 1940, 230 refugees, including many children, perished when the tramp steamer 'Salvador' foundered in the Sea of Marmara. They had hoped to proceed overland from Istanbul, but no visas were available. In March, 1941, 793 refugees, mostly fleeing from the massacres in Rumania, arrived on board the 'Darien'. In view of the vessel's condition they had to be landed, but for 17 months they were kept in detention under the threat of deportation .On the 24th of February, 1942, came the 'Struma' tragedy. That boat had stood in the port of Istanbul for nearly two months waiting for Palestine visas. In the end only children were allowed to proceed, but the decision came too late. The Turkish authorities had turned the vessel back into the Black Sea, where it sank. Of its 764 passengers, only one survived.

"'In Palestine,' writes an American Jewish author, 'over half a million Jews waited with open arms for their tormented and hopeless kin

. . . *while over the Mediterranean and Black Seas unclean and un-seaworthy little cargo boats crept from port to port, or tossed about on the open waters, waiting in vain for permission to discharge their crowded human cargoes. Hunger, thirst, disease and unspeakable living conditions reigned on those floating coffins . . . There is a list of mass tragedies already available; incomplete though it certainly must be, it is sickeningly long.'*

"After the 'Struma' disaster the rules were relaxed. It was decided to admit and gradually release all refugees from Europe who got to Palestine on their own. At the same time it was made clear that nothing would be done to help them get there. In a communication to the Jewish Agency in May 1942, the British Government said: 'In pursuance of the existing policy of taking all practical steps to discourage illegal immigration in Palestine, nothing whatever will be done to facilitate the arrival of Jewish refugees in Palestine.'

"It should be borne in mind that at that time no facilities existed in the Balkans for obtaining visas to Palestine. The only way for a refugee to seek legal admission to Palestine was to reach Istanbul and apply to the British Consul there. But at Istanbul he was already considered 'illegal'!

"Late in 1942 authentic reports about the wholesale extermination of the Jews became public. Under their impact the Government, in the middle of 1943, agreed to facilitate the journey to Palestine of all refugees reaching Istanbul. Yet this decision, of which the Jewish Agency was informed confidentially, was not published, nor was it, for a further nine months, communicated to the Turkish Government. This robbed it of much of its value.

"There can be little doubt that substantial numbers who are dead today, certainly tens of thousands, might have been alive if the gates of Palestine had been kept open."

On September 1, 1939, Hitler attacked Poland, having first entered into a non-aggression pact with the USSR. Britain and France came to the defense of their ally. And World War II was launched.

On December 7, 1941, Hitler's ally, Japan, attacked Pearl Harbor; the U.S. was plunged into war.

Exposure of Hitler's plan for the extermination of the Jews of Europe by the American Jewish Congress and World Jewish Congress, and cor-roboration of it by the U.S. State Department, was to come only in 1942. But from 1939 on the program itself was being enacted, preceded *by denial of rights, including the right to work, seizure of Jewish property, ghettoization and physical attack, which was to pile up the horrendous record of Hitler's deportation and destruction of 6 million Jews in crematoria, gas chambers and extermination centers designed for this sole purpose.*

*   *   *

One of the most extraordinary chapters in civilized history, also written in this period, was the behavior of the free Jewish communities toward Britain in the face of Jewish disaster and the closing of the doors of Palestine.

In Palestine, and in the United States, Jews rallied to the defense of Britain long before the attack on Pearl Harbor.

In Palestine, 146,200 Jews registered, immediately after the war's outbreak, for service with the British forces, among them 50,400 women. Refusing them at first, Britain ultimately accepted 33,000 volunteers, 26,000 of whom saw active service on all the Allied fronts in the British Army, Navy and Air Corps. Half of them perished.

Lipsky summarized this record to the Committee on Foreign Affairs of the House of Representatives on July 19, 1951:

> *"There were 60 units of Royal Engineers, Transport, Ordnance Mechanical Services. Selected civilian volunteers carried out secret raids in the Middle East and parachute missions in enemy Europe. Half of them lost their lives. Army orders totaling over £36 million in the economic field were executed by Jewish industry. The Hebrew University, the Technical Institute at Haifa and the Sieff Scientific Institute at Rehovoth performed technical and scientific services of special value. The armed services, in Palestine and outside, relied on skilled Jewish labor for important tasks of construction and repair. Jewish contractors, engineers, and skilled personnel helped to enlarge the oil refineries in Abadan, Iran, bridged the Euphrates, covered Syria with a network of roads and camps and built maintenance airdromes in Iran, Bahrein and Cyprus."*

The Arab community in Palestine was indifferent to the Allied war effort. Most of the Arab States were pro-Axis, while the Grand Mufti of Jerusalem was an active ally of the Axis.

A total of 12,445 Arabs were recruited into the British services from three Arab States, Transjordan, Lebanon, Syria, coming to Palestine for this purpose. Half of them deserted or were discharged before the war ended.

Of seven Arab States, only Transjordan, under the British Mandate, declared war on the Axis in 1939. Egypt, Syria, Lebanon, Saudi Arabia, after first making certain that the Nazis were losing, declared war three months before its end, in order to qualify for membership in the organizing conference of the United Nations. Iraq declared war in 1943 after the defeat of a pro-Nazi revolt.

In the United States, many American Jewish leaders were in the forefront of support for Britain, beginning in 1939, through the William Allen White Committee for the Defense of the Allies, Short of War.

An American section of British War Relief was organized in 1939 through the initiative of the American Jewish Congress, led in this endeavor by Stephen Wise, Dr. Israel Goldstein and Lipsky.

Simultaneously, the American community at large was being educated out of its isolation by the American Jewish Congress leaders to understand that the crimes of Hitler against the Jews and against Britain were crimes against civilization which would engulf civilization if not halted.

While this movement in support of Britain continued, a continuous effort went on:

1. To secure international action to rescue European Jews, and to open the doors of Palestine while rescue was still possible;

2. To secure recognition of Jewish Palestine as an ally of the United Nations and reassurance of a return to the intent and purpose of the Balfour Declaration, at the war's end;

3. To stimulate raising of funds to accelerate the development of Palestine;

4. To mobilize the American Jewish Community to speak as a united community in support of a Jewish Commonwealth in Palestine.

A principal in this many-faceted effort—on the one hand, in support of the British War effort, and on the other to force Britain to face up to her obligations to create a Jewish State, was Louis Lipsky.

His platforms were the American Jewish Congress, of which he was a Vice-President; the Zionist Organization of America, of which he was Honorary President; the United Palestine Appeal, of which he was Co-Chairman, and the Jewish communities of the country, where he was a coveted speaker.

Some of the speeches of that period, dealing with the The Record of British Betrayal; Palestine as a Haven; The Search for Recognition of the Jewish People as an Ally of the Free World are reprinted in the succeeding pages.

The Editor

THE BRITISH CABINET TURNS AGAIN TO THE MUNICH LINE*

As these lines are being written the Chamberlain Government has not yet made public its formal decision on the policy it intends to impose in Palestine. Reports are coming in hourly from all parts of the world—agitated and appealing—warning that the die has been cast. A Cabinet meeting on Wednesday, May 10th; a public announcement on Monday, May 15th; or, as the latest report has it, on May 23rd; and then a Command Paper is to be laid before Parliament. The momentous announcement may be made at any moment, it is cabled. We sense a great deal of excitement; and there is good reason for such excitement; but no clear image of the situation in London is indicated in the varying reports.

What do these contradictions mean? Are they all false and misleading? Have the wires been entangled in transmission?

Not at all. All the reports are both right and wrong. They are details of a larger picture. Put the reports in their proper sequence, read them in a certain order, and they tell us a consistent story. They reveal the "mind" of the Chamberlain Government. It has not yet made its detailed plans public, but in its own mind the policy is settled. It is resolved to cancel the Balfour Declaration, to take steps to nullify the Mandate, and to replace the authority under which it has been operating in Palestine with an arrangement which, in effect, will subordinate the Jewish National Home ultimately to a sovereign Arab State and give British imperial interests great latitude in action. It will do it if it is able. It is preparing all the necessary steps to effectuate its scheme. It has given Mr. MacDonald a free hand on that line.

The Time Table guiding the sickening procedure of committing this political larceny is subject to change. The details are subject to change. But it needs no political specialist to draw the conclusion that the stage is being set in London for a sharp turn back to the Munich line, and that at the other end of the line now stand not only Hitler and Mussolini but the sinister figure of the former Mufti of Jerusalem.

* *The New Palestine*, May 12, 1939.

The hesitations of the Time Table reflect, however, one illuminating fact: The Chamberlain Government is still wrestling with its Conscience; the sad, disappointed, worried eyes of that Conscience still disturb the men in whose hands Fate has placed the government of the British Empire.

The Chamberlain Government is now wrestling with its Conscience and it pauses before making the fateful announcement. Why does it hesitate to do the evil that is in its heart? Why has it hesitated all these weeks?

It fears the adverse effect of a repudiation of its covenant with the Jewish people upon the liberal groups in the United States. It wishes to avoid offense to the American Government and its great President, who has interceded in the name of Honor and Fair Play on their behalf.

It hesitates to alienate American public opinion. It hesitates to alienate its own liberal democratic opinion, which turns from the fabricated "realities" Mr. Chamberlain pretends are his guides, and still has notions of British Honor, of the sanctity of covenants; which still believes England should cease placating its enemies at the expense of its friends. It hesitates to make an alliance with venal Arab states, entrusting important lines of imperial communication to their loyalty, which is purchasable in the open market. It balances the benefits that may accrue against the opprobrium that will be earned. It is prepared to do a shameful wrong if convinced that the crime would pay.

That is what makes the Chamberlain Government hesitate to publish the details of its "imposed" policy. It is not sentiment or morality or principles, but a balancing of interest. It is wrestling with Conscience in order to silence it, and Conscience, in all likelihood, is about to get the worst of the struggle, as it did at Munich, as it did in Prague, as happened in Spain, and as it may also happen again with regard to its most recent pledge to Poland.

At the last moment, seeking to placate the outraged, it clutches at a preliminary report on British Guiana as a place for the settlement of refugees, without even looking into its cautious recommendations, and proposes, as compensation for the closing of the doors of Palestine to Jewish immigration, a vague offer of opportunities in that undeveloped country for Jewish settlement. This hypocritical gesture is an insult to Jewish intelligence. It assumes that a wronged people will be pressed by necessity to take what may be offered, regardless of substance of immediate or future value and that such an acceptance could be displayed as proof of the virtue of the Government making the offer. The plan is as yet no definite proposal. The betrayal is blatantly clear and definite.

The unpublished plans of the Chamberlain Government, decided upon in secret, representing a congealed attitude toward the problem of Palestine, have a number of hurdles to take before they can be realized. They are to be submitted to Parliament, and Parliament may be relied upon to put up a courageous, effective fight against the Government's scheme. If approved in Parliament, they are to be placed before the League of Nations, and the Permanent Mandates Commission may be relied upon to pass judgment. An outraged Jewish people will endeavor to save the Chamberlain Government from this betrayal not only of Jewish right, but of English interests, by appealing to Parliament against its Government. It will marshal the forces of democracy the world over to protest the action in the councils of the League. It will make that League which was chloroformed into inaction by Mr. Chamberlain, rise from its sleep and hear the protest of the wronged. It will not allow, without petition and demonstration, the commission of this last act of perfidy. Should the Government succeed in getting by these hurdles, it will then face the last and most difficult barrier to the success of its scheme.

It will have to face the 500,000 Jews of the Yishuv, who, as one man, will resist the setting up of the so-called government it intends to establish in Jerusalem with the aid of the Mufti and his murderous band recalled from their exile. The men and women who came to Palestine to build the Jewish National Home, invested on the strength of a British promise not only their means, not only their moral and intellectual resources, but their future and the future of their children. They performed their part of a contract. They worked and suffered privation. They reclaimed the soil and endured the endemic diseases of a neglected land. They made the realities of whatever State is visible in Palestine, and they will not allow a usurping authority, without legal or moral right, to rule them. These 500,000 Jews in Palestine represent performance on a covenant, and they will defend their possessions and their rights. Their defense will be given the moral and financial and political support of the great American Jewish community, as well as of other free Jewish communities.

Despite our feeling that the Chamberlain Government is committed to the policy of taking away the Jewish right to Palestine without compensation, there is a possibility that before it reaches the end of the road, many things may happen that may completely alter the appalling conditions that face us these days.

ENGLAND DISHONORED*

The results of the vote in Parliament were anticipated but it was felt that the Government would at least make a show of response to the storm of protest that greeted the White Paper last week. Mr. Chamberlain is now engaged in a heroic effort to retrieve the position lost at Munich and to achieve good will and confidence for England in the negotiations being conducted in many European capitals. There are vital English interests to be served in America which are in danger of being lost. The office of the Prime Minister must have felt the reverberation of the thunderous moral indignation that was being expressed in every segment of the Anglo-Saxon world, and especially in the United States. It must have heard the many voices of England, the England of the better days, the England that had felt outraged by Munich and Prague. It must have felt the spiritual significance of the Jewish protest at the Wailing Wall where the White Paper was torn into shreds in a symbolic gesture of disdain and contempt. All of this, it was thought, would bring from the leaders of the Government some reply; a persuasive defense; a recital of the mitigating circumstances that were forcing betrayal; some explanation that would take into account the morality of the protest.

But the victory of the Chamberlain Government was achieved without explanation or defense. It was a weak contradictory case; it was misleading in statement of fact; it was tricky in argument and evasive; it was unworthy of the high standards of the British Parliament. As a performance in pleading, the lawyer for the defense would have had his case thrown out of court.

The victory of the Government was achieved, however, without convincing explanation because it was determined to win the English people and their representatives in the House not by appealing to reason or to a sense of justice, or to morality, but by appealing to fears that had been craftily nurtured by the Government itself ever since the days preceding the Munich pact. These fears have been the principal stock in trade of the Government for quite some time. It was the war just around the corner. It was the bugaboo of Communism. It was the aggression of Hitler and Mussolini. The victory was not achieved on the moral plane by invoking a higher patriotism or loyalty. It was achieved through the use of petty, legalistic method, working upon the fears of the Conservative class in England.

* *The New Palestine,* May 26, 1939

COUNTERFEIT FOR STERLING

And at the end of a journey of less than twenty years, the Government that had accepted the Mandate with exalted faith and purpose, that had set out to pay a debt and to fulfill a promise—that Government proposes to exchange its sacred promise and its international pledge for the appeasement of its own anxieties and fears, to use its sacred promise as consideration in a sale, and to set up a state in Palestine which it dares call an independent state, to be guided not by the builders, the peace-makers, the redeemers, but a state in which the destroyers shall be established in positions of power and authority. And this intention to betray and dishonor is cloaked under the pretense of a sacrifice for the sake of peace and the organization of the democratic world.

Throughout the years, faith in the sincerity of England's promise had been maintained among us, despite the double-dealing administration, the low level of political negotiation, and even when it seemed that the Mandatory Government was determined to earn for England the epithet of "perfidious." It was felt that while there remained a field in which the National Home could grow, while there was still opportunity for development, faithless administration could merely alter the time-schedule or affect the tempo of the national enterprise. There was always the prospect of better days to come. Under the oppression of injustice, and in spite of the obstacles, the population grew, labor expanded, land was acquired, experience in nation-building matured and extended over an ever-growing field. And ever the soft words of reassurance were being offered by ministers and high commissioners. How could one disbelieve these courteous gentlemen?

The most striking demonstration of that loyalty was revealed in the last trying years of disorder and terror. The entire Yishuv stood as a wall of self-restraint. It refused to engage in retaliation even though scores of our best sons and daughters died at the hands of the terrorists. They held themselves in check, biting their lips and clenching their fists. They refused to mar the quality of their enterprise by the shedding of innocent blood. It was a magnificent display of moral courage—this long period of self-restraint. It was a striking act of enlightened states-manship.

It was a naive thought that such high morale would affect the English official mind. It was disregarded. It was taken as evidence of weakness of the cause for which the self-restraint was a demonstration. What did impress the rulers of Palestine and the occupant of the Colonial Office was the policy of the murderer who flung dynamite into kindergartens and cinemas, the acts of bandits and saboteurs, of bomb-throwers and snipers. Loyal self-restraint was sacrificed to placate the claimant who disdained the softness of the Jewish approach. "Appeasement" was not won by loyalty and cooperation; it was won by intimidation, defiance and terror.

Today, the advocates of aggression seem triumphant. It is not with Guardians of Law and Justice that we are dealing. They are political gamblers who are using their special position in Palestine, acquired through covenant and treaty, as a pawn in a game that is being played on a larger board. It is not inefficiency or lack of understanding that was responsible for the adoption of a zig-zag course of policy. It was part of an imperial plan, designed or patterned in advance, changing with circumstances, but always true to its course, which has unmasked itself this week in the House of Commons.

It is not a Balfour who speaks for England today. It is the Chamberlain of the Munich pact, the Chamberlain who sacrificed the Czechoslovakian Republic, who has pursued a consistent policy of abandonment of the high ideals of the British people. It is the loyal son of Ramsay MacDonald who makes public the policy that for the first time mirrors the truth of the proposed dishonor of the authors of the Balfour Declaration. The Great Betrayal, prematurely described a decade ago, is officially confirmed in May, 1939. It is proposed to deposit that Black Paper in the archives of the League of Nations, provided the English people allow this confession of dishonor to be sealed and delivered.

What is nullified is the Promise, and what is cancelled is the recognition of Right. But the Promise we have clung to and believed in for 2,000 years, and for the fulfillment of which we have labored these forty years, does not need English sanction to continue to live. It had its sanction long before the English Empire was set up. Recognition may be cancelled and nullified, but the Right which was the substance of the Recognition continues in full force and will abide with us so long as Jewish hearts beat and the Jewish spirit lives. For this Promise and recognition cannot be withdrawn by any act of the English Government. Cancellation and nullification arrive too late. The Promise is no longer merely a scrap of paper, the declaration of an intention. It has been incarnated in a living National Home. It drew its first natural breath when that covenant was made in 1922. Life was born of the Promise, and it cannot be called back. It has given birth to a growing, expanding, articulate Jewish National Home. It is a small Home, but young and strong, colorful, enterprising, courageous. It is strong enough to break any chain that may be forged to be imposed upon it. It will refuse to be strangled or suffocated to serve the interests of a misguided and faithless Government.

DECEIT AND DISHONOR

That National Home—backed by all of us, far and wide, Jews the world over who have aided in giving it life—will declare the new British policy null and void, and of no effect. Our eyes will refuse to see or recognize it. It was born in deceit and dishonor. It has no moral or legal sanction for its edicts. Its authority rests upon usurpation. The Government that issues it is like a defaulter who proposes to occupy the property of his creditors. It is like the faithless guardian taking possession of the resources of the ward whom he has defrauded, and who impudently asks the ward to give sanction and consent to the fraud. The Government thus operating has no authority to declare who are legal and who are illegal immigrants; it cannot prohibit or sanction the sales of land it does not rule by consent. If it wishes to rule, it will have to do so by force and violence.

Against that force and violence, the Jews of Palestine cannot be called upon to exercise the self-restraint of the past years. They will resist the setting up of the structure of the new government. They will stand as an invincible phalanx against any government that denies their basic right as a people. They will refuse to be parties to the destruction of their national home. It is not their national home alone but it is to be held open to the thousands of homeless and stateless who pour into the land from all European shores.

The policy announced by the Government will inevitably cause the shedding of innocent blood. There are wrongs so flagrant that they cannot be calmly endured, that arouse the passions, that create an overwhelming indignation that cannot be controlled. Authority will endeavor to moderate the expression of righteous indignation and resistance, but for all the blood shed, the usurping Government will be accountable and responsible. The Chamberlain Government, engaged in forming alliances to stop the Madman who rules in Germany, will be hard put to it to explain why, at the same time, it seeks to destroy the only Sanctuary left to an oppressed people; and why the land they have made to live again shall now be only another land in which they are to be admitted on sufferance and not as of right. The Government headed by Mr. Chamberlain has unloosed a force of righteous indignation and protest, which will be heard by the democratic states that Mr. Chamberlain of all men, is calling to defend democratic world order.

And thus Mr. Malcolm MacDonald, the "friend" of the Jewish cause, with no case worthy of the name, was given authority to proceed to execute a plan for the government in Palestine which not only involves perfidy and dishonor, but which is repudiated and rejected by the Jews of Palestine, by the Arabs of Palestine, by the best moral forces of England, by an overwhelming official and unofficial American public opinion, and which has the single virtue of satisfying Mr. Chamberlain, Lord Halifax, Mr. MacDonald and Aly Maher Pasha of Egypt, and perhaps Nuri Pasha of Baghdad.

Thus, the road of betrayal leads England further and further and further into the mire of the Munich pact, into a continuation of the double-dealing, up-and-back policy, which has become synonymous with the name of Mr. Chamberlain. Principles and ideals are being laid aside ostensibly to organize the democratic world against aggression and violence. But the course of appeasement is not halted and the appeaser comes to resemble more and more the aggressors whom he seeks to encircle.

It seems that Mr. Chamberlain is not disturbed by the fact that the vote in the House registered a minority and not a majority in favor of his proposal. He seems not to be worried by the fact that fear, not conviction, determined the action of those who stood with him. It does not matter that nowhere will the Government find support for the new policy. In grim earnest it will have to be imposed by force. But Mr. Chamberlain and his Colonial Secretary, Mr. MacDonald, are perfectly satisfied to be able to say at long last that the Government has ceased to vacillate, it has come to a decision, it has a policy, which has been ratified and confirmed; and that is the end of it.

But just as it seemed to have a policy when Ormsby-Gore two years ago stood up in the House and claimed to have a policy in the partition plan and only a few months thereafter announced its abandonment, so too Mr. MacDonald may have a policy signed and sealed, technically and legally endorsed by Parliament, but when his High Commissioner girds up his loins to enforce that policy, the same indecision and vacillation and doubt may return and he may hesitate even as did Ormsby-Gore to enforce what he might have a legal right to enforce, but which it might become disadvantageous to the Government to proceed with any further. Parliament may give him the right to go on, but as Mr. MacDonald himself assured the Jewish delegation in London in February this year, a state or a policy cannot be maintained in Palestine without the consent of the Jewish people. Whatever there is of organized responsible society in Palestine is represented by the life created and maintained in that part of Palestine which is occupied by the Jewish National Home. No Government can survive without the consent of that National Home.

That consent the English Government will never have. Those whom the Government has betrayed will regard any administration the High Commissioner will endeavor to set up as usurpation of authority, as illegal and as immoral. Only the Mandate gives England a place in the life of Palestine. A repudiation of the Mandate, a basic violation of its objective, means a cancellation of all English authority in Palestine. The Government may, as a substitute for the legal position it has under the Mandate, decide to maintain authority through force, through oppression, through denial of right. But in that case England will be occupying Palestine in exactly the same way as Mr. Mussolini is occupying Albania.

Against that occupation of Palestine the protesting voice of the Jewish people will be heard and it will not be silenced. And against that usurpation the Yishuv will be organized: every Jew capable of service will be registered and mobilized to carry out the program of non-cooperation and resistance to usurpation of rights. It will regard as null and void every infringement of the rights accorded to Jews in the Mandate. It is prepared to endure privation, to make any sacrifice to uphold and maintain what the Jewish people have achieved in Palestine.

They must not be allowed to stand alone. They are engaged in the defense of the Jewish National Front. They occupy the trenches of the Jewish national defense. The rights they are fighting for are the rights that were guaranteed to the whole Jewish people. They are fighting for the right of Jewish refugees to enter the Promised Land. It becomes our duty with all our moral and material resources to stand by the Yishuv, to provide it with the means to maintain the struggle, and to regard the conflict into which they have been thrust by a faithless government as a conflict which engages the honor and prestige and interests of the whole Jewish people.

A VIOLATION OF COVENANT*

The British Government authorizes the issuing of regulations to place the sale of land by Arabs to Jews under strict government control. The regulations follow the report of the Woodhead Commission. They enact one of the proposals of the MacDonald White Paper, the first

* *The New Palestine*, March 1, 1940.

having been the restriction of immigration regardless of absorptive capacity, and the third and last being the constitutional changes intended to be introduced in order to transform Palestine into an Arab-dominated land, and to reduce the Jewish people to the position of a minority. Regardless of all moral and social considerations, indifferent to the claims of justice and fair play, the British Government seems determined to make effective a policy which was challenged by the best opinion in England when it was first proposed; temporary approval of which it secured only under pressure of the imminence of war; and which, even now, the most powerful voices in England condemn as unwise and futile.

What was announced this week with regard to the regulation of land sales is in line with the policy of that White Paper which aims, through various restrictive measures, to set up and maintain artificial barriers between Jews and Arabs; through governmental intervention to keep Jews and Arabs from living side by side throughout the land; and further, as far as possible, to keep Jews within the environs of the cities. The aim is separation and segregation. It is to break Palestine into two parts, zig-zagging from north to south, from east to west, so that these artificial barriers shall always stand in the way of the normal development of the land. It eliminates all the vestiges of the idealism that animated the Government which issued the Balfour Declaration. The announcement of this week is another step in the direction of effectively annulling both the Mandate and the Declaration.

Why this action was taken at this time is obscured by the reticences of diplomatic and political intrigue. It was the general impression that the policy of the MacDonald White Paper had been congealed by the intervention of war. Whatever may have caused the adoption of that policy, the fears the English Government may have had arising out of Nazi influence among the Arabs, the anxieties as to what the Arab States might do, the war had radically altered all these circumstances and rendered the policy of the White Paper inoperative, obsolete and irrelevant. The motivations given by Mr. MacDonald last year in London had become meaningless. The Colonial Office had become a subordinate department of a war cabinet. In the face of that war, in which Palestine was destined to occupy an important strategic position, in which the Jews were prepared to play an important part, the policy of the White Paper was reduced to the expression of a petty ambition of a frustrated Colonial Secretary. It had been detoured into a blind alley. It was confidently expected that when the war would end, a wholly different set of circumstances would confront the British Empire and, in fact, the whole civilized world, and new issues would have to be dealt with, a new orientation would have to be worked out for the Near East, and the relations between Jews and Arabs might be completely altered by these circumstances and through their devotion to a common cause. But, we regret to say, all these ideas seem to have been given no weight in the decision of the Government made public this week.

Nor is the urgency of the action explained. Unrest among the Arabs is reported to have disappeared. Many sprigs of cooperation have become evident and have been reported in the press. Common economic interests have drawn Jews and Arabs together as never before. They both face common dangers. They both appear in the military contingent that landed in France this week. They are both concerned in the economic and military defenses of Palestine. The arrival of the Australian troops in Palestine seems to have made clear to all concerned that the intransigent Arab elements have taken to cover, and that Arab-Jewish relations cannot now be regarded as one of the insoluble problems the Mandatory Government has to deal with.

Surely, Mr. MacDonald does not expect to have his *ex parte* statements accepted without demur. The resurrection of the exploded myth of landless Arabs reveals the fact that Mr. MacDonald still depends upon the formal case prepared for him by his legal experts to see him through, and that he is still unwilling to, and rather fearful of submitting his case to an impartial tribunal. In what way the restriction of land sales will help Arab cultivators to maintain their existing standards of life is very hard to understand, since only in such areas where Jews and Arabs have worked side by side have the standards of living of the Arabs improved, and only in such areas where the Arabs are segregated have their standards of living gone down. Why does not Mr. MacDonald rest his case upon facts and not upon the conclusions of commissions which have followed Government instructions as policy?

The action of the British Cabinet has no justification on legal, moral or economic grounds. It serves no discernible, legitimate interest of the Empire. It is an infringement of the civil rights of both Jews and Arabs —the right of Jews to buy; the right of Arabs to sell. It denies Jewish access to the soil, and forces the creation of two pales of settlement—one to be occupied by Jews, the other by Arabs—the boundaries of which are not to be crossed. It violates the letter and spirit of the Mandate and flouts the authority of the League of Nations, whose Mandates Commission has given its opinion that the whole White Paper is incompatible with a reasonable interpretation of the Mandate.

Is it necessary to remind the English Government at this time that Palestine is not a free, unencumbered chattel of the British Empire, to be disposed of as England by itself may decree? The Mandatory Government was named by an international, legal act as guardian of a land which was to be governed in accordance with the terms of an international covenant. How England has discharged its obligations is subject to the scrutiny of a League of Nations, and should that League be inoperative for a time, there is still operative a world public opinion which has a right to review the situation and to express its judgment, especially so at this time when England seeks the sympathy and cooperation of neutral states in a struggle to maintain international justice.

While, on the one hand, the English Government is associated with the French in the fight for the preservation of international morality and against racial and religious persecution, in which they have the sympathy of all democratic states and all liberal people; on the other hand, it violates its own international covenant with the Jewish people and proceeds, contrary to the moral judgment of the civilized world, to impair the foundations of the Jewish Homeland at a time when the Jewish people are pressed, as never before, to protect themselves against the very enemies who, at the same time, are the enemies of the democratic states. It is a betrayal of one of its loyal Allies—the victims of the war, humble but cooperative and loyal—by a great Empire engaged in the defense of the inviolability of international covenant and treaty.

There is no other recourse but for us to enter our protest against, and condemnation of, the step taken by the Mandatory Government, and to call upon the moral forces in the civilized world to register their rejection of an act that undermines confidence in the cause for which the Allies are fighting, and which is a betrayal of the ideals of justice and fair play. We call for the suspension of the new land regulations and of the White Paper policy as a whole for the duration of the war, pending which the Mandatory Government should use its best endeavors to stimulate and foster good relations between Jews and Arabs, allow for free intercourse between both peoples, interpose no artificial barriers between them, so that when peace finally comes and the Allied cause triumphs—as it is our prayer that it should triumph—it may be possible, in the new world to be created, to fulfill the pledges made to Jews, with adequate recognition of those rights to which the Arabs of Palestine are entitled under the terms of the Mandate.

THE PERVERSITY OF THE BRITISH GOVERNMENT*

The Imp of the Perverse continues to play havoc in our relations with the Mandatory for Palestine. These relations are never smooth for long. That is the fate of the Jewish National Home. Within the Colonial Office—the source of all perversity—there sit minds busily at work, stirring up difficulties by everlastingly redefining what has already been defined—shifting the balances, relentlessly irritating the situation whenever peace seems to be in the ascendant. They conceive government to be the arm of prohibition; that administration is a series of "Don'ts" —of petty interferences with liberty—which must be employed if government is to prove its value. Read the long list of delimiting definitions: the Churchill White Paper, the Passfield White Paper, the MacDonald White Paper, (all white), and the reports and investigations and their conclusions. The plain Mandate, based upon the simple Balfour Declaration, has been "done in" by the overzealousness of Government.

In the days of Ormsby-Gore the conclusion was reached that the Mandate was unworkable and that the doubly Promised Land would have to be divided into two parts in order to liquidate the promises made to each of the interested parties. But it was not until February, 1939, that the successor of Ormsby-Gore tackled the problem of finally disposing of the certified corpse. Mr. MacDonald hit upon a shrewd plan and proposed to bring together both Jews and Arabs at a round table, and to bid them iron out their differences. They came as summoned, but sat at two different round tables, with the agile peacemaker moving from one to the other. Finally, patience exhausted, Mr. MacDonald warned those who lingered around St. James' Palace that they had better come to some agreement. The clenched fist held what has become the White Paper of May, 1939. It will be labelled in history as the Mac-Donald White Paper, not quite as white as its predecessors.

That the peacemaker was not a disinterested party, and that the gist of the White Paper had been prepared in advance for use in an emergency, that it protected the Government's own interests chiefly, is beside the point. But it seemed that Mr. MacDonald was in a hurry to get results and to win the goodwill of the Arab states, because he was afraid that at any moment the long predicted European war would become a

---

* *Address as Presiding Officer, Mass Demonstration Protesting Land Restrictions in Palestine,* Carnegie Hall, March 4, 1940.

reality, and all his efforts to dispose of the Mandate would be lost. A substitute had to be found, and without delay. The London Conference led to no agreement, and the White Paper had to be issued.

But this White Paper, like other declarations of policy before it, was soon enveloped in a fog of legal discussion, and before the discussion was ended the Germans had invaded Poland, and England was in a state of war. Now, it was thought, Mr. MacDonald would be resigned to the passive role of Colonial Secretary, and leave government to the abler hands of the War Cabinet, and his White Paper would be put on ice for the duration of the war.

As an important segment of the Empire, Palestine was now also in the war. Normal business gave way to emergency. The land had to be put on the defensive. The economy of the land had to be reorganized. Preparations had to be made to utilize Palestine as the military base of an Eastern development. Jews by the tens of thousands offered their services. Arabs also came forward. Troops and materiel were being accumulated, and the military authorities became de facto the representatives of governmental authority. All civil matters, it was assumed, would become auxiliary to the military need.

As a matter of course, therefore, the conclusion was that the White Paper could have no meaning or significance in the light of events. For it represented policy discredited by the Mandates Commission. It had created division in Parliament. It was defended only by the Colonial Secretary. Lastly, it was policy incapable of being translated into reality. It had been born out of the spirit of appeasement and fear. Once the die was cast, and the menace of Europe had been courageously challenged, it would be covered up and returned to, if at all, later on, when the war had been disposed of.

But Satan—it is said—often finds mischief for idle hands to do. And the Colonial Office began laboring with the blueprints of the discarded plans of previous years. In their darkened offices, the White Paper looked like material to work on; and they were not content to remain idle.

With the war developing gradually, inevitably, it was expected that the thousands of victims fleeing from the zones of war would be regarded as an emergency and that if the stream of Jewish life was forced into Palestine, the routine procedure of peacetime would be abandoned and every victim would be received and given shelter and, if possible, made to be of service in his new home. They would be regarded like the Belgians in the last War—after the Germans had invaded their land—as the debris of warfare, entitled to fraternal treatment.

But the Colonial Office undertook to regard this Jewish immigration as subject to regular procedure—the schedules and visas of the past. They were treated as if they were violators of law. The conscience of the world was stirred by the spectacle of a great Empire at war, harrying for "illegality" and driving from the seas the victims of the barbaric European power which was the Empire's enemy as well. It was not content to stand watch in the Mediterranean, to halt and search and turn back vessels heavy with the fleeing victims, but it went to the length of taking steps to warn governments not to allow ships to be chartered for use by so-called illegal immigrants.

That was one section of the MacDonald White Paper which the Colonial Office was unable to overlook. Now comes another diversion from the tragic incidents of war—the land regulations. They shed no blood; they destroy no cities; they further no war aims. They are just an innocent piece of legislation, designed as a contribution to good will and peace. But their introduction will do more to impair English prestige than the loss of many battleships and battalions.

It is essentially an act of wanton injustice, profitable neither to its authors nor to any of the parties it is assumed to serve. It is unwarranted by any of the circumstances of the economic or political life of Palestine. It does not serve the cause of internal peace, nor strengthen the defenses of Palestine. It violates the expressed terms of the Mandate by drawing racial lines of discrimination between the citizens of Palestine. It completely nullifies the preamble of the Mandate.

It is a senseless intrusion upon a situation which should have been used by Government to bind together the Jewish and Arabic communities and not to promote their further division. It is an interference with the civil right of both Jews and Arabs to carry on free commerce between themselves. It arbitrarily segregates Jews and Arabs in several zones or spheres of influence, and provides no method for overcoming the barriers thus erected. The division of Palestine into segments prohibited to Jews, segments permitted to Jews, segments dependent upon the good will of the High Commissioner, places the land not under the rule of law—as we understand law—but under the rule of an official not responsible to any mandate either from the League of Nations or of the people he undertakes to govern.

What is the reason advanced for this action at this time? Mr. MacDonald has thus far condescended to refer once more to the landless

Arabs. This is a category mentioned on a number of occasions in several official reports, but no alert investigator has ever been able to find a substantial number of such landless Arabs. It is impossible to produce such alleged victims. The Jewish development in Palestine has enabled more Arabs to remain bound to the soil than any of the government schemes that have been suggested from time to time. But is it necessary at this time, for the sake of the mythical landless Arabs, to dislocate the economy of Palestine, the growing good will between Jews and Arabs, and to undertake a scheme which, even taken at its face value, with all its fictions, could not effectively change conditions even after a lapse of many, many years? What presses action now, when all of Palestine is practically under martial law?

Informed foreign correspondents suggest that Mr. MacDonald has other reasons for insisting just now upon the implementation of his policy. Hints are given—as were given in February 1939—that there are the Arab states in the offing. They threaten to make trouble. They must be appeased. No specifications are given, but may be mentioned in the same subtle way—as has been done on previous occasions—in Parliament on Wednesday, when the representatives of the English Government will be called upon to review the difficult situation the Colonial Secretary has created for them.

It is important to eliminate the Arab states in whose name, and out of fear of whom, the Colonial Secretary ventures to speak. Those Arab states are more in need of England today than England is in need of them. They were constituted with England's aid, and are maintained by English support. They become active when the Colonial Office sounds the alarm, and subside when the signal is given. They have their own private grievances, in which Palestine plays no part. These private grievances are not to be satisfied with legislation which penalizes the Arabs of Palestine and freezes their land. Their grievances are to be satisfied in such values that have some relation to their own interests. They stay on the sidelines of all the problems England is dealing with in Palestine.

In spite of Mr. MacDonald's performance, we do not believe that English statesmanship is dead. There are men in England who are thinking of how the world is to be constituted when peace comes. In that new world it is inconceivable that the diplomacies and strategies, the legalisms and the dialectics of the leaders of English Government in the past twenty years will survive the cleansing processes of war. In that new world, the fictions and the mockeries of justice that have been built up in and around Palestine—that have destroyed the effectiveness of the Mandate—are bound to be burned away, and the truth about both Arabs and Jews will be revealed. In that new world the Jewish relation to the Arabic world will be seen in the mirror of reality; the traditions that bind us together will obliterate the seeming differences that have been distorted by interested politicians and if in that New World there are to be judges between us, these judges will have to come into the court with their purposes and interests honestly placed on record, not smothered in specious "double talk."

Against this act of the British Government we protest not only as Jews, but as well-wishers of the English people intimately concerned in the victory of its arms. We protest in the name of that sensibility to justice which the English people have done so much to spread in the modern world. We protest against the shortsightedness, the ineptness and lack of vision, the callousness to justice and fair dealing, which this act of government has placed on the record of history, to the discredit of the cause of England and the humiliation of all its friends and well-wishers.

DISREGARDING REALITIES*

The Government of Palestine still holds that a state of war may exist in every part of the Empire, but not in Palestine. It proceeds along the old line of policy with regard to immigration, and announces with precision that for the next six months 9,060 certificates will be issued in three installments; that of these certificates 1,850 will be capitalist certificates, 3,000 for youths, children and students, 3,000 for dependents of immigrants, and 200 for laborers. It takes great pains to point out that the new immigration schedule is being issued in accord with the provisions of the MacDonald White Paper.

The schedule and the statement given out in connection therewith ignore everything that has happened in European affairs since the outbreak of war. Mr. MacDonald views the Government of Palestine as engaged in a civil job unrelated to the war scene, although right under the nose of High Commissioner MacMichael the whole of Palestine is being placed on a war footing, and elaborate preparations are being made for military expansion on a large scale.

Will it be necessary, here as elsewhere, for the realities of the war

---

* *The New Palestine*, May 3, 1940.

situation utterly to destroy this pretense before the English Government begins to adjust itself to the realities? The field of war is indivisible and extends from Canada to India, and includes all Imperial possessions and wardships. Palestine cannot, on the one hand, be maintained as a community under civil government, and on the other hand, be used for the purpose of preparing the Eastern front of the Allied armies.

Since Munich, the English Government has moved reluctantly, step by step, in the direction of facing the inevitable conflict with the Nazi Terror. Action always lagged after resolution. It came too late to the defense of Poland. It realized too late the implications of the attack on Finland. It is now struggling heroically—and, we hope, successfully—to overcome its tardiness and lack of preparation in the defense of Scandinavia. It pays heavy penalties for its tardiness, and interest charges mount high.

It still refuses to abandon the official policy in Palestine and to be reconciled with the development there, although every day lost means the loss of opportunities that could be immensely helpful to the Allied cause. It regards the Jews in Palestine as wards of a civil obligation, whose proffer of service in the war must be conditioned by prewar policies. The service Jews can render on the Eastern front is scrutinized and questioned. It is undecided what to do with the tangled skein of prewar promises, broken but still legible in protocols of Government.

And there is still no sense of realization of the fact that the Jews seeking sanctuary in Palestine are not merely refugees, accidents of life, unrelated to the conflict. The Jewish refugees hammering at the gates of Palestine are victims of the war in which the Allies are engaged. They are the victims of the same barbarous enemy whom the Allies must destroy if democratic freedom and international justice are to prevail in the world. They are the men and women who, standing in the way of the enemy, have been trampled underfoot, and they are entitled to receive generous shelter in Palestine just as the war victims are being received generously in France and England. They cannot be regarded as uninvited guests entitled to a conditional reception. As a matter of war duty and responsibility, Palestine must be regarded as one of the fields of war in which all the victims of war are entitled to equal consideration. Until the old policy of Mr. MacDonald is completely abandoned, immigration schedules of whatever size, containing whatever categories there may be, issued in three installments or six installments, will appear as fantastic and unreal, and not entitled to serious consideration.

MOMENTOUS CHANGES*

It had to be serious reverses on the war front to force the retirement of the Chamberlain Government. A Government that had succeeded in reducing the prestige of the British Empire to a level never reached in modern history, managed to hold on to the reins of office with a strange tenacity, even though dangers threatened the very foundations of the Empire, and although it must have realized for some time that it was riding for a catastrophic fall. It had reached the depths of duplicity and stupidity in the Munich pact, and did not have the courage or vision to resign even when it discovered the tragic error of its conduct, but held on for several years with a dogged resistance unworthy of the great interests involved, zigzagging between Munich and glimpses of a great day, until the defenses of the Empire literally began to crumble under the savage and inhuman blows of Teutonic aggression. It even hesitated about retirement after a decisive vote in Parliament, but finally was forced into resignation by the rising indignation and protest of the English people. That chapter of tragic muddling through is closed. A new, resolute Government from now on directs the struggle against a Germany once more on the warpath. Mr. Churchill—bold, resourceful, determined, clearheaded—is a welcome relief. Standing with him are other men like Mr. Amery, Mr. Morrison, Mr. Eden and Mr. Duff Cooper, who may be relied upon, in war or peace, to stand for policies of a nobler England.

The radical change in the British Government included the retirement of Mr. Malcolm MacDonald and the appointment of Lord Lloyd as Colonial Secretary. This is a decided change for the better.

A word in passing about Mr. MacDonald. He came into office a friend of the Jewish cause, and left it after he had pursued a course that did infinite harm to the Jewish position in Palestine. In the last few years he seemed to be definitely an opponent of the Jewish National Home, determined to liquidate the Balfour Declaration and the Mandate. He succeeded in alienating both Jews and Arabs by his devious behavior. He was led into a policy that brought about the shameless violation of the implications of the Mandate, and finally was responsible for the introduction of an Administration that ruled Palestine without law and without justice, governed almost exclusively by interests entirely foreign

* *The New Palestine*, May 17, 1940.

to the purposes of the Mandate. He flouted the authority of the League of Nations, and without the shadow of a legal right proceeded to enforce the policy of his White Paper which he had assured Parliament he would not do until the League had passed upon it. The conduct of his office was such as to add heavily to the burden of the Chamberlain Government, damaging its reputation and making its tasks more difficult. He was a man of mediocre talent, adroit in speech, cunning and clever, but devoid of political integrity. His place should have been vacated a long time ago.

Of Lord Lloyd it may be said that he is first of all a frank, clear-spoken man. There is no shiftiness or circumlocution in his action or manner of speech. Should he be an opponent, he would make it clear without hesitation or ambiguity. When he served as High Commissioner of Egypt (1925–29), it was said that he was definitely pro-Arab in his attitude toward Palestine problems, but in the course of recent years he has indicated that his mind is open to the consideration of plans that would enable England to fulfill its pledges to the Jewish people and, at the same time, deal justly with the Arabs. He recognizes a dual obligation, but would be the last man to favor the annulment of the one in order to fulfill the other. He sees a Palestine in which Trans-Jordan must be included, in order to enable the Mandatory Government to satisfy the national ambitions of both Jews and Arabs.

Lord Lloyd has represented his Government in Turkey and Persia, as well as in Egypt, and he saw service in the World War at Gallipoli, in Mesopotamia and the Hedjaz. He speaks Arabic and Turkish, and is deeply grounded in the problems of the Near East. It is impossible to foretell what policy he will pursue in connection with Palestine, but one thing is certain: The miserable, half-hearted, double-crossing methods of the MacDonald regime will no longer prevail in the government of Palestine. There is further reassurance in the fact that in the cabinet of Mr. Churchill there are many forthright friends of the Zionist cause and that the new Prime Minister himself is a resolute man who has definite and comprehensive views about a Palestine in which the Jewish people are to play an important part.

The circumstance that served to bring about the fall of the Chamberlain Government was not the disastrous retreat in Norway. It was the lightning invasion of Holland and Belgium by the Nazi hordes. Here was revealed the savage features of the so-called Nazi revolution, undecorated by masks, lies and hypocrisies. The invasion of Holland was an objective in and for itself, but it is to prepare the way for that attack upon England which was the sinister purpose of Hitler even when discussing "peace in our day" with Chamberlain at Munich. The reckless air attacks, the parachutists descending upon the peaceful streets of Holland with machine guns, the bombardment from the air of the unprotected cities of Belgium—served to arouse in every city and hamlet in the United States and the world over, memories of the awful days of the World War, more intense, more destructive, more insane than in the previous era of world disorder. The furious onslaught on these neutral states corroborated the impression of German war guilt in 1914. Here was being repeated, twenty-six years later, the same brutal aggression, on the same soil, with the same strategic purposes (but with death coming from the air) as was begun on that fateful day in August 1914. It seemed as if the German dead of the World War had risen from their graves grimly determined to finish the tasks they were unable to achieve in their previous incarnation.

So far as we Jews are concerned, there is one difference here. In 1914, Jews were in the armies on all fronts, fighting under the flags of the states in which they were citizens—at least equal in the right to bear arms. In 1940, all the Jews of these lands are now merely victims of the war, and wherever the black flag of Hitler is raised, there Jews have lost all their rights and are being treated with the mercy and compassion accorded by wild Indians to their captives. Whatever may happen to others who lose in the war—the Poles, the Danes, the Norsemen, the Dutch, the Belgians—Jews for the time being are the debris of war, to be removed as speedily as possible, entitled to none of the considerations of humanity. It is an hour of tragedy unrelieved for all Jews caught in the vise of Nazi barbarism. And the field occupied by the destroyers of civilization may yet be extended before the Nazi fury will be broken on the resistant arms of the Allies.

The center of our special concern, naturally, is the Jewish National Home. It is the hope around which all of Jewish life in distress now revolves, drawn more closely and intimately to it in these days of adversity than in the days of comparative peace and security. It is still calm in the Mediterranean. The Dictator of Italy has not yet decided to abandon the role of "neutral" and to enter the war on the side of his partner in aggression. Although his minions make demonstrations as he dictates, to impress both friend and foe, he remains undecided.

Palestine continues to receive new settlers every week, and the economic structure of the haven of refuge is strained to the limit by the task of integrating the newcomers in the normal life of the community. There is abundance of activity due to the growth of the military encampment, but there is anxiety and apprehension as preparations are being made for the inevitable defenses that will be required once the fury of Nazi and Fascist violence bursts over the land. Whenever the storm breaks, today or tomorrow, it will find a land prepared and resolute, but it will need all the support we can humanly give the courageous defenders of our Homeland to enable them to maintain their positions.

It would be confirmation of our hopes in the new Government of England, and would be regarded as both gesture and deed of high significance, if a way should now be found—while the seas are still calm—for bringing the thousands of Jewish victims of the war to the cities and farms of Palestine, disregarding the worthless policy of immigration schedules. *The Jewish National Home should be regarded by the Mandatory Government as the natural and inevitable Sanctuary for the thousands of Jews who are fleeing from persecution and war.* Every effort should be made to bring them there. The Jews in flight can as well be concentrated in the Jewish National Home as in any part of Europe. Both as workers and as armed soldiers, the refugees can become of great value in strengthening the war equipment of the Allies on the Eastern front. The act of opening the gates of Palestine to Jews in flight would serve immediately to raise the prestige of the new English Government in the eyes of both Jews and neutral sympathizers the world over.

What is left for us to do is to watch and wait, to give support to the building of the National Home to the extent of our capacity, and to be prepared for any eventuality, confident in our faith that ultimately the arbitrament of war will result in the victory of the cause for which the Allies are fighting.

APPEASEMENT IS UNTHINKABLE*

With the world turning violent somersaults—all news nowadays is incredible, fantastic. But the report from Haifa that 1771 Jewish refugees have been denied sanctuary in Palestine, and are to be deported to an island near Martinique, takes the palm for political absurdity. A war to prevent the domination of the world by Nazi Germany—millions

* *The Jewish Day,* November 27, 1940.

of Jews in Europe the victims of that war, seeking refuge on the territory of a belligerent power; and when they find their way, after cruel suffering, to the land promised to the Jewish people by the chief adversary of Hitler, the English representative in Palestine invokes rules and regulations which were born in the last miserable days of appeasement to prevent their landing!

(The intention was frustrated, however, by an "act of God." An explosion in the engine-room of the steamer hurled all the refugees into the sea. About 25 were killed and several hundred were wounded. Hundreds of them eluded capture in the confusion of the sinking of the ship. Palcor reports that 1592 have been transferred to detention camps. This accident, however, does not alter the fact that it was the intention of the High Commissioner to deport all these "illegal" immigrants.)

The High Commissioner does not seem to know that Chamberlain and appeasement are dead, and that Churchill and repudiation of Munich are carrying on the defense of England.

It is obvious that there is a clear-cut, radical discrepancy in policy between the administration in Palestine and the Government in London. The line will have to be straightened out. Official stupidity in the Near East sticks out like a sore thumb in contradiction of the policies of the Empire. Mr. Churchill is struggling against great odds to create through the growing defense of England a program based on foundations of justice, freedom and democracy; to begin to piece together a new world and to forget Chamberlain and his disastrous management.

But the voices of the near past have not all been silenced. In Bombay, in Jerusalem, even in London they are still heard. The High Commissioner in Jerusalem does not know the changes that have been wrought in London. He does not appreciate the new spirit of the reborn England which now, relentless in defense, is determined to become relentless in attack. The High Commissioner is isolated in Jerusalem, nursing the fragments of the old order, and is guided by the code which the Battle for Britain is smashing to a pulp. He relies upon the feeble, obsolete words of Malcolm MacDonald—the last White Paper of June, 1939—the old clichés and the old prejudices. He will probably stick to the rules and regulations until the voice of Mr. Churchill penetrates his ears, when he will realize that appeasement is as dead as a doornail so far as England is concerned.

That the rigid High Commissioner is unaware of the "new line" was shown not long ago when the Jews of Palestine registered to the number of 136,000 for military defense service. They wanted to serve in a Jewish army, under British officers. But the High Commissioner could not conceive how he could accept a Jewish division unless it was balanced by an Arab division. Men were needed for defense. The Jews offered their service, but to take them would disturb the established policy. The High Commissioner met the dilemma by deciding to take as many Jews in as many divisions as would balance the enlistment of Arabs. But the Arabs are not keen to help England. The Arabs are not keen about serving in an English army. Very few of them came forward to serve. The Jews of Palestine, on the contrary, offered all kinds of military service. They outnumbered the Arabs ten to one. There is no question of their loyalty; not even the High Commissioner would question it. There is every reason to doubt the loyalty of the Arabs of Palestine. But the High Commissioner was interested in maintaining "administrative policy" and subordinated the interests of the war to that policy. The White Paper of June, 1939, stands higher than the British flag. In the end, when the High Commissioner saw that his formula of fifty-fifty did not serve, he found a way to have Jews enlist in special services, leaving out of consideration the numerical support of the Arabs.

It is a narrow, pettifogging point of view to assume that in the present state of world affairs, immigration can be regulated by fixed law of the old order. All humane countries are now engaged in finding ways to circumvent the "law" in the interests of humanity. This has been done in a number of South American republics. This was done by France before France fell. This was done by England time and again in order to mitigate the cruelties and inhumanities practiced in this war upon civilian populations. The High Commissioner of the mandated territory of Palestine wishes to keep Palestine—the Jewish National Home—isolated from humanitarian sympathy and non-cooperative especially with regard to Jewish refugees.

But all Jewish wanderers today are the direct victims of the war which the German Nazis are urging against the Jewish people, as well as against the Western democracies. The Jewish wanderers coming to Palestine are not immigrants "moving in." They are refugees driven to find sanctuary; a haven of security. Any port is a lawful port of entry in storm and gale. How much more so are they entitled to enter a port of one of the combatants in the war of which these refugees are the victims? And again, how much more so in the port of a belligerent which in time of peace had engaged itself to utilize Palestine for the building of their National Home?

There may be difficulties in allowing these refugees free entry and freedom of movement in Palestine, in view of the preparations that are being made for active warfare. It is said that among the refugees on the two ships that have been turned back are spies planted by the German Gestapo. But this difficulty could be met by internment. All 1771 could be interned. What is reprehensible in the whole proceeding is the fact that at this time, when all Jewish sympathies are being poured out in favor of the cause for which England is fighting, an English Administration should turn away Jewish war refugees from the doors of the Jewish National Home. If as much ingenuity was spent by the High Commissioner in finding a way to do the humane and right thing as he devotes to finding ways of avoidance, England would not have to suffer the shame of Haifa, in London proclaiming that it is fighting for justice and democracy, and acting in Palestine as if the spirits of Chamberlain and Malcolm MacDonald still controlled the policies of England.

The statement issued from Jerusalem by the Palestine Administration, in explanation of its inhuman action, is not convincing. It is reminiscent of the form of diplomatic evasion of prewar days. It is "well-known to the law of the land" that illegal immigration is prohibited. That would seem to suffice as an explanation. But then it is added that "it would be a menace to British interests in the Middle East." But the admission of legal immigrants also would be a menace to British interest, and all Jewish immigration should be stopped. There are still a few thousand immigrants with legal certificates who have a right to be admitted. But it is recognized that this press explanation is a subterfuge. It is the reiteration of the old "line." It is the echo of the double-crossing methods of prewar times.

For the war has driven England to change many of its well-known laws and practices. The difference between Chamberlain and Churchill is to be found in the fact that Churchill is determined that habit and prejudice and formality shall not be allowed to sabotage the progress of the defensive war. Necessity knows no law, and necessity does not recognize rules and regulations that are born out of the boredom of civil servants. England's success in defense is due to the courageous overriding by Mr. Churchill of the red tape and the tail-chasing practices of a civil service protesting its tenure and security. The new Government in London has been bold enough to flout tradition. It has overhauled the army and substituted youth for the old-type generals of the past day. The clumsy machine of government has been overhauled, and antiquated regulations have been thrown into the wastebasket. Malcolm MacDonald strained legal casuistry to the breaking point in order to dress up his last line of policy and to break the Mandate. What came of it, so far as Palestine is concerned, was of no substantial importance in the life of the population. The last line of policy did not work. English interests have not been protected in the Near East. The sanctity of the law was not furthered in the eyes of the Arabs. The High Commissioner of Palestine seems to forget that something higher than law has come into the English world. It is the use of that "higher" law that has made possible the regeneration of the youth of England and has given vigor, intelligence and self-sacrificing zeal to all of England in fighting against the poisonous advance of the enemy of democracy and justice. With the world in flames, with refugees seeking havens of security wherever they may be found, with Jews, and not Arabs, coming forward in loyalty and with determination to the aid of England, the discredited laws of Malcolm MacDonald cannot be made helpful in the Near Eastern situation where England must build up a formidable military machine.

The cause England is fighting for is the cause for which Jews the world over are prepared to make sacrifices. They recognize in that cause their own cause. All Jews are involved in the war against Hitler. Appeasement is unthinkable among Jews.

But we would be unworthy of the respect of the civilized world—the world of justice and democracy—if, for whatever reason of tact, we overlooked the insult to our prestige and the derogation of our position as allies in the war, which is involved in the treatment of Jewish war victims as if they were the wastage of the world, as is implied in the statement presumptuously issued by the Palestine Administration in the name of "His Majesty's Government."

CIVIL WAR IN PALESTINE

Within Palestine a state of virtual civil war prevails. The Mandatory Power is acting the part of Controller and Inspirer of the Peace. As once in Ireland, the Government has enacted martial law and is ruthlessly enforcing it. Habeas corpus has been suspended; arrests and detentions without trial are the order of the day; military courts are in constant session. On the other side, acts of political defiance occur daily; police stations are attacked; railway lines are blown up.

But with all that, the bulk of the population is anxious for peace. The common man, whether Jew or Arab, does not want any conflagration. The Jewish community as a whole condemns terrorist crimes. This attitude is also shared by Haganah, the responsible self-defense organization of the Jewish community, built up during the period of the prewar Arab attacks on Jewish life and property.

What factors have produced this singular situation? The Jews of Palestine are essentially a peaceable, constructive and orderly community. Their record of non-violence is unique in the history of colonization. During the three years of the prewar disturbances when, day after day, their settlements were being attacked, their homes set on fire, women and children kidnapped and travellers on the road assassinated in cold blood, they maintained strict self-discipline and abstained from retaliation. It was the outcome of those riots, the victory of the Arab terrorists as embodied in the British White Paper of May, 1939, which first injected into that peaceful community of workers and peasants the dangerous conviction that violence pays. As a result of three years of murder and arson, the Arab extremists had gained their aim: Jewish immigration had been reduced to a small trickle and was to come to an end permanently after five years; Jewish land settlement was limited to a narrow strip of the country, 1/20 of the total area; Palestine under the dispensation of the White Paper was within a few years to become an independent state governed by the Arab majority, to whose tender mercies the Jewish National Home was to be delivered.

A wave of fierce resentment passed through the Jewish community. Force had triumphed. Had not the time come, asked young and fiery spirits, for Jews too to resort to violence? Had not experience shown that the peaceable methods of the Jewish Agency, the memoranda to the Government, the representations in London, the appeal to reason and to Britain's pledged word had utterly failed? Moreover, what remained to be lost? Would it not be better to challenge the White Paper regime immediately, rather than await slow strangulation by its ruthless application?

It was along these lines that minds had begun to work when the war broke out. But the war completely changed the situation. Jews felt that the fight against Hitler took precedence over everything else. That was the line taken by the Jewish Agency and it was approved by the greater part of the community. Jews by the thousands volunteered for service in the British forces. They demanded recognition of their effort on a national basis. This was refused. It was only when the campaign in North Africa assumed serious proportions and there was urgent need for mobilizing skilled personnel on the spot that, step by step, Jewish units were formed. A national flag was denied to them. At the same time the Jewish Agency succeeded in gearing Jewish propaganda and industry to the war effort. Under their guidance, food was grown and canned for the British armies fighting in North Africa, while the young industries of Palestine, established during the preceding decade without any Government help, undertook the repair job of the British military machine in North Africa. It was by these efforts that the Jewish Agency succeeded in canalizing the pent-up bitterness of the prewar years into the constructive channel of the struggle against Hitler. The White Paper was not forgotten, but the war effort was prosecuted as though there were no White Paper.

Then came the terrible news of the mass murder of the Jews in Europe. It produced fierce, frantic bitterness. Had it not been for the Palestine White Paper, Jews felt, how many of the parents, brothers and sisters and young children that were being gassed and burned in Poland might have been saved and brought over to Palestine? The tragic episodes of the refugee boats that came from Europe and were denied access to Palestine added oil to the fire. These boats, unseaworthy craft, each carrying a few hundred fugitives from the Nazi terror, were seized by British control vessels, brought into Haifa and their passengers sent into exile to far-off Mauritius where hundreds died from tropical diseases. Another refugee boat, the Struma, reached Istanbul, only to be refused admission to Palestine by the British Government. The boat was turned back by the Turks and went down in a storm in the Sea of Marmara with all hands lost save one.

It was at that time and under these circumstances that the first acts of Jewish violence occurred in Palestine. They were organized by a small group of fanatics—the so-called Stern Group; the bulk of the community and all the Jewish public bodies condemned them from the depth of their hearts. It was not, as the British were wont to declare, mere lip service. The Jews were deeply convinced that this was the wrong way. They fully realized the dangers, moral as well as political, inherent in that course. The Jewish Agency continued its efforts to gain national recognition for the Jewish war effort, young men continued to flock to the British colors and in the end the Jewish war effort received national recognition through the creation of the Jewish Brigade Group which fought in the final stages of the war on the Italian front.

But those who believed in resorting to force were not deflected from their course. Step by step the two terrorist groups, the Irgun Zvai Leumi and the Stern Group, built up their organizations. In November, 1944, the latter struck its first blow. Lord Moyne, the British Minister for the Middle East, resident in Cairo, who was regarded as responsible for the iniquities of the White Paper, and in particular for turning back the Jewish refugee boats, was assassinated in Cairo.

A wave of fierce resentment against the misguided fanatics passed through the Jewish community. It was felt that a fatal blow had been struck at the moral foundations of Jewish Palestine, that its good name had been besmirched. The eyes of the Jewish community were more than ever centered on Europe, where the Jewish Brigade Group was now taking active part in the final campaign in Northern Italy, where Jewish refugees were every day being freed by the advancing Allied armies and where the Jewish troops were taking a more active part in helping the Jewish survivors of the Nazi terror. As reports came in, the actuality of the Jewish position in Europe became more and more clear. It turned out that about one and one half million had survived the great slaughter. Their position was appalling. Thousands were dying day after day, even after help had been brought to them. Their bodies had suffered so much that even liberation could not bring them new life.

No issue has so deeply affected the emotions and the attitude of the Jewish community in Palestine as the fate of these survivors. If nothing could be done during the years of the Nazi terror to rescue them, if the Palestine White Paper had prevented any significant number from being brought over to the Jewish National Home, surely now that the war was over, the old specious arguments against their admission would no longer prevail; quick action, so it was hoped, would be taken to bring the survivors from the area of the dread concentration camps and give them the chance of a new life among their kith and kin in Palestine. There were few families in Palestine that had not lost close relatives in the great holocaust. There were a good many who had relatives among the survivors. The offices of the Jewish Agency were besieged day after day by thousands clamoring for certificates. *But the British Government remained adamant.* The White Paper stood and its provisions were ruthlessly applied. A new argument was put forward in defense of that iniquitous policy. The war with Japan was not over, it was said, and nothing must be done to disturb the Middle East, which was a vital line of communications to the Far East. The war with Japan came to an end much more quickly than anyone had foreseen, yet there was no change. The White Paper still held.

Then came the elections in England. The Jews were advised that they must await the results, for the Government in power could not, at such a moment, decide on new policies. The elections were held. The results were announced. It turned out that the party which had all along given

strong support to the Zionist cause had won an overwhelming victory
and was for the next five years to control the Government of England.
Expectations ran high. It is well known that the Arab States had, in
those weeks, reached the conclusion that nothing further was to be
gained from Great Britain as regards Palestine, seeing that the new
Government was so deeply committed to the support of the Jewish
National Home policy, and that the Arab States should extract concessions from Great Britain in other spheres. But gradually reports became
current both in London and in Palestine that the Labor Government did
not regard itself bound by the pledges of the Labor Party and that the
permanent officials of the Foreign and Colonial Offices would continue
to maintain control under the new Government, and would pursue the
old policies. It was not long before these apprehensions were confirmed
officially. Mr. Bevin's statement on Palestine, delivered at the beginning
of November, was perhaps the greatest shock that Zionism had experienced since the Mandatory regime was introduced in Palestine. It
showed that the new Government had thrown to the winds the traditional
pro-Zionist policy of British Labor and had accepted and even exceeded
the anti-Zionist policies of its predecessors. The Bevin statement went
beyond the White Paper. It denied categorically that Palestine offered a
solution of the Jewish problem. It officially endorsed assimilation and
dispersal of the Jews as a solution of the Jewish problem. This was
soberly stated after assimilation had been shown up as never before,
during the Hitler regime, as a hollow mockery.

It was fantastic and cruel beyond words for the British Government to
deprive the Jews of their only hope of national salvation and to tell them
that their future lay in renewed dispersal all over Europe, where anti-
Semitism was now more rampant than ever before. Bevin's statement
broke the camel's back. Jews, in particular younger Jews, came to see
that there was no reliance on Great Britain whether its Government was
of a Conservative or of Labor complexion. Dismay seized the community. In that atmosphere of despair and utter disillusionment, the
extremists in the Jewish camp had little difficulty in undermining the authority of Zionist bodies and winning followers for their desperate course.

Such is the background of the present acts of Jewish violence in
Palestine. The situation has deteriorated from month to month. The
arrest of the Jewish national leaders, the search by British Forces for
arms in the Jewish settlements—arms bitterly needed for their defense
against Arab attack—and finally the sending back of the refugee boats
and the internment of the refugees in Cyprus, have created an appalling

situation. Jewish leadership, however bitter it may feel about the recent acts of terrorist violence, can do little to stop the drift toward extremism as long as the British Government continues along its desperate path of disentangling itself from its commitments to the Jewish people.

THE PRESENT POLITICAL SCENE*

The Labor Party took over the Government of the British Empire last August. It was several months after the collapse of Hitler and just about the time the Japanese surrendered. An international Zionist conference was then being held in London. The Labor Party did not expect the overwhelming vote it received and was engaged in distributing the important offices hurriedly. Mr. Attlee became Prime Minister; Mr. Bevin, the Foreign Secretary; George Hall took over the Office of Colonial Secretary, with Mr. Greech-Jones as Undersecretary. Many of the offices were still vacant when Zionist representatives tried to get an expression of the views from the new Government as to the retention of the White Paper of 1939, which the Labor Party had vehemently rejected at its spring convention, and which had been made an issue in the political campaign.

The Government pleaded with the Zionists to give them a little time and not to press for an immediate decision. As the Zionists knew, the Labor Party was not committed to Zionism in merely a formal way. Many of its leaders were active participants in Zionist propaganda. Many of its leaders were friends of long standing. A majority of the Zionists therefore felt that it would be wiser to forego an immediate expression of views in order not to embarrass the new leaders of the British Government. What good would it do to make the hard road of the friends of many years harder still?

It was never suspected at that time that the withdrawal of pressure would be used by the Labor Government to maneuver itself into a better position to become the active instrument of deep-rooted, malevolent anti-Zionist policy in Palestine; to become the protagonist, instead of the opponent, of the White Paper of 1939; to become the spokesman in England of an anti-Zionist and even an anti-Jewish policy.

That is what the British Government is today.

---

* *Address to Bnai Zion Convention,* June 22, 1946. Published in *Bnai Zion Voice,* June, 1946.

What was masked and hidden at the beginning by smooth talk, by legalistic quibble, by procedural evasions, has become today an obviously hostile situation.

While the British Empire sits as a member of the United Nations, one of the Big Five, presumably cooperating in making order out of a disorderly world; while it is pretending to be the arbiter in a Jewish-Arab controversy in Palestine, it is in fact at this moment engaged in laying the foundations of a war in Palestine against the Jewish people. It is not defending Jewish interests. It is making war for the protection of its own interests. It is a selfish war of aggression; not open and above board, but pretending to have other objects.

There are, according to some reports, over 100,000 British soldiers encamped in Palestine. It is a complete army, with planes, with naval protection, with tanks, with all the essential equipment for an army prepared to march into battle. Its objective, where it is going to, is not mentioned. It pretends that the Jews are "rebels" and calls the defense of their rights "terrorism." The Mandatory Government has for all practical purposes established a regime of martial law, making military order superior to civil procedure. Exercising the right of search, penalizing whole villages, abolishing due process of law, it makes the law as it goes along the road to achieve its imperial purposes.

Its main concern seems to be not the development of peace, but the defense of the White Paper of 1939. It is concerned with keeping Jews out. It is concerned with keeping all goods, except English goods, out. It is concerned with making the White Paper whatever the White Paper should be to protect its own shaking interests. It has placed Palestine in a sort of "no man's land" where no law prevails, except the law of the General and the High Commissioner. In the United Nations the British representative speaks of peace and law and order, of justice and agreements, but in Palestine all these things have been banished.

It is in the light of this background that the foreign policy conducted by Mr. Bevin must be regarded. In Palestine it is producing a hatred and indignation which has transformed a friendly Jewish people into a people compelled to take up arms to defend its rights.

It would be unworthy of this assembly of Zionists if we did not associate ourselves without any restraint or hesitation with the Jewish resistance movement in Palestine. It is that resistance movement which gives dignity and spiritual significance to what the Jewish people have built in Palestine. They are not prepared to give their lives merely for the sake of their own comfort, of their own freedom, of their own welfare. They are prepared to give their lives for the right of those who are stateless or homeless, wherever they may be, and who need the Homeland which they have prepared for them. We applaud the organized Jewish resistance movement and greet with gratitude their defense of Jewish rights in Palestine.

It is this Jewish resistance, this movement for Jewish freedom, which may have provoked the extraordinary behavior of Mr. Bevin, the British Foreign Minister. He has a difficult task to perform. It is he who is called upon to defend the indefensible. It is he who is called upon to make plausible that which is incredible as a matter of justice and fairness. It is he who is called upon to reconcile untruths that cannot be reconciled. Jewish resistance is a challenge which he is unable to meet fairly in rational discussion. It causes his blood to boil, his anger to burn, his speech to become incoherent.

That Government which started last August and pleaded for time to consider plans and decisions, has made any number of decisions during the course of the year. There was not one promise that was kept—not only promises made to the Jewish people, but assurances given to the American Government. The appeal of President Truman for the admission of 100,000 Jews into Palestine without delay, was met with a delaying tactic calling for the appointment of a Joint Anglo-American Committee. The promise that was made by the Foreign Minister that a unanimous report of that Committee would be accepted by the British Government, was rejected by the promisor when the unanimous report was issued. The issuing of the Anglo-American Committee report was met by the proposal to have the matter considered once again by representatives of governments, and then while the question of another conjoint committee on a lower level was being considered, Mr. Bevin took the occasion of a vacation at Bournemouth, where the Labor Party was meeting, to violate all promises made and to recreate a new British policy in a blaze of enthusiastic oratory.

This great oration of Mr. Bevin has disturbed international affairs. It is not that Mr. Bevin's speech is vulgar and disregards facts and indulges in low-bred prejudices and is unworthy of the technique of members of the British Cabinet. His speech has not created a tempest because of etiquette. It is because that speech reveals the adoption by a Foreign Minister of the British Empire of a policy based upon deliberate political lying as the way to conduct international affairs.

The British Empire has suffered many blows. It lost a great deal in the First World War. It lost a great deal more in the Second World

War. It has many redeeming features which must go to its credit in both wars. But in the field of international relations the British Empire has suffered no greater blow than that which was delivered by its Foreign Secretary, Mr. Bevin. He has helped to reduce the England of Balfour to the stature of a Balkan state.

PALESTINE AS HAVEN

PALESTINE AS SALVATION*

It is now five years since Dr. Weizmann last visited the United States. With great patience and devotion he had completed the task of drawing into the responsibilities of the Jewish Agency that influential group of American friends of the Palestine enterprise, then led by Louis Marshall. He returned to London, and the summer of 1929 saw the formal launching of the extended Jewish Agency at Zurich, under the most promising auspices, with program enlarged and budgets increased.

Almost instantly the clear sky was overclouded by a succession of disasters. The death of Louis Marshall shortly after the adjournment of the Council of the Jewish Agency, bereft the Jewish people of one of their most distinguished and capable leaders. The outbreak of Arab violence a few weeks thereafter dislocated the constructive plans of the Jewish Agency and threw the Zionist world into turmoil and confusion. The various acts of evasion and repudiation by the Mandatory Government aroused the entire Jewish world to protest and denunciation, controversy and clamor, which paralyzed creative effort and confused thought and plan. The Shaw investigation, the Passfield White Paper, the letter of Prime Minister MacDonald to Dr. Weizmann (calculated to calm the troubled waters, which were not calmed) are the headings of the chapters of disappointment and blockade of progress which characterized those years.

The Jewish communities in lands of dispersion suffered similar concussions and disappointments, which had even more far-reaching effects. The universal economic depression, finally reaching out to the United States, caused the undermining of the institutions of Jewish

---

* Address as Chairman of United Palestine Appeal at Reception for Dr. Chaim Weizmann, June 28, 1933.

life, and turned attention to local and individual difficulties, excluding, to a very large extent, consideration of the larger problems of the Jewish people. An epidemic of anti-Semitism—the by-product of political confusion and material hunger, the postwar convulsions of organized society—progressively seized all of Eastern Europe and reached its tragic climax in the ruthless form of anti-Semitic barbarism now on exhibition in the German Reich.

Once more the whole problem of the anomalous position of the Jewish people within the structures of organized nationalities clamors for international attention. A condition that permits, without intervention or check, exclusion of large segments of its native-born citizens from the economic life of any people, forces their emigration and flight without even providing facilities for exodus; creates a forced congestion of aliens in various lands that are grappling with their own economic and political problems; and, as in the case of Germany, permits the dissemination of intolerance, hate and prejudice against a whole people throughout the world by the use of modern methods of communication—is not the concern of any one nation but, beyond the shadow of a doubt, is a matter which demands the attention of such associations or alliances of nations as are interested in preserving international peace and re-establishing economic prosperity in the world.

At the Peace Conference, in that time which now seems distant and dim, two political advantages were gained by the Jewish people. American Jewry, united in the delegation sent to Versailles by the American Jewish Congress, played an important part in securing the insertion in the peace treaties of minority group rights, which were made applicable to the Jewish people. Realizing the grave international problems involved in the fact that in no place in the world have the Jewish people an inalienable right to establish themselves as a people and to give free expression to their own ideals and culture, the allied nations gave their sanction to the Balfour Declaration, and subsequently, through the League of Nations, gave a mandate to Great Britain to cooperate with the Jewish people in the establishment of their National Home in Palestine.

The nations who were responsible for the granting of these minority rights as affecting the Jewish people, and who gave recognition to the historic right of the Jewish people to establish their National Home in Palestine, cannot now fail to consider the grave situation that has arisen within recent years and which requires their united intervention. If the grind of race prejudice, if the force of economic discrimination plays havoc with justice and does massive injury to Jews not only in one land but in many lands, if it creates problems not only for one nation but for many nations, the wrongs done must find remedy and reparation, if it is intented that there be such a thing as international justice in the world.

In mentioning incidents affecting our status in Palestine, I have not referred to one important item. The failure of the Mandatory Government to support the peaceful, constructive plans and the moderate views of Dr. Weizmann with effective aid, led to his retirement from the Presidency of the Jewish Agency. In this time of stress and change, his absence from the official leadership of the Jewish Agency is a loss of great magnitude. Nevertheless, his absence from the Presidency has not in the slightest restrained him from taking a leading part in Zionist activities. He has been a faithful servant of the Keren Hayesod, and was responsible for the great success achieved in South Africa. He has given his personal cooperation to the Executive of the Jewish Agency in many political matters of outstanding importance. Although Dr. Weizmann has come to the United States to be the guest of honor at Jewish Day in Chicago, he intends to use his presence in the United States to further plans which he carries with him, approved by the Executive of the Jewish Agency, which are of the greatest importance in the solution of the problem of the future of the Jews of Germany. It is to be hoped that these plans will be given wholehearted support by all groups and elements in American Jewry. The time has come for us to consider not the usual makeshift program, the hand-to-mouth method in dealing with serious Jewish questions, but to tackle the problem with plan and continuous consecration to the end that out of the misery imposed upon us, there shall come something of permanent value that may serve in part to help in the emancipation of the Jewish people from the continuing thraldom of the Galut. What was good enough ten years ago may be invalid in the new world which has been created since the World War. The facts and circumstances of Jewish life, the experiences of the past decade, must be taken into account. It would be fatal to proceed as if nothing new had happened, and as if all the old slogans and methods still had power, although all of Jewish life stands in contradiction to such slogans and methods.

Unlike other periods in 1914, in 1918 and in 1929, today Palestine looms as a tangible, practical and immediate factor of considerable dimensions in any plan that may be devised that has to do with the salvation of the oppressed among the Jewish people, and especially of the Jews of Germany.

In this situation of tremendous unrest and divergence of opinion, many will agree that Dr. Weizmann is destined to play an important part. In every stage of the development of the Zionist movement since 1914, his tact, his good sense, his ability to adjust differences and maintain continuity of policy within a prescribed course, his talent for retaining the kernel of an idea while throwing away the shell, his ability to win men and harness them to the proposed action, have been of the greatest historic value and represent his unique contribution to our great cause. It was due to his leadership that within the form of the extended Jewish Agency there were joined together forces of varying ideas in support of one constructive program. The experiences of the past few years have given that union a jolt and there are many fractures in the edifice, vacancies have to be filled, and much will have to be done to rehabilitate that which was created in Zurich in 1929. A great deal of passion and zeal was expended, controversy fought out, leadership put in jeopardy, in order to establish a united Jewry behind the work of upbuilding in Palestine. Our partners should not let the union fail in fairness to themselves and those in the Zionist leadership who fought for it.

It is a source of personal satisfaction to a large group of American Zionists that Dr. Weizmann is once more actively engaged in the leadership of our affairs.

The times are trying; the situation is perilous; parties and factions are rampant in controversy. What is needed is a union of constructive leadership to bring order out of our tangled affairs; that out of the tragic circumstances, it may be made possible that Jewish life be strengthened, the National Home in Palestine extended, and Jewish honor and dignity in the world maintained.

LOOKING FAR WHEN ZION IS NEAR*

All the days of the Zionist movement it has been dogged by attempts to divert Jews away from thoughts of Palestine by proposing alternative territories. When the movement was young, these diversions intruded

---

* *The New Palestine*, October 18, 1935.

even into the councils of the Zionist Organization—there were El Arish and Uganda. The open doors of many lands beckoned at that time, and Zionism had to content itself with an appeal to sentiment and to the ideals of Jewish life. Zionism was referred to as the fulfillment of an age-long dream. You had to be an unworldly sentimentalist to be a Zionist.

But times have changed. The boot is on the other foot. All the open doors have been slammed shut and tight. Palestine has moved out of the fog of dream and sentiment. It is now the only open door—for an immigration that grows from 40,000 to 60,000 per year—for as many as 100,000 per year for some years to come, if we only fix our minds upon it. It is the only land both available and accessible. It is next door to the barbarian lands that are now forcing the exodus. It is a land of growing economic opportunity. It enjoys prosperity when the whole world is struggling with an unparalleled economic depression. It is a field of comparative peace surrounded by a growing area of war.

And just as in olden times, so in this day of grace, when Palestine and Zionism have conquered not only the field of reality but also the field of immediate practicality, the same unrepentant stubborn elements, nursing old grudges, again rise to battle against what seems inevitable destiny, and bob up once more with a varied assortment of territorial plans.

They seem to be frantic about it. Some land must be found, and that, soon. They leap over oceans and continents, find faraway places scarcely known to civilization, and rush them up for consideration by the "practical" men in Israel, who are impractical only when they are called upon to deal with matters of Jewish life. The purpose is to relegate Palestine to the background.

There is a place called Ecuador in South America. You could not get further away from Palestine than Ecuador. It is over six thousand miles from Warsaw. A step beyond and you fall off the rim of the globe. Nobody knows what it is, whether it is actually available, how much money would be required, do the people over there want Jews, could you get Jews to go there? In spite of absence of information, Ecuador is projected with superb impudence as a counter-proposition to the bustling and thriving realities of Palestine.

Letters are being circulated about Birobidzhan. Articles about it are being inspired in the press. It is becoming a two-faced symbol, one face turned toward Communism and the other toward high-class Jewish philanthropy. Birobidzhan is over 3,000 miles away from Moscow; about 4,000 miles away from Warsaw. It has been variously described; some declare it can be developed and provide a living for thousands of people; others claim that it is malarious and unfit for habitation. Everybody seems to be agreed that to colonize it will require the investment of millions of dollars.

At first Birobidzhan was projected as a form of salvation for Russian Jews. It was to be used for Jews of Russia dissatisfied with work in the cities, who wanted to establish themselves in an agricultural autonomous state. That idea has collapsed. All citizens in the Soviet Union are equal, and there is no reason why the Jews should voluntarily segregate themselves in such a forsaken place as Birobidzhan. It is now said that the Soviet Government may be willing to consider placing this land at the disposal of Jewish refugees from other lands—from Germany or Poland. The economic system imposed upon all Russians by the Soviet Government will also prevail in Birobidzhan. The New Friends of this territory argue, however, that Birobidzhan would be a good place for refugees from Germany or Poland. It is assumed that the Jews of Germany, advocates of assimilation for many generations, are anxious to establish a Jewish autonomous state, if possible, even in Soviet Russia. The best feature of Birobidzhan seems to be that it is close to the Chinese frontier.

For this fantastic project those who regard Palestine as poison are expected to make many sacrifices, and already a movement is on foot, committees are being formed, articles are being written in the press, leading philanthropists are beginning to issue interviews, and another counter-movement against Palestine is in the process of being organized.

It will probably take at least ten years for Birobidzhan to begin to look like an inhabited place. It will take years of experience and the investment of millions of dollars to make it capable of absorbing from 5,000 to 10,000 Jews a year. It is doubtful whether there are any Jews in Germany who consider Birobidzhan as an answer to any of their prayers. It is at best an extremely difficult enterprise.

But those who cannot abide Palestine are not concerned about these difficulties. They have lost their sense of practicality. They are operating now with a prejudice and an intuitive fear. What is involved here is not their love for Birobidzhan or Ecuador, but their hatred of Palestine, and what a National Home implies. There is not a Jew in his right senses who will not admit that Palestine is a practical investment which will pay the Jewish people more in return than any other investment that now lies before them. It pays more in opportunity, in freedom, in Jewishness, in stability and permanence than any other land that has been mentioned. If all Jews were united in a love of Zion, tens of thousands of Jews could be added to the annual record of Palestine each year. Within the next ten years we could build a citadel of Jewish strength that would abide for generations. But this seems to be one of the inevitable habits of many Jews. They won't go the way God points, and then curse their stars when they break their necks in following their own stupid adventures.

MCDONALD'S RESIGNATION*

It was suggested soon after Mr. James G. McDonald was appointed as High Commissioner for Refugees, in October, 1933, that he should have resigned at once, for it was quite evident that the League was making a mere gesture in handing him the appointment as High Commissioner, and that it did not have the slightest intention of providing the Commissioner either with financial support or the normal cooperation of the States who were members of the League.

In effect, Mr. McDonald was being given the privilege and responsibility of doing what he could do to mitigate the sufferings of victims of racial and religious persecution—the victims of criminal action on the part of a country at that time still a member of the League—and of knocking at all doors for help, with the certainty that none of the members of the League, responsible for his appointment and capable of helping, would be home when he called.

But it was worth the time devoted by Mr. McDonald to his fruitless task to be in a position to write the splendid document which was made public with his letter of resignation this past week. In his efforts to relieve the victims of German oppression he accumulated a knowledge not only of the Jewish situation in every land; he not only acquired vivid information with regard to the lands that may be available for Jewish immigration, but he got to know the real value of the ideal sentiments expressed by important Governments, and to appreciate that the duties assigned to him were a fundamental problem that belonged to the League of Nations. The League cannot hope to have moral authority unless it is prepared to tackle such problems at their source, instead of thinking that it can avoid responsibility by the devices of diplomatic and legalistic negotiation.

Mr. McDonald's resignation is couched in words of bitter reality. It deals with facts. It gives ample figures to support his conclusions. It

* *The New Palestine*, January 3, 1936.

tells a story of German cruelty, which has seldom come to light in an international public document. It is a scathing indictment of the League of Nations and of the nations that control its destinies.

Mr. McDonald pays tribute to the cooperation of Jewish and other bodies in helping to meet the problems of the refugees. But he points out that the new Nuremberg Legislation has altered the entire complexion of the problem. Now it is known, without any uncertainty, that at least half a million people have been permanently deprived of their political rights, their civil status has become that of guests or wards of the State, and a threat of even more drastic action against them has been pronounced before the Reichstag. The insane program of the Nazi Party has become the relentless policy of the German Government. He concludes that this is a problem that cannot be met effectively by the efforts of private organizations or of any League organization for refugees. These efforts can only mitigate a problem of growing gravity and complexity, which must be tackled at its source if disaster is to be avoided. This problem must be met by the League itself with all the authority of international morality. It can no longer shunt the consequences of German criminality by keeping the matter involved in the field of diplomacy.

The concluding paragraph of his letter of resignation is a personal note, in which Mr. McDonald declares that he is convinced that desperate suffering in the countries adjacent to Germany, and an even more terrible calamity within the German frontier, are inevitable unless present tendencies in Germany are checked or reversed; and therefore he cannot longer remain silent. He concludes with the following sentences, which deserve to be quoted here:

"When domestic policies threaten the demoralization and exile of hundreds of thousands of human beings, considerations of diplomatic correctness must yield to those of common humanity. I should be recreant if I did not call attention to the actual situation and plead that world opinion, acting through the League and its Member States and other countries, move to avert the existing and impending tragedies."

In the discharge of his difficult task, Mr. McDonald has given distinguished and effective service to the cause of humanity and to the cause of the Jewish people. He has done whatever could be done under the circumstances, and with the powers he possessed, to mitigate the suffering of Jewish and other refugees from Hitler Germany. He has spoken his mind with restraint and with deep appreciation of the amenities required by the situation. In his descriptions of the service performed by

Palestine in connection with the refugee situation, he has been objective, unprejudiced and deeply mindful also of Jewish ideals and the powers of the Jewish people for sacrifice in their own defense. He has written a very fine page in modern Jewish history, and will be always regarded as a friend of the Jewish people of whom they may well be proud.

JEWISH EXODUS FROM GERMANY
(Whence Comes Our Salvation)*

The cabled report in the New York Times on Monday, giving what seemed to be an analysis of all projects being considered in connection with the emigration of from 100,000 to 250,000 Jews whose existence is threatened in Germany, turns out to be an interesting piecing together of various unrelated ideas swimming about in London with regard to the fate of German Jewry.

The delegation whose coming here is announced (Sir Herbert Samuel, Viscount Bearsted and Mr. Simon Marks, representing British Jews, to consult with American leaders), seems not to have anything substantially to do with the story of the Times correspondent. They are gratuitously, it seems, interwoven in the story. Mr. Marks, in communication with American Zionist leaders, has disclaimed any connection with those features of the report that relate to pressure and threats from the German Government, that relate to institutions that are to be established for the disposal of German goods, that relate to fixed ideas as to program. It is fairly certain that there is no comprehensive plan which the delegation is bringing with it, except the hope that funds will be forthcoming from American Jewry to supplement financial support given by British Jewry for the emigration of German Jews to Palestine. It is certain that the delegation will propose a pool of capital, to be contributed in the course of four years, be formed jointly by British and American Jews. It seems to be the intention to appeal to circles of wealthy Jews who in addition to an interest that may be expressed through the United Palestine Appeal or the Joint Distribution Committee, might be willing to finance a well thought-out large-scale economic enterprise that would make possible such an extensive emigration. The contributors to the pool would be expected to regard these subscriptions as a super-tax over and above their contributions to the program in Palestine of the Jewish Agency, or to the program of the Joint Distribution Committee.

* *The New Palestine*, January 10, 1936.

For the time being, the Times cable may be removed from the agenda. Some of the ideas in it may return in discussion, but as a whole, it is too much of a conjecture and deduction. Yet it has had a depressing and disturbing effect upon all Jews and friends of Jewish interests. This effect has not been removed by subsequent explanations that have been offered. For, while the Times cable lacks the elements of political reality, it did reveal, with horrifying directness, the cruel position in which the Jews of Germany find themselves. It brought out in a clear form, the place the Jewish tragedy occupies in the thinking of the civilized world.

There is yet to be heard a voice of authority and influence giving endorsement to the views expressed by Mr. James G. McDonald last week. These views have been circulated throughout the civilized world. They are registered in the protocols of the League of Nations. They have appeared in the leading newspapers of all nationalities, and there have been editorial comments on Mr. McDonald's proposals. But in all the descriptions of events, the daily record which is being made of the inhumanity of the Nazi Government, the shameless disregard of the principles of humanity, the brutal attacks that accompany the enactment of barbaric laws, there is nothing to give the slightest indication that those who are writing about these Nazi acts regard the matter as something which deserves not merely their comment, but their active intervention.

In the analysis given by the Times correspondent, he seems to be discussing a crime which has been committed and which is daily being renewed by the Archcriminal, with the whole civilized world as witnesses, and the question that he seems to be considering is: What is going to be done by the relatives of the victims to get them out of the clutches of their assailant? Already, so many tens of thousands have been dispersed. Pressure is being brought to bear upon tens of thousands of others to bring about their enforced emigration. The environment of Jewish life in Germany is becoming a suffocating experience from which thousands of children will flee, from which all those who have physical vigor and means to carry them will run. New laws are to be enacted, further poisoning the life of those who remain. A callous disregard for Jewish suffering suffuses the conscience of the whole of Germany.

And at Geneva, and in London, and in Paris, and in Washington, there are statesmen who read the reports (which probably shock and disturb them; they spoil the morning's coffee) but in the last analysis none feels the slightest need for raising a voice of protest or taking up the matter of the crime as a duty that rests upon the forces of justice and right in the world. All of them, in a casual way, as if they were interested spectators of a rather brutal scene, are curious to know what the Jews are going to do to extricate themselves from the consequences of the unequal struggle.

Time and again we have said:

The freedom of the Jewish people must be won through the sacrifices of the Jews themselves. The land of the Jewish hope must become the National Home of the Jewish people through the organized determination and constructive ability of the Jewish people themselves. No freedom is worthy of the name unless it is achieved through the efforts of those who feel the humiliations of servitude. Jews must break the chains that shackle their spirit and their rights. They must act for themselves.

But the time is coming for the nations of the world to appreciate that the freedom we are fighting for requires a field for the exercise of our powers, a world in which at least a semblance of justice prevails. The crimes that are committed against the life and property of the Jewish people in Germany, and in other lands, can no longer be perpetrated without bringing evil consequences also to those lands whose doors seem to be closed to the forms of injustice and cruelty that have been adopted in anti-Semitic lands. The efforts of the Jewish people to extricate themselves from the difficulties that have arisen in Germany spill over into various lands and create difficult questions that can be solved only with the cooperation of the enlightened governments of those lands. If they are not ready to raise their arms to bring to a halt the inhumanity of the German Government, then they must unite in order to protect themselves against the consequences that flow out of the situation that will be created outside of Germany by the persecution and dispersion of the Jews of that land.

The resettlement of the Jews of Germany is a matter that cannot be carried out solely by Jews. The emigration of 100,000 or 250,000 Jews to Palestine is not a matter that can be undertaken and carried through with success, in the first instance, without the direct cooperation of the British Government. Questions that have to do with the transmission of funds from one country to another may involve violation of laws which may have to be modified in order to meet the difficulties of a large emigration of Jews, if they are to take some part of their hard-earned property with them. There are questions of balance of trade, tariffs, economic reciprocity, that are connected with this tremendous job.

Nor can the Jewish people ever give its consent to a procedure with regard to the Jews of Germany, involving the abandonment of their fundamental human rights and involving also an intimation that similar barbaric treatment of Jews on the part of other nations may follow the line of precedent. Coupled with any large-scale emigration of Jews from Germany must be assurances by governments of their interest in, and concern for, the protection of the human rights of Jews, no matter where they may reside. Nor can we Zionists concede that we propose the building of the Jewish National Home in Palestine, and the development of our right in that land, upon a voluntary repudiation of our hard-won human rights in Western civilization.

The Times cable should stimulate the discussion of the fundamental human questions involved in the whole matter of the exodus of Jews from Germany. It was a disturbing introduction, in which for the first time not only Jews but friends and sympathizers of Jewish life were made to feel the broad interests of humanity and justice that are directly affected by what is going on in Germany.

Those who are responsible for a pro-Nazi agitation in the United States in connection with the Olympics, may well hang their heads in shame at the revelation contained in that article of what is known to be the despicable purpose of the German Government to profit, if possible, from its own criminal and inhuman acts. Those who have been thinking that the situation in Germany is a purely local matter, may well reconsider their conception of the whole situation. The Times has done a service by the publication of this correspondence. It has done no service to the delegation which is to come to the United States, by seeming to attribute to them ideas and explanations that emanate from evil sources with which they have no connection.

But it has undoubtedly served to present the issue in the clearest possible way to the leaders of American thought. It compels consideration by the American Government of what part it is bound to play in the solution of a question in which are involved the principles of justice and the principles of humanity. It makes clear that unless England and America, the two great democracies of modern times, unite to aid the Jewish people in their unequal struggle, the civilization they are concerned to maintain will suffer irreparable injury.

Is there not one good Samaritan among the Christian nations?

PARTITION*

Once more we gather from the North and the South, from the East and the West, gravely troubled but hopeful, to begin—in our ceremonious Washington way—another hard year in the building of the Homeland in Palestine.

It is a disturbing prospect. The Heavens darken over the entire House of Israel—in the lands of Dispersion and also in the Land of Promise. Clouds gather, storms threaten and break, gales of hate and destruction sweep all highways, "Darkness covers the earth, and gross darkness the people." The World, burdened with sin and iniquity, is in labor. What will issue from its pain, none can foretell. The purge brings upheaval and convulsion and blurred vision. But the wages of iniquity must be cleared off, worked out.

Beneath the debris of the seething revolution, Jewish life is trampled underfoot without remorse. It lives in houses without roofs or windows or doors. On all sides it is exposed, without privilege or right. Slaves of yesterday enslave it and heap insult upon it—pour salt upon open wounds they have inflicted. The cries and protests of the victims are drowned out by shameless boasting and wild cries, and no voice is raised in censure or reproof or even in sympathy.

The people of Poland, who for generations aspired to freedom and found support in all Western lands, celebrate their first decades of liberty by depriving their Jewish neighbors of the right to live in the republic they helped to establish. The once great German people, who complained, after the World War, of calumny and ill-will through misrepresentation, raised its voice against the injustice of the Treaty of Versailles and won the sympathies of the liberal world; has now turned to the mad sport of dictators not only to persecute its Jewish citizens, but to insult and libel the whole Jewish people. Rumania, which was patched together of many races and nationalities, receiving a portion from Hungary, another from Austria, and a third from Russia; today, without shame or remorse or explanation, proclaims to the world that has lost the power of protest and remonstrance, that its Jewish citizens are unwanted and should be provided for by others.

It is a mad, wicked world we are living in. And it is in this world that

* *Address as Chairman of United Palestine Appeal to National Conference for Palestine,* January 23, 1938, Washington, D.C.

our struggle for Jewish national freedom—our effort to establish a home —must be enacted.

Once, when Zionism was young and impudent, the Galut looked at us with disdain and we returned it with indifference. We hated the ease and comfort of the Galut, its sailing with any wind that blew, its falling into the lap of any local loyalty or culture, its shameless avoidance of the noble patrimony of the Jewish people. But today we are all bound together in destiny, rise and fall, take insults and humiliations together— the Galut and Zion inseparable, one line, one chain; the same Destination determined for all of us.

The operation could be made. The settlement of 425,000 Jews in Palestine could make its peace with the Arabs and live on and grow, extend itself to the East and South; cut itself off from the concerns of the Galut. The lifeline could be severed; the covenant of brotherhood could be broken; but that treason would poison the bread of generations to come; the meaning of the life in Zion would go out. For good or ill, all Israel is one brotherhood. It has a common Jewish destiny.

Long before the Pandemonium of modern civilization began, it was our fond hope, in the fullness of time, gradually, without haste, to establish our Sanctuary in Zion. For 40 years we have been pleading with a hardnecked generation, preparing the way for freedom, asking that in the day of comparative ease they put aside, in advance, some portion of their gains for the day of adversity. But only the few heard our words and responded. We were seeking not a Utopia, not freedom from the normal ailments of organized society, but surcease from that peculiar malady of Jewish life, its homelessness and lack of freedom. Only the few turned to hear the appeal, the warning, and joined in making a path to Zion.

The world's disorders come too soon. The distemper of the times, the loss of its sense of justice, the abandonment of ideal for the material, the clash of warring selfishnesses, have caught us in the midst of building our Sanctuary which has also become an open field where the winds of hate and prejudice and injustice have free sweep.

In the building of the Sanctuary, we always lagged far behind Opportunity, which we always expected would knock again. Overwhelmed by adverse conditions of life, we sought to propitiate ill-fortune with gifts to the less fortunate among us, but when the sun shone again and the harvests again were good, it was found that nothing had been laid aside for the dark years.

It was a weak vessel at first, almost like a sieve. When the Biluists came, they were utter strangers in the land, feeble in the arts of living, ignorant of soil and climate, looking up abjectly to authority. At the beginning of the war, there were colonies in which Arab peasants labored. At the end of the war, 20 years after the first Basle Congress, the movement had deposited a remnant of 65,000 Jews, with some schools, with some colonies, with little industry, with Hebrew just becoming the language of the nation, and the foundation of the Hebrew University about to be laid on Mount Scopus. With the setting up of the Keren Hayesod, the coming of a civil administration in Palestine, the pace quickened. When Poland made its first attack upon the Jews, and thousands of them had to leave, Palestine was already prepared to hold many of them, but their zlotys evaporated, they still did not know how to force circumstances, and many of them returned to the Galut.

But when the German Jews began their return, that sieve had become a copper-lined vessel, and everything poured into it by dogged labor was held. The Sanctuary was prepared to retain and absorb more than 60,000 a year. Its roots had been watered with the sweat of labor, its trees had been nurtured with the care of pious children returning home, and there was every prospect that thousands upon thousands could be taken back into the bosom of the Homeland. In these 40 years, the Land of Promise has had good and bad times, and we should remember both.

Whatever the Guardian makes of the Mandate, liquidates it, tears it to shreds, we recall the day of its issuing with high satisfaction and pride. They may have forgotten, but we remember that when Mr. Balfour was told by Dr. Wise that a Congress of the Jews of America had urged by unanimous vote that England become the trustee for the Homeland, that great English statesman, in words of humility, expressed his appreciation of the compliment to his country.

They may forget, but we remember the words òf Lloyd George, who said that England had merely opened the door for the Jewish people; that they themselves would have to build the Homeland. It was upon the sincerity of the words of Balfour, Lloyd George, Robert Cecil, that we entered and built. Whatever there is of National Home in Zion has been made by the labor and sacrifice of Jews, with confidence in the pledged word of England. It was England that closed its eyes and shut that door in the face of the thousands clamoring to enter. They may forget, but we shall remember that, in spite of obstacle and devious policy, the 65,000 after the War became the 425,000 of 1937, that a land was reclaimed and revived, a people was reborn that had discovered its patrimony, and that revenues were placed at the disposal of Government to provide the needs of all the inhabitants of Palestine, including Trans-Jordan. We remember the Balfour Declaration as the charter of Jewish national rights, the pledge of a great Empire; that 52 nations of the world gave recognition, through the Mandate, to the historic right of the Jewish people to their Homeland.

From that land we learned the ways of nature and discovered how to live in harmony with it; how to cleanse the swamps of their noxious poisons, how to build the roads; how to build cities and homes; the intricate arts of industry and commerce; how to become immunized against the ills of soil and air, how to eradicate long-standing, chronic ailments.

All these things we learned in Zion. All these things we have been able to overcome, but not the hostility of Ishmael, not the disloyalty of the trustee. Alone, facing God and His mountains, we could have made Zion a land flowing with milk and honey—all of Zion, extending beyond the Jordan, into the Negev, and to the North. But the friend that should have aided went astray in friendship. The trustee that should have kept the faith, dissolved the pledge into its verbal elements and then went on to wash the slate clean. We thought that England would know how to appreciate friendship and loyalty, but instead, it has served deceit and violence, rejecting the confidence of an ancient people, frustrating its hope and dashing the cup of fulfillment from its lips.

England has shaped the life of modern Europe. Its culture and civilization have dominated on all the continents. It has written many brilliant chapters in modern history. Its conquering armies, followed by civil administration, have brought with them the arts of peace, of industry, of science and government. It is the Mother of Parliaments and pragmatic democracy. Its Imperialism has been mitigated by liberalism. Its rule has given freedom to the mind and to the spirit. It still controls an empire that encircles the globe. But when the story will be told of how England played the Good Samaritan to a people of high morality, the founders of a great mother religion, a people persecuted for its faith through the ages; how, professing to aid in the Fulfillment of prophecy, in righting an ancient wrong, it accepted the guardianship of Jewish hope, and how it met its sacred obligation—the sons of the England of today who will read that story will not find cause for pride or moral satisfaction.

It promised Fulfillment, and by devious ways wandered so far from the covenant that in the end it landed (20 years after the Balfour Declaration) in the blind alley of virtual bankruptcy. It promised Fulfillment and now, necessity driving it to default, asks to settle all claims under the covenant by a Token Payment. It thus follows the way of the world.

The debts of Germany, accepted in the Treaty of Peace, have been disowned and cancelled. The debt of Poland to its minorities (among its other debts) is ignored and repudiated. Even the debts between the Allied Powers have been placed in suspense. Why should not the covenant of the Great Empire with a humble and defenseless people also be abrogated by the so-called realities of a difficult political situation? Why should it observe in Zion what has been evaded by all powerful nations, everywhere, under the New Code of international justice?

There should be gratitude for the proposed Token Payment. If the Mandate is to be liquidated (it being impossible to establish the Jewish National Home by the gradual process there prescribed), let the Jews take a Jewish State in a part of Palestine and call it quits. Cancel the balance! Give the Trustee release from its covenant.

For us it is the choice of necessity. It is the balance of several disadvantages. It is taking the least of several evils, the most of the good in them. Some are not inclined to bow to this necessity, but would take up the Torch of Protest and abide as intransigents. The large majority, as always, would and must make the most of the situation.

But let the Token be genuine and real. Let the words used mean what they say. If it is to be a free Homeland, it should not be hemmed in by crippling limitations. Self-government should be real. Let not the heart of Jewish hope, the symbol of all that is holy in Zion, be extracted by a pettifogging device, and the Holy City of Jerusalem find itself in the territory of a foreign state. If consideration is to be given to realities, let not the Good Samaritan forget the growing army of exiles from Germany and Poland, and perhaps tomorrow from Rumania, but give us land sufficient to satisfy Jewish need. Let there be no mockery of the thing that is offered by so reducing its opportunity for economic growth that the free land offered will frustrate the ideal which has sustained us. And at least let not the Token Payment be so delayed by the wiles of Government as to serve as a screen, behind which the Mandate is to be liquidated and the Jewish National Home sabotaged and reduced to ruin, and the Mufti of Jerusalem to be given possession of the Promised Land.

If the task assumed by Zionism had been a short haul, the present period of trouble would cause despair. It was foretold that years would elapse before the exile of 2,000 years could be transformed into an enduring self-emancipation. For that long journey we need endurance, patience, ability to retreat as well as to advance, to profit through defeat and to learn from our weaknesses. The way to self-emancipation is filled with disappointment, turns and twists in the road, advance and retreat, jubilee and lamentation. The forest is filled with unseen enemies. Therefore, the life line of Jewish solidarity must be maintained, without interruption, with faith and confidence.

At the front, where the fortress of defense has been established, where almost half a million Jews (men, women and children) have taken their stand, an amazing, an unparalleled heroism prevails. In the midst of disorder, in the midst of uncertainty, they plant and build and protect themselves and look forward without fear. They know what they want, and they will endure until it is achieved. They stand there to make space for more Jews, room for freedom. They hold that line, awaiting re-enforcement, the supplies we can send them, the encouragement and the support we may give them. They maintain not only their own heroic spirit, but the example of their nobility gives encouragement and spiritual strength to those who support the line in the Dispersion. They hold up the banner of Jewish honor.

Let us not fail them, for through them we shall also free ourselves.

PALESTINE FOR THE REFUGEES*

There will be several thousand Jewish visitors in Washington on Saturday and Sunday, January 14th and 15th, among whom there will be, of course, a large number of Zionist and non-Zionist representatives of the Jewish communities of the United States. They will come to hear reports, listen to important addresses, adopt such resolutions as may be required, discuss the problems of the Zionist movement, and, not of the least importance, to exchange informally (in committee rooms, at lunches and dinners and in the lobbies of the Mayflower Hotel), their local experiences in the field of fund-raising for Palestine during the year 1938. They will carry home with them, we have no doubt, a message that will inspire their local and regional fellow-workers. A much larger public will participate in the Conference than is here indicated. Many of the addresses will be broadcast over the radio with national

* *The New Palestine*, January 13, 1939.

hookups. The general press will undoubtedly carry the more weighty utterances. What will be said and done at Washington will be the subject of discussions in pulpits and at meetings throughout the country for weeks to come. The United Jewish Appeal of the Joint Distribution Committee and the United Palestine Appeal will thus be given its first official introduction to the American Jewish community at the Washington Conference.

All elements in Jewish life are today tremendously moved by the immediate problems of Jewish life. The vulgar phrasing is the problem of Jewish refugees. The term refugee implies a running away in the dead of night under a cloud of suspicion. But these are innocent men, women and children plundered and despoiled in broad daylight, driven from their homes by merciless governments, and seeking sanctuary in the territory of civilized states. The democratic states have taken official cognizance of their plight; not for the purpose of arresting the destructive activities of the gangster governments, but exclusively to deal with the problem of taking care of their victims; and the number of victims increases from day to day. The civilized world takes notice of international outrage, but confesses impotence in checking the reign of lawlessness.

The problem is under consideration by the Intergovernmental Committee. Mr. Rublee is scheduled for discussions in Berlin. Plans are under consideration—some real, some fantastic—and Berlin still maintains its extortionist policy. But in all these plans, the burden of responsibility is assumed to rest upon the shoulders of the Jewish people. The cost of salvaging the victims is to be borne largely by Jews, the kinsmen of the army of impoverished and helpless. Thus far, no great power has included in its budget any appreciable provision for the cost of salvaging the victims of German barbarism. Preparations are therefore being made, wherever there are Jewish communities, for the collection of funds to alleviate immediate distress, to rehabilitate the despoiled, to provide homes for the homeless (temporary or permanent) and to get immediate political protection for those who have lost the protection of the states to which they had belonged.

The problem is the problem of the Jewish people. In the treatment of that problem the best thought of Jewish leaders will have to be organized and coordinated. While immediate relief is the order of the day, it would be folly to avoid consideration of broader implications and a long-distance view of the issues. There should be order and plan in the work of relief, but it would be tragic if, in the work of relief, there would not appear also the qualities of statesmanship and vision. The soup kitchen, the refugee camp, barracks for children, food and clothing, are of the greatest importance, but in the matter of salvaging tens of thousands of human beings who have been uprooted, turned into exile, and compelled to begin life anew, consideration will have to be given to plans and projects calculated ultimately to resolve the soup kitchen and the refugee camp and the children's barracks into forms of permanent settlement under conditions that will enable those provided for to begin living their own lives on a self-sustaining basis.

It will not be possible to solve the entire problem merely by adding up all wants and needs and dividing the income upon a pro rata basis. It is a long distance operation. Permanent homes will have to be found. There can be foreseen suffering extending over months and years. Large financial resources will have to be forthcoming. To refuse to look at a problem in its totality would be to pursue a shortsighted, improvident policy.

Into the glass of the immediate future all Jews will have to look, without flinching, without fear or prejudice, and with deep understanding of the opportunities the Jewish National Home in Palestine offers. These opportunities are not only material; they have tremendous moral value as well. They represent creativity, freedom, recovery, the building of a national future. Palestine is the front where pressure can transform political reality, and economic strength force political change. That is the front where Jewish relief can create for itself the conditions of its own freedom. That is the front where the quintessence of the so-called refugee problem will receive its permanent solution. There we face a wall, but that wall can be made to yield to Jewish determination and Jewish faith. *In any budget of relief and reconstruction that may be set up, impartially (without prejudice, without fear, with deep understanding of Jewish values), the uses of the Jewish National Home in the emergency problem that faces us will have to be given intelligent and adequate consideration.*

The program of the Washington Conference is designed to make a contribution to this appreciation of the values represented by the Jewish National Home. It is intended to project the totality of Jewish interest in the appalling conditions that confront us. It will proclaim the United Appeal. But at the same time, it will give expression to a determination that, in the propaganda set in motion to enlist the largest possible support for the *United Fund,* proper emphasis, appreciation and support shall be inspired for the Jewish National Home in Palestine, both haven and hope.

WHY NOT PALESTINE?*

The executive members of the Intergovernmental Committee have been meeting in Washington this week under the chairmanship of Lord Winterton. A preliminary statement has been issued to the press. An official meeting is to be held this week, which may be expected to give definite form to the plans they intend to pursue in dealing with the problem of refugees.

With all due respect, it cannot be said (from what has been announced in the press) that the Committee has made substantial progress in coping with even the limited aspects of the problem. It stands today practically where it stood five months ago.

The blame for the slow progress may be laid to the conditions of the war, but it is nearer the truth to say that from its inception, the Intergovernmental Committee has not been free to act. It has had to deal with a general disinclination to grapple effectively and comprehensively with the problem, lest it run counter to the restrictive immigration policies of the cooperating states. But without some disturbance in that direction, all that was left for the Committee to do was to find some undiscovered territory, as distant from their interests as possible, where a colonization scheme might be attempted. This accounts for the continuous search for new territories—the naming of British Guiana, Tanganyika, Northern Rhodesia, San Domingo, and the Philippine Islands.

President Roosevelt delivered an address at the opening of the meeting. He divided the program into two parts. He spoke of a short-range program which involves 200,000 to 300,000 refugees, "who are in dire need and who must as quickly as possible be given opportunity to settle in other countries where they can make permanent homes." This, the President said, was not an insoluble task. He ruled out the cooperation of Great Britain and France because they are engaged in a major war and can only give a continuance of their sympathy and interest in these days which are so difficult for them. This would mean that upon the neutral nations rests an obligation to carry on the work.

But then there is the larger, far-range program which will arise when

_____
* *The New Palestine*, October 20, 1939.

the present war comes to an end. This program will affect, in the judgment of the President, from 10,000,000 to 20,000,000 human beings. The Intergovernmental Committee would have to prepare itself for this larger task. It will involve study, investigation, organization, experimentation.

We would be the last to take a critical attitude toward the Intergovernmental Committee and, least of all, toward the views of President Roosevelt, whose sympathy and friendship toward the Jewish problem are generally known. But it is quite clear that the suggestion of the larger program does not serve to stimulate interest or enthusiasm for the disposition of the short-range and immediate program, nor do the constant references to the generosity of the Jewish relief organizations serve to raise any desire on the part of any Government to lend a helping hand with the substance of relief. The effect upon a hesitating committee will be an inclination to delay all action for the time being, long as well as short range.

The Zionist organizations of America felt it their duty once more to attempt the task of placing Palestine on the agenda of the Intergovernmental Committee in the consideration of its immediate and distant program. They submitted the facts and figures. They have not yet succeeded in their effort. There may be diplomatic or political reasons that stand in the way of discussing Palestine as a means for serving the immediate program of 60,000 Jewish refugees in Holland, Switzerland and Belgium, as well as the large number of 300,000 Jews who are to be found scattered in various parts of Central Europe, and whose numbers are being continuously augmented as the war of destruction progresses.

Any conception of settlement for refugees that does not take into account the human factors, that does not seek a form of settlement in which there is an instinctive cooperation on the part of the refugees themselves, is bound to lead to ineffective results. From the point of view of either the short-range or the long-range program, Palestine cannot be excluded. It serves with an immediacy which is not contained in any of the projects that have been discussed. It will take millions of dollars and a number of years to make San Domingo, for example, a place for Jewish settlement of any considerable numbers. It will take millions of dollars and many years to make the Philippine Islands available for a reasonable number of Jews.

Here we have in Palestine a land already prepared. It is capable today of finding permanent homes for from 50,000 to 100,000 per annum. It contains a Jewish population of 500,000 eager to cooperate. Every refugee going to Palestine becomes activized into cooperative service and self-support. Refugees go to Palestine willingly, while they will go to San Domingo or the Philippine Islands only as a last resort. It goes without saying that Palestine cannot serve for the solution of the problem of the vast number of refugees that may arise at the end of the war. But Palestine is available without delay, today. Resources are at hand that make it an outstanding opportunity to serve the refugee problem.

Why, then, *is Palestine,* the land assigned by the League of Nations as the Jewish National Home, *consistently and persistently kept off the agenda of the Intergovernmental Committee* called into being for the express purpose of serving refugees' needs? Why is all reference to Palestine taboo, in the public announcements of the Committee as well as at the luncheon given by Mr. Myron Taylor on Thursday in honor of Lord Winterton and Sir Herbert Emerson? The avoidance of any reference to Palestine cannot be accepted by Jews interested in the welfare of their people, nor does it raise the prestige of the Intergovernmental Committee which has had the confidence thus far of all classes and elements of American Jewry.

THE NEW BARBARISM*

Days of growing evil descend upon us.

The sins of a turbulent past, buried deep in the sub-consciousness of the human race, have burst into life again; and the corrosion of their influence spreads over the face of the earth. An organized assault, unparalleled in form and intensity, is being made upon the ideals of justice and freedom, and the sanctity of human life. A New Barbarism, not wild and untutored, but trained in the science of destruction, breaks through the barriers of civilization. We face the utter ruin of that world which was our heritage from sacrificial ancestors. It seems to be sweeping on uncontrolled to the fulfillment of its destiny; and as yet there seem to be no effective defenses against the epidemic which moves forward with mechanical precision to a terrifying climax.

The Jewish struggle for national freedom, based on our ancient traditions, was stirred to new life by the ideals born of the French Revolution, which for the first time proclaimed and fought for the rights of man on a world scale. These ideals were carried into every corner of the

---

* *Address to the 43rd Annual Convention of the Zionist Organization of America,* Pittsburgh, July 1, 1940.

civilized world. They set the pattern for new states, gave birth to dreams of Utopias, and the fulfillment of prophecy. As a consequence of that Revolution, the ideals of democracy and human freedom became dominant in the larger part of the Western world. The Jewish people, treasuring their own traditions and culture, living in a world of their own creation, awoke from their national slumber and slowly moved forward, profiting from the awakened influence of democracy. The Dream of Zion ceased being merely the substance of prayer and hope, and in our own day was thrust into the arena of political realities.

But movements have their birth and death, their rise and fall—they spend their force and shrivel and die. They fulfill their purpose, and are absorbed in peace and in new struggles. Today, the Jewish struggle for freedom—as all other struggles similarly inspired—faces a counter-revolution—a revolution in the reverse—that seeks to destroy the foundations upon which modern society has been established and maintained. It is a revolution that finds its strength and stimulations in the power of primitive concepts of a fantastic mythology; that arms itself to destroy this old world in order to create a new world fashioned in the fantastic image of its savage gods. It is a revolution that grows with lightning rapidity, but does not know clearly where it is going, and what monstrous form will ultimately greet it when its energies have been spent in blood and destruction.

The battle now being fought out on the war-scarred fields of Europe absorbs our minds, shatters our nerves, confuses the normal calendar of life, shortens our days and lengthens our nights. It casts shadows of fear and apprehension in the hearts of all men, transforming life into an unbroken nightmare that transcends the wildest imaginings of minds disordered. The waste of the wealth of generations, the reckless shedding of human blood, the fall of communities that have symbolized ancient cultures, the enemy's arrogant contempt for all the refinements of life—all of this is involved in what we read and hear morning, noon and night. Who can escape the clamor? Where shall we turn to escape its confusion? Who can be deaf to the cries of distress and pain?

On this side of the ocean we stand as shuddering witnesses, capable for the time being only of lending a hand to maintain and relieve, sending a word of comfort wherever communications are still unbroken, feeling deep in our hearts that the day will soon come when we too shall be directly involved in the sanguinary struggle and that then bad may become worse. Upon the outcome of that great battle depends the future of the human race, from which our Jewish future is indivisible. For we are no longer separated from the generality of life, our problem lies in the very heart of the struggle.

If the Destroyers are victorious, it will mean that darkness has fallen and God is obscured, and His Law has been silenced. It will mean that the morality of the past will be purged from human society, and the rule of the steel fist will be unchallenged. Dreams of the millenium, of the better day, will be driven to cover, and all of life will be savagely competitive, filled with hate, subject to the perverse eccentricities of masterminds who are taking over the affairs of the world. The virtues of kindness and good-fellowship will be forbidden and youth will be trained into hardness of muscle and heart. The Good Samaritan will be a symbol to be derided. All of the records of how man has lifted himself out of the mire of savagery, all conceptions of justice and right, will be torn out of the books and new records will be written by order. Already, in a large part of the world, the figure of Jesus on the Cross, that once aroused universal sorrow, has become the symbol of weakness that should be eradicated by blood-sacrifices. The quest for justice, the striving for the better life (never realized but always coming nearer) will be abandoned as an adventure not worthy of the heroes of bombing planes. In the world which the German hordes are now creating, the ideals of the prophets and of the humanists and of the French Revolution will be effaced to make room for ambitions oozing from the dark caverns inhabited by the carnal gods of forgotten faiths.

But the Destroyer, moving on with growing savagery as victories accumulate, will himself, in the end, be destroyed by the hates and the evils he has aroused. The soul of the German people will not be able to carry the weight of iniquity that it is accumulating, and which isolates it from the rest of the world. The aggressor may destroy in anger and vindictiveness, but when his appetite is sated, the ghosts of a nobler past will rise to haunt him and stir his slumbering conscience into revolt.

When the present revolution comes to its predestined end, it will mean not only the end of fears and the beginning of days of peace. The day of peace will bring with it a revaluation of the ideals of the past. It will have to be greeted with the determination to purge out of our hearts the sins that have caused the epidemic that now threatens to overwhelm us. The false diplomacies, the wrong perpetrated by man against his fellow-man, the pursuit of selfish group interests, the easy-going disloyalty to ideals and virtues will have to be confessed and expelled from our lives. The day of peace will be a day of repentance and contrition.

Cast down by the daily record of events that seem to move toward tragedy, let not despair capture our minds and wills. Behind the war fronts there are engaged in the struggle not merely planes and tanks and battleships; there are involved the collision of moralities and the power of ideals that have for generations been incorporated in human character, and that resist destruction. The battle fronts are, in a certain sense, false fronts of boast and gesture. Behind them, will and spirit and traditions wrestle for mastery. The issue is not yet decided. The struggle continues, although one by one the democratic states fall and the aggressor strides over the map of Europe, mangles the prostrate body of republican France, and now roars his challenge to the British citadel on the Thames. Practically alone, sin-laden England with its powerful Dominions bares its breast to the aggressor, girds itself for enduring battle, invokes its martial tradition to sustain its youth—corroded by dialectics and amoralized by skepticism—and still hopes for the support of allies who prepare reluctantly for the struggle into which they will inevitably have to plunge.

Distant from the battlefield, the Republic of the United States, to which we owe our deepest loyalty, begins to sense its own peril, the approaching danger to its own way of life, to its own peace. The valorous President of the United States, cautious in decision and sensitive to the responsibilities of Government, has spoken what is in the hearts of his countrymen, pointing the way the American people will have to go to preserve the freedom they cherish. Although France has given up its struggle, weakened by perfidy and overwhelmed by force, today is not the day on which the bankruptcy of democracy is to be proclaimed. May that day never come.

What we stand for also makes its contribution to the decisive situation. We are the carriers of the ideals of the Hebrew prophets and the experiences of a people inured to suffering. In our veins courses the blood of martyrs and saints who died that these ideals should be preserved and that their way of life should be perpetuated. Justice and peace have been the pillars of our religion and the aspiration of our lives. It is against those ideals and against us as a people that the spearhead of aggression is directed. We were the first to feel the impact of the attack on modern civilization. We were the first victims to take the road of exile, now crowded by hordes of men and women from the lands that have fallen under the heels of tyranny. We stand with the forces of human progress for human rights and human freedom—the freedom of peoples and the freedom of man. We fall or rise with the victory or the defeat of the aggressor, and as all free peoples of the earth are now organizing to meet the challenge, gathering their material and moral resources, readjusting their lives to meet the unparalleled emergency, inculcating loyalty and sacrifice in the hearts of their citizens, so we too must prepare for heavy burdens and sacrifices to preserve our freedom in this world, to play our part in the great struggle in a manner worthy of our ancestry.

At all costs, what we have we should resolve to hold tenaciously, no sense of defeat entering our hearts up to the last moment of life; no part of our national front in the Homeland given up without a defensive struggle; no position we occupy here or in any other sector of the Diaspora to be abandoned without resistance.

To this end we Zionists, the remnant that forty years ago pledged itself to the national salvation of the Jewish people, the vanguard of the organized forces engaged in fighting for freedom in their own land, are called upon to mobilize all our forces and to close our ranks under a united and effective leadership in order to meet the grave responsibility of the moment.

Our greetings go forth to the Jewish commonwealth in Palestine, to its builders and defenders, to whom we pledge our fraternal support. It is cities and towns they have built with their own hands that they stand organized to defend. At long last it is a Jewish National Homeland they are defending and for which they are prepared to die. It is their culture and their organized society, the structure that reflects their own will to live, which they stand ready to protect. To the legal guardian of the Homeland, they have offered their arms. They have laid aside all their just grievances, and are prepared to sacrifice all they possess in this life in defense of the frontiers of the land which was promised to them. Their petition for the privilege of organizing their service in the cause of a fighting democracy, we here—in the name of all American Jews—re-enforce with our appeal to the British Government that the right to arm in their own military units be given to the Jews of Palestine. A denial of this right is an offense to the cause for which the World War is being fought.

THE WORLD IN TORMENT*

The like of what we are witnessing was never seen as far back as remembrance goes. There are no records that reveal such a desperate threat to the stability of the world as is reflected in the amazing attack

* October, 1940.

that has transformed Europe into a shambles, and free peoples into slaves of an insatiable despotism; that aims to destroy the intellectual and spiritual bases of our lives and to substitute a way of life that means reversion to an incredible barbarism.

In the olden times they never ceased to grope for the light, to seek the better life. In this day, having seen the light, it is proposed to extinguish it and bring back darkness. The new Conqueror comes to achieve an end which cannot be formulated in terms. He conquers for the sake of domination, to work his will on an enslaved civilization. His empire will have no boundaries. He will be halted by no inner compulsion or sense of justice or humanity. He can be restricted only by the force of arms and the power of moral resistance. Either a strait jacket or utter destruction will end his struggle for power.

The maneuvers of the Saboteurs of the world are on an amazing scale. They involve the encirclement of the globe, no less. The masterminds in Berlin find the map of Europe insufficient for the planning of their attacks. They use the globe, turning on a pivot, which marks all the highways of land and sea and air. No place is too remote for their vision. They move from Norway down to the North Pole, down to Alaska, to China, down to the Indian Ocean. They include the Americas—North and South. These are not secret plans. What is even more amazing is the fact that the book written by the Master Destroyer has been read by millions in all languages, in all lands; and that although the scheme of conquest is easy to follow, instead of a union against the aggressor, one by one the smaller nations have been broken and subjugated, and now only England (and its Dominions) stand ready to resist the Destroyer while the others still remain unconvinced. They open their doors to spies and saboteurs, their press and radio stations are saturated with enemy propaganda, and they talk of defense and preparation "when the time comes"—each for itself—awaiting the day of attack, and all the while still doubting that such diabolism is possible, and all the while wondering whether defense will be really needed.

In this world we Jews continue to be, as in the past, an incident of the struggle—hard substance that gets in the way. Certain aspects of the propaganda of hate implicate Jews as if they were the chief cause of the unrest that compels violence and destruction. But that is one of the many camouflages of the destroyers of the "falsities of liberty and equality." The Jewish participation, insofar as it appears under its own banner, is largely passive defense. In fact the greater part of Jewish life is now devoted not to the affirmation of rights, not to the filing of demands, not to the making of protests, but simply to the alleviation of a universal misery that depresses and absorbs every Jewish heart. The Jews of every land, with the coming of the Scourge, must prepare for flight, and all those not in flight find their only consolation the possibility, in an insignificant measure, to find crevices of escape where the victims may find temporary shelter.

All Jewish overseas relief is a program for finding havens of refuge for the tens of thousands—first of Germany, and in rapid succession of Austria, Italy, Czechoslovakia, Poland, Denmark, Norway, Belgium, Holland, France, now of Rumania and Hungary. It is an appalling sight, and more particularly so to the kinsmen of the hundreds of thousands who have been displaced and who are constantly forced to move from one haven to another. It is a terrible responsibility for the remnant of Jews living in security to carry alone, for it is upon their shoulders that the whole responsibility rests. Whatever interest others take in the Jewish tragedy is incidental—kind words and acts in passing. The old plans of reconstruction and rehabilitation of the Joint and the ORT have had to be discarded. The HIAS and the National Refugee Service stand in the foreground with their programs of elementary succor. The prospect is overwhelming in its magnitude.

Even in Palestine, where the status of Jewish life remains as recognizable as it was before the war began, and where we stand shoulder to shoulder with the defenders of England, day by day it becomes harder to maintain the program of building, the program of extension, and more and more the basic problems arising out of the coming of refugees—their safety and immediate living—take precedence over all other tasks. We are maintaining the Jewish National Home in the full knowledge that sooner or later it will be part of the terrain on which Nazi and Fascist bombs will explode, and the things created with so much labor and sacrifice will be devastated by the same powers that are now blasting in their fury the democratic life the English people have maintained on their island for so many centuries.

It is our good fortune that in this struggle not only are we physically to be counted among the forces arrayed against Hitler—in the armies and navies and air fleets of every land in which we are loyal citizens—that we have the support of the victims of Nazi oppression—but that all our hopes and the confirmation of our age-long faith are represented by the force disrupting the progress of the Nazi destroyers.

It is our duty to serve that cause without hesitation, and generously.

Whatever we can do, here in this land of liberty, for the defense of the democracies and the defeat of Hitler, should be done not only individually and as American citizens, but as Jews and collectively. It is our primary duty as Americans and as Jews to serve that cause. Here, there is no contradiction in interest or loyalty. Our American and Jewish interests are one unequivocal patriotism.

And what we are doing, or should do in greater measure, to strengthen the Jewish National Home in Palestine is a direct contribution to the defense of human freedom. Every refugee settled in Palestine means that a liability becomes an asset for democracy. The more Jews in Palestine, the more defenders of the Eastern Front of England. The stronger our economic life in Palestine, the stronger the position of the military organization in the Near East, which is not only a defense of Palestine but a preparation for an advance against Nazi forces.

The successes of Nazi Germany are illusory; they are seeming victories. There is no moral force behind them to retain loyalty or maintain discipline. The hidden resources of the civilized world cannot be destroyed by bombing planes, but, buried under the physical ruin of the world, will rise again to confound and destroy the Slave Empire which Hitler aims to construct. On the day his Empire collapses—as it certainly will—our faith in justice and morality will be vindicated, and a new day will dawn not only for the Jewish people, but for humanity at large.

THE UNNAMED ALLY

THE FALL OF ENGLAND*

In May, 1939, the British Government, weakened by a decade of moral and political defeats, performed the last desperate act in the rout of a Great Empire. It sealed the Jewish National Home in Palestine within the folds of a new Arab State. It traded a loyal friend to purchase the seeming friendship of a potential enemy. It broke its pledge to the one on the ground that it had made a pledge to the other. It aimed to serve both itself and an enemy in the same act. The document of 1939 was, however, the final episode of the British tragedy in which Munich was an intermediate stage.

This White Paper was England's last tribute to a tragic situation of its own creation. It was the last gesture in the progressive decline of England's position in the Middle East. Step by step, it had bartered away its heritage and could give no more. England's honor could not continue to live in the suffocating atmosphere of an appeasement that never could be made adequately to appease. It could not breathe in such a world. No sooner was Malcolm MacDonald's proposal for the breach of the covenant with the Jewish people approved by a Parliament sitting under the darkening pall of war, than the England of Baldwin and Chamberlain threw up its hands and expired in hopeless despair; and a new, desperate, resolute leadership was born. War—in preparation since 1918 and long overdue—had to be declared forthwith. Unequipped, practically unarmed, England took its stand against a powerful and unscrupulous enemy, prepared to do the best with the poor weapons it had. It could look to only one neighbor for support. That neighbor had become a disunited France, a France consumed by cancerous politics, from which all nobility of character and national devotion had been

---

* *Address to Annual Z.O.A. Convention,* September 12, 1943, Columbus, Ohio (Published in *New Palestine* as "Camouflage of a Tragedy," Oct. 8, 1943).

scooped out by the political maggots in its midst bribed by its traditional enemy. Degenerate France was the only foreign arm it had to rely upon. But it collapsed without resistance. Within a few months, England stood alone, its back to the wall, while its leadership undertook as a last measure to organize the democratic world into a second line of defense against the onrushing Invader.

Out of its adversities and defeats, purified by fire, a new England came to life which appreciated for the first time the long, terrible ordeal it had yet to pass through if the Empire was to survive; and prepared to die rather than submit to the will of the prospective ruler of earth. With amazing courage, it faced the blasting storms that poured down from the skies on its cities and towns. It met appalling disaster at Dunkirk. It survived defeats in Libya and Greece. It evacuated outposts of imperial strength in the Far East. It saw its great naval protection battered and broken by the undersea weapons of the enemy. Its banners went up and came down and were raised again. And none defaulted in duty, and none defaulted in sacrifice. This grand spectacle of an aroused people fighting for its life will never be forgotten.

Over and above the roar of battle, the clash of planes, the silence of the thousands of graves in which the heroic dead were enshrouded, the resonant voice of one valiant man was heard, awakening self-reliance and courage, inspiring tenacity and faith and finally gathering around the Banner of England the freedom-loving and freedom-defending peoples of all lands.

History, resting on a stable perspective, will give its estimate of the great service rendered by this man not only for England and the Empire, but for the great free world that is to emerge out of the terrible conflict in which we are now engaged. He has spoken out of the heart of the sturdy people whom he so vividly represents. In his words are heard the majestic tones of Shakespeare, the rotund verse of Milton, the martial songs of Kipling; they reveal the courage and resourcefulness of a gallant people, the stamina of a great race, whose vigor has not abated. Winston Church-ill, leader of England's Government, Chief of its armed forces, organizer of the democratic world, raised England to its old classical stature, redeemed its immediate past and transformed what seemed to be a beaten people into a people of valor, endurance and faith, worthy of respect and reverence.

It was indeed fortunate that on this side of the Atlantic there was found a brother-in-arms and in-purpose, equipped by breeding, by character and experience, to stand by the side of Winston Churchill in leadership. While England was struggling to its feet, seeking a prop for its back, arms and food for its defense, the power and influence of the President of the United States were heard in clear, resonant words, becoming progressively stronger and more determined from month to month, clarifying the issues of the war, indicating the dangers ahead and preparing the united front of the Western democracies. It was the great moral influence and farsighted vision of President Roosevelt that molded a divided people into an effective national union for the defense of the democratic way of life and international justice. In short, this momentous crisis in human history found two extraordinary men in the position of effective leadership.

Thus a world on the brink of destruction, facing the imminent danger that everything held dear for a thousand years was to be set in reverse, was saved for a more secure future in which the seeds of freedom and justice and tolerance, planted by our predecessors, might again come to life in the days to come. There was heard the proclamation of the Four Freedoms. Plans for a nobler destiny of the human race were freely enunciated in all the capitals of the democratic world. Charts of the future were circulated and discussed, once again raising thoughts of world union, world federation, world justice, world equality. These messages of hope, carried to the four corners of the earth, were heard; wherever slaves labored for a master race, wherever men and women were rotting in prison camps, wherever it was possible for the oppressed to look up to the stars, these messages gave them hope to live on. The march of Democracy's soldiers was paced by the drumbeats sounding the call of freedom and equality and justice. Who will deny that there is now becoming visible the dawn of that new day, that better day, and that a fair future awaits the civilization we are fighting for?

But while this amazing recovery has thrilled all those who have lived through it and witnessed the transformation, and while every trace of that macabre world which was about to overwhelm us is being burnt away in struggle, a strange, inexplicable phenomenon forces itself upon our wondering attention. We who sit in this Convention considering the problems of our people, depressed by its present and anxious for its future, are unable to avoid reference to it. The world's recovery excludes the faintest reference to a people vitally, totally involved, but strangely missing in all plans for today and tomorrow. A successful camouflage has obliterated the physical and spiritual presence of an ancient people whose tragedy is the very core of the tragedy of the world.

When the planners of tomorrow speak of a free world, they include as the component parts of that world all sorts and conditions of men—all states and territories and peoples, all servitudes, all wrongs, all inequalities. They take into account, as a matter of course—they need no urgent reminders—all the victims of conquest and refer to each of them by name and place and unequivocal identification. But the people against whom war was declared from the start, who have been expropriated and rendered stateless en masse, who were marked for death from the moment the Nazis took power, who have been systematically killed in all lands occupied by Nazis, who are set aside for death until the very last shot is fired, are looked at with a blind unrecognizing glance, seemingly without place in the picture. These scarred remnants are not included in the inventory. These wrongs are not to be accounted for under an identifying name. These people cannot be included in any category, in any classification. They are summarized in the generality. They are disposed of by evasive references. The brand of inequality and inferiority imposed upon them by their cruelest enemy is not to be touched or removed until the rest of the world has been reorganized and rearranged. With regard to them—their wrongs, their hopes—there is nothing to talk about, nothing to explain, nothing to apologize for. There is to be no accounting. There is to be no word of comfort. There is to be no decision or judgment—memory is to be suspended—no word is to be uttered, *until the nightmare of war has become a matter of the past.* At which time, in all probability, there will be no point in saying anything except to repeat the words of the Kaddish.

That is the general approach. Reflecting that situation, isolated from it yet looming large in the consequences, it is suggested that the same procedure follow in connection with the problem called the Jewish National Home—by oblique reference Palestine—which involves the tiniest notch of land, the slightest disturbance of the rights of others, but which implicates international obligations that have been on the record twenty-five long disappointing years. There was a promise and a covenant made then. It was part of the realities of political and physical life. It was bound up with present and future, but it is intimated that this covenant should be cancelled out for the time being. In the light of vexatious world problems, why should we present that scrap of paper for review now? Why should we remind Great England of an episode it wants to forget? Why should we trouble a troubled world with it? It is, relatively, a piece of business of no great importance. It is a slight item on a bulging agenda. The whole world is to be subjected to overhauling, readjustments, new alliances, new federations. War is to be outlawed. States and peoples are to be reconciled. World trade and industry are to be coordinated. In ways no one can describe at this time, it is intended that that great act of sentiment and magnanimity, that great act of piety, known as the Balfour Declaration, conceived by great English spirits, shall be honored in due course at its discounted value and disposed of when it will not disturb the March to Victory, or the building of the New World.

The perpetration of this monstrous wrong goes on in the midst of the war for freedom and justice. In its effort to smother remembrance of the evasion of responsibility assumed, the violation of a contract performed in good faith by the party of the second part, the Uneasy Conscience of England gives expression to the strangest contradictions in action. It seems to be conscious of sin, but it lacks the moral courage to make confession and reparation. The sight of a living people, standing in protest and refusing to be silenced, provokes auxiliary wrongs, not deliberately intended, perhaps. It is the irritation our moral indignation creates that has made it possible for England to exclude Jewish victims of the war from the Promised Land, to deny Jews the right to bear arms in its defense, to use a lawless White Paper as the instrument for the factual betrayal of a wronged people, *at a time when they are unable to chasten betrayal because of their vital interest in the winning of the war.* It is only in the Jewish National Home that the Munich aberration still has validity.

Is it not pertinent to ask, why do not the grand words of Churchill find response in the English Administration which rules in Palestine? Is the High Commissioner—who sits in Jerusalem and makes and executes laws—an authentic symbol of the fighting Empire reborn under Mr. Churchill's inspiration and guidance? The Administration in Palestine seems to be rigging a situation which is intended to be presented when the war ends as the complete implementation of the White Paper of 1939.

The Jewish Agency is being ignored and oppressed and made the object of organized calumny and slander. The structure of cooperative economy created by Jewish labor is being supplanted by Government institutions in which Jews of Palestine are to be allowed to play no part. The contribution of the Jews of Palestine to the armed forces, and their support of the war effort in general, is being made the subject of prejudiced inquisition, reports of which—under government franchise

—are circulated in all parts of the world to condition world opinion against Jewish rights in Palestine.

Nor is this enterprise born in Jerusalem unknown to London and Washington. It is not a policy conducted in secret. It is a well-planned, self-revealing enterprise which finds support in the London press, in some of the American press and, to our great regret, receives effective aid and support in our Department of State. In this respect, there seems to be a remarkable accord between London and Washington. The plans in Washington fit in smoothly with the plans of the Colonial Office. In Cairo, an official group, animated by a common interest, composed of Englishmen and Americans and servile Arabs, with its contacts in Jerusalem, in London, in New York and in Washington, is engaged in directing a sinister plot to frustrate and nullify Jewish hopes.

The pawns of a projected Arab Federation are being arranged and assigned their respective positions. Emissaries hostile to Jewish aspirations travel from the United States for discussion with King Ibn Saud in Riyadh, and a royal reception is being prepared here for Crown Prince Faisal. Is it intended that Jerusalem shall be governed from distant Riyadh, whose King only yesterday snatched his scepter, dripping with blood, from the hands of old King Hussein? Or is Jerusalem to be ruled from Cairo, the city of bazaars, the venal city, where all things can be bought and sold, including journalists and statesmen, honor and loyalty? In effect, it seems that during the silence we are called upon to observe, an amazing dramatic intervention in a far distant land is being prepared, which is to be used to subordinate Jewish rights in Palestine and remove them from the chart of political information.

To lower our defenses through silence and supineness while our rights are thus being thoroughly emasculated would be not only a crime against ourselves and the future of our people. It would be a betrayal of the principles of democracy and justice which are to be the foundation of the new world.

The time has come for a more natural human approach of Government to the desperate problem of the Jewish people. This moment of decision demands that the Government in Washington, as well as in London, pay us at least the tribute of candor. We have no armies or navies or flying fortresses. We have no gold mines or oil wells. We have none of the powers or authorities of government. We are a people greatly hurt and greatly wronged. We emerge out of this war, out of the Valley of Death, broken as never before. We have a right to demand that the play of diplomatic formalities be discarded with relationship to Jewish suffering and Jewish oppression and Jewish right, and that there should be frank dealing in Washington, as well as in London. There is needed an assurance in plain speech that the covenant made is intended to be kept; that the principle of equality declared for all shall be applied also to us; that the National Home about which America and England have made definite and oft-repeated statements and declarations shall not be left in doubt, shall not be abandoned for other interests, shall not be treated as a trivial incident in the remaking of the world, and that Jewish suffering and Jewish rights shall be treated with respect.

Pages of history are now being written with the blood of our generation. Like the generation that went forth in 1914, many will soon return expecting that a Temple of Justice is being created, where all nations shall meet as equals and all shall be free. It would be a travesty of a holy ideal, if after this great war has passed, its scars healed and its sufferings a matter of memory, in which struggle millions of Jews have suffered, in which Jewish honor has been offended most cruelly, that in that Temple of Justice the cause of the Jewish people shall not be accorded its rightful place, and that Jerusalem shall be forgotten.

NO MORE ANONYMITY*

In the first World War Jews fought on all fronts, but not as Jews. There were two minor exceptions: Jews fought as Jews in the Zion Mule Corps at Gallipoli and in the Jewish Legion against the Turks in Palestine. In every other instance Jews fought as citizens of the State they were part of; they wore various uniforms and died under various flags. They hoped that by sharing in the common defense they would be defending their equal status as citizens. No matter under what disabilities they lived, as Jews they had to subordinate their own interests to the interests of their States. They were loyal, they were patriotic. They wanted to believe that in the peace that was to come, Jewish rights would not be overlooked. Promises calculated to win universal Jewish sympathy were then made by both the Allies and Germany. The Germans offered —if they were the victors—full emancipation to the Jews in Poland, even minority group rights. The Allies issued the Balfour Declaration. But these pledges were unrelated to the fact that the Jews of Poland were fighting with the Russians, the Jews of Germany with the Germans, and

* *The Congress Weekly*, November 15, 1940.

so forth. Whatever came at the end of the war for Jews, it would be a gratuity, an act of kindness, a handout—nothing acknowledged as earned.

A case could be made to show that all was not gratuity; that our political position in Palestine had been created through labor and sacrifice; the foundation of a homeland had been laid—schools set up, swamps drained, colonies settled, a national culture had been revived; the Jewish Legion had been sent to Palestine. All of this had become the substance of demands related to the Balfour Declaration. But not even the vestige of a case could be put together in all of Europe. What we got out of that war was allocated to justice and humanity. The ideal of making the world safe for democracy was subordinated to the high political strategy of the victorious powers.

The world set up at Versailles broke into fragments; not a vestige of it remains alive today. The League of Nations was allowed to die a long drawn-out, servile death. Even before the League passed out, the constitutions of the new states which included equality of rights for Jews had become scraps of paper, mocked and derided. Even the Mandate for Palestine was on the verge of being liquidated; England had in effect announced its intention to congeal the status quo in Palestine and place the Jews under the domination of the Arabs.

Not only had all Jewish rights been disregarded and our position reduced to levels lower than ever before, but there was unloosed, with the connivance and encouragement of the leading western democracies, an organized crusade of hate and prejudice against all Jews, which aimed to sweep Jewish life from the continent of Europe. The devastations of the Nazis have made five million Jews homeless and stateless, and through Nazi aggression anti-Semitism has become a burning issue in every land where Jews live. Whereas in former generations Jews found defenders and protectors, in our day the Jewish people found themselves without defense or protection. Justice and humanity were flouted and eliminated from the field of political action. Even in the United States under great leadership, it became almost impossible to persuade government to raise its voice against the unholy crusade of which the Jews were victims.

The capitulation of the democracies at Munich registered the bankruptcy of the world that had developed out of the French Revolution. For the Jewish people, however, Munich removed the ground under our feet and left us hanging in midair; with no court to appeal to and without opportunity for self-defense. The whole world could adjust itself in case of need to the Nazi way of life; but for the Jews, life in a world made by Hitler was inconceivable. Once that world would be established, Jewish life would be liquidated.

Fortunately, Munich was the last step in retreat. It was realized that the democracies could go no further in the direction of appeasement. The declaration of war issued by England and France was the beginning of resistance. When they offered to defend the sovereignty of Poland, that meant the end of the unchecked crusade of the Nazis. The resistance of England and France opened the door for Jewish participation in their own emancipation and their own defense.

The French Republic has collapsed. It is the victim of its own inner demoralization—of venal politicians, traitorous generals and a mercenary press. It has been disloyal to the ideals of the French Revolution and treacherous to its own partner in the conflict. England now stands alone and interposes the will and self-sacrifice of its people against a desperate aggressor. It is forging a weapon of attack out of its heroic measures of defense. Together with England, as day passes day and the purposes of the world aggressor become more and more apparent, the American people are being drawn closer to the battlefield. It is realized that as goes England, so goes the whole American continent—its freedom, its way of life, its ideals and hopes. It is a source of deep satisfaction to us that the American people are now engaged in preparing their defense, summoning their men to the colors, steeling themselves to the eventualities of war. The American sentiment against Hitler is manifest throughout the country. There is no division on this point between the parties. Subversive movements—including anti-Semitism—have been driven to cover by the resurgence of a determined American patriotism. Americanism is taken today to be synonymous with hostility to the aggressions of the Nazis and all they stand for, including anti-Semitism. It seems to be generally agreed that the American Republic is destined to lead in sacrifice to save democracy and to lead subsequently in the framing of policy that will come with peace.

What part are Jews to play in the struggle fateful for themselves and for the world? Wherever they are free, how are they going to use their freedom in the service of this cause? What are we Jews in America going to do to show that we appreciate that an opportunity faces us to act both as Americans and as Jews?

In the second World War—which will finally determine the unsettled issues of the first—it would be suicidal for Jews to play the part of the Unknown Soldier. In this life and death struggle, we must refuse to be merely the victims, the passive, the impotent, the people without a name.

To serve under all flags but not under our own would serve no useful purpose. It would be quixotic without even symbolic value, it would give us no credit anywhere at any time. It would bring us to another peace conference with Jewish delegations again speaking of justice and rights and humanity. It would repeat an old futile performance. It would maintain an old tradition of Jews as the everlasting suppliants for relief, humbly pleading for the right to live, resigned to being pushed around at will. There would be no record of any contribution that Jews have made to the winning of the war—no matter what we may have done anonymously in any part of the world.

This flagrant misrepresentation must not be allowed. Enlightened Jewish leadership must not let it happen.

At least in Palestine no such prospect is visible. There are over 500,000 Jews who occupy a strategic military position of great importance, which they will not allow to be reduced to anonymity. They know that they can serve as the nucleus of the Near East front, the strength of which is vital to England. They are in a position to supply men and material for the army organized to repel the Italian invasion of Egypt. Practically every able-bodied man has registered for military service. But they are asking for the right to fight under the Jewish flag, in their own units, in their own companies, brigades, divisions; according to the number of men they contribute. The insistent demand of the Palestinian Jews for the right to participate in the Near Eastern defense as Jews has been rejected for months by the stupid British reactionaries in Jerusalem. But what they ask for is so just, their enthusiasm for service is so impressive, that many Zionists are convinced that Prime Minister Churchill will soon be able to remove the Jerusalem obstruction to the formation of a Jewish Army; and Jews the world over will soon have the satisfaction of knowing that on that front Jews appear on the field of battle in their own uniforms, under their own flag, with their own officers, as part of the British Expeditionary Force.

But what are we American Jews doing or proposing to do, in the way of registering our Jewish as well as our American patriotism in this connection? There has been little or no discussion of the problem. I have found in both Zionist and non-Zionist circles a definite fear of organizing any action by American Jews in their own name in any way at all. There is a general unwillingness to face the realities.

The fact is that in many American circles a practical aspect has been given to the idea of aiding England "short of war." Groups have been formed to provide equipment to be shipped to England—ambulances, first aid material, and even planes if they can be purchased. Many of these groups appeal to all citizens. There are quite a number of Jews associated with the William Allen White Committee, with Bundles for Britain, and so forth, but great care is being taken to avoid the impression that the Jews, as Jews, are interested in contributing to the defense of England. Anonymity is preferred. There are some Jews who get excited when they hear of Jews being in the forefront of any of these activities. It is the height of folly for Jews to pursue this course. It is important that we show that as Jews we are not satisfied to do only that which is expected of all Americans. We have a much deeper interest in the defeat of Hitler than any other American citizens. The defeat of Hitler means the victory of Jewish ideals as well as the defeat of the enemy of democracy. We should demand the right to make our own identifiable sacrifice to the cause of Jewish freedom and democracy. It is of extreme importance that in every city Jewish groups—men and women—collect funds, collect materials and send them—in case no Jewish address is known—to any one of the recognized groups, but to ask that their contributions be booked in the name of the Jews of America.

When the time comes—and it may come soon—and a Jewish Army for service in the Near East is given public recognition, it may be possible to send American Jewish men of military age to join that army provided, of course, an agreement can be made with the American Government allowing such young men to cross the seas to help England.

At this time when all America is beginning to realize the important service it has to render to the cause of world democracy—when the best elements are beginning to speak and to assume leadership, let us not show lack of confidence in the moral strength of the American people and lack of faith in the power of American ideals. Let us not be fearful that the Republic based on the Bill of Rights will succumb to alien ideals and misinterpret our desire to serve as Jews in the great struggle. Let us not hesitate to do our duty also as Jews; in doing that we shall be making a significant contribution to the idealism of America and at the same time help to restore the honor of the Jewish people.

THE NEW EMANCIPATION*

The world is in a seizure of appalling disorder. Violence and destruction are the order of the day. Immense physical forces are interlocked in deadly struggle. The sealed caverns that held primitive hatreds and prejudices have been broken open, and barbarities we thought had been purged from our civilization are again unleashed. The whole world is the battlefield—the land, the sea, the air; the frozen regions of the North, the blazing deserts of the torrid zones; all continents and all peoples; the foundations of great civilizations are shaken by a worldwide collision of tremendous forces.

The plan of battle has now become integrated and composed in a kind of order. Today, the Aggressor occupies the larger part of Europe. There is his arsenal. There he maintains his commissary department. It is a fortress in which enslaved peoples are forced to supply labor for aggression. From that point of advantage he sallies forth to conquer, to loot and destroy. After he had overcome the Lowlands, he made his assault from that fortress on the British Isles, encountered a stubborn and heroic resistance, and retreated to his den to lick his wounds and revise his plans. Then he turned his attacks to the East, trampled over many states, seemingly intended to break through further in the direction of Syria, Palestine, the Suez Canal and Egypt. In a moment of fatal decision, he turned his planes and panzers to attack his erstwhile friend in Russia. There he now stands, battering his head against a stubborn opponent, sacrificing many divisions of his strength, unable to break through and incapable of preparing an alternative attack. But slowly the wall of encirclement is extended. It is now almost completed. Russia, Persia, Syria and Iraq, Egypt and Abyssinia to the East; and to the West, England still mistress of the sea, reinforced by an America no longer isolated and neutral. The circle of resistance has become a stout cordon of mechanized armies, of air fleets and sea-craft. The free action of the Aggressor is hampered and interfered with, and he faces the possibility of a furious general assault on all his fronts. He who set out with pomp and brag on an adventure to encircle the world and to make it Prisoner to his will, finds himself slowly being encircled. His doom is marked on the map, and the form of his doom has become discernible. Much of life will have to be spent; the material resources of generations will have to be sacrificed. But this Madness can and will be eradicated.

* *Address to 44th Z.O.A. Convention*, September 7, 1941, Cincinnati, Ohio.

It is to be regretted, however, that what the free world is fighting for is not equally discernible. The Enemy intended to reorganize the world and to establish a New Order. It was based upon the death of democracy, the enslavement of the smaller peoples, the dominance and the rule of the Herrenvolk. The creation of this New Order is to be prevented; that is the purpose of the armies of the free states; that is the determined will of all free peoples. But the issue is not only the frustration of the Nazi hope, but also what kind of world is to emerge when the war is ended. The old world, shaken to its foundations, can never be made to look the same or to be the same in spirit or in form. The causes that lead to periodical outbursts of distemper and insanity and destruction must be eradicated. The flagrant injustices that dominate the organization of our life must be removed. The diplomacy of the forked tongue, the fraud and deception of international dealings, will have to be replaced by a new language and a new spirit. The status quo ante cannot be reintroduced and maintained. The leaders of the war may not evade speaking the truth and acting justly even in wartime. They are called upon to show by conduct that those who raise the banner of freedom and justice even now in the midst of war reject the way of life of the Enemy.

It is tragic that nothing has been said clearly, sincerely, directly, to indicate the intentions of the fighting democracies, the quality and form of the New Order they intend to set up. "Justice," "freedom," the "rights of man" are words repeated, knowing that these words have always been used while perpetrating the grossest offenses against the rights of man and the rights of people. Unless these words are defined, they have no meaning. The world is nauseated by the mechanical repetition of high-sounding slogans. It is waiting for a new content to be placed into these much-abused, old words. This has yet to be spoken. This presses for utterance. Enlightened statesmanship cannot avoid a statement of principles, purposes and ideals—in honest speech, in words that go directly to the heart of the New Man the war is creating.

It is this situation which disturbs the contemplation of our specific problems. We draw comfort from the fact that the Jewish tragedy, which at first seemed to be an isolated and unrecognized incident, has finally been included as an integral part of the tragedy of the world, into which the Barbarism of aggression has plunged it. All of Jewish life has been subjected to a furious, inhuman attack. Hundreds of thousands of human beings have been subjected to the basest cruelties. The institutions of life they had created in the course of generations were plundered and devastated. They have been treated as less than human. All this was regarded by the Western democracies as the recurrence of an unrelated barbarism. It was the Eternal Wanderer again being set upon, despoiled and driven forth. It was a repetition of an old, medieval practice.

To a large degree, it is Jews, through their own actions, who have created the altered situation. They figure no longer as Victims, merely. They have answered the Roll Call and appear in person as active participants in the War. Jewish cooperation is not hidden under cover. It appears more and more as a distinctive, mentionable factor. It has been admitted to the membership of the fighting fraternity. Jews have risen out of the dust and dirt to take up arms in defense of their freedom, of their status in the world. In every free state Jews are fighting valiantly against the common enemy—in the battalions of free Czechoslovakia, of the free Poles, the free French and the free Greeks. Jews have given their lives with outstanding bravery and self-abnegation in the defense of Greece, of Poland, in France, in Crete, in Syria and Abyssinia. The 10,000 Jews enlisted in Palestine have served on all fronts. Now, also, Marrano-Jews hidden away in Soviet Russia are appearing as the most valiant among the defenders of invaded Russia.

It is now impossible for statesmanship to regard Jews as Aliens in the war against Hitler. The pressure of Jewish indignation and protest may still be required to persuade a reluctant England to give place on the battlefield to Jewish divisions, carrying the Jewish flag. But that indignation—and the English sense of justice—will ultimately force the reactionaries in the British Government to concede our demand for equality among the free peoples engaged in the war.

In the preliminary discussions of the New Order, going on simultaneously with the developments of the war, we have earned the right to speak in the discussion, to be considered as voting members of the Fraternity, not suffered, but welcomed. We are not merely a stray people wounded in the accidents of war, but direct and honorable participants in all forms of combat and struggle.

It is not compatible with justice that the status thus acquired should be ignored at this time and that we, of all people, should be asked in the interests of the War to adjourn the consideration of the question of our right to equality. It belies the general professions of devotion to principle and ideal to propose such disregard of our human rights at the very moment when Jewish blood is being spilled on all battlefields. We have the right to express the suspicion that if we are not being greeted as equals in wartime, we shall not be treated as equals when Peace comes.

It is disconcerting, to say the least, to find in all the propaganda of the

562 Memoirs In Profile

war, high and low, a studied avoidance of reference not only to the status of the Jewish people, but also a reluctance even to express sympathy with the sufferings of the Jewish people. The impression is made that Jews are the Unmentionables. Their tragedy, the cruelties practiced upon them, the sufferings they endure, the courage they manifest in battle, are regarded as matters not to be spoken of.

After all, the quintessence of Jewish demands is Equality of rights and status, not favor. It is a denial of Equality to avoid reference to the sacrifices and sufferings of Jews while appreciations are extended toward the sacrifices of other people. It is a denial of Equality to pass by with indifference the claims of Jews in a New Order which is to be based upon justice and democracy. It is a denial of our Equality to pass unobserved and uncensored the worldwide propaganda against Jews, conducted by the Aggressor States. It is a denial of our Equality to propose that our rights, in particular, shall be subordinated, in discussion and in fact, to the rights of any other people, to assume our status to be inferior to the status of any other people. Human beings are equal in the sight of God and before the law. Peoples are equal, whether large or small, in a just political world. There are inalienable rights acquired by Jews in every land under law, and they cannot be made the subject of adjustments and balances without our direct participation in the discussions. We are not prepared to endure any offense to our status without protest and complaint. In every discussion in which Jewish interests are involved, the Jewish people are entitled to be self-represented. It is unfair and unjust to ask us, in the interests of the War, to postpone consideration of this fundamental principle in order to relieve friendly governments of what they regard as political embarrassment they must be prepared to face if they honestly have in mind to deal justly with our cause.

It is implicit in our demand for Equality the world over to insist that during the wartime, the right of the Jewish people to establish a free Homeland in Palestine shall not only be acknowledged, but that nothing shall be done during the war to frustrate or to impair that right. The pleadings of the old diplomacy have lost their convincing power. That diplomacy retains only a historical value. It has no validity in a world torn by passions and interests, a world in upheaval, in which a New Order is being created. The existence of the Homeland in Palestine and all it signifies, all it implies, cannot be ignored and its status must not be treated as secondary or auxiliary under the plea of political necessity.

The Jewish Homeland in Palestine is not a recent discovery. It represents unbroken loyalty to an ancient ideal which, in our own time, we have succeeded in making real, substantial, effective. The 500,000 Jews now rooted in the soil of their Promised Land came there under pledges made by responsible governments at a time when they were sober, far-seeing and desirous of being helpful to a just cause. They did not settle there surreptitiously, without title. Their title was validated by law and guaranteed by 51 free states. The implications of their settlement were known and appreciated. They have driven their stakes deep into the soil and cannot be uprooted, nor can they be made pawns in political contracts with third parties. Their title cannot be turned into leaseholds, nor can they be made subject to alien rules. It was known in advance that the purpose of their entry into Palestine was to establish a self-governing Jewish Commonwealth, and that Commonwealth cannot be placed under alien subjection or impaired in plan and scope to suit the exigencies of the changing political situation. The Key to the Homeland in Palestine belongs to the Jewish people, and it cannot in justice be taken away under the plea of serving the vital necessities of the war.

This position the Jewish people must defend with all their strength and influence. In the chaos that prevails in Jewish life generally, in the disorder of Jewish organization, it is important that we remind ourselves, and the Jewish world at large that the Zionist Organization, the instrument of redemption founded by Theodor Herzl, has assumed and possesses, in a formal way, the corporate right to represent the interests and the destiny of the Jewish people.

There are Jews who aspire to avoid the appearance of Jewish solidarity. They pursue a course of avoidance and denial. The amazing advice is given that it might be wiser strategy to deny the unity of Jewish destiny, and to appear in unrelated fragments, as a variety of claimants in the Court of International Justice. This advice would be fatal to our cause and fatal to Jewish survival. As Zionists, we seek a manifestation of the solidarity of all Jews, here and abroad, in a common responsibility for Jewish life. We seek a status of equality now, during the war, and confirmation of that status later, when peace comes.

THE UNNAMED ALLY OF THE UNITED NATIONS*

The vast economic resources of the American people are at last being absorbed in the grim business of warfare. A great effort in propaganda

* *Free World*, September, 1942.

and organization was required to make America aware of the fact that it is directly involved in the most destructive struggle of all history. The nerves of the American people have been racked by excited comment (through press, radio and forum) on the developing strategies of the battlefield. The scene does not suffer a lack of clamor, alarm, and wild speculation. It will take some time to toughen Americans and make them feel in a killing mood. That dreadful task must be prepared for and resolutely faced. Enormous progress in that direction has been made. It is visible throughout the land.

As we become accustomed to this state of affairs, discussions of how the fighting is being organized become franker and more realistic. The amenities of a debating society cannot be maintained in the face of a rapid reorganization of our economic life, radical changes in daily habit and outlook—civilian defense, rationing, dim-outs and blackouts, the mounting record of destruction and death. It will not take long for war to destroy established refinements in public speech and manners. The approach to the problem of peace will also have to become as real and brutal. Man-to-man talks are in order. The old diplomats have nothing further to contribute to the creation of the world of tomorrow. The wretched parts they have played have fallen out of the drama of life. A new routine will have to be invented and employed. Peace also will have to be made with iron and steel. The white heat of justice will have to consume the diplomatic approach and the legalistic technique of the past.

Candor and truth should dominate at least one part of the world scene where peace is being prepared. The discussions in London and Washington between leaders of the governments-in-exile play an important part in war and in peace. These men have seen the destruction of their homelands and the enslavement of their kinsfolk. They now taste the bitterness of exile and gather in foreign lands to see what they can do to redeem the broken world. They are encouraged by the democratic welcome accorded their hopes and aspirations. They have formed associations and agencies of propaganda to strengthen the morale of their exiled compatriots here, in England, and in South America. Their stimulating influence reaches out to the prisoners in the concentration camps of their homelands. They influence directly and indirectly the underground movements that are shaking the soil under Hitler's feet. They organize legions on foreign soil to join under their own national banners on every front. And they are engaged in talking of the future.

In these discussions there is accord on the unrelenting desire to see

Hitler destroyed. There is unanimity in the deep loathing of all he stands for. That about exhausts the scope of harmony. With regard to other subjects, the qualities of courage and directness and clarity are still lacking. Those who take the floor skirt the edges of all prickly difficulties. They make vague allusions to things that are admittedly vital but which it would not do to mention now. There are too many subjects taboo. Reference to old feuds and racial disputes must be suppressed in order to concentrate undisturbed on the chief business of defeating the aggressor. The show window must be arranged to display a united front. Nothing must be allowed to spoil the public impression.

This state of affairs is ominous. The new world cannot be based merely upon hatred of Hitler. It cannot be balanced on that narrow platform. Many inter-group hatreds and prejudices will have to be consumed in the fires of this war in order to establish a lasting peace. Now is the time for the democratic nations to rip off the masks of politeness and etiquette and get down to the rough business of eradicating the cankers of old feuds and rivalries and prejudices. It is easier to break the complacent mood when men are drawn together in adversity than later, at the end of the war, when selfish interests and ambitions again begin to reassert themselves. A lasting fraternity can be created when the victims of Hitler's crimes suffer a common exile and common misfortune. Comrades in arms can more easily come to an understanding when the fighting is hot, than when each one goes his own way and pursues his own interests. Now is the time for national error to be confessed and past sins forgiven. Peace is not served by making believe that these matters can be tackled later. The representatives of governments-in-exile should seal pacts of lasting friendship, conscious of historic realities, while they are in a common exile. It would do them all good to acquire the habit of frankness and friendliness with those who, yesterday, may have been the stealers of their territory, the oppressors of their minorities, miniature imitators of an execrated Hitler.

Included in these reservations is the problem of the Jewish people. This seems to be the blind spot in all discussions. The facts that reveal the active and passive presence of Jews in every corner of the fighting world are not given any place on the agenda. The use Hitler makes of anti-Semitism as the entering wedge of his Fifth Column invasions is overlooked; and no attention is paid to the vicious propaganda that the Jews are responsible for preventing the Democracies from making peace with the peace-loving Hitler. The policy seems to be: Don't make any replies in which Jews are implicated. The case of the Jews seems doomed to be dimmed out for the duration. Not that it is wholly suppressed. It is sensed in the overtones of all conversation. It overshadows the discussion of other problems. But it has no integrated existence of its own. Jews may be invited to sit in at informal round-table conferences, but, at these conferences, not even an oblique reference is made to what place, if any, they are to occupy in the world of tomorrow. In no part of the political field are they qualified to speak as parties in interest. There are good friends who suggest the tactfulness of not even pressing this point. Is not equal justice promised for all when peace comes?

The whole world is undergoing revolutionary changes. The Jews are the objects of an incredible crusade aiming at their extinction. They are defending themselves as far as it is humanly possible. But the traditional attitude toward them is still being maintained in all political circles. The status of the Jewish people is to be determined by competent authority at the end of the war. From a formal point of view, they have not been, and they are not now, members of any recognized group of states, nations, or peoples. When the day comes, they may apply for admission and their credentials will be scrutinized and passed upon. Consideration of their case will come up only after all of the other states and peoples have agreed to the order of business. The tragedy of the Jews is an incident in the domestic affairs of the peoples among whom they have found protection. Let the Poles and the Czechs dispose of their Jews; the English and the Americans have no Jewish problems of their own. It is considered sufficient merely to say that "the world of tomorrow will not know the shame of anti-Semitism." Indignation may be expressed on occasion about racial persecution. The terrible plight of the refugees may find sympathy. It is better, however, to avoid too much emphasis even upon Jewish suffering. For the time being, what ails Jews should be fragmentized or isolated. The world problem of the Jewish people will be taken up by the international club after the registry has been agreed to and the constitution adopted.

The peace that dated from Versailles gave Poland its freedom and set up the new republic of Czechoslovakia. It dismembered the Austrian Empire, gave Hungary its independence, handed over Bessarabia and Bukovina to Rumania. It set up Finland, Estonia, Latvia, and Lithuania. All its unfinished business it transferred to a League of Nations, which was hamstrung by constitutional limitations and an amazing system of checks and balances. What is forgotten is that the same authority also confirmed and established the rights and status of the Jewish people. The decisions affecting the Jews are as valid as all other treaties and agreements created by the peace after the first World War. The makers of the new order do not propose to start from scratch, to take over the world Hitler has destroyed and regard that as the *status quo*. They will begin with the scraps of the era after Versailles and patch up what is reclaimable or remake what is beyond repair. Whatever remains of the rights given to Jews at Versailles, therefore, cannot be overlooked either during the war or when peace comes, if the principles of justice and equality are to be applied without prejudice or discrimination.

Out of the first World War came recognition of the equality of Jews as such, in lands where lingual, cultural or religious rights were accorded to minorities. The historical connection of the Jewish people with Palestine was recognized and it was agreed to give them an opportunity under international guardianship to rebuild their national home in that land. It gave the Jewish people a national habitation as a matter of international justice. With the debacle of the states in which they were to be exercised, Jewish group rights have now disappeared. In the course of twenty years, the Mandatory Government, using Palestine as a pawn in a larger political game, reduced the meaning of the Mandate to the nullifying policy of the MacDonald White Paper, which proposed to place the Jews in Palestine in the status of a permanent minority. But whatever the implications of these destroyed rights, the United Nations, fighting for international justice, cannot in justice proceed on the theory that the Jewish people must start with those desiccated rights they had when Hitler began his conquest of the world.

The savage efforts of the Nazi gangsters to destroy the Jews in Europe have not succeeded. Jews are available as substantial assets in the global war effort. They have not lost their courage or their hope. Equally with all other conquered peoples, they are enslaved and oppressed, but wherever possible they make an effective resistance. In spite of the destructive efforts of Hitler, a substantial remnant of Jews carries on the active struggle.

The Jewish part in the fight of the countries now overrun by the Nazis is a record of heroism and valor. Wherever they could, Jews have stood up and fought to the last against the invading German armies. Poland was the first country to give battle to Hitler's hordes; the Polish Jews were the first to take up arms against the common enemy. The Polish Government had no time to mobilize more than a small part of its reserves. In addition to some 30,000 Jews serving normally with the Polish standing army, authoritative estimates indicate that only an additional 20,000 were called up at the outbreak of the war. At the same time many Polish Jews resident abroad enlisted with the Allied armies. It is estimated that in France alone by February, 1940, some 7,000 Polish Jews had registered for service. In the recent reconstruction of the Polish armies on Soviet soil, Jews have contributed a high percentage which, according to the estimate of General Anders, has brought up the Jewish ratio to 15 per cent of the new Polish force raised in Russia.

The number of Jews serving in the French Army and Foreign Legion before the collapse of France is estimated as high as 60,000. This represents the majority of Jewish adults of military age in France. A number of Jews later joined the Free French Forces in Syria and elsewhere. In the Greek fight Jews took a valiant part, which has been acknowledged by the Greek authorities. The number of Jews serving with the Greek armies is estimated at some 20,000. Jewish participation in the heroic guerilla warfare now being conducted in Yugoslavia, Greece and elsewhere should not be overlooked. In particular, their part in the Partisan units in Soviet Russia is a stirring chapter of which the world at present knows too little. The heroic fight of the Jews of Poland, Greece and Russia on the front and behind the lines is an epic story of amazing courage and daring.

Jewish volunteering in Palestine forms a chapter by itself. The sixteen thousand Jewish men and women who have volunteered for service with the British Army have provided pioneer companies which saw fighting on many fronts, including France; they supplied the personnel of drivers' companies, artillery units, R.A.F. ground staff, etc., etc. These Jewish soldiers have been cited for extraordinary bravery and gallantry in action by the commanding officers in the campaigns of Tobruk, Greece, and Crete. The Jewish National Home has not only been able to place in the field volunteers for the army and technicians for its specialized services at times when they were most needed, but it has also furnished a body of several hundred thousand men and women, absolutely loyal to the cause of the United Nations, at a point of strategic importance where they render the greatest service to the war effort.

In addition to providing this foothold of a dependable population on the approaches to vital empire communications, the Jewish National Home gave outstanding service through the contribution of its industrial, scientific, and technical resources. It is worth noting that Jewish Palestine has been able to make some contribution to the vital battle of the seas. Many Jewish seamen have already given their lives for the common cause in Jewish ships that have been lost both on Atlantic routes and in local coastal navigation. Many other Jewish seamen are serving with the

Royal Navy, the R.A.F. marine stations, and the merchant navy.

A discussion of the war effort made by the Jewish people throughout the world would be incomplete without reference to the many contributions, apart from that of combatant manpower, made in the struggle against the forces of Nazism. The Jewish people of many countries, particularly the five million Jews in the United States, have played a notable part in the moral rearmament of the Democracies. As the first victim of Nazi aggression, Jewry has been most sensitive to the true character and real aims of Nazism. It recognized the Nazi designs against all free peoples; from the first it threw all its spiritual and material strength against the Nazi tyrants. Jews served as awakeners of the forces of democracy and perhaps their outstanding contribution has been to aid in the slow but growing awareness by democratic peoples of the Nazi bid for world mastery, which was at the same time an awareness of the futility of isolationism and of the necessity for collective security. They stressed these principles and they warned the Democracies of the increasing strength and danger of Hitler when these acts brought upon them the odium of warmongering. They braved this criticism when the cup of prejudice against them was already spilling over because they felt that it was their duty to play this part in mankind's struggle for freedom.

Why has it not seemed in order to speak of these facts and to mention the Jews as active factors in the war? Has it been due to a subconscious desire to avoid arousing a sleeping anti-Semitism in the Democracies themselves? Or is it a remnant of the fatal wish to appear not to cross Hitler which lingers in the thoughts of many European statesmen? Or does this studied oversight mark a desire not to have Jews raise their heads as a people when the war ends?

In no way has this policy of evasion seemed more fantastic and inexplicable than in the attitude assumed toward the Jewish appeal to be allowed to form a Jewish Army in Palestine which would fight with the United Nations under its own flag to strengthen the defenses of Palestine and the Near East. From the beginning of the war an earnest effort has been made by recognized spokesmen of the Jewish people to persuade English authority, but decision has been stalled and the effort has failed. It was urged that the Arabs might be offended; that equipment was not available; that the Jews might, through such recognition of the right to arm themselves, make political demands at the end of the war. But common sense rejects all these explanations. They are not truthful explanations. Equipment could have been made available had the value of Jewish participation been recognized and appreciated. The Jewish people are the only people in the Near Eastern territory upon whose loyalty and devotion there can be absolute reliance. The Jews are the only inhabitants of Palestine pleading for the right to be registered among the recognized defenders of their land, which they regard as the bulwark of the democratic front. They stand alone as the unequivocal enemies of Hitler in a sullen sea of Arab treachery. The Arabs are not being appeased by refusing to allow Jews to be armed; the real appeasement of the Arabs would require the English evacuation of their positions in the Near East. From Cairo to Bagdad, the Arabs are waiting to spring to the aid of the Nazis and the Fascists at the first sign of collapse of the defenses of the United Nations around the Suez Canal.

The suppression of the facts of Jewish participation in the war is therefore unwarranted by any of the interests in the political field or in the war effort. To intimate that it is premature to raise the question is a denial of the general conclusion that present discussion of the pattern of the new world, in all its aspects, is an imperative preliminary to a just peace after the war. It is not proposed to construct the new world out of new material or newly discovered principles of justice and right-eousness. These old principles have not been discarded. The reaction to the Nazi revolution will produce a better understanding of these ideals, which are to be translated anew into the material of the new structure of international society. A sincere effort will have to be made once again to see whether justice and righteousness can overcome the depravity of the human race.

The rights Jews have acquired in the modern world have come after generations of struggle against tremendous odds. Their medieval status as aliens was altered with the French Revolution, the ideals of which were carried by Napoleon's legions all over Europe. Their recognition as citizens in the French Republic was the beginning of their emancipation in Europe. The last hundred and fifty years has witnessed a continual struggle to have their rights extended to their brethren in other lands; and they have had a fair measure of success. In 1918, they were accorded rights in every state in which democratic equality was given to individuals and to groups united by ties of race, religion, language or culture. The Balfour Declaration, as subsequently integrated in the Mandate, recognized their right to establish their national homeland in Palestine. The concept of their nationhood was thus enlarged. Through the exercise of their rights in Palestine for over twenty years they have displayed their capacity for national life and self-government. Through the rights given to them as groups, the Committee of Jewish Delegations, an association representative of all European Jewish communities, took an important part in the development of the rights of minorities in the League of Nations. That accumulation of legal action and representation under international sanctions cannot now be regarded as of no importance and entitled to no consideration. The disregard of their acquired status is at variance with the professions of the United Democracies as enunciated by their leading statesmen.

The Jewish people are entitled to a place in the world order now, as a matter of justice and fair play. There can be no interregnum in an obvious case of justice so far as the United Nations are concerned. The Jewish people are entitled to be heard now. Not as fragments, not as individuals, but as a people. They have a stake as interested parties in the world's unfinished business. The points of order that are raised stem from practices which the new world is called upon to do away with for all time. Hesitation or equivocation will contribute to the impairment of the morale of the democratic forces. It is a flagrant violation of right that in the concert of nations now rallying to reassert the authority of justice in the modern world, the Jewish people—the carriers of the Hebraic conception of justice and righteousness—should be shoved back into what is tantamount to their medieval status, as if they were a horde of hapless refugees entitled to the charity of the world, but not to their inalienable rights. Least of all is it becoming for the smaller peoples now suffering oppression and exile to refuse to make room in their councils for the national representatives of the classic exiles of the world. Between these small peoples and the Jewish people, there is one distinction: the Jews have suffered more and for a longer time. They should cease to be the unnamed ally of the democratic nations.

STILL ON THE WAITING LIST*

Rumors had been circulated in Washington before the President left for the Crimea Conference that the problem of the Jewish people and Palestine would come up for discussion by the Big Three. It may be that the wish was father to the thought. The wish was substantiated by what seemed to be sources of authorized prophecy. The Jewish question was about ripe for discussion in an official way. American opinion favorable to a Jewish Palestine had expressed itself generously in the press, on the

* *Palestine*, March 1945 (Editorial).

radio, in the halls of Congress. The desirability of disposing of the matter without further delay was being urged by men high in authority. The President himself had given indication of a desire to follow the matter through at the earliest opportunity. There was every reason to think, therefore, that a preliminary discussion might take place at any rate between Mr. Churchill and Mr. Roosevelt when next they met.

The reports on what was achieved at these conferences have now been recorded. Many of the controversial issues were settled. Announcement was made that a conference would be held in San Francisco on April 25, 1945, where, it is expected, the foundation will be laid for the international organization which is to succeed the League of Nations.

The only reference to the problem of the Jewish people and Palestine was made by Mr. Churchill in his address to the House of Commons on February 17th:

"Although we did not reach a solution of the problems of the Arab world and of the Jewish people in Palestine, I have hopes that when the War is over, good arrangements can be made for securing the peace and progress of the Arab world and generally of the Middle East."

Mr. Roosevelt's address to Congress on March 1st was even less revealing than Mr. Churchill's. His only reference to Jews was a facetious remark which did not appear in the advance copy of his speech that went to the press. In a reference to his meeting with King Ibn Saud, Jews were alluded to. It would appear from official reports, therefore, that the Jewish question was not even discussed between the Big Three. It was laid over for the duration.

Once again, by accident or design, the Jewish question seems to have been relegated to the rear and Jews are bidden to await the end of the war. A claimant for justice, again sent back to the end of the line, might have been favored with some public assurance that justice would ultimately reach him. But the official reports contain no balm for the wounds of the Jewish people, no words of general consolation and no promise on which hope could be based. The Jewish interest in Palestine was blacked out by the pomp and ceremony attendant upon the task of establishing good relations with the Arab kings.

Attempts will now be made, as always, to establish another account of "off-the-record" conversations which, for various reasons, could not be included in the official versions. Guesses have been ventured as to what actually was talked of between Mr. Churchill and Mr. Roosevelt. One rumor has it that it was practically agreed to set up a Jewish State in a partitioned Palestine. Another rumor was that the ban on Jewish immigration would be lifted and that the Arabs had been persuaded to consent to this action in order to show the world that they were not utterly lacking in the milk of human kindness.

It is crystal-clear, however, that the United Nations officially are not ready for a statement on Palestine and that their present intention is to avoid a decision "for the duration," which may mean until Germany is defeated or until Germany and Japan are disposed of.

It will now be urged by non-Jewish friends of the Jewish cause that the Jews should not be disturbed by what has taken place. They will be advised to be patient for a little while longer. What cannot be done now, whatever the reason may be, will be done in due course. The makers of the peace, the organizers of the New World, have enormously difficult tasks before them which they must dispose of first. You may rely upon the assurances given by your friends in authority, that there is no ground for disquiet. They have not forgotten you. Very soon your turn will come.

We confess that although there was no ground for believing that consideration would be given at Yalta to the Jewish cause, nor that a preliminary discussion would take place to be ripened into a decision later on, nevertheless there is cause for disquiet in the utter silence of the reporters on the nature of the Jewish problem, in the absence of a consoling word, or of an assurance that the Jewish case is being considered with an eye to an ultimate just decision. Why should the Jewish people be the last on the list? Why is it regarded as subsidiary to all other problems? Do not the sufferings of Jews entitle them to a kindly word from the Court of Justice? The repetition of these obvious questions becomes tiresome.

Under conditions as they are, such friendly advice might be followed if in the waiting period the position of the Jewish people with regard to Palestine would not be prejudiced, and during the interim the status quo would be maintained; if Jews would be confident that at the end of the period their position would not be worsened; if they could afford to wait.

Last month we attempted, upon the basis of news reports, to indicate the hopeless situation of hundreds of thousands of Jews in the liberated areas. It will be almost impossible for the vast majority to find a place in the economic field in view of the prejudiced conditions that still prevail and will continue for a long time to come. Tens of thousands of them are doomed to perish of neglect and privation. They see no future for themselves in the lands soaked with the blood of millions of their brethren. They sense with acute pain that there is no place for them in these lands where, as soon as the war ends, a terrible struggle for survival will ensue in which they will be crushed between rival interests. For that reason, the vast majority look to Palestine as the land of their future and they cannot wait until the last acre of Germany is taken and occupied. Action deferred increases the number of victims of a long-endured martyrdom.

Nor does our position vis-à-vis the Arab world remain in status quo. While the Jews patiently wait, the political friends of the Arabs are actively engaged in strengthening the position of the Arab world, which is organizing itself against Jewish interests. The Arab League (designed and promoted by England over a period of many years) now features a Greater Syria in which Palestine is to be absorbed. The outlines of this combination are already visible. A broader federation of Arab states to serve as the spearhead of collective Arab aggression was recently formed in Cairo. This larger federation has the blessing of both England and the United States.

While the Jews are waiting, the prestige of the Arab states is being raised by propaganda organized by the British Foreign Office and our own State Department. Their kings are being flattered and the good will of these potentates is being solicited at a time when it is well known that their only common interest is a desire to strengthen their autocratic powers and to frustrate Jewish hopes. Mr. Roosevelt's reception of King Ibn Saud was more than a social event. It was an act of political significance. His conversations with King Farouk serve to give Egypt a clear bill of health and paved the way for the acceptance of Egypt as a member of the United Nations. It was the signal for declarations of war against Germany from the "sovereign" Arab states, and preparations for their admission on the basis of their war declarations as member states at the San Francisco Conference.

Thus these erstwhile enemies of the Allies—saboteurs and obstructionists—will take their seats in the international Conference but the interests of the Jewish people with regard to Palestine will not be represented at all.

In other words, while the Jews wait, the Jewish National Home is being encircled by recognized and registered Arab states introduced to the society of nations by their political friends who advise us to wait for a decision with regard to our own case after the war is over. For our own good, they should not commit themselves on the Jewish question.

And while we are waiting, the Mandatory Government seals the doors of Palestine to Jewish immigration and within thirty days, no more visas for Palestine will be available for the thousands of Jews clamoring for them in France, in Belgium, in Switzerland, etc. The intent of the White Paper is being achieved while we are waiting. The land promised the Jews will be closed to them in the moment of their greatest distress. In effect, for all practical purposes, the judgment we are advised to wait for with patience and confidence will have been rendered against us. After the enemy is defeated, decisions already incorporated in terms of reality will be proclaimed.

THE GRIEVANCES OF THE JEWS*

In the world-wide discussion of United Nations plans for the promotion of international justice and security, we, as Americans and as Jews, are impelled once more to ask for just consideration of the tragic position of the Jewish people and their vital interest in the postwar world.

American opinion has been advised not to expect from San Francisco anything more than the draft of a constitution. Only the framework of international relations and of procedure for maintaining an international organization should be anticipated. No effective decisions on policy or declarations of general principles are to be made. The terms of peace are to be left to the Fighting Allies. Any expression of views of matters that agitate the heart of mankind have been declared by technicians as irrelevant to the prescriptions set for the guidance of the Conference. The Council Chamber is to be conditioned for utter silence on controversial questions. There must be no clamor for the righting of fundamental wrongs.

It would be a stultification of the great cause for which millions have died if the first public assembly of free states, after the devastation which has impaired the foundations of modern civilization, were to ignore the mood and temper of the world and pass without comment or consideration the grievances that have to be registered, the injustices that must be protested, the universal conditions that make for peace or war, and would regard as relevant only the bare bones of a new world structure.

The Dumbarton Oaks proposals, influenced by what are called realistic considerations, sought to avoid the use of abstract principles

* *Address, Rally for Jewish Rights,* under the auspices of the American Jewish Conference and American Zionist Emergency Council, April 29, 1945, Lewisohn Stadium, N.Y.

and gave only passing expression to sentiments of justice and human rights. The intention was to isolate the form from the substance. But the vital questions that press heavily upon the conscience of the world will not so easily be excluded from an international gathering assembled at this time.

The printed agenda may exclude them, but the conscience of men of vision and justice will refuse to be arbitrarily confined to formalities. What the war was fought for cannot be waived aside on the ground that it may interfere with routine or convenience, or may provoke embarrassment.

The great army of the dead will be looking over the shoulders of the statesmen, admonishing them to live up to the ideals for which so many sacrifices have been made.

What is to be done to insure a brighter future for human rights; what kind of world is to be established; how peace and brotherhood and equality are to be achieved; what fundamental wrongs have to be considered before the proceedings begin—must find a place in the record of San Francisco, even if it will not be incorporated in final decisions.

When the roll was called at San Francisco this week, a basic question immediately arose, which goes beyond the rules of order: *Ab initio*—who are its members and who has a right to appear? The names of all states allied in the war (and present in San Francisco) have been called and their accredited delegates have received credentials. Even the names of states which sabotaged the war and remained enemies until the last day of grace (and which came to San Francisco with pomp and colorful decorations) were called and their accredited delegates were handed their credentials.

But the people who submit an international covenant, subscribed to by fifty-two nations, under which they were accorded recognition as a people; who, in the first act of the Hitler tragedy, appeared as disfranchised aliens, homeless and stateless, and were abandoned to their fate by the democratic world; who, in the second act, were a people in flight everywhere, stripped of dignity, everywhere hunted and destroyed, serving only as human barricades against the aggressor; and who, in the last act, were the victims of a mass extermination unparalleled in history— this people has not been called or named or given tickets of admission. Its representatives are not present. There are no credentials for them. On the register of living peoples with rights and status, their name does not appear.

Nor will they be heard to present their bill of particulars—who wronged them and how, what they ask to be done to repair injuries, to give them security and freedom. They are compelled to wander about in the lobbies, without identification, barred from entrance to official councils, passing their memoranda, sending letters to the authorities, seeking a friend at court to speak for them. Only that greatly wronged people has found every door closed, every window barred, every crevice sealed, and every legal technicality invoked to deny it the right to appear among the free peoples of the world and to speak on its own behalf.

It is repugnant to our sense of justice that the first formal step in the creation of a new world federation should, by indirection or omission, by legal definition, congeal a fundamental wrong which radically affects the status of a people.

The first League of Nations gave recognition to the historic association of the Jewish people with Palestine, their ancestral home, and to all the implications of that relationship. It gave national status to an Agency of the Jewish people and charted the course that was expected to lead to the establishment of Palestine as a free Commonwealth. The Jewish people were given the opportunity, under law, to set in motion the processes of Jewish return and liberation. Sanction was given to their beginning the creation of their own self-governing State. How this State was to be created was described and approved in the Mandate.

What the League of Nations approved and sanctioned, the trustee of the Mandate nullified by illegal action. It was the violation of the intent and purpose of the Mandate which made it impossible for the Jewish people to proceed with their national redemption, and thus made it impossible under the rules to appear in court in person to demand redress. Against procedure which subordinates a fundamental human right to formal definition, which rules out in advance the right of a people to plead its own case, which establishes a people as an "outsider" in the society of peoples, this great assembly in New York's Stadium registers its protest and addresses itself to San Francisco, to take cognizance of its protest in the name of international justice.

For twelve heart-rending years the Jewish people have endured a systematic persecution that has moved with mounting speed and ferocity to a dreadful climax, the horrible details of which are now being given in the press. It has become apparent that the problem of the Jewish survival as a people was coming to an unavoidable climax and demanded a radical and immediate solution. Appeals for the rescue of the millions of Jews trapped in Europe were not heard by the Allied nations during all these years. Demands for the abrogation of the British White Paper and the opening of the doors of Palestine to Jewish immigration received only a formal hearing and a practical denial. A great variety of protest meetings on all occasions have been held and the record is filled with resolutions adopted. Volumes of memoranda have been submitted to various nations, pointing to legality and justice and humanity. Assurances have been given that when the war is over, it would be possible to consider the question. Many words of sympathy were uttered, many declarations were made, but in effect, the whole question of Jewry's suffering and survival has not yet come within the range of the agenda of the nations gathered to deal justly with the problems of the new order and to establish a permanent peace.

The eyes of all the world have therefore turned to the great assembly meeting in San Francisco, with the hope that not only the universal problems of peace and justice shall be solved but that the forty-six nations gathered together would not allow the moment to pass without giving thought to the tragic plight of the Jewish people and to their demands for justice, hitherto denied them.

We are a small people with a long history of suffering. Down through the ages we have been the classical victims of continuing crucifixion. Destiny forces us to hold high and unfalteringly the torch of justice and peace, to suffer for the right, and to maintain the brotherhood of man. It is our duty to demand that justice be established as the pervading principle in the future structure of organized society. Until justice is done, even unto the Jewish people, the work begun in San Francisco, to be continued elsewhere later, will not be well done; the foundations will not hold, and those who have died on the battlefields will have died in vain.

OUTSIDE THE UNITED NATIONS*

The task completed by the United Nations at San Francisco has been accepted with relief by a grateful world. The delegates surmounted all the hurdles of methods and interests and emerged with an instrument of greater promise than was foreshadowed in the Dumbarton Oaks proposals. The opening of the proceedings was imbued with what seemed

* *Palestine*, July–August 1945 (Editorial).

to be a mood of collective dedication. Before many days had passed, however, the Conference came up against the elimination by death, suicide, and surrender of the Nazi leaders and the collapse of the German front. With the cessation of hostilities there came to the fore, growing in volume from day to day, the old habits of sparring for place and power, as if all parties concerned were interested in returning as quickly as possible to the practices of the prewar world. It was like the morning after a nightmare. The delegates at San Francisco began to wonder how they could have been overcome—what magic had been used—to accept the stirring slogans of the critical days before and after Dunkirk. They wanted to get rid of the implications of a perfectionist world, and began to think and work in prewar fashion, determined, however, to move along this time with greater caution and deliberation.

Fearful of any discussion of basic questions, the leadership of the Conference had insisted that the agenda should be limited to the drafting of a charter for a new world organization. It should not have anything to do with the peace settlements. It should lay over for another day consideration of all knotty problems. It should avoid precise definitions. It should be devoted merely to "drafting" a document. The procedure at San Francisco did hew to this formal line, but the realities could not be hidden for long by debate about the text of a document. Motives and interests were exposed through the transparencies of strategy. Each of the Big Three had its satraps, and the votes showed the existence of blocs, of spheres of influence, of far-reaching combinations for economic advantages. In the last analysis, the Conference was not so formal as it seemed to be at the beginning. In fact, the pattern of the future was being woven into the text of the Charter through discussion, controversy, press statements, press comments, so that the whole world could see what the future was to be in spite of the attempt to camouflage it.

One wondered why the delegations of the United States and England were so interested in having Peron's Argentina included among the charter members of the United Nations at this first session. What political purpose would it serve that could stand the scrutiny of justice? Why could not Argentina be asked to wait a while? The Fascist state of Argentina had written a shameless record of collaboration with the Axis during all the years of the war; even while the Conference was being held, it was engaged in proving its enduring friendship for Nazi Germany by providing a haven of refuge for the Nazi criminals and their stolen property. It served no political purpose to ignore the criminal past of Argentina and to accord it a place among the peace-loving nations without scrutiny of its intentions. In fact, the admission of Argentina did for Argentina what it was unwilling to do for itself. The Conference washed away its sins without requiring even a gesture of repentance from the sinner.

One may also wonder why it was necessary—for what urgent political purpose—to call the five Arab states to San Francisco. During the entire period of the war not one of them fought by the side of the Allies. Not one of them sympathized with the war aims of the Allies, and every one of them had conspired to sabotage the war effort, even to the extent—as in the case of Iraq—of organizing a German-supported revolt against England; and, as in the case of Egypt, of standing by sullenly and resentfully while England defended Egypt's territory.

The emergence of both Syria and Lebanon from the status of mandated territories had taken place only yesterday. They were occupied by the armies of the Allies; their dispute with France had not been ironed out; they were in the midst of domestic controversies. But without the slightest hesitation the two of them were accorded permanent equal status as sovereign states in an international conference to draft a constitution for the government of the world.

Great interest, especially in the American newspapers, was centered in Saudi Arabia, thanks to a splendid job of press-agentry by interested oil companies. But if Saudi Arabia is a sovereign state, why has the overburdened budget of England subsidized King Ibn Saud for the past twenty-five or thirty years? The revenue of the "independent" state of Saudi Arabia is derived from three sources: England, the oil concessions owned by American companies, and the pilgrims going to Mecca.

The five Arab states—five votes in the assembly, five votes in the commissions—did what the English expected them to do at San Francisco. They registered in an international conference the collective opposition of the Arab League to the recognition of the Jewish National Home in Palestine; their refusal to accept Jewish cooperation in the redemption of the Holy Land; their indignant rejection of any scheme that would allow Jews to settle in Palestine. Their proposals with regard to the Palestine Mandate were defeated several times in different forms. That did not matter. They came to San Francisco to register a threat, and that threat was noted in the press and in the minutes of the committees. It is no exaggeration to say that that threat is a menace to peace and justice, to democracy and law, in the Near East.

Although, in return for their admission to the Conference, the Arab colleagues of the British delegation did their duty in this respect, their performance in other fields was not creditable to their sponsors. Their anti-Jewish views were brutal and tactless. It was hardly politic for them not to indicate in the slightest degree an interest in the problem which the Western world had agreed must in conscience be settled with some respect for existing rights and common humanity. Not only the million and a half homeless and stateless Jews of Europe were involved in the problem but also the rights of 600,000 Jews in Palestine, who cannot in justice be disposed of by placing them under the rule of an Arab community which has in recent years not given evidence of toler-ance, kindness, and justice to peoples of other religions or races. The Arabs took the position that it was not their business to make a contri-bution to the solution of the Jewish problem. They were cynical about it. They pretended it was unrelated to their own interests. They repudiated sentiments uttered during the first World War by a great Arab Prince who spoke of Jews as kinsmen of the Arabs, and who wrote that "We Arabs look with the deepest sympathy on the Zionist movement and will do our best to help them."

When San Francisco learned that these five Arab states with five votes in the Conference were so exercised about the claim of the Jewish people to a "little notch" in the territory they occupy—six tenths of 1 per cent of the Arab lands—and that they were cold to any reasonable argument for a fair deal, it was realized that the Western world had to deal with a mentality and a morality reminiscent of the old Sultan Abdul Hamid, who regarded all the territory within the Arab states as his personal property. The modern Arabs seemed relics of an isolationist era, untutored in Western ways and resentful of the fact that the West had begun to in-trude upon their world. They relied for political success upon the exaggeration of intransigence and the repetition of mendacities. They seemed to have no conception of the extent to which the future of humanity and civilization was involved in the World War, and they made no appreciable contribution to the larger questions of the Conference.

In other words, their first appearance in Western society did not give encouragement to the thought of their development in the future. But they are now members in good standing of the United Nations. They will use that advantage to the hilt. They may be relied upon to come forward with greater self-assurance, and with better advisers, in the days to come. The Arab League fostered and supported by England and the United States is now one-tenth of the organized world. That is a dis-concerting fact. The Arabs will not let the world forget that fact.

Undoubtedly the Charter of the United Nations is a good beginning on which the world may build an enduring structure. When the wars are at an end and we settle down to peace, we shall have to abandon not only the methods of appeasement that prevailed since 1918, but we shall have to resist the piling-up of unsolved problems that fester in darkness and uncertainty and that are vitiated by the avoidance of just decisions. We shall have to reject the amoral methods of the old diplomacy which has been bankrupt ever since Hitler appeared on the world scene. To think that Truth and Justice may be avoided for the day, to be considered later on, is a snare and a delusion. Justice delayed is Justice betrayed.

BALFOUR DECLARATION IN THE BALANCE*

Whatever the unrevealed political motives may have been, the Balfour Declaration stands out as the wholesome human reaction of a great people to a colorful ideal which had stirred their emotions and imagination. It was not forced by immediate political difficulties or by extreme Jewish needs. A great war had been fought and won by the Allied Nations. A powerful enemy had been defeated. The world had been shaken, but the processes of law and order had not been dislocated. Jews had served in the armies of the countries where they were citizens and lost much in lives and property; but they were in no greater distress than were many of their brothers-in-arms.

The Declaration was the response to a potent moral appeal which awakened memories reaching down to the foundations of Christian civilization. Read the comment on the Balfour Declaration when it was issued. Much of it tried to recapture the apocalyptic vision of the Hebrew prophets. Many believed that they were rectifying long-standing historical wrongs and fulfilling what had been foretold; and that they were the instruments of an overdue Redemption.

The Balfour Declaration aroused the ardor and devotion of a generation of Jews. When that miracle occurred, our doubts were chiefly directed not as to the utterances of statesmen, but with regard to our own people. Had they the capacity to throw themselves into the ancient land where the hardships of pioneers awaited them? Would they take advantage of the opportunity history had placed in their hands? Had they the stamina and the fortitude to recreate their national life? Were they ready to redeem Zion and rebuild Jerusalem?

The answers to these queries are indelibly recorded in what Jews have

* *Bnai Zion Voice*, October, 1945.

created in Palestine in the last twenty-five years. The doubts were not justified. They built better than was anticipated. They overcame great hardships. They faced difficulties unflinchingly and conquered them. They have shown beyond doubt that, latent in the Jewish soul—in spite of dispersion, assimilation, persecution and oppression—there burns an unquenchable determination to establish and maintain an authentic Jewish life in a state of freedom. The soil of the Land is now saturated with their blood and sweat, and they are prepared to defend what they have built against all injustice and wrong dealing.

Twenty-eight years after the Declaration, the Jewish position in Europe discloses an appalling transformation. It is unrecognizable as the succession of what was Europe in the earlier days. It is ruin in every area—physical, social and political. An endemic anti-Semitism spreads the poisons of hatreds and prejudices, unrestrained by law, or ethics, or tradition or even by self-interest, though the Master Race has been defeated and crushed.

Now, the protection of elementary rights—the right to live and to work, to be unmolested, to congregate with their own—claims the first pressing priority. Greater rights on the higher level are to be relegated to the nebulous future—they have no relation to the issues of the day. The most important urgent task, after six months of peace, is to assure the bare existence of the survivors of the massacres, the maimed and wounded left on the battlefields. The living remnants of millions of ghosts must be banished from the scene as speedily as possible, so that the new order in Europe may not be troubled by their presence.

It is this cause that now calls with sharp insistence upon the conscience of the world for effective action. There are no references now in the speeches of statesmen to the apocalyptic vision of the Hebrew prophets, nor is there anybody bold enough to regard himself as the instrument of an overdue Redemption. It is stark reality, brutal, bleeding fact, life that demands breathing space, life that disintegrates before your eyes, and pleads for immediate attention. When the Allied Victors gather after the second round of world war to endeavor to organize a just order in a disorderly world—thinking perhaps of the third war now in the making—the Jewish question intrudes, shorn of its sentiment and romance, its ethical fervor and religious vision, and asks that bare justice be done; that there be no more delay; that judgment be issued. Life cannot wait much longer. It is not Redemption that is called for, but the healing of wounds, the salvaging of life.

The destiny of every displaced, homeless or stateless Jew is involved in the destiny of the Promised Land. The 600,000 in Zion and the 2,000,000 displaced and stateless in Europe cannot be regarded as unrelated facts to be considered in separate compartments of political policy. This land and these people are of one piece. The problem of the one is the problem of the other. They are driven on to one road. It leads to that corner of the world which is the beacon attracting all the homeless wanderers of the House of Israel. The area of the Jewish world has contracted to a narrow space and there is only a narrow outlet. If there is security and peace for Jews, it is to be found only in the Promised Land, for the Jewish people will achieve only in that land the strength and power to guarantee their security and freedom. If the 600,000 Jews now in Palestine are to be ruled and dominated by ruthless enemies, encircled by a desert that rejects civilization and democracy, the Jews will be compelled to stand their ground to the point of death. In that struggle they will not stand alone.

Again, as in 1917, England holds the immediate destiny of the Zionist cause in its hands. It cannot, while retaining the advantages of possession through trusteeship, building its Empire on that tiny strip of land, using the Mandate as the stepping stone to claiming title in its own name, expect to find sentimental partners to share responsibility without equal advantages. The explanation given for the disavowal of the Covenant, which is incorporated in the White Paper of 1939, was that England had to face the growing aggression of the totalitarian states, that it had to maintain the balances in its far-flung Empire by concession and bribe and acquiescence, because it was unprepared for war and had to gain necessary time to organize its defenses. The White Paper of 1939 was to be its last sacrifice on the altar of appeasement. It pretended that it would have kept the covenant had not the Arabs made difficulties. But when England and France turned to face the enemy with armed force and subsequently were joined by the United States and Russia, it advanced other excuses for the continuance of the same policy. The alleged exigencies of war now made it impossible to consider a revision of the White Paper. The same reason was given for turning away to perish in the sea the thousands of Jewish victims who sought shelter in Palestine; why the mantle of anonymity had to cover the part played by the Jewish people in the war; why for almost the entire period of the war the inalienable right of Jews to fight as Jews against the common enemy was rejected; why the process of implementing the White Paper had to continue. These excuses for betrayal became an obvious patter, deceiving nobody; and there was always the smooth and persuasive assurance that when the war would end a just decision would be rendered, that firmness and resoluteness would take the place of the evasions of twenty-five years, that the word of honor of England should not be impugned because in the end the right thing would be done. When the war was finally won, however, Winston Churchill, a sponsor of Zionism, was no longer the head of the British Government.

Instead of what was alleged to be a worn-out, visionless, opportunistic, conservative party, learning nothing from the revolutionary changes in life, laboring with the burdens of a bankrupt imperialism—the resolute, fresh, idealistic party of labor took over the destinies of the Empire. The Labor Party, working cautiously over the years to lay the foundations of a cooperative state, adjusted to the temperament and the character of the English people, represented the hope that under its guidance a new England could be born out of the fires of the devastating conflict that had come to an end. It would speak and act for the rights of labor, for social justice, for a collective nationalism, for a revision of imperialism and a new order. It would enter the concert of nations not as the protagonist of balances and blocs, but as the enlightened arbiter in the impending struggle between the East and the West.

The test of the Labor Government came through the letter of President Truman, urging the opening of the doors of Palestine for the admission of 100,000 of the displaced Jews of Europe.

All America has paid tribute to the purpose and sentiment of our President. This was the act of a man of heart, moved by an obvious human impulse. His conscience could not resist the conclusions of Mr. Earl G. Harrison, the American representative who saw what was contained in the concentration camps. His letter was the response of an American President following an American tradition, who would not allow the procedures of diplomacy or the temporary interests of higher international politics to prevent the salvaging of the lives of hundreds of thousands of human beings. The President's letter gave the new English Government an opportunity to act under a similar human impulse and at the same time with political vision, under a moral responsibility jointly shared with the American Government.

But the leadership of the new English Government lacked both courage and vision. It hesitated to give way to its natural feelings. It gave heed to the whisperings of the Colonial Office, to the cautions of its legal advisers. It rejected, after weeks of hesitation and doubt, the invitation to join President Truman in an act of humanity, which would be regarded as the symbol of a new trend. It rejected the invitation as if it were anxious to impress the world with the fact that the advent of a Labor Government in England did not mean that the long-awaited revolution had arrived, that in international affairs the standards of the old regime still prevailed, and that proletarian Mr. Bevin could be relied upon to continue the practices of aristocratic Mr. Eden.

The Labor Government of England met the moral issue with the courage and vision and ethical understanding which led Neville Chamberlain to the catastrophe of Munich. It seemed as if it were not in the mood for righteousness and justice, for fair play and humanity. It hid its intentions for a time under the plea that decision should be postponed. It summoned the Colonial officials of the Near East for expert advice, knowing in advance what that advice would be. The Labor Party had advice expert enough to determine its own action last Spring, but it thought it very shrewd now to take cover behind that arm of government which is responsible in large measure for the continued decline and decay of the British Empire. It contrived a bartering solution, reminiscent of old time, suggesting a limited concession to humanity in return for the continuation of the White Paper for another year. It proposed to liquidate a pressing human debt by the payment of one cent on the dollar, overlooking the fact that the debt involved what has been left over of millions of human beings murdered according to plan, and hundreds of thousands still scattered on the battlefield after victory has been won and abandoned by the Victors.

At the same time the propaganda offices of the Empire were set in motion to defend Government. The five Arab States admitted to membership in the United Nations Organization, stimulated to form a Federation dedicated to fighting Jewish claims to Palestine, came to life with renewed subventioned vigor in London, in Washington and in Cairo, and uttered threats of civil war and of injury to American oil interests. England was again presented as the innocent peacemaker and arbiter, the unselfish agent of civilization, unable to arrive at a just decision because of the extremists in both national groups.

This is a government that does not lead. This is not a great power destined to play a dominant part in the reconstruction of a democratic world. This is not a government creditable to the ideals of the Labor movement which seeks to find place for the common man in the organization of world affairs. This is not a government that can command the restless hopes of the English people, seeking to rebuild their lives upon secure foundations and hoping to play a decisive part in the establishment of justice and democracy in the world.

I regret to say that this is a government of trimmers and opportunists, confused leaders without conviction or feeling for humanity. It is a government which, failing to act its part in this crucial situation, will speedily have to make way for others more competent for the task.

The final decision of the Labor Government of England, fateful for the British Empire as well as for the Jewish people, is being awaited with a dull impatience and uneasiness.

MISCELLANY

Stephen Wise and Louis Lipsky were contemporaries. Together with Chaim Weizmann and Shmarya Levin, Stephen Wise was perhaps the deepest attachment of Lipsky's life.

Wise's death in 1949 ended forty-nine years of comradeship in the fight for the establishment of the Jewish National Homeland in Palestine, the defense of Jewish rights at home and abroad, and the fight for the organization of free and democratic Jewish institutions in America.

That comradeship was highlighted by fundamental differences in temperament between the two men and enlivened by their debates in the Zionist movement and in the American Jewish Congress—rarely over end objectives, but over form, method, time and place. But at every crisis affecting the Jewish National Homeland, or the rights or welfare of Jews anywhere, or the exercise of free, democratic rights, the two mounted the hustings, each in his own way, but united in purpose.

It was Stephen Wise who opened the door for Lipsky to the official Zionist family when he invited him to become editor of The Maccabean.

In turn, Louis Lipsky, in 1916, 1917, 1918, 1920, 1933, 1938, helped to build and rebuild the American Jewish Congress, providing what was to become the principal forum for Stephen Wise from 1925 to 1949.

The two parted company in 1921 over the establishment of the Keren Hayesod. Stephen Wise resigned from the Zionist Organization. But his departure was brief.

For ten years, through the darkest days of Hitlerism, Lipsky stood at the side of Stephen Wise in the American Jewish Congress in the great undertakings against the Nazi peril.

Symbolic of their relationship was the difference between them on the timing of a World Jewish Congress. In 1934 Lipsky, fearing competition with the World Zionist Organization, opposed it and held up its formation. But in 1935 that did not prevent Lipsky from fighting the American Jewish Committee attack on it and upholding the right of such an organization to come into being.

Events having convinced Lipsky within a year of the urgent need for such an international body, it was he who formulated the organizational structure of the World Jewish Congress and the election procedure by which democratic elections for it were held in the United States in 1936.

The respect, admiration and affection each had for the other had its rare public articulation on October 31, 1939, at the Palestine Pavilion of the World's Fair. The occasion was Stephen Wise's 65th birthday and the presentation to him of Jacob Epstein's portrait bust. Lipsky's presentation speech follows.

The Editor

ODE TO STEPHEN WISE*

I have been given a mandate by a group of your friends to hand over to you in their name your portrait in bronze. It is the work of a distinguished sculptor, Jacob Epstein, and has been on exhibition in the Palestine Pavilion these past six months. It has been acclaimed as a great work of art by tens of thousands. It enhances the deserved reputation of a great Jewish artist.

It is the object of the artist to seek to capture, in the eye of his truth, the essence of the subject under observation. He tells what he sees and feels—not the moment's flash, or the quick reaction to the transitory event; not the smile or the glance of scorn—but that which seems to be the impress of personality that endures, the wholeness of the subject. He seeks to immobilize the ever-changing; to congeal the living object in a mold that symbolizes the subject he is aiming to catch in the material he uses. But at best, what is taken down never seems to tally with the living, changing truth which contemporaries of the subject see in him, for they are always aware of the dynamic which the artist strives to reduce to the static.

Nothing on canvas, nothing in bronze, will ever—to those who have lived with you in the struggles of your life—fully reveal the picture of your vibrant personality which they have in their minds. You are a vivid player in the exciting drama of our lives. From the days of youth

---

* *Address on presentation of Jacob Epstein's bust of Dr. Wise,* October 31, 1939 (at Palestine Pavilion Dinner at World's Fair, N.Y.)

to the days of your maturity, in all your moods—playful, ironic, devastating in humor and invective, ubiquitous in service—it is all one piece, but never the same. There are no still pictures that can hold your ever-moving mind and spirit. It is constant agitation. It is constant restlessness and dissatisfaction. It is burning indignation and protest. Your life has been dominated by an irrepressible desire to serve the great cause of our day. You have raised your voice, in season and out, on behalf of the oppressed and the wronged. You have barged in, uninvited, upon the slothful and the complacent and have disturbed their indifference with the lashings of your eloquence. You have transformed a routinized pulpit into a vibrant pulpit, constantly alive to all human problems. No wrong—no matter where or by whom perpetrated—has been refused place on your unlimited agenda.

In our Jewish life, you have denounced those who are hostile to your ideal, almost unconscious of the lacerations you have inflicted. You have fought to force the ideal of Zion into hearts that have refused to give it place. You have berated and denounced and excoriated those who would not see the light. In the long, unended fight for the dignity and freedom of Jewish life, you have never failed to speak out courageously with all truth, refusing to countenance the tyranny of wealth or station among us. It is true that you have been inconstant in method, but you have never failed to be faithful to the ideal. After forty years of self-sacrificing service, you stand out in our contemporary life as a figure built on heroic, classical lines.

The task of the sculptor is finished. Here you have the bust which we hope will ultimately find an honored place in the national gallery of the free Judean State. Mr. Epstein has given shape and form to what he has seen; he will be unable to add another stroke or line to the work of his hands.

But you have passed out of his studio, and, day by day, month by month, and for many years to come, you will be making important additions to the portrait of a great Tribune of an ancient people struggling for its place in the sun. You will be adding significant colorful detail to the portrait. You will find new battles to wage; you will find new causes to espouse; you will spend your energies, thinking that there is an inexhaustible source of strength to sustain you; and nothing will hold you back.

As in 1914, as in 1925, as in 1939, when you were in the vanguard of the great struggle for Jewish rights, in the effort to maintain the rights we had acquired in the Jewish National Home, so in the years to come your unquenchable spirit will be found among those fighting to secure a place for your people in the gallery of nations. Nothing in your repertory of interests will be permitted to lie fallow, unexercised, unexpressed. It is the hope of all of us that *that* portrait will not be finished for many, many years to come. May you live to see the fulfillment of your cherished hopes.

TREES AND REMEMBRANCE OF ZION

In January 1947, World War II, which had witnessed the Hitler extermination of six million Jews, had been over almost two years.

And still the pitiful survivors of Hitler's savagery were huddled in D. P. camps and had found haven nowhere.

Britain still kept closed the doors of Palestine. President Harry S Truman's urging of the immediate admission of 100,000 Jews to Palestine had been rejected by British Foreign Minister Bevin.

Palestine was in ferment, and world opinion was being mobilized on all sides. Three months later, Britain was to place the Palestine question on the agenda of the United Nations—leading to the November 29, 1947 U. N. resolution on the Partition of Palestine.

In this atmosphere of terror and turmoil, Lipsky was able to see with clarity the urgency of maintaining, uninterrupted, the building for the redemption of Zion. The following is his exhortation, delivered at a meeting of the Jewish National Fund.

The Editor

The same theme recurs in variations at all Zionist gatherings. Those who fight for their lives in the Dark Forest find their strength in the Vision of what is to be tomorrow, which they will never see. But there is one Vision that has always sustained them in the hour of trial. It is reflected in the dream of freedom and rebirth. It is chanted in various keys. It is heard in the slow measures of the dirge, the stirring cries of battle, the songs of labor and creation. It is heard in all our efforts to accumulate strength and power for our enduring defenses.

Down through the ages, the Jewish people have never forgotten Zion. They thought of its body as well as its soul. They remembered its ancient glories—its battlefields and its seminaries of learning, its vines and trees, its rivers and lakes, its valleys and hills. They remembered the cradle where the Jewish people was born. All their hopes were concentrated in the amazing experiences of an ancient people who were sustained in a long exile by memories of an ancient land, which now gives them strength to endure the greatest trials in their history.

But in their thoughts of Zion, its Earth had a peculiar fascination. All that was holy in God's world was incarnated in that Earth. They remembered its aroma and fecundity, its softness and warmth, the bigness of its trees, the perfume of its flowers, the coolness of its evenings and the heat of its sun. Nowhere in the world was the perfection of God's creation so vividly manifested as in the land and earth where God had placed the people to whom He had revealed Himself. Because they had sinned in that holy land, their punishment was beyond the measure of ordinary justice. For their sins, they were cast under a spell. They became the dust on the highway; they became the spurned of all lands and peoples. A curse had been laid on Zion. It was withered and parched, its earth dry and brittle. The soil had been washed away by the rains and it was bled to death. Its highways were abandoned to jackals and the hot winds drove the desert sand over orchard and field. But when once the enchantment would be lifted, the exiles would be re-called and once more they would stand erect and free. And on that day, the Earth of Zion would be given back its youth and beauty. Its rivers would begin to run; its lakes would begin to sparkle in the sun; its mountains would be adorned with green. This would not be a natural event. It would require a miracle. The Jews had faith in that miracle.

All this time, although Zion was remembered in prayer, its earthly symbol was the deed of piety that touched the body of Zion. Gifts were sent to the poor and the feeble who came to die in Jerusalem. Messengers went out to all parts of the Diaspora to remind the exiles of the duty of piety. Strange emissaries, speaking the ancient language, received the token of piety and brought it back to those who had gathered in Zion to die. Fortunate were they who were destined thus to be enfolded in the bosom of their fathers. For Zion was the nearest earthly door that opened on the other world. It was the threshold where you discarded pain and humiliation and put on garments of gold and silver and stepped into the light of God's Heaven. The Chalukah was the deed of piety and token of faith. The coin in the box, the mite of the poor, the gratuity of the rich, went into the Chalukah. It made no urgent demands; it offered no difficulties; it called for no struggle. It was a passive tribute to a far-off hope. It was the routine of piety. The road to Zion, in their eyes, ended at the door of the undiscovered country from whose bourn no traveller ever returned.

The Keren Kayemeth symbolizes a new relation toward Zion. It is piety pulsating with life. The new Zion was not a threshold. It was not a closed door. It was the theatre of self-liberation in which once more Jews were to be the living witnesses of God's truth, the bearers of His light in a world of darkness. These living witnesses were not to rely on miracle, but were to go forth and achieve miracle through labor and sacrifice. The tears of their lamentation were to be dried in the warm sun of Zion. The grains of sand that once closed the eyes of the dead were to be quickened to sustain the living. Zion ceased to be the hand-maiden of decay and death and the end of things. The road to Zion became the pathway to life. And the Keren Kayemeth was its instrument. The old symbol of the Chalukah passed into oblivion.

When the crusaders of old forced their way into Zion, they left a trail of Jewish blood on their march through Europe. The Jews were innocent bystanders, but their innocence did not protect them. The modern builders of empire saw Zion as a convenient road to the markets of the East. But the Jewish builders of the new Zion came with the tools of labor, with plowshares, with the seeds to plant in the unused soil. They wanted to make Zion live again and everything in it renewed in spirit and hope. They wanted the land to be holy with life. It was to be no longer a threshold, but a window looking into the everlasting.

The Keren Kayemeth is the symbol of redemption. It is the redeemer of the land. It is the builder and the rebuilder. It sought and found the hidden waters and satisfied the long endured thirst of the frustrated soil. The pores of the earth were opened for the heat of the sun. It covered the bare spaces with green trees. It gave a living meaning to the ancient places. It made a new Jerusalem on the hill that looked out upon three continents. It made a land for Jewish feet to walk on. It gave Jews a sky they could call their own. It recovered the memories of a people long estranged from Earth.

The Redemption was sanctified by the ideal that was their guide through the darkness of ages. It was the sanctuary of escape from in-justice, intolerance, and inhumanity. It was the opportunity to recover the way of life that had been denied and derided. The return to Zion meant freedom. All that which had been rejected was summoned back to refreshing service. It was not their function to create a world imitative of what had been abandoned. In the world they were called to create, the words of the prophets would live again, all men would be equal, labor would be raised to dignity, and land would cease to be the object of barter and sale. The Jews, too, were crusaders; but their crusade aimed to bring life to the abandoned land, restore the holiness of Jerusalem and to re-establish the law and the word of God as a living force in a confused world.

It is amazing that this great effort, reflecting the rebirth of an oppressed people, the civilized world should refuse to see or to appreciate. They preferred to think of the decay and desolation of the old Zion and regarded its displacement as incongruous and unwelcome. The new Zion blurred the picture with which Christian piety was familiar. Fulfillment was not within the jurisdiction of a regenerated Jewish people. They were conditioned in religious faith against the new Zion, the living, growing, changing Zion. They preferred the desert and the sepulcher. They preferred the goats browsing in the streets of decaying cities. They preferred the filth and the squalor that reminded them of an ancient day. They preferred the picturesque outlaw of the desert, covered with vermin, living on violence and spoilation. The ancient plowshare was more picturesque than the modern tractor. They wanted to preserve a decaying, religious museum piece, which had provided space for the returning Messiah. The return of the exiles was an unwanted miracle. Much more compatible with their ideal of the Holy Land seemed to be the un-Samaritan behavior of the sons of Ishmael who turned upon the exiles to frustrate the restoration.

The spectacle of redemption should have quickened the sympathies of the civilized world. For were they not the witnesses of miracle that had been prophesied? Was this not the triumph of faith and loyalty over 2,000 years of grief and tragedy? But the Return threatened their own plans and ambitions. It contradicted the dogmas of the Church which wanted to dominate the world. It crossed the line of empire development. It raised fears that the fulfillment of the Jewish hope, even in miniature, might require imperial rearrangements, the change of habit. Even when they saw a helpless people murdered and the survivors fleeing for their lives, they closed the door and prevented the return of the exiles. The Miracle seemed to blind and paralyze their conscience.

How can the truth we stand for be made to penetrate the heart of a world now being reconstructed in the struggle which is drenching the earth with the blood of the youth of our generation? How shall the mist of tragic error be lifted from the eyes of the makers of the new world?

It is our duty to renew in deeds our professions of faith and thus proclaim the validity of our truth. The record of Jewish frustrations is long. We of today are not dismayed by the holocaust nor by the heartless indifference of the world. It is the historic fate of the Jewish people to be the scapegoats for the sins of those who dominate and rule. And the greatest act of faith is reflected in our effort, in spite of all discouragement, in spite of all disloyalties and deceptions, to recover the soil of Palestine and to defend the land of promise—redeem it for life, redeem it for the Jewish people, and to see to it that every day some little part of that soil is saved to serve Jewish destiny. Let the world see that we at least have a faith which cannot be destroyed, and that there will come a Day of Days when His power will be manifest on earth.

HERZL AND THE JEWISH NATIONAL FUND*

It is fitting on this occasion to join in memory and reverence both the 50th anniversary of the death of Theodor Herzl and the record of the Jewish National Fund, which started as a poor relation in Zionism but grew in scope and power and later kept pace in Zionist history with the challenging ideal of the political State.

It was the startling advent of Herzl, boldly raising the banner of a Jewish State, and his obsessive personal dedication to an overwhelming task, which aroused the Jewish people and made them aware of the Destiny which awaited them and the imminence of Fulfillment. It was his dramatic call for action, his incessant plea for international recognition, his faith and confidence, his understanding, that persuaded the Firstlings of the movement that if they willed it, the dream could become a reality.

The brochure he wrote in feverish haste, and rewrote again and again, sensing an unseen hand guiding his pen, evoked a reaction utterly beyond all expectations. There was magic in its title and timeliness in the moment he spoke his exciting words. In spite of its inadequacies as literature, its looseness of form, its improvisations, the brochure served to make Jews conscious of their origins and destiny, aware of their perilous status and of the necessity to take measures to ensure their survival. It raised the Jewish spirit from the humiliations of exile and gave them confidence in their hope of ultimate liberation.

* *Address, Jewish National Fund Land for Security Assembly*, March 12, 1954, Washington, D.C.

In the first years, his loyal partisans refused to admit as integral to his program the practical aspects of the Return, reserving as his objective only the forensic political design. They insisted that the political task should have exclusive priority; they were jealous of rival gods. They claimed that Herzl's exclusive purpose was to win international opinion in support of the right of the Jewish People to return to the Promised Land. For that they must have a Charter of Right. It was important to concentrate on the Charter and consider all other forms of national activity as premature or contradictory, or, at any rate, as wasteful of time and effort. You cannot return to the Promised Land without a license from its present owner. To assume that you may invoke your own inherent moral right, and fight your way through would vitiate the appeal of the Zionist leader and remove the platform from under his feet. A people that had waited 2,000 years for the fulfillment of the Promise could not be asked to work their way back underground to their Sanctuary. They would have to return in ordered ranks with passports and visas, with reserve banks for their capital, with blueprints of their enterprise, and the possibility to correct the program if it did not work.

When the Congress legalized the Jewish National Fund in 1901, Herzl was already being driven into the blind alley of East Africa. He did not know that his subconscious awareness of the Land of Israel was influencing his thoughts and stirring his slumbering memories. The vague outlines of the New Zion were taking shape in the workings of his mind and became entangled with his political mission, which he could not acknowledge on the platform.

For over a decade the issue of practical versus political Zionism was the bone of contention in Zionist circles with varying degrees of intensity. In retrospect, it was largely a verbal dispute, a partisan controversy, an academic discussion. How the movement was to start was determined in fact by Herzl's illuminating analysis of the Jewish problem and by the dynamism of his propaganda. It was not a matter of deliberate choice. He went on his hazardous way because it was the only path open to him. What was workable had priority, and all schemes had to be tested in the field of possibility. He could not waste time—his was limited—in the long-term discussions and disputes. In fact, however, the real distinction between practical and political gradually lost its meaning at an early date. Weizmann expounded his familiar formula of synthetic Zionism in 1907 but the discussions went on. After the death of Herzl, David Wolffsohn pursued a course against which few practical Zionists had real cause for complaint. Arthur Ruppin was sent to

Palestine; Franz Oppenheimer was interested to organize a cooperative colony of his own design; the Anglo-Palestine Company opened a number of branch offices in Palestine and established itself as a sound financial institution. The Jewish National Fund was buying various tracts of land. But the party conflict continued without abatement. It was kept alive as an issue with a strange obstinacy until David Wolffsohn retired from office; and echoes of the controversy were heard even after the end of the First World War.

In spite of the fact that political Zionism was Herzl's contribution to the modern Zionist movement, the records show how deeply Herzl was affected by the mystical attraction of Zion. He was not allergic to the same love of Zion which obsessed the East European Zionists. His political failures were the source of impatience and irritation and boredom. He took refuge in that world largely unknown to him which was called Zion. Thoughts of the Holy Land were provoked by his frustrations and were a living continuous pressure in his imagination for years before the novel *Altneuland* was published in 1902. Here was revealed for the first time the nature of his gropings for the realities. He tried— not too successfully—to reconstruct his memories of a distant past. Here was revealed his spiritual kinship with the Land of Israel; the alien returning home, remembering what had been lost on the long journey, recapturing names and places long forgotten and beginning to understand the value and significance of the Jewish National Fund when it was created.

The Fund was the comfort of the last years of his life. He considered it as the practical instrument of redemption in which the Jewish masses would participate and through which they would live their Zionist lives. It was not, as he first thought, merely an idea brought up from the past by a Professor of Mathematics. It was the basic ideal of national memory and tradition and an essential factor in the building of the New Zion. It was the moral tie that bound the Jew in exile, (landless and without rights), to the Land of Promise. The land must be redeemed from alien hands. It must not be taken by force but should be bought and paid for, and once title is taken, must be the everlasting possession of the whole Jewish people—Jews in exile as well as Jews who have already made their Return. In this respect, at least, the Jewish people were one.

With his passion for details, Herzl devoted himself to the Fund from 1901 to the day of his death in 1904. It was his intervention that assured the vote for the Fund in the Congress. He organized and directed the practical work of the first few years of its existence. He made the first subscription in the Golden Book. When the father he so dearly loved died in 1902, he inscribed his name in the Golden Book and made it a practice to honor friends and persons he sought to win for Zionism by inscribing their names in the immortal book of the National Fund. It was his practice personally to sign all Golden Book certificates. At one of the Congresses he passed his top hat around and pouring the collection on the table, called attention to his empty hat and said: "You can see, gentlemen, I withhold nothing from you." He was always delighted whenever his collections exceeded expectations. His was the most effective influence in the creation of the Fund in its formative years. He gave the Fund that aspect of immortality which later it was to gain for itself through its own efforts.

It has not been so well known that he was personally concerned in the first negotiations for the redemption of land in Israel. He directed the Anglo-Palestine Company to purchase land in Palestine for the Fund in advance of its having acquired the stipulated capital of 200,000 pounds. He was aware of the proposal to buy Ben Shemen and Hulda on the basis of a survey by Eliahu Sapir and Joshua Hankin. He suggested the purchase of 10,000 dunams of land for a colony in accordance with Franz Oppenheimer's plan from which came Merhavia. It is also a fact that he started the negotiations for the purchase of the Emek, which was fully consummated later by Ussishkin. A representative of the Sursuk family, the largest landowners in Palestine at the time, came to Vienna offering the Emek for sale. The offer was referred to by Herzl in the following words: "We have been offered land in the Valley of Jezreel by a certain Mr. Sursuk of Beirut." Herzl died while negotiations for Hulda and Ben Shemen were in progress.

The Fund is the first-born of Zionism and is distinguished in that its integrity has been maintained with loyalty throughout the years to a degree not evidenced by any other Zionist institution. Its quality could not be diluted. Its objective could not be diverted. Its appeal was never mangled by fuzzy words and huckster methods. The love of the Jewish people for the Fund of Land Redemption, and for those who worked for that Fund, grew from year to year. It spoke of redemption, recovery, rebirth and appeals to the consciousness of all self-respecting Jews who have a memory of national pride. It has avoided mergers, partnerships and alliances and remains true to its Trusteeship. In the tangled forest of Zionist enterprises it stands out as a Holy Temple, sanctified by the unselfish sacrifices of a large army of devotees.

The Fund provided the first outlet for Zionist action in which all Jews were able to participate, each in his own way. It was the first to teach Zionists how to work for redemption. In a period when so much time was spent in argument, in making the ideal understood and acceptable, in resisting theories that impaired Zionist hope, the National Fund workers were made conscious of their national duties. In its service all Zionists felt at home. Here they were dealing with a tradition that touched the heart, that bound one up with tradition and history and endless memories. Under its influence a union of humble workers was created who made the soil the object of their piety. It introduced the Golden Book, the tree certificate, the National Fund Stamp, the blue and white box. Behind all the ideological procedures, the battles of the slogans, the partisan bickerings, the silent tangible work of the Jewish National Fund went on, accumulating dunams of land, slowly enlarging its domain, covering the barren soil with green forests, bringing water to the arid land, draining the sick soil of its impurities and fostering the growth of settlements.

In a manner hard to describe, the spirit of Herzl set its mark on the features of the Fund. The Fund is the obverse of the ideal of the State to which Herzl gave the glamor of his personality. In the Fund you will find simplicity, the love of people, the smell of the soil, dignity and humility, boundless love of the Holy Land. These were qualities associated with Herzl.

David Wolffsohn appreciated the heart of Herzl's personality. He was the executor of his estate. He was a loyal friend. He therefore sent to the Fund in Jerusalem with unerring instinct the furnishings of his office in Vienna, his books, pictures and manuscripts, and subsequently a room was built in the Keren Kayemeth building in Jerusalem in accordance with the design of his Vienna office; and there, under the loving care of the Fund he founded, his workshop is being maintained. Whoever comes to Israel will not only make a pilgrimage to the Memorial Shrine where his dust lies buried, but will also visit Herzl's workroom in the Keren Kayemeth building.

LIPSKY AND THE ZIONIST LABOR MOVEMENT

David Ben-Gurion, first Prime Minister of Israel, was a Labor Zionist. His Party, Mapai (Labor Party) has led in every election in Israel since the first in January 1949.

For fifty years before the Jewish State was recreated, the Labor Zionist movement had played a central role in the development of Jewish Palestine. Under the Mandate, it provided a large proportion of the new immigrants to Palestine, trained them as settlers, working the soil; developed a powerful Labor Federation which organized schools, hospitals, and a substantial sector of the basic economy.

Himself a General Zionist, Lipsky, nonetheless, had a close association with Labor Zionists in the United States as well as abroad.

On May 1, 1955 he was a principal speaker at a rally in Carnegie Hall marking the fiftieth anniversary of the Second Aliya (immigration into Palestine) organized by the Labor Zionists. This is his tribute.

The Editor

ALIYA OF LABOR*

It would have been a lapse of memory or gross ingratitude to have regarded the celebration of the 50th anniversary of the Second Aliya as an exclusive Party event. The heroic men and women who initiated the 1904 historic labor trend within Zionism were the providential reinforcements of a movement, which had reached the end of an era. It was this group that picked up the remnants of the Herzlian adventure and raised the ideal of a State based on Jewish labor as the alternative road to national freedom.

They did not stand alone then when they entered the front trenches, nor do they stand alone today, when they face the tormenting problems of statehood and security and adjustment to radically new conditions; and when they are being subjected to an undeserved barrage of partisan depreciation and misunderstanding.

Many of us—not of their party—shared their hopes and their vision

* *Address at Poale Zion Rally*, May 1, 1955, Carnegie Hall, New York.

from the start. They were the intrepid beginners. We rejoiced in their strength, courage and loyalty to great Hebraic traditions, and their devotion to the Jewish people. We regarded ourselves the comrades of all who threw themselves into the task of redeeming the soil with their own hands, and laying the foundations of the State in harmony with Jewish social ideals and the vision of the prophets of Israel. We were envious of their audacity and proud of their achievements. They were the brave advance guard blazing a path for others to follow. They gave living proof for our faith in ultimate success. Without their labors we would have continued to wander in the wilderness of uncertain goals, and would have remained for a long time to come Idealists whose Vision could not be brought down to earth.

I speak for many Zionists of the early days when I say that although not parties to the controversies of the factions, or sympathetic to their ideological differences, their obstinacies and prejudices, we saw what they were doing for the redemption of the land, the recovery of the ancient language, the rejuvenation of thought and spirit, the collective solidarity they were able to create; and we were uplifted and refreshed and encouraged; and our gratitude went out to them in full measure; and continues to issue with warmth and deep concern also to those who have inherited the Torch of Collective Labor and are struggling in the face of difficult circumstances to maintain their inspiring ideals in the new day of Israel's freedom.

The first efforts of the Chovevei Zion must be included in our memories of the early days with gratitude and appreciation. They also had a passionate devotion to the ideal of national rebirth. They too created as best they could a Hebraic environment in their way of life. They too were filled with nostalgia for the past and grand dreams for the future. But they were not equipped by training or aptitude or interest for the hard tasks of pioneer enterprise in a land that had been ravaged and left desolate; and which required more than sentiment or nostalgia to spark the dynamism of Redemption. They had no conception of how soil could be made productive and agriculture could be organized, and suffered from the continuing disabilities derived from Galut life. Their Zionism did little to transform or redeem them. They brought with them too much baggage from the Galut and could not rid themselves of it. Their colonies resembled Russian villages where they functioned as lords of the manor, resting on Arab labor. The committee in Odessa was soon unable to provide the budgets to cover the deficits and they had to turn for relief to the Great Father in Paris. They were unable to hold their children on the land, many of whom wandered away into exile, frustrated and empty.

When Herzl raised the banner of statehood and called a halt to proceeding in Palestine without a Charter of Right and created the Congress, the Chovevei Zion lost their prestige and potency, the élan of a glamorous ideal, and their leadership. Arthur Ruppin traversed Palestine as a tourist in 1907. What depressed him most was the lack of courage and energy and enterprise in the first colonies. They gave the impression of premature old age. The young men who had founded them were worn out in hard and futile labor. The spirit of heroism and dedication had been extinguished. Dr. Ruppin was convinced that without fresh young blood imbued with the spirit of self-regeneration through labor, the situation was hopeless. A new Aliya was called for.

The Second Aliya was the response to a provocative call for reinforcements. The new group, young and bold, became the carriers of Zionist destiny. They started a revolution in the life of the Yishuv and set new sights for all Zionist enterprises. The exile had weaned Jews away from a healthy, normal interest in soil and manual labor and had made them city dwellers not integrated in the economic life of the Galut, hovering about the fringes of economic society or as middlemen in order to survive. The Second Aliya proposed the return of Jews to Zion as a people of workers. They were the first to raise labor to the dignity of sanctification. They were the first to speak of the transformation of the Jewish personality, freeing their way of life from the captivity of old habits. They were the first to assert the right to take over the defense of Jewish possessions. They drove out the lethargic and passive and produced a generation of self-assertive, self-defending, self-revealing Jews. They gave self-emancipation a new meaning. They made real the Jewish tradition that the land was the heritage of the whole Jewish people and must be redeemed not only by paying for it, but also by bringing it back to full life through Jewish labor.

They invoked the spirit of cooperation and community of interest without which, in those days, pioneer organization work would not have been possible. The individual would have found it difficult to settle on the land but the group (bound in common ideals and interests, sharing equally in tasks and rewards, working shoulder to shoulder in service) was a concentration of corporate power that might be able to overcome great difficulties. They made Jewish labor an army of brotherhood and poured their blood into the common stream of productive life and were content to be used up in the process for the sake of the nation and its future.

It was with this background of consecration that they began their amazing contribution to the national home. They did not remain merely a back-to-the-soil movement. They were persuaded that they were called upon to forge the pattern of the rebirth. They became the stonebreakers and the roadbuilders. They took over the transportation services. They were the pioneers of industries. They ventured in every area of economic experience. It was their supreme moral duty to take over self-defense and they became the founders of Haganah. They organized chains of cooperative agencies for interrelated communal services. They provided medical services for their constituents.

Nor were they limited to the primitive ideals of labor. They exercised a large influence on the Renaissance. They made the Hebrew language a vigorous, colorful expression of their way of life, the essential national tie that bound them to universal Jewish redemption. They provided their constituents with their own newspapers, their own books, their own forms of art, their own theatre. Through them the folk music and the dance lived actively in the national home. The mind and spirit of the whole movement were bound in kinship and in destiny through the workman, and through the workman the nation was reborn. There is no parallel in modern history to match the quality of this pioneer group. They were raw in experience when they came, ignorant of the tasks that faced them, with scant resources. And yet, they built on such firm foundations that they were able to clear a path for tens of thousands to follow them.

Who can say what they might have fashioned had they been able to concentrate in freedom on their dream of fulfillment and had they not been diverted to defensive measures to ward off attack not only on themselves, but against Jews in other lands who were at no time without crisis or emergency or tragedy. They lived under governments not of their creation. They endured the corruption and ignorance of the Turkish regime. They greeted the coming of the English, but the English betrayed their expectations. They felt the coming of Hitler many years before he took over the German Reich and began his career of carnage and destruction, which changed the course of Jewish history and unbalanced the trend of Zionist development; it forced a revision of strategy and entangled all thought, all planning, in the consequence of the horrifying nightmare.

Out of the incredible disorders of this situation, miraculously, the sovereign State of Israel was born. No sooner was its birth proclaimed than it was called upon to fill the vacuum caused by the English evacuation, to fight a defensive war on several fronts against the Arabs, and at the same time to tackle the problem of the refugees who were now pouring through the open door. How was the State to be financed? How were the hundreds of thousands of refugees to be healed and housed and settled? How were the ties of brotherhood with the Diaspora to be cemented and a solid Aliya of men and means promoted and organized?

They were coming into a land which had already established its own way of life, its own language and culture, its own economy and an unparalleled social solidarity. There had been established in Israel a sound labor organization bound together in social and political traditions, with routines of its own, with a discipline which had become habitual.

In the face of this revolutionary change, the old order cannot be maintained. The State must engage in a financial struggle to maintain its solvency. It must command support of the Jewries of the world. It must call upon Jewish free enterprise to provide funds for large industrial enterprises which its own resources are unable to provide. The accumulation of labor capital and its investment in far-reaching enterprises must be balanced against a new form of capital investment for which the nation is thirsting.

The loyalties of the heirs of the Second Aliya will be tested in the adjustment of their lives and their institutions to the changed and changing conditions, to the growing need for a new form of economic democracy, to the urgency of stabilizing the turbulent sea in which Israel now struggles for survival.

In their struggle to meet that test, the heirs of the Second Aliya will not lack the good will and support of all who remember the ardent days of their youth, the daring of their adventure, the range of their vision, and who will not forget the new emancipation they brought to Jewish life. Whatever forms the State of Israel may take, it will not go back to ideals that have been outlived. The new democracy of Israel will not reinstate social injustices that have been discarded—there and elsewhere. It will find its destiny in the core of progressive life created and rooted in Israel by the sacrifices of Jewish labor.

The peace of Israel—its present and future—lies with you. I am confident that you will remember who your teachers were and what they lived and died for. You will not be the slaves of doctrine. You do not have to be told which road you are called upon to take. It is not the road of a rigid, intolerant dogmatism—political or economic. It is the road of brotherhood and of subordination to the highest interests of the nation.

AMERICAN JEWISH CONFERENCE

Two years before the end of World War II, on August 29, 1943, an American Jewish Conference assembled at the Waldorf-Astoria Hotel in New York, after seven months of preparation, to formulate Jewish demands at the Peace table, in the knowledge that "American Jewry, which will be required in large measure to assume the responsibility of representing the interests of our people at the Victory Peace Conference, must be ready to voice the judgments of American Jews along with that of other Jewish communities of the free countries, with respect to the postwar status of Jews and the upbuilding of Jewish Palestine."

Thus, for the second time in American Jewish history, democratically elected representatives of a united community had been assembled to discuss and plan postwar solutions.

The Conference's predecessor, in 1918, had been the American Jewish Congress.

The Conference adjourned on September 12, 1943 with the adoption of a number of resolutions, the principal one being support for the establishment of a Jewish Commonwealth in Palestine at the war's end in accordance with the pledge of the Balfour Declaration and the Mandate for Palestine.

Five hundred and one delegates attended the sessions of the American Jewish Conference; all but four voted for the resolution, with the American Jewish Committee in opposition, which it expressed by leaving the Conference. Nineteen delegates abstained, 16 representing the Jewish Labor Committee; three, the National Council of Jewish Women.

Of these 501 delegates, 379 had been elected in 78 local and 58 regional conferences in every state of the Union, based on an allocation of one delegate for each 10,000 Jewish inhabitants.

The local or regional conferences were constituted by delegates elected *by local Jewish organizations or branches of national organizations on the basis of membership, one delegate for the first fifty members, and thereafter one delegate for each 75 members. According to the American Jewish Conference these delegates represented some 2,225,000 persons.*

In addition, 123 delegates represented 65 national organizations, with an estimated membership of one million.

The convener of the American Jewish Conference was Henry Monsky, President of the Bnai Brith, who had been a delegate to the first American Jewish Congress, supported subsequently by 32 national Jewish organizations, with a membership of one million. Like the first American Jewish Congress, the inspiration for the American Jewish Conference came from the Zionists.

The British White Paper of 1939, Hitler's destruction of six million Jews, the failure of the Western powers to rescue any substantial numbers of Jews, and an increase in anti-Zionist sentiment in the U.S. aroused the fears of the Zionists and renewed the determination to recreate the Jewish Homeland at the end of the war.

In May 1942, at a conference of Zionists called by the Zionist Emergency Council, all branches of the movement united behind a resolution attacking the 1939 British White Paper and demanding "that the gates of Palestine be opened, that the Jewish Agency be vested with control of immigration and the necessary authority for upbuilding the country" and that Palestine be established as "a Jewish Commonwealth integrated in the structure of the new democratic world."

The next test was to bring into being an organization which would represent a consensus of organized Jewish opinion in support of this view, able, effectively, to register this support with the American Government and influence American action to this end.

The American Jewish Conference became that organization.

Union in 1943, as in 1918, was preceded by opposition; and as in 1915–1917, in the first American Jewish Congress, the principal opponent was the American Jewish Committee.

Once again the specter of "dual loyalty" was raised by the American Jewish Committee to ward off democratic elections. Once again it failed. Once again compromises were made, principally changing the name of the organization from Assembly to Conference, with some modification of the election procedure, and, as in 1917, the American Jewish Committee finally agreed to be represented.

But, on September 1, 1943, Judge Joseph Proskauer, then President of the American Jewish Committee, walked out of the Conference in opposition to the resolution supporting the establishment of a Jewish Commonwealth in Palestine, patterned after the resolution of the Biltmore Conference. This secession was subsequently approved by the Executive Committee of the American Jewish Committee on October 24, 1943.

Lipsky played a formidable role in the organization of the American Jewish Conference and in its activities throughout the seven years of its existence.

He was the chairman of the National Board of Elections, which formulated the basic election procedure for the Conference.

At the 1943 sessions of the Conference he served as chairman of the General Committee, the guardian of the Conference reports and resolutions.

Thereafter, he was a co-chairman of its Interim Committee and chairman of its Executive Committee from 1945 until the dissolution of the Conference in 1949.

In the latter role he headed the efforts of the Conference to secure support for a Jewish State at the 1945 Organizing Conference of the United Nations at San Francisco, where the Conference was a consultant to the U.S. Delegation; represented the Conference in its submissions to the Anglo-American Commission of Inquiry in 1946; to the United Nations in 1947; to the U.S. Congress and the U.S. Administration from 1945 to 1949.

In 1949 the American Jewish Conference disbanded, its mission accomplished. An effort to establish a permanent body failed.

The following articles delineate the course taken by the Conference.

The Editor

RAISON D'ETRE OF THE AMERICAN JEWISH CONFERENCE
(He Spoke the Mind of American Jewry)*

There were two preludes to the American Jewish Conference. The Pittsburgh meeting of January 1943 was the second. It came about as a result of the failure of an antecedent effort to establish a program of cooperation through negotiation and private conference. Dr. Chaim Weizmann was responsible for persuading the American Jewish Committee to discuss the Jewish problem in relation to the peace that was to

* *1943 Report by Louis Lipsky (published in The Congress Bi-Weekly, Oct. 13, 1958).*

come. The negotiations were designed to clear up misunderstandings and to arrive at a program for united action in the Councils of Peace at the end of the war, which, it was expected, were to follow the pattern of Versailles at the conclusion of World War I. But the discussions brought no definite result, no agreed formulas, no agreement at all. It seemed that the American Jewish Committee could not reconcile certain internal differences of opinion. Finally, the Committee issued a statement of its own, in which views in direct contradiction of the Zionist program were advanced. This was taken to mean a rejection of the Zionist proposals. It registered the failure of the negotiations.

Unable to find a way through negotiation for united action by American Jewry, it was decided to appeal to Jewish public opinion and to invoke democratic procedure; to submit the question to judgment by vote. The point was, who would issue the call? It is to the credit of Henry Monsky, then President of the Bnai Brith, that he stepped into the situation and convened the Pittsburgh meeting. And this conference, supported by all national Jewish organizations (with the exception of two), decided to initiate action for summoning an American Jewish Assembly. Although the American Jewish Committee was not present at Pittsburgh, it subsequently agreed to enter the committee for the organization of an American Jewish Assembly, provided two conditions it presented were accepted. One condition was that the name be changed; the second, that any organization entering the Assembly (later called the Conference) and expressing its dissent on any question had the right to withdraw and publicly state its views.

The Zionists at a conference held at New York's Biltmore Hotel in 1942, adopted what later became known as the "Biltmore Program," calling for a Jewish Commonwealth in Palestine. Thus the term Commonwealth was formally introduced into the political discussion. It was not a new term. It had been used by President Wilson. It was included in the text of the Palestine resolution of the first American Jewish Congress in 1918. It was a familiar term in Jewish history. It had been absorbed in the terminology of the Balfour Declaration. It was translated in the official documents and became "National Home." Being evoked in 1942, it revealed the determination of the Zionists to avoid the ambiguities connected with the term "National Home" and to project the idea of Commonwealth as the expression of the ultimate political goal.

This bold utterance was employed with full knowledge that it would alienate many Jews who had been drawn to Zionism and Palestine as defined in the Balfour Declaration and the Mandate. It was felt, however, that this boldness was warranted by political conditions and by Jewish needs the world over. The Biltmore resolution was subsequently endorsed by practically all functioning Zionist bodies throughout the world.

Nevertheless, there were fears that if this unequivocal resolution would be pressed in the American Jewish Conference—*in the state of non-Zionist opinion existing at that time*—many friends would be lost and a unanimous vote would become impossible. In spite of that possibility, Zionists seemed to be determined to go ahead with this line. But there were many who felt that when the delegates of the American Jewish Conference came together, no matter how many of them were Zionists, how few were non-Zionists, the logic of the situation would compel some form of compromise in order to avoid the withdrawal of the minority.

The trained observer of Jewish life was struck, during all this time, by the strange disparity between what was being said on Zionist platforms and printed in the Zionist press and what was being done in actual encounters with the "opposition" of various grades. Bold statement and suggestion of compromise went hand in hand. The louder the asseveration of Zionist "maximalism," the readier the asseverator seemed to be to find a way to the reconciliation of opposing views.

Many concessions were made to bring the American Jewish Committee within the Conference. They were made in the framing of the call, in the rules of election, in the precise limitation of the program, in the lifespan of the Conference. It was suggested that the Conference might even be postponed out of deference to certain views of men associated with the Committee. The first session might be an innocuous general debate, with the real decisions and the election of a delegation to take place later. Why not give time for adjustments to be made? Why could not, ultimately, the obnoxious terms of the Zionist resolution be dissolved in a happy circumlocution that would be palatable to the non-Zionists? In fact, at the last minute, an effort was made to have the Conference laid over out of deference to views alleged to have been expressed in official Washington.

But all these matters never reached a climax. The "off-the-record" never became a matter of record anywhere. The date for the opening of the Conference drew near. The elections were over. Delegates began pouring into the Waldorf-Astoria and it became obvious that whatever was to happen would have to happen within the Conference itself.

The lobbies were filled with delegates and their friends as early as Thursday, three days before the opening of the Conference. The time was consumed in animated caucuses of delegates under various auspices, but chiefly by the delegates grouped under the banner of the American Jewish Congress. The General Zionists avoided any caucus on matters of program and did not hold their meeting until Sunday morning, but they were very busy with the issue of "committee placements," which they seemed to regard as of the highest political importance. The Labor Zionist group developed a strong feeling about the permanence of the Conference and went about advocating that cause with great fervor, following the precedent they had made in the first American Jewish Congress. In the caucus of the Congress delegates, only postwar problems were discussed. It was taken for granted that the problem of Palestine would be taken care of by a small committee of the Zionist Emergency Committee, which was engaged in formulating the draft of the Palestine resolution and was still going through the tortures of editing and re-editing.

But there were no discussions with the non-Zionists in advance of the Zionist decision. There seemed to be nobody with whom discussions could be held. The only other resolution visible was the one submitted by the Union of American Hebrew Congregations, which had been deposited in the "hopper" waiting for something to be done with it, but no Zionist representative accosted a delegate of the Union with the suggestion for a heart-to-heart talk about the matter. So far as was known, the American Jewish Committee had no prepared resolutions of its own. It had a large bundle of negatives. It suggested that resolutions satisfactory to them should be presented, but gave no hint as to what might be satisfactory. No Zionist seemed to have the temerity to open conversations on his own with the other side in order to provoke reactions. And yet, all the indications were that something would have to happen pretty soon to break down the walls of difference and establish something "in between" that would get unanimous support.

There were many difficulties in setting up the Conference as a formal body. The foundations of a new institution were being laid. The procedure had to be agreed to by groups that had never before cooperated on a democratic basis. At the opening session the organization of the Conference was still in a state of flux. The report on elections had to be formally presented by the delegates. The procedure agreed to unofficially by the groups or blocs comprising the Conference had to be ratified by the delegates. The relative strength of the groups had yet to be officially established. The procedure remained in a state of confusion even after the Conference had been opened. The groupings did not follow party lines. Many non-Zionists could not be persuaded to enter "like-minded" groups and finally entered "unlike-minded" groups solely to secure representation on committees. The result was that general agreement had to be given at the first session to the proposal that the plenary sessions on Sunday evening and on Monday should be devoted to general debate. The subjects were Saving the Jews, Palestine, and Postwar Europe. The first general debate was held on Sunday evening.

Here, Dr. Stephen S. Wise, who was the first Zionist speaker in the general debate, found himself in an awkward situation. He was expected to devote his address to the problem of saving the Jews of Europe, but he was preceded by Judge Joseph M. Proskauer with a political address, in which the attitude of the American Jewish Committee was revealed for the record. Had Dr. Wise followed his natural impulses he would have replied to Judge Proskauer with his own bold exposition of the Zionist program. But he was uncertain as to his function. He was not prepared to open the Zionist case. He took refuge in his impression that a clash of opinion on the platform at that time should be avoided. At any rate, he was not inclined to start what might become the first controversy of the Conference. He was hoping to be a peacemaker. He bypassed the issue and thus unwittingly helped to maintain the impression that the Zionists were reserving their adjustments for the committees, but in the meantime would not disturb the atmosphere of goodwill and peace. Dr. Wise, usually a good judge of forensic timing, bypassed his historic and histrionic opportunity.

When the plenary session adjourned on Sunday evening and the delegates scattered, meeting in clusters at various coffeehouses, there was a dead certainty in their minds that the much-discussed bold attack, the "maximalist" program, was in the process of deflation. This was confirmed the next day when "the rights of the Jewish people with reference to Palestine" was under specific discussion by speakers officially representing various groups.

The general debate on Palestine was introduced by Dr. Nahum Goldmann who, representing the Jewish Agency, considered that it was his duty to present a thesis in which polemics would be avoided and the formal aspects of the Zionist problem would be elucidated. That he should have avoided creating the controversy was quite understandable. But the position taken both by Dr. Solomon Goldman (speaking for the General Zionists) and by Dr. James Heller (speaking, strangely enough, for a "non-partisan" group) continued the general impression made by Dr. Wise the evening before. They rejected the role of provocateurs. They preferred to sail the sea of generalities about which there could be no division of opinion, no acrimony, no ill-will.

Dr. Heller used the occasion to make an appeal for the avoidance of an "insensate partisanship." Dr. Solomon Goldman could not bring himself to approach anywhere near the political aspects of the situation. He looked for signs of agreement. He had found among the delegates an agreement as to the peoplehood of the Jews, that the British White Paper should be abrogated, that Jewish achievements in Palestine had been considerable, and that there should be unlimited immigration to Palestine. But he made no reference to the Jewish Commonwealth, to Jewish control of immigration, to any idea in dispute. He contented himself with saying that "Israel must be restored to nationhood."

At this halting moment, with the Zionists greatly troubled, with the non-Zionists uncertain as to where this confusion would lead, the man destined to play the part of *deus ex machina* revealed himself, in the person of Abba Hillel Silver, who was the next speaker—representing not the Zionists, but the American Jewish Congress which named him as their spokesman.

He rose from his seat in the second row on the platform. He moved somewhat clumsily and with uncertain steps in the direction of the speaker's desk. He leaned his hands on the desk and braced his shoulders. His voice rang out resonant, fresh and arrogant. He was the debater, the pleader, the rebuker. He was interested in making a case and winning it and used all the arts of the advocate who wanted to convince and win a verdict. He sought the right word to describe what he wanted to say. He was not evasive. He was not tactful. He gave a moving, penetrating analysis of the prevailing conditions of Jewish life and what Zionism meant and wanted.

He disdained reference to the Jewish Commonwealth as an ideology. He asked:

Is the natural, normal instinct of a homeless people to find a home for itself after centuries of homelessness and to lead a normal, natural existence, *an ideology?* Is it an ideology for an Englishman to want an England, or for a Frenchman to want a France? Is it an ideology for the people of Israel to want the land of Israel? We are not insisting on ideologies. We are insisting on the faithful fulfillment of obligations internationally assumed toward our people and on the honoring of covenants made with us. If we surrender our natural and historic claim to Palestine and rely solely on the refugee appeal, we shall lose our case as well as do violence to the historic hopes of our people. To ask, therefore, the Jewish people to abdicate the political positions which after centuries they had finally acquired in Palestine, or by remaining silent about them to suggest to the world that we have abandoned them, on the vain assumption that this would lead to the opening of the doors of Palestine to large-scale Jewish immigration, is utterly fantastic.

Any summary of this remarkable address would be inadequate to convey the public impression it made upon the audience that heard it. The electric excitement it created seemed to bind every syllable uttered by the speaker to the nervous system of every listener. It was indeed the climax of a great moment. It brought back the Zionist groups to the mood of unswerving loyalty to their cause, to a refusal to bandy words and make compromises. It made the Zionist program vividly clear. It strengthened the conviction of the Zionists that they could carry the whole Jewish people with them on the wings of their faith in the great struggle in which the Jewish people were immersed. It was in effect a reaffirmation, in more realistic terms, of the Palestine resolution of the first American Jewish Congress. It voiced the authentic feelings of democratic American Jewry.

The question of Palestine then passed over into the hands of a committee of which Dr. Silver was selected as chairman. In the committee meeting he adopted the reverse of his platform method. He was the moderator directing the discussion of forty-six speakers, keeping "the table" clear for the discussion of the resolutions, adding nothing to his presentation in the plenum. All the Zionist speakers in the committee, as if at last released from their inhibitions and fears, forgot whatever idea they may have had of conciliation and compromise, of adjustment and avoidance, and stoutly held the line laid down. The vote in committee for the Commonwealth resolution was sixty to two. The vote in the plenum recorded only four against and about twenty not voting.

Thus the drama was played competently and brilliantly and came to its predestined conclusion. Dr. Silver had given a great performance. The spokesman for the opposition contented himself with a small part, well-mannered, urbane, but ineffectual. He was content to express his dissent and later to announce the withdrawal of the American Jewish Committee from the Conference.

The proceedings in the plenum when the resolution was adopted were brief, the mood was one of hushed suspense, and the delegates broke into prolonged applause when the vote was announced.

And the Conference proceeded to other matters of importance, heard many addresses, adopted many resolutions. But nothing equalled the impression made by Dr. Silver's address.

ON THE EVE OF ARMISTICE*

In August, 1943, in the city of New York, the foundation was laid of what may be called the organized respectability of the American Jewish community within specified areas of the postwar Jewish problems. There the forms and precedents were created and a broad base of agreements was established—agreements which have served to guide the Conference during the past fifteen months.

The First Session gave authority to an Interim Committee of fifty-six members to implement the decisions and agreements entered into, without, however, a clear notion at the time, of the grave difficulties surrounding the effort that would have to be made to establish effective cooperation among the various elements within the union. As if sensing that the Interim Committee would soon be compelled to renew and clarify its mandate, the delegates gave it the authority to call a Second Session to be held not later than twelve months after the First. The exigencies of war transportation made the holding of the Second Session at the date first fixed impossible. The period of operation was thus extended by three months, and today we are meeting in Pittsburgh to review our position, to chart our further course in the light of the new objective, which was first formulated in general terms in Pittsburgh in January, 1943.

It is not the same world we saw a year ago. The growing armies of the United Nations are now pushing forward on all sides against a retreating and defeated enemy. The aggressors have been driven out of many of the lands they had occupied and desecrated. The whole of North Africa has been liberated, the larger part of Italy, Rumania and the Baltic States; France has been restored to freedom and status in the democratic world; and now the combined armies of the Americans, the French, the English and the Canadians are pounding away at the crumbling German West Wall, while Russia pierces further and further to the heart of the enemy who is fighting desperately, without hope.

With the advance of the victorious forces of democracy, the surviving

---

* *Address as Co-Chairman of Interim Committee and Chairman of Executive Committee to Second Session of American Jewish Conference*, Pittsburgh, December 4, 1944.

Jews in the liberated areas are having their elementary human rights gradually restored. But as the curtain rises on the great devastation, it is obvious that the survivors of the Jewish communities will have to have the protection and the cooperation of representatives of their own people if their rights are to be fully restored, if their property is to be returned, if their status is to be acknowledged, and if the criminals responsible for the agony they have endured are to be punished for their crime.

Last year, we were thinking of the organization of a delegation which, in due course, was to go overseas to attend a Peace Conference, to which would be submitted the carefully considered demands of the Jewish people.

Today, it is evident that instead of such a delegation, provision will have to be made for representatives to attend a series of conferences on various aspects of the problems of peace, held from time to time. These representatives will have to speak in the name not only of one or two of the organized Jewish groups, but on behalf of a union for all free Jewish communities which, prepared in advance, must be ready to submit from day to day, from month to month, the argument of facts and experiences, the precedents, the laws, the moral directives, that constitute the Jewish case.

The duty of organizing such a Council of Jewish Representatives and of securing public recognition of its status, is not now to be postponed. It must be undertaken without delay. It is the paramount and unavoidable responsibility of this Session to arrive at decisions with regard to this matter.

At the first Session our program was formulated. At this Second Session we cannot delay the implementation of the resolutions adopted. We were then speaking of an agency to represent the Jews of America. That agency must in turn now take the initiative in the formation of that Council of Jewish Representatives, which is to speak and act for the Jews of all lands.

THE STATE IS BORN*

It is my great privilege in opening this session to make an important statement. It was announced a few hours ago, that at Flushing Meadows the United Nations Assembly by a vote of 33 for, 13 against, 10 abstaining and one absent, gave official recognition to the Jewish State in Palestine.

* *Address as Chairman, Executive Committee, to Fourth Session of American Jewish Conference,* November 30, 1947, Chicago.

(The audience rose and burst into "Hatikvah.")

May I add that this great historical event, which stirs the heart of every Jew throughout the world, is an occurrence of far-reaching significance to the civilized world as well as to the Jewish people. It marks the vindication of the long-cherished national aspirations of a people whose national integrity has been denied for 2,000 years. It opens a door through which the Jewish people will pass in untold numbers into freedom and creativeness.

The gratitude of the delegates of this Conference, representing the great American Jewish community, will be expressed at the conclusion of this Session in an appropriate address to be delivered by Dr. Stephen S. Wise.

It is fitting at the opening of this Session of the American Jewish Conference, which is to see the birth, we hope, of a permanent body representing the great Jewish community, that the first name uttered here should be the name of a man whose life is linked with the creation of the American Jewish Conference, and whose memory lingers and is cherished by every part of this Conference, and by the Jews of America. The man is Henry Monsky. The memorial address will be given by his distinguished successor, the president of Bnai Brith, Mr. Frank Goldman.

With this Session, the American Jewish Conference enters its final phase. It has been a long session—four years long. It has maintained to the end the procedures so clearly formulated at the beginning. It has kept to the terms of its directives with rare integrity. It has successfully resisted the temptation to blaze new paths and to detour from the prescribed course. In all its procedures, on all levels, it has retained its representative quality, never aspiring to powers not authorized and never misrepresenting those from whom its specified authority was derived. It has laid, I think, the foundation upon which a successor organization may well be based. Should such an assembly be called to life, the Conference will hand over to it the record of an invaluable experience in the advocacy of Jewish interests, in the art of internal coordination, and in democratic management. It is our hope that the lessons of the past four years will not be dropped into the archives as dead records, but will serve as guidance in the organized development of a democratic American Jewish community.

The postwar world is not what we expected it to be. It is a shocking caricature of the hopes that uplifted us in the dreadful years of the conflict. The whole world has been left scarred and broken. The larger part of it is in a state of chronic hunger and need and seems to be unable to help itself. The old social structure cannot be restored. The wheels of industry seem unwilling to turn, no matter how hard one tries. A paralysis of energy, a distrust of the future, a lack of confidence in life itself, has spread over the face of the earth. Nothing normal or stable or rational has taken the place of what has been swept away. There were protestations that a new spirit was to come once the evil of the day was removed. There were fervent orations and comprehensive plans of universal scope. This has been followed in a most amazing way by the growth of hates and rivalries, by cold and vicious aggressions, which have transformed many of the small nations into the terrorized subordinates of contentious great powers. It is impossible to tell the difference between the Victor and the Defeated. The enemy has scattered and is to be found everywhere. He is called by various names, but all descriptions add up to the "new Fascist." He has changed his costume, taken his place right next to the heroes of the war and talks loudly of "our victory" and of law and justice and democracy. He is even speaking in the United Nations in a loud voice of these principles, while he prepares to rise again to power.

The pattern of the future is as yet a formless blur. The scars of recent battles have not yet healed. The ruined cities have not yet been rebuilt. The roads of commerce have not yet been repaired. But sovereign states, members of the United Nations, are now preparing for another struggle for power and dominance, returning to the tactics and stratagems of the past, preparing for the collisions that will inevitably lead to war. An inventory of the cost of the past war has been made. What new weapons of war may be able to do, is suspected. But the fighting nations of to-morrow seem unaware that the next war may be a scramble over dead spoils, that place and power will have no meaning in a world reduced to shambles.

When the American Jewish Conference was born in 1943, it was believed that the procedure after the First World War would be followed after the Second World War. The Victors would sit at the head of the table and summon their defeated enemies to the conference room and dictate the settlement. As at Versailles, the Jews would contrive to submit their case through authorized representatives in the main hall or in a side room. They would be given—we hoped—a respectful hearing and be told to wait outside for judgment. It was our hope to be present. The American Jewish Conference would aid in the organization of a Jewish delegation representing as many communities as possible, and presenting a united front. But this was not the course of events.

There was not one peace conference, but many, each session dealing with an agenda drawn to meet emergencies as they arose. The United Nations was organized at San Francisco just as the war with Germany came to an end. The organization of its functioning committees went on from month to month, and finally the United Nations settled down to a regular life at Lake Success or Flushing Meadows. The treaties of peace were the sole concern of the Big Powers who had fought and won the war. They were meeting as a Council of Foreign Ministers in various capitals of Europe. They first tackled the peace treaties with the ex-enemy satellite countries. They then went over to the consideration of the treaties with Austria and Germany. The meetings of the Council of Foreign Ministers were the battleground where interests were fought out, and long drawn-out and sensational discussions ensued with many disagreements and few accords. The Austrian and German Treaties are now being considered in London. The treaties with the ex-enemy satellite states were ratified only this September.

It was clear from the start that in the United Nations and in the drawing up of the treaties a marked change had come about in the relation of the war allies. They had lost the mood of cooperation. They had lost their confidence in the possibility of establishing an ordered world. At San Francisco, before the news of the collapse of Hitler had arrived, a mood of exultation and dedication prevailed. But immediately after victory was definitely announced, the cold relation of freezing friendships came to the surface. Every encounter between the parties evoked new suspicions and antagonisms. There were threats and menaces and an endless barrage of propaganda from all sides that made the postwar years an endless provocation of hatreds and prejudices and disorder. The One World foreseen in the midst of the war and preached by many apostles of peace, seemed to be breaking up into fragments. Even the preachers of peace are no longer heard.

The climate of the postwar world was thus not calculated to make the task of Jewish advocacy easier. In the lobbies of a world unable to maintain calm and objectivity, with its "sovereign" states thinking of peace only in terms of their own aggressive interests, the cause of the outsider could not so easily get on the agenda. It was always a bit out of order; it was irrelevant and annoying; it was related to ideals of justice and fair dealing; and why should such matters be brought up?

It was obvious that our task in 1945 would not be as simple as it appeared in 1943. The way to reach authority had to conform to the new international procedure. The time at our disposal had to be extended. We would not be able to submit our case at one hearing and return to the next session of the Conference with a final report, and a final adjournment. We had to move with the international conferences from one capital to another, giving attention to the issues as they came into the discussions. This made Jewish representations necessary in Washington, in San Francisco, in Paris, in Montreal, and in London, and finally at Lake Success. The Jewish position had to be expressed in the form of communications and formal memoranda to governments, to the press, and to influential personalities. The situation compelled the Conference to become a functioning body, requiring a staff of expert personnel and day-by-day activity.

Being limited in time and scope, the Conference was not concerned in accumulating credits and assets of its own for use in later years. It would have no later years. It was to be the temporary servant of the emergency. This was a handicap and an advantage. The advantage was that the Conference could serve disinterestedly as the coordinator of Jewish endeavor, as the symbol of Jewish unity, with no reservations and no ulterior purposes. It had no interest to use the power of majority. It had every reason to rely upon persuasion and appeal, being concerned in having a real influence on the situation. Its policies were therefore a blend in which distinction between majority and minority faded away, in which pride of organization was forgotten. The Conference aimed to avoid domination and seek good will and common understanding. It had to create a place for itself in a crowded field. The banner of union had to be raised in the midst of rivals and competitors. Many instruments were being played. The Jews of America realized that what was needed was not instrumentalists, but an orchestra in which all were to play in unison and harmony. What was more important than tactics or relative positions of groups was the creation of a sense of Jewish solidarity, the molding of an organized people into a workable union. That seemed to emerge as the chief mission of the Conference.

The first step in the fulfillment of that mission was the partnership formed with the World Jewish Congress and the Board of Deputies of British Jews. The Congress is the authorized representative of a large range of communities in all parts of the world. During the war period it had become an effective agency serving the scattered Jewish communities. It had developed a staff of experts of wide knowledge and technical ability, recruited from among the exiles of the affected European countries, so that it became, in time, a clearing house and general agent for all the distant communities and interests within the range of its influences. The Board of Deputies is the traditional representative body of British Jews. For decades it had been recognized as such, both by its Government and the Jews of England. The Congress aspired to universal jurisdiction. The Board was conditioned by the Anglo-Jewish tradition of self-sufficiency. But in spite of this, we were able to overcome their special claims and reservations and to form and maintain our union without interruption and with substantial success. In spite of the problem of geography, the Board and the Congress joined with us in San Francisco. We prepared the material together in advance and conferred on every problem. Together we proceeded to Paris where the Council of Foreign Ministers met to consider the treaties with the ex-enemy satellite states. There we found other Jewish groups from many countries, each intent upon making its own special contribution to the Jewish cause in its own way. The three of us agreed to invite all these groups, large and small, old and new, democratic and undemocratic, to explore the possibility of preparing a memorandum to reflect the common views of all parties, to pool the experience of all our experts, and to establish a common council for the transaction of all business. It became possible for the experts to agree on one document. The document, thus approved and signed, was submitted to the Council of Foreign Ministers as the expression of the views of the whole Jewish people. No other Jewish document was submitted in connection with these treaties. This was an achievement of which we may well be proud. It showed that differences that had been dividing us were superficial and of no great importance. It showed that Jews could agree and act together once they removed the inhibitions engendered by prejudice and group isolation.

By unanimous consent the rescue of Jews was added to the program of the Conference at its First Session. It has had a large share of our attention. As the Nazis moved eastward, the Jews involved were hidden behind walls that could not be penetrated. What was happening behind these walls was surmised but not known with certainty. Wild rumors and terrifying warnings broke the blockade of silence even then, and revealed a picture incredible to the human mind. As the intentions of the Nazis became known, thousands could have purchased their way to freedom, but the Allies were concerned with the great difficulties of a perilous war. They were not able to give even slight attention to a relatively small act of humanity which might affect the destiny of a large number of people. The true story is now being told by persons who had a great deal to do with these liberating efforts. It is now abundantly clear that a burden of guilt rests upon the Allies—including branches of our own Government —for having turned their backs upon the doomed captives of the Nazis.

With the end of the war, the survivors became known as Displaced Persons. They were the living witnesses of the horrors practiced by the Nazis. They continue to be dealt with practically as prisoners-of-war. They are kept in concentration camps on the poisoned soil of Germany. They have no right to leave the place of their detention. They have no haven to welcome them. A great empire still blockades the highways to freedom. Their case history is a long, complicated and utterly revolting story of senseless inhumanity. Why it is not possible to provide 250,000 people with freedom and a home is something future generations will never understand. After all the memoranda, the negotiations, the speeches, the letters written by high officials, the problem of the Displaced Persons is regarded by statesmanship as almost hopeless.

In our interventions in connection with this problem, the Conference established a working union of all groups concerned—the Jewish Agency for Palestine, the Joint Distribution Committee, the World Jewish Congress, the American Jewish Committee, and the Board of Deputies of British Jews. Our chief emphasis and the emphasis of all parties concerned has been on the political action to be taken in Washington and overseas to relieve the condition of the Displaced Persons. We have been able to keep the frontiers of the American Zone open, thanks to the fine cooperation of the Military Command, first General McNarney and now General Clay. Our union had the privilege of suggesting the names of the Jewish Adviser appointed by the American Military Command.

The same pattern of cooperation was followed in the field of Reparations and Restitution. There was no central authority in the whole of Germany. Germany was occupied by the Big Powers and agreement between them had not been established. Our concern was with the American Government, which had adopted from the start a generous and humane attitude toward the Displaced Persons. The first draft of the American Restitution Law was ready in the fall of 1946. Detailed comment on the proposed law was submitted jointly by the Joint Distribution Committee, the Jewish Agency for Palestine, the World Jewish Congress, the American Jewish Committee and the American Jewish Conference. We were successful in having many amendments of the proposed law included within the final draft.

It was evident that the United States would have to enact the law for enforcement only in the U.S. Zone. On November 10, 1947, General

Clay promulgated the law designed to name the Jewish Restitution Commission as the successor of heirless property and the property of the destroyed Jewish communities. The principle on which the law was based was stated: "That looters shall not be permitted to hold on to their loot." To deal with the enforcement of the law, a Jewish Restitution Commission was incorporated in New York in June, 1947. It includes among its incorporators a large range of Jewish groups. It is to be an international body representative of Jewish interest without parallel in history. So far as America is concerned, it represents the totality of American Jewish interests. Efforts are still being continued to secure the enactment of a similar law in the zones of the other Allied Powers.

The program of the Conference has not been disposed of. It is a matter of daily business, of changing events, of fulfillment and disappointment. There is an accumulation of unfinished business. The responsibilities are still there. Nothing has been finished off satisfactorily. Obligations have been assumed that will have to be taken up by others. Jewish rights under the treaties—such as they are—will not enforce themselves without Jewish advocacy. The new Jewish State will have a rocky road ahead of it. It will have to take up a task unparalleled in modern history. It will be surrounded by many enemies and its friends will be far away. It will require the material and the moral support, especially of the large Jewish community of America. The question of Jewish survival has become more acute than ever. The poisons of anti-Semitism have spread over a universal area. Many small Jewish communities now find themselves in hostile environments. The Jewish right to survive on our own terms will have to be defended wherever possible. The Jewish capacity to survive will have to be strengthened and reinforced. We have lost so much and gained so little. Our resources in influence and strength must be pooled and not scattered. The luxury of waste is denied us.

The question arises: Shall we now, after the great blood losses we have suffered, relapse into the status of scattered unrelated communities bound together only by abstract ties of ancestry—by the threads of a common religion? Shall each fragment of the Jewish people seek to battle alone under its own banner, or shall we recognize the great value of universal union, not alone American union, and make the sacrifice of subordination to the will and interests of all concerned?

This is the gist of the problem to which you are asked to give your serious thought. The Conference has created a function which no other agency in American Jewish life is in a position to perform. Its passing will leave a vacuum which will have to be filled, if not today then in years to come. Your decision may lay the issue on the table and avoid action; or you may have the privilege of initiating forces in American Jewish life that will create through persistent effort and through union an invaluable instrument for the survival of Jewish life.

FINALE: AND THE CHALLENGE AHEAD*

The Conference was the second attempt of American Jews to organize a representative body to deal with postwar Jewish problems. These attempts did not clearly express the purpose behind the public effort. Always, there was the thought of creating a permanent body representing American Jewry, to deal with its common problems. Frankness at the beginning would have nipped in the bud the whole enterprise. Perforce, unity was established on a narrow plane. Attempts made to broaden the field, at various times, brought about inevitably a paralysis of the effort.

The first American Jewish Congress was based upon an agreement requiring its adjournment *sine die* after its delegation to the Versailles Peace Conference had rendered its final report. The American Jewish Conference likewise was limited to operations in the foreign field and prohibited from undertaking activities at home; it was stopped from undertaking any long-term obligations lest it become a permanent body.

In both cases, a powerful minority made freedom of action impossible. The first Congress was reconvened at once by a small group of adherents who set up what they called the American Jewish Congress, knowing full well that what they were doing did not have at that time the full support of all the parties concerned. The American Jewish Conference adjourned, however, in orderly fashion, observing all the rules. The record of the American Jewish Conference is completed with the publication of the minutes of the last meeting of its Executive Committee. These minutes wind up the affairs of the Conference. There is appended a last accounting of its budget and a report on how its assets were disposed of. There are no debts unpaid. All commitments have been discharged. The record is contained in the four volumes reporting the proceedings of the annual sessions of the Conference. In these volumes will be found the complete story of how the Conference was organized and maintained, what it did, what were its problems and how it ended its life. The sessions of the Conference were unique in that they maintained a parliamentary proce-

* *Final Report as Chairman to American Jewish Conference Executive Committee,* January 31, 1949.

dure of high democratic grade from its first sesssion to its last. In the record will be found the blueprint for a permanent American Jewish body.

There is a larger commitment, however, which the Jews of America will have to deal with in the days to come. It is universally admitted that the problems the Conference was called upon to solve have not yet been solved. New problems show themselves from day to day. A revolution is taking place in Jewish life. A Jewish State is in being. The relations between Galut and Zion call for serious thought. Are the Jews outside of Israel to be organized in isolated communities unrelated to one another? Are the grave problems of American Jewry to be met by a fragmentized, discordant community? How is Jewish life to survive if we are unable to face its problems together? Shall anarchy prevail or shall an attempt be made to establish democratic order?

We hand over all that remains of the American Jewish Conference to the new generation which will be called upon to face unparalleled conditions in Jewish life.

TO THE DEFENSE OF ISRAEL: 1956

Eight perilous years followed the proclamation of the Jewish State in 1948.

From the very first day of its existence, Israel was compelled to fight a war on two fronts:

1. *The war launched against her by the armies of the Arab States on May 15, 1948; victory was won in 1948–1949.*
2. *The battle in the U.N. where, under Arab and British pressures, various attempts were made to postpone implementation of the 1947 Partition resolution; to truncate Israel; to prevent Israel's development of its water resources.*

From 1949 to 1956, despite armistice agreements, Israel was subject to constant, heavy Arab harassment on all its frontiers, with resultant loss of life.

An Arab boycott of Israel goods was extended to firms doing business with Israel, whatever their nationality.

Israel ships were denied freedom of passage through the Suez Canal.

Israel's own port of Elath was immobilized by armed Egyptian encampments on Sharm el-Sheikh which debarred the Gulf of Aqaba from free use.

All efforts to proceed with peace discussions were resisted by the Arabs, despite specific provisions of the Armistice Agreements.

Arab marauders, based in Egyptian-held Gaza, known as Fedayeen, raided Israel settlements day and night.

No action to end this situation had been taken by the United Nations, up until the Fall of 1956.

On October 31, 1956, Israel forces launched a surprise attack, pushed through the Sinai Peninsula, occupied Egyptian-held Gaza, captured Sharm el-Sheikh and destroyed the military installations there and on the islands of Sanafir and Tiran, the approaches to the Gulf of Aqaba.

Britain and France entered the foray, with announced intent to occupy the Suez Canal which had been seized by Nasser in July 1956. Landings were made by the French and the British. But, before they could accomplish their purpose, the Security Council of the U.N. moved in.

Russia threatened to bomb Britain and France; to send in "volunteers" to destroy Israel.

Under threat of sanctions the U.N. produced a cease-fire.

Britain, France and Israel became the targets of bitter attack and pressure in the U.N. led by Secretary-General Hammarskjold, buttressed by full support from the United States and the Soviet Union.

In the face of American opposition, Britain and France withdrew their forces at the deadline set. Israel refused to budge without specific guarantees.

Ignored by the U.S. and the U.N. were the acts of Egypt against Israel and Egypt's continued insistence that it enjoyed the right to exercise belligerency despite its debarment by the Armistice Agreement.

Secretary of State John Foster Dulles went so far as to threaten economic sanctions against Israel if Israel did not withdraw from Gaza and Sharm el-Sheikh.

The public reaction to this threat, and Israel's determination not to yield, produced results. The U.N. agreed to form an International Police Force to protect the approaches to the Gulf of Aqaba. Israel withdrew from Sharm el-Sheikh in March 1957, when this International Police Force took over, and also from Gaza.

At the same time, the Gulf of Aqaba was declared to be an international waterway with freedom of passage for all ships, and with a U.S. guarantee of action if this freedom was curtailed. Such a pledge was made directly to Israel by Secretary of State Dulles and announced in the U.N. by U.S. Ambassador Henry Cabot Lodge and supported by a number of other countries, members of the United Nations.

Only after the most heated debates inside and outside the U.N. were these agreements reached. A formidable opposition was developed which made its weight felt in Washington.

Among the leaders of the opposition were the American Zionist Council, formerly called the American Zionist Emergency Council before it was reorganized under the Chairmanship of Mr. Lipsky in September, 1949, (a post in in which he served until early 1954) and the American Zionist Committee for Public Affairs, of which he was the Founding Chairman in 1954.

On November 29, 1956, at a rally of protest at Manhattan Center, Louis Lipsky made the following policy address.   *The Editor*

TO THE DEFENSE OF ISRAEL: 1956*

From day to day the danger of war increases and apprehensions grow that the promises of our American Government are floundering in a mood of double purpose. There is amazing political unrest in the Middle East. Preparations for war are quite evident, but the savage boasts of revenge by the Arab states are greeted in silence and inaction by the Western Powers.

How is the State of Israel to meet the attacks by jet bomber planes, supplied with speed by agents of Russia, if it is not provided with appropriate weapons of defense which many of our friends have in surplus?

Never before in Israel's short life has it been threatened by such a situation, and never before have the Jews of America, in their support of the Homeland, had to face the embarrassment of not knowing what are the real intentions of their own Government, what it is prepared to do to break the encirclement of Israel by its enemies. For the first time Washington seems to have abandoned Israel to chance. It has joined with others in treating Israel as an expendable pawn in a game of chess.

In this grim climate the Jews of America are being advised that it should be their patriotic duty to keep silent on what is called a "foreign" policy to which our Government is committed, the course of which is set; and that we should not challenge the wisdom of the State Department.

Is it really a foreign issue in which only the kinsmen of Israel are concerned? No! It is an issue in which the United States is directly, morally and politically implicated ever since the Balfour Declaration, the beginning and the end of the Mandatory Regime, the Partition Decision of the United Nations, and the recognition of the State of Israel by the United States. The American Congress on two occasions adopted resolutions favorable to the creation of a Jewish Homeland in Palestine, and on the record was an active dedicated integral factor in the creation of the Jewish State. The acceptance of Israel in American foreign policy is a matter of record. It is a commitment which cannot, at this time, with Israel facing attack by a conspiracy of Arab states, be shifted to the shoulders of the Jewish State alone, taking the attitude of a bystander in a far-off local fight and warning its own "Americans of the Jewish persuasion" to be neutral and keep silent or to evacuate the threatened territory.

This strange advice given to American Jews—and only to Jews—

* *Address, Protest Rally,* November 29, 1956, Manhattan Center, New York City.

might be entertained, cruel as its implications may be, if the United States were involved in war, imminent or actual, or if the policy claimed to be American were in fact clear and undisputed. There is no war in the Middle East yet. What America's policy should be is now being discussed in Congress and in the press, on radio and TV, with a great deal of heat and partisan interest and ignorance in high places. At best the policy is in flux. It changes from week to week. The vocabulary of its official utterances confuses the thinking of the Nation and arouses indignation and distrust. It is not accepted at home or abroad. It even meets with dissent from the Arab states who are expected to be pleased. There must be something wrong with this disrupted policy, which only public discussion may cure.

I am sure that the Jews of America will not give heed to the advice of their enemies who are trying to fence off encircled and besieged Israel from their chief support in the American Jewish Community. Literally, they would like Israel to be isolated and to face its enemies alone so that in the agony of its need it may be forced to accept the secret terms of peace the Western Powers seem to have prepared for it. Mr. Eden has the blueprint of a compromised plan in his pocket.

All of us recall with contrition and humiliation the fact that nothing was done by us to stay execution when Hitler's Reich drenched the world in blood and destroyed millions of Jews. The callousness of the civilized world then made public action impossible, but we ourselves were culpable in not understanding in time and in not doing what should have been done if the hand of the executioner would not be stayed. The crime of silence and inaction facing impending tragedy will not be repeated in this day. We remember the past horrors and see before us a living structure of Jewish National life, after the travail of fifty years. We have created a Homeland of peace and justice amidst a people who threaten us with the fires of destruction now, as they did in the earlier days when there was no State, but only the beginnings of a Jewish Homeland.

AFTER THE STATE: WHITHER ZIONISM?

The congealment of Zionist forms of authority as an end in themselves was always opposed by Lipsky.

In 1929, Dr. Chaim Weizmann succeeded in persuading distinguished non-Zionists to join an extended Jewish Agency and to cooperate in rebuilding Jewish Palestine.

A great controversy ensued in Zionist circles, where fears were expressed lest the power of the Zionist Organization be curtailed.

Lipsky, then the President of the Zionist Organization of America, took his place by the side of Dr. Weizmann. In an article written in Jerusalem in 1929 he called upon the Zionists to broaden their horizons and accept cooperation in order to accelerate the achievement of their goals.

Just twenty-eight years later, nine years after the creation of the State of Israel, Mr. Lipsky was to make one of the most devastating attacks on the organization he had spent a lifetime in building, for its failure to recognize that its goals had been accomplished—i.e., a thriving Jewish State, Israel; and for its refusal to reorganize itself in a way that took account of the new era created by that great and dramatic reality.

The article and the address are presented here.

The Editor

THE NEW BIRTH*

I speak first of Palestine—the hub of our national adventure, our fortress, the barometer of our achievements, the test of our ideals and theories, the source of our anxieties and spiritual satisfactions. How

* *Message from Jerusalem of the President to the 32nd Annual Z.O.A. Convention in Detroit, June 5, 1929.*

difficult it is for us who linger in Galuth—beguiled by its diverting influence—to appraise the distance in time and space which separates us from the processes of renaissance in which both the Land and the Pioneers are now struggling.

The theatre of our national experiment is immeasurably far in every respect from the consuming, everyday life of Galuth. The handicaps (or opportunities) of the national home are strangely alien. Its form and standards are so different. It is a growing world foreign to most of our acquired habits of living and thinking. There life tends to revert to the encrusted primitive—into which the lingering desires of the still unforgotten West grotesquely intrude. The receding West looks down upon the freshly turned loam of the East. Atavistic restraints come into play—new appetites and self-denials long unpracticed. The returning Wanderer finds himself going through the throes of a new birth with the old consciousness still pulsating. He is apprehensive of the social and mental implications. The old Galuth skin has not yet been shed but the new skin of Redemption forms underneath. Why wonder then—or complain—that we in Galuth, enmeshed in quite another world, find it hard to appreciate how Redemption is being achieved, and that we should so easily fall into habits of hasty judgments and impatience; measuring, quite naturally, the fresh creation by the banal, obsolete standards of a disintegrating Galuth?

A degree of humility should be ours. It is they—and not we—who have stood under the glaring sun, floundered about in the poisonous morasses, tortured their bodies with grinding physical labor, torn themselves away from the fixed habits of Galuth for the sake of our national future. We have not shared their experiences—their privations or the pangs of their adjustments. While they were climbing the steep hill of the new life, we have lingered afar, giving of our surplus (merely of our sentiment and good wishes!), looking on while they made the grade of national living. Excess of praises would be bad taste, but it is the extreme of ingratitude to underestimate what our pioneers have done for the recovery of our national life and our land.

It is literal Truth: a new Land comes to life, rising painfully out of the submerged Past. It is as if in the far years past Palestine had slumbered in a trance and the Magic Spell now has been broken. Is this a figure of speech? Do you call it fantasy?

When God saw His people driven forth by the Romans from the Land He had promised them as their heritage forever, compassion overcame Him and He set His seal on the Land to hold it until they should return—

as He had promised they would! His finger of mercy touched it and it fell into a sleep that has endured for over nineteen hundred years. Empires rose and fell; conquerors came and conquerors departed; but the Land lay prostrate in fearful slumber and was not disturbed.

The middle sea was reduced to paralysis. Its circulation was inhibited and it became the Dead Sea; a strange useless appendix, absorbing the riches of the soil; a bottomless pit, a cistern of Death. And all the waters of the Jordan poured into that sinister vessel and left their wealth there and poured into the Great Sea to the west. The rivulets that gave their life to the Jordan felt no urge to feed a useless instrument and wandered aimlessly about, losing themselves finally in swamps and morasses. Deprived of perennial renewal of water, the forests decayed, were destroyed by predatory tribes and the roots of what was left of them were nibbled away by hordes of goats driven by impoverished Bedouins. The extinction of the trees left the mountains bare—forbidding skeletons of their former state. The hills of Judea were left unprotected, abandoned by Nature and by man. The coastal plain, once Nature's storehouse, became desert sand. Dust covered the ugly decay of the cities. Centuries of progress passed the deserted land and made not a mark upon its features. Commerce turned to other ports. Ships, passing, saw a strip of sand from Gaza to Acco, topped by the range of devastated rocks of the Judean hills. Upon that bleak ridge the ancient city of Jerusalem rested. Within its creaking gates old rites and customs were being lazily repeated by derelict remnants of many races, who seemed to have taken a vow to await unchanged the Deliverance that had been promised the favored son. A darkened capital—a land left forgotten by its children—sightless people moving about, going through prescribed motions like automata; the wind blowing the sand forever further toward the hills. The Bride was awaiting the coming of the predestined Groom. She kept her beauty hidden. For protection against unwelcome suitors she had donned unsightly garb; had become unkempt, ugly, lethargic, morose, lacking grace and beauty—a tragic spectacle of desolate mourning and hopeless lamentation. . . .

Now, the Veil of Ages is being removed! The Magician has spoken the word and many hands have responded to reveal the Truth. The Land is being remade, refurnished, cleansed, set in order, debris removed, new roots planted. *Palestine is being reborn.* The hands of love touch its soil and that which seemed dead beyond recall comes to life. It recognizes the touch of the Beloved One. It reciprocates remembrance and love. It rises to meet the Groom with unexpected gifts.

If you come too close to the scene you may not see the Bride or the Groom. If you lose yourself in details the larger picture will be blurred. Take all the astounding changes in the Land; observe all that has been achieved with sympathy, put yourself in their places—get the right perspective—and it will speak but one word: New Birth!

What do you think is the truer meaning of the reclamation of the Dead Sea? They speak of millions of tons of chemical deposits. It is going to release the wealth that has poured into it through the centuries. They speak of industrial enterprises, of cheap fertilizer. But the Dead Sea is the physical heart of Palestine; the heart that had stopped beating. The quickening of its life means the removal of a cancer that had eaten into the physical life of the Land. It had been a clog; it had been a drain. It had taken all and given nothing in return. When Novomeysky opens the veins of this cancer, creates an exit for the waters of the Jordan, he restores Nature's normal circulation in Palestine's physical Life. The good news will be carried to the creeks and rivulets and wadis, into every swamp and morass. Every artery will be prepared to function when once the heart resumes its healthy beat.

Pinchas Rutenberg came before Novomeysky, but there is a direct connection between the harnessing of the Jordan and the exploitation of the Dead Sea. Rutenberg is bracing the walls of the river. He is cleaning its bed, regulating its flow, clearing the way for the converging streams. He is creating an adequate receiver for an enlarged waterfall that will hold and use all the water that is poured into it. The river will at last have both a normal beginning and a healthy exit. The strengthening of the Jordan—now in process of execution—means bringing to life the hidden currents of water in the Land. It is contributing to the making of a dependable system of circulation. A physical abnormality is being removed. The Land is being helped to awaken.

Along the coastal plain from Rehovot to Haifa, reaching back into the Emek, there are now long stretches of green. It is a remarkable transformation. Orange groves, green trees, water service, a tried industry and a successful branch of agriculture. Ten years of experiment, disappointments—mistakes—finally an industry. But beyond the business side of it looms the fact that long stretches of useless sand have become fertile; no longer dead, no longer ugly, no longer unresponsive to the human touch.

What a change has come over the cities! They have burst their cerements and stretch themselves out sleepily as if gladly responding to the summons. They have distinctive features that already foretell their future. Tel Aviv has grown like an awkward child. It is unformed and lacks grace. But the traits of its origin continue in its adolescence. It is the creation of the first flush of national energy and daring. It is the first city made by émigrés from the Galuth before the deeper springs of the Land had been touched. Its streets are open, as if they did not know which way they were going. You trample the sand under your feet and it turns into a sidewalk. Architecture knows no restraint; it pays tribute to no tradition. Tel Aviv has the strength and the faults of the parvenu; it is ready to be remade every day. The new settler need not fear that he will have no share in its building; the city hates mere duplication and monotony. This is the city which is going to be the dynamic, revolutionary center of the country.

Haifa leaps ahead of all imaginative prophecy. What was yesterday a walled-in dust heap has become the city of largest promise. It is to be the cosmopolitan center of commerce. Who will set his imprint upon it? The tradesmen of all nations, the mariners of all lands, and those who are able to be the interpreters of the East to the West. Haifa is likely to take after Alexandria. It will be the market place of Palestine, gathering together the awakening commerce of the East into one organic knot. The port—the pipeline to Bagdad—industrial plants—the city on Mount Carmel and its terraced slopes—the Emek as its backyard—and all of the East using its terminal facilities. Who is responsible for the bursting of this chrysalis? Fumbling, untutored, ill-equipped, pioneer Jews, with their national madness, their financial recklessness, their disregard for form and balance. They dominate the hill. They stir the commercial life of the old city.

No such familiarity as one observes in Tel Aviv is possible with relation to Jerusalem. The ancient city takes you captive and you had better not struggle against the conditions it imposes. You cannot so easily remake the rocky hills, nor can you subjugate the old, walled-in remnant. There are ancient spirits loitering about its darkened streets holding converse in the moonlight. It is a hard city. It is an arrogant city, making no compromises. You may bring in modern hotels (which is being done), and water and pave the streets; but its granite lines cannot so easily be disposed of. Our presence will be indicated most effectively by the edifice which is being constructed on Mount Scopus. The Hebrew University will make Jerusalem the Jewish City. The meaning of our presence will be explained by that noble institution which is assembling all Jewish knowledge, bringing form into what seemed to be a disordered mass and beginning already to speak of the wisdom of the past in terms of the present and the future. Not the Wailing Wall around which lamentation gathers; not the spirit of weeping at the graves of ancestors; but the Light of Learning and Wisdom for which the Jewish people shall be responsible. The light of Jerusalem has been rekindled.

It is not only the Land which is coming to life. The Galuth Jew has been transformed into a free Jew, who draws upon his inner strength, who is fearless and creative. He is the resurrection of the Jewish peasant and the Maccabean warrior. Just as the young trees come to life on the Judean hills, so the sprigs of new character, new habits of life, new ways of thinking, new sources of physical strength, become apparent in those who are laying the foundations of the physical life in Palestine. The layers of alien manners are falling away. The narrow vision of men and women long immured within city walls is being broadened and deepened by the hardships and experiments of the pioneer enterprise.

There is so much of the Galuth which has to be given up. The wastefulness of Western civilization is being replaced by an enforced primitive thrift. They have learned to do without things as a matter of national duty. The climate and the soil; the inherent difficulties of both; the remarkable effects upon them of the recovery of our own language—these have made for dignity and self-respect. The physical qualities of their bodies undergo change and develop a new kind of resistance. The weaknesses of Galuth are being purged out of them by the life-giving power of the Sun, by the hard toil conquest of the soil imposes upon them. The forms and tempo of the East become their second nature. Shall not the land that made a priest people out of slaves once more produce a revolutionary change in character and qualities when the prodigal returns?

This miraculous rebirth of Land and People is due to the sustained effort of a remnant of the House of Israel, who have carried the burden during the many years of preparation. It was the Zionist understanding of the Jewish problem—their intellectual contempt for the conditions of Galuth—that brought the Ideal to active Life and kept it effective during the period when the Jewish people were committed to a studied avoidance of national obligation.

Through the agitation we set in motion; the dissatisfaction we created; the unrest we engendered; through the life we brought into the national home, the Balfour Declaration was finally achieved. During the past ten years (here in Galuth and there in the Land to which our historic right has been recognized) we of the Zionist Organization have been responsible for the organized, sustained, unremitting effort to meet the heavy national burden that had been placed upon the whole Jewish people by the ratification of the Mandate. Years of great hope and enthusiasm; of despair and vacillation; of inadequate achievement; committing mistakes and struggling along with their consequences; making a great noise to awaken the sleepers and being rebuked for exaggerations; but whatever the conditions, standing firm and loyal and faithful to duty, refusing to acknowledge defeat, refusing to compromise with pedantry or with counsels of caution or of perfection; moving along with our burden until this day, when Palestine itself comes forward to greet us with its message of life and of hope.

The instrument created by Theodor Herzl has yet to receive a just appreciation for what it has done for the destiny of the Jewish people in carrying the burden of responsibility unto this day.

The way has been prepared for a union of all Jewish elements in the building of the national home. It will not be denied that what has been accomplished in Palestine and the beneficent influence Zionist education has had upon Jewish life in Galuth have finally awakened the conscience of the whole House of Israel to its duty toward the national home.

They may not accept or understand the Zionist vocabulary—there may be verbal discords—but they seem to be in earnest with regard to the part they expect to play in the establishment of a national home that shall be worthy of the Jewish people. We look forward to their entering the house we have built as partners in the great enterprise.

There will in all likelihood be differences of opinion; but just as Zionist differences have always been ironed out in the council chamber and unity has been preserved through the give and take of discussion, so it may be anticipated that with good will and mutual confidence the extended Jewish Agency will become an instrument not only for large-visioned constructive work in Palestine, but also for strengthening the bonds of unity and peace among all elements of the Jewish people. The Zionist cause has everything to gain and nothing to lose by the contemplated partnership. Just as we are remade by what is being created in Palestine —the balance of power and influence always being with Palestine—so we may anticipate as between our partners and ourselves a growing harmony and understanding with regard to both the problems of Palestine and of Jewish life in general.

It is our aim to redeem Israel and Zion, to rebuild not only the Land of Israel but also the House of Israel—in order to explain and justify the historic persistence of the Chosen People and to make them once more the bringers of light and guidance to the peoples of the earth.

The achievement of Jewish unity with regard to Palestine will doubtless require a thorough reconsideration of our methods of Zionist propaganda. It is plain, however, that we should not be diverted to the intellectual pleasures of controversy. Our interest lies in winning for our ideals and principles, *as they express themselves in works,* the understanding and cordial support of Jews who are not in agreement with us.

There are Zionists who fear that the new policy will undermine the authority of the Zionist Organization. This fear is based upon the notion that the Zionist Organization is to cease to function as the corporate expression of Zionist aims; and that the extended Jewish Agency is to take its place. This is an unfounded fear. The Zionist Organization remains the agency that carries the Zionist ideal. It is the guardian of Jewish national interests; its powers are derived from no external authority, but only from its own inner will to act. A sharing of responsibility does not alter its status. If anything, the acquisition of partners who are potentially capable of strengthening our position in Palestine will give added prestige and influence to the Zionist Organization both in Palestine and in Galuth.

In other words, it is our duty to strengthen the authority of the Zionist Organization. But there is no need for involving the bogey of the extended Jewish Agency to depress Zionists and to make them overlook the power that lies in their hands at the forthcoming Zurich Congress.

If there was any Magic used to bring Zion back to life and to galvanize the Wandering Jew into active resistance to Galuth, that Magic was born out of the spirit and enthusiasm of Zionists. We had been infected by the wild hope that the Miracle was possible, and with that hope we lived, and labored and sacrificed. Now that Reality stalks in our midst, moving about under a Sun that blinds the eyes; now that Mystery seems to have disappeared and the Prosaic is pushed into the foreground, let us not forget that as we dig into the roots of Jewish life, and as we build high on the Judean hills, we may yet recover the real Magic which produced prophets and seers in Israel, and breakers of new paths, and makers of new wisdom.

"WHITHER ZIONISM?"

The Zionist Movement encountered the revolution caused by the birth of the Jewish State without adequate realization of its grave consequences. It was drawn into the vortex of the desperate struggle of the new

* *Address to National Founding Assembly of American Jewish League for Israel,* May 1957, New York City.

State for survival, and was plunged into the process of its birth, and emerged to find two organic concepts occupying its vision, where formerly there was one. Zionism gave help in the birth of the State, which has had to fight for its life and destiny. In the confusion and shock of the struggle, Zionism, thus liberated, was unable to see where it was going. It knew only that its primary duty was to serve the State through the years of its trial, and thus, in preoccupation with that grave task, it lost its initiative and the compass of its direction.

In the few years of its existence, Israel has made an amazing record. It welcomed and settled and integrated masses of Jews forced by persecution to find their redemption in Israel. It kept an open door through which poured victims of many lands. It admitted them even when it had to fight a desperate war for its survival at birth, and continues to admit them even now, under the most difficult and trying circumstances. It set up and maintains an effective democratic government. It organized a substantial, competent army of defense and offense. It is a respected member of the United Nations. It has established close, friendly relations with many foreign countries. It is developing the culture and scientific experience of the new State with great vision and ability. It sends its own emissaries to the Jews of the Diaspora, and influences their thought and action. It has taken over completely all the political responsibilities formerly assumed by the Zionist Organization. It is the free state dreamed of by Herzl and Weizmann, and prepared by half a century of Zionist creative work. It is the glowing symbol of the national renaissance.

But the Zionist Movement—the creator—has not yet found the center of its own being under the new conditions. There are warm and generous relations between the Movement and the State. There is a deep maternal concern as to the future of the State that now lives in accordance with the developing laws of its own being. But as time goes on, it is recognized that each is bound to find its own characteristic life grooves, form its own communal habits, deal with its own peculiar needs; struggling for its own security, culture and survival, in its own environment, in its own self-chosen ways.

The birth of Israel left an open wound close to the heart of the Zionist Movement, which remains unhealed; to a large extent, Zionism continues its old ways, unable to appreciate that it cannot live and retain its previous status under the shadow of the growing State. It carries on its discussion of old problems, despite the fact that many of them have become irrele-

vant and obsolete. It refuses to acknowledge that the revolution demands
a severance of certain basic relations, fundamental readjustments,
the beginning of a new era. It drags its feet to its Congresses, to its
Actions Committee meetings, burdened by statutes and procedures and
party memories. It engages in futile duels with the Israeli Government on
jurisdictional rights. It wrestles with old definitions and old concepts.
Most Zionists who are spectators of these grand discussions, wonder
why these storms and stresses should have struck them in the midst
of what seemed to be the national triumph, the fulfillment of an ancient
hope, and left them gasping helplessly at the climactic spectacle of Israel's
struggle for freedom, in which they are now, perforce, reduced to the
dimensions and functions of an auxiliary influence. It is disturbed by a
large variety of Israeli-based fund-raising agencies, delegations and
instructors of parties bringing with them their own slogans and inspirations, which drain away from specific Zionist jurisdiction the energies and
interests that should have their center in the Diaspora life of the Zionist
Movement. It no longer occupies a commanding position in Jewish life.

What is most appalling is the fact that the Zionist movement seems
not only to have lost the ability to exercise its freedom, but also its
desire to be free. It has allowed its independence of thought to be suffocated by traditions and external authorities, without protest or dissent.
It continues to invoke the democracy of its first years, but all of that is
now reduced to the scrutiny of votes, to the rights of parties, to the search
for organizational power, to the struggle for survival as an organized unit.

In short, the vacuum in Zionism created by the birth of the State has
not been filled with dynamic creative power. Its scattered activities leave
no deposit of wisdom or direction or spiritual satisfaction. What passes
for discussion is trapped in conversations within a charmed circle where
tradition must be maintained at all costs, and in which no fresh concept
finds admission. Events in Zionist life which were once regarded as
miracles are retained in a state of rigid memorial. It is fettered by statutes,
by party rights, by sacred formulas, by the conclusions of ideological
discussions that now seem like a jungle of dead words to be deciphered
by the learned scholars of recorded history.

It is tragic that parties in Israel should control their counterpart in the
Diaspora. There are controls in the Jewish Agency which dominate the
parties in the Diaspora. There are controls in the Government of Israel

that fetter the Jewish Agency in the Diaspora as well as in Israel. It is an interlocking chain of controls to the last outposts of influence. The supremacy of the sovereignty of Israel is conceded; but the Jewish Agency has its own sovereignty, and so in their way the parties have sovereignty in their veto power. One looks in vain to find provision for the freedom of the local group, or the individual, or the unattached, or the territorial division, in matters that directly concern them, where they live, where their Zionist life should be concentrated.

The New Jews, recently awakened to the realities and the vision of the State of Israel, have yet to find their appropriate place in the fraternity of the Jewish people allied with Israel. Most of us look upon the New Jews, so deeply dedicated, with peculiar suspicion, and would like to have them undergo an inquisition of their faith, to have them affix their signatures to their pledges, to give an assurance of enduring tenure of commitment. Their loyalty is questioned, although in any census of workers for the State of Israel, or for Jewish interests at large, the New Jews enormously outnumber the enrolled members of the Zionist organizations, matching them in service and sacrifice, in tenacity of faith and emotional fervor. In order to qualify for inclusion in the new army for Israel, the New Jew is expected to pass the test of "Shekel" and Party, and give satisfactory replies to the Zionist catechism sanctified by sixty years of Zionist history.

This state of indecision cannot drag on indefinitely. The pressure of historic events requires that the House of Zionism open its windows wide and let fresh air in, and refuse to be confined as a prisoner behind the old walls of habit, regurgitating old slogans and clichés, and wrestling with procedures and statutes that have been the source of Zionist controversy and education since the beginning of Zionist time. The birth of the State has swept away these accumulations. Zionism is struggling for its identification and life in a whirlpool of revolutionary change, and if it is to remain alive, it must revise its relations with its past and find a new concept of life, that will enable it to give expression to its own ideals and aspirations and respond to the lessons of its own experience. It must abandon the general debate and look at the realities. It must regard the records of the Zionist past as revered deposits in the national archives—in reality, the museum of our colorful past. Zionism must find its own life elsewhere.

A reconstruction of Zionism is obviously called for, but the catalyst of revolution has not yet been found. All forms of Zionist groupings avoid the problem and take refuge in repetitious debates and evasions of truth, as if the sanctity of Zionism is likely to be soiled by freedom of speech. They are held enthralled by nostalgia and fears. A spark of free initiative, lighting up one corner of the scene, might kindle a flame and bring life to the tired bones and lethargic spirit of the organization, and start it on a new round of struggle and give exciting stimulation to the desire for freedom, and introduce a new era of creativity. A declaration of independence might be the first step toward such a renaissance: but the existing groups seem content to linger on with a vanishing form of life, becoming more desiccated from year to year, hysterically protecting their past, bemoaning the cruelty of history that has fastened that problem on their weary shoulders.

I speak with grief of the Zionist Organization of America, which was the center of my own Zionist life for over fifty years, and which should have been a conspicuous instrument of liberation. It has preferred to ignore the challenge, and even resents its intrusion on public attention or its own private discussions. It makes its chief contribution to the *new* Zionist Day by taking shelter in a political party of Israel, as if under the wings of that party, stewing in its own partisan disputes, it may become a part of Jewish life in the Land of Promise—unconscious of the fact that thus it is living a full life neither here nor there. It refuses to make permanent landing anywhere, preferring to float in the air for decades to come.

I submit that the new Zionist group may become the catalyst in the liberation of the Zionist Organization. At any rate, it is the first step in the renaissance and reconstruction of the Zionist Movement. It is that step—painful but necessary—we propose to take. The New Group will endeavor to create new forms of organized action. It will introduce standards of selected operations, the concept of qualifications for leadership. It will avoid the ambitions and controversies of parties. It will seek the specific, rather than the universal task. It will think of the place where we live, rather than of the universe, which is an abstraction. It will seek fraternal relations with all Jews—the New Jews, to whom the wonders of the *new* Zion have only been recently revealed, as well as the old Zionists, who need a new revelation. It will avoid muttering over the resurrection of the untenable status quo that clutters the way to rebirth—and give a warm welcome to all forces in Jewish life prepared to contribute to revival and recreation.

"The New Day calls for a new bold approach." Out of the loins of the great historic movement which brought Israel to life must come a new will to live, a strong desire to rise to the great responsibilities of the Jewish people, emanating from the obligations of statehood. Only through rededication, through freedom of thought, through faith and initiative, through sacrifice, through absence of fear and through love for Jewish peoplehood, will it be possible for Zionism to be as inspiring and creative in the days to come as it was in the days of the Founding Fathers, the pioneers of labor, the builders of the National Home.

With our help and our faith, Israel will become the everlasting foundation of the living Jewish people, free and unafraid, exercising its own sovereignty, and respectful and considerate of the sovereignty of others.

NEW SIGHT OF ISRAEL

Israel's march on the Sinai Peninsula to destroy the Fedayeen nests, responsible for continuous sudden death on its borders, was in full progress when Lipsky arrived in Israel in November 1956.

This was his second visit to the Jewish State, the first since his retirement from office in the movement for a Jewish State for whose creation and survival he had fought for more than half a century.

At the Weizmann Institute of Science at Rehovot he was made an Honorary Fellow. The citation reads:

"In recognition of the luminous gifts he has brought to the service of Zionism and Israel over the course of half a century and more—unswerving disciple of Chaim Weizmann, sharer of his vision, inspirer of the Louis Lipsky Exchange Fellowships for the enrichment of Science in Israel through the Weizmann Institute."

On November 12, 1956, Mr. Lipsky presented a summation of his Zionist philosophy, in the Chaim Weizmann Memorial Lecture.

That lecture is reproduced here.

The Editor

HERZL, WEIZMANN AND THE JEWISH STATE*

The years through which many of us have walked on the long journey toward Zion have left a record difficult to recall. Our memories are burdened with heavy baggage, much of it excess to present thought. It is hard to discern how the obstacles encountered were transformed from their primitive beginnings to the vibrant exciting Present. It is like the

* *The Chaim Weizmann Memorial Lecture,* delivered at Rehovot, Israel, November 12, 1956.

apotheosis of a long Dream in which the present and the past are mingled; and the clue as to which was the beginning and which the end has been lost. Time measurements have no meaning. Think back to the earliest days of the modern Awakening. Pause at each step up the ladder, look around, and see the panorama of burgeoning life revealed about you. It is a Miracle in which the living and the dead are interlocked in the turbulent processes of a birth which seems to have no end. Life has become so varied and strong that all anxieties and tensions, apprehensions of danger to come, are dominated by the amazing revolution which gave Israel its first fighting chance for survival in freedom.

I heard the first living summons of Zion through the voice of Theodor Herzl. I heard it in the distant American city where I was born. I read his first words in a stray copy of the London *Jewish Chronicle*. At that time his voice was thrilling and confident. He gave the impression of having made a startling discovery which the world must be made to know about. It was an old story, but he gave tone and power to an ideal Jews had nurtured over the centuries, which they had murmured in their prayers and which they had retold to their children, again and again, but had never dared to address, formally or informally, to strangers living in another world and speaking a language Jews had not yet learned to speak. The naiveté of Herzl gave him courage and audacity, and provided him with a new vocabulary to describe the ancient hope and made it possible to force his way into the anterooms of kings and statesmen, into the presence of men of letters and molders of public opinion; and, even as a stranger, as he was then, to reach down into the heart of his own people and to evoke from them a new expression of their hidden passion and cherished hopes.

What I knew of Jews in those days related to communities of emigrants brought from a distance across the sea and encumbered with the memories and traditions of the past, whose chief absorption was the problem of their provincial Jewish life and how to make their way in peace in the land of freedom. But I had been reading books about Jews in English (there were not many) and heard their repetitious legends and their wayward dreams, wondering when their awakening would come, and whence would arise their redemption and how they would be able to return to the Promised Land through the wilderness of man-made obstacles. In the clarion words of Herzl, in his dramatic plays on the international stage, in his "Jewish State" and the first Congresses, in the furiously indignant denunciations of Max Nordau, the old hope came to life with startling resonance, and its echoes stirred the faithful in dispersion and made them conscious of their living peoplehood.

Time has given a deeper meaning and a sharper reality to the familiar image of Theodor Herzl, as to other legendary figures of the Jewish renaissance. To those who were thrilled when he came, he is now not merely the Hero beating his wings against unyielding walls. He is not the diplomat in a frock coat. He is not the propagandist in the world press. He is not only the organizer of his people. The legend has been greatly enlarged. It is the story of an eager man of letters, young and ambitious and arrogant who, by a miracle of imagination, found himself dedicated to an ideal plucked from Jewish tradition, animated by confidence and faith and proclaimed with the bravado of an angry prophet. When he fell he was like an eagle stricken in flight. When he was buried in the old Vienna cemetery, he had served his destiny and registered the climax of a tragic adventure. When he was finally entombed on the hill facing Jerusalem from the west—no longer a stranger—his dust was laid to rest in the bosom of his people, where they with their own hands were building the State his imagination had described before he knew what the plot of the story was to be, and which they were then defending, for the first time, with their own arms and under their own command.

It seemed that his mission would die with him. The leader had vanished and with his death Zionism seemed to pause to catch its second wind and to consider how to rise again and what form the resurrection should take. But the movement did not expire with its leader. A spark had been ignited. The flame could not be extinguished. It spread slowly among the oppressed in body and spirit. It renewed itself through language and new vision and new legends carried over into a new generation. It passed out of the hands of the beginners. The search for political adventure was abandoned, and instead of pursuing the prospects of a diplomacy that never pierced the source of power, it began to take root in the soil of the Promised Land. Action in depth followed the exciting sweep of political maneuver and debate.

The first wave of pioneers, whose love was greater than their creative abilities, was followed by others who in turn were succeeded by bolder and more resourceful men and women, who had armed themselves with the ideals and tools of labor to undertake the hard task of conquering the soil and to strike up a working arrangement with the unknown land which had been promised but had yet to be conquered. They became the builders of roads, the planters of trees, the drainers of swamps, the breeders of cattle, the builders of colonies, the founders of schools, the revivalists of an ancient culture incorporated in an ancient language. It was a herculean struggle against great difficulties. The debris of past erosions had to be removed. The arid soil had to be recreated to receive the blessed seed that would give forth the food required to sustain life. The swamps had to be cleansed and their poisons absorbed and drained away. Where the old soil vanished under the new soil cannot be distinguished. What came first—what was last—who were the victors—who were the vanquished? These struggling waves of creative life are now integrated in a sovereign nationhood. Only those who were sweating partners in the struggle are able to tell the story of the rebirth. The pioneers of all grades and levels clasp hands in a common past. They are now all joined as brothers in the historic memory of the State, in which their first labors are the foundations on which it was established.

As we turn to him who rests in Rehovot, I am strangely aware of his presence hovering restlessly over the land, observing his people, sharing their anxieties and tensions, troubled in spirit as they are troubled. He has not found peace. The greater part of his life was spent in finding the ways to build the National Home, and to lay the foundations of the State. He lives in the memory of his people, associated with the totality of the creation. He carried his burden without intermission from the earliest days until the State was proclaimed. He had his triumphs and his frustrations, his days of joy and his days of agony. He is still the Witness inseparable from the destiny of his people. He is no longer a controversial figure. The controversies he labored with, which often confused his relations with his people, are no longer relevant to the present scene.

He is now more real and explicable than he was in life. All the facets of his personality are mirrored in balance in our recollections. He is the brooding student at the university. He is the alert and sagacious debater in the Zionist Congresses. He conceived of science as one of the essential features of a modern state. He was among the first to dream of a Hebrew University and kindred institutions of learning. He was the leader often at odds with his people, the rejected and the rehabilitated, growing from strength to strength, and winning in the course of a long life the reverence and affection and respect of a generation of creative Jews, chiefly on account of his great love for Zion and his great devotion, and his identification with its great struggles.

Redemption did not come to Dr. Weizmann as a discovery. Its seed was born in him at his birth. It was nurtured by his Jewish environment. It was the atmosphere of a family life in which the Law and the Prophets were ever present. It was refreshed by the books he read. It was the fulfillment of prophecy. It was not born of persecution. It was predestined. It had the glow of the Messianic hope, which was the mantle that enfolded his Vision.

He saw the Jewish State as the organic creation of a dedicated Jewish people. It was to be cleansed of the dross accumulated in the Dispersion. It was to bring back the first memories, refine and redeem them, and make them live in the bosom of a people whose heartbeat they would become. It was to rest on foundations of peace and justice and brotherhood. It was to incarnate a way of life that would be the authentic expression of the foretold destiny of the Jewish people. Because he had such deep faith, he was not driven by the pressures of time. The ingredients of the national life would have to be found and cultivated, allowed to germinate, to create an organic life of its own. Out of this arid strip of rocky and swamp-infested land on the edge of a desert, a land brimming with milk and honey would have to be brought alive by patient labor, by cautious progress, by clearing a way through the jungle of civilization, and finally reaching the highway of freedom.

He had faith that peace and progress would inevitably lead to fulfillment. That faith shackled his imagination and when it became evident that the road was being diverted—that the map of progress was being altered—he could not retrace the route of his thoughts. His restraints, his hesitations, the weight of the burden of his responsibilities as leader, became unbearable. He clung, in spite of all the evidence against it, to the concept that historical events would lead to the emergence of a greater and a better reality. He believed in agreements—not in conflicts—and that in the processes of creation, foundations would be laid that could hold organic life in spite of all oppressions and diversions. He preferred to avoid battle and move around an impasse rather than risk destruction through pressure to break it. He did not reckon on the awakening of Arab chauvinism that would bring a rebirth of ancient feuds. He did not anticipate British disclaimer of the covenant. He did not foresee the disintegration of the Germany of Goethe, Schiller and Kant, and the ruthless effectiveness of a reborn German barbarism. In the light of the great Reversal he had to face, which forced his people to turn from the ploughshare to take up arms against a world that seemed intent on destroying Israel's hope, he stands out as a personality of great tragic and moral significance in the history of our time.

The National Home was the first appearance of the Jewish State. The world was unable to right the wrongs of the Jewish people in one sustained effort. Regret seemed to follow at once on the act of benevolence and political courage. The drafting of the Mandate under which Israel was to live, absorbed several years of cautious political hesitation. Second thoughts rushed with speed to restate the objective of the Declaration. The Mandate was amended and reinterpreted. It was sent back to the drafters of legal documents. The revisions came out in the open in formal statements, in debates in Parliament, in White Papers. The grand premises of statesmen were reduced to bland legal formulas. The scrutineers of phraseology found that what was meant by a National Home was not clear. Was all of Palestine to become the National Home or was the National Home to be an enclave in Palestine? What was meant by absorptive capacity? Was it an economic or political concept? It took them years to project their forms and to state their conclusions. In the course of time, the National Home became a flexible instrument of stumbling authority, reflecting eclectic views on interests as they arose, but always slanted toward the original intention. All doubts were cleared, however, when the White Paper of 1939 settled the issues in favor of the Arabs. Unfortunately, the flight of Jews from Europe, their clamor for admission to the National Home, the war that was being prepared by the Nazis against Europe gave the 1939 document the sinister aspect of sabotage. It was an unfortunate moment for the Mandatory to rid itself of its alleged double obligation. It was the most unfavorable time to cut the Gordian knot and to confess the utter defeat of the Declaration and the Mandate. It seemed like the tragic epilogue to the Hitler story.

The second encounter of the Jewish people with international law and justice took place in the United Nations in 1947 when the State of Israel, in a specified part of Palestine, was established. All the formalities were executed—the vote in the Security Council, the vote in the Assembly, the first recognition of Israel by the President of the United States and Israel's admission as a member of the United Nations.

The record has no flaw. Israel is a nation among nations. Its delegates appear and speak at the sessions of the United Nations; they are assigned to committees. It is visible in the sight of world opinion. Its voice is heard. But after eight years of struggle against great odds, Israel stands in a moment of great peril and it is again being tested by the grueling processes of second thoughts. What should now be an area of peace and

tranquility, has been transformed by external pressures into an encampment of alerted defenders. Grim-visaged war looks out at Israel on all
its frontiers. It is being maneuvered into a position of grim isolation. It
extends the hand of friendship to the aggressors and asks for the completion of the armistice agreements in peace. But pressures for peace seem
to be outmoded. It finds no active sponsors. Action for peace must be
avoided in order not to disturb the appeasements being devised to win
the vagrant friendship of the Arab states. There are no points of order
raised when the Arab states in the United Nations use its platform to
traduce Israel, and to give vent to threats of destruction. Nor is notice
taken of the plans of the Arab states to act in concert in aggression
toward Israel. The conspiracy is not being conducted in secrecy. It is
being shouted from the housetops. It is taken down in the records of the
United Nations. It is the national theme song of every Arab state. It
makes use of the mail and cables freely to circulate their war cries. It
issues interviews to press associations to circulate Middle East attacks
on Israel. Israel is blocked in the Suez Canal and at Elath. The boycott
of Israel is conducted through ambassadorial agents who use their
immunity with impudent bravado. Not only have the armistice agreements been transferred to the guardianship of an international police
force on the spot to protect the peace, such as it is, but the agreements
themselves have become the source of litigation and irritations. They
provide incidents to be brought by the Arab states to the Security Council,
whose discussions are material for the press inflaming public opinion,
giving the Arabs an opportunity to challenge history and to libel a
neighboring state without being called to book in any court of law or
justice.

In effect Israel, recognized as a free state, admitted to the United
Nations, enjoying its rights and privileges, is practically under siege. The
violation of its rights under the Charter is being conducted in full view
of an international audience without protest or remonstrance. It seems
to be regarded as the illegitimate child of the United Nations; it is an
orphan in a rising storm. Under the pressures contrived by the Arab
states, the United Nations avoids consideration of the basic problems
of the Middle East. The peace of Israel is the last item on its agenda.

The faith that sustained us in the darkest days of Hitler and the war
in Israel, that blessed the sacrifices of our people and enabled us to
overcome unparalleled obstacles, will abide with us in these days of
grave peril, for Israel is stronger today than it was a decade ago. It has

had the experience of freedom, democracy and self-defense. It has received within its limited territory over 800,000 kinsmen and settled them in their own homes and introduced them to the Israeli way of life. It is more knowledgeable in the ways of National living. It has brought the Jews of the world together in a renewed covenant. Wherever there are Jews, Israel has forged a bond of unbreakable brotherhood with them. It has established fraternal relations with nations, great and small, and won their individual respect and sympathy. It has created a modern state that is mindful of Jewish tradition and appreciative of Jewish culture. It has incorporated into its way of life the achievements of modern science and technology and made amazing progress in the fields of agriculture and industry and commerce. It is at home on the sea, in the air, and in the military skills of defense. It is a democratic state in the best sense of the word. It may boast of a labor movement which is the envy of free labor in every land. It is, in fact, a symbol of the ideal that should animate the civilized world. It is the only steadfast beacon of light and progress and peace in the Middle East.

Its foundations are secure, and any reckless aggressor planning an open attack against this national creation will find not only a people equipped for defense, but one that will fight with capacity for self-sacrifice and endurance worthy of the Maccabeans in whose footsteps they walk.

Nor, in any inventory of the strength and resources of Israel, should the kinsmen of the people of Israel be overlooked or underestimated or misunderstood. They represent a reserve force of great value and significance. They cannot be dismissed by definition because they do not belong to the category of Zionists. Their love for their Land and its freedom admits them without question to the Brotherhood of Israel.

When the Nazis attacked the Jewish communities of Europe and sought to raise anti-Semitism to an international crusade, they aroused Jews everywhere as nothing had stirred them before in Jewish memory. The attacks strengthened the ties of kinship that had long slumbered, created the spirit of identification through sacrifice and redemption and gave meaning to the lives of hundreds of thousands of Jews who had never thought that they would ever be swept off their feet by what they had regarded as a chimerical Jewish hope. It brought to life a newborn love for Zion, for Jewish peoplehood and its dignity. It evoked a genuine concern for Jewish survival and forced participation in the struggle. Jews began to look to the Promised Land as the battlefield of their own defense and their own self-emancipation, as well as the haven of refuge for the victims of persecution. They responded with the anger of a people outraged beyond words against a civilization that could allow without intervention or protest a wholesale massacre of their brethren. In the light of this fiery indignation, the Zionist propaganda of words and controversy is reduced to a secondary level of interest and importance.

An awakened Jewish people, scattered in the Dispersion, now occupies dynamic areas of Jewish life. The Germans gave them an object lesson of what could happen to a people unorganized and unequipped for defense and survival. Generations to come will remember that tragic lesson. It will haunt their subconscious selves as well as their immediate life. What Zionists have been talking about for sixty years is now the living foundations of the Jewish people. It is Israel which must be defended and maintained. It is the starting point for the building of a common future: you at the center; we kinsmen encircling the Promised Land; with free commerce of persons and things between us; the Hebrew language becoming ours more, not less; your aspirations ours, fusing in a natural way as common experience grows; your State, our Homeland.

The communities we were urged to conquer have been conquered by the tragic events of Jewish life. Their deeds proclaim their faith. All aspiring Jews march side by side, not wearing the same uniforms or displaying the same badges, responding to different names but sharing in the common sacrifices, seeking the same way of life, rejoicing together and mourning together, all concerned in the survival of the Jewish people and the fulfillment of their destiny.

They are the long awaited reinforcements who are now being woven into the fabric of Jewish destiny. Theirs is not a foreign or a passing interest. They are bound with us in a covenant restored and strengthened by the generations of martyrs who died undefended on the battlefields of Europe. At home and abroad—in Zion or in the Dispersion—they stand with interlocked faith and spirit to defend the Land of Israel, its freedom and its future.

IMPORTANT DATES IN THE LIFE AND CAREER OF LOUIS LIPSKY

November 30, 1876   born in Rochester, New York

1876 to 1900   Grew up in Rochester, attended public and high schools, became a voracious reader, followed the theatre avidly, wrote amateur plays, tried his hand at journalism, taught night school, read for the law

1899   Founded, edited and published *The Shofar*, an Anglo-Jewish weekly; 13 issues published

1899   Took competitive examination for the post of corporation counsel for the City of Rochester

1900   Invited by Philip Cowen to become Managing Editor of *The American Hebrew* in New York

1900   Left Rochester for New York to assume *American Hebrew* post; never returned

1900   Invited to become a corporation counsel in Rochester, after notification that he had passed examination at the top of the list. Declined the offer

1900   Entered Columbia University for an eclectic course

1900 to 1914   In continuous service as editor of *The American Hebrew*

1900 to 1914   Became a devotee and authority on the theatre in New York— Yiddish, American, German

1901   Invited by Gustave Gottheil and Stephen S. Wise to become first Editor of *The Maccabean,* the first Zionist publication in English in the United States, an unpaid post

1901 to 1918   Served as Editor of *The Maccabean*, with brief intermissions

1902 to 1913   Wrote short stories, essays, plays, book reviews, drama critiques. Translated from the Yiddish the stories of I. L. Peretz. From 1910 to 1913 was on the staff of the *New York Morning Telegraph*, writing on the theatre, contributing fiction, book reviews and drama criticism.

For two years he contributed a weekly article to the *Sunday Telegraph*

He wrote articles, essays and fiction published by *The Reader Magazine* of which Louis Howe was the Editor and Sinclair Lewis the Associate Editor

His articles appeared in *The New York Press* and *The Associate Magazine*, Sunday publications, the latter supplement of a national chain of newspapers, which included *The New York Herald Tribune*

1903	Became Secretary to Leo N. Levi, President of the Bnai Brith, and ran a Boy's Club on the Lower East Side for the organization
1906	Married Charlotte Schacht, who bore him three sons
1912	Became Chairman of the Executive Committee of the Federation of American Zionists
1913	Attended, in an official capacity, the World Zionist Congress in Vienna; made a trip to London and encountered the English Zionists; made his first acquaintance with the London theatre. This was his first trip abroad
1913 to 1946	Attended all subsequent World Zionist Congress meetings with the exception of the 1939 Congress in Geneva.
1914	Accepted first paid post in Zionist Movement; became Secretary of the Federation of American Zionists
1914	Resigned his post as Editor of *The American Hebrew*
1914	On eve of World War I, together with Dr. Shmaryahu Levin called for Extraordinary Conference of Zionists. This conference united all Zionist parties and established a Provisional Executive Committee for General Zionist affairs. Louis D. Brandeis came officially into the Zionist Movement then as head of the Executive Committee of the Zionist Provisional Committee
1915	Named Chairman of the Executive Committee of the Federation of American Zionists
1915 to 1921	Served as Chairman of the Executive Committee of the Zionist Movement; from 1915 to 1918 for the Federation of American Zionists; 1918 to 1921 for the Zionist Organization of America which replaced the Federation
1915	Initiated support by the Zionist Movement for the establishment of a democratically elected American Jewish Congress to register

support of American Jews for the re-establishment of the Jewish national homeland in Palestine and to secure protection of the rights of minorities abroad. Helped secure the support of Louis D. Brandeis

1915 through 1949 — Led struggle for right of American Jews to organize locally and nationally by democratic procedures and to name their own spokesmen instead of using self-appointed spokesmen. Defined this concept as in the American tradition, against those who periodically charged that democracy when applied to organization of Jewish life, invited the charge of dual loyalties

1916 — Acted as Zionist negotiator to secure the participation of the American Jewish Committee in the American Jewish Congress. (The American Jewish Committee was the chief antagonist of the Congress concept on grounds that it subjected the American Jews to charges of dual loyalty)

1916 — Attended preliminary meeting of American Jewish Congress in Philadelphia, piloted through concessions limiting purposes of Congress, thus assuring participation of American Jewish Committee

1915 to 1917 — Active participant in all undertakings, with Louis D. Brandeis, Stephen Wise and Felix Frankfurter, to secure American support for the Balfour Declaration, eventually issued on November 2, 1917 after President Wilson's support had been assured

1918 — Participated in first American Jewish Congress elected by direct democratic votes of American Jewish Community, the first such practice in democracy in the history of the American Jewish Community. Helped in election of delegates to the Peace Conference to seek endorsement of Balfour Declaration in peace treaties and protection of minority rights, together with other Jewish delegations joined in the Comité des Délégations Juives

1918 — Formulated and secured adoption of District Organization Plan substituting individual membership for organizational membership which continues to be the organizational basis of the Zionist Organization of America to this day

1918 — Assumed also the responsibilities of organization for the Zionist Organization of America then headed by Louis D. Brandeis as Honorary President and Judge Julian W. Mack as President

1920 — Attended session of the American Jewish Congress where delegation reported on successful efforts which produced the Palestine Mandate and inclusion of minority rights in the peace treaties.

When the session, in accordance with prior agreement, adjourned sine die, presided at meeting which decided on organization of new American Jewish Congress to continue its work

1920   Attended Conference in London summoned by Dr. Chaim Weizmann; joins with him in establishing the Keren Hayesod as the fund raising instrument of the World Zionist Movement to develop Palestine as the Jewish National Homeland in accordance with the Mandate terms

1920   Split with Louis D. Brandeis, Judge Julian W. Mack, Stephen S. Wise, Justice Felix Frankfurter, over the Keren Hayesod which they opposed, preferring independent, autonomous plan for territorial organization

1920   Resigned his offices in the Zionist Organization of America in order to prepare and lead fight for support of the Keren Hayesod at the forthcoming Zionist Convention

1921   Brought Dr. Chaim Weizmann to the United States for the first time in connection with the impending Keren Hayesod battle

1921   Successfully led fight at the Cleveland Convention of the Zionist Organization of America which endorsed the Keren Hayesod. Defeated Louis D. Brandeis and his supporters, causing a split in the movement and the resignation of Brandeis (since 1916 a Justice of the U.S. Supreme Court), Frankfurter, Mack, Wise and a majority of the Executive Committee

1921   Founded *The New Palestine* as instrument for supporting the fight for the Keren Hayesod. This periodical became the official publication of the Zionist Organization of America. Was its first editor, continuing in that capacity intermittently until 1928

1921   Headed coalition group which governed the administration of the Movement until elected President of the Zionist Organization of America in 1926

1921   Attended the World Zionist Congress in Prague, the first since World War I, where Dr. Chaim Weizmann was elected President for the first time

1922   Elected Chairman of the National Executive Committee of the Zionist Organization of America at its convention

1923   Attended World Zionist Congress at Carlsbad

1923   Elected a member of the World Zionist Executive Committee

1923   Participated in the reconvened session of the American Jewish Congress which reorganized and elected a new administration

1924	Named head of the Organization Department for the World Zionist Executive Committee
1924	Went to London twice to carry forward missions for the World Zionist Executive
1924	Founded in London *The New Judaea*, as the official organ of the World Zionist Organization; named J. Hodess as editor
1924	Visited Palestine for the first time
1926	Summoned to London twice by Dr. Chaim Weizmann to confer on problems of the Zionist Movement
1926	Elected for the first time as President of the Zionist Organization of America
1926 to 1930	Re-elected annually as President of the ZOA
1926	Brought to the United States for the first time *The Habimah*, under the auspices of the Zionist Organization of America— a theatre group founded after the Russian Revolution by a group of Jewish actors
1927	As President of the ZOA paid the expenses of the troupe to Palestine where they established Israel's national theatre, but creating a furor in the U.S.A. which almost cost him the presidency
1927	Re-elected a member of the Executive Committee of the World Zionist Organization, with an assignment in London, the international headquarters of the Movement.
1927	Collected writings were published in three volumes including a partial reminiscence of his Zionist work, stories and plays
1929	Helped Dr. Weizmann to establish the enlarged Jewish Agency bringing in, for the first time, important non-Zionists, after considerable opposition within and without the Zionist Movement
1930	Left the Zionist Organization of America as a paid official
1930 to 1954	Served the Zionist Movement, on call without pay, as propagandist, speaker, planner, organizer, travelling throughout the United States and Europe
1930	Accepted post as President of the Judaea Life Insurance Company, later the Eastern Life Insurance Company
1930	Elected as President of Eastern Life Insurance Company
1933	Elected as American member of the Executive Committee of the Jewish Agency for Palestine
1933 to 1946	Served continuously as American member of Jewish Agency Executive
1934	Elected Vice President of the American Jewish Congress; served

	also as Chairman of its Governing Council and head of its National Administrative Committee
1934 to 1945	Actively associated with Stephen Wise in American Jewish Congress in rousing and organizing America against Hitler; for the rescue of Jews and forging American Jewish Congress into leading democratic spokesman of organized Jewish community
1934 to 1945	Became leading American propagandist for opening doors of Palestine to Jewish immigration and honoring by Britain of its Mandate pledges
1936	Was a co-founder with Dr. Stephen S. Wise and Dr. Nahum Goldmann of the World Jewish Congress. Formulated the election procedure in U.S. for American representation
1936	Elected Chairman of the Central Committee at first session of World Jewish Congress in Geneva
1936	Co-Chairman of the United Palestine Appeal—the fund-raising campaign name of the Keren Hayesod and the Keren Kayemeth (the Jewish National Fund)
1938	Co-Chairman of the UPA
1938	Led fight for a national public referendum on the organization of a single Jewish Agency for the defense of Jewish rights as proposed by the American Jewish Congress and opposed by the American Jewish Committee and the Anti-Defamation League of the Bnai Brith
1938	Formulated procedure whereby the American Jewish Congress was reconstituted by direct democratic vote through national elections
1939	Served as National Chairman of the Keren Hayesod, the Palestine Foundation Fund, principal fund-raising arm of the World Zionist Movement
1939 and 1940	Chairman of the Board of Directors of the Keren Hayesod by annual election
1939 through 1941	Chairman of the Administrative Committee of the UPA by annual election
1939	Helped with Dr. Stephen S. Wise and Dr. Israel Goldstein to organize the American Section of British War Relief
1940 through 1943	National Chairman of the Keren Hayesod by annual election
1941–1942	Chairman of the Executive Committee of the UPA
1941	Was a principal leader in the fight to secure from the national

funds recognition of the place of Palestine in the work of rescuing Jews. Co-Chairman with Dr. Silver of the United Palestine Appeal and also Chairman of the Keren Hayesod, he led the fight against the referendum on national budgeting of the Welfare Funds. Although the Welfare Funds won by one vote, thus splitting the United Jewish Appeal, they later capitulated. This fight led to the subsequent parity and later dominant position won for Palestine undertakings at the end of the war.

1942   Incorporated United Jewish Appeal of New York City

1943   Named Chairman of the Board of Elections for the American Jewish Conference, devising the rules of procedure whereby Jewish communities through democratic elections and national organizations through designated delegates formed an American Jewish Conference as the spokesman of a united Jewish Community with respect to the postwar status of Jews and the up-building of Jewish Palestine

1943   Served as Chairman of the Committee of Five which devised the agenda and rules of procedure of the first Session of the American Jewish Conference

1943   Served as Chairman of the General Committee at the first Session of the American Jewish Conference which supervised the conduct of the three-day sessions

1943 through 1947   Through the American Jewish Conference became a principal factor in mobilizing American opinion to be registered with the American Government for the opening of doors of Palestine to survivors of holocaust in the camps of Europe and in Cyprus and Mauritius, for recognition of Jewish rights to a State, and support for partition of Palestine

1944   Elected Co-Chairman of the Interim Committee of the American Jewish Conference together with Henry Monsky and Dr. Israel Goldstein

1944 through 1949   Served as Chairman of the Executive Committee of the American Jewish Conference

1945   Before World War II had ended, twice made the dangerous journey to London and Palestine to confer with Dr. Weizmann and other Zionist leaders on preparations for rescuing the holocaust survivors and bringing them to Palestine

1945   Headed delegation of American Jewish Conference at the organizing conference of the United Nations in San Francisco to press forward claims for creation of Jewish State in Palestine

1947 to 1949   Headed movement, through American Jewish Conference, to prevent rescinding of American support of partition as a result of the Arab war on the U.N. partition resolution

1949   Presented final report concluding mission of American Jewish Conference which then disbanded

1949 to 1954   Chairman of the American Zionist Council, representing all branches of Zionist Movement in the U.S. There mobilized action, through American support, to protect new State of Israel against its would-be destroyers

1950   Visited the State of Israel for the first time after its establishment

1954   Chairman of American Zionist Committee for Public Affairs, later American Israel Committee for Public Affairs, an important instrument for making known Israel's peaceful aims and concentration on building a viable state

1956   Visited the State of Israel as guest of the Weizmann Institute of Science, arriving in Israel at the height of the Sinai Campaign. On November 12, 1956, he delivered the Chaim Weizmann Memorial Lecture at Rehovot. There he was made an Honorary Fellow of the Institute.

1956   Published a Gallery of Zionist Portraits, a résumé of the Zionist Movement, its founders and its early and later leaders

1959   Retired as President of the Eastern Life Insurance Company after 29 years in that office

1959   Became Chairman of the Board of the Eastern Life Insurance Company

1960   Became Honorary Chairman of the Board of the Eastern Life Insurance Company

1962   Published *Tales of The Yiddish Rialto*, stories of the Yiddish Theatre, the leading Yiddish playwrights and actors at the turn of the century

INDEX

Page numbers of biographical sketches are denoted in *italics*.
Academic and other titles are given only where this facilitates identification.